HIDDEN PACIFIC NORTHWEST

Including Oregon, Washington, Vancouver, Victoria & Coastal British Columbia

Eric Lucas

NINTH EDITION

Ulysses Press

EXPLORING THE HIDDEN REALM

From Seattle's glittering cityscapes to Vancouver's windswept shores, the Pacific Northwest presents a staggering array of choices for the modern traveler. The key to finding your own perfect adventure is to experience the realm the way the locals do, visiting unique and uncommon places off the beaten tourist path. While *Hidden Pacific Northwest* also covers many well-loved and famous spots in the area, its true goal is to guide you on an unforgettable visit, discovering treasures most visitors never see. With highlighted listings, detailed maps and easy-to-follow directions, you'll find secluded hiking trails, rocky, tidepool-rich beaches, luxurious boutique hotels and quirky bed-and-breakfast inns, along with waterfront seafood stands and venerable Chinese restaurants. As you continue through the guide, your adventure will follow the trail of Northcoast American Indians, lead you through lush old-growth forests, enchanting winter wonderlands and tranquil lakeside campgrounds, and help you create your dream itinerary.

Crashing Sol Duc Falls cascade into a misty river on an enchanting, hemlock-shrouded trail in the Olympic Peninsula.

NORTHWEST INDIAN ART

From elaborately handcarved wooden dance masks to intricately woven grass baskets, Northwest Indian artworks represent not only the skills of native tribes (called First Nations people in Canada) but also the cultural traditions that continue throughout the Northwest today. Featuring highly stylized bears, ravens, orcas and other natural and supernatural beings, traditional designs are still used to decorate everything from small boxes and canoes to building façades and towering totem poles. While you may encounter any number of American Indian–inspired items while in this region, visit a local museum, shop or park that illuminates these fine native works to truly appreciate them.

Victoria's diminutive Thunderbird Park boasts huge and colorful handcarved totem poles.

Authentic First Nations artwork is showcased at the Bill Reid Gallery of Northwest Coast Art in Vancouver.

A scenic stroll will bring you face to face with the impressive First Nations totem poles that watch over Victoria's **Thunderbird Park** *(p. 587)*. In Vancouver, the celebrated **Bill Reid Gallery of Northwest Coast Art** *(p. 539)* showcases 19th-century American Indian works in an intimate museum setting. The gift shop at the **Makah Cultural and Research Center** *(p. 184)* near the Canada/Washington border specializes in handcrafted jewelry and basketry. Just outside of Seattle is the **Burke Museum of Natural History and Culture** *(p. 64)*, which displays an expansive collection of native carvings. For an unusual exhibit of hand-fashioned lava heads, stop by the **Maryhill Museum of Art** *(p. 361)*, near the Columbia River Gorge.

FORESTS AND FOLIAGE

Bountiful forests were what brought early settlers to the Pacific Northwest, and today more than three million acres of ancient evergreens still exist in Washington alone. The thick groves of redwoods, Western hemlocks and white pines stretch high into ethereal canopies while buttercups, huckleberries and azaleas color the ground below. With such an abundance of natural beauty, there is no shortage of secluded forests and gardens to explore away from tourist crowds. Walking amidst wild irises and glossy madrone trees, you'll discover a tranquil region you can't find anywhere else.

The Sol Duc River Valley within the **Olympic National Forest** *(p. 177)* is a wooded wonderland with numerous creeks and rivers. The **Hoh Rainforest** *(p. 187)* on the west side of Olympic National Park is a rare, temperate, emerald paradise. On Bainbridge Island, you can tour 150 acres of picturesque meadows, gardens and forests at the **Bloedel Reserve** *(p. 73)*. Near Florence, Oregon, the small **Darlingtonia Botanical Wayside** *(p. 402)* boasts unusual native cobra lilies amid a woodland picnic area. **Lost Forest** *(p. 309)* in the Cascades is a little-traversed, beautiful 9000-acre ponderosa-pine grove.

The lush Hoh Rainforest is one of the wettest destinations in the contiguous states, averaging more than 145 inches of rainfall a year.

In the Olympic National Forest, the serene Sol Duc River washes over moss-cloaked boulders and stream-smoothed stones.

BEACHES

Like its dense forests, the Pacific Northwest's multitude of beaches creates a varied and picturesque landscape. Along the coast there are tiny coves blanketed with sands undisturbed by visitors. Some beaches are alluring for their rich tidepools and rocky trails, others for secluded woodsy camping or spectacular swimming spots. At these hidden locales you can lazily hunt for sand dollars or shells while the cool ocean water laps at your feet. Locals converge at beaches for crabbing, clamming and community, so you will have a chance to watch everyday life unfold while you relax—overall, a splendid Northwest experience.

Wave-polished stacks of driftwood dot the sands at **Rialto Beach** *(p. 187)* near the Quileute River in Washington. Nearby, the **Olympic National Park Coastal Unit's Ozette Beach** *(p. 188)* features tranquil rocky shores great for exploring. Forty miles of sand abutting forested bluffs make up the locally loved **Oregon Dunes National Recreation Area** *(p. 403)*. **Teddy Bear Cove** *(p. 128)* along the Northern Puget Sound offers a secluded strip of white sand bordered by thick trees.

Ocean waves crash onto sweeping sands along 40 acres of the Oregon Dunes National Recreation Area outside of Florence.

Ozette Beach, a rocky strip teeming with tidepools, is one of six beaches within the Olympic National Park Coastal Unit.

BED & BREAKFASTS

As elegant as they are charming, B&Bs offer cozy accommodations along with the one exceptional detail large hotels can't provide—individualized hospitality. Whether providing fresh-cut flowers, in-house massage or homemade cookies, the innkeepers at Pacific Northwest B&Bs are dedicated to bringing guests all the comforts they desire. These delightful spots are full of character; some are Victorian estates brimming with antiques, others are country clapboard mansions decorated with warm floral prints. Whether they're set on a hillside or nestled on a city street, these unique affairs offer sincere generosity and thoughtful amenities.

Evening hors d'oeuvres are served in the plush library at **Abigail's** *(p. 590)*, a Tudor inn located in downtown Victoria. **O Canada House** *(p. 546)* in downtown Vancouver is a Victorian home that serves a gourmet three-course breakfast and afternoon sherry. In Leavenworth, Washington, **All Seasons River Inn** *(p. 242)* provides complimentary bicycles for guests who want to explore the surrounding forest. Visitors can relax in a garden hammock under a cedar tree at Hood River's **Inn at the Gorge Bed & Breakfast** *(p. 363)*, a 1908 inn with a wraparound porch.

In Victoria, European-inspired Abigail's boasts well-kept gardens, vaulted ceilings and antique furnishings.

BOUTIQUE HOTELS

A burgeoning trend throughout metropolitan areas in the Pacific Northwest, boutique hotels offer a unique getaway experience. With their hand-chosen style, these individualized retreats provide a glimpse into the heart of the region and its varied past. Whether they are styled in vineyard decor with burgundy walls and dark cherry-wood furniture or are former seafarer bordellos with vintage red-light detail, these accommodations offer one-of-a-kind themed lodgings with exceptional attention to design.

Overlooking the Methow River, cozy, Western-spirited **Hotel Rio Vista** *(p. 232)* is decked out in bright, homey prints and is an ideal family spot. Chic, contemporary style pervades Portland's vibrant and richly appointed **Heathman Hotel** *(p. 331)*. Once a luxury apartment building, the 1912 **Sylvia Hotel** *(p. 544)* in Vancouver boasts minimalist elegance with soft peach hues. A short walk from Victoria's Inner Harbour, the stately **Bedford Regency Hotel** *(p. 590)* is reminiscent of England, complete with its own pub. Seattle's **Sorrento Hotel** *(p. 44)* is filled with European romance, including plush linens, decadent fabrics and gold accents.

Luxury accommodations meet Northwest style at the posh Heathman Hotel.

SUCCULENT SEAFOOD

From Dungeness crab to Charleston salmon to Penn Cove shellfish, the seafood on the Northwest coast is as fresh and delicious as it gets. The harbors here set the standard to which other states ascribe. A trip to this region would not be complete without a sample of succulent sea fare pulled straight from the depths and prepared by local chefs who know how to do it best. Rich, buttery scallops, creamy clam chowder and savory alder salmon are at their most exquisite when enjoyed on an oceanfront patio overlooking the waters from whence they came.

Generous plates of crispy fish and chips are served in the seaside dining room at the **Ship Inn** *(p. 391)* in Astoria. Stop at **Kokanee Café** *(p. 455)* in the Oregon Cascades for sesame crab fritters with rose-scented orange and carrot salad. Looking down at Pike Place, **Matt's in the Market** *(p. 46)* offers steamed mussels with saffron butter and wild salmon with Bing cherry vinaigrette. Nearby, **Place Pigalle** *(p. 46)* serves outstanding calamari in dijon-ginger cream sauce at tables over Elliott Bay. Pepper-stewed oysters and fried halibut add to the long list of fresh items at Vancouver's **The Only Seafood Café** *(p. 547)*.

Seafood doesn't get fresher than it is at Matt's in the Market, where entrées such as salmon with figs on gnocchi set the bar.

ETHNIC EATERIES

Zaina, a lively Greek taverna in downtown Seattle, offers outstanding traditional favorites to local crowds six days a week.

While the Pacific Northwest is known for its seafood-rich restaurants, there are equally outstanding eateries throughout the region that present cuisines as culturally diverse as their chefs. Seattle and Vancouver are home to some of North America's largest Asian populations, so it's no surprise there are exquisite Chinese, Korean, Thai and Japanese dining rooms all along the coast. You will also find premier Mexican menus offering fresh salsa and steaming-hot tortillas and tiny Greek tavernas serving handwrapped dolmas and crispy moussaka. To get a true taste of the local scene, make a point to reserve a table at one of these little-known gems.

Outside of Salem, locals line up to get a table at **Amador's Alley** *(p. 492)* where the generous portions of *huevos con chorizo* spill off the plates. For Tahitian-style meals, head to Portland's Pacific Island delight, **Saucebox** *(p. 332)*. An array of Asian cuisine is served at **Siam Palace** *(p. 282)* in Grand Coulee, east of the Cascades. Downtown Seattle's International District boasts **Zaina** *(p. 45)*, a friendly Greek eatery with all the traditional favorites. Indulge in the curry buffet at Victoria's **Bengal Lounge** *(p. 593)*.

WINTER WONDERLAND

Jack Frost spends plenty of time in the Pacific Northwest, sugaring the mountaintops and creating a wide range of cold-climate activities. From alpine skiing in the Washington Cascades to snowboarding on the Oregon slopes to watching snowflakes float outside fireside lodges in Vancouver, there's a variety of opportunities to experience this winter wonderland the way the locals do. Aside from big resorts and major mountains, little-known retreats and less-snowshoed trails allow you to take in the landscape and still have a secluded getaway.

The snow-covered slopes at Mt. Baker-Snoqualmie National Forest make for perfect alpine skiing.

Cross-country and downhill skiers will love the snowy expanses at **Mt. Baker-Snoqualmie National Forest** *(p. 252)*, which begins at the Canadian border. The eastern slope of the Blue Mountains includes the remote 792-acre **Field Spring State Park** *(p. 299)*, a sparkling area great for tubing and snowshoeing. More than 200 marked runs are available at the resort at **Whistler-Blackcomb** *(p. 576)*, offering prime winter opportunities. In Oregon, hit the slopes at **Deschutes National Forest** *(p. 459)* amid frosty ponderosa pines. The highest peak in the Cascade and Coast mountain ranges is **Mt. Ashland** *(p. 518)*, rising 7500 feet into the sky.

Snowboarders launch off the majestic peaks at Whistler-Blackcomb.

For cross-country skiers, the Deschutes National Forest in the Oregon Cascades provides premier powder through five wilderness areas.

HIKING

Sometimes putting foot to earth is the best way to get to know an area, getting off the busy roads and finding an intimate, personal connection to the land. From the snowy peaks of Mt. Hood to the thick forests along the Puget Sound to the coastal bluffs of Vancouver, the Pacific Northwest's hiking opportunities are as varied as its landscape. You can trek through a towering evergreen grove, breathing in the natural essence, and stroll along a secluded shore of the Pacific, reveling in the quiet crash of the waves. While wild cobra lilies bloom on the trail and shorebirds soar overhead, you'll be mesmerized by the natural beauty—and the details you'll discover miles from the tourist crowds. Few other places in the world offer the chance to explore tranquil lakeside trails and steep summit treks in the same day.

The **Pacific Crest National Scenic Trail** *(p. 265)* traverses wildflower-strewn meadows and rugged mountain heights. Winding all the way around Mt. Rainier, the **Wonderland Trail** *(p. 267)* extends for 93 miles for an amazing trek. An enchanting hike to numerous waterfalls, the **Ten Falls Loop Trail** *(p. 522)* lies within Silver Falls State Park outside of Salem. The **Dungeness Spit Trail** *(p. 218)* on the Olympic Peninsula snakes around the longest natural sandspit in the U.S. In Vancouver, the **Juan de Fuca Marine Trail** *(p. 628)* follows the coast for 14 miles, lacing through gravel beaches and towering fir forests.

At times a challenging trek, the Pacific Crest National Scenic Trail rewards hikers with wildflower-filled meadows and snowy slopes.

Winding around gigantic Mt. Rainier, the Wonderland Trail laces old-growth forests and sparkling glaciers for more than 90 miles.

CAMPING

Known for its lush evergreen forests and vast sweeping shorelines, this area is brimming with campgrounds, ranging from lakeside coves to beachfront stretches to spots tucked deep in the woods. You can venture to the Pacific Northwest's camping havens and still avoid the packed tent-to-tent sites: Beyond the major mountain ranges are other idyllic and remote parks, some barely intruded upon by humans. Sneak to one of the little-known gems ensuring that you won't have to share that nearby babbling creek or huckleberry-lined trail. For a uniquely peaceful outdoor experience, seek out one of these oases you can have all to yourself.

The serene sites around the **Okanogan-Wenatchee National Forests** *(p. 240)* provide prime overnight locales, some near the aptly named Enchantment Lakes. At unfrequented **Palouse Falls State Park/Lyons Ferry State Park** *(p. 300)* in Southeastern Washington, you can set up camp then walk to thundering waterfalls. The sandy, log-strewn crescent at **Willingdon Beach Municipal Campsite** *(p. 570)* offers both riverside and forested spots. Ten miles outside of Olympia is 842-acre **Millersylvania State Park** *(p. 103)*, which includes miles of primeval conifer forests. **Cape Lookout State Park** *(p. 397)* boasts a variety of options, from cabins to yurts to tents.

Campgrounds bordering tranquil Snow Lake in the Okanogan-Wenatchee National Forest are ideal for secluded getaways.

HIDDEN®
PACIFIC
NORTHWEST

Including Oregon, Washington, Vancouver, Victoria & Coastal British Columbia

NINTH EDITION

"An excellent guidebook."
—*Seattle Times & Post-Intelligencer*

"Uncovers the true spirit of this unique region."
—*Tennessean*

"*Hidden Pacific Northwest* lives up to its name
with its tips on finding attractions that are off the beaten path."
—*Edmonton Sun*

"Written with an eye for the off-beat, the book is the perfect
companion for a jaunt up the Oregon coast, a camping trip
on the Olympic Peninsula or even a visit to Vancouver. . . .
Fun to read for both the casual visitor and the intrepid traveler."
—*Our World*

Ulysses Press
BERKELEY, CALIFORNIA

Published by: ULYSSES PRESS
                 P.O. Box 3440
                 Berkeley, CA 94703
                 www.ulyssespress.com

ISSN 1522-1172
ISBN: 978-1-56975-618-8

Printed in Canada by Transcontinental Printing

20 19 18 17 16 15 14 13 12

AUTHORS: Eric Lucas, Richard Harris, Stephen Dolainski, John Gottberg Anderson
UPDATE AUTHOR: Richard Harris
MANAGING EDITOR: Claire Chun
PROJECT DIRECTOR: Elyce Petker
COPYEDITOR: Emma Silvers
EDITORIAL ASSOCIATES: Lauren Harrison, Abigail Reser, Kate Kellogg, Katy Loveless
PRODUCTION: Judith Metzener
CARTOGRAPHY: Pease Press
HIDDEN BOOKS DESIGN: what!design @ whatweb.com
INDEXER: Sayre Van Young
COVER PHOTOGRAPHY: front © Joel Rogers; back © Russ Bishop
COLOR INSERT: *page i* © Terry Donnelly; *page ii* © Terry Donnelly; *page iii* top © Kenji Nagai; bottom © Mark Gibson; *page iv* © Andrew Palazzari; *page v* © Mary Liz Austin; *page vi* © Steven L Pierce; *page vii* © Larry Ulrich; *page viii* © Abigail's; *page ix* top © Heathman Hotel; *page x* © Bryan Yoo; *page xi* © Robbie Augspurger; *page xii* top © 2006 David Gómez-Rosado & Lorena Fernández-Fernández, gomez-rosado.com; bottom © istockphoto.com/Faulknor Photography; *page xiii* © Joel Rogers; *page xiv* © Taylor Westphal; *page xv* © Andrea Johnson; *page xvi* © Forrest Cook

Distributed by Publishers Group West

HIDDEN is a federally registered trademark of BookPack, Inc.

CONTENTS

MAPS

OUTDOOR ADVENTURE SYMBOLS

The following symbols accompany national, state and regional park listings, as well as beach descriptions throughout the text.

🏕	Camping	🏄	Surfing
🥾	Hiking	🎿	Waterskiing
🚲	Biking	⛵	Windsurfing
🐎	Horseback Riding	🛶	Kayaking/Canoeing
⛷	Downhill Skiing	🚤	Boating
🎿	Cross-Country Skiing	🚤	Boat ramps
🏊	Swimming	🐟	Fishing
🤿	Snorkeling/Scuba Diving		

HIDDEN LISTINGS

Throughout the book, listings that reveal the hidden realm—spots that are away from tourists or reflect authentic Pacific Northwest—are marked by this icon:

There are also special maps at the start of each section that guide you to some of these hidden listings. Each place is identified with this symbol:

THE PACIFIC NORTHWEST

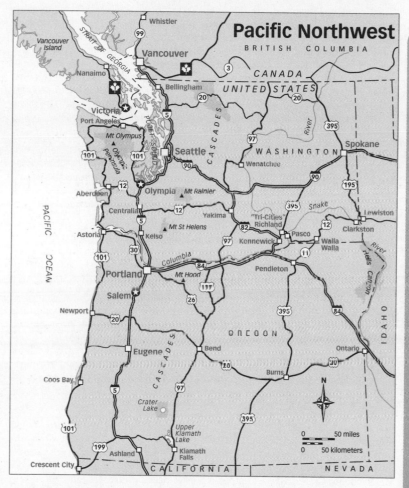

Pacific Northwest

The Pacific Northwest goes by many names, but perhaps "The Evergreen Playground" best captures its enchanting appeal. This is a land of intense beauty: gossamer mists on towering evergreens, icy summits that cast shadows on pastoral valleys and bustling cityscapes, wind-sculpted trees on wave-battered capes and inlets, warm breezes through juniper boughs. Powerful volcanoes, wondrous waterfalls, glistening waterways, even shifting desert sands.

The heavy rainfall for which the Pacific Northwest is famous truly gives the region its majestic soul. The drizzle and clouds that blanket the coastal region during much of the winter and spring nourish the incredibly green landscape that grows thick and fast and softens the sharp edges of alpine peaks and jagged sea cliffs. But there's a flip side: Over half the region (meaning points east of the Cascade Range) is actually warm and dry through the year.

"The Evergreen Playground" fairly begs to be explored. While much of it remains undeveloped, vast expanses of wilderness are close by metropolitan centers. Almost without exception, each city is surrounded by countless outdoor recreational opportunities, with mountains, lakes, streams and an ocean within easy reach. It's no surprise that residents and visitors tend to have a hardy, outdoorsy glow. After all, it is the proximity to nature that draws people here. That remains especially true in Oregon, where development of the land is allowed only in certain areas close to a city center within an "urban growth boundary." The areas outside the towns are protected from the ugly suburban sprawl that has spread throughout much of the West Coast.

Asian populations lend an exotic feel to the bustling commercial centers of Seattle, Portland and Vancouver, while the distinctly British aura of Victoria imparts an entirely different foreign appeal. A montage of tiny ghost towns, towering totem poles, aging wooden forts, Scandinavian and Bavarian communities, stage stops and gold-mining boomtowns, and old-time fishing villages adds a frontier feel to the Vancouver region.

This book will help you explore this wonderful area, tell of its history, introduce you to its flora and fauna. Besides taking you to countless popular spots, it will lead you to off-the-beaten-path locales. Each chapter will suggest places to eat, to stay, to sightsee, to shop and to enjoy the outdoors and nightlife, covering a wide range of tastes and budgets.

The book starts in Seattle, taking visitors in Chapter Two through this popular city and the surrounding communities spread along Southern Puget Sound. Chapter Three heads up the Sound, taking in some small and some not-so-small coastal towns and the San Juans, an archipelago of evergreen-clad islands. Chapter Four covers the moss-laden rainforests and historic port towns of Washington's Olympic Peninsula and southwestern coast while Chapter Five explores the numerous parks, forests, wildernesses and removed resort communities of the Washington Cascades.

Chapter Six heads to the arid plateau and desert region east of the Cascades in both Washington and Oregon. Portland, the "City of Roses," and the windy Columbia Gorge are the subject of Chapter Seven. Next we go on one of the nation's most scenic drives along the Oregon Coast in Chapter Eight and on to Mt. Hood, Mt. Bachelor, Crater Lake and other majestic peaks of the Oregon Cascades in Chapter Nine. Chapter Ten covers the cultural, learning and political centers lining the Heart of Oregon.

In Chapter Eleven we visit British Columbia, Canada's most westerly province, with stops in enticing Vancouver and the famous Whistler ski resort, followed by a motoring trip up the sleepy Sunshine Coast, an outdoors-lover's paradise. Chapter Twelve rounds out the book with a ferry trip to unspoiled Vancouver Island, its coasts lined with bucolic fishing villages, and to the very proper, very English Victoria, capital of the province.

What you choose to see and do is up to you, but don't delay; things are changing here. The Pacific Northwest is no longer the quiet backwater of a couple of decades ago. Growth and expansion continue in the major population centers strung along the long, black ribbon of Route 5. While Northwesterners are vociferous advocates for preserving nature, rapidly increasing population and growing economic demands are taking a toll.

Sadly, it's becoming difficult to miss the horrid clear-cut swaths through the evergreen background, evidence of the logging industry that feeds the local economies. Salmon that once choked the many streams and rivers have dwindled in number, as have numerous forest creatures such as the spotted owl.

Tourism has also had an impact. As the beauty of the area has been "discovered" by travelers who've taken home tales of this don't-spread-it-around secret vacationland, it's become a hot destination, especially among international visitors. It's getting harder and harder to find those special hidden spots—go soon before "hidden" no longer applies.

THE STORY OF THE PACIFIC NORTHWEST

GEOLOGY

Between a billion and 200 million years ago, magma erupting from the earth's core led to spreading oceanic ridges in the Pacific and Atlantic oceans. As the oceans widened, the continents broke apart and what is now the Pacific Northwest made its first appearance. Washington and southern British Columbia grew again, beginning 100 million years ago, when island continents floating in the Pacific Ocean began to collide with North America and attach themselves to the mainland as microcontinents. Today, the North Cascades range, which spans the international boundary between northwestern Washington and British Columbia, is the best place to see the eroded remains of these nonvolcanic, island-formed terrains.

Washington and Oregon's ancestral volcanoes began to emerge 40 million years ago, but the modern Cascades appeared only about a million years ago with the pumice and lava eruptions that built Mount Rainier. Younger volcanoes like Mount St. Helens, the youngest and most active in the range, formed only 70,000 years ago and remain highly active today.

Unrelated to the volcanic Cascades, the Olympic Mountains began as lava flows along the continental shelf about 50 million years ago, mingling with ocean sediments and forming a thick offshore sedimentary delta. When the Cascades were pushed up by the subduction of the Pacific plate beneath the lighter North American plate, scientists think part of the oceanic plate, the Juan de Fuca plate, got hung up in the vicinity of Vancouver Island. The submerged offshore delta may have been forced to ride back to the North American continent and got rammed below lava basalts, forcing up a new nonvolcanic range: the Olympics.

During the last Ice Age, 2 million years ago, massive ice sheets from Canada covered the region, and glaciers sculpted the peaks, valleys and fjords of the distinctive Northwest landscape. By 10,000 years ago, the warmer climate had melted much of the ice, flooding Puget Sound, Hood Canal, the Strait of Juan de Fuca, and other glaciated troughs.

Six million years ago, the Columbia River was being pushed north from its course by mile-deep basaltic lava flows that formed the Columbia Plateau. Catastrophic floods—the most extensive in history—carved the Columbia Gorge between 19,000 and 12,000 years ago, when a 2000-foot-high ice dam that impounded glacial Lake Missoula failed. The Bretz Floods buzzed vertically through Cascade basalts, sculpting Channeled Scabland terraces, coulees (side canyons) and dry falls, and left boulders and gravel high and dry.

HISTORY

THE FIRST PEOPLE The first migrants may have come from Asia across the Bering Strait land bridge some 25,000 years ago. From the diverse background of those earliest inhabitants descended the many American Indian tribes that populated the North American continent. Kwakiutl, Haida, Bella Coola, Tlingit, Salish, Yakima, Nez Perce, Paiutes, Shoshone, Umpqua and Rogue are but a few of the Northwest tribes.

The verdant land of the Pacific Northwest both provided for and dictated the lifestyles of the various tribes. Those that lived inland east of the mountain ranges lived a hunter-gatherer lifestyle, harvesting wild foods throughout the year as they became available. When the Spaniards reintroduced horses to North America, Columbia Plateau people traveled farther afield, paddling up the Columbia to attend huge annual rendezvous near The Dalles to trade, socialize and intermarry.

The mild climate and abundant resources of the valley and coast led to a fairly sedentary lifestyle for the tribes that lived west of the mountain ranges. They constructed permanent villages of communal red-cedar longhouses, fished the rich waters of the coast and mouths of rivers, and developed complex ritual arts, ceremonies and other cultural pursuits. Social status was recognized through the potlatch, a ceremony that emphasized eating, dancing and the redistribution of gifts, such as blankets and carved cedar boxes, by chiefs to prove their power and prestige.

Arrival of the white man brought many changes to the generally peaceful natives. Introduction of the horse made life easier for a period, facilitating hunting and travel for the nomadic tribes. However, disease, drugs (namely alcohol) and distrust accompanied the newcomers and eventually added to the decline of the American Indian population. Land grabbing by European settlers forced the tribes onto ever-shrinking reservations.

Resurgence in American Indian arts and crafts is evident in galleries and museums throughout the Northwest. While most natives no longer live on the reservations but have integrated into white society, many have banded together to fight for change. Tribal organizations are now reclaiming lands and fishing rights; nations such as the Sechelt Band in British Columbia have won the legal right to independent self-government. There are even a growing number of native-owned and -operated resorts such as Ka-Nee-Tah, a hot spring and golf retreat in central Oregon.

EARLY EXPLORATION   In terms of white exploration and settlement, the Pacific Northwest is one of the youngest regions on the continent. The Spanish began to arrive in the Northwest by sea as early as the mid-1500s; the Strait of Juan de Fuca, Heceta Head, Fidalgo Island, Cape Blanco, Quadra Island and other prominent landmarks bear witness to Spanish exploration and influence. Spanish interest waned when other pressing matters required the attention and money needed to chart the Northwest, and all claims to the area were dropped in 1819 as part of the negotiations regarding Florida.

The Russians also made their way into the region, beginning with the explorations of Vitus Dane in 1741. Soon afterward, Russian trappers trekked from Siberia down through Alaska and into the Northwest. As a result of losses brought on by the Napoleonic Wars, Russia renounced all claims to the area south of 54°40' in 1824.

Sir Francis Drake passed briefly along the Northwest Coast in 1579, but it was explorer Captain James Cook's expedition in 1778 in search of the legendary "Northwest Passage" that resulted in British claim to the region. When passing through China on their homeward-bound trip, he and his men discovered the high value of the pelts they carried, leading to an intense interest on the part of the British government in the profitable resources of the Northwest.

The government later commissioned Captain George Vancouver to chart the coastal area between 45° and 60° north latitude, which includes Oregon, Washington, British Columbia and Alaska. Mt. Baker, Whidbey Island, Puget Sound, Vancouver Island, Burrard Inlet and many other geographical features retain the names he gave them on his meticulously drawn maps completed between 1791 and 1795.

Captain Robert Gray was also plying Northwest waters at this time, making certain that the United States could lay claim to parts of the lucrative new territory. During his journey, he discovered the mighty Columbia River while searching for the same fabled waterway between the Pacific and Atlantic oceans.

Early explorers like Alexander McKenzie and Simon Fraser were actually the first Europeans to explore land routes, but it was not until Meriwether Lewis and William Clark explored and mapped overland passages, returning with stories of the area's beauty and natural bounty, that interest in settling the Northwest began in earnest.

THE NEWCOMERS   Trading posts were established to facilitate the fur enterprises; large firms like the Hudson's Bay Company and the North West Company vied for control of the profitable region. Settlements sprang up around these posts and continued to grow as the trickle of pioneers swelled into a wave with the opening of the Oregon Trail in the mid-1800s.

Tensions left over from the War of 1812 and the not-yet-forgotten American Revolution caused friction between the Americans and British in the Northwest. The American/British Treaty of 1846 failed to define the border of the British territory, so the Americans and British agreed to use the 49th parallel. However, this latitude divided the San Juan Islands in two, leaving British and American soldiers staring each other down across the makeshift border. The entente was preserved until a lone British pig wandered into the garden of an American settler, who shot and killed the pig—the only bullet fired during the 13-year dispute, a diplomatic struggle for the islands that came to be called the "Pig War." Ultimately the islands were awarded to the United States by a German arbitrator in 1872.

Homesteading, fishing, logging, ranching and other opportunities kept the flow of settlers coming, as did a series of gold strikes. Stage routes were established, and river traffic grew steadily. There were enough residents to warrant separation of the Oregon Territory by the 1850s, and Washington and Oregon attained statehood by the turn of the 20th century. British Columbia was officially accepted as a Canadian province in 1871. Railroads pushed into the region, reaching Portland and Puget Sound by 1883 and British Columbia in 1885, ushering in the modern age.

Rapid industrial development came with the world wars, and the Northwest emerged as a major player in the shipbuilding and shipping industries. Expansion in lumber, agriculture and fishing continued apace; Washington State fisheries catch more than 1.3 billion pounds of fish and seafood annually, more than half the nation's total edible catch. Growth industries today include banking, high technology and Pacific Rim trade. Modern residents are for the most part rugged individualists, fiercely proud of their natural setting and protective of the environment.

FLORA

While it's generally the coniferous trees that everyone equates with the Pacific Northwest, there is much more to the flora of the region than its abundance of redwoods, Western hemlock and white pine, red cedar and other evergreens. Each of the distinct geologic zones hosts its own particular ecosystem.

In the moist woodlands of the coastline, glossy madrone and immense Coast redwoods tower over Pacific trilliums and delicate ladyslippers.

Bogs full of skunk cabbage thrive alongside fields of yellow Scotch broom and hardy rhododendrons in a riot of color. Unique to the region are pristine rainforests with thick carpets of moss and fern beneath sky-scraping canopies of fir, cedar and spruce.

In the lowland valleys, alders, oaks, maples and other deciduous trees provide brilliant displays of color against an evergreen backdrop each spring and fall. Daffodils and tulips light up the fields, as do azaleas, red clover and other grasses grown by the many nurseries and seed companies that prosper here. Wild berry bushes run rampant in this clime, bringing blackberries, huckleberries, currants and strawberries for the picking. Indian paintbrush, columbines, foxglove, buttercups and numerous other wildflowers are also abundant. These valleys also host hundreds of hazelnut orchards. In fact, Oregon grows 99 percent of the entire U.S. commercial crop of hazelnuts. (That's why the hazelnut coffee is so delicious here!)

The verdant parks and forests of the mountain chains contain some of the biggest trees in the world, holding records in height and circumference, with fir, pine, hemlock and cedar generally topping the charts. Thick groves filter the sunlight, providing the perfect environment for mushrooms, lichens, ferns and mosses. The elegant tiger lily, bear grass, asters, fawn lily, phlox, columbine, valerian and a breathtaking array of alpine wildflowers thrive in high meadows and on sunny slopes.

With the dramatic decrease in rainfall in the plateaus and deserts zone comes a paralleling drop in the amount of plantlife, although it is still rich in pine, juniper, cottonwood and sagebrush. Flowers of the area include wild iris, foxglove, camas, balsam root and pearly everlasting.

FAUNA

It was actually the proliferation of wildlife that brought about white colonization of the Pacific Northwest, beginning with the trappers who came in droves in search of fur. It turns out that beaver and otter pelts were highly valued in China during the 1800s, so these creatures were heavily hunted. Nearly decimated colonies, now protected by law, are coming back strong. Playful otters are often spotted floating tummy up in coastal waters. Once endangered, bald eagles can be seen frequently wintering on the Skagit River and feeding on returning salmon.

The Dungeness crab was the first commercially harvested shellfish on the Olympic coast, and fish, especially salmon, were a major factor in the economic development of the region. They remain so, though numbers of spawning salmon are dropping drastically. Nonetheless, fishing fanatics are still drawn here in search of the six varieties of Pacific salmon, along with flounder, ling cod, rockfish, trout, bass and other varieties of sportfish. Those who don't fish will still be fascinated by the seasonal spawning frenzy of salmon, easily observed at fish ladders in Washington, Oregon and British Columbia.

Among the more readily recognized creatures that reside in the Pacific Northwest are the orca, porpoises, dolphins, seals and sea lions often spotted cavorting in the waters just offshore. Twice-yearly migrations of gray whales on the trip between Alaska and California are much anticipated all along the coastline. Minke whales are more numerous, as are Dall's porpoises, often mistaken for baby orca because of their similar coloration and markings.

Of the varieties of bear living in the Northwest's remote forests, black bear are the most common in Oregon and southern Washington. Weighing upwards of 300 pounds and reaching six feet tall, they usually feed on berries, nuts and fish and avoid humans unless provoked by offers of food or danger to a cub. Grizzly bears are more prevalent farther north in the North Cascades range, which spans the international boundary between Washington and British Columbia. Big-game herds of deer, elk, antelope along with moose, cougar and mountain goats range the more mountainous areas. Scavengers such as chipmunks, squirrels, raccoons, opossums and skunks are abundant in the area as well. Also watch for the Pacific giant salamander in fallen, rotting logs: it is the largest of its kind in the world, growing up to a foot in length and capable of eating small mice.

Over 300 species of birds live in the Pacific Northwest for at least a portion of the year. Easily accessible mud flats and estuaries throughout the region provide refuge for tufted puffins, egrets, cormorants, loons and other migratory waterfowl making their way along the Pacific Flyway. Hundreds of pairs of bald eagles nest and hunt among the islands of Washington and British Columbia and winter along the Oregon coast, along with great blue herons and cormorants. You might also see red-tailed hawks and spotted owls if you venture quietly into the region's old-growth zones.

Northern spotted owls are the fifth largest of the 19 owl species. They have been the center of controversy in recent years, the focus of the recurring nature-versus-commerce debate. As logging companies cut deeper into the old-growth forests, which have taken 150 years or more to grow, the habitat for this endangered owl grows smaller. (These nocturnal birds need thousands of acres per pair to support their indulgent eating habits.) The old-growth forests of the Pacific Northwest provide adequate nesting spots in the protected snags and broken branches of tall trees that shelter their flightless young. However, within the last hundred years, these glorious forests have been reduced to ten percent of their former range.

With a proliferation of protected refuges and preserves providing homes for great flocks of Canada and snow geese, trumpeter swans, great blue herons, kingfishers, cranes and other species, birdwatchers will be in seventh heaven in the Pacific Northwest, one of the fastest-growing birder destinations on the continent.

Twenty-three species of slug thrive in the 100-percent humidity of the Olympic rainforest and leave behind telltale viscous trails everywhere. The bane of gardeners, they are regarded as a mascot of the region, along with geoducks (pronounced gooey-ducks), a type of razor clam found in Hood Canal. Souvenir shops stock plush toy replicas of slugs and gag cans of slug soup.

WHERE TO GO

The number of tourists visiting the Pacific Northwest continues to grow as the secrets of its beauty and sunny summer and fall weather get out. Because the landscape is so widely varied, each area with its own appeal, here are brief descriptions of the regions presented in this book to help you decide where you want to go. To get the whole story, read the more detailed introductions to each chapter, then delve into the material that interests you most. We begin in Washington, head to Oregon, then up to cover British Columbia.

Seattle offers a comfortable mix of cultural sophistication and natural ruggedness. The clustered spires of its expanding skyline hint at the growth in this busy seaport, the shipping and transportation hub of the Northwest. Nearby communities stretched along the **Southern Sound**, including Tacoma, Olympia (the state's capital) and the Kitsap Peninsula, are also covered.

The **Northern Sound & the San Juans**, regarded in this book as the coastal area stretched between Seattle and Blaine on the Canadian border, is completely enchanting, from sea-swept island chains to pastoral coastline. The entire region is punctuated by rich farming tracts, picturesque, forest-covered islands, quaint fishing villages and a shoreline of sloughs and estuaries. The arts are strong in the region, perhaps because of the preponderance of artists drawn by its natural beauty to live here.

American Indians were the first people to discover the beauty and bounty of the **Olympic Peninsula & Washington Coast**, with lush rainforests, stretches of driftwood-cluttered beach, tumbling rivers and snow-capped mountains. Several tribes still live in the area on the outskirts of the massive Olympic National Park alongside fishing villages such as Sequim and Port Angeles and the Victorian-style logging town of Port Townsend.

National parks, forests and wildernesses, including the North Cascades, Snoqualmie and Wenatchee national forests, Mt. Rainier National Park and the Mt. St. Helens National Volcanic Monument, make up the bulk of the spectacular **Washington Cascades**. Fascinating Leavenworth, a Bavarian-style village, and several small resort towns are also important features here.

The majestic Cascade Range parallels the West Coast running through Oregon and Washington and up to British Columbia. Once past the slopes, you'll find sagebrush-filled high desert country with shoot-'em-up Western towns and quiet Indian reservations scattered through Washington and Oregon in the **East of the Cascades** zone. Commercial Spokane, pastoral Yakima and industrial Pendleton (home of the famous Pendleton Wools) are also described in this section.

Bounded by an evergreen forest, productive greenbelt and the mighty Columbia River, **Portland & the Columbia River Gorge** remain as close to nature as a growing metropolis can be. Portland, the "City of Roses," reflects a pleasant mix of historic buildings decorated in glazed terra cotta and modern structures of smoked glass and brushed steel. These buildings lie in the downtown core intersected by the Willamette River and numerous parks. The sense of hustling enterprise falls away as you head east into Columbia River Gorge National Recreation Area, a particularly scenic 80-mile stretch of the Columbia River. Here you'll find gorgeous natural scenery such as Multnomah Falls and Beacon Rock; the charming town of Hood River, the Windsurfing Capital of the World; and The Dalles, a historically important town at the end of the gorge with an excellent museum.

The awe-inspiring beauty of the **Oregon Coast** includes 400 miles of rugged coastline dotted by small, artsy communities such as Yachats and Bandon and larger fishing villages such as Astoria, Newport and Coos Bay, all connected by Route 101, one of the most beautiful drives in the nation. Foresight on the part of the state legislature preserved the coast from crass commercial corruption, so great stretches remain untouched and entirely natural.

The **Oregon Cascades** hold a bevy of treasures including world-famous rivers like the Rogue and the Umpqua (fishing haunt of Zane Grey), the Mt. Hood and Mt. Bachelor ski resorts and the sapphire splendor of Crater Lake, the deepest lake in the country. As with the Washington Cascades, it is a region of national forests and wildernesses.

Cradled between the Coastal and Cascade mountain ranges is the **Heart of Oregon**, a pastoral valley of historic stage stops, gold-mining boomtowns and small farming communities. Sheep-covered meadows, cloud-shrouded bluffs and striped pastures line Route 5, the primary artery traversing the valley. Salem, the state capital, Eugene, home of the University of Oregon, and Ashland, site of the celebrated Shakespeare Festival, are included in this section.

Stretched above Washington and the United States border, British Columbia boasts delights that are hard to match. Extraordinary natural beauty surrounds **Vancouver & the Sunshine Coast**, seen in the caressing Pacific, soaring, protective mountains and vast tracts of forest. Bustling Vancouver sparkles and excites, with more than enough sightseeing, shopping, dining and entertainment opportunities to please one and all. The scenic Sunshine Coast entices with a broad range of recreational opportunities including hiking, biking, boating, camping, diving and fishing. The glacier-covered peaks of Garibaldi Provincial Park and alluring Whistler resort round out the territory.

Visitors to **Victoria & Vancouver Island** will find civility, gentility and a bit of pomp surrounded by one of the greatest outdoor vacation destinations around. Managing to retain the stately air of the British Empire outpost it once was, charming Victoria, the capital of British Columbia, rests at the southernmost tip of the island. Few roads connect the scattered seaport settlements and rugged provincial parks strewn across the remainder of the island, which is rather wild and wooly.

WHEN TO GO

SEASONS

The Pacific Northwest isn't the rain-soaked, snow-covered tundra many imagine it to be. In fact, summer and fall days (June through September) are generally warm, dry and sunny. Overall temperatures range from the mid-30s in winter to the upper 80s in summer, except east of the Cascade range, where summer temperatures average in the mid-90s. There are distinct seasons in each of the primary zones, and the climate varies greatly with local topography.

The enormous mountain ranges play a major role in the weather, protecting most areas from the heavy rains generated over the Pacific and dumped on the coastline. Mountaintops are often covered in snow year-round at higher elevations, while the valleys, home to most of the cities, remain snow-free but wet during the winter months. East of the mountain ranges are temperature extremes and a distinct lack of rain. Travelers spend time at the rivers, lakes and streams during the hot, dry summers and frolic in the snow during the winter.

The mountainous zones are a bit rainy in spring but warm and dry in summer, when crowds file in for camping, hiking and other outdoor delights. Fall brings auto traffic attracted by the changing seasonal colors, while winter means snow at higher elevations, providing the perfect playground for cold-weather sports.

The coastal region is generally soggy and overcast during the mild winter and early spring, making this the low season for tourism. However, winter is high season among Northwesterners drawn to the coast to watch the fantastic storms that blow in across the Pacific. Be forewarned that these coastal mountain roads can be treacherous, especially in winter. When driving in snowpacked conditions, let someone know your itinerary and stick to it. Travel early in the day and keep simple signaling devices such as mirrors and whistles in the car. Summer offers easier travel and is typically warm and dry in the coastal valleys and along the crisp, windy coast, making it the prime season for travelers. And visitors *do* show up in droves, clogging smaller highways with recreational vehicles.

CALENDAR OF EVENTS

Festivals and events are a big part of life in the Northwest, especially when the rains disappear and everyone is ready to spend time outdoors enjoying the sunshine. Larger cities throughout the region average at least one major event per weekend during the summer and early fall. Below is a sampling of some of the biggest attractions. Check with local chambers of commerce (listed in the regional chapters of this book) to see what will be going on when you are in the area.

JANUARY

East of the Cascades   In addition to catching a dog-sled ride, you'll hear carillon bells and perhaps munch wiener schnitzel at the **Bavarian Ice Fest** in Leavenworth.

Vancouver & the Sunshine Coast   A quick plunge into frigid English Bay during the **Polar Bear Swim** on New Year's Day is said to bring good luck throughout the year.

FEBRUARY

Seattle & the Southern Sound   The **Seattle Print Fair** offers the chance to see and buy rare prints. The **Lunar New Year Celebration** is a day-long community event, with crafts, music, food and live entertainment. **Wintergrass** in Tacoma features bluegrass music and a street dance. Authors of all ethnicities converge for the **Rainbow Bookfest**, a literary extravaganza showcasing readings, book displays and fun children and teen areas celebrating writers of all backgrounds.

Olympic Peninsula & Washington Coast   The **Seafood and Wine Fest** in Newport, the oldest and largest wine fest in the Northwest, promises plenty of seafood, wine and live entertainment.

Oregon Coast   Munch crustaceans to your heart's content at the annual **Crab Feed** in Charleston.

Vancouver & the Sunshine Coast   **Chinese New Year** lights up Vancouver's Chinatown with fireworks, food and a boisterous dragon parade.

MARCH

Seattle & the Southern Sound   **St. Patrick's Day** is celebrated by the Irish Heritage Club with a parade, film festivals, lectures and music.

Washington Cascades   There are world-class aerial ski jumpers and snowboarders, snow castle and sculpture competitions, workshops, races and fireworks at the **White Pass Winter Carnival**.

Portland & the Columbia River Gorge   Collectors flock to the Portland Expo Center for **America's Largest Antique & Collectible Show**, where over seven acres of goods are on display.

Oregon Coast   Events in Lincoln City and all along the coast celebrate the northward migration of gray whales during **Spring Whale Watch Week**.

Victoria & Vancouver Island   The **Pacific Rim Whale Festival** in Ucluelet and Tofino showcases local marine art, dancing and a parade.

APRIL

Seattle & the Southern Sound   Enjoy some of the first blossoms of spring at the **Daffodil Festival Grand Floral Parade**, which passes through Tacoma, Puyallup and nearby communities.

The Northern Sound & the San Juans   If you'd rather catch those early-spring colors in all their natural glory, queue up for the drive through the rich farmlands of La Conner and Mount Vernon during the **Skagit Valley Tulip Festival**.

Washington Cascades Enjoy over 40 different apple-oriented events during the **Washington State Apple Blossom Festival** held in Wenatchee.

Portland & the Columbia River Gorge Delicate pink-and-white apple blossoms of the area orchards steal the show during the **Hood River Blossom Festival**.

Victoria & Vancouver Island There's a lot of toe-tapping going on as top entertainers perform at the **Hot Jazz Jubilee** in Victoria.

MAY

Seattle & the Southern Sound Bring your umbrella to watch contestants lure gulls in Port Orchard's **Seagull Calling Festival**. Running into June, the **Seattle International Film Festival** showcases a huge variety of screenings, lectures and programs about cinema. Live music and a beer garden are featured at the **Pike Place Market Festival**.

The Northern Sound & the San Juans A salmon barbecue is held in conjunction with the 85-mile **Ski-To-Sea Relay Race** between Mt. Baker and Bellingham.

East of the Cascades The ten-day **Spokane Lilac Festival** features a carnival, bed race, torchlight parade, food booths and more. There's also a **Hot Air Balloon Stampede** with over 50 balloons in Walla Walla. The **Maifest** in Leavenworth celebrates spring with Bavarian maypole dancing, a grand march and oompah bands.

Heart of Oregon A hydroplane boat race, waterskiing show and parade are part of the fun at **Boatnik** in Grants Pass.

Vancouver & the Sunshine Coast Vancouver International Children's Fest, with food and festivities geared to please the little ones, takes place in Vancouver.

Victoria & Vancouver Island Victoria Day is the big event of the season, topped off by a grand parade in mid-May.

JUNE

Seattle & the Southern Sound You'll enjoy hearty servings of strawberry shortcake and performances by dancers, magicians and bands at the **Strawberry Festival** in Marysville.

Olympic Peninsula & Washington Coast Booths sell sausage, doughnuts, ice cream, baskets and dolls made of garlic at the **Northwest Garlic Festival** in Ocean Park (Long Beach Peninsula).

Portland & the Columbia River Gorge Portland's biggest festival of the year, the **Rose Festival** is a month-long celebration with parties, pageants and a "Grand Floral Parade" second only to California's Rose Parade.

Oregon Coast Participants from around the globe come to create a world of perishable marvels at the **Cannon Beach Sandcastle Contest**, ranked one of the top competitions in the world. The **Astoria Scandinavian Festival** celebrates the area's heritage. The **Summer Kite Festival**

takes off in Lincoln City, the "Kite Capital of the World" with demonstrations and activities.

Oregon Cascades   The High Cascades play host to the **Sisters Rodeo** in Sisters.

Heart of Oregon   Outstanding jazz, bluegrass and gospel performances, as well as classical concerts, mark the month-long **Oregon Bach Festival** at the University of Oregon in Eugene. A similarly outstanding event is the **Peter Britt Music Festival** near Medford that features an array of music, dance and theatrical performances and runs through early September.

Vancouver & the Sunshine Coast   Vancouver pulls out all the stops in June with the colorful **Dragon Boat Festival** on False Creek and the ten-day **International Jazz Festival** with performances by world-class musicians. Vancouver's Granville Island hosts the **Vancouver New Play Festival**, which features experimental productions and new plays by Canadian playwrights.

Victoria & Vancouver Island   Not to be outdone, Victoria has its fair share of summer events in June, including the **Oak Bay Tea Party** and the **Jazz Fest**.

JULY
Seattle & the Southern Sound   Get ready for alder-smoked salmon and live music at the **Ballard SeafoodFest**. Northwest talent is showcased in Bellevue at the **Bellevue Festival of the Arts**, host to over 300 artists, craftspeople and performers. Scottish roots are celebrated with pipe bands, athletic events and food at the **Pacific Northwest Highland Games and Clan Gathering**.

East of the Cascades   The **Sweet Onion Festival** is a celebration of Walla Walla's famous produce, with food booths, arts and crafts and onion contests. Cowboys and Indians turn out in force to take part in the rodeo and American Indian exhibition that are the centerpieces of the **Chief Joseph Days** in Joseph, Oregon.

Portland & the Columbia River Gorge   The **Robin Hood Festival** in Sherwood hosts a parade, live music and—what else?—an archery competition.

Oregon Coast   Coos Bay, North Bend and surrounding towns join forces to present the **Oregon Coast Music Festival**.

Heart of Oregon   The **International Pinot Noir Celebration** attracts top winemakers from around the world to McMinnville.

Vancouver & the Sunshine Coast   The first of the month brings **Canada Day Celebrations**, which take place throughout the country. The Sunshine Coast pulls out all the stops during July with the **Sea Cavalcade** in Gibsons, both good, old-fashioned fairs with booths, games, competitions and parades.

AUGUST
The Northern Sound & the San Juans   Many of the Northwest's finest artists display their work at top local shows like the **Coupeville**

Arts and Crafts Festival on Whidbey Island. Friday Harbor is the site of the **San Juan County Fair**, with arts and crafts, agricultural and animal exhibits, a carnival and food booths featuring the bounty of the islands.

Olympic Peninsula & Washington Coast Canoe races, traditional dancing and a street fair are just part of **Makah Days**, the largest American Indian celebration in Washington. World champions descend on Long Beach to compete in the **Washington State International Kite Festival**.

East of the Cascades The **Steens Rim Ten-Kilometer Run** is followed by live music, kids' activities, food and fun at the **Frenchglen Jamboree**, both in Frenchglen, Oregon.

Portland & the Columbia River Gorge The renowned **Mt. Hood Festival of Jazz** in Gresham is an eagerly awaited weekend of big-name musicians performing in the great outdoors.

Oregon Coast Fresh blackberries and quality arts and crafts draw large crowds to the **Annual Blackberry Arts Festival** held in Coos Bay.

Heart of Oregon A carnival, agriculture and craft exhibits, lots of entertainment and plenty of junk food await at Salem's **Oregon State Fair**, which spills over into September. Junction City's Danish roots are celebrated during the **Scandinavian Festival** with folk dancing, food and crafts.

Vancouver & the Sunshine Coast The **Fair at Pacific National Exhibition**, a massive agricultural and industrial festival with everything from top-name entertainment to lumberjack contests, happens from mid-August through Labor Day in Vancouver. The Sunshine Coast also puts on **Roberts Creek Daze**, a fun-filled fair with games and booths.

Victoria & Vancouver Island The **Canadian Open Sand Sculpting Competition** takes the spotlight in Parksville.

SEPTEMBER

Seattle & the Southern Sound **Bumbershoot** brings music, plays, art exhibits and crafts to Seattle Center. "Do the Puyallup" is the catch phrase of the **Puyallup Fair**, one of the country's largest agricultural fairs. Olympia Harbor Days, one of the largest arts-and-crafts fairs in the Northwest, also offers a fascinating tugboat race.

Olympic Peninsula & Washington Coast Many of Port Townsend's grand Victorian homes are open to the public during the town's **Historic Homes Tour**.

East of the Cascades Bronco busting awaits at the **Ellensburg Rodeo**, ranked among the top 25 rodeos in the nation. Tour the *biergarten* and German food circus at the **Odessa Deutschesfest**. See prize-winning livestock, produce and crafts, nibble cotton candy and enjoy a ride or two at the **Central Washington State Fair** in Yakima. In Oregon, the main event is the **Pendleton Round-Up**, a major rodeo along with a historical parade of covered wagons and buggies and a pageant of American Indian culture. Leavenworth is ablaze during the **Washington State Autumn Leaf Festival**, complete with oompah bands and Bavarian costumes.

Portland & the Columbia River Gorge   Portland's **Art in the Pearl** shakes up the city with dance, music, visual-art displays and theater performances.

Oregon Coast   Vast quantities of salmon are slow-baked over an open fir-and-alderwood fire at the **Indian Style Salmon Bake** in Depoe Bay. The Bandon Cranberry Festival in Bandon celebrates the autumn harvest with a cranberry foods fair, crafts and a parade.

Vancouver & the Sunshine Coast   Alternative performance arts take center stage during the **Vancouver Fringe Festival**.

Victoria & Vancouver Island   On Labor Day weekend there's a flotilla of pre-1955 wooden boats in the **Classic Boat Festival** in Victoria's Inner Harbour. Salmon is king at the **Salmon Festival** in Port Alberni.

OCTOBER
Seattle & the Southern Sound   The **Issaquah Salmon Days Festival** features a salmon bake, races, live entertainment, arts and crafts, and a parade.

Olympic Peninsula & Washington Coast   There's plenty of seafood and entertainment along with a shucking contest at the **Oyster Fest** in Shelton.

Vancouver & the Sunshine Coast   Celluloid delights brought from around the world are the focus of the **Vancouver International Film Festival. Oktoberfest** brews and oompah bands seem right at home in Whistler's Bavarian-style village.

NOVEMBER
Oregon Coast   Artists, musicians, writers and craftspeople gather for the **Stormy Weather Arts Festival** in Cannon Beach.

Vancouver & the Sunshine Coast   **Cornucopia**, Whistler's wine and food celebration, features wine workshops, tastings, gourmet food events and live jazz.

Victoria & Vancouver Island   Boat tours of local oyster farms, a costume ball and lots of oyster-inspired cuisine highlight Tofino's **Clayoquot Oyster Festival**.

DECEMBER
Seattle & the Southern Sound   **Zoolights** lends a festive spirit to Tacoma's famous Point Defiance Zoo & Aquarium from late December through early January. Seattle Center is all decked out with an iceskating rink, Christmas train display and a few arts-and-crafts booths during **Winterfest**, which runs through New Year's Eve.

East of the Cascades   The Bavarian village of Leavenworth looks like a scenic Christmas card during the **Christmas Lighting Festival**.

Heart of Oregon   Roseburg celebrates the holiday season with its **Umpqua Valley Festival of Lights**, which features Christmas lights formed into a variety of shapes, from Santa Claus to dragons.

Vancouver & the Sunshine Coast   On December 31st there's the alcohol-free **First Night**, a New Year's Eve bash with entertainment on the village square at Whistler.

Victoria & Vancouver Island   **Butchart Gardens** puts on the holiday finery with Christmas light displays throughout the month.

BEFORE YOU GO

VISITORS CENTERS

WASHINGTON STATE TOURISM ✉ *P.O. Box 42525, Olympia, WA 98504-2525* ✆ *800-544-1800* ✑ *www.experiencewashington.com, tourism@ctcb.wa.gov* Log onto the state tourism website for information on Washington.

OREGON TOURISM COMMISSION ✉ *670 Hawthorne Avenue SE, Suite 204, Salem, OR 97301* ✆ *800-547-7842* ✑ *www.traveloregon.com Travel Oregon Magazine* is available free of charge from the state tourism commission.

TOURISM BRITISH COLUMBIA ✉ *P.O. Box 9830, Station Provincial Government, Victoria, BC V8W 9W5* ✆ *800-435-5622* ✑ *www.hellobc.com* This office has travel information and reservation services.

Both large cities and small towns throughout the region have chambers of commerce or visitor information centers; a number of them are listed in *Hidden Pacific Northwest* in the appropriate chapter.

WELCOME CENTERS   For visitors arriving by automobile, Washington and Oregon provide numerous Welcome Centers at key points along the major highways where visitors can pull off for a stretch, grab a cup of coffee or juice and receive plenty of advice on what to see and do in the area. The centers are clearly marked and are usually open during daylight hours throughout the spring, summer and fall.

PACKING

Comfortable and casual are the norm for dress in the Northwest. You will want something dressier if you plan to catch a show, indulge in afternoon tea or spend your evenings in posh restaurants and clubs, but for the most part your topsiders and slacks are acceptable garb everywhere else.

Layers of clothing are your best bet since the weather changes so drastically depending on which part of the region you are visiting; shorts will be perfectly comfortable during the daytime in the hot, arid interior, but once you pass over the mountains and head for the coastline, you'll appreciate having packed a jacket to protect you from the nippy ocean breezes and damp chill, even on the warmest of days.

Wherever you're headed, during the summer bring some long-sleeve shirts, pants and lightweight sweaters and jackets along with your shorts, T-shirts and bathing suit; the evenings can be quite crisp. Bring along those warmer clothes—pants, sweaters, jackets, hats and gloves—in spring and fall, too, since days may be warm but it's rather chilly after sundown. Winter calls for thick sweaters, knitted hats, down jackets and snug ski clothes. Also remember that the maximum amount of liquid permitted in carry-on luggage is 3 oz. per container; all liquids must be sealed in a quart-sized Ziploc bag.

It's not a bad idea to call ahead to check on weather conditions. Sturdy, comfortable walking shoes are a must for sightseeing. If you plan to explore tidal pools or go for long walks on the beach, bring a pair of lightweight canvas sneakers or waterproof river sandals that you don't mind getting wet.

Scuba divers will probably want to bring their own gear, though rentals are generally available in all popular dive areas. Many places also rent tubes for river floats and sailboards for windsurfing. Fishing gear is often available for rent as well. Campers will need to bring their own basic equipment.

Don't forget your camera for capturing the Pacific Northwest's glorious scenery and a pair of binoculars for watching the abundant wildlife that live here. Note that if you're arriving by plane and you're not using a digital camera you'll want to buy your film once you arrive in the Pacific Northwest and have it developed before you leave to prevent x-ray damage. Never carry undeveloped film in your checked luggage. Pack an umbrella and raincoat, just in case, and by all means don't forget your copy of *Hidden Pacific Northwest*!

LODGING

Lodging in the Northwest runs the gamut, from rustic cabins in the woods to sprawling resorts on the coastline. Chain motels line most major thoroughfares and mom-and-pop enterprises still vie successfully for lodgers in every region. Large hotels with names you'd know anywhere appear in most centers of any size.

Bed and breakfasts, small inns and cozy lodges where you can have breakfast with the handful of other guests are appearing throughout the region as these more personable forms of accommodation continue to grow in popularity. In fact, in areas like Ashland in southern Oregon and the San Juans in Washington, they are the norm rather than hotels and motels.

Whatever your preference and budget, you can probably find something to suit your taste with the help of the regional chapters in this book. Remember, rooms are scarce and prices rise in the high season, which is generally summer along the coastline and winter in the mountain ranges. Off-season rates are often drastically reduced in many places. Whatever you do, plan ahead and make reservations, especially in the prime tourist seasons.

Accommodations in this book are organized by region and classified by price. Rates referred to are for two people during high season, so if you are looking for low-season bargains, it's good to inquire. *Budget* ($) lodgings are generally less than $90 per night and are satisfactory and clean but modest. *Moderate*-priced ($$) lodgings run from $90 to $150; what they have to offer in the way of luxury will depend on where they are located, but they often offer larger rooms and more attractive surroundings. At a *deluxe* ($$$) hotel or resort you can expect to spend between $150 and $300 for a homey bed and breakfast or a double; you'll usually find spacious rooms, a fashionable lobby, a restaurant and a group of shops. *Ultra-deluxe* ($$$$) properties, priced above $300, are a region's finest, offering all the amenities of a deluxe hotel plus plenty of extras.

Whether you crave a room facing the surf or one looking out on the ski slopes, be sure to specify when making reservations. If you are trying to save money, keep in mind that lodgings a block or so from the waterfront or a mile or so from the ski lift are going to offer lower rates than those right on top of the area's major attractions.

DINING

Seafood is a staple in the Pacific Northwest, especially along the coast where salmon is king. Whether it's poached in herbs, glazed in teriyaki sauce, or grilled on a red-cedar plank, Indian-style, plan to treat yourself to this regional specialty often. While each area has its own favorite dishes, its ethnic influences and gourmet spots, Northwest cuisine as a whole tends to be hearty and is often crafted around organically grown local produce.

Within a particular chapter, restaurants are categorized geographically, with each entry describing the type of cuisine, general decor and price range. Lunch and dinner are served, except where noted. Dinner entrées at *budget* ($) restaurants usually cost under $10. The ambience is informal, service usually speedy and the crowd a local one. *Moderate* priced ($$) restaurants range between $10 and $20 at dinner; surroundings are casual but pleasant, the menu offers more variety and the pace is usually slower. *Deluxe* ($$$) establishments tab their entrées from $20 to $30; cuisines may be simple or sophisticated, depending on the location, but the decor is plusher and the service more personalized. *Ultra-deluxe* ($$$$) dining rooms, where entrées begin at $30, are often gourmet places where the cooking and service have become an art form.

Some restaurants change hands often while others are closed in low seasons. Efforts have been made to include in this book places with established reputations for good eating. Breakfast and lunch menus vary less in price from restaurant to restaurant than evening dinners. If you are dining on a budget and still hope to experience the best of the bunch, visit at lunch when portions and prices are reduced.

TRAVELING WITH CHILDREN

The Pacific Northwest is a wonderful place to bring the kids. Besides the many museums, boutiques and festivals, the region also has hundreds of beaches and parks, and many nature sanctuaries sponsor children's activities, especially during the summer months. A few guidelines will help make travel with children a pleasure.

Many Northwest bed and breakfasts do not accept children, so be sure of the policy when you make reservations. If you need a crib or cot, arrange for it ahead of time. A travel agent can be of help here, as well as with most other travel plans.

If you're traveling by air, try to reserve bulkhead seats where there is plenty of room. Take along extras you may need, such as diapers, changes of clothing, snacks, toys and books. When traveling by car, be sure to carry the extras, along with plenty of juice and water. And always allow extra time for getting places, especially on rural roads. Also note that child restraint laws vary from state to state. In Oregon, children weighing less than 40 pounds must be in a car seat; children weighing more than 40 pounds and who are less than 4'9" tall must be in a booster seat. In Washington, children under 7 years old and less than 4'9" tall must be in a child restraint; those under 12 years old must be in the back seat if possible. In British Colombia, children under 40 pounds must ride in a booster seat unless than are 9 years old or taller than 4'9".

A first-aid kit is a must for any trip. Along with adhesive bandages, antiseptic cream and something to stop itching, include any medicines your pediatrician might recommend to treat allergies, colds, diarrhea or any chronic problems your child may have.

When spending time at the beach or on the snow, take extra care the first few days. Children's skin is especially sensitive to sun, and severe sunburn can happen before you realize it, even on overcast days. Hats for the kids are a good idea, along with liberal applications of sunblock. Be sure to keep a constant eye on children who are near the water or on the slopes, and never leave children unattended in a car on a hot day.

Even the smallest towns usually have stores that carry diapers, baby food, snacks and other essentials, but these may close early in the evening. Larger urban areas usually have all-night grocery or convenience stores that stock these necessities.

Many towns, parks and attractions offer special activities designed for children. Consult local newspapers and/or call the numbers and check the websites in this guide to see what's happening where you're going.

WOMEN TRAVELING ALONE

Traveling solo grants an independence and freedom different from that of traveling with a partner, but single travelers are more vulnerable to crime and must take additional precautions.

It's unwise to hitchhike and probably best to avoid inexpensive accommodations on the outskirts of town; the money saved does not outweigh the risk. Bed and breakfasts, youth hostels and YWCAs are generally your safest bet for lodging, and they also foster an environment ideal for bonding with fellow travelers.

Keep all valuables well-hidden and clutch cameras and purses tightly. Avoid late-night treks or strolls through undesirable parts of town, but if you find yourself in this situation, continue walking with a confident air until you reach a safe haven. A fierce scowl never hurts.

These hints should by no means deter you from seeking out adventure. Wherever you go, stay alert, use your common sense and trust your instincts. If you are hassled or threatened in some way, never be afraid to yell for assistance. It's also a good idea to carry change for a phone call, or better yet, carry a cell phone, and know a number to call in case of emergency.

For more helpful hints, get a copy of *Safety and Security for Women Who Travel* (Travelers' Tales).

Women alone will usually feel safer in more conservative British Columbia, especially in the well-populated areas, but Vancouver and Victoria are major havens for drug addicts, so be cautious and stay alert in downtown areas. However, it's a good idea to remain cautious just the same.

Most major cities have hotlines for victims of rape and violent crime. In case of emergency in Seattle, contact **King County Sexual Resource Center** (P.O. Box 300, Renton, WA 98057; 24-hour crisis line 888-998-6423; www.kcsarc.org). In Portland contact the **Portland Women's Crisis Line** (503-235-5333, 888-235-5333; www.pwcl.org). The **Sexual Assault Support Services** offers assistance in Eugene (541-484-9791, 541-343-7277 [24-hour crisis line], 800-788-4727; www.sass-lane.org).

GAY & LESBIAN TRAVELERS

Information hotlines and social and support groups for gay and lesbians exist in several of the Northwest's larger cities and towns.

GAY CITY HEALTH PROJECT ☎206-860-6969, 206-461-3222 (24-hour crisis hotline) ⬦www.gaycity.org, info@gaycity.org Information on gay services and events in the Seattle area can be obtained from this organization, which also has an emergency crisis hotline.

PFLAG INFORMATION REFERRAL LINE ☎509-489-2266 ⬦www.pflagspokane.org, info@pflagspokane.org PFLAG offers support and information in Spokane.

GAY MARRIAGE ⬦www.gayvancouver.net/marriage.htm Same-sex marriages have been legal in British Columbia since 2003 and more recently have been legalized throughout Canada. You don't have to be a Canadian resident. In fact, more than half of the same-sex weddings in British Columbia to date have been between U.S. citizens. Marriage licenses are issued by private firms, often insurance agencies; there are nine authorized marriage license issuers each in Vancouver and Victoria, and at least one in most other towns. Civil ceremonies are performed by official marriage commissioners. A list of gay-friendly marriage commissioners is available at the above website. Curiously enough, Canadian divorce laws are limited to "marriage between a man and a woman," so technically at least, gay divorces are not allowed, though at least one judge in British Columbia has recently ruled otherwise.

SENIOR TRAVELERS

The Pacific Northwest is a hospitable place for senior citizens to visit, especially during the cool, sunny summer months that offer respite from hotter climes elsewhere in the country. Countless museums, historic sights and even restaurants and hotels offer senior discounts that can cut a substantial chunk off vacation costs. The large number of national parks and monuments in the region means that persons age 62 and older can save considerable money with an America the Beautiful–National Parks and Federal Lands Senior Pass, which allows free admission for the pass holder plus all passengers in a non-commercial vehicle (or three additional adults at per-person entrances). Apply for one in person at any national park unit that charges an entrance fee. Many private sightseeing attractions also offer significant discounts for seniors.

AMERICAN ASSOCIATION OF RETIRED PERSONS (AARP) ✉*601 E Street Northwest, Washington, DC 20049* 📞*800-424-3410* ✐*www.aarp.org, member@aarp.com* AARP offers membership to anyone age 50 or over. Check their website for member discounts and escorted tours.

ELDERHOSTEL ✉*11 Avenue de Lafayette, Boston, MA 02111* 📞*800-454-5768* ✐*www.elderhostel.org* This company offers reasonably priced, all-inclusive educational programs in a variety of Pacific Northwest locations throughout the year.

Be extra careful about health matters. In addition to the medications you ordinarily use, it's a good idea to bring along the prescriptions for obtaining more. Consider carrying a medical record with you—including your medical history and current medical status, as well as your doctor's name, phone number and address. Make sure your insurance covers you while you are away from home.

DISABLED TRAVELERS

Oregon, Washington and British Columbia are striving to make more destinations accessible for travelers with disabilities.

INDEPENDENT LIVING RESOURCES ✉*2410 Southeast 11th Avenue, Portland, OR 97214* 📞*503-232-7411 (ask for Kathe Coleman)* 📠*503-232-7480* ✐*www.ilr.org, info@ilr.org* For information on the areas you will be visiting, contact this organization.

TOURISM BRITISH COLUMBIA ✉*P.O. Box 9830, Station Provincial Government, Victoria, BC V8W 9W5* 📞*800-435-5622* ✐*www.hellobc.com* For more specific advice on traveling in the Pacific Northwest, turn to *B.C. Accommodations*, available from the tourism office, which lists many wheelchair-accessible lodgings in British Columbia.

SOCIETY FOR ACCESSIBLE TRAVEL & HOSPITALITY ✉*347 5th Avenue, Suite 605, New York, NY 10016* 📞*212-447-7284* ✐*www.sath.org, sath travel@aol.com* SATH has general information regarding traveling with disabilities.

MOBILITY INTERNATIONAL USA ✉P.O. Box 10767, Eugene, OR 97440
📞541-343-1284 💻www.miusa.org This organization provides more information and services for international exchange travel programs.

FLYING WHEELS TRAVEL ✉143 West Bridge Street, Owatonna, MN 55060
📞507-541-5005, 877-451-5006 💻www.flyingwheelstravel.com Flying Wheels is a travel agency specifically for disabled people.

FOREIGN TRAVELERS

PASSPORTS AND VISAS Entry into Canada and the U.S. calls for a valid passport, visa or visitor permit for all foreign visitors. U.S. visitors are not technically required to show a U.S. passport to gain entry to Canada—proof of citizenship (voter's registration, birth certificate, driver's license), including two pieces of photo identification, are all that's required—and may visit without a visa for up to 180 days. However, since 2007, tighter U.S. Department of Homeland Security regulations now mandate that all those traveling to the U.S. by air, land or sea (including ferries) must show a valid passport to enter or reenter the U.S. So, in a nutshell, everyone, including U.S. citizens, should now carry a valid passport at all times if they plan on visiting British Columbia and returning to the U.S. Because one of Washington's 18 daily San Juan Islands ferry sailings also goes to Vancouver Island, B.C., Homeland Security requires all passengers returning from the San Juans to Anacortes to show their passports, including U.S. citizens who have not left the U.S. at all.

CUSTOMS REQUIREMENTS Foreign travelers are allowed to bring in the following: 200 cigarettes (1 carton), 50 cigars or 2 kilograms (4.4 pounds) of smoking tobacco; one liter of alcohol for personal use only (you must be at least 21 years of age to bring in alcohol); and US$100 worth of duty-free gifts that can include an additional quantity of 100 cigars (except Cuban). In carry-on luggage, all containers with liquids must be enclosed in a one-quart Ziploc bag and the maximum amount of liquid permitted in each container is 3 oz. You may bring in any amount of currency (amounts over US$10,000 require a form). Americans who have been in Canada over 48 hours may take out $400 worth of duty-free items ($25 worth of duty-free for visits under 48 hours). Carry any prescription drugs in clearly marked containers; you may have to provide a written prescription or doctor's statement to clear customs. Meat or meat products, seeds, plants, fruits and narcotics are not allowed to be brought into the United States. The same applies to Canada, with the addition of firearms.

DRIVING If you plan to rent a car, an international driver's license should be obtained prior to arrival. United States driver's licenses are valid in Canada and vice versa. Some rental car companies require both a foreign license and an international driver's license along with a major credit card and require that the lessee be at least 25 years of age. In Washington, laws restrict drivers from using a hand-held cell phone or text-messaging while driving. Seat belts are mandatory for the driver and all passengers. Note that child restraint laws vary from state to state. See "Traveling with Children" for more information.

CURRENCY   American and Canadian money are based on the dollar. Bills in the United States come in six denominations: $1, $5, $10, $20, $50 and $100. Every dollar is divided into 100 cents; in Canada the $1 coin is generally used. Coins are the penny (1 cent), nickel (5 cents), dime (10 cents) and quarter (25 cents). The exchange rate between U.S. and Canadian dollars has traditionally been quite stable at about US$1 = Can$0.80. But beginning with the two countries' economic crises in late 2008, the exchange rate has fluctuated dramatically, sometimes changing by as much as 20 percent in a matter of weeks. If you're planning to spend more than a couple of days north of the border, it can pay to keep an eye on the daily rate. Half-dollar and dollar coins are used infrequently. (Incidentally, Canada's $1 coin, which bears the image of a loon, is called a "loonie"; there's also a $2 coin, sometimes called a "toonie.") You may not use foreign currency to purchase goods and services in the United States and Canada. Consider buying traveler's checks in dollar amounts. You may also use credit cards affiliated with an American company such as Interbank, Barclay Card, VISA and American Express. Bank debit cards issued in the U.S. will work in ATMs at Canadian banks, dispensing the requested amount in loonies and charging your account in U.S. dollars at the prevailing exchange rate. However, the nonbank ATMs found in many Canadian hotel lobbies, gas stations, casinos and such will not accept debit cards from the U.S.

ELECTRICITY AND ELECTRONICS   Electric outlets use currents of 110 volts, 60 cycles. For appliances made for other electrical systems, you need a transformer or adapter. Travelers who use laptop computers for telecommunication should be aware that modem configurations for U.S. telephone systems may be different from their European counterparts. Similarly, the U.S. format for videotapes and DVDs is different from that in Europe; U.S. Park Service visitors centers and other stores that sell souvenir videos often have them available in European format.

WEIGHTS AND MEASUREMENTS   The United States uses the English system of weights and measures. American units and their metric equivalents are as follows: 1 inch = 2.5 centimeters; 1 foot = 0.3 meter; 1 yard = 0.9 meter; 1 mile = 1.6 kilometers; 1 ounce = 28 grams; 1 pound = 0.45 kilogram; 1 quart (liquid) = 0.9 liter. British Columbia uses metric measurements.

OUTDOOR ADVENTURES

CAMPING

Parks in the lush Pacific Northwest rank among the top in North America as far as attendance goes, so plan ahead if you hope to do any camping during the busy summer months. Late spring and early fall present fewer crowds to deal with and the weather is still fine.

WASHINGTON STATE PARKS AND RECREATION COMMIS-
SION ✉P.O. Box 42650, Olympia, WA 98504 ☎360-902-8844 (general information), 888-226-7688 (reservations only) ⌕www.parks.wa.gov, infocent@parks.wa.gov Though much of Washington's scenic coastline is privately owned, there are a few scattered parks along the shore and even more situated inland in the mountains. Reservations for campsites in state parks are recommended during the busy summer months; contact the parks and recreation commission for details.

OREGON PARKS AND RECREATION DEPARTMENT ✉725
Summer Street Northeast, Suite C, Salem, OR 97301 ☎503-986-0707, 800-551-6949 ⌕www.oregonstateparks.org You'll find a multitude of marvelous campsites along Oregon's protected coast and in its green mountain ranges. Some of the state parks with campgrounds are open year-round. Reservations are accepted at 28 parks and are essential if you hope to get a spot during July and August; reservations are accepted from two days to nine months in advance. This state department maintains **Reservations Northwest** (800-452-5687) to provide updated campsite availability.

OUTDOOR RECREATION INFORMATION CENTER ✉REI
Building, 222 Yale Avenue North, Seattle, WA 98174 ☎206-470-4060 ⌕www.nps. gov/ccso/oric/htm Contact this office for information on camping in the various national parks and forests in the Puget Sound area. Closed Monday in fall and winter.

B.C. PARKS ✉1610 Mount Seymour Road, North Vancouver, BC V7G 2R9 ☎888-
549-8820 ⌕www.bcparks.ca Many of British Columbia's prime wilderness areas, both marine and interior, are protected as provincial parks. Except for those that are day-use only areas, most parks are set up with some sort of camping facilities, from primitive sites with pit toilets to pull-through recreational vehicle pads (with nearby sani-stations but no electrical, water or sewage hook-ups). There is a minimal fee for use of the campsites available on a first-come, first-served basis year-round. Reservations can be made through **Discover Camping** (604-689-9025, 800-689-9025; www.discovercamping.ca; closed September 16 through March 31). For further information, contact B.C. Parks. Or try the **Outdoor Recreation Council of B.C.** (47 West Broadway, Vancouver, BC V5Y 1P1; 604-873-5546; www.orcbc.ca, outdoorrec@orcbc.ca).

PARKS CANADA ☎905-566-4321, 877-737-3783 ⌕www.pccamping.ca For
information on camping at the Pacific Rim National Park on Vancouver Island's western shore and other national parks in British Columbia, contact this agency.

PERMITS

Wilderness camping is not permitted in the state parks of Oregon and Washington, but there are primitive sites available in most parks. Permits (available at trailheads) are required for wilderness camping in parts of the Alpine Lakes wilderness area of the Mt. Baker–Snoqualmie and Wenatchee national forests in Washington and in the Mt. Jefferson, Mt. Washington and Three Sisters wilderness areas of Oregon between May 15 and October 31; permits are available at the ranger stations.

Campers should check with all other parks individually to see if permits are required.

Follow low-impact camping practices in wilderness areas; "leave only footprints, take only pictures." When backpacking and hiking, stick to marked trails or tread lightly in areas where no trail exists. Be prepared with map and compass since signs are limited to directional information and don't include mileage.

OUTDOOR RECREATION INFORMATION CENTER ✉️*REI Building, 222 Yale Avenue North, Seattle, WA 98174* ☎️*206-470-4060* Some guidelines on wilderness camping are available here. Closed Monday in fall and winter.

B.C. PARKS ✉️*1610 Mount Seymour Road, North Vancouver, BC V7G 2R9* ☎️*604-924-2200* 🖱️*www.bcparks.ca* In British Columbia, wilderness camping is allowed in Garibaldi, Manning, Strathcona and Cape Scott provincial parks. No permit is required, but it's always best to check in with a ranger station to let someone know your plan before heading into the backcountry. B.C. Parks regulations vary from park to park. Check individual park web pages if you plan on staying overnight as building campfires and bringing pets may not be permitted. Contact B.C. Parks for further details.

PARKS CANADA—BRITISH COLUMBIA ✉️*P.O. Box 129, Fort Langley, BC V1M 2RS* ☎️*604-513-4777* 🖱️*www.parcscanada.gc.ca* Wilderness camping is also permitted in British Columbia's national parks. Contact this office for more information.

BOATING

With miles of coastline and island-dotted straits to explore, it's no wonder that boating is one of the most popular activities in the Northwest. Many of the best attractions in the region, including numerous pristine marine parks, are accessible only by water and have facilities set aside for boaters.

WASHINGTON STATE PARKS AND RECREATION COMMISSION ✉️*P.O. Box 42650, Olympia, WA 98504* ☎️*360-902-8844* 🖱️*www.parks.wa.gov, infocent@parks.wa.gov* Write, call or visit this agency's website for a boater's guide to the Evergreen State.

OREGON STATE MARINE BOARD ✉️*P.O. Box 14145, Salem, OR 97309* ☎️*503-378-8587* 🖱️*www.osmb.state.or.us, marine.board@state.or.us* This office will furnish information on boating statewide.

CANADA CUSTOMS ☎️*604-666-5607* 🖱️*www.tc.gc.ca* Boaters heading into B.C. waters from the U.S. must clear customs at the first available port of entry; Canada Customs can provide more information on specific policies.

RIVER RUNNING

Whitewater rafting is one of the best-known adventure activities in the region, with challenging rapids on the Lewis, Snoqualmie and White rivers in Washington, the Rogue, Deschutes and McKenzie in Oregon and the Fraser and Green rivers in British Columbia. If you aren't acquainted with these rivers join a guided trip or chat with outfitters who know the treacherous spots to look out for.

NORTH WEST RAFTERS ASSOCIATION ✐*www.nwrafters.org* This company is a good source for more information.

KAYAKING & CANOEING

Kayaking and canoeing are also popular ways to shoot the rapids. Paddlers ready to take on the open ocean gain access to spectacular places like the various marine parks in British Columbia (Desolation Sound and the Pacific Rim National Park) and Washington (numerous

High Adventure in the Northwest

Whether you're an expert or a novice, a fanatic or simply curious, there's a sport here with your name written on it. Remember, the Pacific Northwest is known as "Evergreen Playground," not "Evergreen Couch Potato." So if what turns you on is dropping through the sky, paddling alongside whales or keeping your feet firmly on the ground, just do it!

For heart-stopping thrills, there's *bungee jumping*. Jumpers strapped into a full-body harness with three to five connecting bungee cords swan dive off a 191-foot-high bridge, the highest commercial bungee bridge in the Western Hemisphere. If this sounds great until you actually eyeball the 20-story drop, **Bungee.com** (P.O. Box 121, Fairview, OR 97024; 503-520-0303; www.bungee.com) will refund the jump fee. Those who make the plunge are awarded membership in the Dangerous Sports Club.

Heli-sports, from skiing untouched powder or blue glaciers to hiking spongy, moss-covered alpine fields, are all the rage in the high reaches of B.C. The copter ride to inaccessible areas is the highlight for many, while others appreciate the ease of having gear packed in for them. **Coast Range Heliskiing** (P.O. Box 16, 1641 Airport Road, Pemberton, BC V0N 2L0; 604-894-1144, 800-701-8744; www.coastrangeheliskiing.com) offers daily tours out of Whistler.

With so many majestic ranges in the Northwest, *mountaineering* abounds. Rock and ice climbing are big draws in both the Cascades and Rocky Mountains. Climbers should be familiar with cold-weather survival techniques before tackling Northwest heights, which are tricky at best. For climbers' guidelines and further information, turn to the **Outdoor Recreation and Information Center** (REI Building, 222 Yale Avenue North, Seattle, WA 98109; 206-470-4060, 800-627-0062 ext 6). The **Outdoor Recreation Council of B.C.** (47 West Broadway, Vancouver, BC 5Y 1P1; 604-873-5546; www.orcbc.ca) also has information. Famous mountaineering clubs like **The Mountaineers** (300 3rd Avenue West, Seattle, WA 98119; 206-284-6310; www.mountaineers.org) in Seattle and the **Mazamas** (909 Northwest 19th Avenue, Portland, OR 97209; 503-227-2345; www.mazamas.org) in Portland conduct classes and lead hiking and climbing trips to Northwest peaks.

protected islands among the San Juans). Other placid bodies of water suitable for kayak and canoe exploration include the Hood Canal in Washington, the Willamette and Columbia rivers in Oregon and the Powell River Canoe Route on British Columbia's Sunshine Coast.

AMERICAN CANOE ASSOCIATION ⊠1340 Central Park Boulevard, Suite 210, Springfield, VA 22401 ✆540-907-4460 ⌂www.acanet.org There are several waterways suitable for extended canoeing and kayaking trips. The ACA can provide more information.

EBB & FLOW PADDLESPORTS LIMITED ⊠0604 Southwest Nebraska Street, Portland, OR 97201 ✆503-245-1756 The folks here can tell you more about the waters and area outfitters.

WINDSURFING

Squeezed between the border of Washington and Oregon, the breezy Columbia Gorge is reputed to be the windsurfing capital of the continent, with championship competitions held annually. English Bay in Vancouver and Washington's San Juan Islands are also popular destinations for the sport, with numerous outfits set up to teach would-be windsurfers or just rent the sailboards and wetsuits.

COLUMBIA GORGE WINDSURFING ASSOCIATION ⊠P.O. Box 182, Hood River, OR 97031 ✆541-386-9225 ⌂www.cgwa.net This group has information on windsurfing opportunities.

UNITED STATES WINDSURFING ASSOCIATION ⌂www.uswind surfing.org This national organization can put you in touch with top schools in the northwest region.

WATER SAFETY

The watery region of the Pacific Northwest offers an incredible array of water sports to choose from, be it on the ocean, a quiet lake or stream or tumbling rapids. Swimming, diving, walking the shore in search of clams or just basking in the sun are options when you get to the shore, lake or river. Shallow lakes, rivers and bays tend to be the most populated spots since they warm up during the height of summer; otherwise, the waters of the Northwest are generally chilly. Whenever you swim, never do so alone, and never take your eyes off of children in or near the water.

FISHING

With its multitude of rivers, streams, lakes and miles of protected coastline, the Pacific Northwest affords some of the best fishing in the world. The waters of British Columbia alone hold 74 known species, 25 of those sportfish. Salmon is the main draw, but each area features special treats for the fishing enthusiast that are described in the individual chapters of *Hidden Pacific Northwest*.

Fees and regulations vary, but licenses are required for salt- and freshwater fishing throughout the region and can be purchased at sporting-

goods stores, bait-and-tackle shops and fishing lodges. You can also
find leads on guides and charter services in these locations if you are interested in trying a kind of fishing that's new to you. Charter fishing is
the most expensive way to go out to sea; party boats take a crowd but
are less expensive and usually great fun. On rivers, lakes and streams,
guides can show you the best place to throw a hook or skim a fly. Whatever your pleasure, in saltwater or fresh, a good guide will save you
time and grief and will increase the likelihood of a full string or a handsome trophy.

WASHINGTON DEPARTMENT OF FISH AND WILDLIFE ✉ *600
Capitol Way North, Olympia, WA 98501-1091* ☎ *360-902-2200* ⌕ *wdfw.wa.gov* For information on fishing in Washington concerning shellfish, bottom fish,
salmon, freshwater and saltwater sportfish, contact this Washington
state department.

OREGON DEPARTMENT OF FISH AND WILDLIFE ✉ *3406 Cherry
Avenue Northeast, Salem, OR 97303* ☎ *503-947-6000, 800-720-6339* ⌕ *www.dfw.state.
or.us* This office can supply information on fishing in Oregon.

FISHERIES BRANCH ✉ *Ministry of Environment, 10470 152nd Street, Surrey,
BC B3R 043* ☎ *604-582-5222* Check here for updated details and regulations
for freshwater fishing in British Columbia.

FISHERIES AND OCEAN CANADA ✉ *Department of Fisheries and
Oceans, 401 Burrard Street, Suite 200, Vancouver, BC V6C 354* ☎ *604-666-5835* ⌕ *www.
dfo-mpo.gc.ca* Try this office for information on saltwater fishing.

SKIING

As winter blankets the major mountain ranges of the Pacific Northwest,
ski season heats up at numerous resorts. Ski enthusiasts head for Mt.
Adams, Mt. Rainier and Mt. Baker in Washington, Mt. Hood, Mt. Bachelor and Mt. Ashland in Oregon and Mt. Seymour, Grouse Mountain
and the Whistler/Blackcomb mountains in southwestern British Columbia. Specifics on the top resorts are listed in each regional chapter.

Cruisin' through the Pacific Northwest

ALASKA SIGHTSEEING CRUISE WEST ✉ *2401 4th Avenue, Suite
700, Seattle, WA 98121* ☎ *800-426-7702* ⌕ *www.cruisewest.com* Nautical adventurers can embark on two week–long cruises through the Northwest offered
by Alaska Sightseeing. The Columbia and Snake Rivers voyage traces Lewis
and Clark's search for the Northwest Passage. Departing from Portland, destinations on this scenic, wildlife-infused journey include Hells Canyon in Idaho,
Washington's wine country and Hood River. The Canada's Inside Passage
cruise follows Captain George Vancouver's expedition along the shore of the
Pacific Northwest, taking in the fjords along the British Columbia coast, the
towering granite mountains surrounding Princess Louisa Inlet, and the sights
and sounds of Victoria and Vancouver.

PACIFIC NORTHWEST SKI AREAS ASSOCIATION ✉*P.O. 1720, Hood River, OR 97031* ✆*541-386-9600* ✎*www.pnsaa.org* Contact this group for additional information on skiing in Washington and Oregon.

TOURISM BRITISH COLUMBIA ✆*800-435-5622* ✎*www.hellobc.com* For information on skiing in British Columbia, obtain a copy of *Outdoor Adventure* here.

BIKING

Mountain bike descents—racing down alpine slopes on two wheels—is a growing sport in resort areas of British Columbia. Participants usually take high-performance mountain bikes on the gondola to the heights, then follow experienced guides down mountain faces that are the winter domain of skiers. Rest assured: There are tamer outdoor adventures here. In fact, many swear that the best way to soak in the region's beauty is to travel slowly by bike or foot.

WHISTLER BLACKCOMB RESORT ✉*4545 Blackcomb Way, Whistler, BC V0N 1B4* ✆*800-766-0449* ✎*www.whistler-blackcomb.com* The experienced guides at this resort can help you learn the thrill of mountain biking.

BACKROADS ✉*801 Cedar Street, Berkeley, CA 94710* ✆*800-462-2848* ✎*www. backroads.com* Extensive guided bicycling and walking tours of the mountains, forests, coastline and islands last anywhere from two days to weeks. Top operators include Backroads.

SIERRA CLUB ✉*Outing Department, 85 2nd Street, Second Floor, San Francisco, CA 94105* ✆*415-977-5522* ✎*www.sierraclub.org* This well-known organization leads bike tours.

SEATTLE & THE SOUTHERN SOUND

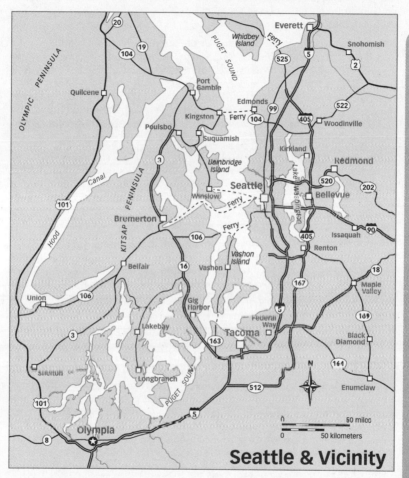

Seattle & Vicinity

Rain city? Not today. Last night's storm has washed the air clean, swept away yesterday's curtain of clouds to reveal Mt. Rainier in all its astonishing glory. From your hotel room window, you can see the Olympics rising like snow-tipped daggers beyond the blue gulf of Puget Sound. Below, downtown Seattle awakens to sunshine, espresso and the promise of a day brimming with discovery for the fortunate traveler.

The lesson here is twofold: Don't be daunted by Seattle's reputation for nasty weather, and don't limit yourself to anticipating its natural setting and magnificent greenery, awesome as they may be. For this jewel surrounded by water, earning it the nickname "The Emerald City," sparkles in ways too numerous to count after a decade or more of extraordinary growth.

Greater Seattle has changed dramatically. The city, squeezed into a lean, hourglass shape between Elliott Bay and Lake Washington, covers only 84 square miles, and its population is still under 600,000. But the greater metropolitan area, reaching from Everett to Tacoma and east to the Cascade foothills, now boasts some 4 million.

While most newcomers have settled in the suburbs, Seattle's soaring skyline downtown is the visual focus of a region on the move. No longer the sleepy sovereign of Puget Sound, Seattle today is clearly the most muscular of the Northwest's three largest cities. Its urban energy is admired even by those who bemoan Seattle's freeway congestion, suburban sprawl, crime and worrisome air and water pollution. Growth has been the engine of change, and although the pace has slowed in the '90s, the challenges posed by too rapid an expansion remain persistent topics of discussion.

Seattle offered no hint of its future prominence when pioneers began arriving on Elliott Bay some 150 years ago. Like other settlements around Puget Sound, Seattle survived by farming, fishing, shipbuilding, logging and coal mining. For decades the community hardly grew at all. One whimsical theory has it that because the frontier sawmill town offered a better array of brothels to the region's loggers, miners and fishermen, capital tended to flow into Seattle to fund later investment and expansion.

Whatever the reason, the city quickly rebuilt after the disastrous "Great Fire" of 1889. Before the Alaska Gold Rush thrust Seattle into prominence at the turn of the 20th century, Tacoma was Puget Sound's leading city. But on July 17, 1897, the ship *Portland* steamed into Elliott Bay from Alaska, bearing its legendary "ton of gold" (actually, nearly two tons), triggering the Klondike Gold Rush. Seattle immediately emerged as chief outfitter to thousands of would-be miners heading north to the gold fields.

Today, Seattle remains tied to its traditions. It's so close to the sea that 20-pound salmon are still hooked in Elliott Bay, at the feet of those gleaming, new skyscrapers. It's so near its waterfront that the boom of ferry horns resonates among its buildings and the cries of gulls still pierce the rumble of traffic. But the city's (and the state's) economy has grown beyond the old resource-based industries. International trade, tourism, agriculture and software giants like Microsoft now lead the way. The spotlight has passed from building ships to building airplanes, from wood chips to microchips, from mining coal to cultivating the fertile fields of tourism.

In the process, one of the nation's most vibrant economies has emerged. You can see that energy in Seattle's highrises, feel it in the buoyant street scene fueled in part by locals' infatuation with espresso. And there is fresh energy beneath your very feet. An "underground" of retail shops (as distinguished from the historic Pioneer Square Underground) has taken shape around the downtown Westlake stations in the Metro Transit Tunnel.

Civic energy has produced a glorious art museum downtown, a small but lively "people place" in Westlake Park, a spacious convention center and additions to Freeway Park. Private enterprise has added hotels, office towers with grand lobbies brimming with public art, shopping arcades, restaurants, nightclubs and bistros.

During the late '80s, as locals struggled with construction chaos, Seattle's downtown briefly suffered the nickname "little Beirut." Now, in the early years of the new millennium, downtown Seattle is once more under construction. But this time the atmosphere is one of urban revitalization, as the city has gained a new symphony hall, a plethora of condominiums and several upscale shopping and entertainment complexes. As vibrant as it is, downtown also exhibits the famed Seattle social courtesy and informality. Drivers on many downtown streets still stop to let waiting pedestrians cross, and it's not considered polite to honk your horn. Ask directions of anyone who looks like they know their way around; they'll almost always do their best to help. Only bankers and corporate executives wear suits to work, and not even all of those do. Casual wear is acceptable in almost every social situation; even the symphony and opera draw fans dressed in jeans. Historically, weather bureau statistics show that mid-July to mid-August brings the driest, sunniest, warmest weather—a sure bet for tourists, or so you'd suppose. But in the last decade or two, that midsummer guarantee all too often has been washed away by clouds or rain. What's the sun-seeking tourist to do?

Consider September. In recent years it has brought modestly reliable weather. Or, simply come prepared—spiritually and practically—for whatever mix of dreary and sublime days that fate delivers. An accepting attitude may be the best defense of all in a region once described in this way: "The mildest winter I ever spent was a summer on Puget Sound."

Have goofy weather, growth, gentrification of downtown neighborhoods and a tide of new immigrants eradicated the old Seattle? Not by a long shot. Pike Place Market's colorful maze is still there to beguile you. Ferry boats still glide like wedding cakes across a night-darkened Elliott Bay. The central waterfront is as clamorous, gritty and irresistible as ever. Pioneer Square and its catacomb-like underground still beckons. The soul of the city somehow endures even as the changes wrought by regional growth accumulate.

It is indeed the changing geography of the wider Puget Sound region that may appear more striking. What nature created here, partly by the grinding and gouging of massive lowland glaciers, is a complex mosaic. From the air, arriving visitors see a green-blue tapestry of meandering river valleys weaving between forested ridges, the rolling uplands dotted by lakes giving way to Cascade foothills and distant volcanoes, the intricate maze-way of Southern Puget Sound's island-studded inland sea.

From on high it seems almost pristine, but a closer look reveals a sobering overlay of manmade changes. Even as Seattle's downtown becomes "Manhattanized," the region is being "Los Angelesized" with the birth of a freeway commuter culture stretching from Olympia on the south to Everett on the north and beyond Issaquah on the east. Some commuters arrive by ferry from Bainbridge Island to the west. Farmlands and wetlands, forests and meadows, are giving way to often poorly planned, hastily built housing tracts, roads and shopping centers. And as the dense vegetation that once held the earth in place is scraped away, huge swathes of the metropolitan area are left naked and exposed to flooding, mudslides, rockfalls and other forms of damaging erosion.

For the traveler, such rapid growth means more traffic and longer lines for the ferry; more-crowded campgrounds, parks and public beaches; busier bikeways and foot trails; more folks fishing and boating and clam-digging. Downtown parking can be hard to find and expensive.

But despair not. The legendary Northwest may take a bit more effort to discover, but by almost any standard Seattle and its environs still offer an extraordinary blend of urban and outdoor pleasures close at hand. And growth seems only to have spurred a much richer cultural scene in Seattle—better restaurants serving original cuisines, more swank hotels, superb opera and a vital theater community, more art galleries and livelier shopping in a retail core sprinkled with public plazas that reach out to passersby with summer noon-hour concerts. In this chapter we will point you to familiar landmarks, help you discover some "hidden" treasures and find the best of what's new downtown as we look at a region that reaches from Olympia to Everett, Bremerton to Issaquah.

DOWNTOWN SEATTLE

When you fly into Seattle, the central part of this lush region looks irresistible. From the air (on a clear day) you'll be captivated by deep bays, harbors, gleaming skyscrapers, parks stretching for miles and hillside neighborhoods where waterskiing begins from the backyard. Central Seattle's neighborhoods offer a seemingly inexhaustible array of possibilities, from the International District to Lake Union and the waterfront to Capitol Hill. Eminently walkable, this area can also be explored by monorail, boat and bike. From the lofty heights of the Space Needle to the city's underground tour, this is one of the Northwest's best bets.

SIGHTS

Downtown Seattle (Pioneer Square to Seattle Center, the waterfront to Route 5) is compact enough for walkers to tour on foot. Energetic folks can see the highlights on one grand loop tour, or you can sample smaller chunks on successive days. Since downtown is spread along a relatively narrow north–south axis, you can walk from one end to the other, then return by public transit via buses in the Metro Transit Tunnel or aboard the Waterfront Streetcar trolleys, each of which have stations in both Pioneer Square and the International District. The Monorail also runs north–south between Westlake Center and Seattle Center.

CITYWIDE CONCIERGE VISITORS CENTER ⊠*Within the Washington State Convention & Trade Center, 800 Convention Place* ✆*206-461-5840* ⊘*www. visitseattle.org* A good place to orient yourself is at this visitors center. Folks staffing the desk will supply you with sightseeing advice, and reservations for ground transportation and area restaurants. Closed Saturday and Sunday November through April.

PIONEER SQUARE This square and its "old underground" remain one of Seattle's major fascinations. It was at this location that Seattle's first business district began. In 1889, a fire burned the woodframe city to the ground. The story of how the city rebuilt out of the ashes of the Great Fire remains intriguing to visitors and locals alike.

UNDERGROUND TOUR ⊠*608 1st Avenue* ✆*206-682-4646* ⊗*206-682-1511* ⊘*www.undergroundtour.com* To learn exactly how the underground was created after the new city arose, then was forgotten, then rediscovered, you really need to take this one-and-a-half-hour tour. Several of these subterranean pilgrimages are offered daily to the dark and cobwebby bowels of the underground—actually the street-level floors of buildings that were sealed off and fell into disuse when streets and sidewalks were elevated shortly after Pioneer Square was rebuilt (in fire-resistant brick instead of wood). Admission.

Above ground, in sunshine and fresh air, you can stroll through 90 acres of mostly century-old architecture in the historic district (maps and directories to district businesses are available in most shops). Notable architecture includes gems like the **Grand Central Building**, 1st Avenue South and South Main Street, **Merrill Place**, 1st Avenue South and South Jackson Street, the **Maynard Building**, 1st Avenue South and South Washington Street, the cast-iron **Pergola** in Pioneer Square Park and facing buildings such as the **Mutual Life and Pioneer buildings**, 1st Avenue and Yesler Way. More than 30 art galleries are located in the Pioneer Square area. Here you can shop for American Indian art, handicrafts, paintings and pottery. (Incidentally, the Pioneer Building houses Seattle's first electric elevator.)

YESLER WAY   Located in the heart of the Pioneer Square area, this street originated as the steep "Skid Road" for logs cut on the hillsides above the harbor and bound for Henry Yesler's waterfront mill, and thence to growing cities like San Francisco. Later, as the district declined, Yesler Way attracted a variety of derelicts and became the prototype for every big city's bowery, alias "skid row."

KLONDIKE GOLD RUSH NATIONAL HISTORICAL PARK ✉319 2nd Avenue South ☎206-220-4240 ⬦www.nps.gov/klse The new city boomed during the Alaska Gold Rush in 1897–98. For a look back at extraordinary times, stop by the Seattle Unit of this park, one of the tiniest National Park Service sites in the lower 48. In this historic red-brick building in downtown Seattle, you can see gold-panning demonstrations (only in summer), a collection of artifacts, films and other memorabilia. Other units of the park are in Southeast Alaska

OCCIDENTAL MALL AND PARK   The main pedestrian artery is this treelined, cobbled promenade running south from Yesler Way to South Jackson Street allowing pleasant ambling between rows of shops and galleries (don't miss the oasis of **Waterfall Park** off Occidental on South Main Street).

SMITH TOWER ✉506 2nd Avenue and Yesler Way ☎206-622-4004 ✆206-622-9357 ⬦www.smithtower.com, info@smithtower.com For an overview of the whole district, ride the historic manually operated elevator to the open-air observation deck of this 42-story tower, built in 1914. Closed weekdays from November through March. Admission.

INTERNATIONAL DISTRICT ✉Yesler Way to South Dearborn Street, 4th Avenue South to Route 5 Sharp ethnic diversity has always marked this district, next door to Pioneer Square to the southeast. The polyglot community that emerged on the southern fringes of old Seattle always mixed its Asian cultures and continues doing so today, setting it apart from the homogeneous Chinatowns of San Francisco and Vancouver, across the border in British Columbia.

MATT'S IN THE MARKET

PAGE 46

Mouthwatering, modern, fresh seafood dishes and a view of the Pike Place food stalls

THE INN AT HARBOR STEPS

PAGE 42

Luxurious boutique hotel overlooking the heart of the waterfront—perfect homebase for exploring Seattle on foot

ZAINA

PAGE 45

Lively Greek taverna packed with locals that serves delicious traditional fare—moussaka, dolmas and gyros

YE OLDE CURIOSITY SHOP

PAGE 37

Eclectic museum of oddities with Northwest Indian art among shrunken heads and three resident mummies

Chinese began settling here in the 1860s, Japanese in the 1890s, and today the "I.D.," as it's commonly known, is also home to Koreans, Filipinos, Vietnamese and Cambodians. For all its diversity, the district clearly lacks the economic vitality, bustling street life and polished tourist appeal of other major Chinatowns. Yet some find the International District all the more genuine for its unhurried, even seedy, ambience. A variety of mom-and-pop enterprises predominates in the I.D.—specialty food and grocery stores, herbal medicine shops, dim sum palaces and fortune cookie factories.

UWAJIMAYA ✉*600 5th Avenue South* ☎*206-624-6248, 800-889-1928* 📠*206-405-2996* 🖱*www.uwajimaya.com* This is the International District's major retail store. It's fascinating to wander up and down the food aisles of this family-owned store, trying to identify the strange and exotic ingredients sold there—many of them bright pink. This retail store is not only the largest Asian grocery and gift store in the Northwest but also a worthwhile experience of Asian culture even if you're not shopping.

WING LUKE ASIAN MUSEUM ✉*719 South King Street* ☎*206-623-5124* 📠*206-623-4559* 🖱*www.wingluke.org, folks@wingluke.org* Around the corner from its original location, the new incarnation of this museum encompasses a building eight times the size of its former home. The expansion includes more space for exhibits offering a well-rounded look at the Northwest's Asian American history and culture. Representing ten groups of Asian immigrants, presentations include historical photography and social commentary on the Asian-American experience. Closed Monday. Admission.

KOBE TERRACE PARK ✉*221 6th Avenue South* ☎*206-684-4075* Named after Seattle's sister city in Japan, this park offers pleasant strolling among Japanese pine and cherry blossom trees. On the hilltop, which affords a view of Mt. Rainier, there is a four-ton, 200-year-old Yuki-midoro stone lantern. An adjacent community garden is tended by local residents.

HING HAY PARK ✉*South King Street and Maynard Avenue South* This park is the scene of frequent festivals—exhibitions of Japanese martial arts, Chinese folk dances, Vietnamese food fairs, Korean music and the like. It's colorful pavilion comes from Taipei, Taiwan.

WATERFRONT The old waterfront beginning at the western edge of Pioneer Square remains one of the most colorful quarters of the city and what many consider Seattle's liveliest "people place." On sunny summer days, it is the most popular tourist draw in the city. The waterfront grows more interesting by the year, a beguiling jumble of fish bars and excursion-boat docks, ferries and fireboats, import emporiums and nautical shops, sway-backed old piers and barnacle-encrusted pilings that creak in the wash of wakes. Here's a sampler of attractions: As you stroll south to north, you'll encounter a harbor-watch facility, a dozen historical plaques that trace major events, a public boat landing, the state-ferry terminal at Colman Dock and the waterfront fire station whose fireboats occasionally put on impressive, fountainlike displays on summer weekends. Ye Olde Curiosity Shop houses a collection of odd goods from around the world, Ivar's is the city's most famous fish bar, and cavernous shopping arcades include pier-end restaurants, outdoor picnic areas and public fishing. **Waterfront Park** is a crescent-shaped retreat from commercialism presenting sweeping views over the harbor.

WATERFRONT STREETCAR This waterfront's action is concentrated between Piers 48 and 60, and again around Pier 70. Poking around by foot remains the favorite way to explore, but some folks prefer to hopscotch to specific sites aboard this streetcar, which runs from the International District to Pier 70. You also can climb into a horse-drawn carriage near Pier 60 for a narrated tour. Still another way to do it is via boat (see "Hey! The Water's Fine" on page 106).

YE OLDE CURIOSITY SHOP ✉*1001 Alaskan Way, Pier 54* ☎*206-682-5844* ⌘*www.yeoldecuriosityshop. com* Dating back to 1899, this shop is a combination souvenir shop and museum that draws crowds with odd displays such as a Siamese twin calf, a four-legged chicken, rare Eskimo walrus-tusk carvings and one of the world's largest collections of shrunken heads. It also boasts a collection of Northwest Indian art, including carved totem poles. The antique, coin-operated games are an easy way to get rid of pocket change.

Downtown Seattle

POINTS OF INTEREST

- Ⓐ Benaroya Hall
- Ⓑ Children's Museum, Seattle
- Ⓒ Citywide Concierge Visitors Center
- Ⓓ EMP-SFM
- Ⓔ Klondike Gold Rush National Historical Park
- Ⓕ Occidental Mall and Park
- Ⓖ Pacific Science Center
- Ⓗ Pike Place Market
- Ⓘ Pioneer Square
- Ⓙ Quest Field
- Ⓚ Rainier Square
- Ⓛ Safeco Field
- Ⓜ Seattle Art Museum
- Ⓝ Seattle Aquarium
- Ⓞ Seattle Central Library
- Ⓟ Space Needle
- Ⓠ Two Union Square
- Ⓡ Victor Steinbrueck Park
- Ⓢ Westlake Park

SEATTLE AQUARIUM ✉1483 Alaskan Way, Pier 59 ☎206-386-4300 📠206-386-4328 ✐www.seattleaquarium.org, aquarium.programs@seattle.gov A visit here allows you to descend to an underwater viewing dome for up-close looks at scores of Puget Sound fish. Other exhibits include an ocean oddities display, a coral reef tank teeming with colorful tropical fish and a giant Pacific octopus. Salmon are born at the aquarium and allowed to migrate to the open sea, returning later to spawn. Admission.

PIKE PLACE MARKET ✉Pike Street and 1st Avenue The Pike Hill climb across Alaskan Way leads up—almost straight up, 155 steps' worth—past several decent restaurants and shops to this famed market. (There's an elevator for the walk-weary. You can also reach the north end of the market from a stairway/elevator complex opposite the Pier

62/63 public wharf.) You'll also pass some piers whose sheds have been leveled to provide public access, the last vestiges of working waterfront on the central harbor—fish-company docks and such—as well as the Port of Seattle headquarters. The venerable market, born in 1907, has proved itself one of the city's renewable treasures. Saved from the wrecking ball by citizen action in the early '70s, the market was later revitalized through long-term renovation.

THE FIRST STARBUCKS ✉*1912 Pike Place* ☎*206-448-8762* Not the oldest coffee company in town but certainly the best known, Starbucks has more than 6000 locations in 44 countries. The "original" location, started by two high school teachers and a freelance writer during the early days of Pike Place Market, is across the street from the market. Historic preservation laws keep the storefront rather plain, with the name in unobtrusive letters above the rain awning that shelters street musicians. It has been in business here since 1976.

PIKE PLACE MARKET NATIONAL HISTORIC DISTRICT ✉*Virginia Street to just south of Pike Street, 1st to Western avenues* ☎*206-682-7453* ✆*206-625-0646* ✐*www.pikeplacemarket.org, info@pikeplacemarket.org* This historic district is, in many respects, better than ever. The main historic market, with its famous neon-lit clock, brass pig and fish-throwing vendors, now offers hundreds of different products in hundreds of categories, from exotic spices, fresh oysters and homemade crumpets to ceramics, fine jewelry and old-fashioned toys. It currently has about 100 regular farmers, 200 craftspeople, 240 shops and restaurants, and 200 musicians and performers, and is visited by nearly 10 million visitors a year. In all, a market experience unparalleled in the nation! To learn more, visit the market's website or stop at the Info Booth at 1st Avenue and Pike Street.

There are so many ways to enjoy the market that we can scarcely begin to list them. Come early for breakfast and wake up with the market (at least a dozen cafés open early). Come at noon for the ultimate experience of marketplace clamor amid legions of jostling shoppers, vendors hawking salmon and farm-fresh produce, and street musicians vying for your contributions. Come to explore the market's lower level, often missed by tourists, a warrenlike collection of secondhand treasures, old books, magazines, posters and vintage clothing. Come to shop for the largest collection of handmade merchandise in the Northwest on handcraft tables at the market's north end. Come to browse all the "nonproduce" merchandise surrounding the main market—wines, exotic imported foods, French kitchenware, jewelry and avant-garde fashions.

PIER 66 Just a bit north of Pike Place Market is the Port of Seattle's Pier 66, the Bell Street Pier. With a small-craft marina, three restaurants, a museum, a conference center and a skybridge leading up to the booming Belltown shopping/restaurant district along 1st Avenue, this recent development has become a popular stop for travelers.

SEATTLE ART MUSEUM ✉*1300 1st Avenue* ☎*206-654-3100* ✆*206-654-3135* ✐*www.seattleartmuseum.org* South of Pike Place Market is this art museum, designed by Robert Venturi and Denise Scott. The five-story, limestone-faced building highlighted with terra-cotta and marble has quickly become a regional, postmodern landmark. You'll enter via a grand staircase, but to see the collections, you'll have to ascend by elevator to the galleries. Known for its Northwest Coast American Indian, Asian and African art, the museum also features Meso-American, modern and contemporary art, photography and European masters. Closed Monday. Admission.

BENAROYA HALL ✉*200 University Street* ☎*206-215-4700, 866-833-4747* 📠*206-215-4701* 🖱*www.seattlesymphony.org, info@seattlesymphony.org* Located across the street from the Seattle Art Museum, this massive hall is home to the Seattle Symphony. The grounds include a memorial garden dedicated to Washington residents who died in military conflicts from World War II to the present.

DOWNTOWN City center has undergone a remarkable rejuvenation. It's a delightful place to stroll whether you're intent on shopping or not. Major downtown hotels are clustered in the retail core, allowing easy walks in any direction.

FREEWAY PARK ✉*6th Avenue and Seneca Street* One way to start your downtown tour is at this park, which offers five-plus acres of lawns, gardens and fountains, and is the nation's first major park to be built over a freeway. The park's many waterfalls and pools create a splashy, burbling sound barrier to city noise. Beds of summer-blooming flowers, tall evergreens and leafy deciduous trees create a genuine park feeling, inspiring picnics by office workers on their noon-hour break and street performers of all kinds. Amble north through the park, and take a short detour beneath a street overpass toward University Street (steps next to more waterfalls zigzag up to Capitol Hill and dramatic views of city architecture).

WASHINGTON STATE CONVENTION & TRADE CENTER ✉*800 Convention Place* ☎*206-694-5000* 🖱*www.wsctc.com, info@wsctc.com* If you continue north, Freeway Park merges with the similarly landscaped grounds of the state convention center, which features impressive architecture and a large collection of public art. Maps and information are on hand at the **Citywide Concierge Visitors Center** (206-461-5888), located on the first level of the convention center.

TWO UNION SQUARE Head west through linking landscaping that leads you past waterfalls and flowers in the main plaza of this square.

US BANK CENTRE ✉*6th Avenue and Union Street* Cross 6th Avenue and enter this center. The handsome building's lower levels contain the City Centre mall, featuring upscale shops, bold sculptures and stunning exhibits of colorful art glass. Wander and admire for a bit, stop for a meal or an espresso, then continue by leaving the building at the 5th Avenue and Pike Street exit.

WESTLAKE PARK ✉*4th Avenue and Pine Street* Cross 5th Avenue past what used to be the striking Coliseum Theater, now renovated and occupied by Banana Republic, then head west on Pike Street to 4th Avenue. Turn right to enter this triangular park, which offers a leafy copse of trees and an intriguing pattern of bricks that replicate a Salish Indian basket-weave design best observed from the terraces on the adjoining Westlake Center.

WESTLAKE CENTER This is an enormously popular, multilevel glass-enclosed retail pavilion, a people place offering espresso bars, flower vendors, handicrafts and access to what's been dubbed downtown's "underground." The marbled, well-lighted, below-street-level arcades were created as part of the city's transit tunnel. Metro buses (propelled electrically while underground) rumble by on the lowest level. Just above it are mezzanines full of public art, with vendors and shops, and underground access to a string of department stores.

RAINIER SQUARE ⊠*Between 4th and 5th avenues and University and Union streets* Walk south on 4th Avenue a few blocks to this square, and discover another burgeoning underground of upscale enterprises. Follow its passageways eastward past a bakery, restaurants and access to the venerable **Fifth Avenue Theatre**. Continue east, up an escalator back to Two Union Square and Freeway Park.

TILLICUM VILLAGE ✆*206-933-8600, 800-426-1205* ✉*206-933-9377* ⌂*www.tillicumvillage.com* Offshore on Blake Island is this village, with a huge cedar longhouse styled after the dwellings of the Northwest Coast American Indians, situated on the edge of a 475-acre marine state park. The village presents traditional salmon bakes and performances by the Tillicum Village Dancers. Tillicum Village charters Argosy vessels from Pier 55 on Seattle's central waterfront year-round.

LODGING

Lodgings vary widely in style and price throughout the Seattle area. Downtown, there's a thick cluster of expensive luxury hotels interspersed with a few at moderate and even budget rates.

PIONEER SQUARE HOTEL hidden
$$–$$$ 75 ROOMS ⊠*77 Yesler Way* ✆*206-340-1234, 800-800-5514* ✉*206-467-0707* ⌂*www.pioneersquare.com, info@pioneersquare.com*
A Best Western property, this hotel combines a prime location with Four-Diamond historic charm. The essence of comfort is captured here by turn-of-the-20th-century decor and remarkably quiet rooms. Rates are quite reasonable by downtown standards. The Pioneer Square Historic District surrounding the hotel is a haven for fascinating restaurants, taverns, art galleries, shops and more. The ferry terminal and Seattle Art Museum are also within a few blocks.

THE EDGEWATER
$$$ 223 ROOMS ⊠*2411 Alaskan Way* ✆*206-728-7000, 800-624-0670* ✉*206-269-4581* ⌂*www.edgewaterhotel.com, contactus@edgewaterhotel.com*
This hotel has changed completely since the days when the Beatles used to fish for sand sharks from the windows, but the location—

directly on the waterfront—is still hard to beat. The property began as a top-flight hotel on Pier 67, built in the 1960s for the World's Fair. It later slid into decay and was renovated in "mountain lodge" style—meaning stone fireplaces and natural-log furniture in the rooms. Half of the 223 rooms and suites have stunning views of Elliott Bay, West Seattle and the Olympic Peninsula. Rooms are comfortable, and the staff is accommodating. The restaurant has a fine water view.

ALEXIS HOTEL

$$$ 121 ROOMS   ✉1007 1st Avenue   ✆206-624-4844, 866-356-8894
☏206-621-9009   ✐www.alexishotel.com, reservations@alexishotel.com

The Alexis is an elegant little haven two blocks from the waterfront and close to downtown stores and business centers. The rooms have rich colors and contemporary furnishings mixed with original pieces of art, all done in good taste. Some of the roomy suites have fireplaces, and others have two-person jetted tubs. The service is unmatched in this renovated historic hotel. Pet-friendly.

THE INN AT HARBOR STEPS ___ hidden

$$$ 28 ROOMS   ✉1221 1st Avenue   ✆206-748-0973, 888-728-8910
☏206-748-0533   ✐www.innatharborsteps.com, inn@harborsteps.com

This luxury hotel has perhaps the best possible location for exploring downtown Seattle on foot. Across the street from the Seattle Art Museum and two blocks from Pike Place Market, the inn occupies the lower floors of a condominium highrise overlooking the heart of the waterfront. Each spacious guest room features a king- or queen-sized bed, a sitting area, a gas fireplace and an oversized jetted bathtub.

W SEATTLE

$$$$ 450 ROOMS   ✉1112 4th Avenue   ✆206-264-6000, 877-946-8357
☏206-264-6100   ✐www.whotels.com, wseattle.whatwhen@whotels.com

For grandeur and luxury check in to this Italian Renaissance–style hotel that was built in 1924 on land that was the site of the original University of Washington. Conveniently located in the heart of downtown close to Pike Place Market, this grande dame is the ultimate statement of refined elegance. The rooms are tastefully appointed, and modern conveniences combine gracefully with the classic furnishings. The public areas, adorned with impressive floral arrangements and crystal chandeliers take you back to another era while the fantasy blown-glass arrangements in the main dining room bring you back to the 21st century. Add a health club with pool and huge jacuzzi and you need look no further.

GREEN TORTOISE HOSTEL

$ 30 ROOMS   ✉105 Pike Street   ✆206-340-1222, 888-424-6783   ☏206-623-3207
✐www.greentortoise.net, info@greentortoise.net

The downtown location for this hostel is convenient to most central-Seattle attractions. With functional private and dorm rooms, 24-hour check-in, a common room and a fully equipped kitchen, it's much like a traditional hostel, with one extra advantage: a free full-service breakfast, including unlimited eggs, fresh fruit, make-your-own waffles and fresh-baked brownies. There are also 11 computers with free internet access. Many guest services, such as tours and discounts at local clubs, pubs and restaurants, add value as well.

43

PENSIONE NICHOLS _____ ⓗidden

$$–$$$ 12 ROOMS ✉1923 1st Avenue ☏206-441-7125, 800-440-7125
☏206-441-7125 ⌨www.pensionenichols.com, info@pensionenichols.com

This charming hotel offers European-style lodging within a block of Pike Place Market. Ten rooms on the third floor of a historic building share three baths and a large common space with a view of the bay, while two rooms share one bath on the second floor. The rooms are painted a cheerful yellow and have antique furnishings; some have windows, while others only have skylights. There are also two ultra-deluxe suites that sleep four and have views of the sound, fully equipped kitchens and private baths. A continental breakfast is served.

INN AT THE MARKET _____ ⓗidden

$$$–$$$$ 70 ROOMS ✉86 Pine Street ☏206-443-3600, 800-446-4484
☏206-448-0631 ⌨www.innatthemarket.com, info@innatthemarket.com

A retreat from the throngs in Pike Place Market, this inn is nestled with several shops and a restaurant in a brick courtyard with an old cherry tree. Light and airy and furnished in contemporary European style, the inn is one of Seattle's best. Guest rooms have views of the city, courtyard or water.

HOTEL MONACO

$$$ 189 ROOMS ✉1101 4th Avenue ☏206-621-1770, 800-715-6513
☏206-261-7779 ⌨www.monaco-seattle.com

Offering stylish, upscale accommodations in funky, plush rooms and suites is the Hotel Monaco. The grand high-ceilinged lobby has columns and pilasters and a white stucco fireplace. Make sure to take advantage of their in-room pet goldfish adoption program.

EXECUTIVE HOTEL PACIFIC

$$–$$$ 150 ROOMS ✉400 Spring Street ☏206-623-3900, 888-388-3932
☏206 623 2059 ⌨www.pacificplazahotel.com, resehp@executivehotels.net

Considered a luxury hotel in the 1930s, the Executive is now a dignified, quiet downtown classic with 150 rooms. Though updated and decorated with modern furniture, it hasn't lost its old-fashioned flavor, with windows that open, ceiling fans and rather small rooms. The concierge is very helpful. Wi-fi access available.

HOTEL ANDRA

$$$–$$$$ 119 ROOMS ✉2000 4th Avenue ☏206-448-8600, 877-448-8600
☏206-441-7140 ⌨www.hotelandra.com, hotelandra@hotelandra.com

Located in a former 1920s apartment building, this hotel provides spacious guest rooms converted from studio apartments. Decorated in earth tones, the rooms include sitting areas with love seats. There's also a fitness room.

SIXTH AVENUE INN

$–$$ 167 ROOMS   ✉2000 6th Avenue   ☎206-441-8300, 888-627-8290
  📠206-441-9903   🖱www.sixthavenueinn.com, sixth.avenue@starwoodhotels.com

Between downtown and Seattle Center is this five-story motor inn. The rooms are a cut above those in most motels. They contain brass beds, desks and large windows. Those on the north and in back are the quietest. There's a restaurant overlooking a small garden, a fitness facility and wireless internet.

SORRENTO HOTEL

$$$–$$$$ 76 ROOMS   ✉900 Madison Street   ☎206-622-6400, 800-426-1265   📠206-343-6155   🖱www.hotelsorrento.com, mail@hotelsorrento.com

The Sorrento is known for its personal service and attention to detail. A historic building that has been remodeled, Sorrento is at the top of what is locally known as "Pill Hill" (for its proximity to the hospital), a few blocks from the downtown area to the north and the International District immediately south. Beyond the quiet, plush lobby are a notable restaurant and an inviting lounge with a fireplace that is a popular spot for a nightcap. The Sorrento has been called one of the most romantic hotels in Seattle. All 76 rooms and suites have a warm, traditional, European atmosphere.

INN AT VIRGINIA MASON

$$–$$$ 79 ROOMS   ✉1006 Spring Street   ☎206-583-6453, 800-283-6453
  📠206-223-7545   🖱www.innatvirginiamason.com

This attractive, nine-story brick building is owned by the medical center next door. On the eastern edge of downtown, it caters to hospital visitors and others looking for a convenient location and pleasant accommodations at reasonable prices. The rooms have dark-wood furnishings and teal and maroon decor. Two suites have a fireplace and whirlpool tub. There's a small restaurant by a brick terrace.

DINING

AL BOCCALINO

$$–$$$ ITALIAN   ✉1 Yesler Way   ☎206-622-7688   📠206-622-1798
  🖱alboccalino@aol.com

The fine dining room here serves some of the city's best Italian meals. Located in a brick building in Pioneer Square, the restaurant's atmosphere is unpretentious and intimate, the antipasti imaginative, and the entrées cooked and sauced to perfection. Saddle of lamb with brandy, tarragon and mustard is a favorite choice. There are daily specials for every course. No lunch on Saturday or Sunday.

IL TERRAZZO CARMINE

$$$–$$$$ ITALIAN   ✉Pioneer Square, 411 1st Avenue South   ☎206-467-7797
  📠206-447-5716   🖱www.ilterrazzocarmine.com

For a romantic dinner, try Il Terrazzo in the Merrill Place Building. For patio diners, a cascading reflecting pool drowns out some of the freeway noise. Entrées include roast duck with cherries or veal piccata with

Seattle's Coffee Wars

It doesn't take long for visitors to notice that Seattle's primary energy source is coffee. Coffee bars, the preferred business and social meeting spots, do a booming business, and it seems as if there's a drive-up espresso kiosk on every block. Conventional wisdom blames the weather for making the steamy, mood-lifting beverage more popular than Prozac, but on sunny summer days, you'll still see people waiting in line for iced lattes and granitas.

In 1971, "fresh coffee" still meant a new five-pound can of Folger's from the supermarket. Then Jim Stewart, with backing from his brother Dave, started Stewart Brothers Coffee, a small stand selling coffee beans in Pike Place Market. Jim first used a peanut roaster he'd bought from a vendor on a southern California beach but soon traveled to Italy to learn the art from master espresso roasters and purchased a real coffee bean roaster. The unfamiliar smell of fresh roasted coffee wafted through the market and made his stand an instant hit. Later that same year, a second coffee bean stand opened in Pike Place Market under the name Starbucks.

Soon the two rivals began buying coffee beans from different parts of the world, developing assorted distinctive blends and adding flavorings. In 1984 Starbucks started its first coffee bar at 4th and Spring streets in downtown Seattle. Meanwhile, Stewart Brothers began selling whole-bean coffee in bulk through supermarkets. Learning that there was another coffee wholesaler named Stewart, the brothers abbreviated the company's name to SBC Inc., which in turn inspired its trade name, Seattle's Best Coffee.

SBC grew to become the world's leading seller of specialty coffee beans, while Starbucks has expanded to nearly 4000 coffee bars, including locations in Tokyo, Beijing, Manila and Kuwait. Starbucks finally bought its in-city rival in 2003 but SBC retains an independent identity. The city now boasts 26 other retail and wholesale coffee-roasting companies as well as five green brokers (importers of unroasted coffee beans).

capers and lemon. The restaurant also features an extensive Italian wine list. No lunch on Saturday. Closed Sunday.

ZAINA _____ hidden

$ GREEK ✉ *108 Cherry Street* ✆ *206-624-5687*

It's impossible not to get thoroughly filled at this friendly, low-key Greek eatery in the midst of the lower downtown business district. The place is packed with office workers at lunch, but the crowd thins out after 1 p.m. The food is filling and flavorful. Closed Sunday.

BOTTICELLI CAFFE

$ DINER ✉ *101 Stewart Street* ✆ *206-441-9235*

A favorite among downtowners is this small café known for its panini—little sandwiches made of toasted focaccia bread and topped with olive oil, herbs, cheeses, meats and vegetables. The espresso and ices are good, too. Breakfast and lunch only. Closed Saturday and Sunday.

JADE GARDEN

$$–$$$ CANTONESE   ✉424 7th Avenue South   ☎206-622-8181

White linen tablecloths, black rattan furnishings and loads of plants await you at this upscale Cantonese restaurant in the International District. In the foyer, the specials—such as hot and smoky crab in a spicy sauce, fresh fish with vegetables or clams in black bean sauce—are posted on the blackboard.

PALOMINO

$$$–$$$$ INTERNATIONAL   ✉1420 5th Avenue, Suite 350   ☎206-623-1300
💻www.palomino.com

Shoppers and theatergoers love this restaurant and its large, airy dining room, which lends itself to prime people watching. The food's good, too—this bustling downtown spot is best known for thin-crust pizzas that barely support the heap of toppings. Also on the menu is a variety of regional American and southern European–inspired salads, pasta and roasted meat and poultry dishes. Though crowded, you can still count on fast and efficient service.

PLACE PIGALLE

$$$–$$$$ SEAFOOD/NEW AMERICAN   ✉81 Pike Street   ☎206-624-1756

Wind your way past a seafood vendor and Rachel, the bronze pig (a popular market mascot), to this restaurant with spectacular views of Elliott Bay. The dark-wood trim, handsome bar and other touches make for a European bistro atmosphere. The restaurant makes the most of fresh ingredients from the market's produce tables. Dine on fresh Penn Cove mussels with bacon in a balsamic vinaigrette, calamari in a dijon-ginger cream sauce, or one of the daily fresh salmon specials. The dishes are artfully presented. Patio dining available in summer. Closed Sunday.

IL BISTRO

$$$–$$$$ ITALIAN   ✉93-A Pike Street   ☎206-682-3049   📠206-223-0234
💻www.ilbistro.net

Tucked into a hillside in Pike Place Market, this is a cozy cellar spot with wide archways and oriental rugs on wooden floors. Light jazz, candlelight and well-prepared Italian food make it an inviting spot on a rainy evening. Several pastas are served; the entrées include rack of lamb, veal scallopine, fresh salmon and free-range chicken. Dinner only.

MATT'S IN THE MARKET

$$–$$$ SEAFOOD   ✉94 Pike Street, third floor   ☎206-467-7909
💻www.mattsinthemarket.com, dan@mattsinthemarket.com

Matt's warehouse-sized windows look down upon the Pike Place food stalls, where the cooks shop twice a day, guaranteeing the freshest possible fish and produce. Typical dishes on the constantly changing bill of fare range from steamed clams and mussels with saffron butter, white wine broth and fresh herbs to wild salmon with Bing cherry–caper vinaigrette or grilled rack of lamb with fig compote, watercress and sweet onion salad. Closed Sunday.

THREE GIRLS BAKERY

$ DELI   ✉1514 Pike Place, Suite 1   ☎206-622-1045   📠206-622-0245

Across the cobbled street from Il Bistro, you can observe the eclectic mix of shoppers and artists in the Pike Place Market at this popular hangout. The tiny lunch counter and bakery with just a few seats serves good sandwiches—the meatloaf sandwich is popular—and hearty soups, including chili and clam chowder. You have more than 50 kinds of bread to choose from. The sourdough and rye breads are recommended. If you don't have room for pastries, buy some to take home.

ORIENTAL MART

$ PACIFIC RIM   ✉1506 Pike Place Market   ☎206-622-8488

The food here is a combination of Filipino and Asian—and it's very good and very inexpensive. Try the pork *adobo* if they have it that day; otherwise, any of the chicken preparations are excellent. There's no better place for lunch at the Market. The lunch counter is in back of the food-and-novelties store.

KELLS

$–$$$ IRISH   ✉1916 Post Alley   ☎206-728-1916   📠206-441-9431
🖮www.kellsirish.com/seattle

In Post Alley, behind some of the market shops, you will find more than just a wee bit of Ireland. This traditional Irish restaurant and pub will lure you to the Emerald Isle with pictures and posters of splendid countryside. A limited menu includes Irish stew and meat pies. From the heavy, dark bar comes a host of domestic and imported beers. Irish musicians play live music seven days a week.

THE PINK DOOR

$$–$$$ ITALIAN   ✉1919 Post Alley   ☎206-443-3241   📠206-443-3341
🖮www.thepinkdoor.net

Talk about hidden—this place doesn't even have a sign. You enter through the pink door off of Post Alley. With its Italian kitsch decor, this spot is lively and robust at lunchtime. Especially good are the *lasagna della porta rosa* and a delicious cioppino. In the evening, the pace slows, the light dims and it's a perfect setting for a romantic dinner. In the summer, rooftop dining offers views of the Sound. Closed Sunday.

CAMPAGNE

$$–$$$$ FRENCH   ✉86 Pine Street   ☎206-728-2800   📠206-448-7562
🖮www.campagnerestaurant.com

Off a brick courtyard above Pike Place Market, this is one of the city's top restaurants. Diners enjoy French country cooking in an atmosphere both warm and elegant. The menu changes six times a year.

Entrées may include pan-roasted beef *onglet* served with Roquefort butter, sautéed greens and *pommes frites* or Southwest French white bean stew with lamb, pork, duck confit and garlic sausage. The simply prepared dishes are usually the best: young chicken stuffed with ricotta, spinach and roasted herbs and served with sage-infused *jus* and rosemary roasted potatoes, for example. Dinner only.

WILD GINGER

$–$$ PAN-ASIAN   ✉ *1401 3rd Avenue*   ☏ *206-623-4450*   📠 *206-623-8265*
🖱 *www.wildginger.net*

The decor is spare and clean here, and the menu is pan-Asian. Dark-wood booths fill the main dining room. There's also a satay bar where skewered chicken, beef, fish and vegetables are grilled, then served with peanut and other sauces. The wondrous Seven Elements Soup, an exotic blend of flavors, is a meal in itself. No lunch on Sunday.

DAHLIA LOUNGE

$$$–$$$$ INTERNATIONAL   ✉ *2001 4th Avenue*   ☏ *206-682-4142*   📠 *206-467-0568*
🖱 *www.tomdouglas.com, office@tomdouglas.com*

Contemporary, international cuisine prepared with imagination is served at this lounge near the shops of Westlake Center. Bright red walls, a neon sign and paper-fish lampshades create a celebratory atmosphere. The chef draws upon numerous ethnic styles and uses Northwest products to develop such dishes as roasted mussels and smoky lamb sausage served with yam soufflé and carmelized apples and ginger. No lunch on weekends.

Just north of downtown, you'll find the thriving Belltown shopping, dining and nightlife scene.

LE PICHET

$$ FRENCH   ✉ *1933 1st Avenue*   ☏ *206-256-1499*   🖱 *www.lepichetseattle.com*

At Seattle's most authentic French bistro, you'll find small plates such as oysters on the half-shell and pork pâté with honey and walnuts served around the clock, accompanied by glasses of surprisingly affordable imported wines. During dinner hours, the menu expands to include a wider range of distinctively French fare. Try, if you dare, the crisp confit of pork belly with cornichon and butternut squash confiture, followed by roast quail on a ragout of flageolet beans with chicken livers and preserved lemon.

MARCO'S SUPPERCLUB

$$–$$$ INTERNATIONAL   ✉ *2510 1st Avenue*   ☏ *206-441-7801*
🖱 *www.marcossupperclub.com*

Dark and intimate, Marco's is a little-known purveyor of fine, eclectic multiregional dishes; the seasonal menu may include ahi tuna with wasabi anglaise, enchilada mole casserole or duck breast with cherry-port sauce. The staff is friendly and experienced, the music is '30s and '40s jazz, and the filling meals are reasonable by Belltown standards. Dinner only. Closed Sunday.

BELLTOWN PIZZA

$–$$ ITALIAN ✉2422 1st Avenue ☎206-441-2653 🖰www.belltownpizza.net, jimmyd09@comcast.net

Scarlet walls, high-backed booths and dim lighting help this place stand apart from your average pizza joint. It helps, too, that the pies here are damn tasty. Also on the menu is a small selection of pasta, salads and focaccia sandwiches. But after 10 p.m. on weekends, expect a hip, lively crowd that's more interested in the bar than the food. Dinner only.

THE TWO BELLS BAR & GRILL

$–$$ AMERICAN ✉2313 4th Avenue ☎206-441-3050 ☎206-448-9626

Artists and others without a lot of money for eats hang out at this bar and grill. Local artwork on the walls changes every two months. This funky bar with ten kinds of draft beer and a host of inexpensive good food is a busy place. You can always find good soups, sandwiches, burgers, salads and cold plates. Some favorites are an Italian sausage soup and the hot beer-sausage sandwich.

SHOPPING

PIONEER SQUARE ANTIQUE MALL ✉602 1st Avenue ☎206 624-1164
The oldest and loveliest structure in Pioneer Square is the Pioneer Building. In the basement is this mall with more than 6000 square feet of space devoted to antiques and collectibles and maintained by some 60 dealers.

PIONEER SQUARE GALLERIES Need a Morris Graves painting or a portrait of grunge legend Kurt Cobain? Several Pioneer Square galleries specialize in local artists, including **Linda Hodges Gallery** (closed Sunday and Monday; 316 1st Avenue South; 206-624-3034; www.linda hodgesgallery.com), **Davidson Galleries** (313 Occidental Avenue South; 206-624-6700; www.davidsongalleries.com) and **Greg Kucera Gallery** (212 3rd Avenue South; 206-624-0770; www.gregkucera.com).

ELLIOTT BAY BOOK COMPANY ✉101 South Main Street ☎206-624-6600, 800-962-5311 🖰www.elliottbaybook.com In the heart of the Pioneer Square district is Elliott Books, featuring over 150,000 titles, including an outstanding stock of Northwest books. You're bound to enjoy browsing, snacking in the on-premises café or listening in on frequently scheduled readings by renowned authors.

UWAJIMAYA ✉600 5th Avenue South ☎206-624-6248 ☎206-405-2996 🖰www.uwajimaya.com Seattle's connection with the Pacific Rim is legendary, and this shop demonstrates the tie with shoji screens and lamps, kanji clocks, gold imari ceramic pieces and Japanese, Chinese, Thai, Vietnamese, Filipino and American canned and frozen foods.

KOBO GALLERY ✉604 South Jackson Street ☎206-381-3000 Housed in the old Higo Variety Store building (a neighborhood institution from the 1920s), the KOBO showcases traditional Japanese handicrafts and contemporary Pacific Northwest.

YE OLDE CURIOSITY SHOP

✉*1001 Alaskan Way, Pier 54* ☎*206-682-5844* ⌂*www.yeoldecuriosityshop. com* Along the waterfront, Piers 54 through 70 are shoppers' delights. You'll love this Seattle landmark where the mummies "Sylvia," "Sylvester" and "Gloria" preside over souvenirs that wouldn't be out of place at Ripley's Believe It or Not. Among the hodgepodge of shrunken heads, Russian folk art and taxidermied animals you'll find a nice collection of native Northwest art. American Indian totem poles, handcarved masks and intricate silver jewelry might seem at odds with some other novelties here, but they just add to the mystique of this museum of oddities.

PIKE PLACE MARKET ✉*85 Pike Street* ☎*206-682-7453* ⌂*www.pikeplace market.org* Called the "Soul of Seattle," this market is a bustling bazaar with nearly 300 businesses (about 40 are eateries), 100 farmers (selling produce and flowers at tables and stalls) and 200 local artists and craftspeople.

PURE FOOD FISH MARKET ✉*1511 Pike Place* ☎*206-622-5765* ⌂*www. freshseafood.com* A notable establishment within the market is Pure Food, which ships fresh or smoked salmon anywhere in the U.S.

In the downtown area, 5th Avenue, Seattle's fashion street, is lined with shops displaying elegant finery and accessories.

NANCY MEYER

✉*1318 5th Avenue* ☎*206-625-9200, 800-605-5098* ⌂*www.nancymeyer. com* This elegant shop specializes in very fine European lingerie. Closed Sunday.

RAINIER SQUARE ✉*1333 5th Avenue Rainier* Prestigious retail establishments dominate this square.

TURGEON RAINE ✉*1407 5th Avenue* ☎*206-447-9488, 800-678-0120* ⌂*www. turgeonraine.com* An exceptionally good, locally owned jewelry store is this one, featuring top-quality gems.

TOTALLY MICHAEL'S ✉*521 Union Street* ☎*206-622-4920* ⌂*www.totally michaels.com* Off 5th Avenue on Union is this shop, which has contemporary, upscale clothing. Closed Sunday.

WESTLAKE CENTER ✉*4th Avenue and Pine Street* At this center there's the **Fireworks Gallery** (206-682-6462; www.fireworksgallery.net), which takes its name from unusually fired sculptures. Also offered are a variety of intriguing home accessories, gifts and jewelry.

MILLSTREAM ✉*400 Pine Street* ☎*206-233-9719* You will find Northwest sculpture, prints, pottery and jewelry by local artisans at this boutique.

ALHAMBRA ✉101 Pine Street 📞206-621-9571 🖃www.alhambranet.com Near the Millstream boutique, this spot offers high-end women's clothing, Indonesian furniture and a variety of jewelry.

NIGHTLIFE

Seattle's nightlife, music and club scene is astounding for a city its size. More than 50 clubs, lounges, restaurants and taverns feature live or deejay-spun music, and dozens more have occasional performances. The offerings run the gamut from folk to punk/metal; dance venues range from midnight raves in port district warehouses to salsa nights at Latin bars.

UNEXPECTED PRODUCTIONS ✉The Market Theater, 1428 Post Alley, Pike Place Market 📞206-587-2414 🖃www.unexpectedproductions.org Check out this venue for comedy performances and workshops in improvisational theater techniques.

COMEDY UNDERGROUND ✉109 South Washington Street 📞206-628-0303 🖃www.comedyunderground.com Comics entertain nightly at this "underground" venue. Cover.

There are many fine nightclubs in Pioneer Square, and on "joint-cover" nights, one charge admits you to nine places within a four-block radius.

DOC MAYNARD'S ✉610 1st Avenue 📞206-682-3705 🖃www.docmaynards.com Heavy on rock-and-roll, this nightclub features live music on weekends. Cover.

NEW ORLEANS CREOLE RESTAURANT ✉114 1st Avenue South 📞206-622-2563 🖃www.neworleanscreolerestaurant.com This restaurant offers live jazz and blues nightly along with Cajun Creole food in an eclectic, laid-back atmosphere. Cover on weekends.

TRINITY NIGHT CLUB ✉111 Yesler Way 📞206-447-4140 🖃www.trinitynightclub.com info@trinitynightclub.com A mixed crowd enjoys deejay dance music at this happening local haunt. Cover.

THE SHOWBOX ✉1426 1st Avenue 📞206-628-3151 🖃www.showboxonline.com This nightclub features local, national and international live bands and all types of music and a full bar. A downtown fixture since 1939, the Showbox has hosted music legends ranging from Duke Ellington and Gypsy Rose Lee to the Ramones and Pearl Jam. A second location, the **Showbox SoDo** (1700 1st Avenue South; 206-652-0444), presents local and West Coast rock bands. Cover.

DIMITRIOU'S JAZZ ALLEY ✉2033 6th Avenue 📞206-441-9729 🖃www.jazzalley.com Dimitriou's is a downtown dinner theater and premier jazz club with international acts. Closed Monday. Cover.

SEATTLE SYMPHONY ✉200 University Street 📞206-215-4700, 206-215-4747 (tickets) 🖃www.seattlesymphony.org, info@seattlesymphony.org The symphony performs at Benaroya Hall. Noted especially for its attention to American composers, the symphony, under the direction of Gerard Schwarz, is one of the top recording orchestras in the United States.

PARAMOUNT THEATRE ✉*911 Pine Street* ☎*206-467-5510* ✐*www.the paramount.com* This elaborate 1920s movie palace now offers diverse events from Broadway musicals to political programs.

SEATTLE CENTER– QUEEN ANNE AREA

Northwest of downtown a familiar landmark rises skyward—the Space Needle. This symbol of the city nestles comfortably among museums, cultural centers and a sports arena at the Seattle Center. Just north of the arts and entertainment complex sits the stunning Queen Anne area, a hilly neighborhood of fanciful homes and great views. This is the part of Seattle where the downtown bustle starts to give way to the more peaceful charms of the outlying neighborhoods.

SIGHTS

SEATTLE CENTER ✉*Two miles north of the downtown core between Denny Way and Mercer Street at 305 Harrison Street* ☎*206-684-7200* ☎*206-684-7342* ✐*www. seattlecenter.com* Once the site of the 1962 World's Fair, this center is now a 74-acre campus with more than a dozen buildings housing a variety of offices, convention rooms and theaters. Locals and visitors continue to flock to the 605-foot-high **Space Needle** (admission; 206-905-2100; www.spaceneedle.com, info@spaceneedle.com) for the view or a meal, to summer carnival rides at the **Fun Forest**, to the **Center House**'s short-order ethnic eateries, to see nearby opera and live theater and to check out wide-ranging exhibits and demonstrations at the **Pacific Science Center** (admission; 206-443-2001, fax 206-443-3631; www.pac sci.org, vs@pacsci.org). The **Seattle Children's Theatre** (206-443-0807, fax 206-443-0442; www.sct.org, info@sct.org) has jovial performances geared to a young audience. The **Pacific Northwest Ballet** (tickets, 206-441-2424, fax 206-441-2420; information, 206-441-9411; www.pnb.org) has its offices and rehearsal space at the Phelps Center (where the public can watch the corps rehearse through a glass wall). For a rewarding, spur-of-the-moment visit, drop by Seattle Center on a summer evening for a contemplative quarter-hour of gazing at the **International Fountain**. The combination of changing lights and waterworks synchronized to music during the first 15 minutes of every hour against a rose-tinted summer sunset can lull you into a dreamy state.

CHILDREN'S MUSEUM, SEATTLE ✉*Seattle Center* ☎*206-441-1768* ☎*206-448-0910* ✐*www.thechildrensmuseum.org* Kids will also enjoy visiting this museum on the ground floor of Center House. The collection features a kids'-sized neighborhood and multicultural global village, a two-story walk-through re-creation of a mountain forest and mechanically oriented displays. There is also a small lagoon for children and a drop-in art studio. Admission.

EXPERIENCE MUSIC PROJECT–SCIENCE FICTION MUSEUM AND HALL OF FAME ✉325 5th Avenue North ✆206-448-9444, 877-367-7361 ✆206-707-2727 ✐www.empsfm.org, experience@empsfm.org

It's obvious from the metallic space-age exterior of this Frank O. Gehry–designed facility that the EMP-SFM is an unusual museum. Half rock-and-roll showroom and half sci-fi gallery, this 140,000-square-foot extravaganza includes an interactive sound stage, an audio history lab, an exploration of extraterrestrials and a display on time-travel technology, along with many other state-of-the-art exhibits. If you've ever dreamed of being a rock star or an astronaut, this one-of-a-kind establishment is well worth your time. Admission.

OLYMPIC SCULPTURE PARK ✉2901 Western Avenue ✆206-332-1377 ✆206-332-1371 ✐www.seattleart museum.org

A nine-acre waterfront park, this newest addition to Seattle's growing art scene showcases ultracontemporary pieces in an outdoor setting. Three smooth eye-shaped figures (which double as benches), a 60-foot-long decaying log in an 80-foot-long greenhouse, a bronze fountain, a glass bridge and numerous skyscraping steel sculptures make up only part of this sweeping public exhibit. The PACCAR Pavilion (closed Monday) within the park houses rotating works by current artists.

KERRY PARK ———— hidden

✉211 West Highland Drive at 2nd Avenue West ✆206-684-4075 For the best possible view of downtown Seattle, search out this tiny (1.6 acres) patch of pavement and emerald-green lawn on the south slope of Queen Anne Hill. It has been used as a background for so many movies and TV news reports that it may evoke a sense of déjà vu. The panorama takes in the Space Needle, all of downtown Seattle, Elliott Bay, Bainbridge Island, the distant Olympic Peninsula and, on particularly clear days, Mt. Rainier. A 15-foot abstract steel sculpture by celebrated Seattle artist Doris Chase crowns the viewpoint.

LODGING

BEST WESTERN EXECUTIVE INN
$$$ 121 ROOMS ✉200 Taylor Avenue North ✆206-448-9444, 800-351-9444 ✆206-441-7836 ✐www.bestwestern.com/executiveinnseattle, info@bwexec-inn.com
Conveniently located two blocks from Seattle Center, half of this inn's rooms offer views of the Space Needle. In the lobby guests enjoy a fitness center with jacuzzi, a full-service restaurant and lounge. A complimentary hot breakfast is offered every morning.

HAMPTON INN & SUITES
$$$ 199 ROOMS ✉700 5th Avenue North ✆206-282-7700, 800-426-7866 ✆206-282-0899 ✐www.hamptoninnseattle.com
On Lower Queen Anne Hill is this inn with standard rooms boasting either a king-sized or two double beds. One- and two-bedroom suites are also available and include fireplaces and full kitchens. Full breakfast buffet included.

Seattle–Queen Anne Area & Capitol Hill

BOREN/INTERLAKEN PARKS

PAGE 60

Secret greenway with views of Lake Washington and miles of trails intertwining moss-covered trees

KERRY PARK

PAGE 53

Tiny patch of emerald green lawn with the quintessential view of Seattle's skyline, including Mt. Rainier

RICE N SPICE

PAGE 55

Fifty-plus authentic Thai dishes rich with flavors of coconut, curry, garlic, peanuts and peppers

DINING

SKYCITY RESTAURANT

$$$$ AMERICAN ✉*400 Broad Street* ☎*206-905-2100* 🖷*206-905-2211*
🖳*www.spaceneedle.com/restaurant, skycitymanagers@spaceneedle.com*

At the Space Needle, the entertainment—from 500 feet up—in either this restaurant or the observation deck is seeing metropolitan Seattle, its environs, Puget Sound, the Olympic Mountains and Mt. Rainier, the Queen of the Cascade Range, as you rotate in a 360° orbit. The restaurant serves various seafood, beef, pasta and poultry dishes, such as honey peppercorn–crusted king salmon and mocha-braised beef short ribs. Weekend brunch. Dress code enforced; no tank tops.

FIVE POINT CAFE

$ DINER ✉*415 Cedar Street* ☎*206-448-9993*

On the plaza at Five Point Square, next to the Chief Seattle statue, this café is a distinctive Seattle landmark. The drinks are stiff, the portions are huge and the ambience is part bar scene, part mom-and-pop diner. The jukebox is usually playing and the lights are dim. Try the meatloaf sandwich or the fish and chips.

MACRINA BAKERY

$$ DINER/BAKERY ✉*2408 1st Avenue* ☎*206-448-4089*
🖳*www.macrinabakery.com, contactus@macrinabakery.com*

For sublime breakfast pastries and delicious Mediterranean-inspired lunch items, head for this cozy European-style bakery and café where the moss green walls are adorned with scrolls, ironwork, paintings and other work by local artists. Breakfast items include house-made coffee cakes, cereals and fruit pastries, while a changing lunch menu may offer such dishes as turkey on ciabatta with aioli, arugula and rhubarb jam.

BOKA

$$$$ PACIFIC NORTHWEST ✉*Hotel 1000, 1010 1st Avenue* 📞*206-357-9000* ✐*www.bokaseattle.com, info@bokaseattle.com*

Hip to the max, BOKA (not a misspelled Spanish word for mouth, but an acronym meaning "bold artistic kitchen artistry") channels old Hollywood for modern Seattle foodies. Here you'll find clever little renditions of the chef's "urban cuisine": sugar cane–skewered Dungeness crab "cupcakes" and pear bruschetta for starters, alongside tuna tartines. Entrées include pan-roasted scallops with spiced carrot mousse and braised pork shank with oven-dried tomato ragout, while the dessert menu boasts pumpkin bread pudding.

RICE N SPICE

$ THAI ✉*101 John Street* 📞*206 205 9000*

Near Seattle Center, this restaurant serves authentic Thai cuisine in a friendly, comfortable setting. There are art objects from Thailand to look at while you wait for your order of Swimming Angel (chicken in a peanut-chili sauce over spinach) or another of the menu's 50-plus items. They vary in hotness and are rich with the flavors of coconut, curry, garlic, peanuts and peppers. No lunch on weekends.

NIGHTLIFE

SEATTLE CENTER ✉*305 Harrison Street* 📞*206-684-8582* ✐*www.seattlecenter.com* Home of the 1962 World's Fair, this center still offers numerous nighttime diversions.

MARION OLIVER MCCAW HALL FOR THE PERFORMING ARTS ✉*321 Mercer Street* 📞*206-389-7676, 800-426-1619* 📠*206-389-7651* ✐*www.seattleopera.org* The Marion Oliver McCaw Hall is the city's opera and ballet companies' glamorous concert hall. Founded in 1964, Seattle Opera is dedicated to producing theatrically compelling, musically accomplished opera. The leading Wagner company in America, the company stages five operas a year.

PACIFIC NORTHWEST BALLET ✉*301 Mercer Street* 📞*206-441-2424* 📠*206-441-2420* ✐*www.pnb.org, tickets@pnb.org* This company's annual production of Tchaikovsky's *Nutcracker*, with fanciful sets designed by famed children's illustrator Maurice Sendak, is a perennial favorite.

SEATTLE SYMPHONY ✉*200 University Street* 📞*206-215-4747, 866-833-4747* ✐*www.seattlesymphony.org, info@seattlesymphony.org* Music director Gerard Schwarz has led the Seattle Symphony to prominence by focusing on baroque and romantic classics and formerly little-known American composers such as Alan Hovhaness (a longtime Seattle resident), David

Diamond and Howard Hanson. Masterworks symphony concerts are Thursday, Friday and Saturday evenings and Sunday afternoons. Tickets are often still available on performance days, which offers visitors the chance to see one of the top orchestral ensembles in the United States. No shows August to early September.

SEATTLE REPERTORY THEATRE ✉*155 Mercer Street between Warren Avenue and 2nd Avenue North* ☎*206-443-2222, 877-900-9285* ✎*www.seattlerep.org* This rep company plays an eclectic mix from musicals to classic dramas at the **Bagley Wright Theatre** and the **Leo K. Theatre**.

INTIMAN THEATRE ✉*201 Mercer Street at 2nd Avenue North* ☎*206-269-1900* ✎*www.intiman.org, intiman@intiman.org* From April to December, this theatre presents plays by the great dramatists, as well as new works.

ACT THEATRE ✉*700 Union Street* ☎*206-292-7676* ✎*www.acttheatre.org, service@acttheatre.org* In the old Eagles Auditorium next to the Convention Center, ACT specializes in works by new playwrights.

CAPITOL HILL

Seattle's sizable gay population and diverse array of gay inns, clubs and meeting places is one of the many reasons travelers are increasingly flocking to the city. While gay activities and nightlife are found throughout the city, the highest concentration is in Capitol Hill, one of Seattle's most cosmopolitan neighborhoods. Take a walk down Broadway in Capitol Hill, and you'll see one of the most vibrant gay communities in the country.

SIGHTS

CAPITOL HILL This mixed neighborhood is a fun place to browse. Within a block or two you can toss back an exotic wheatgrass drink at a vegetarian bar, slowly sip a double espresso at a sidewalk café, shop for radical literature at a leftist bookstore or hit a straight or gay nightclub. If you can't find it on Capitol Hill, Seattle probably doesn't have it. Broadway Avenue is the heart of this region known for its boutiques, yuppie appliance stores and bead shops.

VOLUNTEER PARK ✉*15th Avenue East from East Prospect Street to East Galer Street* Home of some of the city's finest Victorians, the Capitol Hill neighborhood also includes this park. Be sure to head up to the top of the water tower for a great view of the region.

SEATTLE ASIAN ART MUSEUM ✉*Volunteer Park, 1400 East Prospect Street* ☎*206-654-3206* ☎*206-654-3191* ✎*www.seattleartmuseum.org* Housed in an Art Moderne–style building, this museum features Japanese, Chinese and Korean collections, but also has works from south and southeast Asia. Japanese folk textiles, Thai ceramics and Korean screen paintings are some of the highlights. Admission. Closed Monday and Tuesday in winter.

SALISBURY HOUSE BED & BREAKFAST

$$–$$$ 5 UNITS   ✉750 16th Avenue East   ✆206-328-8682   ✇206-720-1019
🖰www.salisburyhouse.com, sleep@salisburyhouse.com

The Salisbury House is a quiet, dignified, gracious Capitol Hill home two blocks from Volunteer Park. The five crisp, clean rooms (all have private baths) are furnished with antiques and wicker; only the fully equipped 600-square-foot suite boasts a television. Fresh flowers, duvets on the beds, a full (meatless) breakfast and thoughtful innkeeper make this a well-done B&B.

GASLIGHT INN

$$ 8 ROOMS   ✉1727 15th Avenue East   ✆206-325-3654   ✇206-328-4803
🖰www.gaslight-inn.com, innkeepr@gaslight-inn.com

In the popular, busy Capitol Hill area, this bed and breakfast is brimming with urban flair. The 1906 house is furnished with oak, maple and glass antiques. Various period styles have been effectively combined with modern amenities in the guest rooms. Most have private baths, and one boasts a fireplace. Gaslight has a heated, outdoor swimming pool (closed in winter) and an outdoor deck that overlooks the city. A continental buffet breakfast is served.

BACON MANSION

$$$ 12 UNITS   ✉959 Broadway East   ✆206-329-1864, 800-240-1864
✇206-860-9025   🖰www.baconmansion.com, info@baconmansion.com

On Capitol Hill near Volunteer Park in the Harvard-Belmont Historic District is this 1909 Tudor stucco home. In addition to the two-story carriage house, which has a living room, dining room and two guest rooms with a private bath in each, there are nine guest rooms in the main house, seven with private bath. The Capitol suite has a sun room with wet bar, fireplace, king-sized bed and a big bathtub.

DINING

611 SUPREME

$–$$ FRENCH   ✉611 East Pine Street   ✆206-328-0292   🖰www.611supreme.com, info@611supreme.com

West of Broadway, on Pike and Pine streets, is a collection of bars and restaurants catering to the hipster population. The 611 is a cheery, comfy café specializing in crêpes both sweet and savory. Try the Gruyere and sautéed vegetables crêpe, or the citron version. No lunch on Monday. Weekend brunch.

AYUTTHAYA

$ THAI   ✉727 East Pike Street   ✆206-324-8833   ✇206-324-3135

A corner restaurant in Capitol Hill, this place is renowned for its Thai cookery. Small, clean-lined and pleasant in light wood, Ayutthaya features plenty of chicken and seafood dishes along with soups and noodles. Flavors blend deliciously in the curried shrimp with green beans, coconut milk and basil. Or try the chicken sautéed in peanut-chili sauce. No lunch on Sunday.

CAFÉ SEPTIÈME
$$ AMERICAN/FRENCH ✉*214 Broadway East* ☎*206-860-8858* 🖷*206-860-0760*
This is a re-creation of the small Parisian cafés that cater to the literati and students. A full-service restaurant, it carries plenty of reading material and turns out cups of good coffee, lattes and light fare. Sandwiches and salads are standard, but the real treat is the mouth-watering display table, loaded with cakes, pies and cookies. Breakfast, lunch and dinner.

SHOPPING

The trendy boutiques of Capitol Hill draw shoppers looking for the unusual, though there are many standard stores, too. You'll see dozens of shops with new and vintage clothing, pop culture items, ethnic wear and artifacts, all interspersed with myriad cafés and coffeehouses.

BABELAND ✉*707 East Pike Street* ☎*206-328-2914* ⌖*www.babeland.com* Yes, it's a sex shop. But Babeland isn't what you'd expect. Plate-glass front windows, plenty of lighting and a comfy bench have turned this purveyor of toys, books and body products into a neighborhood hangout. Come here to feel empowered, admire the tasteful-albeit-pornographic glass art and meet more locals than at the corner café.

BROADWAY MARKET ✉*401 Broadway East* ☎*206-322-1800* This Capitol Hill market is filled with popular shops like **Urban Outfitters**, which features casual urban wares, offers new and vintage clothing, jewelry, housewares and shoes for the hip crowd.

BAILEY/COY BOOKS ✉*414 Broadway East* ☎*206-323-8842* ⌖*www.bailey coybooks.com* Check out this shop, which is well-stocked with reading material, including gay and lesbian literature.

NIGHTLIFE

In the "Pike-Pine corridor," west of Broadway, a string of stylish (and stylized) bars stretches toward downtown. East of Broadway, the clubs along Pike and Pine drop down a notch on the scene scale and gain in loungeability.

EL CORAZÓN
✉*109 Eastlake Avenue East* ☎*206-381-2094* ⌖*www.elcorazonseattle.com*
Formerly known by various names, this small, loud live music venue has been a staple of the Seattle Sound for decades. In 1990, Pearl Jam performed for the first time in public here. Through all its changes, the club has kept its focus on grunge, punk and metal rock music. Mexican bar food is served.

BALTIC ROOM ✉*1207 Pine Street* ☎*206-625-4444* ⌖*www.thebalticroom.net*
With its mohair booths and starry ceiling, this glamorous retro cocktail

lounge sets the standard. Music (both live and deejayed) ranges from jazz to hip-hop to Bollywood. Cover.

NEUMO'S CRYSTAL BALL AND READING ROOM

✉925 East Pike Street ☎206-709-9467 🖱www.neumos.com
Known in the early '90s as ground-zero for the Seattle grunge scene, this spot reopened as Neumo's in 2003 and is now a proving ground for a new generation of Seattle Sound bands. What's new now? Check it out and hear for yourself.

BARÇA ✉1510 11th Avenue ☎206-325-8263 🖱www.barcaseattle.com This slinky lounge, although less crowded than the Baltic Room, lacks in live music. Prime viewing is from the balcony.

SEATTLE INTERNATIONAL FILM FESTIVAL ☎206-324-9996 (box office), 206-464-5830 🖱www.siff.net, info@siff.net Robert Redford's Sundance Festival may be more famous, but this International Film Festival is actually the longest-running, largest and most highly attended film festival in the country. Each spring, SIFF draws hundreds of thousands of cinema lovers for its 25-day run, usually in Capitol Hill and downtown theaters, and each year at least one of the SIFF favorites goes on to national acclaim. Admission.

Gay Scene
Capitol Hill offers a number of popular gay and lesbian clubs and bars, including the following:

R PLACE BAR & GRILL ✉619 East Pine Street ☎206-322-8828 🖱www.rplaceseattle.com, rplace@qwest.net Depending on your mood when you're here, you can plunk down at the sports bar, throw darts, enjoy a music video, shoot pool, enjoy tunes from the jukebox or deejay, take advantage of the dancefloor or feast on quesadillas and taco salad. Weekly events include karaoke.

NEIGHBOURS ✉1509 Broadway ☎206-324-5358 🖱www.neighboursonline.com, neighbours@guest.net This hotspot offers deejay dance music from retro disco to Latin. Closed Monday. Cover.

WILD ROSE ✉1021 East Pike Street ☎206-324-9210 🖱www.thewildrosebar.com Founded in 1984, this venue claims to be the oldest women's bar on the West Coast, offering food and drink, pool tables and video games as well as camaraderie. Monday is reserved for trivia and Wednesday for karaoke. Occasional live music.

MADISON PUB ✉1315 E. Madison Street, 206-325-6537 This pub is a laid-back neighborhood local. It's just the place to enjoy a few pints, a game of pool or darts, and watch the game.

SEATTLE GAY NEWS 🖱www.sgn.org For a comprehensive list of Seattle's gay arts and entertainment scene, pick up a copy of this weekly paper.

PARKS

BOREN/INTERLAKEN PARKS ___ hidden

✉ *Entry points are on 15th Avenue East across from the Lakeview cemetery and at East Galer Street and East Interlaken Boulevard.* ☎ *206-684-4075*

A secret greenway close to downtown is preserved by these neighboring parks on Capitol Hill; it's just right for an afternoon or evening stroll. With miles of intertwining hiking and biking trails, you'll get lost in the densely packed, moss-covered trees and be so dazzled by the sunlight filtering through the leaves that you'll forget your anywhere near the city. Jogging paths treat visitors to panoramic views of Lake Washington.

OUTLYING NEIGHBORHOODS

While downtown is the city's magnet, some of Seattle's best parks, sightseeing and nightlife can be found in its nearby neighborhoods. Arboretums and science museums, lakeside dining and shopping worth a special trip are all in this region.

SIGHTS

LAKE UNION   The six miles or so of shoreline circling this lake present a varied mix of boat works and nautical specialty shops, street-end pocket parks, boat-in restaurants, seaplane docks, rental-boat concessions, ocean research vessels, houseboats and flashy condos. You could spend a day exploring funky old warehouses and oddball enterprises. The lake's south end offers extensive public access to the shore behind a cluster of restaurants, a wooden-boat center and new park.

LAKE WASHINGTON SHIP CANAL   Few guidebooks look at this canal as a single unit. Yet it ties together a wondrous diversity of working waterfront and recreational shoreline along eight miles of bay, lake and canal between Puget Sound and Lake Washington. Construction of the locks and canal began in 1911 and created a shipping channel from Lake Washington to Lake Union to Puget Sound. Along its banks today you can see perhaps the liveliest continuous boat parade in the West: tugs gingerly inching four-story-tall, Alaska-bound barges through narrow locks; rowboats, kayaks, sailboards and luxury yachts; gillnetters and trawlers in dry dock; government research vessels; aging houseboats listing at their moorings; and seaplanes roaring overhead.

All in all, the ship canal presents a splendid overview of Seattle's rich maritime traditions. But you'll also discover plenty that's new—rejuvenated neighborhoods like Fremont and south Lake Union's upscale shoreline, a renovated Fisherman's Terminal and a handful of trendy,

Outlying Neighborhoods

DAYBREAK STAR CULTURAL CENTER

PAGE 62

Gallery featuring rich, vibrant, contemporary art and the legends of the Northwest's deep history

PONTI SEAFOOD GRILL

PAGE 66

Mediterranean-style seafood dishes served with spectacular canal views from flower-filled patios

FOSTER ISLAND TRAIL

PAGE 63

Intriguing hike through marshy wetlands teeming with fish and fowl at the edge of Lake Washington

waterside restaurants. Amid the hubbub of boat traffic and ship chandlers, you'll also encounter quiet, street-end parks for birdwatching, foot and bike paths, the best historical museum in the city and one of the West's renowned arboretums. Here's a summary, west to east.

HIRAM M. CHITTENDEN LOCKS ☎206-783-7059 ☎206-782-3192 This waterway in Ballard is where all boats heading east or west in the ship canal must pass and thus presents the quintessential floating boat show; it's one of the most-visited attractions in the city. Visitors crowd railings and jam footbridges to watch as harried lock-keepers scurry to get boats tied up properly before locks are either raised or lowered, depending on the boat's direction of passage. Terraced parks flanking the canal provide splendid picnic overlooks. An underwater fish-viewing window gives you astonishing looks at several species of salmon, steelhead and sea-going cutthroat trout on their spawning migrations (June to November). Lovely botanical gardens in a parklike setting offer yet more diversion. The visitors center offers free guided tours from March through November. The center is closed Tuesday and Wednesday from October through April.

FISHERMAN'S TERMINAL ✉On the south side of Salmon Bay about a mile east of the locks ☎206-728-3395, 800-426-7817 ☎206-728-3393 ⌂www.portseattle.org, ft@portseattle.org Home port to one of the world's biggest fishing fleets (some 700 vessels, most of which chug north into Alaskan waters for summer salmon fishing) is Fisherman's Terminal. You'll always be able to see boats here—gill-netters, purse-seiners, trollers, factory ships—and working fishermen repairing nets, painting boats and the like. Here, too, are net-drying sheds, shops selling marine hardware and commercial fishing tackle. One café opens at 6:30 a.m. for working fish-

Outlying Neighborhoods

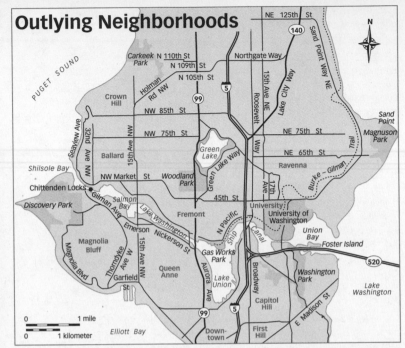

N

NE 125th St

140

NE 75th St

NE 65th St

Northgate Way

5

99

Carkeek Park

N 110th St

N 109th St

N 105th St

Crown Hill

NW 85th St

NW 75th St

Green Lake

NW Market St

Woodland Park

Fremont

45th St

University

University of Washington

Ballard

Shilsole Bay

Chittenden Locks

Discovery Park

Salmon Bay

Gilman Ave

Magnolia Bluff

Magnolia Blvd

Thorndyke Ave W

Garfield St

Queen Anne

Gas Works Park

Lake Union

Emerson

Nickerson St

N Pacific

Ship Canal

Aurora Ave

Broadway

Capitol Hill

Down-town

First Hill

Lake Washington

Washington Park

E Madison St

520

Union Bay

Foster Island

Ravenna

Burke – Gilman Trail

Magnuson Park

Sand Point

Sand Point Way NE

Lake City Way

15th Ave NE

Roosevelt Way

Seaview Ave

32nd Ave NW

15th Ave NW

Holman Rd NW

17th Ave

Green Lake Way

Lake Washington

15th Ave NW

PUGET SOUND

Shilsole Bay

Elliott Bay

0   1 mile

0   1 kilometer

ermen; there's a fish-and-chips window and one good seafood restaurant (Chinook's) overlooking the waterway.

DAYBREAK STAR CULTURAL CENTER ⬭ⓗidden

✉*Discovery Park, 3801 West Government Way* ☎*206-285-4425* ✑*www.unitedindians.org, info@unitedindians.org* Located on 20 acres in Discovery Park, this center operates as a cultural meeting place for American Indian communities in the Seattle area. The art gallery here is a testament to this group's dedication to preserving native Northwest culture. The permanent collection features works by artists from around the country, but several pieces use rich Washington woods and vibrant colors to convey the legends of the Pacific Northwest.

FREMONT DISTRICT ✉*North 34th to 36th Streets North around Fremont Avenue; Take Aurora Avenue North (Route 99) to North 34th Street and turn west just before the bridge across the canal.* A few decades ago, this district was a run-down warehouse zone. Now a lively public arts program and a grass-roots public relations effort touting the district as "Far from Normal" have helped transform it into an active artists' colony, and gentrification has begun to set in. Besides the array of art galleries and studios, antique shops and specialty stores, the Fremont District's economy has diversified to include the 17,000-square-foot Fremont Fine Arts Foundry, which includes a major art gallery. Tours of the district are available with local artist Roger Wheeler (206-634-1569; maskman@nocharge.zzn.com).

GAS WORKS PARK ✉️*2101 North Northlake Way* 📞*206-684-4075* This park occupies property that dangles like a giant green tonsil from Lake Union's north shore. Until 1956, the park's namesake "gas works" produced synthetic natural gas from coal and crude oil. Some of the rusting congeries of pipes, airy catwalks, spiraling ladders, tall towers and stubby tanks were torn down during park construction, but enough remains (repainted in snappy colors) to fascinate youngsters and old-timers alike.

WASHINGTON PARK On the south side of Union Bay, this 230-acre park at Lake Washington Boulevard East and East Madison Street presents enough diversions indoors and out to fill a rich day of exploring in all sorts of weather.

WASHINGTON PARK ARBORETUM ✉️*Visitors Center: Arboretum Drive East* 📞*206-543-8800* 📠*206-616-2871* 🌐*www.wparboretum.org, uwbg@u.washington.edu* The most famous attraction in the neighborhood is this park arboretum (which occupies most of the park with 10,000 plants), at its best in the spring when rhododendrons and azaleas—some 10 to 15 feet tall—and groves of spreading chestnuts, dogwoods, magnolias and other flowering trees leap into bloom. Short footpaths beckon from the Visitors Center. But two in particular deserve mention—Azalea Way and Loderi Valley—which wend their way down avenues of pink, cream, yellow, crimson and white blooms. The arboretum's renowned Japanese Garden (admission, 206-684-4725) is especially rewarding in the spring months, and both arboretum and garden present splendid fall colors in October and early November. In the Winter Garden, everything is fragrant, and the Woodland Garden highlights the arboretum's acclaimed collection of Japanese maples.

FOSTER ISLAND TRAIL
Miles of duff-covered footpaths lace Washington Park. For naturalists, the premier experience will be found along this one-and-a-half-mile (each way) trail at the north end of the park on Foster Island behind the Museum of History and Industry (see later in this section). The footpath takes you on an intriguing bog-walk over low bridges and along boardwalks through marshy wetlands teeming with ducks and wildfowl, fish and frogs and aquatic flora growing rank at the edge of Lake Washington.

FOSTER ISLAND In summer, you can join the canoeists paddling the labyrinth of waterways around this island, sunbathers and picnickers sprawling on lawns, anglers casting for catfish and trout and the swimmers cooling off on hot August afternoons. Canoes are for rent through the University of Washington.

MUSEUM OF HISTORY AND INDUSTRY ✉️*2700 24th Avenue East* 📞*206-324-1126* 📠*206-324-1346* 🌐*www.seattlehistory.org, information@seattlehistory.org* On rainy days, this museum is a fitting retreat. It's the city's best early-day collection and pays special tribute to Puget Sound's rich maritime history, as befits any museum located next door to this vital waterway. In 2008 a new permanent exhibit opened detailing 150 years of Seattle history. Admission.

UNIVERSITY OF WASHINGTON Exceptional architecture, a garden setting and easy access make a campus tour of this university (locals call it U-dub) a highlight of a Seattle visit. The university began downtown in 1861; in 1895, it was moved to its present site. The Alaska–Yukon–Pacific Exposition of 1909 was held on the campus, and several of its fine buildings date from that event.

The campus borders the canal north of Montlake Cut (part of the waterway) and is a haven for anyone who enjoys the simple pleasure of strolling across a college campus. It boggles the mind to think of what awaits you on its 693 acres—handsome old buildings in architectural styles from Romanesque to modern; Frosh Pond; the **Henry Art Gallery** (closed Monday, 206-543-2280, fax 206-685-3123; www.henryart.org) with its marvelous textiles and contemporary exhibits; red-brick quads and expanses of lawn and colorful summer gardens; canal-side trails on both sides of the Montlake Cut; access to the Burke-Gilman Trail; and a lakeside **Waterfront Activity Center** (206-543-9433; h2ofront@u.washington.edu) with canoe and rowboat rentals. Pick up a free walking tour map at the visitors center (206-543-9198) in Odegaard Undergraduate Library on George Washington Lane.

BURKE MUSEUM OF NATURAL HISTORY AND CULTURE

✉️*University of Washington, at 17th Avenue Northeast and Northeast 45th Street* 📞*206-543-5590* 📠*206-685-3039* 🌐*www.burkemuseum.org, the burke@u.washington.edu* Boasting the fifth largest collection of Northwest Coast Indian art in the country, this museum within the university offers a study in the region's indigenous cultures through jewelry, sculpture, instruments, weapons and tools. Nearly 10,000 items comprise the collection, and rotating exhibits feature specific types of works, such as dance masks and wood carvings. Towering totem poles greet visitors upon arrival. Admission.

A mile or so north of the ship canal, Woodland Park and Green Lake Park straddle Aurora Avenue North (Route 99) and together offer more than 400 acres of park, lake and zoo attractions.

WOODLAND PARK ZOO ✉️*Fremont Avenue North and North 50th Street* 📞*206-548-2500* 📠*206-548-1536* 🌐*www.zoo.org, webkeeper@zoo.org* The star of the parks is Woodland, which has won praise for its program of converting static exhibits into more natural, often outdoor environments. Most notable are the African Savannah, Gorilla Exhibit, the Willawong Station, the Jaguar Exhibit and the Elephant Forest. There's also a Tropical Rain Forest, heralded as a "journey through different levels of forest," and a seasonal contact yard and family farm. Admission.

GREEN LAKE PARK   Enormously popular with all ages and classes of Seattleites, this park is simply the best outdoor people-watching place in the city. Two loop trails circle the shore (the inner trail is 2 miles long, the outer 3.2 miles) and welcome all comers. On summer days, both paths are filled with strollers and race-walkers, joggers and skaters, bikers and nannies pushing prams. On the lake you will see anglers, canoeists, sailboarders, swimmers, birdwatchers and folks floating in inner tubes.

LODGING

Seattle's neighborhoods offer several hotels and numerous bed-and-breakfast accommodations. A bed and breakfast can be a great value, offering a casual atmosphere, home-cooked food included in the room rate and personal contact with an innkeeper who usually knows the city well.

PACIFIC RESERVATION SERVICE 206-439-7677, 800-684-2932 206-282-1351 www.seattlebedandbreakfast.com, information@seattlebedandbreakfast.com This company can help book rooms at a variety of bed-and-breakfast accommodations, including cabins, cottages and traditional inns. Closed weekends.

CHAMBERED NAUTILUS BED AND BREAKFAST INN
$$–$$$ 10 UNITS   5005 22nd Avenue Northeast 206-522-2536, 800 545-8459 206-528-0898 www.chamberednautilus.com, stay@chamberednautilus.com
A favorite of visitors to the University of Washington, both gay and straight, this inn is only four blocks from the campus. Games and books, soft chairs by the fireplace and all-day tea and cookies create a sense of homeyness. All guests rooms have private baths and four feature private porches; two have gas fireplaces, and four offer kitchens. A business room with printer, computer and fax machine is always open. A full gourmet breakfast is served, sometimes on the sun porch.

HOTEL DECA
$$$–$$$$ 158 UNITS   4507 Brooklyn Avenue Northeast 206-634-2000, 800-899-0251 206-547-6029 www.hoteldeca.com, reservations@hoteldeca.com
In the University District is this 16-story tower with 155 corner rooms and three suites with balconies. All units have views of the mountains or the lake and cityscape. Standard hotel furnishings adorn the spacious rooms, decorated in Art Deco style. A handsome restaurant and lounge are on the floor below the lobby.

DINING

SANTA FE CAFE
$$ SOUTHWESTERN   5910 Phinney Avenue North 206-783-9755
This café is more upscale than what you may expect, offering a fussier version of Southwestern cuisine, more avocados and cilantro than beans and tortillas. Chile-flavored beer, anyone? Wags might call it Northwest/Southwest Contemporary cuisine; it's worth a visit after a trip to the Woodland Park Zoo.

35TH STREET BISTRO

$$–$$$ FRENCH   ✉709 North 35th Street   ☎206-547-9850   🖱www.35bistro.com, info@35bistro.com

When you're nostalgic for a neighborhood restaurant with an upbeat, casual flavor, head for this bistro. Set in the unpretentious Fremont District, it has high windows, a friendly atmosphere, music, and a seasonal southern European–inspired menu. Try the white wine and truffle–poached chicken or the grilled steak with horseradish and hand-cut french fries. No lunch on Monday. Weekend brunch available.

PONTI SEAFOOD GRILL

$$$$ SEAFOOD/EUROPEAN FUSION   ✉3014 3rd Avenue North ☎206-284-3000   🖷206-284-4768   🖱www.pontiseafoodgrill.com, info@pontiseafoodgrill.com

This grill is near the Fremont Bridge on the Lake Washington ship canal. The Mediterranean-style restaurant offers spectacular views of the canal from flower filled patios. The menu features mostly seafood—fresh seafood—though there are creative pasta, steak and chicken dishes as well. Dinner only.

ELEMENTAL

$$ PACIFIC NORTHWEST   ✉3309 Wallingford Avenue North   ☎206-547-2317 🖱www.elementalatgasworks.com, elemental@gasworks.com

Located in the bottom of a condo complex overlooking Gas Works Park, this is a tiny *bijou* eatery that lives up to its own billing as "an eclectic culinary endeavor." The free-form menu changes every Tuesday and draws inspiration from whatever is organic, fresh and local that week. Entrées range from the delightfully unusual (espresso roast duck with grape flatbread) to the frankly far-out (pickled lamb tongue with onion strudel). For $10 a head, owner Phred Westfall, a wine connoisseur, will select a glass of wine for you to accompany each course. This is adventurous eating at its best. Closed Monday.

IVAR'S SALMON HOUSE

$$–$$$ SEAFOOD   ✉401 Northeast Northlake Way   ☎206-632-0767 🖱www.ivars.net, webmail@keepclam.com

Touristy though it may be, the great view, alder-grilled fish and historic photos of native Salish people in old-time Seattle combine to make Ivar's a great Seattle restaurant. The restaurant is a replica Northwest American Indian longhouse, complete with an open-pit barbecue, and features views of the kayak, canoe, tugboat, windsurfer and yacht activity on Lake Union. The menu includes Northwest American Indian–style alder-roasted salmon, pork loin and halibut.

FARESTART

$$ AMERICAN   ✉7th Avenue and Virginia Street   ☎206-443-1233 ext. 6210 🖱www.farestart.org, reservations@farestart.org

In 1992, a group of star chefs from some of Seattle's best-known restaurants got together to create a unique training program aimed at teaching commercial kitchen skills to the homeless. Since its inception, Fare-Start has trained over 1500 homeless people and now prepares meals for local shelters and also serves daily lunch and Thursday-night dinners in their own Lake Union building. Most popular are the Guest Chef Dinners, where 200 lucky diners get to sample what the young trainees have been learning. An assortment of soups, salads and sandwiches are served. The meals are a frequent sellout, so book well in advance.

KINGFISH CAFÉ

$$ SOUTHERN ✉602 19th Avenue East ☏206-320-8757
🖫www.thekingfishcafe.com, kingfishcafe@aol.com

You don't have to travel to the Deep South to get a taste of gourmet soul cookin', but expect to wait in line at this stylish café, where sepia-tinted family-album photos (including one of cousin Langston Hughes, the great African-American writer) adorn the walls. Miss Choo Choo's Company's Commin' Steak is a menu favorite, along with the buttermilk fried chicken, the barbecued pork, and the crab and catfish cakes (served Benedict style at Sunday brunch).

ROVER'S

$$$ PACIFIC NORTHWEST ✉2808 East Madison Street ☏206-325-7442
📠206-325-1092 🖫www.rovers-seattle.com

In a small house surrounded by gardens, this restaurant specializes in multi-course meals of Northwest cuisine with a French accent and is just the place for those romantic occasions. Chef Thierry Rautureau creates the ever-changing menu based on locally available, fresh produce. In addition to seafood in imaginative sauces, entrées might include rabbit, venison, pheasant and quail. A good selection of Northwest and French wines is available. Service is friendly and helpful. Lunch is only served on Friday. Closed Monday.

CACTUS

$$ SPANISH/SOUTHWESTERN ✉4220 East Madison Street ☏206-324-4140
🖫www.cactusrestaurants.com, comments@cactusrestaurants.com

A colorful and lively Spanish-eclectic restaurant in the Madison Park area, Cactus serves a cuisine representative of many different cultures, but mostly influenced by Southwestern food. Start with a salad of baby field greens topped with grilled steak, bleu cheese, pico de gallo and chipotle-balsamic vinaigrette or orange jalapeño-marinated prawns with pineapple salsa. No lunch on Sunday.

SHOPPING

ARCHIE MCPHEE'S ✉2428 Northwest Market Street, Ballard ☏206-297-0240
🖫www.mcphee.com This toy and novelty store primarily for grown-ups with a strange sense of humor is the place to go if you're in the market for a Jesus bobblehead doll, a Jane Austen action figure, the world's largest champagne glass or an inflatable fruitcake. Look for the trademark giant lizard head on the building's exterior.

WASHINGTON PARK ARBORETUM VISITOR CENTER GIFT SHOP ✉2300 Arboretum Drive East ☏206-325-4510 At this gift shop are gardening books, cards, china, earrings, necklaces, serving trays and sweatshirts. You can also buy plants from the arboretum greenhouse.

LA TIENDA/FOLK ART GALLERY ✉2050 Northwest Market Street, 206-297-3605 ✐www.latienda-folkart.com Dominated by the UW campus is the University District, a commercial neighborhood overflowing with a vast array of retail shops. At this one you'll find handpicked craft items, jewelry and textiles from all over the world, including those made by 200 selected American artisans. Closed Sunday.

NIGHTLIFE

CONOR BYRNE'S ✉5140 Ballard Avenue Northwest ☎206-784-3640 ✐www.conorbyrnepub.com In Ballard, this pub has live music, specializing in Irish, folk, bluegrass and blues five nights a week. The Old World building has exposed bricks, high ceilings, original art and low light. Weekend cover.

THE TRACTOR ✉5213 Ballard Avenue Northwest ☎206-789-3599 ✐www.tractortavern.ypguides.net, schedule@tractortavern.com This tavern offers a mix of live rock, country, Celtic, jazz and alternative music five to seven nights a week. Cover.

GIGGLES COMEDY CLUB ✉5220 Roosevelt Way Northeast ☎206-526-5653 ✐www.gigglescomedyclub.com There are cocktail service, full dinner and comedy shows Thursday through Sunday at Giggles. One-drink minimum in addition to cover on Friday and Saturday.

BIG TIME BREWERY & ALEHOUSE ✉4133 University Way Northeast ☎206-545-4509 ✐www.bigtimebrewery.com, comments@bigtimebrewery.com Located just barely off campus, the happening student hangout in the University District is Big Time, which offers beer, pizza and a rowdy young crowd. Seattle's oldest brewpub (c. 1988), it has an antique bar, shuffleboard in the back room and a museum-like collection of beer bottles, cans, signs and memorabilia. Closed Sunday.

ZOO TUNES ✉Fremont Avenue North and North 50th Street ☎206-615-0076 ✐www.zoo.org, concerts@zoo.org One of Seattle's most eagerly anticipated and fun summer events is this evening concert series, held in the zoo's North Meadow with festival seating. Bring a picnic and the whole family and enjoy great music by artists like the Indigo Girls, Little Feat, Leo Kottke, Shawn Colvin, David Wilcox and others (with a little bit of lions, tigers and bears, oh my! chorusing in the background). All proceeds benefit the zoo.

BEACHES & PARKS

DISCOVERY PARK

✉Located a quarter-hour drive north of downtown in the Magnolia district. The main entrance is at 3801 West Government Way and 36th Avenue West. ☎206-386-4236 ✐discover@seattle.gov

🚶 🚲 With two miles of beach trail and nine miles of footpaths winding through mixed forest and across open meadows, this bluff-top preserve (Seattle's largest at more than 550 acres) protects a remarkable "urban wilderness." Here are sweeping vistas, chances to watch birds (including nesting bald eagles) and study nature, the **Daybreak Star Cultural Center**, an interpretive center (closed Monday), four miles of road for bicycling and an 1881 lighthouse (oldest in the area). Fort Lawton Historic District includes Officers' Row and military buildings surviving from the park's days as an Army fort. There are areas suitable for picnics; restrooms and a visitor center are at the park's east gate.

CARKEEK PARK

✉ *950 Northwest Carkeek Park Road. Take 3rd Avenue Northwest to 110th Street Northwest, turn and follow the signs.* 📞 *206-684-0877* 📠 *206-364-4685*

🚶🚴 Tucked into a woodsy canyon reaching toward Puget Sound, this 216-acre wildland protects Piper's Creek and its resurrected runs of salmon and sea-going trout. Signs explain how citizens helped clean up the stream and bring the salmon back. Trails lead past spawning waters, to the top of the canyon and through a native-plant garden. Follow wooded paths to the bluff overlooking the beach for magnificent views of the Sound and the Olympic Mountains. There are also shorter walks perfect for families with small children. You will find picnic areas, restrooms, play areas and beachcombing (as long as you take nothing home with you), a pioneer orchard as well as an educational learning center (closed weekends).

WARREN G. MAGNUSON PARK

✉ *Located on Lake Washington, northeast of downtown Seattle, at 7400 Sand Point Way Northeast and 65th Avenue Northeast* 📞 *206-684-4946* 📠 *206-684-4997* ✏ *parksinfo@seattle.gov*

🚴 ⛵ 🚤 🏊 This 350-acre site carved from the Sand Point Naval Air Station presents generous access to Lake Washington and wide views across the lake. It's a favorite place to launch a boat, swim or toss a frisbee. You'll find picnic areas, restrooms, softball fields, tennis courts, swimming beaches with summer lifeguards, a community center and garden and a wheelchair-accessible wading pool. Adjacent to the park is the National Oceanic Atmospheric Administration's **Sound Garden**, which is full of sculptures that move and chime when the wind blows. The melodic garden gave the Seattle multiplatinum rock band its name. (Visitors who want to tour the garden must show picture ID at a checkpoint entrance at 77th Street and Sand Point Way.)

SEWARD PARK

✉ *5902 Lake Washington Boulevard South; Located on the west shore of Lake Washington, southeast of downtown, at South Orcas Street* 📞 *206-684-4075* 📠 *206-684-4853* ✏ *parksinfo@seattle.gov*

🚶🚴 ⛵ 🚤 🏊 🛶 On Bailey Peninsula, this 300-acre park jutting into Lake Washington encompasses Seattle's largest virgin forest. Walking through it on one of several footpaths is the prime attraction, but many come to swim and sunbathe, launch a small boat, fish or visit a fish hatchery. Seward Park offers a rare opportunity to see nesting bald eagles in an urban setting. The best introductory walk is the two-and-a-half-mile shoreline loop stroll; to see the large Douglas firs, add another mile along the center of the peninsula. The swimming beaches' gentle surf is ideal for children, and there are lifeguards in summer. You can fish from the pier for crappie and trout. There are tennis courts, picnic areas, restrooms and play areas.

SEATTLE NORTH

Heading north from Seattle, you'll cross the county line (into Snohomish County) toward the less urban and more maritime cities and villages lining Northern Puget Sound. You don't have to travel far to catch a glimpse of the region's past, before Seattlemania lured businesses and families to relocate here. North of Seattle you'll find a slower pace and strong reminders of Washington's history.

SIGHTS

EDMONDS North of Seattle, this long-time mill town has a lot of charm and provides a link to the Olympic Peninsula.

PORT OF EDMONDS ⊠*336 Admiral Way* ☎*425-775-4588 (marina operatons)*, *425-774-0549 (main office)* ⏎*www.portofedmonds.org* Ferries leave hourly from this lively marina located on the east side of Puget Sound. With about 50 businesses, including restaurants and shops as well as a beach park and a long fishing pier, it makes a great boardwalk destination. There is also an underwater park that is popular with divers. The park teems with marine life that swims around sunken structures: boats, a dock, a bridge model and others. On shore, the **Edmonds Discovery Program** (425-771-0227, fax 425-771-0253; www.ci.edmonds.wa.us, lider@ci.edmonds.wa.us) hosts summer beach walks. Closed Sunday.

EDMONDS CHAMBER OF COMMERCE ⊠*121 5th Avenue North, Edmonds* ☎*425-670-1496 (chamber), 425-776-6711 (visitor information)* ☎*425-712-1808* ⏎*www.edmondswa.com, chamberofcommerce@edmondswa.com* The local chamber of commerce wins the prize for quaintness. Its information center is housed in a pioneer log cabin that looks like a storybook house. Closed Sunday.

EDMONDS HISTORICAL MUSEUM ⊠*118 5th Avenue North, Edmonds* ☎*425-774-0900* ⏎*www.historicedmonds.org* A visit to this museum with its working shingle-mill model, maritime heritage exhibits and collections of logging tools and household furnishings gives a better understanding of the pioneer heritage and industrial history of Edmonds. Rotating exhibits and a giftshop are upstairs on the second floor. Closed Monday and Tuesday.

LODGING

BEST WESTERN EDMONDS HARBOR INN

$$ 91 ROOMS ⊠*130 West Dayton Street, Edmonds* ☎*425-771-5021, 800-441-8033* ☎*425-672-2880* ⏎*www.bestwestern.com, harborinn@seanet.com*
Just a few blocks from Port of Edmonds is this three-story traditional-style inn with a spacious lobby featuring a towering stone fireplace.

Rooms and suites are decorated with natural earth tones, bright wood tables and flatscreen TVs; some boast fireplaces and kitchenettes. Amenities include a fitness center, a hot tub, laundry facilties, free wi-fi and a continental breakfast.

DINING

LA GALLERIA

$$ ITALIAN   ✉546 5th Avenue South, Edmonds   ☎425-771-7950
🖰www.10000flavors.com

If you venture up to Edmonds, you must try this local favorite. A small, comfortable restaurant, it boasts a romantic interior and an excellent Italian menu. Best choices include pollo *modena* (chicken breast sautéed with mushrooms in creamy balsamic vinegar sauce) and penne with rock crab. Brunch is available Friday through Sunday.

ANTHONY'S HOMEPORT EDMONDS

$$–$$$ SEAFOOD   ✉456 Admiral Way, Edmonds   ☎425-771-4400
📠425-771-2331   🖰www.anthonys.com, edmonds@anthonys.com

For waterfront dining on the marina, Anthony's fits the bill. This upscale eatery decked out in nautical decor is the place locals come to celebrate and sink their teeth into fresh, local seafood. Specialties include mahi mahi tacos with cabbage, fishermen's cioppino, and pan-fried Willapa Bay oysters. Come early on Sunday night for your share of the all-you-can-eat Dungeness crab extravaganza. Dinner and Sunday brunch only. **Anthony's Beach Café** on the ground level provides a more casual dining experience for lunch Monday through Saturday. Sit outdoors for a waterfront treat.

SHOPPING

AMERICAN EAGLES ✉12537 Lake City Way Northeast ☎206-440-8448 📠206-363-6569 This is simply the largest hobby shop in the United States, with an inventory of more than 87,000 different items—one-fourth of them miniature soldiers. The specialty is plastic models and military books. Closed Sunday.

RESIDENT CHEESEMONGER

✉405 Main Street, Edmonds ☎425-640-8949 🖰www.residentcheese monger.com Say cheese! This specialty shop in downtown Edmonds features more than 120 cheeses, from sharp white cheddar to triple cream brie to barrel-aged feta. Varieties from around the world are represented here, but the star selections are from regional farms. Wine, crackers, tapenade and salami (look for the renowned Salumi salami) are also well-stocked. Take a minute to check out the unusual artwork in the back of the store too. Closed Monday.

AURORA ANTIQUE PAVILION ✉24111 Route 99, Edmonds ✆425-744-0566 ⌨www.auroraantiquepavilion.com More than 150 dealers sell their wares here. You will find European-style furniture, crystal, glass figurines, vintage artwork and thousands of unusual knick-knacks.

SEATTLE WEST

Seattle West offers some rare treasures such as a company town operating in the time-honored manner, a fascinating Indian cultural show, a marine science center and inns that look like they were created for a James Herriott book. From the islands of Puget Sound west to Hood Canal, this is also a region rich in parks and natural areas. You'll also want to tour the Kitsap Peninsula, Bremerton's Naval Heritage and the parks of Southern Puget Sound.

SIGHTS

VASHON ISLAND _____ Since you can reach this pastoral island by state ferry from the Fauntleroy dock in West Seattle (a 15-minute crossing), we include it in this section of the book. However, Vashon stretches south for 13 miles toward Tacoma (accessible by another 15-minute ferry from Tahlequah), creating a lovely Seattle-to-Tacoma country-road alternative to Route 5. The ferry to Tacoma lands next to one of the city's highlights, splendid Point Defiance Park (see "Tacoma and Olympia" Sights).

COUNTRY STORE AND GARDENS ✉20211 Vashon Highway Southwest ✆206-463-3655, 888-245-6136 ✉206-463-3679 ⌨www.vashoncountrystore.com, info@countrystoreandgardens.com The Vashon Island Highway will take you fairly directly down the island, through the town of Vashon. Just south of town is this local sundries shop, where you can peruse merchandise grown or produced on the island—fruit and syrups, berries and preserves, a nursery stocked with perennials and a variety of gardening tools, natural-fiber clothing, kitchenware, books and such.

POINT ROBINSON COUNTY PARK Side roads beckon from the highway to a handful of poorly marked state beaches and county parks. Point Robinson on Maury Island (linked to Vashon via an isthmus at the hamlet of Portage) is easier to find and particularly interesting since it's next door to the Coast Guard's picturesque Point Robinson Lighthouse (not open to the public).

BAINBRIDGE ISLAND To the north, this island offers a much more attractive destination than Maury Island for most travelers, and you can see it on foot. The picturesque town is located on an island of the same name, just a 35-minute ferry ride from Coleman Dock. To see more than obvious attractions (restaurants, shops, a winetasting room), head for the mile-long waterfront footpath called **Walkabout** to the left of the ferry landing. Follow it along the shoreline, past shipyards and hauled-

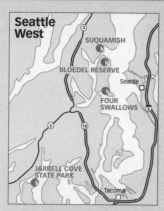

Seattle West

SUQUAMISH
BLOEDEL RESERVE
Seattle
FOUR SWALLOWS
JARRELL COVE STATE PARK
Tacoma

SUQUAMISH

PAGE 75

Historic town with a museum portraying the region's allied tribes—a rich source for American Indian heritage

BLOEDEL RESERVE

PAGE 73

150 acres of lush meadows, ultraserene forests and placid ponds on idyllic Bainbridge Island

FOUR SWALLOWS

PAGE 78

1880s farmhouse with a menu featuring innovative Northwest dishes like veal chops with porcini mushrooms and *brodetto*

JARRELL COVE STATE PARK

PAGE 76

Swimming, waterskiing and clamming at a rocky stretch of beach perfect for setting up camp

out sailboats under repair, to **Eagle Harbor Waterfront Park** and its fishing pier and low-tide beach. Carry on to a ship chandler and pair of marinas. Return as you came, or through the town's business district.

BLOEDEL RESERVE

⊠*7571 Northeast Dolphin Drive, Bainbridge Island* ☎*206-842-7631* ⊜*206-842-8970* ⊘*www.bloedelreserve.org, email@bloedelreserve.org* If you enjoy gardens, don't miss a tour of this famous reserve. Once a private estate, the reserve has 150 acres of forest, meadows, ponds and a series of beautifully landscaped gardens. Reservations are required for all visits. Closed Monday and Tuesday. Admission.

BREMERTON   Another interesting loop trip west of Seattle begins in this Navy town. You can explore some of the region's history, as well as the remote reaches of southern Puget Sound.

PUGET SOUND NAVAL SHIPYARD ⊠*Burwell Street and Pacific Avenue, near the ferry dock, Bremerton* ☎*360-476-7111* ⊜*360-476-0937* ⊘*www.psns.navy. mil* If you take the ferry or drive to Bremerton, you'll pass by this Puget Sound scene. The best way to get here is the Washington State Ferry (cars and walk-ons; one hour) or state foot-ferry (50 minutes) or the passenger-only fast ferry (35 minutes) from Seattle's Colman Dock

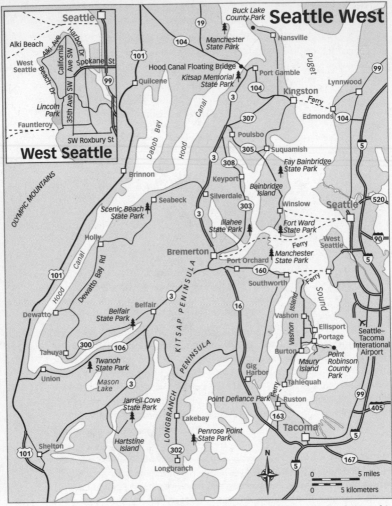

West Seattle

Seattle West

(Pier 52) through Rich Passage to Bremerton. Although the shipyard is not open for public tours, it's an amazing sight even from a distance.

BREMERTON NAVAL MUSEUM ✉ *402 Pacific Avenue, a half-block north of the ferry dock, Bremerton* ☎ *360-479-7447* ✒ *bremnavmuseum@aol.com* Also known as the Naval Museum of the Pacific, this institution looks back to the days of Jack Tar and square-riggers and includes a wood cannon from 1377 along with more than 600 naval items.

NAVAL UNDERSEA MUSEUM ✉ *610 Dowell Street, Keyport* ☎ *360-396-4148* ✒ *underseainfo@kpt.nuwc.navy.mil* In the small town of Keyport, off Route 308 between Poulsbo and Silverdale, you'll find this museum. Historical exhibits here focus on the Navy's undersea activities from the Revolutionary War to the present. Diving and defense displays explore such subjects as nautical archaeology and the history of the submarine. There's also an interactive installation on the ocean environment. Closed Tuesday from October through May.

KITSAP PENINSULA   Only an hour from the heart of Seattle, this site is framed on the east side by Puget Sound and the west by Hood Canal. Historic company towns, naval museums and remote parks make this area a fine retreat from the city.

SUQUAMISH

✉15838 Sandy Hook Road off Route 305, Suquamish ☎360-598-3311 ✆360-598-6295 ⌂www.suquamish.nsn.us/museum A good place to learn about the region's American Indian heritage is this historic town. Chief Seattle and the allied tribes he represented are showcased at the **Suquamish Museum**. There's an outstanding collection of photographs and relics, along with mockups of a typical American Indian dwelling and the interior of a longhouse. Two award-winning video presentations are shown in a small theater. Closed Monday through Thursday in winter. Admission.

CHIEF SEATTLE'S GRAVE   Set under a canopy of dugout canoes, this monument, in a hillside graveyard overlooking Seattle (his namesake), is just a few miles down Suquamish Way. Follow the road signs.

POULSBO   "Velkommen til Poulsbo" is an oft-repeated phrase in this community, also known as "Washington's Little Norway." Looking like a lane in faraway Scandinavia, the main street is lined with wonderful galleries and boutiques. There are some wonderful samples of historic architecture on a walking tour of town; the **Greater Poulsbo Chamber of Commerce** (19351 8th Avenue, Suite 108, Poulsbo; 360-779-4848, fax 360-799-3115; www.poulsbochamber.com, admin@poulsbochamber.com) can provide more information.

MARINE SCIENCE CENTER ✉18743 Front Street Northeast, Poulsbo ☎360-598-4460 ⌂www.poulsbomsc.org At this educational center, you can learn about the marine life that inhabit the waters of Southern Puget Sound; they even have touch tanks of friendly sea creatures. Closed Monday through Wednesday.

PORT GAMBLE

Situated on a bluff at the intersection of Admiralty Inlet and Gamble Bay, this century-old community is owned by the Pope and Talbot lumber firm, making it one of the West's last company towns. The oldest running lumber mill in the United States (operating since 1853) was closed in 1995. Although all the sawmill workers were laid off, Pope and Talbot announced that they will keep the town running. The town had long been home to about 150 sawmill workers and their families, who rented homes by the company. Picturesque frame houses, towering elms and a church with Gothic windows and a needle spire give the community a New England look.

PORT GAMBLE HISTORIC MUSEUM ✉*Route 3, Port Gamble* ☎*360-297-8074* ✆*360-297-7455* ⌕*www.portgamble.com, portgamble@orminc.com* Don't miss the mock-ups of Captain Talbot's cabin and A. J. Pope's office at this historic museum. Closed Monday through Thursday from November through April. Admission.

SOUTHERN PUGET SOUND   On a map, this area looks like a fistful of bony fingers clawing at the earth. The maze of inlets, peninsulas and islands presents plentiful saltwater access and invites days of poking around.

LONGBRANCH PENINSULA ———
South of Bremerton is this peninsula, a showcase of Southern Puget Sound's outdoor treasures. Quiet coves and lonely forests, dairy farms, funky fishing villages with quiet cafés, shellfish beaches and oyster farmers, a salmon hatchery, fishing piers and wharves all await leisurely exploration. Take Route 16 to Route 302, proceeding west until you reach Key Center. The Key Peninsula Highway, running south from this community, is the main road bringing you to most attractions.

LAKEBAY   To visit this hamlet on Mayo Cove, turn east from Peninsula Highway three and a half miles south of Home (the town, not your Home Sweet) onto Cornwall Road and follow it to Delano Road.

PENROSE POINT STATE PARK ✉*Off Delano Road at the foot of 158th Avenue, Lakebay* ☎*253-884-2514* ✆*360-753-1594* With 152 acres of forest on the south side of the cove, this park has more than two miles of beaches, hiking trails, fishing, picnicking and camping.

LONGBRANCH   At the end of the highway is this bayside village on the shores of Filucy Bay, one of the prettiest anchorages in these waters.

HARSTINE ISLAND ———
✉*Northeast of Shelton via Route 3 and Pickering Road* This island is connected to the mainland by a bridge, providing auto access to a quintessential Southern Puget Sound island experience.

JARRELL COVE STATE PARK ———
✉*Foot of Wingert Road, off North Island Drive* ☎*360-426-9226* Many of the island's public beaches are poorly indicated, but the 3500 feet of shoreline at this state park and a marina on the other side of the cove are easily found at the island's north tip. Although you won't find soft sand to spread your towel on, the rocky beach that extends around long docks makes a perfect home base for swimming, waterskiing and clamming. You'll see plenty of boats from both sides of the cove, and at the park you can stroll docks, fish for perch, walk bits of beach or explore forest trails. Main roads

loop the island's north end, or head for the far southern tip at
Brisco Point near Peale Passage and Squaxin Island.

HOOD CANAL

The eastern shore of this canal is located a mere mile or two from
the western side of the channel, but in character it's worlds
apart. Beach access is limited, but views across the canal to the
Olympic Mountains are splendid, settlements few and quiet and
back roads genuine byways—few tourists ever get here. This is
also where the canal bends like a fishhook to the east, which has
been nicknamed the "Great Bend."

To see the east shore in its entirety, begin at Belfair, leaving Route 3 for
Route 300. At three miles, watch for Belfair State Park on the left. The
road now narrows and traffic thins on the way to the modest resort
town of Tahuya; shortly beyond, the canal makes its great bend. The
road dives into dense forest, bringing you in about 11 miles to a T-
junction; bear left, then left again to the ghost town of Dewatto. Take
Dewatto Bay Road eastward out of town, then turn north and follow
signs 12 miles to a left turn into the little town of Holly, or continue
north 15 miles more to **Seabeck**, founded in 1856 as a sawmill town and
popular today with anglers, scuba divers and boaters.

LODGING

HOLIDAY INN EXPRESS
$$–$$$ 175 ROOMS   ✉19801 7th Avenue Northeast, Poulsbo   ☎360-697-4400,
800-465-4329 ☎360-697-2707 ⌨www.hiexpress.com/poulsbowa,
poulsbo_hax@hotmail.com
Guest rooms at Poulsbo's Holiday Inn are modern and comfortably
furnished with big beds, individual air conditioning and other basic
amenities; a few are equipped with kitchenette or jacuzzi. There is a
seasonal outdoor jacuzzi, and a continental breakfast is included.

VILLA HEIDELBERG
$$–$$$ 6 ROOMS   ✉4845 45th Avenue Southwest, West Seattle
☎206-938-3658, 800-671-2942 ☎206-935-7077
⌨www.villaheidelberg.com, info@villaheidelberg.com
Located on a corner hillside is this Craftsman-style bed and
breakfast. The inn has a wide wraparound porch that overlooks
gardens of roses and rhododendrons. Inside, the atmosphere is
comfortable and relaxed. The house features leaded glass windows, beamed ceilings and the original 1909 gaslight fixtures and
embossed wall coverings. The six guest rooms feature brass or
oak beds and oak dressers. Some have views of the Puget Sound
and the Olympic Mountains. A full breakfast is served.

ALKI CAFÉ BEACH BISTRO

$$ SEAFOOD/AMERICAN ✉2726 Alki Avenue Southwest, West Seattle ☎206-935-0616 ⌨http://alkicafe.home.comcast.net

Spend a perfect summer day at Alki Beach in West Seattle, then take in dinner at this bistro, where a well-rounded menu includes great salads (that change seasonally), seafood, meat, chicken and pasta dishes. Specials of the evening are listed in the dining area.

ALKI BAKERY

$ BAKERY ✉2738 Alki Avenue Southwest, West Seattle ☎206-935-1352 📠206-935-1749

Just down the street from the Alki Café, this bakery offers up a host of muffins and cinnamon rolls, scones, coffee, espressos and lattes. If you've overindulged, you can always take another stroll on the beach.

SPRING HILL

$$$ PACIFIC NORTHWEST ✉4437 California Avenue Southwest, West Seattle ☎206-935-1075 ⌨www.springhillnorthwest.com, info@springhillnorthwest.com

This narrow and sleek polished wood restaurant owned and operated by husband-and-wife team Mark and Marjorie Fuller—he's a locally legendary chef and she's the most gracious of hostesses—has become one of Seattle's most talked-about restaurants in spite of its out-of-the-way location. The house specialty is handmade tagliatelle pasta tossed with hen-of-the-woods and wild chanterelle mushrooms and delicata squash. Weekend brunch features such intriguing breakfast items as duck's eggs Benedict and a quinoa waffle with apple-quince compote.

BISTRO PLEASANT BEACH

$$ MEDITERRANEAN ✉241 Winslow Way West, Bainbridge Island ☎206-842-4347 📠206-842-6997 ⌨www.bicomnet.com/bistropb, ramadanbistro@aol.com

The white linen tablecloths and low lighting here bespeak a comfortable island elegance. The chef specializes in Mediterranean seafood but includes a couple of succulent chicken dishes, pastas and aged beef entrées. The leg of lamb, served with roasted garlic, fresh herbs and shallot–rose cabernet sauce, comes recommended. Made-to-order pizzas are baked in the wood-fired oven. When the weather's nice, patio seating is available. Sunday brunch. Closed Monday.

FOUR SWALLOWS

$$–$$$ PACIFIC NORTHWEST ✉481 Madison Avenue, Bainbridge Island ☎206-842-3397 ⌨www.fourswallows.com

Exotic flavors and innovative sauces are what you'll find at this upscale Italian restaurant located in a spacious 1880s farmhouse. The kitchen staff, utilizing fresh Northwest ingredients, whips up gourmet, thin-crust pizzas and zesty pastas. The entrées show the chef's creativity, and include grilled veal chops with porcini-mushroom sauce and *brodetto*, a fresh fish-and-shellfish stew in a rustic saffron-tomato-fennel broth. Dinner only. Closed Sunday and Monday.

CASA DE LUNA

$ MEXICAN/AMERICAN ✉18830 Front Street Northeast, Poulsbo ☎360-779-7676 Here you'll find fast and cheap traditional Mexican favorites. Diners are treated to colorful murals and sweet ballads while munching on tacos and burritos and sipping Negra Modelo.

SLUYS BAKERY ✉18924 Front Street Northeast, Poulsbo ☎360-779-2798 Get
your fill of Norwegian strudels, bear claws, breads, pastries and cookies at this irresistible bakery.

SHOPPING

VERKSTED CO-OPERATIVE GALLERY ✉18937 Front Street Northeast,
Poulsbo ☎360-697-4470 ✐www.verkstedgallery.com In Poulsbo, you'll find paintings, pottery, weavings, cards, rosemaling, baskets, woodturnings and even food products created by local artists at this gallery.

POTLATCH GALLERY ✉18830-B Front Street Northeast, Poulsbo ☎360-779-
3377 ✐www.potlatchgallery.com Here you'll find a fine selection of prints, glasswork, pottery and jewelry by Northwest artists.

BEACHES & PARKS

MANCHESTER STATE PARK
✉Located at the east foot of East Hilldale Road off Beach Drive, east of Bremerton
☎360-871-4065 ☎503-378-6308

This one-time fort overlooking Rich Passage includes abandoned torpedo warehouses and some interpretive displays explaining its role in guarding Bremerton Navy Base at the turn of the 20th century. The park is infamous for its poison oak—stay on the two miles of hiking trails, or try the 3400 feet of beach. The rocks off Middle Point attract divers. Fishing yields salmon and bottomfish. There are picnic areas, restrooms and showers. Day-use fee, $5.

▲ There are 35 standard sites ($19 per night), 3 primitive walk-in sites ($14 per night), 15 RV hookup sites ($36 per night). Sites are first come, first served from mid-September through mid-May. Reservations: 888-226-7688.

FAY BAINBRIDGE STATE PARK
✉At Sunrise Drive Northeast and Lafayette Road about six miles north of the town of Bainbridge Island ☎206-842-3931 ☎360-902-8844

A small park (17 acres), it nevertheless curls itself around a long sandspit to present some 1400 feet of shoreline. The only campground on Bainbridge Island is here. Facilities include picnic areas, restrooms, showers, a play area, horseshoe pits and volleyball courts.

▲ There are 10 standard sites ($19 per night), 26 RV hookups ($26 per night) and 13 primitive walk-in sites ($14 per night). Closed mid-October to mid-April.

OLD MAN HOUSE STATE PARK

✉ *On the Kitsap Peninsula north of Agate Pass off Route 305* ☎ *206-842-3931*
📠 *206-385-7248*

🚶 This day-use-only facility was once the site of a longhouse. Check out the interpretive and historical displays. A small, sandy beach overlooks the heavy marine traffic that cruises through Agate Passage. You'll find pit toilets and picnic tables. Closed in winter.

BUCK LAKE COUNTY PARK

✉ *6959 Northeast Buck Lake Road; Take Route 104 from Kingston to Hansville Road and follow it north.* ☎ *360-337-5350* 📠 *360-337-5385*

🚶 🐎 ⛵ 🚣 Near Hansville on the northern tip of the Kitsap Peninsula, picturesque Buck Lake is a good spot for quiet, contemplative fishing or a relaxing summer swim. Trout fishing is excellent on the lake or from the shore. Facilities include restrooms, picnic tables, a baseball diamond, a volleyball court, barbecue pits and a playground.

SALISBURY POINT

✉ *North of Hood Canal Floating Bridge, turn left on Wheeler Road and follow the signs* ☎ *360-337-5350* 📠 *360-337-5385*

⛵ 🚤 🚣 This tiny, six-acre park with a small stretch of saltwater beach is next to Hood Canal Floating Bridge and gives views of the Olympic Mountains across the canal. Shrimping is popular here. There are restrooms, picnic shelters and a playground.

KITSAP MEMORIAL STATE PARK

✉ *From Kingston take Route 104 (which turns into Bond Road) to Route 3, then follow it north until you reach the park* ☎ *360-779-3205* 📠 *360-779-3161*

🚶 🚤 🚣 This 58-acre park four miles south of Hood Canal Floating Bridge has a quiet beach well suited for collecting oysters and clams. Between the canal, beach and playground facilities there's plenty to keep the troops entertained, making this a good choice for family camping. Restrooms, showers, a shelter, tables and stoves, boat moorage buoys, a playground and a volleyball court are available; some facilities are wheelchair accessible. Day-use fee, $5.

⛺ There are 21 standard sites ($19 per night); 18 sites with hookups ($26 per night); and a trailer dump ($5). A blufftop log cabin with full bedding, bath towels and a kitchenette (no stove) is also available; $156 per night in peak season. To reserve the log cabin call 800-360-4240.

ILLAHEE STATE PARK

✉ *Located at the east foot of Sylvan Way (Route 306) two miles east of Route 303 northeast of Bremerton* ☎ *360-478-6460* 📠 *360-792-6067*

🚶 🚲 ⛵ 🎣 🚤 🚣 Wooded uplands and 1700 feet of saltwater shoreline are separated by a 250-foot bluff at this site. A steep hiking trail connects the two park units. On the beach is a wheelchair-accessible fishing pier where anglers can cast for perch, bullhead and salmon; at the south end are tide flats for wading. Facilities include a picnic area, restrooms, showers, a baseball field, a play area and horseshoe pits.

⛺ There are 24 standard sites (no hookups); $18 per night; one utility space ($25 per night).

TWANOH STATE PARK
Route 106, eight miles southwest of Belfair *360-275-2222*

With many amenities of a city park, Twanoh's 182 acres also include the forests, trails and camping of a more remote site. A two-mile hiking trail takes you through a thick forest of second-growth conifers next to Twanoh Creek; nearly a half-mile of saltwater beach attracts divers. Fishing yields cutthroat, salmon and trout. There are picnic areas, restrooms, showers, tennis, horseshoe pits and a concession stand.

There are 25 tent sites ($19 per night) and 22 full hookup sites ($26 per night).

BELFAIR STATE PARK
Route 300, three miles west of Belfair *360-275-0668*

Two creeks flow through this 63-acre park en route to Hood Canal, affording both fresh and saltwater shorelines. Along its 3720 feet of beachfront the saltwater warms quickly across shallow tide flats, making ideal swimming conditions. Fishing affords salmon, steelhead and trout. Shellfish are usually posted off-limits. There are picnic areas, restrooms, showers, two volleyball fields and two horseshoe pits.

There are 137 tent sites ($19 per night) and 47 full hookup sites ($26 per night); dump station ($5). Reservations: 888-226-7688.

SCENIC BEACH STATE PARK
Located just west of Seabeck on Miami Beach Road Northwest, about nine miles northwest of Bremerton *360-830-5079* *360-830-2970*

Nearly 1500 feet of cobblestone beach invites strolls; scuba divers also push off from here. Every year in May, 88 acres of native rhododendrons burst into bloom. Anglers try for salmon and bottom fish at the nearby artificial reef, and there's a boat launch less than a mile from the park. There are picnic areas, restrooms, showers, a play area, two horseshoe pits, two volleyball areas and a community center.

There are 52 standard sites ($19 per night); no hookups. Closed in winter. Reservations: 888-226-7688.

PENROSE POINT STATE PARK
Off Delano Road at the foot of 158th Avenue, near Lakebay on the Longbranch Peninsula *253-884-2514* *253-884-2526*

With more than two miles of saltwater shoreline, this 152-acre park provides some of the most accessible public beaches on Southern Puget Sound. You can swim at the park's sandy, shallow-water beaches, hike along two miles of trail, launch a canoe or kayak, fish for bottomfish and salmon, picnic and camp. The entire park closes for the winter. Restrooms, showers, restaurant and grocery store are close by.

There are 82 standard sites ($19 per night). Reservations: 888-226-7688.

SEATTLE EAST

Seattle East, extending from the eastern shore of Lake Washington to the Cascade foothills, blends the urban and rural assets of this metropolitan region. Here you'll find wineries and archaeological sites, prime birdwatching areas and homey bed and breakfasts.

SIGHTS

WOODINVILLE   This small, forest-shrouded town, just east of Bothell off Route 522, is the center of Washington's burgeoning wine industry, with 40 wineries and not much else. The wine grapes—a full range of varietals, including chardonnay, pinot noir, riesling, meritage, ottimo, sauvignon blanc and others—are actually grown in vineyards on the dry side of the Cascades in the Columbia River Valley. Then the juice is extracted and transported in tanker trucks more than 200 miles to Woodinville for fermentation, aging, blending, fining, filtration and bottling.

Woodinville is famous for its wineries. Bucolic Chateau Ste. Michelle and Columbia Winery are the main draws for oenophiles, along with the smaller boutique wineries such as DeLille Cellars, Facelli and Matthews Cellars that are quickly gaining in popularity.

CHÂTEAU STE. MICHELLE _hidden_

✉14111 145th Street Northeast, Woodinville ℡425-415-3300 📠425-415-3657
🖰www.ste-michelle.com, info@ste-michelle.com   The place to start any Woodinville wine tour is this château, the original Woodinville winery that started it all and still the largest winery in Washington. The elegant mansard-roofed French-style headquarters and lavish gardens create an ideal tasting and picnic spot. Tours are available (fee), providing information about the property's history, which spans more than a century, and the Columbia Valley winemaking region. Summer concerts here feature big-name musicians like the Neville Brothers, Lyle Lovett and John Legend.

SILVER LAKE   ✉1500 Vintage Road, Zillah ℡509-829-6235 🖰www.silverlake winery.com   This winery keeps gaining new fans. The Zillah tasting room stands on a hill overlooking the winery's acres of grapes. They have two other tasting rooms in the area; one is in Leavenworth (715 Front Street; 509-548-5788) and the other is in Woodinville (15029 Woodinville-Redmond Road; 425-485-2437).

BELLEVUE   Renowned as Seattle's foremost suburb, this community boasts a surprisingly diverse network of parks embedded within its neighborhoods. Getting there will most likely take you over **Evergreen Point Floating Bridge**, the world's longest floating bridge at 1.5 miles. **Mercer Slough Nature Park**, stretching north from Route 90 off Bellevue Way with the entrance at 2102 Bellevue Way Southeast, is the big-

CHÂTEAU STE. MICHELLE
PAGE 82

Elegant French-style building with lavish gardens perfect for a picnic—*the* place to start a wine tour

IZUMI
PAGE 86

Extra-fresh ingredients, friendly service and a top-notch sushi bar—one of Puget Sound's best Japanese spots

MAPLE VALLEY BED & BREAKFAST
PAGE 85

Quintessential Northwest inn with open-beamed ceilings, cedar walls and rooms opening on a rooftop garden

gest and may be the best with some 300 acres of natural wetland habitat and four miles of trails.

WILBURTON HILL PARK ✉*12001 Main Street off 116th Avenue Northeast, Bellevue* ☎*425-452-6885* 📠*425-452-7221* ✐*parksweb@bellevuewa.gov* This park, between 120th Southeast and 118th avenues on Main Street, centered around the **Bellevue Botanical Garden** (425-452-2750; www.bellevue botanical.org), is filled with native and ornamental Northwest plants. The park covers over 100 acres and has more than three miles of hiking trails as well as softball and soccer fields.

OLD BELLEVUE To see what Bellevue used to be like before freeways, commuters and office towers, stroll this short stretch of shops along Main Street westward from Bellevue Way Northeast.

GREENWOOD MEMORIAL PARK ✉*350 Monroe Avenue Northeast, Renton* ☎*425 255 1511* Seattle's rock legend Jimi Hendrix is buried south of Bellevue. A caretaker can show you the guitarist's grave here.

LODGING

WILLOWS LODGE
$$$$ 84 UNITS   ✉*14580 Northeast 145th Street, Woodinville* ☎*425-424-3900, 877-424-3930* 📠*425-424-2585* ✐*www.willowslodge.com, mail@willowslodge.com*
This sumptuous resort on the Sammamish River adjoins the wineries, making it the perfect base for Wine Country touring. The elegant rooms and suites in this rustic retreat have balconies and patios overlooking the gardens. Other amenities include stone fireplaces, DVD/CD players, French press coffee, beds with 300-thread-count sheets and down

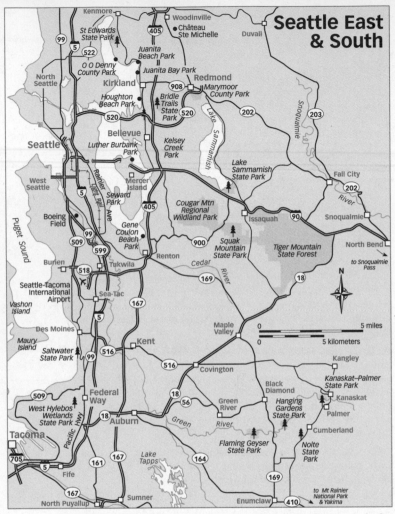

comforters, and large soaking tubs. There is also a pool, a spa and a fitness center. Pet-friendly.

A COTTAGE CREEK INN

$$–$$$ 4 ROOMS   ✉12525 Avondale Road Northeast, Redmond   ✆425-881-5606
✆425-881-5606   www.cottagecreekinn.com, innkeepers@cottagecreekinn.com

Set on three-plus acres, this inn has its own creek, pond, waterfall and gazebo on the grounds. The English Tudor house features four rooms, one with a brass bed, one with an antique bed, all with their own bathrooms and highspeed internet access. There are full jacuzzis in the two larger rooms and a communal outdoor hot tub. There's a pleasant sitting room with a piano, which guests are encouraged to play. Full breakfast included.

THE WOODMARK HOTEL

$$$$ 100 ROOMS   ✉1200 Carillon Point, Kirkland ☎425-822-3700,
800-822-3700 📠425-822-3699 💻www.thewoodmark.com,
mail@thewoodmark.com

This handsome, four-story brick structure is located on Lake Washington's shore. Its small scale, residential-style lobby, and comfortable bar with a fireplace and shelves of books create the ambience of a welcoming, stylish home. The rooms have all the amenities: mini-bars, flatscreen TVs, soaking tubs, robes and hair dryers. Ask for a room on the west side—they have lake views.

MAPLE VALLEY
BED AND BREAKFAST

$$ 2 ROOMS   ✉20020 Southeast 228th Street, Maple Valley ☎425-432-1409, 888-432-1309 💻www.maplevalleybnb.com, wildlifepond@hotmail.com

In a quiet, wooded area southeast of Seattle is this two-story stone home with open-beamed ceilings, peeled-pole railings, cedar walls and detailed wood trim. Guests like to relax on the antique furniture in the sitting room. The guest rooms are individually decorated and color coordinated with French doors that open onto a roof garden. Both have log beds. On cool nights, heated, sand-filled pads ("hot babies") are used to warm the beds. A full breakfast is served on country-stencil pottery in a dining area that overlooks trees, wandering birds and ponds with ducks.

DINING

ANDRE'S EURASIAN BISTRO

$$ ASIAN/CONTINENTAL   ✉14115 Northeast 20th Street, Bellevue
☎425-747-6551 📠425-747-4304 💻www.andresbistro.com

The open kitchen at Andre's is as entertaining as the food. This restaurant offers a menu with Vietnamese specialties like chicken with lemongrass, as well as Continental selections, such as lamb with garlic. No lunch on Saturday. Closed Sunday.

POGACHA

$$ PACIFIC NORTHWEST/CROATIAN   ✉119 106th Avenue Northeast,
Bellevue ☎425-455-5670 💻www.pogacha.com

You wouldn't expect to find a good restaurant in this little shopping strip, but here it is. At this spot, a Croatian version of pizza is the mainstay. The pizzas, crisp on the outside but moist inside, are baked in a clay oven. Because the saucing is nonexistent or very light, the flavor of the toppings—pesto and various cheeses, alone or over vegetables or meat—is more apparent. Other entrées include Adriatic-inspired grilled meats and seafood, salads and pastas. No lunch on weekends.

IZUMI

$$–$$$ JAPANESE   ✉12539 116th Avenue Northeast, Kirkland
✆425-821-1959   🖰www.izumikirkland.com

One of the best Japanese restaurants in all of Puget Sound is hidden in the Totem Lake West shopping center in suburbia. Here you'll find an excellent sushi bar. Entrées are fairly standard—beef, chicken sukiyaki and teriyaki and tempura—but the ingredients are especially fresh and carefully prepared. Service is friendly. No lunch on weekends. Closed Monday.

SHAMIANA

$$–$$$ PAKISTANI   ✉10724 Northeast 68th Street, Kirkland   ✆425-827-4902
🖰www.shamianarestaurant.com, shamianarestaurant@msn.com

A couple of local residents who grew up in Pakistan and Bangladesh have opened this restaurant. The food is cooled to an American palate but can be spiced to a full-blown, multistar *hot*. A buffet of four curries, salad, *naan* and *dal* is offered at lunch. Dinner is à la carte, and includes entrées such as lamb curry with rice *pulao*, chicken *tikka* and prawns in "velvet butter" (a rich cumin tomato sauce).

SHOPPING

BELLEVUE SQUARE ✉Northeast 8th Street and Bellevue Way Northeast, Bellevue 🖰www.bellevuesquare.com In Bellevue, this area has 200 of the nation's finest shops, department stores and restaurants.

ALVIN GOLDFARB JEWELER ✉305 Bellevue Way Northeast, Bellevue ✆425-454-9393 🖰www.alvingoldfarbjeweler.com One of the most elegant shops in Bellevue is Alvin Goldfarb. Specializing in 18-carat platinum and gold pieces crafted by an in-house goldsmith who also works with precious and semiprecious gems, this is a mecca for discriminating people who desire a one-of-a-kind item. Closed Sunday.

ANTIQUE MART AT KIRKLAND ✉151 3rd Street, Kirkland ✆425-827-7443 Hunters of antiques appreciate the selection here. The mall has nearly 70 dealers selling antiques and collectibles.

LAKESHORE GALLERY ✉107 Park Lane, Kirkland ✆425-827-0606 Excellent Northwest ceramics, jewelry and blown glass make this gallery a fine place to stop even if you have no intention of buying. The carved woodwork is especially well done.

GILMAN VILLAGE ✉317 Northwest Gilman Boulevard, Issaquah ✆425-392-6802 🖰www.gilmanvillage.com Refurbished farmhouses, a barn and a feed store are stocked with handicrafts and artful, designer clothing at this charming shopping village. Among the 40-plus shops clustered in these historic structures is **The Revolutionary Gallery** (425-392-4982; www.revolutiongallery.com), an artists co-op featuring fun and functional artwork fashioned from recycled materials.

BOEHM'S CANDIES ✉255 Northeast Gilman Boulevard, Issaquah ☎425-392-6652 ☏425-557-0560 ✐www.boehmscandies.com Satisfy your sweet tooth at Boehm's, where hundreds of chocolates are hand-dipped every day. You can view the factory on a free, self-guided tour (year-round) or reserve a guided tour (fee) during the summer (no tours on Wednesday) and watch the skilled workmanship that goes into making candies of this quality.

NIGHTLIFE

FORECASTERS PUBLIC HOUSE AT THE REDHOOK ALE BREWERY ✉14300 Northeast 145th Street, Woodinville ☎425-483-3232 ✐www.redhook.com Enjoy live tunes on Friday and Saturday at this local pub set on a huge grassy amphitheater.

DANIEL'S BROILER ✉Bellevue Place, 10500 Northeast 8th Avenue, 21st Floor, Bellevue ☎425-462-4662 ✐danielsbellevue@schwartzbros.com Daniel's has a live pianist playing contemporary hits seven nights a week.

0/8 SEAFOOD GRILL AND TWISTED CORK WINE BAR ✉900 Bellevue Way Northeast, Bellevue ☎425-637-0808 ✐www.08seafoodgrill.com There is live music Wednesday through Saturday nights at this wine bar, located in the Hyatt Regency Bellevue.

VILLAGE THEATRE ✉303 Front Street North, Issaquah ☎425-392-2202 ✐www.villagetheatre.org Good things come in small packages, and this theatre proves it. The local casts here will tackle anything, be it Broadway musicals, dramas or comedy.

BEACHES & PARKS

MARYMOOR COUNTY PARK
✉Located on West Lake Sammamish Parkway Northeast off Route 520, just south of Redmond city center ☎206-205-3661 ☏206-296-1437 ✐marymoorpark@kingcounty.gov

🏃🚴🐎 This roomy, 640-acre preserve at the north end of Lake Sammamish in Redmond is a delightful mix of archaeology and history, river and lake, meadows and marshes, plus an assortment of athletic fields. A one-mile footpath leads to a lakeside observation deck, and there's access to the ten-mile Sammamish River Trail. The circa-1904 Clise Mansion, near a pioneer windmill, was built as a hunting lodge. Facilities include picnic areas, restrooms, play areas, baseball and soccer fields, tennis courts, a model-airplane airport, a bicycle velodrome with frequent races, a climbing wall, an archaeological site and an off-leash pet area.

SAINT EDWARDS STATE PARK
✉Located on Lake Washington's northern shore, on Juanita Drive Northeast in Kenmore ☎425-823-2992

🏃🚴🛶⛵🏊🚣 This former Catholic seminary still exudes the peace and quiet of a theological retreat across its 316 heavily wooded acres and 3000 feet of Lake Washington shoreline. Except for a handful of former seminary buildings, the park is mostly natural, laced by miles of informal trails. To reach the beach, take the wide path just west of the main seminary building. It winds a half mile down to the shore, where you can wander left or right. Side trails climb up the bluff for the return loop. You'll also find picnic areas, restrooms, a horseshoe pit, soccer and baseball fields, basketball, volleyball, badminton, a gymnasium (fee) and an indoor pool (fee).

LUTHER BURBANK PARK

✉ *Entrance is at 2040 84th Avenue Southeast and Southeast 24th Street, via the Island Crest Way exit from Route 90 on Mercer Island, east of Seattle* ☎ *206-236-3545* 🖥 *206-275-7867*

🚶 🛶 🚤 ⛴ 🎣 At the northeast corner of Mercer Island in Lake Washington, this little jewel presents some 3000 feet of shoreline to explore along with marshes, meadows and woods. The entire 77-acre site is encircled by a loop walk. You can fish from the pier for salmon, steelhead, trout and bass, and in summer swim at the beach. Among the facilities are picnic areas, restrooms, a play area, tennis courts and an amphitheater with summer concerts.

GENE COULON BEACH PARK

✉ *Bordered by Lake Washington Boulevard North in Renton, north of Route 405 via Exit 5 and Park Avenue North* ☎ *425-430-6700* 🖥 *425-430-6603*

🛶 🚤 ⛴ 🎣 At the south tip of Lake Washington in Renton, this handsomely landscaped site is most notable for the loads of attractions within its 55 acres: one-and-a-half miles of lakeside path, the wildfowl-rich estuary of John's Creek and a "nature islet," a lagoon enclosed by the thousand-foot waterwalk and "Picnic Gallery," the famous seafood restaurant Ivar's, a fast-food restaurant, and interesting architecture reminiscent of old-time amusement parks. A logboom-protected shoreline includes a fishing pier. There's a boat harbor with an eight-lane boat launch and good fishing from the pier for trout and salmon. The bathing beach is protected by a concrete walkabout with summer lifeguards. There are two restaurants, picnic grounds and floats, restrooms, play areas, and volleyball and tennis courts.

LAKE SAMMAMISH STATE PARK

✉ *2000 Northwest Sammamish Road* ☎ *425-649-4275*

🚶 🚴 🛶 🎣 🚣 🚤 ⛴ 🎣 A popular, 512-acre park at the southern tip of Lake Sammamish near Issaquah, it offers plenty to do, including swimming (no lifeguard), boating, picnicking, hiking and birdwatching along 6858 feet of lake shore and around the mouth of Issaquah Creek. Look for eagles, hawks, great-blue heron, red-wing blackbirds, northern flickers, grebes, kingfishers, killdeer, buffleheads, widgeon and Canada geese. Picnic areas, restrooms, showers, soccer fields, five horseshoe pits and a jogging trail are the facilities here.

SEATTLE SOUTH

Meander from the heart of the city and you'll find one of the world's great aviation museums. Inviting saltwater beaches provide a convenient retreat from urban living. Seattle South serves as the city's back door to the wilderness.

Where Are They Now?

GRAVESITE OF BRUCE LEE ✉*1554 15th Avenue East, Seattle* ✆*206-322-1582* Nearly 30,000 visitors each year make pilgrimages to Seattle to visit the gravesites of deceased superstars. The headstone of martial arts film hero Bruce Lee (1940–1973), engraved in English and Chinese, is found in Lake View Cemetery on Capitol Hill, just north of Volunteer Park. Alongside, another headstone marks the final resting place of his son, **Brandon Lee** (1965–1993), who died in a freak gunshot accident while filming *The Crow*.

Lake View Cemetery is also the final resting place of several Seattle historical figures—among them founding fathers **Henry L. Yesler** (1830–1892) and **David "Doc" Maynard** (1808–1873), and Chief Seattle's daughter **Princess Angeline** (1820?–1896).

GRAVESITE OF JIMI HENDRIX ✉*350 Monroe Avenue Northeast, Renton* ✆*425-255-1511* Legendary guitarist Jimi Hendrix (1942–1970), who reigned as Seattle's most famous rock musician until his fatal drug overdose a year after his landmark appearance at Woodstock, is interred at Greenwood Memorial Park in suburban Renton. Because of the large number of fans who still visit the grave, a large open-air family mausoleum has been built on the site.

MEMORIAL FOR KURT COBAIN ✉*151 Lake Washington Boulevard East, Seattle* Don't look for the grave of Seattle's other deceased rock superstar, Kurt Cobain (1967–1994), lead singer and guitarist of the grunge group Nirvana. His remains were cremated and the ashes scattered in the Wishkah River near the south boundary of Olympic National Park. The river provides the water supply for the city of Aberdeen, Washington. If you can't make the pilgrimage out to Aberdeen, head for Seattle's Viretta Park instead. This tiny park, due south of Cobain's former home, has become an informal memorial site, complete with flowers, candles and graffiti left by fans.

SIGHTS

MUSEUM OF FLIGHT ✉*9404 East Marginal Way South, Seattle* ✆*206-764-5720* 🖷*206-764-5707* About ten miles to the south of downtown Seattle, off Route 5 at Boeing Field, you'll encounter this soaring museum. Centered in a traffic-stopping piece of architecture called the Great Gallery, the museum is a must. In the glass-and-steel gallery, 22 aircrafts hang suspended from the ceiling, almost as if in flight. In all, more than 135 air- and spacecraft (many rare) trace the history of a century of aviation. You'll see the world's first fighter airplane, the first airliner to carry flight attendants, the first presidential jet Air Force One and the only existing M-21 Blackbird spyplane.

One part of the museum, the 1909 Red Barn, was originally a boat-building factory on the banks of the nearby Duwamish River. Later Bill Boeing bought it and turned it into the original headquarters for the Boeing Corporation. Relocated several times, the Red Barn now houses exhibits on Boeing's early days in the airplane business, a far cry from today's mammoth factories.

EL TRAPICHE PUPUSERÍA & RESTAURANT

PAGE 91

Homespun restaurant serving authentic Salvadoran dishes like *pupusa de chicharron, pescado frito* and *pollo asado*

WEST HYLEBOS WETLANDS PARK

PAGE 93

120 acres of rare urban wetlands, including remnants of an ancient forest and over 100 species of birds

GREEN RIVER GORGE

PAGE 90

Spectacular natural site cutting through layers of solid rock, flanked by state and national parks

Like Boeing, Seattle's other economic giant, Microsoft, also has its own museum, but it only exists in cyberspace. Look it up at www.microsoft.com/mscorp/museum.

BLACK DIAMOND HISTORICAL SOCIETY MUSEUM ⊠*32626 Railroad Avenue, Seattle* ✆*360-886-2142, 253-852-6763* ✑*wwwblackdiamond museum. org* Black Diamond (about 35 miles southeast of Seattle on Route 169) has the odds and ends of its mining, logging and railroading history on display at this museum. It is housed in an 1884 railroad depot. Open Thursday and weekends or by appointment.

BLACK DIAMOND BAKERY ⊠*32805 Railroad Avenue, Seattle* ✆*360-886-2235* ✑*www.blackdiamondbakery.com* The real reason most folks stop in Black Diamond—on their way to Mt. Rainier, the Green River Gorge or winter ski slopes—is this famous bakery, which opened in 1902. At last count, the bakery and its wood-fired brick ovens produced some 30 varieties of bread.

GREEN RIVER GORGE   ⓗidden

This spectacular natural site is less than an hour from downtown Seattle but is worlds away from the big city. Just 300 feet deep, the steep-walled gorge nevertheless slices through solid rock (shale and sandstone) to reveal coal seams and fossil imprints and inspire a fine sense of remoteness. The heart of the gorge covers only some six miles on the map but is so twisted into oxbows that it takes kayakers 14 river miles to paddle through it. State and county parks flank the gorge (see "Parks" below).

SEATTLE MARRIOTT

$$$ 459 ROOMS . ✉3201 South 176th Street, Seattle ✆206-241-2000, 800-314-0925
📠206-248-0789 ✐www.marriott.com

A stone's throw from Sea-Tac Airport, this wonderfully luxurious hotel features a 20,000-square-foot tropical atrium five stories high. A restaurant, lounge, whirlpool, health club with massage therapy (by appointment) and gameroom round out the amenities. Airport shuttle is provided.

DINING

BAI TONG

$ THAI   ✉16876 Southcenter Parkway, Tukwila ✆206-575-3366,
206-431-0893 ✐www.baitongrestaurant.com

This excellent eatery in Tukwila is known for its steamed curry salmon, grilled beef with Thai sauce and marinated chicken. The Zen-inspired dining room is lush with potted plants.

EL TRAPICHE
PUPUSERÍA & RESTAURANT

$-$$ CENTRAL AMERICAN   ✉127 Southwest 153rd Street, Burien
✆206-244-5564 📠206-242-2120

For an unusual experience in low-priced dining, head west of the airport to the increasingly Latino suburb of Burien, where you'll find El Trapiche. This homespun, unpretentious little restaurant serves authentic Salvadoran specialties such as *pollo asado* (a skinless, boneless chicken breast chargrilled in annatto-seed marinade), *pescado frito* (whole deep-fried tilapia) and *pupusa de chicharrón* (cornmeal rounds stuffed with shredded pork and served with spicy slaw). Practically the only Central American eatery in the greater Seattle area, El Trapiche's novelty draws a growing clientele from all parts of the city.

CAVE MAN KITCHEN

$$ SMOKEHOUSE   ✉807 West Valley Highway, Kent ✆253-854-1210
✐www.cavemankitchen.com

You won't find many out-of-state cars in the parking lot, but southside locals love this mostly take-out eatery, run by the same family since 1971. The Cave Man specializes in whole or half-chickens and French bread sandwiches heaped high with beef, pork and sausage. The meats are hardwood-smoked slowly for weeks before they're grilled over alder coals. All the smoking is done on the premises. In true Northwestern style, the sauce is as bland as barbecue sauce can get without being ketchup.

WILD WHEAT BAKERY CAFÉ & RESTAURANT

$-$$ CAFÉ ✉️202 First Avenue South, Kent 📞253-856-8919

Tucked away in the southeastern suburb of Kent, not too far from Sea-Tac International Airport, this chic yet unpretentious café has a cheerful attitude and walls hung with local artists' paintings, as well as the best breakfasts in metro Seattle, or so claim many devotees. Try a smoked salmon and cream cheese omelet or a crab and asparagus omelet, served with home fries and freshly baked bread. There's also a tempting lunch menu, including such creative fare as a duck, mango and caramelized onion wrap. No dinner.

PARKS

GREEN RIVER GORGE CONSERVATION AREA

This conservation area includes the county and state parks that flank the 12-mile gorge. Here we pick the two developed parks at the entrance and exit of the gorge and one nearby state park on a lake.

SEAHURST PARK

✉️Southwest Seahurst Park Road, Burien 📞206-988-3700

🏃 🛶 🎣 🚣 ⛵ A well-designed, 178-acre site where landscaping divides 4000 feet of saltwater shoreline into individual chunks is just right for private picnics and sunbathing. A nature trail and some three miles of primitive footpath explore woodsy uplands and the headwaters of two creeks. Other facilities include picnic areas, restrooms, and a marine laboratory with a small viewable fish ladder.

FLAMING GEYSER STATE PARK

✉️23700 Southeast Flaming Geyser Road, Auburn; Off Green Valley Road
📞253-931-3930 📠253-931-6379

🏃 🚵 ⛵ 🚣 Once a resort, this 480-acre park downstream from the exit of Green River Gorge offers four miles of hiking trails and nearly five miles of riverbank. Originally, the flaming geyser area was a test site for coal samples, but miners found natural gas instead, which, when lit, produced a 20-foot flame. The "flaming geyser" is only eight inches high now, and can be seen off one of the trails. Pick up a trail map and brochure at the main office. Fish for rainbow trout and steelhead in season (check the posted regulations). The Green River is a good choice for whitewater rafting and tubing. There are picnic areas, restrooms, play areas, volleyball courts, a horseback riding area (but no stables) and horseshoe pits.

KANASKAT-PALMER STATE PARK

✉️32101 Cumberland-Kanaskat Road Southeast, Ravensdale; 11 miles north of Enumclaw and Route 410 📞360-886-0148 📠360-886-1715

🏃 🚵 ⛵ 🚣 Lovely walking on riverside paths, especially in summer, is the hallmark of this 320-acre park upstream from the entrance to Green River Gorge. During fishing season, try for steelhead and trout (check posted regulations). Picnic areas, restrooms, showers, volleyball courts and horseshoe pits are the facilities here.

⛺ There are 31 standard sites ($19 per night) and 19 with partial hookups ($25 per night). Reservations: 888-226-7688.

NOLTE STATE PARK
✉ *36921 Veazie-Cumberland Road Southeast, Enumclaw* ☎ *360-825-4646*

🚶 🚴 🚤 🎣 ⛵ ⛴ Surrounding Deep Lake, this 117-acre park is famous for its huge Douglas firs, cedars and cottonwoods. A one-and-a-quarter-mile path circles the lake taking you around nearly 7200 feet of shoreline and past the big trees; a separate nature trail interprets the forest. You can swim at the lake (no lifeguards); motorboats are prohibited. The lake is open for fishing, offering trout, bass, crappie, catfish and silvers. There's a minimal picnic area. Closed October to mid-April.

WEST HYLEBOS WETLANDS PARK
idden

✉ *411 South 348th Street, Federal Way; Just west of Route 99 and Exit 142*
☎ *253-835-6901* 📠 *253-835-6969*

🚶 A rare chunk of urban wetland tucked between industrialization and subdivisions, this 120-acre park offers examples of all sorts of wetland formations along a one-mile boardwalk trail—springs, streams, marshes, lakes, floating bogs and sinks. You'll also see remnants of ancient forest, plentiful waterfowl, more than a hundred species of birds and many mammals. Facilities are limited to portable toilets.

TACOMA & OLYMPIA

The Tacoma/Olympia region southwest of Seattle is rich in history, parks, waterfalls and cultural landmarks. Tacoma features numerous architectural gems; nearby villages like Gig Harbor are ideal for daytrippers. One of the nation's prettier capital cities (and here you may have thought Seattle was the capital of Washington!), Olympia is convenient to the wildlife refuges of Southern Puget Sound, as well as to American Indian monuments and petroglyphs.

Despite a lingering mill town reputation, Tacoma, the city on Commencement Bay, has experienced a lively rejuvenation in recent years and offers visitors some first-rate attractions. Charles Wright, president of the Great Northern Railroad, chose it as the western terminus of his railroad, and he wanted more than a mill town at the end of his line. Some of the best architects of the day were commissioned to build hotels, theaters, schools and office buildings.

SIGHTS

HISTORIC DISTRICTS Today, Tacoma is the state's "second city" with a population of 179,000. The city jealously protects its treasure trove of turn-of-the-20th-century architecture in a pair of historic districts overlooking the bay on both sides of Division Avenue. The 1893 **Old City Hall** at South 7th and Commerce streets was modeled after Renaissance Italian hill castles. The 1889 **Bostwick Hotel** at South 9th Street and Broadway is a classic triangular Victorian "flatiron."

NO CABBAGES BED AND BREAKFAST

PAGE 98

Charming inn with eclectic folk-art decor, water views, and grounds populated with deer and foxes

POINT DEFIANCE PARK

PAGE 95

Fifty miles of trails winding through a spectacular saltwater park jutting dramatically into the Sound

NORTHWEST MUSEUM STORE

PAGE 101

Handmade silver jewelry by local artists continuing the traditions of the region's diverse history

GARDNER'S SEAFOOD & PASTA

PAGE 100

Popular with locals, a cozy seafood spot with fresh dishes like Dungeness crab casserole

PANTAGES THEATER ✉Broadway Center, 901 Broadway, Tacoma ☎253-591-5894 (general information), 800-291-7593 (tickets), 253-591-5890 (tours) 📠253-591-2013 ✐www.broadwaycenter.org, tickets@broadwaycenter.org This exquisitely restored 1918 masterpiece of the vaudeville circuit is the centerpiece of Tacoma's thriving theater district. A classic of the vaudeville circuit (W.C. Fields, Mae West, Will Rogers and Houdini all performed here), this theater offers dance, music and theater. The Pantages is worth visiting simply to gawk at its glittering grandeur.

TACOMA ART MUSEUM ✉1701 Pacific Avenue, Tacoma ☎253-272-4258 📠253-627-1898 ✐www.tacomaartmuseum.org, info@tacomaartmuseum.org Both Northwest art and international-class shows are presented here; past exhibits have featured Picasso's ceramics and works on paper. The permanent collection focuses on the early glass works of Tacoma native Dale Chihuly. Closed Monday. Admission.

UNION STATION ✉1717 Pacific Avenue, Tacoma ☎253-572-9310 ✐www.chihuly.com/installations/unionstation The 70-foot diameter rotunda dome here rises 60 feet above ground level; the Beaux Arts neoclassical–style building dates from 1911. The rotunda holds one of the world's finest exhibits of glass art made entirely by Tacoma native Dale Chihuly, the renowned founder of the Pilchuck School of blown-glass art.

WASHINGTON STATE HISTORY MUSEUM ✉1911 Pacific Avenue, Tacoma ☎253-272-9747, 888-238-4373 📠253-272-9518 ✐www.wshs.org Next door to Union Station is this museum, offering a comprehensive view of the state's human cultures, from the original inhabitants dependent on salmon to the logging, fishing and farming that first brought settlers to the Northwest. Interactive exhibits allow visitors to sit in the driver's seat of a covered wagon, take a stab at separating wheat from chaff and experience a coal mine cave-in. Closed Monday. Admission.

MUSEUM OF GLASS ✉1801 Dock Street, Tacoma ✆253-284-4750, 866-468-7386 📠253-396-1769 ✐www.museumofglass.org, info@museumofglass.org The **Chihuly Bridge of Glass**, a tunnel of light and color created by the renowned Tacoma glass artist Dale Chihuly, connects the Union Station to this museum. Dedicated to showcasing glass art from around the world, the museum also features a hands-on studio for visitors and a store specializing in glass. Most exciting is the Hot Shop, a glass workshop where a resident team of glass blowers plies its trade. Closed Monday and Tuesday between Labor Day and Memorial Day. Admission.

JOB CARR CABIN MUSEUM ✉2350 North 30th Street, Tacoma ✆253-627-5405 ✐www.jobcarrmuseum.org This museum is a reconstruction of the first permanent settlers' log cabin, and it commemorates Tacoma's founding with original artifacts, photos and historical displays. Closed Sunday through Tuesday.

W. W. SEYMOUR BOTANICAL CONSERVATORY
✉316 South G Street, Tacoma ✆253-591-5330 📠253 627 2192 ✐seymour@tacomaparks.com Without a doubt, Tacoma's prettiest garden spot is this graceful Victorian-style domed conservatory constructed at the turn of the 20th century with over 3000 panes of glass. Inside is a diverse collection of more than 250 plants, including birds of paradise, ornamental figs, orchids, cacti and bromeliads, accented by a koi pond. Closed Monday.

POINT DEFIANCE PARK
✉5400 North Pearl Street, Tacoma ✆253-305-1000 ✐www.metroparkstacoma.org A treat for both kids and adults is this park, set on a sloping peninsula above the south Puget Sound shore. The 702-acre urban park has an outstanding **zoo and aquarium** (253-591-5337; www.pdza.org) with a Pacific Rim theme. You can watch the fish from above or through underwater viewing windows. You'll also see an outdoor logging museum with steam trains; Fort Nisqually, a reconstruction of the original 1850 Hudson's Bay Company post (closed Monday and Tuesday except in summer); rhododendron, rose, Japanese and native Northwest gardens; and numerous scenic overlooks (see "Beaches & Parks" below).

GIG HARBOR Situated across the Tacoma Narrows off Route 16 is this classic Puget Sound small town. The community that arose around the harbor was founded as a fishing village by Croatians and Austrians. Today you're more likely to see every sort of pleasure craft here; it's one

Tacoma & Olympia

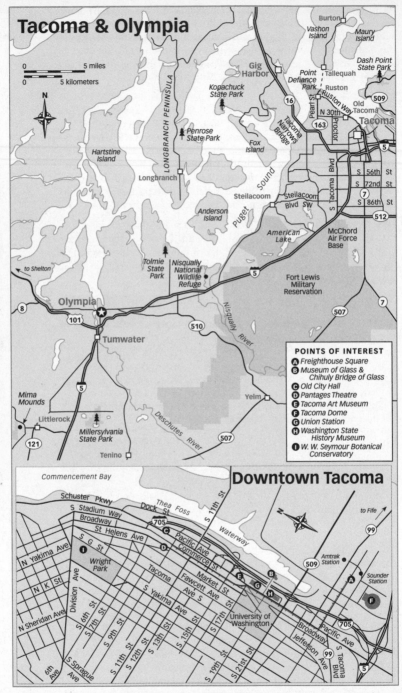

0 — 5 miles
0 — 5 kilometers

N

Burton

Vashon Island

Maury Island

Gig Harbor

Dash Point State Park

Kopachuck State Park

Point Defiance Park

Tallequah

Ruston

Old Tacoma

509

LONGBRANCH PENINSULA

Penrose State Park

Fox Island

16

Tacoma Narrows Bridge

Pearl St

Ruston Way

N 30th

Proctor

163

Tacoma

5

Hartstine Island

Longbranch

Steilacoom

S Tacoma Blvd

S 56th St

S 72nd St

S 86th St

7

512

Anderson Island

Steilacoom Blvd SW

Puget Sound

American Lake

McChord Air Force Base

to Shelton

Tolmie State Park

Nisqually National Wildlife Refuge

5

Fort Lewis Military Reservation

507

7

8

Olympia

101

510

Nisqually River

Tumwater

Mima Mounds

5

Littlerock

Millersylvania State Park

Deschutes River

Yelm

121

Tenino

507

POINTS OF INTEREST

A Freighthouse Square
B Museum of Glass & Chihuly Bridge of Glass
C Old City Hall
D Pantages Theatre
E Tacoma Art Museum
F Tacoma Dome
G Union Station
H Washington State History Museum
I W. W. Seymour Botanical Conservatory

Downtown Tacoma

Commencement Bay

Schuster Pkwy

S Stadium Way

Broadway

Dock St

Thea Foss Waterway

S 11th St

705

to Fife

99

St Helens Ave

C

Pacific Ave

N

S G St

D

Commerce St

509

Amtrak Station

N Yakima Ave

I

Wright Park

Tacoma

Market St

E

B

A

Sounder Station

N K St

Division Ave

Fawcett Ave S

G

H

F

N Sheridan Ave

S 6th St

S 7th St

S Yakima Ave

117th St

University of Washington

Broadway

99

S Tacoma Blvd

705

6th Ave

S Sprague Ave

S 9th St

S 11th St

S 12th St

S 13th St

15th St

S 17th St

S 19th St

S 21st St

Jefferson Ave

Pacific Ave

5

of the best boat-watching locales on Puget Sound. The tight harbor entrance funnels boats single-file past dockside taverns and cafés where you can watch the nautical parade. Or, rent a power boat or kayak from **Gig Harbor Rent-A-Boat** (8829 North Harborview Drive, 253-858-7341; www.gigharborrentaboat.com, gigharborrentaboat@comcast.net) and join the flotilla.

STEILACOOM

About five miles south of Tacoma is this quiet counterpoint to Gig Harbor's bustle. Founded by Yankee sea captains in the 1850s, it exudes a museum-like peacefulness and preserves a New England look among its fine collection of clapboard houses. Get a brochure at **Steilacoom Historical Museum** (1801 Rainier Street, Steilacoom; 253-584-4133; www.steilacoom historical.org). The self-guided tour features the **Pioneer Orchard**, which surrounds the **Nathaniel Orr Home** (1811 Rainier Street), one of the town's most noted buildings, dating back to 1857.

OLYMPIA At the southern tip of Puget Sound, the state capitol dome rises boldly as you approach on Route 5, a tempting landmark for travelers and an easy detour from the busy freeway. But this community of some 45,000 offers visitors more to peruse than government buildings and monuments. Nevertheless, the capitol campus may be the best place to begin your explorations.

You can take a daily guided tour seven days a week through the marbled halls of the Romanesque **Legislative Building** and see other buildings on the grounds—**Temple of Justice**, **Executive Mansion** and **State Library**.

STATE CAPITOL MUSEUM ⊠211 Southwest 21st Avenue, Olympia ☎360-753-2580 ☏360-586-8322 ⊘www.wshs.org This museum includes a fine collection of Northwest Coast Indian artifacts. Closed Sunday through Tuesday. Admission.

OLD CAPITOL Downtown, this handsomely restored building, at 7th Avenue and Washington Street across from stately Sylvester Park, will catch your eye with its fanciful architecture. But most of downtown is a potpourri of disparate attractions—the **Washington Center for the Performing Arts** at 512 Washington Street Southeast, galleries, the **Capitol Theater** at 5th Avenue and Washington Street with its old films and local theater, and a bit of Bohemia along 4th Avenue West.

PERCIVAL LANDING ⊠217 Thurston Avenue Northwest, Olympia This is an inviting, harborside park with observation tower, kiosks with historical displays, picnic tables, cafés and boardwalks next to acres of pleasure craft.

CAPITOL LAKE ⊠From Percival Landing, head south on Water Street, cross 4th and 5th avenues, then turn west and follow the sidewalk next to the Deschutes Parkway. The park-dotted shores of this manmade lake, which is two and a half miles from the town of Tumwater, make for a pleasant stroll.

TUMWATER HISTORICAL PARK ✉777 Simmons Avenue, Tumwater ☎360-754-4160 🖷360-754-4166 🖳www.ci.tumwater.wa.us **Tumwater** marks the true end of Puget Sound. Before Capitol Lake was created, the sound was navigable all the way to the Deschutes River. This historical park, at the meeting of river and lake, is rich in both history and recreation. One of two pioneer houses here was built in 1860 by Nathaniel Crosby III (Bing Crosby's grandfather). Down by the river you can fish, have a picnic, explore fitness and hiking trails, watch birds in reedy marshes and see more historical exhibits. Across the river, a handsome, six-story, brick brew house built in 1906 marks an early enterprise that lives on in a 1933 brewery a few hundred yards south

TUMWATER FALLS PARK ✉Deschutes Way and C Street, Tumwater ☎360-943-2550 🖷360-943-2550 🖳otf@olytwnfoundation.org Follow Deschutes Parkway south to Tumwater Falls Park (not to be confused with Tumwater Historical Park), a small park that's a nice spot for a picnic lunch and whose main attraction is the namesake "falls," twisting and churning through a rocky defile. Feel the throb of water reverberating through streamside footpaths. Listen to its sound, which the Indians called "Tumtum." You'll find plenty of history in the headquarters exhibit, including a monument recounting the travails of the first permanent settlement north of the Columbia River here in 1845.

MIMA MOUNDS ✉Wadell Creek Road, Littlerock ☎360-577-2025 Ten miles south of Olympia are an unusual group of several hundred hillocks spread across 450 acres. Scientists think they could have been created by glacial deposits or, believe it or not, busy gophers. There is a self-guided interpretive trail offering a close look at this geologic oddity, as well as several miles of hiking trails. Wildflowers paint the mounds yellow, pink and blue from April through June.

LODGING

CHINABERRY HILL

$$$–$$$$ 5 ROOMS   ✉302 Tacoma Avenue North, Tacoma ☎253-272-1282
🖷253-272-1335 🖳www.chinaberryhill.com, chinaberry@wa.net

Chocolates left on my pillow are but one of the reasons I have sweet dreams when I stay here. This luxurious 1889 Victorian bed and breakfast offers three spacious romance suites with bay windows, double jacuzzis, private baths with showers and harbor views or a fireplace. The adjacent two-story carriage house, with its cabin atmosphere, is ideal for families featuring a queen-sized curved iron canopy bed, a double bed loft and a jacuzzi alcove. Appointed with period antiques and surrounded by gardens, the inn is an inviting retreat.

**NO CABBAGES
BED AND BREAKFAST**

$$$ 4 ROOMS   ✉10319 Sunrise Beach Drive Northwest, Gig Harbor
☎253-858-7797 🖳www.nocabbages.com, info@nocabbages.com

A lovely home with a view of the water and access to the beach, this bed and breakfast has three guest rooms with both private and shared bathrooms, and a suite with its own private entrance. The house is laden with eclectic, primitive folk art and interesting conversation. The grounds feature deer, fox, woodpeckers and a prayer labyrinth for introspection and walking meditation. The innkeeper serves an outstanding breakfast.

LIGHTHOUSE BUNGALOW

$$$ 3 UNITS   ✉1215 East Bay Drive, Olympia   ☎360-754-0389
⌐www.lighthousebungalow.com, info@lighthousebungalow.com

This beachfront property includes a beautifully restored 1920s-era bungalow with waterfront access to Budd Inlet on Puget Sound. The four-bedroom, four-bath upstairs unit sleeps ten comfortably and is furnished with antiques, hardwood floors, a full kitchen, two fireplaces and views of the Sound and Olympic Mountains from its deck. The cozy two-bedroom, lower-level unit includes a sitting room and sleeps up to four. The owners lend bicycles, kayaks and a canoe.

DINING

SOUTHERN KITCHEN

$$ SOUTHERN   ✉1716 6th Avenue, Tacoma   ☎253-627-4282

If you've a hankering for barbecued ribs, fried chicken or catfish, try this delicious spot. This is no antebellum mansion, just a plain, well-lit café with good food. Just as good as the entrées are the greens, grits, yams, fried okra, biscuits, homemade strawberry lemonade and melt-in-your-mouth corncakes served up alongside. The cooks are Southern stock themselves, so you can count on this fare being authentic. Breakfast is served all day.

FUJIYA

hidden

$$–$$$ JAPANESE/SUSHI   ✉1125 Court C, Tacoma   ☎253-627-5319
⌐www.fujiyatacoma.com

Do you enjoy good tempura? Then don't walk, run to this restaurant in downtown Tacoma. Masahiro Endo, owner and chef, is a great entertainer with his knife at the sushi bar. In addition, the chicken sukiyaki is delicious. Closed Sunday; no lunch on Saturday.

FALLS TERRACE

$$–$$$ CONTINENTAL/SEAFOOD   ✉106 Deschutes Way, Tumwater
☎360-943-7830   ✆360-943-6899   ⌐www.fallsterrace.com

One of the best views in Olympia is from the huge windows in this dining room, which overlooks Tumwater Falls on the Deschutes River. A good way to start your meal is with some fresh oysters. The menu features pasta dishes, an excellent bouillabaisse and an array of chicken and beef entrées. Reservations recommended.

GARDNER'S SEAFOOD AND PASTA

$$$ SEAFOOD   ✉111 West Thurston Avenue, Olympia ✆360-786-8466
⊲www.gardnersrestaurant.com

Gardner's is no secret to locals, who flock to this small restaurant. While seafood is the specialty here, there are several pastas that are very good, too. Try the pasta primavera. The Dungeness crab casserole is rich with cream, chablis and several cheeses. Homemade ice cream and other desserts fill out the meal. Dinner only. Closed Sunday and Monday.

MCMENAMIN'S SPAR CAFÉ

$$ DINER   ✉114 East 4th Avenue, Olympia ✆360-357-6444
⊲www.mcmenamins.com

Patrons don't usually go to a restaurant for the drinking water, but at McMenamin's it truly is exceptional because it comes from the eatery's own artesian well. Once a blue-collar café, the restaurant features large photographs of loggers felling giant Douglas firs. On the menu are thick milkshakes, giant sandwiches, prime rib and ale-battered fish and chips.

URBAN ONION

$$ INTERNATIONAL   ✉116 Legion Way, Olympia ✆360-943-9242
⊲www.theurbanonion.com

In downtown Olympia, this eatery serves sizable breakfasts, good sandwiches and hamburgers and a hearty lentil soup. Dinners include chicken, seafood and *gado*—a spicy Indonesian dish of sautéed vegetables in tahini and peanut sauce, along with Mexican entrées. They also offer several vegetarian specials. The restaurant is part of a complex of shops in the former Olympian Hotel.

SHOPPING

PACIFIC NORTHWEST SHOP ✉2702 North Proctor Street, Tacoma ✆253-752-2242, 800-942-3523 ⊲www.pacificnorthwestshop.com In the Proctor District in north Tacoma you can find Northwest foods, gifts and clothing here.

THE HARP & SHAMROCK ✉2704 North Proctor Street, Tacoma ✆253-752-5012 Fine Irish imports are in stock at this festive shop.

OLD HOUSE MERCANTILE ✉2717-A North Proctor Street, Tacoma ✆253-759-8850 ⊲www.oldhousemercantile.com The Old House offers gifts for the kitchen and garden as well as a selection of teapots, soaps and jewelry.

TEACHING TOYS ✉2624 North Proctor Street, Tacoma ✆253-759-9853 ⊲www.teachingtoysandbooks.com Educational toys (what else?) are found at this kid-friendly store.

NORTHWEST MUSEUM STORE _____

✉*1911 Pacific Avenue, Tacoma* ☎*253-798-5880, 800-593-6773* ⌨*www.indian blanket.com* This gift shop in the Washington State History Museum is a treasure trove of art that reflects the diverse history of the Pacific Northwest. Here you'll find books on American Indian history and the stories that shaped the region, as well as a wide variety of silver jewelry made by local artists whose patterns and designs come from the traditions of the area's past. Closed Monday.

FREIGHTHOUSE SQUARE ✉*2501 East D Street at East 25th Street, Tacoma* ☎*253-305-0678* ⌨*www.freighthousesquare.com* Near the Tacoma Dome downtown, this square boasts a thriving collection of shops and eateries in an old railroad warehouse. Dozens of shops offer local crafts, jewelry, ethnic gifts, flowers and food items.

THE BEACH BASKET ✉*1102 Harborview Drive, Gig Harbor* ☎*253-858-3008* In Gig Harbor, this aptly named place features, of course, baskets as well as women's clothing and other gifts.

STRICTLY SCANDINAVIAN ✉*7803 Pioneer Way, Gig Harbor* ☎*253-851-5959* ⌨*www.strictlyscandinavian.com* Jewelry, utensils, books and gifts from Sweden, Denmark and Norway can be found here.

MOSTLY BOOKS ✉*3126 Harborview Drive, Gig Harbor* ☎*253-851-3219* ⌨*www.mostlybooks.com* Mostly Books stocks books (you're kidding), bookmarks and postcards.

JUICY FRUITS ✉*111 Market Street, Suite 103, Olympia* ☎*360-943-0572* In Olympia, at this shop you'll find contemporary women's clothing and accessories.

OLYMPIC OUTFITTERS ✉*407 East 4th Avenue, Olympia* ☎*360-943-1114* ⌨*www.olympicoutfitters.com* Housed in a restored, brick-and-metal building, this store is stocked with everything from bicycles to backpacking and cross-country ski gear.

NIGHTLIFE

THE SWISS PUB ✉*1904 South Jefferson Avenue, Tacoma* ☎*253-572-2821* ⌨*www.theswisspub.com* For drinks and live music, this longtime favorite is at the top of a flight of stairs connecting the State History Museum with the campus of the University of Washington—Tacoma. It's renowned for its collection of Chihuly glass, not a common thing for a college pub.

KATIE DOWNS TAVERN ✉*3211 Ruston Way, Tacoma* ☎*253-756-0771* ⌨*www.katiedowns.com* Katie Downs is an adults-only pub overlooking Commencement Bay with a menu featuring local microbrews, seafood and pizza. Flatscreen plasma TVs broadcast sporting events, if the waterfront view isn't enough entertainment.

ALE HOUSE PUB ✉*2122 Mildred Street West, Tacoma* ✆*253-565-9367* ⌐*www.alehousepub.com* Boasting one of the largest selections of draught beer in the state, this jolly tavern also has a handful of activities, including shuffleboard, darts and interactive trivia.

TACOMA LITTLE THEATRE ✉*210 North I Street, Tacoma* ✆*253-272-2281* ⌐*www.tacomalittletheatre.com* This community theater produces five plays a year.

THE TIDES TAVERN ✉*2925 Harborview Drive, Gig Harbor* ✆*253-858-3982* ⌐*www.tidestavern.com* The Tides features live bands on Saturday nights playing '50s and '60s rock and some rhythm-and-blues.

BEACHES & PARKS

DASH POINT STATE PARK _____

✉*Located just northeast of Tacoma on Southwest Dash Point (Route 509)*
✆*253-661-4955* 📠*253-661-4995*

🚶 🚴 🏊 🦀 ⚓ Nearly 400 acres of forested wildland with 3300 feet of saltwater shoreline preserve a bit of solitude just barely outside the Tacoma city limits. Eleven miles of trails ramble through a mixed forest of second-growth fir, maple and alder. The park's beach is one of the few places on Puget Sound where you'll find enjoyable saltwater swimming—shallow waters in tide flats are warmed by the summer sun. Tides retreat to expose a beachfront nearly a half-mile deep. There's fishing from the pier at Brown's Point Park south of Dash Point State Park, and swimming in tide flat shallows (no lifeguard). Facilities include picnic areas, restrooms and showers.

▲ There are 114 developed sites ($19 per night) and 27 sites with hookups ($26 per night). Reservations: 888-226-7688.

POINT DEFIANCE PARK _____ hidden

✉*The entrance is at 5400 North Pearl Street* ✆*253-305-1000*
📠*253-305-1098*

🚶 🚴 🦀 ⛴ ⚓ Jutting dramatically into Puget Sound, this 702-acre treasure is hailed by some as the finest saltwater park in the state, by others as the best city park in the Northwest. Here are primeval forests, some 50 miles of hiking trails, over three miles of public shoreline and enough other attractions to match almost any visitor's interests. Five Mile Drive loops around the park perimeter with access to trails, forest, beach, views, attractions and grand overlooks of Puget Sound. The park is also known for its zoo and aquarium, particularly the shark tank (fee). Popular with boaters, there's a fully equipped marina with boat rentals, a boathouse (253-591-5325) and a restaurant. You can fish from the pier or in a rented boat. You'll find picnic areas, restrooms, play areas, tennis courts and a snack bar at the boathouse.

KOPACHUCK STATE PARK

✉Located on Kopachuck Drive Northwest at Northwest 56th Street, about seven miles west of Gig Harbor and Route 16 ☎253-265-3606
✆360-644-8112

🚶🚴🚤⛵🎣🏕🚣⛴🚗 Spectacular views across Carr Inlet toward the Olympic Mountains from a half-mile of shoreline gives this 109-acre park much to boast about. Many car-top boaters launch from the beach near the park to fish for bottom-fish and salmon or paddle out to Cutts Island Marine State Park (also known as Dead Man's Island) a half-mile away. No lifeguard is on duty. There are picnic areas, restrooms and showers. ⛺ There are 41 sites for tents and RVs ($19 per night); no hookups are available.

NISQUALLY NATIONAL WILDLIFE REFUGE

✉Route 5 Exit 114, about 25 miles south of downtown Tacoma
☎360-753-9467 ✆360-534-9302 ⌨www.fws.gov/nisqually

🚶🥾🚗 This 3000-acre refuge's ecosystem is a diverse mix of conifer forest, deciduous woodlands, marshlands, grasslands and mud flats and the meandering Nisqually River (born in Mt. Rainier National Park). Here, the river mixes its fresh waters with the salt chuck of Puget Sound. The refuge is home to mink, otter, coyote and some 50 other species of mammals, over 200 kinds of birds and 125 species of fish. Fishing yields salmon, steelhead and cutthroat. Facilities include a visitor center and restrooms. Day-use fee, $3 per family.

TOLMIE STATE PARK

✉Hill Road Northeast, northeast of Olympia via Exit 111 from Route 5 ☎360-456-6464
✆360-456-6464

🚶🚤⛵🎣🥾🚣🚗 A salt marsh with interpretive signs separates 1800 feet of tide flats from forested uplands overlooking Nisqually Reach. The sandy beach is fine for wading or swimming; at low tide you may find clams. A three-mile wheelchair-accessible perimeter hiking trail loops through the park's 105 acres. An artificial reef and three sunken barges 500 yards offshore and almost-nonexistent current make the underwater park here popular for divers. Fishing yields salmon, cod, steelhead and trout. You'll find picnic areas, restrooms and showers.

MILLERSYLVANIA STATE PARK

✉Exit 95 just east of Route 5, ten miles south of Olympia ☎360-753-1519
✆360-664-2180

🚶🚴🚤⛵🚣🚗 Some 842 acres of primeval conifer forest and miles of foot trail are this park's big appeals. But visitors also come to enjoy its 3300 feet of shoreline along Deep

Lake, where you can swim, launch a small boat (no wake) or fish for trout, bass, perch and crappie. Facilities include picnic areas and restrooms.

▲ There are 120 standard sites ($19 per night) and 48 sites with hookups ($26 per night). No reservations necessary October to May. Reservations: 888-226-7688; res.nw@state.or.us.

OUTDOOR ADVENTURES

SPORTFISHING

Salmon, of course, is the big draw for anglers on Puget Sound. State hatchery programs see to it that the anadromous fish are available year-round, but the months from midsummer to midfall bring the bulk of salmon—and anglers—to these waters. From mid-July to late August, chinook salmon are king; by Labor Day coho take over, until October. Then chum arrive, but since they tend to be plankton eaters they don't bite. Pink salmon return in odd numbered years, in August, and are most plentiful in the Sound north of Seattle, near Everett. Sockeye can be found in Lake Washington as early as late June until August.

Several charter companies operate fishing trips on the Sound. The cost, which can range from $35 to $80 and up, usually includes everything except lunch and the fishing license (which you can purchase through the charter company).

Seattle Area

Downtown, you can drop your line right into Elliott Bay at Waterfront Park (Piers 57-61). But for the real deal, head to Ballard, where the city's commercial fishing fleet is based (at Fisherman's Terminal) and sportfishing tours can be chartered.

ADVENTURE CHARTERS ✉ *7001 Seaview Avenue Northwest, Shilshole Bay Marina* ✆ *206-789-8245, 800-789-0448* ✐ *www.seattlesalmoncharters.com* This company offers full-day salmon fishing trips year-round. Afternoon tours are offered in summer, and all gear is provided.

Seattle North Area

ALL SEASONS CHARTER SERVICE ✉ *Port of Edmonds, 300 Admiral Way, Suite 102* ✆ *425-743-9590, 877-943-9590* All Seasons operates two boats for salmon or bottomfish.

KAYAKING & SMALL BOATING

If your nautical know-how extends no further than a good row across a lake, then head for Lake Union, on the northern edge of Seattle's downtown center. On a bright summer day, the waters of Lake Union are dotted with kayaks, small wooden rowboats and sailboats.

NORTHWEST OUTDOOR CENTER ✉*2100 Westlake Avenue North* ☎*206-281-9694, 800-683-0637* ⌨*www.nwoc.com* To rent a single or double kayak, call this outfitter to reserve ahead. Kayaking on Lake Union is very popular, and it's not unusual for all the center's 100-plus kayaks to be rented on a nice day. Classes and guided trips from one day to five days are available. There's also a special nighttime kayak trip.

CENTER FOR WOODEN BOATS ✉*1010 Valley Street* ☎*206-382-2628* ☎*206-382-2699* ⌨*www.cwb.org* Not only can you rent one of several different kinds of classic wooden rowboats here, you can also learn a bit about their history. There are also several small sailboats for rent, but only experienced boaters can rent them. The center is a nonprofit, hands-on museum that also offers sailing instruction and other heritage maritime skills such as knot-tying, navigation and boat building.

Tacoma & Olympia Area

BOATHOUSE MARINA ☎*253-591-5325* Located near the tip of the peninsula in Point Defiance Park, this marina has twenty 14-foot dinghies for rent. Most of the time they're rented by anglers, but you can take them out to explore the Sound if you prefer. Also for rent are motors to power the boats.

SCUBA DIVING

Although the water temperature in Puget Sound averages a cool 45° to 55°, diving is quite popular, especially from October through April, when there's no plankton bloom because of reduced sunlight during those months. With several dive clubs in the Seattle-Tacoma area, there are usually many dives scheduled each weekend: a wall dive off Fox Island perhaps, or a shore dive at Three Tree Point (near Federal Way) or Sunrise Beach (near Gig Harbor). Southern Puget Sound and the area around Vashon Island are considered the best places to dive—you'll see starfish, crabs, ling cod, scallops and many more species. Be prepared, however: Currents are extremely strong south of Seattle, so you'll need to check the tides and currents carefully before diving. The dive shops listed below can provide details about these hazards as well as information on local dive spots. If you're not an experienced diver, you can arrange lessons with these shops, although it takes several days to complete training for certification.

Seattle North Area

UNDERWATER SPORTS INC. This outfitter has eight shops between Everett and Olympia. The Everett store is closed Sunday and Monday. Seattle (10545 Aurora Avenue North; 206-362-3310, 800-252-7177). Edmonds (264 Railroad Avenue; 425-771-6322). Everett (205 East Casino Road #4; 425-355-3338; www.underwatersports.com).

LIGHTHOUSE DIVING CENTERS This diving center offers outposts in Seattle (8215 Lake City Way Northeast; 206-524-1633) and Lynnwood (5421 196th Street Southwest #6; 425-771-2679).

Hey! The Water's Fine

Even if you're a diehard landlubber, do not fail to go sightseeing here by boat at least once. Simply put, if you leave Seattle without plying its surrounding waters, your trip will be incomplete. So don't hesitate: Head to the downtown central waterfront and make some waves.

WASHINGTON STATE FERRIES ✉*Pier 52* ☎*206-464-6400* 🖰*www.wsdot.wa.gov/ferries* On a clear day you can see forever, or so it would seem aboard one of the state ferries. Headquartered at Colman Dock, the ferries make frequent departures to Bremerton and to Bainbridge Island, both across Puget Sound to the west. From deck you'll be treated to grand views of Mount Rainier, Mount Baker and the Olympics Range, and you may even catch a glimpse of a killer whale. To Bremerton, you can ride the car-and-passenger ferry, the passenger-only boat or the high-speed ferry for pedestrians. At Pier 50 next door, you can board a passenger-only ferry to Vashon Island.

ARGOSY CRUISES ✉*Pier 55* ☎*206-623-4252, 800-642-7816* 🖰*www.argosycruises.com* This is your captain speaking. That's just part of the show on Argosy, which offers at least two tours every day year-round. On the harbor spin you'll get grand mountain views and see boat traffic like you won't believe: freighters, tugboats, sailboats, ferries, you name it.

GRAY LINE WATER SIGHTSEEING ✉*Pier 55* ☎*800-426-7532* 🖰*www.graylineseattle.com* Argosy Cruises joins forces with this company for a great "locks tour." The tour goes north to Shilshole Bay, eastward through the Hiram M. Chittenden Locks into the Lake Washington Ship Canal and then on to the south tip of Lake Union. You return to the waterfront by bus. Going through the locks is an experience in itself.

TILLICUM VILLAGE-BLAKE ISLAND ✉*Pier 55* ☎*206-933-8600* 🖰*www.tillicumvillage.com* An American Indian performance is included in this four-hour excursion to 475-acre Blake Island Marine State Park.

S.S. VIRGINIA V ☎*206-624-9119* 🖰*www.virginiav.org* This is the last authentic operating steamboat of the legendary "Mosquito Fleet," the motley flotilla of steamboats that once carried foot passengers and cargo around Puget Sound before the coming of highways and autos.

LET'S GO SAILING CHARTERS ✉*Pier 54* ☎*206-624-3931, 800-831-3274* 🖰*www.sailingseattle.com* A quieter, more peaceful way to see Elliott Bay is with this company's sailboat tours. Pick a daytime or sunset tour and float gracefully past motorboats, ferries and tankers from May to mid-October.

Seattle South Area

NORTHWEST SPORTS DIVERS INC. ✉*8030 Northeast Bothell Way, Suite B, Kenmore* ☎*425-487-0624* 🖰*www.nwsportsdivers.com* A full-service scuba shop, Northwest Sports rents any equipment you might need. They also offer scuba certification classes.

Seattle East Area

UNDERWATER SPORTS INC. You'll find local branches of Underwater Sports in Bellevue (12003 Northeast 12th Street; 425-454-

5168) and Kirkland (11743 124th Avenue Northeast; 425-821-7200; www.underwatersports.com).Both closed Sunday and Monday.

SILENT WORLD ✉13600 Northeast 20th Street ✆425-747-8842, 800-841-3483 🖱www.silent-world.com In Bellevue, contact this company for classes, gear and rentals. There are beach dives on Sunday, as well as some one-day and two-day trips to the San Juans, Canada and tropical destinations. The shop is closed Sunday.

Tacoma & Olympia Area

LIGHTHOUSE DIVING ✉2502 Pacific Avenue, Tacoma ✆253-627-7617 📠253-627-1877 🖱www.lighthousediving.com In Tacoma, this group takes divers to Canada, the San Juan Islands and other destinations for trips that range from one to two days. Night dives are available. Lighthouse pros meet divers at designated locations. They use one tank per dive. Closed Sunday.

TAGERT'S DIVE LOCKER ✉205 Bethel Avenue ✆360-895-7860 In Port Orchard, contact Tagert's for diving, camping trips and holiday dives, such as an Easter egg hunt underwater. Night dives are available. Trips are no more than a half day and use two to three tanks per dive.

UNDERWATER SPORTS INC. This company offers shore and boat dives as well as dives abroad—both tropical and night dives. They repair gear. Dives are a day long and use two or three tanks. Closed Sunday. Tacoma (9606 40th Avenue Southwest; 253-588-6634). Olympia (1943 4th Avenue East; 360-493-0322; www.underwatersports.com).

GOLF

Except when the occasional snowstorm closes them down, golf courses in the area are open year-round.

Seattle North Area

KAYAK POINT GOLF COURSE ✉15711 Marine Drive Northeast, Stanwood ✆360-652-9676 🖱www.golfkayak.com Kayak Point, about 30 miles north of Seattle, is hilly and overlooks the Olympic Mountains and Puget Sound. This public championship course with a double fairway is worth the drive. Amenities include an 18-hole putting course; shoes, clubs and carts for rent, and a restaurant in the same building.

Seattle East Area

BELLEVUE MUNICIPAL GOLF COURSE ✉5500 140th Avenue Northeast ✆425-452-7250 🖱www.bellevuepgc.com Bellevue is one of the most active courses in the state, probably because it's a good walking course with moderate hills. This public course has 18 holes and cart rentals.

Tacoma & Olympia Area

LAKE SPANAWAY GOLF COURSE ✉15602 Pacific Avenue, Spanaway ✆253-531-3660 This course is in Pierce County Park. The 18-hole public course was cut out of a forest, so it's treelined but fairly open. It has a putting green and a pro shop and rents power and pull carts.

TENNIS

Northwest precipitation practically turns tennis into an indoor sport. You'll have to call a few days in advance to reserve an indoor court at one of these public facilities.

Seattle South Area

AMY YEE TENNIS CENTER ✉2000 Martin Luther King Jr. Way South ✆206-684-4764 Ten indoor courts.

Seattle East Area

ROBINSWOOD TENNIS CENTER ✉2400 151st Place Southeast at Southeast 22nd Street ✆425-452-7690 Four indoor and four lighted outdoor courts. Fee.

Tacoma & Olympia Area

SPRINKER RECREATION CENTER ✉14824 South C Street at Military Road, Tacoma ✆253-798-4000 Four public indoor courts. Fee.

RIDING STABLES

Take off on a guided ride to the top of a mountain east of Seattle or a slow meander through a wooden tract near Tacoma.

Seattle East Area

TIGER MOUNTAIN OUTFITTERS ✉24508 Southeast 133rd Street, Issaquah ✆425-392-5090 On a clear day, you can see more than 100 miles atop Tiger Mountain near Issaquah. This outfitter will get you there in a three-hour trail ride that will let you see Mt. Rainier 65 miles away in the distance and possibly black bear, deer and cougar within several yards. Call for reservations.

Tacoma & Olympia Area

SU DARA RIDING ✉8104 Canyon Road East, Puyallup ✆253-531-1569 ✑www. sudara.com Su Dara offers a "tranquil, peaceful" one-hour ride for up to seven people through woodland thick with firs and maples. On a clear day there are views of Mt. Rainier. Su herself says, "We ride rain or shine."

BIKING

It's no surprise to learn that Seattle has earned a nod from Bicycling magazine as one of the top bicycling cities in the country. Bicycle programs are administered by state, city and county transportation agencies, which has resulted in a network of bicycle lanes and trails throughout the region, many of them convenient for visitor recreational use.

BICYCLE HOTLINE ✉P.O. Box 47393, Olympia, WA 98504 ✆360-705-7277 ✑www.wsdot.wa.gov/bike Helpful information, including bicycle route maps, is available from several agencies. The Washington Department of Transportation operates this hotline from which you can request a route map and informative brochure.

THE SEATTLE BICYCLING GUIDE MAP ✉ *600 4th Avenue, Room 708, Seattle, WA 98104* ✆ *206-684-7583* This Seattle Department of Transportation map can usually be found in bike stores and public libraries, or ordered online at www.seattle.gov/transportation/bikemaps.htm.

KING COUNTY This region publishes a bicycling guide map; it's distributed free at bike shops countywide and at Metro Transit centers, or online at www.kingcounty.gov/bike. Or call the King County Bike Hotline at 206-263-4723.

CASCADE BICYCLE CLUB ✆ *206-522-3222* ✍ *www.cascade.org, info@cas cadebicycleclub.org* This is an all-purpose club for riders of all skill levels. The club operates a hotline, which provides general information about bicycling in the area and club-sponsored weekend rides.

Seattle Area

Although the central city is fairly hilly, especially if you're biking in an east–west direction, there are trails within Seattle that run near the water and on lower and flatter terrain that are ideal for recreational bicyclists. The most famous, of course, is the multi-use **Burke-Gilman Trail**, popular with bikers, walkers and joggers. It's flat, paved and, following an old railroad right of way, it extends from Gas Works Park on Lake Union, through the university campus, past lovely neighborhoods next to Lake Washington and on to Kenmore. In Kenmore, it links up with the **Sammamish River Trail**, which winds through Woodinville (and its wineries) and on to suburban Redmond. It's a lovely city-to-farmlands tour. In West Seattle, the **Alki Bike Route** (6 miles) offers miles of shoreline pedaling—half on separated bike paths— from Seacrest Park to Lincoln Park. Besides changing views of the city and Puget Sound, you should have great views of the Olympic Peninsula mountains.

Tacoma & Olympia Area

When it comes to bicycling in Tacoma and Pierce County, "things are just getting going," according to one of the city's public works planners. The area does not yet have the extensive network of lanes and trails that they have up in Seattle, but continues to develop its bicycle and pedestrian plan. Meanwhile, the **Pierce County Department of Public Works** (2702 South 42nd Street, Suite 201, Tacoma; 253-798-7250) puts out a bike route map. The **Tacoma Wheelmen's Bicycle Club** (253-759-2800; www.twbc.org) operates a recorded Ride Line.

Among the more popular and convenient places to ride in the city is a two-mile lane along the **downtown waterfront**. Beginning at Schuster Parkway and McCarver Street, this multi-use lane (it's separated from traffic, however) extends to Waterview Street along Ruston Way and Point Defiance Park. Within **Point Defiance Park**, a shoulder lane of Five Mile Drive loops around the peninsula. Call the **Metropolitan Park District** (253-305-1000; www.metroparkstacoma.org) for more information.

Bike Rentals

BICYCLE CENTER OF SEATTLE ✉4529 Sand Point Way Northeast ✆206-523-8300 ⤵www.bicyclecenterseattle.com Near the Burke-Gilman Trail, this store rents mountain bikes, hybrids and tandems from May through September.

ALKI BIKE & BOARD COMPANY ✉2606 California Avenue Southwest, Seattle ✆206-938-3322 ⤵www.alkibikeandboard.com This is the place to rent, buy or repair a bike on Alki Beach.

HIKING

Nearly every park mentioned in the "Beaches & Parks" sections of this chapter offers at least a few miles of hiking trail through forest or along a stream or beach. Some are outstanding, such as Nisqually National Wildlife Refuge, Green River Gorge, Point Defiance Park in Tacoma and Discovery Park in Seattle. All distances listed are one way unless otherwise noted.

Downtown Seattle Area

FREEWAY PARK For short strolls in downtown Seattle, try this park and the grounds of the adjoining Washington State Convention Center (.5 mile) and **Myrtle Edwards** and **Elliott Bay parks** (1.25 miles) at the north end of the downtown waterfront. Just across Elliott Bay, West Seattle offers about four miles of public shoreline to walk around Duwamish Head and Alki Point.

Seattle North Area

BURKE-GILMAN TRAIL For a longer walk, this 12-mile trail extends from Gas Works Park in Seattle to Logboom Park in Kenmore and on to Redmond. Full of walkers, joggers, skaters and bike commuters, this well-used corridor offers both urban and wooded stretches, highlighting why the Emerald City is one of the nation's top cycling cities.

SHELL CREEK NATURE TRAIL This .5-mile trail, in Edmonds' Yost Park at 96th Avenue West and Bowdoin Way, is an easy walk along a stream. Contact Edmonds Parks and Recreation (Edmonds Parks Department: 700 Main Street; 425-771-0227) for a guide to the area.

Seattle East Area

WILDERNESS CREEK, WILDERNESS PEAK AND WILDERNESS CLIFFS TRAILS ⬤**h**idden ✉ The trailhead is 3.3 miles south of I-90 exit 15 on Route 900 (17th Avenue Northwest/Renton–Issaquah Road Southeast). ✆206-296-4145 These three trails form a 3.2-mile loop that interconnect to provide hiking access to the remote southeastern sector of Cougar Mountain Regional Wildland Park, King County's largest park, with resident deer, porcupines, bobcats, coyotes and black bears and several spectacular scenic overlooks. The roadless park contains a total of 36 miles of hiking and equestrian trails.

MT. TENERIFFE TRAIL ⓗidden

✉*To get there from Seattle, follow I-90 east for 30 miles to North Bend, then follow 436th Avenue Northeast through town, turn left on North Bend Way and then right on Southeast Mount Si Road, and drive three miles, passing the big Mt. Si parking lot, to the Mt. Teneriffe Trailhead, with a small parking area. The trail starts as a gated, abandoned logging road.* ☎*206-470-4060* In Mt. Baker–Snoqualmie National Forest, less than an hour's drive from Seattle, this trail starts just up the road from the trailhead for the enormously popular climb up Mt. Si. Longer and steeper than the Mt. Si Trail, the 14-mile roundtrip hike has far fewer hikers and better views of the surrounding mountains as it makes its way up rocky abandoned logging roads and then rock-scrambles to the 4788-foot summit. Higher elevations may be snowbound at high elevations until late spring.

Seattle South Area

BIG SOOS CREEK The 4.5-mile trail along the creek, now protected in two parks, is an inviting ramble on a blacktop path next to one of the few wetland streams still in public ownership hereabouts. The trail winds from Kent-Kangley Road to Gary Grant Park. In Kent, south of Seattle, follow signs off Route 516 (Kent-Kangley Road) at 150th Avenue Southeast.

Tacoma & Olympia Area

BROWN FARM DIKE TRAIL ⓗidden

✉*From Highway 5 take exit 114 between Tacoma and Olympia. Turn west under the freeway and follow signs to the refuge.* ☎*360-753-9467* A wonderful river-delta walk, which starts on the Brown Farm Road, this 5.5-mile trail loops through the Nisqually National Wildlife Refuge. You may see bald eagles, coyotes, great blue heron, redtail hawks and a variety of waterfowl such as wood, canvasback and greater scaup ducks, as well as mallards and pintails. Views stretch from Mt. Rainier to the Olympics. You'll also see many of the islands in the south, Steilacoom and the Tacoma Narrows Bridge. No pets. Closed October to January for hunting season.

TRANSPORTATION

CAR

Seattle lies along Puget Sound east of the Olympic Peninsula in the state of Washington. **Route 5**, which carries most of Seattle's intra-city traffic, enters Seattle from Olympia and Tacoma to the south and from Everett from the north. It is one of the busiest freeways in the Interstate Highway System. When there's a major sporting event going on downtown, drivers on Route 5 quickly (or slowly) learn why Seattlites average more time in their cars than people in any other American city. **Route 99**, a surface street also known as Alaskan Way downtown and Aurora Avenue in north Seattle, is often a faster alternative to Route 5 despite the many stoplights. **Route 90** from Eastern Washington goes near Snoqualmie and through Bellevue on its way into Seattle. **Route 405** serves the Eastside suburban communities of Bellevue, Kirkland and Redmond. **Route 169** leads from Route 405 southeast of Renton to Maple Valley, Black Diamond and Enumclaw.

AIR

SEATTLE-TACOMA INTERNATIONAL AIRPORT *www.port seattle.org/seatac* About 20 miles south of downtown, Sea-Tac is served by AeroMexico, Air Canada, Air France, Alaska Airlines, American Airlines, Asiana Airlines, British Airways, Continental Airlines, Delta Air Lines, EVA Air, Frontier Airlines, Hainan Airlines, Hawaiian Airlines, Horizon Air, JetBlue Airlines, Northwest Airlines, Scandinavian Airlines, Southwest Airlines, Sun Country Airlines, United Airlines, United Express, US Airways, Virgin America and several smaller charter airlines. For general information, call 206-431-4444. There's a **visitors information center** on the baggage level of Sea-Tac International Airport.

FERRY

WASHINGTON STATE FERRY SYSTEM *206-464-6400* *www.ws dot.wa.gov/ferries* The state ferries serve Seattle, Port Townsend, Tacoma, Southworth, Vashon Island, Bainbridge Island, Bremerton, Keystone, Kingston, Edmonds, Mukilteo, Clinton, the San Juan Islands and Sidney, B.C. All are car ferries.

VICTORIA CLIPPER *206-448-5000, 800-888-2535* *www.clippervacations. com* This passenger catamaran service operates daily trips (a two-and-a-half-hour trip) between Seattle and Victoria, B.C.

BUS

GREYHOUND BUS LINES *811 Stewart Street* *800-231-2222* *www. greyhound.com* Greyhound serves Seattle from the terminal.

GRAY LINE OF SEATTLE *206-624-5077, 800-426-7532* *www.graylineof seattle.com* Gray Line provides inexpensive bus service from the airport to hotels and the downtown area.

TRAIN

AMTRAK *800-872-7245* *www.amtrak.com* Rail service in and out of Seattle is provided on the "Empire Builder," "Coast Starlight" and "Amtrak Cascades." Call for more information on connections from around the country.

CAR RENTALS 113

Most major car-rental businesses have offices at Seattle-Tacoma International Airport. Rental agencies include **Avis Rent A Car** (800-331-1212), **Budget Rent A Car** (800-527-0700), **Dollar Rent A Car** (800-800-4000), **Hertz Rent A Car** (800-654-3131) and **Thrifty Car Rental** (800-367-2277).

PUBLIC TRANSIT

METRO TRANSIT 206-553-3000, 800-542-7876 www.transit.metrokc.gov
Bus transportation provided by Metro Transit is free in downtown Seattle. Metro Transit provides service throughout the Seattle-King County area.

MONORAIL 206-905-2600 www.seattlemonorail.com Deemed transportation for the future, the Monorail was built for the 1962 World's Fair. It costs less than a dollar to ride, and it runs between downtown and the Seattle Center every ten minutes and zips between Seattle Center and Westlake Center in two minutes.

The downtown hub for both the Monorail and the bus system is at Westlake Center, on Pine Street between 4th and 5th Avenues. The Monorail arrives on an elevated platform above the street-level mall, while buses load in an underground terminal. The buses are uniquely designed so they can switch from diesel to electric power when they enter the subterranean tunnels.

WATERFRONT STREETCAR 206-553-3000 www.transit.metrokc.gov
These trolleys run from Seattle's historic Chinatown to Pier 70.

TAXIS

In the greater Seattle area are **Farwest Taxi** (206-622-1717), **North End Taxi** (206-363-3333) and **Yellow Cab** (206-622-6500).

SEATTLE & THE SOUTHERN SOUND TRANSPORTATION

THE NORTHERN SOUND & THE SAN JUANS

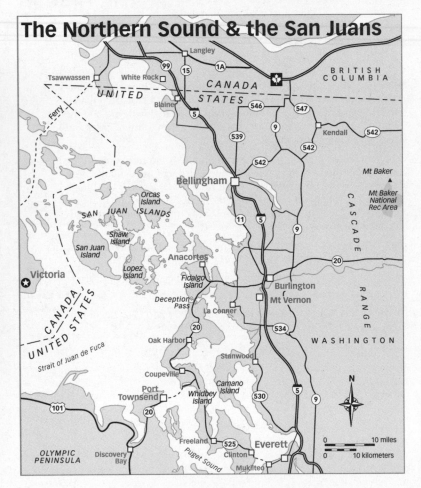

The Northern Sound & the San Juans

Langley
99
15
1A
Tsawwassen
White Rock
CANADA
BRITISH COLUMBIA
UNITED
STATES
Ferry
Blaine
546
547
5
Kendall
542
539
542
9
542
Bellingham
Mt Baker
Orcas
Island
11
5
Mt Baker
National
Rec Area
SAN JUAN ISLANDS
Shaw
Island
9
San Juan
Island
CASCADE
Lopez
Island
Anacortes
20
Victoria
Fidalgo
Island
Burlington
Deception
Pass
Mt Vernon
CANADA
La Conner
UNITED STATES
20
534
RANGE
Oak Harbor
WASHINGTON
Strait of Juan de Fuca
Stanwood
Coupeville
Camano
Island
Port
Townsend
Whidbey
Island
530
5
9
20
N
Freeland
525
Everett
OLYMPIC
PENINSULA
Discovery
Bay
Puget Sound
Clinton
Mukilteo
10 miles
0
10 kilometers

"Every part of this land is sacred to my people. Every shining pine needle, every sandy shore, every mist in the dark woods, every clearing and humming insect is holy in the memory and experience of my people... We are part of the earth and it is part of us. The perfumed flowers are our sisters; the deer, the horse, the great eagle, these are our brothers. The rocky crests, the juices in the meadows, the body heat of the pony, and man—all belong to the same family." This was part of Chief Seattle's poignant reply when, in 1854, the "Great White Chief" in Washington pressed to purchase some of the land around Puget Sound then occupied by several Northwest Indian tribes. And those sentiments still ring true today as the natural beauty and appeal of Northern Puget Sound and the San Juan Islands remain undiminished.

This awe-inspiring land supported the American Indians, providing for all their needs with verdant woods full of deer and berries and crystal waters full of salmon, letting them live in peaceful coexistence for hundreds of years. Even the weather was kind to them here in this "rain shadow," shielded by the Olympic and Vancouver mountain ranges.

Things slowly began to change for the Northwest Indian tribes and the land with the arrival of Juan de Fuca in 1592, who came to explore the coastline for the Spanish. The floodgates of exploration and exploitation weren't fully opened, however, until Captain George Vancouver came in 1792 to chart the region for the British, naming major landmarks such as Mt. Baker, Mt. Rainier, Whidbey Island and Puget Sound after his compatriots.

Establishment of trade with the American Indians and the seemingly inexhaustible quantity of animals to supply the lucrative fur trade drew many pioneers. Before long, industries such as logging, mining, shipping and fishing began to flourish, supporting the early settlers (and still supporting their descendants today).

Geologists who have studied the record say that a now long-disappeared continent moving eastward out of the Pacific Ocean eons ago collided with, or "docked" against, the Puget Sound mainland, laying the foundation for the multiplicity of land forms—islands, estuaries, mountains, coastlines—that characterize the northern Puget Sound region today.

The geographical layout of the 172 islands of the San Juan Archipelago made for watery back alleys and hidden coves perfect for piracy and smuggling, so the history of the area reflects an almost Barbary Coast type of intrigue where a man could get a few drinks, a roll in the hay and be shanghaied all in one night. Chinese laborers were regularly brought in under cover of night to build up coastal cities and railroads in the 1800s. This big money "commodity" was replaced by opium and silk, and then booze during Prohibition.

Smuggling has since been curbed, and while things are changing as resources are diminished, logging and fishing are still major industries in the region. However, current booms in real estate and tourism are beginning to tilt the economic scale as more and more people discover the area's beauty.

The area referred to as Northern Puget Sound begins just beyond the far northern outskirts of Seattle, where most visitors first arrive, and extends northward up the coast to the Canadian border. Coastal communities such as Everett, Bellingham and Blaine tend to be more commercial in nature, heavily flavored by the logging and fishing industries, while other small towns such as La Conner and Mt. Vernon are still very pastoral, dependent on an agriculturally based economy. When heading east from Mt. Vernon, for every mile traveled toward the Cascade Mountains, the average annual rainfall increases by one inch. Consequently, springtime along this stretch of land is particularly lovely, especially in the Skagit Valley when the fields are ablaze in daffodils, iris and tulips. The world's biggest single grower of tulip bulbs—Washington Bulb Company—is based in the Skagit Valley.

Of the 172 named islands of the San Juans, we concentrate on the four most popular. These also are very pastoral, with rich soil and salubrious conditions perfectly suited to raising livestock or growing fruit. The major islands are connected to the mainland by bridges or reached by limited ferry service, an inhibiting factor that helps preserve the pristine nature here.

Although it's not considered part of the San Juans, serpentine Whidbey Island, with its thick southern tip reaching toward Seattle, is the largest island in Puget Sound. Situated at Whidbey's northern tip is Fidalgo Island, home of Anacortes and the ferry terminal gateway to the San Juans. Lopez is by far the friendliest and most rural of the islands, followed closely by San Juan, the largest and busiest. Shaw Island is one of the smaller islands, and lovely Orcas Island, named after Spanish explorer Don Juan Vincente de Guemes Pacheco y Padilla Orcasitees y Aguayo Conde de Revilla Gigedo (whew!) rather than orcas, is tallest, capped by 2400-foot Mt. Constitution.

The ferry system is severely overtaxed during the busy summer season, when the San Juans are inundated with tourists, making it difficult to reach the islands at times and absolutely impossible to find accommodations if you haven't booked months in advance. The crowds drop off dramatically after Labor Day, a pleasant surprise since the weather in September and October is still lovely and the change of seasonal color against this beautiful backdrop is incredible.

NORTHERN PUGET SOUND

Stretched along the fertile coastline between the Canadian border and the outer reaches of Seattle, communities along Northern Puget Sound are dependent on agriculture, logging and fishing, so the distinct pastoral feel of the area is no surprise. Verdant parks and vista spots taking in the beauty of the many islands not far offshore head the list of sightseeing musts here. But islands and shorelines are just part of the scenic and geographic mix in this region, which also includes rivers and delta wetlands, forests and picturesque farmlands.

SIGHTS

As you drive north from Seattle along Route 5, you'll cross a series of major rivers issuing from the Cascade Mountains. In order, you'll pass the Snohomish River (at Everett), the Stillaguamish (not far from Stanwood), the Skagit (at Mt. Vernon/Burlington) and the Nooksack (Bellingham). The lower reaches of these streams offer wetlands and wildlife to see, fishing villages to poke around in, a vital agricultural heritage in the Skagit and Nooksack valleys, and small towns by the handful.

MUKILTEO LIGHTHOUSE ✉Mukilteo ☎425-513-9602 If you plan to catch the Mukilteo ferry to Clinton on Whidbey Island, be sure to allow enough time to visit this historic lighthouse, built in 1906. There are picnic tables above a small rocky beach cluttered with driftwood and a

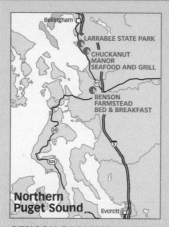

Northern
Puget Sound

LARRABEE STATE PARK
PAGE 128

Fourteen miles of hiking trails, including paths leading to mountain lakes perfect for trout fishing

CHUCKANUT MANOR SEAFOOD AND GRILL
PAGE 124

Scenic restaurant on Samish Bay serving house specialty of clams, mussels, scallops and crab in herbed butter

BENSON FARMSTEAD BED AND BREAKFAST
PAGE 123

Hearty meals and cozy country rooms at a quaint 80-year-old farm in the heart of Washington

big grassy field for kite-flying adjacent to the lighthouse in little Mukilteo Lighthouse Park. A gift shop is located in the former assistant lighthousekeeper's home. Open April through September, weekend and holiday afternoons only.

BOEING FACTORY ✉️*8415 Paine Field Boulevard, Mukilteo* 📞*425-438-8100, 800-464-1476 (reservations)* 📠*425-265-9808* 💻*www.futureofflight.org* Mukilteo is the home of Boeing's largest aircraft assembly plant—in fact, the largest building in the world by volume at 472 million cubic feet. As the largest aerospace business in the U.S., Boeing employs nearly 80,000 people in the Puget Sound area alone. Begin a visit at the **Future of Flight Aviation Center**, located at the western edge of Paine Field 30 miles north of Seattle. Hourly tours of the assembly plant are available (reservations recommended). The factory visit begins with a video of how airplanes are built, then leads past assembly lines for the 747, 767, 777 and 787—in various stages of assembly, manufacture and flight testing. Children must be four feet tall to take factory tours. Admission.

MARINA VILLAGE ✉️*1728 West Marine View Drive, Everett* In Everett you'll find your best vantage point from the dock behind this sparkling complex of upscale shops, microbreweries and restaurants located in the second-largest marina on the West Coast.

JETTY ISLAND 📞*425-257-8300* In summer, a free boat ride will shuttle you from the 10th Street boat launch to this picturesque island for guided nature walks, birdwatching, campfires, a hands-on mudflat safari program to teach children about small marine animals and one of the only warm saltwater beaches on the Sound.

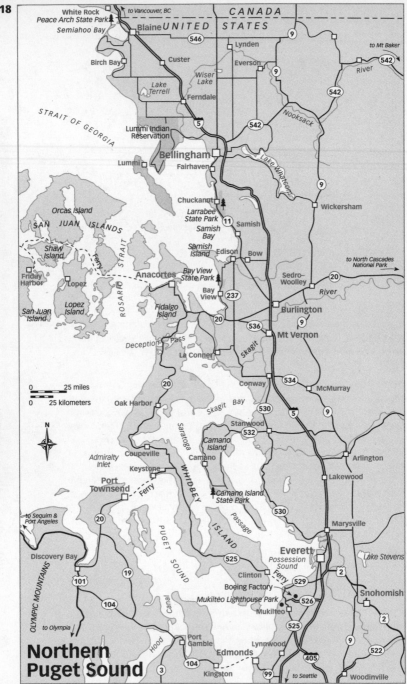

to Vancouver, BC

C A N A D A

White Rock
Peace Arch State Park
Semiahoo Bay
Blaine U N I T E D   S T A T E S

546

Lynden

9

to Mt Baker

542

Birch Bay
Custer
Everson

9

Wiser
Lake

Lake
Terrell
Ferndale

5

River

542

Nooksack

STRAIT OF GEORGIA

Lumini Indian
Reservation

542

Bellingham

Lake Whatcom

9

Lummi
Fairhaven

Chuckanut

9

Orcas Island
Larrabee
State Park

Wickersham

S A N   J U A N   I S L A N D S

11

Samish

Shaw
Island

Samish
Bay

Bow

to North Cascades
National Park

Ferry
Friday
Harbor
Lopez

Samish
Island
Edison

Sedro-
Woolley

20

Anacortes
Bay View
State Park

River

R O S A R I O   S T R A I T

San Juan
Island
Lopez
Island
Fidalgo
Island
Bay
View

237

20

536

Burlington

9

Mt Vernon

Deception   Pass

La Conner

Skagit

534

0   25 miles
0   25 kilometers

20

Conway

McMurray

5

9

Skagit   Bay

530

N

Oak Harbor

Stanwood

532

Arlington

Saratoga

Camano
Island

Admiralty
Inlet

Coupeville

Camano

W H I D B E Y

Lakewood

Keystone

Port
Townsend

Ferry

Camano Island
State Park

530

to Sequim &
Port Angeles

20

I S L A N D

Passage

Marysville

P U G E T

S O U N D

525

Everett
Possession
Sound

Lake Stevens

Discovery Bay

101

19

Clinton

Ferry

529

2

O L Y M P I C   M O U N T A I N S

104

Boeing Factory
Mukilteo Lighthouse Park

526

Snohomish

Mukilteo

525

2

Hood   Canal

to Olympia

Port
Gamble

104

Lynnwood

405

9

522

3

Edmonds

99

Woodinville

Kingston

to Seattle

Northern
Puget Sound

EVERETT AREA CHAMBER OF COMMERCE ✉2000 Hewitt Avenue, Suite 205, Everett ☎425-257-3222 📠425-257-2074 🖰www.everettchamber.com, info@ everettchamber.com Stop by the chamber of commerce for information about Everett and local events. Closed Saturday and Sunday.

MANSIONS On the hillside above the marina, ornate mansions of the lumber barons that once ruled the economy here line Grand and Rucker streets from 16th Street north. None are open to tour, but a slow drive up and down these avenues will give you a feel for the history of the city.

SKAGIT VALLEY This has become a year-round retreat for city visitors, as nourishing to the soul in winter as it is inspiring to the adventurous spirit in summer. Indeed, artists and writers have been gathering in the Skagit for decades, including members of the famed "Northwest School" beginning in the 1930s—Mark Tobey, Morris Graves, Kenneth Callahan, Clayton James, Guy Anderson and many others. They were drawn by the Skagit's enchanting blend of meandering river levees and farm fields, bayous and bays, nearby islands and distant, misty mountains, along with the extraordinary quality of the valley's ever-changing light.

MOUNT VERNON Though this town is situated on the broad banks of the Skagit River, it has done little to capitalize on its superior riverside location. But it does claim the liveliest "main street" in the valley. The true main street is signed as 1st Street here; it is lined with a variety of vintage architecture in both brick and wood dating to the turn of the century. Preservation or recycling of old buildings is in full swing.

THE SKAGIT VALLEY TULIP FESTIVAL OFFICE ✉311 Kincaid Street, Mount Vernon ☎360-428-5959 📠360-428-6753 🖰www.tulipfestival.org, info@ tulipfestival.org Each spring, the fields of the Skagit Valley are alive with color as the tulips and daffodils begin to appear. This office provides a guide to the festival that runs the entire month of April; the guide lists events and includes a tour map of the fields, children's activities and display gardens.

ROOZENGAARDE ✉15867 Beaver Marsh Road, Mount Vernon ☎360-424-8531, 866-488-5477 📠360-424-4920 🖰www.tulips.com, info@tulips.com There are interesting gardens to view in the Skagit Valley year-round but this is the prettiest. It features a three-acre display garden of tulips, daffodils and irises and a great little gift shop.

LA CONNER West of Mount Vernon, across the channel from the Swinomish Indian Reservation, La Conner is in the running for the title of quaintest little seaside town in the Puget Sound area. Built on pilings above the bank of Swinomish Channel, La Conner got its start in the 1880s as a market center for farmers in the Skagit Flats. Now a historic district, this small village of fewer than 800 people is easy to explore on foot and, with its many well-preserved homes and buildings, offers a glimpse of turn-of-the-20th-century life. For more information, head to the **La Conner Chamber of Commerce** (606 Morris Street; 360-466-4778, 888-642-9284; www.laconnerchamber.com).

SKAGIT COUNTY HISTORICAL MUSEUM ✉*501 4th Street, La Conner* ☎*360-466-3365* 🖷*360-466-1611* ⊘*www.skagitcounty.net/museum, museum@co.skagit.wa.us* Park your car at the chamber of commerce and walk a short distance up 4th Street to the top of the hill to visit this museum. You'll find three separate galleries, which include historical items such as a collection of farm and fishing equipment, vintage clothing, household furnishings, dolls and photographs. There is also a video theater and a section for temporary exhibits with kids' activities throughout. Closed Monday. Admission.

GACHES MANSION ✉*703 South 2nd Street, La Conner* Follow Calhoun Street downhill toward the channel for two blocks to this mansion. The grand Victorian home was built in 1891 by a local merchant who wanted the finest house in town. In the early 1900s the mansion was used as a hospital, then it came under the care of the Federal Historical Preservation Fund. Today, it serves as an international quilt museum

LA CONNER QUILT MUSEUM ✉*Gaches Mansion, 703 South 2nd Street, La Conner* ☎ *360-466-4288* 🖷 *360-466-1051* ⊘ *www.laconnerquilts.com, info@laconnerquilts.com* Within the Gaches Mansion is this museum, the only one of its kind in the Pacific Northwest and one of 12 in the whole U.S. Rotating exhibits feature quilts from around the world. Closed Monday and Tuesday, and the first two weeks of January. Admission.

MAGNUS ANDERSON CABIN ✉*2nd and Douglas streets, La Conner* Stroll a block south of the Gaches Mansion to see this historical cabin next to city hall. The oldest structure in Skagit County, the 1869 cabin was moved here from a solitary location on the north fork of the Skagit River to save it from decay.

1ST STREET ✉*La Conner* Walk one block west from the Magnus Anderson Cabin to this time-capsule waterfront street. It has been gentrified with boutiques, galleries and restaurants yet still retains a palpable air of history.

MUSEUM OF NORTHWEST ART

✉*121 South 1st Street, La Conner* ☎*360-466-4446* 🖷*360-466-7431* ⊘*www.museumofnwart.org* Two longish blocks up 1st Street you'll find this museum, which exhibits the works of regional artists. Exhibits present a cohesive look at the distinctive school of visual arts that has developed in the Pacific Northwest—an often surrealistic blend of Northwest Coast Indian and Asian motifs. Admission.

BAY VIEW, EDISON AND BOW These country hamlets (located in the northern valley across Route 20), are treasures of the old way of life and are rarely discovered by the average tourist. Here, you'll see century-old farmhouses rising behind white picket fences, boatworks (some still active) that once turned out fishing boats, country taverns alive with the rustic merriment of farmers, loggers, truck drivers and dairymen. Here, too, are a smattering of art galleries, antique shops, country cafés and upscale eateries.

PADILLA BAY NATIONAL ESTUARINE RESEARCH RESERVE ___ 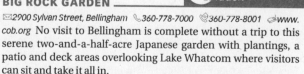 ⓗidden

✉10441 Bay View–Edison Road, Mount Vernon ☎360-428-1558 ⓕ360-428-1491 ⌨www.padillabay.gov, alex@padillabay.gov Located just north of Bay View, this reserve is the place to find bald eagles, great blue herons and dozens of other species of waterfowl and raptors. The interpretive center offers exhibits on the region's natural and maritime history. The center is closed Monday and Tuesday.

BELLINGHAM Early growth in this city centered around the industries of mining and logging. To this day, the city retains an industrial nature with thriving ports that are home to a large fishing fleet and, more recently, the Alaska Marine Highway Ferry System terminal, tempered by a firm agricultural base. Perhaps it is because of this outward appearance that visitors are often amazed at the array of cultural arts and international dining experiences to be enjoyed here.

WHATCOM MUSEUM ___ ⓗidden

✉121 Prospect Street, Bellingham ☎360-676-6981 ⓕ360-738-7409 ⌨www.whatcommuseum.org, museuminfo@cob.org The red-brick Victorian architecture of this museum is as interesting as the fine collections of contemporary American art, Northwest Indian art (including a permanent exhibit on Inuit culture) and regional history featured inside. It's also a good point to start a walking tour of the many outdoor sculptures scattered around downtown. The museum offers a Sculpture Walk route guide. Closed Monday. Admission for special shows.

BELLINGHAM WHATCOM COUNTY TOURISM ✉904 Potter Street, Bellingham ☎360-671-3990, 800-487-2032 ⓕ360-647-7873 ⌨www.bellingham.org, tourism@bellingham.org Local information and a guide to sculptures on the Western Washington University campus are available here.

MARITIME HERITAGE PARK ✉1600 C Street, Bellingham ☎360-778-7000 At the Maritime Heritage Park you can observe outdoor hatchery tanks, watch fish make their way up the ladder (recommended in October and November), learn about the life cycle of salmon, or just toss a line (with the proper license and only in October) into the abutting creek for steelhead or chinook salmon.

BIG ROCK GARDEN ___ ⓗidden

✉2900 Sylvan Street, Bellingham ☎360-778-7000 ⓕ360-778-8001 ⌨www.cob.org No visit to Bellingham is complete without a trip to this serene two-and-a-half-acre Japanese garden with plantings, a patio and deck areas overlooking Lake Whatcom where visitors can sit and take it all in.

WESTERN WASHINGTON UNIVERSITY ✉*McDonald Parkway, Bellingham* ✆*360-650-3900* ⌨*westerngallery.wwu.edu/sculptures.html* Don't miss the opportunity to stroll through the grounds of Western Washington on the Western Sculpture Tour to enjoy the many fountains, sculptures and rich variety of architecture on this green campus. Brochures are available at the visitors information center on campus or at the Western Gallery.

SEHOME HILL ARBORETUM ___ ⓗidden

✉*25th Street at Bill McDonald Parkway, Bellingham* ✆*360-778-7000* ⌨*sha@ cc.wwu.edu* Immediately adjacent to the campus is this arboretum, which includes 180 acres laced with six miles of hiking trails and fern-lined footpaths under a cool green canopy of moss covered trees; only the hum of traffic and the view from the observation tower remind you that you are in the city rather than some forest primeval.

HOVANDER HOMESTEAD PARK ✉*5299 Nielsen Avenue, Ferndale* ✆*360-384-3444* North of Bellingham in Ferndale, this park features a handsome Victorian residence and a cheery red farmhouse alive with cows, goats, pigs, horses, donkeys, sheep and even peacocks (May to October). Laced by the Nooksack River, the 720-acre park also includes **Tennant Lake**, where you'll find a boardwalk leading out over the swamp and marsh habitats that border the edge of the lake, and a fragrance garden with braille signs. There's also an interpretive center. Admission.

PIONEER PARK ✉*2004 Cherry Street, Ferndale* ✆*360-384-6461* To see the largest collection of original log homes in the state, stop here. Each of the 12 buildings is a minimuseum. You'll see a post office, a stagecoach inn, a granary, a veteran's museum, a schoolhouse and a residence. Look for the little log church. Closed Monday and from October through April. Admission.

PEACE ARCH STATE PARK ✉*Follow the signs to the park off Route 5, Exit 276, Blaine* ✆*360-332-8221* ⌨*www.peacearchpark.org, peacearch@parks.wa.gov* The large white arch here, flanked by American and Canadian flags, is surrounded by bountiful formal gardens with sculptures throughout and symbolizes the ongoing friendship between the two neighboring countries. The park is meticulously groomed and spills across the international boundary.

LODGING

HOGLAND HOUSE BED AND BREAKFAST

$$ 2 ROOMS ✉*917 Webster Street, Mukilteo* ✆*425-742-7639, 800-681-5101* ⌨*www.hoglandhouse.com, romance@hoglandhouse.com* Book one of two Victorian-style rooms in this 1906 Craftsman bed and breakfast, located just six blocks from the Mukilteo ferry landing, and enjoy the quiet comforts of a family-owned inn. Both rooms (the Lilac and the Rose) include queen-sized brass beds with color-themed flo-

ral patterns, small dining tables, kitchenettes and DVD players. Five wooded acres surround the inn, which also features a white gazebo, perfect for looking out on the water. A full breakfast is included, but reduced rates are available without it.

THE HOTEL PLANTER

$$–$$$ 12 ROOMS   ✉ *715 1st Street, La Conner*   ☎ *360-466-4710,*
800-488-5409 📠 *360-466-1320* 🖳 *www.hotelplanter.com,*
hotelplanter@aol.com

Originally built in 1907, this hotel is right in the thick of things when it comes to shopping and dining in downtown La Conner. The rooms have skylights, light paint and carpeting, floral chintz comforters and pine furnishings. There's also a jacuzzi under the gazebo on the garden terrace out back. Free wi-fi is available.

BENSON FARMSTEAD
BED AND BREAKFAST

$$ 6 UNITS   ✉ *10113 Avon Allen Road, Bow*   ☎ *360-757-0578,*
800-441-9814 🖳 *www.bensonfarmstead.com*

Built in 1914, this B&B is a charmer in the heart of "the Skagit Valley" farms. Some guests come for the big farm breakfasts and cozy rooms full of country antiques, each with a private bath and queen bed. Others come for the chance to stay on a working crop farm that's been in operation for more than eight decades. Still others stay for the proximity to some of the state's best country bicycling. Or perhaps they seek the English garden and the garden of flowers filled with antique machinery. There is also the barn cottage, which can sleep up to ten people and the nearby beach house, which sleeps six. Closed in the winter except to groups.

ANDERSON CREEK LODGE

$$–$$$ 5 ROOMS   ✉ *5602 Mission Road, Bellingham*   ☎ *360-966-0598*
🖳 *www.andersoncreek.com, andersoncreek@msn.com*

A soaring Northwest-style, glass-and-wood inn on 60 wooded acres near Bellingham, this lodge offers the privacy of a hotel with the intimacy of a bed and breakfast. Each of the five lodge rooms has a king or queen-sized bed, a tiled shower, wi-fi access, hair dryers and large view windows. Two of the rooms have fireplaces. The sitting area in the great room has comfy couches around a massive stone fireplace. Amenities also include a hot tub and full breakfast. Trails wind around Anderson Creek and lead to the inn's own llama herd.

BIRCH BAY HOSTEL & GUESTHOUSE

$ 40 UNITS   ✉ *7467 Gemini Street, Blaine*   ☎ *360-371-2180*
🖳 *www.birchbayhostel.org, hostelmanager@birchbayinfo.org*

Housed in the old Blaine Air Force Base a few miles from the Canadian border and Birch Bay State Park, the Birch Bay offers family- and dormitory-style rooms with three or four beds. The common room is equipped with a television and a DVD/VCR player. From November through April the hostel is open for groups only.

SEMIAHMOO RESORT-GOLF-SPA

$$$$ 194 ROOMS   ✉*9565 Semiahmoo Parkway, Blaine*   ☎*360-318-2000,* *800-770-7992*   📠*360-318-2087*   🖱*www.semiahmoo.com, hotel@semiahmoo.com*

There is something for everyone at this sumptuous resort, located on the tip of the sandy spit stretched between Semiahmoo Bay and Drayton Harbor. History buffs will enjoy browsing through the resort's collection of early photography, romantics will delight in a walk on the beach or a leisurely sunset meal in one of the restaurants or lounges, and sports fanatics will flip over the array of activities, including tennis, golf at two of the top-rated courses, and biking and hiking throughout an 1100-acre wildlife preserve. Treat yourself to a massage at the full-service European spa. The guest rooms are spacious and nicely appointed; some rooms have decks or patios, and others have woodburning fireplaces.

DINING

ANTHONY'S HOME PORT

$$$–$$$$ SEAFOOD   ✉*1726 West Marine View Drive, Everett* ☎*425-252-3333*   📠*425-252-7847*

Anthony's is the spot for seafood when it comes to waterfront dining in Everett. Prime picks on the seasonal menu include Whidbey Island mussels, roasted garlic prawns sprinkled with gremolata and a variety of fresh oysters. Their four-course Sunset Dinner (served Monday through Friday from 4:30 to 6 p.m.) is a bargain and includes everything from appetizers to dessert. You can dine alfresco on the deck or pick a spot in the considerably less breezy dining room or lounge.

CHUCKANUT MANOR
SEAFOOD AND GRILL

$$$ SEAFOOD   ✉*3056 Chuckanut Drive, Bow*   ☎*360-776-6191* 📠*360-766-8515*   🖱*www.chuckanutmanor.com*

Midway between Anacortes and Bellingham, this peaceful restaurant lets you dine on fresh seafood while watching through big picture windows as egrets, gulls and sometimes even eagles soar over the grassy shore of Samish Bay. With an atmosphere that is both upscale and casual, Chuckanut serves oysters fresh from the bay, either breaded and grilled or on the half shell with garlic and wine, as well as wild salmon and halibut, seafood pasta entrées and the house special, a seafood sautée of clams, mussels, prawns, scallops, crab and fish in herb butter. There's a seafood smorgasbord on Friday, and the Sunday brunch makes for a perfect intermission on a scenic drive from Seattle.

CALICO CUPBOARD

$ DINER   ✉720 1st Street South, La Conner   ☎360-466-4451
🖰www.calicocupboardcafe.com

The best bet for breakfast or lunch in La Conner is this cozy café at the south end of the main drag, where they serve hearty and wholesome baked goods, soups, salads, sandwiches and vegetarian fare as good for the heart as for the taste buds. Don't be surprised if there is a line to get into this modest café. No dinner.

FARMHOUSE RESTAURANT

$$ AMERICAN   ✉13724 La Conner–Whitney Road, Mount Vernon   ☎360-466-4411
📠360-466-4413   🖰www.thefarmhouserestaurant.net

A large eatery with country decor dominated by heavy oak tables and chairs, the Farmhouse believes in serving solid, old-country-style portions of meat and potato classics—pot roast, turkey potpie, New York steak and baked potatoes—along with a hearty selection of daily baked goods like their famous pies thrown in for good measure. The lunch buffet and kids' menu are great bargains. Breakfast, lunch and dinner.

BOUNDARY BAY BREWERY & BISTRO

$$ STEAK/SEAFOOD   ✉1107 Railroad Avenue, Bellingham   ☎360-647-5593
📠360-671-5897   🖰www.bbaybrewery.com, info@bbaybrewery.com

At Boundary Bay, bare woodplank floors and simple wooden tables and chairs create an unpretentious setting for "Northwest pub fusion food." What's that, you ask? In this case, it means eclectic offerings such as olive tapenade and yam ale *chiladas*. Wash it all down with a sampler of small glasses of all seven beers and ales they make in plain sight on the premises. In the summer watch a movie in the beer garden while enjoying your meal.

HARRIS AVENUE CAFE

$ DINER   ✉1101 Harris Avenue, Bellingham   ☎360-738-0802

In addition to coffees and teas, this café serves up fresh daily soups, salads, sandwiches and pastries to an eclectic crowd of regulars. It's almost too bohemian, but the cocoa mocha makes it worth the trip. No dinner.

DUTCH MOTHER'S FAMILY RESTAURANT

$$ DUTCH/AMERICAN   ✉405 Front Street, Lynden   ☎360-354-2174
📠360-354-8440

Dutch Mother's is *the* place in Lynden for traditional (that's to say, hearty) Dutch cuisine such as pot roast, meatloaf, beef cutlet, sausage and pierogies. Waitresses sport Dutch dress and often can be overheard speaking Dutch with locals. Closed Sunday.

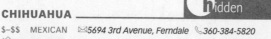

CHIHUAHUA

$–$$ MEXICAN   ✉5694 3rd Avenue, Ferndale   ☎360-384-5820
📠360-384-0644

For Mexican dining, try this festive restaurant. Decorated with Mexican murals, paintings and parrot sculptures, the dining room offers booth and table seating. There's also dining in an enclosed patio. Popular specialties are fajitas, *carne asada* and a wide variety of combination plates.

STARS

$$$–$$$$ SEAFOOD/AMERICAN   ✉*Semiahmoo Resort, 9565 Semiahmoo Parkway, Blaine* ☎*360-318-2000, 800-770-7992* 📠*360-318-2087* 🖥*www.semiahmoo.com, f&b@semiahmoo.com*

For romantic waterfront dining, it's hard to beat this elegant dining room in the Semiahmoo Resort. Soft piano music fills the room as diners feast on grilled king salmon, seared sea scallops, filet of beef Oscar, herb-crusted rack of lamb and other rich entrées. For lighter fare, try the livelier, moderately priced **Packers Lounge** just down the corridor for clam chowder or classic seafood gumbo, a salmon sandwich, crab caesar salad or homestyle burgers. No lunch at Stars; closed Sunday and Monday in off-season.

SHOPPING

STAR CENTER ANTIQUE MALL ✉*829 2nd Street, Snohomish* ☎*360-568-2131* 🖥*www.myantiquemall.com, myantiquemall@gmail.com* Antique hounds will want to make the quick 15-minute trip east of Everett to Snohomish, home to this five-level mall with over 200 dealers and dozens of other antique shops to browse through.

EVERETT PUBLIC MARKET ✉*2804 Grand Avenue, Everett* ☎*425-304-1000* In Everett, this is the prime browsing spot for antiques as well as Northwestern arts and crafts. The market also houses a natural foods co-op that offers organically grown fruits and vegetables.

Shopping is a major drawing card of little La Conner, with most of the boutiques and galleries concentrated along 1st and Morris streets.

EARTHENWORKS ✉*713 1st Street, La Conner* ☎*360-466-4422* 🖥*www.earthenworksgallery.com* Focus on this gallery, established in 1977, for contemporary mixed-metal and glass art works.

THE SCOTT COLLECTION ✉*Pier 7 Building on 1st Street, La Conner* ☎*360-466-3691* 🖥*www.scottcollection.com* This gallery has a selection of fine art, including dozens of original Northwest art prints.

BUNNIES BY THE BAY ✉*623-A East Morris Street, La Conner* ☎*360-293-8037* 🖥*www.bunniesbythebay.com* Stop by Bunnies for collectibles and unique gifts.

ROSABELLA'S GARDEN BAKERY ✉*8933 Farm to Market Road, Bow* ☎*360-766-6360* 📠*360-766-6365* 🖥*rmerritt@wavecable.com* Rosabella's is the perfect place to pick up unique vintage gifts as well as supplies for a picnic. The shop, located on a working farm and 50 acres of fruit orchards, sells apples, baked goods, wine and lunches. Their five-pound apple pies and homemade hard cider are not to be missed. Closed in winter.

The best shops and galleries in Bellingham are generally located in the Fairhaven District.

ARTWOOD ✉*1000 Harris Avenue, Bellingham* ☎*360-647-1628* ⏚*www.artwood gallery.com* This is a co-op gallery of fine woodworking by Northwest artists. Works range from custom furniture to intricately carved boxes and gifts.

INSIDE PASSAGE ✉*355 Harris Street, inside the Bellingham cruise terminal, Bellingham* ☎*360-734-1790* For gifts made in Pacific Northwest, check out this local shop.

DUTCH VILLAGE MALL ✉*655 Front Street, Lynden* ☎*360-354-4440* This is a collection of 12 shops specializing in imported Dutch lace, foodstuffs, wooden shoes and the like. The "mall" is built around a 150-foot-long canal to re-create a typical Dutch street scene.

NIGHTLIFE

ANTHONY'S HOME PORT ✉*1725 West Marine View Drive, Everett* ☎*425-252-3333* ⏚*www.anthonys.com* Things are jumping at Anthony's, with great happy-hour prices and a nice sheltered deck overlooking the marina. Outdoor seating is only available during the warm months.

LA CONNER PUB AND EATERY ✉*702 South 1st Street, La Conner* ☎*360-466-9932* Housed in a waterfront structure that was at one time Brewster's Cigar Store, this is the primary watering hole in La Conner and does a booming business through the wee hours of the morning. There are always at least six microbrews on tap.

There are a half-dozen other country taverns scattered across the Skagit Valley, well known to locals but nearly unknown to tourists, which also serve up terrific burgers, microbrewery ales and bitters and weekend jazz and dancing.

CONWAY PUB AND EATERY ✉*18611 Main Street, Conway* ☎*360-445-4733* The Conway is a great local spot for karaoke and a late-night burger.

OLD EDISON INN ✉*5829 Cains Court, Edison* ☎*360-766-6266* ⏚*www.the edisoninn.com* For fresh oysters, drink specials and live music (Sunday nights), head for this rockin' tavern in sleepy Edison.

THE BLACK CAT ___ *hidden*
✉*1200 Harris Avenue, Sycamore Square, Suite 310, Bellingham* ☎*360-733-6136* You'll find great happy-hour specials and the best sunset views in this little bar.

BEACHES & PARKS

MUKILTEO LIGHTHOUSE PARK
✉*Take the Mukilteo exit off Route 5 and follow the signs to the ferry* ☎*425-355-4141* ☎*425-347-4544*
🏖 A swath of beach adjacent to the Whidbey Island–Mukilteo

Ferry facilities on Puget Sound, this park is a day-use-only facility known primarily as a prime salmon-fishing spot with seasonal public boat launch (fee). Noble little Elliott Point Lighthouse, also known as Mukilteo Lighthouse, on the tip will keep shutterbugs happy; it's also a fine spot for beachcombing or picnicking while waiting for the ferry to Whidbey Island. There are restrooms, picnic grounds and seasonal floats. Boat launch parking fee.

BAY VIEW STATE PARK

✉*Exit 230 off Route 5 in Burlington, follow Route 20 west to Bayview–Edison Road. Turn right, then follow the signs to the park.* ☎*360-757-0227*

🚶 🚵 ⚓ ⛵ ⚓ ⚓ This tiny park on the north side of the town of Bay View overlooks the **Padilla Bay National Estuarine Research Reserve**, an ecological pocket with over 11,000 acres of marsh and tidelands tucked between the north Skagit Valley at Bay View and March Point. The Breazeale Padilla Bay Interpretive Center, half a mile north on Bay View–Edison Road, is a good place to get better acquainted with the many forms of wildlife that inhabit the area. A nature trail winds through parts of the wildlife habitat area just beyond the center. Restrooms, showers (fee), fireplaces, picnic tables and shelter, and a kitchen are some of the facilities here.

▲ There are six cabins ($60 to $72 per night), 46 standard sites ($20 per night) and 30 RV hookup sites ($26 to $31 per night). Reservations: 888-226-7688.

LARRABEE STATE PARK

✉*On scenic Chuckanut Drive (Route 11), seven miles south of Bellingham* ☎*360-676-2093* 📠*360-676-2061* 📧*larrabee@parks.wa.gov*

🚶 🚵 🏇 ⚓ ⚓ ⛵ 🚣 This 2683-acre park on Samish Bay offers 14 miles of hiking trails, including two steep trails to small mountain lakes (Fragrance and Lost lakes), and a one-and-a-half-mile stretch of beach with numerous tidepools for views of the local marine life. There's good freshwater fishing for trout in either of the mountain lakes and crabbing (with a license), clamming and saltwater fishing in Chuckanut and Samish bays and newly acquired Clayton Beach. You'll find restrooms, showers, picnic tables, a playground, barbecue grills and two shelters with sinks.

▲ There are 51 standard sites ($19 to $26 per night), 26 RV hookup sites ($26 to $31 per night) and eight primitive sites ($14 per night). Reservations: 888-226-7688.

TEDDY BEAR COVE

✉*There's a well-signed parking lot along Chuckanut Drive, Route 11, at the intersection of California Street. The trail to the beach is marked with signs at the parking lot and meanders down a steep bank for 100 yards or so from the road.* ☎*360-733-2900* 📠*360-676-1180*

⚓ This secluded, narrow stretch of white sand bordered by thick trees just south of the Bellingham city limits is a public beach that lacks facilities—and the water is very cold in case you're thinking of swimming. The beach area curves out around the shallow cove, like a thumb jutting out toward Chuckanut Bay.

BIRCH BAY STATE PARK — **h**idden

✉ *Eight miles south of Blaine off Birch Bay* 📞 *360-371-2800* 📠 *360-371-0455*

🏃 🚶 ⛵ ♿ 🛶 The highlight of this 192-acre park with 6000 feet of shoreline is the warm, shallow bay, which is suitable for wading up to half a mile out in some spots. The bay is bordered by a mile-long stretch of driftwood and shell-strewn beach edged by grassland. Swimming, clamming and crabbing are popular here. The camping area is inland in a stand of cedar and Douglas fir; nestled in the lush greenery it's hard to tell that the park sits in the shadow of BP's Cherry Point Refinery. Birdwatchers frequent the park to visit the marshy estuary at the south border that attracts over 100 varieties of birds. Facilities include restrooms, fireplaces, picnic tables, shelters and trails; some facilities for the disabled.

⛺ There are 147 standard sites ($19 per night), and 20 RV hookup sites ($25 per night) and 2 primitive hike- or bike-in sites ($10 per night). Reservations: 888-226-7688.

SEMIAHMOO PARK — **h**idden

✉ *Located near Blaine. Take the Birch Bay–Lynden Road exit west off Route 5, turn north onto Harbor View Road then west onto Lincoln Road, which becomes Semiahmoo Parkway and leads into the park.* 📞 *360-733-2900* 📠 *360-676-1180*

🚴 🛶 This long, slender spit dividing Semiahmoo Bay and Drayton Harbor is a favorite among beach lovers, who can stroll sandy, narrow beaches on both sides of the spit, and of birdwatchers who come here to observe bald eagles, loons, herons and others supported by this protected, nutrient-rich habitat. Kite flying is also ideal here. The spit has been an important site for native peoples of the United States and Canada. It was also the site of a fish cannery, the history of which is reviewed in the park's museum. Restrooms, picnic tables, and a bike path are found here.

WHIDBEY ISLAND

Whidbey Island, stretching north to south along the mainland, is the longest island in the continental United States aside from Long Island. This slender, serpentine bit of land is covered in a rolling patchwork of loganberry farms, pasturelands, sprawling state parks, hidden heritage sites and historic small towns. The artistic hamlet of Langley near Whidbey's southern tip is a current hotspot for weekend escapes from Seattle.

SIGHTS

LANGLEY Most of the sights in this town are concentrated along 1st and 2nd streets, where falsefront shops house small galleries, boutiques and restaurants. There's a lovely stretch of public beach flanked by a concrete wall adorned in Northwest Indian motifs just below **Seawall Park** (look for the totem pole on 1st Street), and a wonderful bronze statue by local artist Georgia Gerber above a second stairwell leading down to the beach.

MEERKERK
RHODODENDRON GARDENS _____ hidden

✉ *3531 Meerkerk Lane; Just off Route 525 south of Greenbank* ☎ *360-678-1912* ✐ *www.meerkerkgardens.org, meerkerk@whidbey.net* ☎ Beautiful greenery typifies Whidbey Island, and one Greenbank area establishment offers visitors a close look at cultivating the landscape. These famous gardens feature hundreds of varieties of rhododendron bushes—with 2000 types spread across 53 acres—which find Whidbey's climate one of the best on earth. Magnolia, maple and cherry trees and exotic conifers add to the beauty of this spot, creating an arboretum. April and May are the peak months for blooms, with daffodils providing additional color. The nursery has rhodies for sale from the end of March through May. Admission.

WHIDBEY ISLAND VINEYARD & WINERY ✉ *5237 South Langley Road* ☎ *360-221-2040* ✐ *www.whidbeyislandwinery.com, winery@whidbeyislandwinery.com* Only a few wine grapes ripen in Puget Sound's cool climate, and this winery specializes in clean, crisp, delicate vintages, such as madeleine angevine and siegerrebe, that are rarely grown elsewhere, in addition to other whites and a full range of reds. Daily tastings are available (fee). Closed Tuesday in summer, and Monday and Tuesday the rest of the year.

EBEY'S LANDING NATIONAL HISTORICAL RESERVE ✉ *Ebey's Landing National Historical Reserve, P.O. Box 774, Coupeville, WA 98239* ☎ *360-678-6084* ✐ *www.nps.gov/ebla* Set aside as the first national historic reserve in the country in 1978, Ebey's Landing lies midway up Whidbey Island. The reserve protects 17,400 acres of beaches, uplands, woods and prairies; historic pioneer farms homesteaded under the Donation Land Law of 1850; Fort Ebey and Fort Casey state parks; Penn Cove, long used by the Skagit Indians from across Puget Sound; and the historic town of **Coupeville**, where falsefront buildings line Front Street above the wharf. Here you'll find Alexander Blockhouse (Alexander and Front streets) and Davis Blockhouse (Sunnyside Cemetery Road), built by early settlers for protection against possible Indian attacks, and a good collection of pioneer agricultural artifacts and historical displays in the **Island County Historical Museum** (908 Northwest Alexander Street, Coupeville; 360-678-3310). Reduced hours in winter. Admission.

ADMIRALTY HEAD LIGHTHOUSE ✉ *1280 Engle Road, Coupeville* ☎ *360-240-5584* ☎ *360-678-4120* ✐ *www.admiraltyhead.wsu.edu, gloria@wsu.edu* Built in

Whidbey &
Fidalgo Islands

SHIP HOUSE INN
PAGE 138

Handcrafted cedar cabins with nautical decor and private decks facing the San Juan Islands

PRIMA BISTRO
PAGE 134

Chic waterfront dining room with a fresh, seasonal Northwest menu

SOUTH WHIDBEY STATE PARK
PAGE 135

Old-growth fir and cedar along a rocky shoreline where waters teem with silver salmon and steelhead

1903, this lighthouse at Fort Casey State Park features an interpretive center offering history on the region's military past. You'll also enjoy excellent views of Admiralty Inlet and the Olympic Mountains. Hours vary; call ahead.

HOLLAND GARDENS ✉*Corner of Southeast 6th and Ely streets, Oak Harbor* In the spring months, you'll find a colorful tulip display at these gardens. During the balance of the year come to see the beautiful floral displays that make this small garden a local favorite.

DECEPTION PASS BRIDGE North of Coupeville, past Oak Harbor is this bridge, which links Whidbey with Fidalgo Island. It spans what has been dubbed the "Grand Canyon of Puget Sound." Most visitors just drive slowly by, taking in the sights. But if you want a little more excitement, stroll out onto the bridge for vertigo-inducing views—straight down into the swift, churning currents of Deception Pass. You can also walk down to the shore on the footpaths of Pass Island to watch the streaming waters up close and personal.

LODGING

There are some 11 hotels on the island, all motel-style and clustered around Oak Harbor. But the big draw on Whidbey has always been bed-and-breakfast inns, over 80 of them at last count. Your choices run the gamut from log cabins in the forest to beach cabins and posh retreats. For a comprehensive list, contact the **Langely Chamber of Commerce** (208 Anthes Avenue, Langley; 360-221-6765, 888-232-2080; www.visit langley.com, langley@whidbey.com).

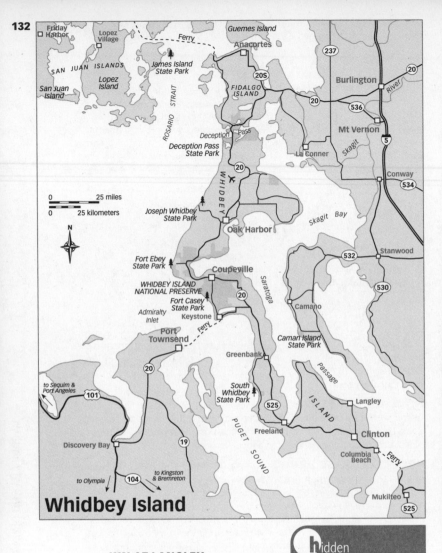

Whidbey Island

INN AT LANGLEY _____ idden

$$$$ 28 UNITS   ✉️400 1st Street, Langley   📞360-221-3033
📠360-221-3033   🖊️www.innatlangley.com, info@innatlangley.com

This beautiful inn has perfected the fine art of hospitality at a polished property worthy of its magnificent waterfront setting. With a decorator's color palette taken directly from the beach, guest rooms in Zen-like shades of gray, cream, tan and brown accented by lots of natural wood are elegant, presenting a delicate balance of modern art and furnishings, and are decked out with every possible amenity (fireplace, jacuzzi, Krups coffee set, wi-fi and large deck to take advantage of the 180° view). A serene oriental garden set in front of the grand dining room is an added touch. If you can afford the tariff, this is the most luxurious selection available on the island. Buffet breakfast.

CLIFF HOUSE

$$$ 2 UNITS   ✉727 Windmill Drive, Freeland   ☎360-331-1566, 800-297-4118
🖰www.cliffhouse.net, wink@whidbey.com

Cliff House is an architecturally stunning two-story structure of wood and sweeping panes of glass set on a wooded bluff overlooking Puget Sound. Guests have the run of the two-bedroom house, with its open central atrium, wonderful gourmet kitchen, sunken sitting area with fireplace and wraparound cedar deck with large jacuzzi. A stairway leads down to miles of empty beach. There is also a separate small cottage with one bedroom.

CAPTAIN WHIDBEY INN

$$–$$$ 18 UNITS   ✉2072 West Captain Whidbey Inn Road, Coupeville
☎360-678-4097, 800-366-4097   🖷360-678-4110
🖰www.captainwhidbey.com, info@captainwhidbey.com

A well-preserved and maintained log inn on Penn Cove, this inn is a fine example of the type of Northwest retreat all the rage years ago and now coming back into fashion. This walk into the past offers several cozy, antique furnished rooms and suites (some with private bath) that boast waterfront views; four wooded private cottages with fireplaces situated around a communal, open-air hot tub are also available. This is one of only a handful of waterside accommodations in the region.

AULD HOLLAND INN

$$ 34 ROOMS   ✉33575 Route 20, Oak Harbor   ☎360-675-2288, 800-228-0148
🖷360-675-2817   🖰www.auldhollandinn.com, dutchvillage@oakharbor.net

This reasonably priced roadside motel has flair, from the flowering window boxes on the European exterior to the immaculately clean, antique-filled rooms. Some units have fireplaces, jacuzzi tubs and princess canopied beds. Continental breakfast.

DINING

CAFE LANGLEY

$$–$$$ SEAFOOD   ✉113 1st Street, Langley   ☎360-221-3090
🖰www.cafelangley.com

Since 1989, this café has served Mediterranean favorites such as spanikopita, moussaka, dolmas and lamb shish kabobs along with fresh seafood (Penn Cove mussels, grilled salmon and Dungeness crab cakes), pastas and steaks. The atmosphere here is airy Mediterranean, with stucco-like walls, exposed beams and an assortment of exotic fish etched on a glass partition. There are often people waiting in the park across the street for a table in this local favorite. Closed Tuesday.

DOGHOUSE TAVERN

$–$$ AMERICAN   ✉*230 1st Street, Langley*   ☎*360-221-4595*

The Doghouse is the place to go for burgers, fish-and-chips and chowder. A totem on the side of this waterfront building points the way to their separate family dining room in case you've got the kids along. Closed Tuesday and Wednesday.

PRIMA BISTRO

$$$–$$$$ FRENCH/PACIFIC NORTHWEST   ✉*201¹/₂ First Street, Langley* ☎*360-221-4060* ⏍*www.primabistro.biz, primabistro@whidbey.com*

For romantic ambience, sit at one of the tables on the heated back patio here, where hanging lights sparkle over the waterfront. Inside, the quaint-yet-chic bistro brims with small-town charm and the kitchen prepares exquisite French-inspired fare with Northwest ingredients. The seasonal menu features entrées such as pan-seared rainbow trout with lemon-caper sauce, house-made fennel and herb sausage, and Oregon country ground beef with watercress and red wine onions. Live music is showcased every Thursday night and wine tastings are held on the first Friday of every month.

TOBY'S TAVERN

$$ AMERICAN   ✉*8 Northwest Front Street, Coupeville*   ☎*360-678-4222* ⏍*www.tobysuds.com, info@tobysuds.com*

Toby's serves up a cheeseburger that was rated tops by actress Kathleen Turner, who starred in the film *War of the Roses*, which was filmed partly in and around Coupeville in 1989. Good fish-and-chips, Penn Cove steamed mussels and an upscale atmosphere add a touch of class to this waterfront watering hole.

CHRISTOPHER'S ON WHIDBEY

$$–$$$ SEAFOOD   ✉*103 Northwest Coveland Street, Coupeville*   ☎*360-678-5480* ⏍*www.christophersonwhidbey.com, christophersonwhidbey@comcast.net*

Christopher's specializes in "creative contemporary cuisine" with a menu that changes seasonally. The emphasis is on fresh, local fare, especially seafood, and runs the gamut from superb Penn Cove mussels, to beef and chicken, vegetarian dishes, and pasta; regional wines and microbrews are also available.

SHOPPING

There's plenty to keep shoppers and browsers busy on Whidbey Island, especially in artsy Langley and historic Coupeville. The best art galleries are concentrated in Langley.

MUSEO ✉*215 1st Street, Langley* ☎*360-221-7737* ⏍*www.museo.cc* This shop specializes in art glass made by local Whidbey Island artists. Closed Tuesday in winter.

SOLEIL ✉*308 1st Street, Langley* ☎*360-221-0383* You will find double-sided aluminum-alloy pieces by Arthur Court here along with silver, bone, pewter and glass jewelry, candles, stationery, photo albums and soaps.

HELLEBORE GLASS GALLERY ⊠*308 1st Street, Langley* ☎*360-221-2067*
This gallery has fine handblown glass created on the premises.

THE STAR STORE ⊠*201 1st Street, Langley* ☎*360-221-5222* ✐*www.starstore whidbey.com* A noteworthy shop in town is this modern mercantile selling fun clothing and housewares.

WHIDBEY ISLAND ANTIQUES ⊠*2nd Street and Anthes Avenue, Langley* ☎*360-221-2393* ✐*www.whidbeyislandantiques.com* This two-part antique shop is full of finely crafted house items and furniture.

There's an array of charming shops in the revitalized waterfront district of Coupeville.

PENN COVE GALLERY ⊠*9 Northwest Front Street, Coupeville* ☎*360-678-1176* ✐*www.penncovegallery.com, info@penncovegallery.com* You'll want to drop by this cooperative where contemporary paintings, sculpture, watercolors, photography, jewelry, ceramics, glass and wood work will be shown to you by the artists who created the work.

BAYLEAF ⊠*101 Northwest Coveland Street, Coupeville* ☎*360-678-0003* ✐*www.bayleaf.us* If it's sunny out and a picnic is in order, stock up at this shop for imported cheeses, cold cuts, olives, wines and rustic, fresh-baked bread. Closed Tuesday.

NIGHTLIFE

HONG KONG GARDENS ⊠*9324 State Route 525, Clinton* ☎*360-341-2828*
This local haunt has a pool table and karaoke every Friday and Saturday night. The occasional band plays on Saturday nights.

TOBY'S TAVERN ⊠*8 Northwest Front Street, Coupeville* ☎*360-678-4222* ✐*www.tobysuds.com* They filmed the bar scene from the movie *War of the Roses* at Toby's, a '60s tavern that still rocks.

BEACHES & PARKS

SOUTH WHIDBEY STATE PARK

⊠*Take Route 525 nine miles north of Clinton to Bush Point Road, which after six miles becomes Smuggler's Cove Road* ☎*360-902-8844* ☎*360-331-5202*
There are 347 acres with 4500 feet of rocky shoreline to explore in this lovely state park. Hikers here will enjoy the one-and-a-quarter-mile loop trail through an old-growth stand of fir and cedar. Anglers seek silver salmon and steelhead, and climbing is popular. Black-tailed deer, herons and osprey are among the many creatures here. Only the hardy will venture into the cold waters of Admiralty Inlet for a dip. There are restrooms, showers, picnic tables, shelter and firepits.
▲ There are 46 standard sites ($18 per night) and 8 RV hookup sites ($25 per night). Closed December and January. Reservations: 888-226-7688.

FORT CASEY STATE PARK

✉At Coupeville turn south off Route 20 onto Engle Road and follow the Keystone Ferry signs to the park. ☎360-678-4519 ☎360-428-1094

🚶 ⛵ 🐟 🏊 🚤 🛶 History buffs and children will enjoy exploring the military fortification of this 467-acre park. While most of the big guns are gone, you'll still find panoramic views of the Olympic Mountains across the Strait of Juan de Fuca from the top of the concrete bunkers built into the escarpment. Wild roses and other flowers line the paths to the museum housed in pretty Admiralty Head Lighthouse (open seasonally) and the beachside campground that overlooks the Keystone Harbor ferry terminal. Scuba enthusiasts swarm to the underwater trail through the park's marine wildlife sanctuary off Keystone Harbor, and anglers try for salmon and steelhead. Facilities include restrooms, showers, picnic tables, fireplaces and an underwater marine park.

▲ There are 35 standard sites ($18 per night) and 3 primitive sites ($12 per night).

FORT EBEY STATE PARK

✉From Route 20 turn west onto Libbey Road, then south onto Hill Valley Drive and follow the signs. ☎360-678-4636 ☎360-678-5136 ✉fort.ebey@parks.wa.gov

🚶 🚴 🎣 🐟 🛶 The massive guns are long gone from this coastal World War II fortification, but there are still bunker tunnels and pillboxes to be explored. The picturesque beach at Partridge Point is the hands-down favorite of the islanders; at low tide it's possible to walk the five-mile beach stretch to Ebey's Landing. Anglers cast a rod for bass on Lake Pondilla. There are restrooms, showers, picnic tables, fireplaces and nature trails.

▲ There are 38 standard sites ($19 to $22 per night), 12 RV hookup sites ($25 to $30 per night) and three primitive sites ($14 per night). The secluded campsites under a canopy of Douglas fir are much nicer than the crowded sites at nearby Fort Casey. Reservations accepted May through September; 888-226-7688.

OAK HARBOR WINDJAMMER PARK

✉Located in downtown Oak Harbor off Pioneer Parkway, east of Route 20; watch for the windmill. ☎360-279-4756 ☎360-679-3902 ✉info@oakharbor.org

🚶 🚴 🐟 🏊 🐟 🚤 🛶 A full-scale windmill is just one of the features of this day-use park on Oak Harbor Bay next to the sewage processing plant (not a deterrent, believe it or not). A sandy beach slopes down from the lighted walking path bordering expansive green fields suitable for flying kites or playing frisbee. Anglers will find salmon, bottomfish, herring, smelt and crab. There are two wading pools in summer and a protected swimming lagoon. There are bathhouses, restrooms, picnic tables, barbecue pits, ball fields, tennis and volleyball courts and a playground.

▲ An RV park with 56 full hookups and hot showers can be accessed at Beeksma Drive or City Beach Street ($20 per night). An overflow area has campsites with no hookups ($12 per night).

✉Take the Mukilteo ferry to Whidbey Island and follow Route 525 and Route 20, or take Route 5 to Exit 230 and follow Route 20 West to the park on the northern tip of the island
📞360-675-2417 📠360-675-8991 ✍www.deceptionpassfoundation.org, deception.pass@parks.wa.gov

🚶 🚴 🛶 ⛵ ⚓ 🚢 🚤 🎣 The most popular state park in Washington, it encompasses over 4300 acres laced with 35 miles of hiking trails through forested hills and wetland areas and along rocky headlands. There are several delightful sandy stretches for picnics or beachcombing. Breathtaking views from the 976-foot steel bridge spanning the pass attract photographers from around the world. There's swimming in Cranberry Lake in the summer (you'll find beaver dams and muskrats on the south shore) and flyfishing for trout on Pass Lake. Facilities include restrooms, showers, bathhouses, picnic tables, kitchens, shelters, fireplaces, a concession stand, a retreat center and an underwater park.

▲ There are 167 standard sites ($19 per night), 137 RV hookup sites ($26 per night) and five primitive sites ($14 per night). Reservations: 888-226-7688.

FIDALGO ISLAND

A two-hour drive northwest of Seattle, Anacortes on Fidalgo Island is a good place to enjoy folk art, ride a charming excursion train and see impressive murals. Quiet inns and waterfront restaurants make this town a pleasant retreat.

But Anacortes is only the beginning of adventures on this charming island. Often called the first of the San Juans, Fidalgo is actually linked to the mainland by the Route 20 bridge over Swinomish Channel in the Skagit Valley, and to Whidbey Island by another bridge. Access is easy. Nevertheless, you can still find quiet beaches and parks to explore. Lonely trails wind through an enormous forest reserve to superb viewpoints. A mini "Lake District" clusters more than half a dozen splendid lakes. And a marvelous resort complex—Scimitar Ridge Ranch—combines a working Northwest horse ranch and a deluxe campground that includes covered wagons outfitted for camping.

SIGHTS

ANACORTES In the late 1800s, this town was referred to as the "Magic City," "Liverpool of the West" and "New York of the West." Today, because of its ferry terminal, it is known as "the gateway to the San Juans," but don't just zip on through because there's plenty to see and do here. One of the best ways to get acquainted with the city and its history is to take a walking tour of downtown to view over 100 life-sized murals attached to many of the historical buildings. As part of the **Anacortes Mural Project**, these murals are reproductions of early-20th-century photographs depicting everyday scenes and early pioneers of the town. A tour map of the murals is available from the

Anacortes Chamber of Commerce (819 Commercial Avenue, Suite F, Anacortes; 360-293-7911, fax 360-293-1595; www.anacortes.org, info@anacortes.org).

W. T. PRESTON ✉*7th Street and R Avenue, Anacortes* ☎*360-293-1916* ✏*coa.museum@cityofanacortes.org* A reminder of earlier days is this drydocked sternwheeler that once plied the waters of the sound and rivers breaking up log jams. Closed weekdays except in June through August. Admission.

ANACORTES MUSEUM ✉*1305 8th Street, Anacortes* ☎*360-293-1915* ✏*coa.museum@cityofanacortes.org* At this museum, you'll find an entertaining collection of art and memorabilia from Anacortes, Fidalgo and Guemes islands, as well as exhibits detailing the history of the islands. In front of the museum there's a highly amusing (but nonfunctional) drinking fountain with varying levels suited for dogs, cats, horses and humans, which was donated to the city by the Women's Temperance Union. Closed Wednesday.

LODGING

HOLIDAY MOTEL
$ 9 ROOMS   ✉*2903 Commercial Avenue, Anacortes* ☎*360-293-6511*
You get what you pay for here, one of the only motels that keeps its prices low even during high season. Aging rooms are very basic but tidy, with nicked furnishings in both the cramped bedroom and separate sitting room.

ANACO BAY INN
$$ 22 UNITS   ✉*916 33rd Street, Anacortes* ☎*360-299-3320, 877-299-3320* ✏*www.anacobayinn.com, anacobay@fidalgo.net*
With 18 spacious, well-appointed rooms all featuring a cozy fireplace, this inn is a step up from the Holiday Inn. Some rooms have kitchens while others offer jetted tubs and fireplaces. Rooms without kitchens have microwaves and mini-fridges. Four two-bedroom suites are also available. A public jacuzzi, a library and laundry facilities round out the amenities. An expanded continental breakfast is included.

SHIP HOUSE INN
$$–$$$ 3 ROOMS   ✉*12876 Marine Drive, Anacortes* ☎*360-293-1093* ✏*www.shiphouseinn.com, info@shiphouseinn.com*
This is an attractive, high-waterfront property facing the San Juan Islands. Handcrafted by the owner in knotty cedar, accommodations are in three pleasant cabins, with nautical bunk-style beds, fridges, microwaves, TVs and private decks. A comfortable gallery room offers guests a place to sip coffee or hot chocolate. Included in the rate is a hot breakfast of French toast, waffles and omelettes.

DECEPTION CAFE & GRILL

$$ AMERICAN ✉5596 Route 20, Anacortes ☎360-293-9250
✎www.deceptioncafe.com, kjlongstreet1954@yahoo.com

Traditional hand-breaded oysters and prawns, grilled burgers and mouthwatering, homemade desserts are the specialty here. Look for this unpretentious roadside establishment on the hill four miles north of Deception Pass. Breakfast, lunch and dinner.

CHARLIE'S

$$–$$$ AMERICAN ✉5407 Ferry Terminal Road, Anacortes ☎360-293-7377
✎www.charliesrestaurant.com

Potted plants, taped light jazz and tablecloths soften the rough edges of this hash house overlooking the ferry terminal and water. Captive diners, here during the long wait for the ferry, choose from soups, salads, sandwiches and seafood at lunch and pasta, steak and seafood for dinner. Closed Tuesday and Wednesday.

SHOPPING

LEFT BANK ANTIQUES

✉1904 Commercial Avenue, Anacortes ☎360-293-3022 ☎360-299-8888
✎www.leftbankantiques.com Most of the great shops on Fidalgo Island are scattered along Anacortes' Commercial Avenue. This one, housed in two floors of a renovated barn, absolutely bulges with American and European antiques and architectural items.

MARINE SUPPLY AND HARDWARE ✉202 Commercial Avenue, Anacortes ☎360-293-3014 ✎www.marinesupplyandhardware.com This historic hardware store is packed to the rafters with nautical antiques and memorabilia, including clothing and hardware. Closed Sunday.

SEABEAR SMOKEHOUSE ✉605 30th Street, Anacortes; Take 22nd Street east toward the Anacortes Marina, turn right onto T Avenue and you'll find the warehouse in an industrial complex a block down on the right. ☎360-293-4661, 800-645-3474 ✎www.seabear.com, smokehouse@seabear.com Resist the temptation to buy smoked salmon to take home until you visit the SeaBear, which has been producing authentic smoked salmons since 1957. Not only does the smokehouse sell smoked salmon, smokehouse chili and smoked salmon chowder, it also offers tours Monday through Friday. Pose with a salmon, learn to fillet, or just taste the goods.

LOPEZ ISLAND

Life on pastoral Lopez Island is slow and amiable; residents wave to everyone and are truly disappointed if you don't wave back. Lopez didn't earn its nickname as the "Friendly Island" for nothing. Even better, it remains much less developed than San Juan and Orcas islands.

SIGHTS

LOPEZ ISLAND HISTORICAL MUSEUM ✉*28 Washburn Place, Lopez Village* ☎*360-468-2049* ✎*www.lopezmuseum.org, lopezmuseum@rockisland.com* The history of the island is colorfully displayed at this museum with its exhibit of pioneer farming and fishing implements, stone, bone and antler artifacts and fairly large maritime collection. While you're here, pick up a historical landmark tour guide to the many fine examples of Early American architecture scattered around the island. Closed Monday and Tuesday, and October through April unless by appointment.

SUNSET VIEWS Stroll out to **Agate Beach Park** on MacKaye Harbor Road to watch the sunset. Another good sunset view spot is **Shark Reef Park** on Shark Reef Road, where you might see some harbor seals, heron and, if you're lucky, a whale or two.

SHAW ISLAND This island is one of only four of the San Juan Islands that can be reached by ferry, but most visitors to the San Juans miss it. You need to stay on the ferry from Anacortes and get off at Shaw, one stop beyond Lopez Island. Those who do make the trip are in for a treat. Stop by the general store and the ferry landing (both are operated by Franciscan nuns) for picnic supplies before heading out to **South Beach County Park** on Squaw Bay Road, two miles to the south.

SHAW ISLAND LIBRARY AND HISTORICAL SOCIETY ✉*Blind Bay Road and Ben Nevis; From South Beach County Park continue east along Squaw Bay Road, then turn north on Hoffman Cove Road and make your way to the little red schoolhouse. Park by the school and cross the street.* ☎*360-468-4068* A tiny log cabin housing a hodgepodge of pioneer memorabilia, this museum features rotating historic exhibits. Open limited hours on Tuesday, Thursday and Saturday.

LODGING

LOPEZ ISLANDER BAY RESORT
$$–$$$$ 38 UNITS ✉*2864 Fisherman Bay Road, Lopez Village* ☎*360-468-2233, 800-736-2864* ☎*360-468-3382* ✎*www.lopezislander.com, desk@lopezislander.com*
The Lopez Islander is fairly upscale. All of the 36 rooms and 2 suites have decks overlooking Fisherman's Bay, perfect for a view of the sunset. Rental houses on the bay are also available. The marina features floats and piers, and a seaplane dock. An ambitious outings program for guests includes opportunities to bike, kayak and fish. Laundry and fitness facilities are on-site, including an island golf course and tennis courts.

EDENWILD _____
$$$ 8 ROOMS ✉*Lopez Village* ☎*360-468-3238, 800-606-0662* ☎*360-468-3238* ✎*www.edenwildinn.com, edenwild@rockisland.com*
This two-story Victorian inn is a welcome addition to the scant list of lodgings on the island. The eight guest rooms are pretty, with carpeted floors and clawfoot tubs; three have romantic fireplaces, one is handicapped accessible and four have views of

Fisherman's Bay or San Juan Channel. Included in the rate is breakfast, served in the sunny dining nook or on the delightful garden terrace. Apéritifs and truffles are served in the rooms.

LOPEZ LODGE

$–$$ 3 UNITS ⊠35 Weeks Point Road, Lopez Village ✆360-468-2816
✍www.lopezlodge.com, needle@rockisland.com

This lodge in the village has two motel-like rooms with microwaves, TVs and wi-fi access that share a bath. An additional studio has a private bath and full kitchen.

DINING

BAY CAFE

$$$–$$$$ AMERICAN ⊠Lopez Village Road, Lopez Village ✆360-468-3700
☎360-468-4000 ✍www.bay-cafe.com, thebaycafe@aol.com

Check out this café, which has an imaginative menu featuring fresh Northwest products. There are always daily specials to choose from, and regular entrées may include duck confit, handmade vegetable ravioli and filet of beef tenderloin. Check out the surprising garlic cheesecake. Reservations are essential, especially during summer. Closed Monday and Tuesday in the winter.

LOPEZ ISLAND PHARMACY

$ AMERICAN ⊠157 Lopez Village Road, Lopez Village ✆360-468-4511
☎360-468-3825 ✍www.lopezislandpharmacy.com, biz@lopezislandpharmacy.com

Set off to one side within this pharmacy is an old-fashioned, red, white and black soda fountain, serving a full breakfast and the best lunch on Lopez. Grab a booth or a stool at the bar and order a sandwich, bowl of soup or slice of pie to go with your phosphate, malt, float or other fountain treat. No dinner. Closed Sunday.

LOPEZ ISLANDER RESTAURANT _____ ⓗidden

$$–$$$ SEAFOOD ⊠Fisherman Bay Road, Lopez Village ✆360-468-2233
✍www.lopezislander.com

A true waterfront restaurant, the Lopez Islander looks west across Fisherman Bay to spectacular evening sunsets. In summer, ask for a table on the outdoor dining patio. Specialties of the house include an award-winning clam chowder and a daily fresh sheet of local seafood—salmon and halibut, for example. The resort's tiki bar stays open later with a limited menu.

SHOPPING

For the most part, shopping here is limited to establishments in Lopez Village.

ARCHIPELAGO ✆360-468-3222 This shop sells cotton T-shirts, women's casual apparel and jewelry made by local artisans. Limited hours during the off-season.

ISLEHAVEN BOOKS AND BORZOI ✉*201 Lopez Road, Lopez Village Center* ☎*360-468-2132* ⊘*www.islehavenbooks.com* Islehaven stocks an admirable selection of new books and regional music. One section of the bookstore is dedicated to local authors.

CHIMERA GALLERY ✉*Lopez Village* ☎*360-468-3265* ⊘*www.chimeragallery. com* For fine art, visit this cooperative that showcases prints, paintings, weaving, pottery, handblown glass and jewelry produced by local artists. Call for seasonal hours and directions.

BEACHES & PARKS

SPENCER SPIT STATE PARK

✉*Take the ferry from Anacortes to Lopez Island, then follow the five-mile route to the park on the eastern shore of the island.* ☎*360-468-2251*

🚲 🛶 ⚓ This long stretch of silky sand on Lopez Island encloses an intriguing saltwater lagoon. The mile-long beach invites clamming, crabbing, shrimping, bottom fishing, wading and swimming during warm summer months. Facilities include restrooms, beach firepits and picnic shelters. Day use fee, $7.

▲ There are 37 standard sites ($20 per night) and seven primitive sites ($14 per night). Closed November through mid-March. Reservations: 888-226-7688.

SAN JUAN ISLAND

San Juan Island, the namesake of the archipelago, is a popular resort destination centered around the town of Friday Harbor. The harbor is named after Joe Friday—an early 1800s settler, not the sergeant of *Dragnet* fame. This 20-mile-long island has a colorful past stemming from a boundary dispute between the United States and Great Britain. The tension over who was entitled to the islands was embodied in American and British farmers whose warring over, get this, a pig, nearly sent the two countries to the battlefield. When an American farmer shot a British homesteader's pig caught rooting in his garden, ill feelings quickly escalated. Fortunately, cooler heads prevailed so that what is now referred to as the "Pig War" of 1859 only resulted in one casualty: the pig.

SIGHTS

SAN JUAN ISLAND NATIONAL HISTORIC PARK ☎*360-378-2240*
☎*360-378-2615* ⊘*www.nps.gov/sajh* The history of San Juan's little-known "pig war" is chronicled through interpretive centers in this historical park, which is composed of English Camp and American Camp. Located on West Valley Road at the north end of the island is **English Camp**, which features barracks, a formal garden, cemetery, guardhouse, hospital and commissary. **American Camp**, on Cattle Point Road at the south end of the island, is where the officers and laundress' quarters, and the Hudson Bay Company's Belle Vue Sheep Farm remain.

San Juan Island

Roche Harbor

DUCK SOUP INN

Friday Harbor

PELINDABA LAVENDER FARM

FOURTH OF JULY BEACH

DUCK SOUP INN

PAGE 147

Rustic restaurant serving regional specialties with an inventive twist—try their namesake dish

PELINDABA LAVENDER FARM

PAGE 144

Organic farm awash in purple that sells everything lavender

FOURTH OF JULY BEACH

PAGE 149

Secluded, gravelly crescent named for the bald eagles that nest in trees along its peaceful shore

SAN JUAN HISTORICAL MUSEUM

hidden

✉405 Price Street, Friday Harbor ✆360-378-3949 ✆360-378-3949 ⌨www.sjmuseum.org, curator@sjmuseum.org This museum is located on the 1891 James King farmstead. The museum complex consists of the original farmhouse, milk house and carriage house, as well as the original county jail. A variety of memorabilia is displayed throughout, including American Indian baskets and stone implements, an antique diving suit, period furniture and clothing. A great place to learn about the region's maritime history, the museum also features an excellent collection highlighting the region's proud past. Hours vary seasonally, so call ahead.

WHALE MUSEUM ✉62 1st Street North, Friday Harbor ✆360-378-4710, 800-946-7227 ⌨www.whalemuseum.org Just east of the history museum is this facility, which details the three resident pods, or extended families, of *Orcinus Orca*, otherwise known as "killer" whales. Because they are so frequently and easily spotted in the protected waters, these gentle black and white giants have been carefully studied by scientists since 1976. A photo collection with names and pod numbers will help you identify some of the 90 resident orcas, distinguished by their grayish saddle patches and nicks, scars or tears in the dorsal fins. There is a collection of artwork, models, artifacts, videos and real whale skeletons. Guests can also listen to the "song" of various species of whales and there are two new intractive exhibits on acoustics. Call ahead for winter hours. Admission.

WESTCOTT BAY SEA FARMS

✉ *904 Westcott Drive, Friday Harbor* ☎ *360-378-2489* 📠 *360-378-6388*
🖰 *www.westcottbay.com, kathleen@westcottbay.com* Oyster lovers and
birdwatchers should make the trip down the dusty road to this
shellfish farm. They'll find saltwater bins of live oysters, mussels and clams (available in spring and summer only) and an
array of birds attracted to the oyster beds that stretch out into
the bay. Closed November through May.

PELINDABA
LAVENDER FARM

✉ *33 Hawthorne Lane, Friday Harbor* ☎ *360-378-4248, 866-819-1911* 🖰 *www.*
pelindabalavender.com The lavender fields here are awash with
color in the summertime, the best time to visit this working organic farm and open-space preservation project. An old farmhouse serves as the general store here, offering all things lavender, from soaps and essential oils to culinary products, baked
goods and household care and pet care products. Self-guided
tours and signage explain the farming and distilling operations. Closed October through April.

AFTERGLOW VISTA ✉ *Roche Harbor Resort, 4950 Reuben Tarte Memorial
Drive, Roche Harbor* This is the mausoleum of one of the region's wealthy
families. The structure itself is fascinating; an open, Grecian-style col-
umned complex surrounds six inscribed chairs, each containing the
ashes of a family member, set before a round table of limestone. A seventh chair and column have obviously been removed, some say as part
of Masonic ritual, others believe because a member of the family was
disinherited or because the seventh member considered life unending.

LODGING

OLYMPIC LIGHTS

$$$ 4 ROOMS   ✉ *146 Starlight Way, Friday Harbor* ☎ *360-378-3186, 888-211-6195*
📠 *360-378-2097* 🖰 *www.olympiclights.com, olympiclights@rockisland.com*
Named for its view, Olympic Lights is a remodeled 1895 farmhouse set on
five grassy, breeze-tossed acres overlooking the Olympic Peninsula
across the Strait of Juan de Fuca. Guests kick off their shoes before head-
ing up to the cream-carpeted second floor with three comfortably ap-
pointed, pastel-shaded rooms; a fourth room on the ground floor is also
available. You'll find no frilly, Victoriana clutter here, just a peaceful night
snuggled under down comforters topped off by a farm-fresh breakfast.

TOWER HOUSE BED & BREAKFAST

$$$$ 2 ROOMS   ✉ *392 Little Road, Friday Harbor* ☎ *360-378-5464, 800-858-4276*
🖰 *www.san-juan-island.com, chris@san-juan-island.com*
This romantic Queen Anne–style B&B is located on ten acres overlook-
ing the San Juan Valley. It features two large suites with private baths
and sitting rooms. Its crown jewel is the tower room with a tufted win-
dow seat and stained-glass window. Popular with honeymooners, the

San Juan Islands

Tower House strives to cater to its guests every need. A large vegetarian breakfast is served on fine china and antique linens. If given notice, the owners will accommodate vegans. Of course, no inn would be complete without a couple of friendly cats.

WHARFSIDE BED AND BREAKFAST

$$$ 2 ROOMS   ⌧Port of Friday Harbor ☏360-378-5661
✐www.fridayharborlodging.com, slowseason@rockisland.com

If you've dreamed of life on the water, you'll appreciate this 60-foot, two-masted sailboat with two guest rooms. The forward stateroom with a queen and bunkbeds feels cozy, while the aft stateroom with queen bed is a little roomier.

BIRD ROCK HOTEL

$$$ 15 ROOMS   ⌧35 1st Street, Friday Harbor ☏360-378-5848,
800-352-2632 ⌨360-378-5848 ✐www.birdrockhotel.com,
stay@birdrockhotel.com

The Bird Rock is an upscale but understated historic inn with individually decorated rooms, all with cool earth tones and minimalist beach-style decor. Some rooms have jetted tubs and fireplaces. Offering prime hospitality, at the Bird Rock breakfast is delivered to your room and beach cruiser bicycles are complimentary. All this romance is conveniently located in the heart of Friday Harbor.

STATES INN & RANCH

$$–$$$$ 9 UNITS   ✉2687 West Valley Road, Friday Harbor   ☎360-378-6240, 866-602-2737 ✎www.statesinn.com, ranch@statesinn.com

Set in the rolling West Valley near English Camp National Park, this is the only working ranch and B&B on San Juan Island. Each of the nine rooms and suites has a decor that hints at its namesake state—tiny Rhode Island comes closest, with shells and brass dolphins on the fireplace mantle, various renditions of ships on the walls and copies of the New England publication *Yankee* to peruse. The friendly and informative innkeepers and the multicourse country breakfasts with prize-winning dishes make up for the slight sulphur odor of the tap water. The inn is also disabled-accessible (hard to find in the islands).

WESTCOTT WOODS

$$$ 1 UNIT   ✉Call for specific directions   ☎206-320-9127 ✎www.westcottwoods.com, sungrebes@gmail.com

Overlooking the water and shrouded by giant trees is one of San Juan Island's best-kept secrets. The rustic two-bedroom cabin was built from reclaimed materials found at historic sites on the island and includes a full kitchen with a wood stove, a laundry area and an herb garden available for guest use. Both bedrooms feature a platform full-sized bed, a deck and a skylight that provides a natural glow throughout the day. Privately owned, this tranquil getaway is perfect for rest and relaxation. Closed November through March. Three-night minimum.

ROCHE HARBOR RESORT ___ hidden

$$$–$$$$ 80 UNITS   ✉248 Reuben Memorial Drive, Roche Harbor ☎360-378-2155, 800-451-8910 ☏360-378-6809 ✎www.rocheharbor.com, roche@rocheharbor.com

This resort has something for everyone. You can check into the 1886 **Hotel de Haro**, where gingerbread trim, parlor beds, antiques and a roaring fireplace bring back memories of the good old days. In addition to this establishment, former workers' **cottages** have been converted into two-bedroom units, ideal for families. The cottages are conveniently located near the swimming pool. Also available are the **McMillin Suites**, with king-sized beds, TVs, a fireplace in the sitting room, a clawfoot iron bathtub, and lovely views of the harbor. For contemporary lodging, choose one- to three-room harbor-view **condominiums**.

THE BLUE DOLPHIN CAFE

$ AMERICAN ✉185 1st Street, Friday Harbor ✆360-378-6116

The Blue Dolphin is an unpretentious diner serving hearty portions of home-cooked breakfast favorites like biscuits and gravy, eggs Benedict, blueberry pancakes and chicken-fried steak. No dinner.

DUCK SOUP INN _____ **h**idden

$$$$ CONTINENTAL ✉50 Duck Soup Lane, Friday Harbor
✆360-378-4878 ⌕www.ducksoupinn.com

Among the best restaurants on the island, the rustic look and rural setting of this dining room hardly hint at the creative bill of fare. Several seafood and beef options are available, but why not try the inn's namesake—duck stew seasoned with chipotle chiles, lime and cilantro or perhaps with African spices and lemon-zest dumplings? For starters, there are appetizers such as Westcott Bay home-smoked oysters or sea scallop ceviche; as well as fine Northwestern and European wines. Dinner only. Closed November through March. Call for hours.

SHOPPING

Most of the shops are located within blocks of Friday Harbor, giving you plenty to do while waiting for the ferry.

COTTON COTTON COTTON ✉165 1st Street, Friday Harbor ✆360-378-3531 ⌕www.cottoncottoncottonline.com Near Sunshine Alley, this aptly named shop sells original screenprint art on organic cotton sportswear, natural-fiber clothing and custom jewelry.

WATERWORKS GALLERY ✉315 Spring Street, Friday Harbor ✆360-378-3060 ⌕www.waterworksgallery.com, info@waterworksgallery.com Waterworks features a collection of contemporary eclectic Northwest art in media such as glass, stone, bronze and ceramic sculpture, oil and watercolor. Limited hours in winter.

THE GARUDA & I ✉60 1st Street, Friday Harbor ✆360-378-3733, 866-488-5294 ⌕www.thegarudaandi.com At this boutique you will find an amazing selection of ethnic arts, beads, crafts, musical instruments as well as jewelry from local artisans.

NIGHTLIFE

HERB'S TAVERN ✉80 1st Street, Friday Harbor ✆360-378-7076 ⌕www.herbstavern.com On San Juan Island, Herb's is the local sidle-up-to-the-bar joint. There are pool tables for everyday recreation, but Wednesdays are devoted to karaoke.

HALEY'S BAIT SHOP ✉175 Spring Street, Friday Harbor ☎360-378-4434 To watch the game on several TVs, visit this sports bar and grill.

MADRONA BAR & GRILL ✉248 Reuben Memorial Drive, Roche Harbor ☎360-378-2155 ⌐www.rocheharbor.com The Madrona has weekend dancing to live music in the summer. Their drink menu includes locally brewed beers, several West Coast wines and the Pig War Martini, honoring the infamous pig that almost caused a war between the United States and Great Britain.

BEACHES & PARKS

SAN JUAN COUNTY PARK
✉On Westside Road just north of Lime Kiln Point State Park ☎360-378-8420
☎360-378-2075 ⌐www.sanjuanco.com/parks, parks@sanjuanco.com

Orca whales frequently pass by the rocky shoreline of this 12-acre park on the western edge of San Juan Island. Because of its location on Smallpox Bay, San Juan County Park is a haven for kayakers and scuba divers who enjoy the easy waters in the shallow bay or the more challenging shelf that drops steeply off about 80 feet out. Swimming is good in the shallow, protected bay; fishing is fair for bottomfish, rockfish, salmon and crab. There are restrooms, picnic tables and fire pits.

▲ There are 23 standard sites ($30 per night), and three premium sites ($35 to $40 per night). Group camping sites for up to 30 people are available. Reservations: 360-378-1842.

LIME KILN POINT STATE PARK
✉Off Westside Road on the western shore of San Juan Island ☎360-378-2044

Situated on a rocky bluff overlooking Haro Strait, this 36-acre park is named for an early lime kiln operation, with remnants of old structures still visible to the north of the lighthouse. The bluff is the prime whale-watching spot on San Juan Island. A footpath takes you to picturesque Lime Kiln Lighthouse, listed on the National Register of Historic Places. Restrooms, picnic tables and interpretive displays are found here. There is no drinking water for the public.

CATTLE POINT NATURAL RESOURCES CONSERVATION AREA

✉Follow Cattle Point Road through American Camp and on to the southern tip of the island. ☎360-856-3500 ☎360-856-2150
⌐www.dnr.wa.gov/reserarchscience/topics/naturalareas

Though it takes a precarious scramble down a rocky ledge to reach it and picnic tables on the bluff above lend little privacy, this gravelly half-moon is arguably the prettiest public beach on San Juan Island. Facilities include picnic tables, shelter, restrooms, interpretive signs and a nature trail.

FOURTH OF JULY BEACH hidden

✉Off American Camp Road, San Juan Island National Historical Park
📞360-378-2240 🖥www.nps.gov/sajh

🚣 ⚓ This secluded, gravelly crescent is where the locals head when they're looking for privacy. There are often bald eagles nesting in the nearby trees, a poignant sign of this aptly named stretch. Griffin Bay extends out a long way and is suitable for wading on hot days. Anglers can try for bottomfish and salmon. There are pit toilets, picnic tables and a fenced grassy area off the parking lot suitable for frisbee.

ORCAS ISLAND

Trendy, artsy-craftsy and lovely to look at, Orcas Island is a resort that caters to everyone from backpackers to the well-to-do. A nature sanctuary pocketed with charming towns, the island also boasts more sun than some of its neighbors.

SIGHTS

ORCAS ISLAND HISTORICAL MUSEUM ✉181 North Beach Road, Eastsound 📞360-376-4849 🖥www.orcasmuseum.org, orcasmuseum@rockisland.com
Of the many small historical museums in the San Juans, this one is our favorite. Six interconnected log cabins of prominent early settlers house a fine assemblage of artifacts representing the culture of the Coast Salish and area homesteaders. Island industry, home and social life, farming and oral histories comprise some of the featured exhibits. Closed Monday and from October through May. Admission.

MADRONA POINT hidden

✉End of Haven Road, Eastsound A pretty madrone tree–dotted waterside park saved from condo development by local residents (especially the Lummi Indians, who consider this site to be sacred), this is a fine spot for a picnic. No dogs are allowed.

LODGING

TURTLEBACK FARM INN
$$$ 11 ROOMS ✉1981 Crow Valley Road, Eastsound 📞360-376-4914, 800-376-4914 📠360-376-5329 🖥www.turtlebackinn.com, info@turtlebackinn.com
A stay at this inn is like stepping into the much-loved story *The Wind in the Willows*, surrounded as it is by acres of forest and farm tracts full of animals as far as the eye can see. Rooms in this lovely, late-19th-century farmhouse vary in size and setup, but all the rooms have a

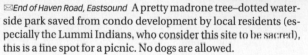

Orcas Island

BILBO'S FESTIVO

PAGE 151

Lively Mexican cuisine like Christmas burritos with tomato and *verde* sauces served in a garden patio

MADRONA POINT

PAGE 149

Perfect picnicking in a madrone tree–dotted landscape considered sacred by American Indians

THE RESTAURANT AT DEER HARBOR INN

PAGE 151

Ultrafresh daily seafood specials at tables nestled in an orchard grove with sunset views over the harbor

charming mix of contemporary and antique furniture, cozy quilts and antique fixtures in private baths. The newer Orchard House offers four spacious rooms with king-sized beds, a sofa sitting area, a gas fireplace, a dining corner, refrigerators, free wi-fi and large decks overlooking the valley. Full breakfast.

WEST BEACH RESORT

$$$-$$$$ 21 UNITS ✉190 Waterfront Way, Eastsound ☎360-376-2240, 877-937-8224 ✐www.westbeachresort.com

Built in 1938 as an exclusive sportfishing camp, this cluster of luxury one- and two-bedroom cabins clusters around the only full-service marina on the west side of Orcas Island. All but two of the cabins are on or near the pebbly beach and have queen-sized beds, fully equipped kitchens, electric heat and wood stoves. Other guest facilities include a fish smokehouse and a hot tub. The waterfront is ideal for fishing, clamming and crabbing. Kayak rentals and tours, sportfishing and wildlife-watching charters, and canoe, motorboat and mountain bike rentals are all available at the marina.

DOE BAY RESORT & RETREAT

$-$$$ 43 UNITS ✉107 Doe Bay Road, Olga ☎360-376-2291 ☏360-376-5809 ✐www.doebay.com, office@doebay.com

Expect a wide variety of accommodations at this funky resort, including hostel beds, camping, yurts and cabins, some of which are fully equipped. There are shared central bathrooms, a community kitchen, free wi-fi and a small seasonal café on the grounds of this large retreat along with a splendid three-tiered sauna and three mineral baths perched on a covered deck. Clothing optional. Be aware of the strict 14-day, advance-notice cancellation policy.

BILBO'S FESTIVO

Hidden

$–$$ MEXICON   ✉North Beach Road, Eastsound   ☎360-376-4728

Bilbo's (so named for the hobbit because the restaurant's owner thought the building looked like it belonged in the shire) specializes in Mexican fare. A margarita or *cerveza* on the tiled garden patio surrounded by adobe walls is a great way to relax. Try the locally popular Christmas burrito, which is topped with both roasted tomato and *verde* sauces. Bilbo's serves dinner only, but opens **La Taqueria**, a lunch outlet in the courtyard, during the summer months. Limited winter hours; call ahead.

THE RESTAURANT AT THE DEER HARBOR INN

Hidden

$$$–$$$$ AMERICAN/SEAFOOD   ✉33 Inn Lane, Deer Harbor
☎360-376-1040, 877-377-4110   ☎360-376-2237
🖥www.deerharborinn.com, stay@deerharborinn.com

This restaurant is tucked away in an expanse of orchard grove peering out over Deer Harbor and the Olympic Range and is where locals come for that special night out. The daily menu is chalked on the board and features the freshest of fresh seafood: wild salmon, halibut, king crab and tiger prawns. Steak and chicken entrées are available as well. For diners on the deck, this is a great spot to watch the sunset. Dinner only; reservations recommended.

SHOPPING

CROW VALLEY POTTERY & GALLERY ✉2274 Orcas Road, Eastsound
☎360-376-4260   ☎360-376-6495   🖥www.crowvalleypottery.com, pottery@crowvalley.com An 1866 cabin houses this long-established studio that got its start making ceramic wind bells inspired by Northwest tribal arts. It has expanded to represent numerous island artists and craftspeople working in pottery, glass, metal sculpture, jewelry, garden art, a variety of printing mediums and more. Closed October to Memorial Day weekend.

ORCAS ISLAND POTTERY

✉338 Old Pottery Road, off West Beach Road, Eastsound   ☎360-376-2813
🖥www.orcasislandpottery.com, orcaspots@rockisland.com Don't spend all your time and money in Eastsound proper because you won't want to miss this shop, which is the oldest existing craft studio on Orcas. You can watch potters at work through the windows of the studio while your kids enjoy the on-site treehouse.

THE RIGHT PLACE ✉️*2915 Enchanted Forest Road, Eastsound* 📞*360-376-4023* 🖥️*www.rightplacepottery.com* This is a family-owned and -operated gallery with pottery strewn about the garden and in the showroom. In the summertime you can try using the wheel yourself (fee).

SALLIE BELL DESIGNS ✉️*140 Sedum Hill Road, Orcas* 📞*360-376-2275, 800-273-4055* 🖥️*www.monkeypuzzle.com* Sallie Bell carries a curious selection of bold and colorful boutique items—jewelry and clothing, both elegant and casual.

ORCAS ISLAND ARTWORKS

✉️*Olga* 📞*360-376-4408* 🖥️*www.orcasartworks.com, info@orcasartworks.com*
At a bend in Horseshoe Highway as you reach Olga is this cooperative art gallery showcasing fine arts, handicrafts and furniture all produced by local hands. Closed January to mid-February.

NIGHTLIFE

LOWER TAVERN ✉️*1 Prune Alley, Eastsound* 📞*360-376-4848* For convivial pub action, step into this tavern and amuse yourself with darts and pool. Beer and wine only.

THE LIVING ROOM

✉️*474 North Beach Road, Eastsound* 🖥️*thelivingroom@orcasonline.com*
This yoga studio/community arts center hosts concerts, poetry readings, storytelling and stand-up comedy.

BEACHES & PARKS

MORAN STATE PARK

✉️*Located near Eastsound, accessible by state ferry from Anacortes*
📞*360-376-2326* 📠*360-376-2360* 🖥️*moran@parks.wa.gov*
🚶🚴 ⛵🎣 ♨️🚣 🐎 Washington's fifth-largest park consists of 5252 verdant acres dotted with five freshwater lakes and crowned by sweeping Mt. Constitution. From its 2400-foot peak, there are beautiful views of the San Juans, Mt. Baker and Vancouver, B.C. There are 38 miles of forest trails connecting the four mountain lakes, numerous waterfalls and five campgrounds. There is fishing for rainbow, cutthroat and kokanee trout on several lakes, with boat rentals available seasonally. Facilities include restrooms, showers, kitchen shelters and picnic tables.

⛺ There are 136 standard sites ($20 to $23 per night) and 15 primitive sites ($14 per night). Reservations: 888-226-7688.

OBSTRUCTION PASS
STATE PARK

hidden

✉ *From the town of Olga follow Point Lawrence Road east, turn right on Obstruction Pass Road and keep right on Trailhead Road until you hit the parking area. From there it's a half-mile hike to the campground.*

📞 *360-376-2326* 📠 *360-376-2360* ✎ *moran@parks.wa.gov*

🏃 ⛰ 🛥 🚣 This primitive, heavily forested locale located on the southeastern tip of Orcas Island is tricky to get to, so the crowds are kept to a minimum, a reward for those who care to search it out. The area has three hiking trails, ten campsites (no potable water) and a beach with cold water for brave swimmers. Anglers will find bottomfish and rockfish. There are vault toilets, picnic tables and trails. Three mooring buoys are available.

△ There are 10 primitive sites ($12 per night); hike-in only.

OTHER PARKS Many of the smaller islands are preserved as state parks including Doe, Jones, Clark, Sucia, Stuart, Posey, Blind, James, Matia, Patos and Turn. They are accessible by boat only and in most cases have a few primitive campsites, nature trails, a dock or mooring buoys off secluded beaches, but no water (except Jones, Stuart and Sucia, in season) or facilities except for composting toilets. Costs are $10 for mooring buoys, $12 for camping, $10 plus $.50 per foot for boats to dock overnight. Washington water trail sites cost $12 per night and must be reached by a beachable human-powered watercraft. For more information, contact Washington State Parks (360-902-8844, infocent@parks.wa.gov).

OUTDOOR ADVENTURES

BOATING

Spending time on the water is a part of daily life here, and certainly something that visitors should not miss. In fact, many of the 100-plus islands of the San Juans are accessible only by boat.

BELLINGHAM BAY COMMUNITY BOAT CENTER ✉ *501 Harris Avenue, Bellingham* 📞 *360-714-8891* ✎ *www.sailpaddlerow.org* On the mainland, contact this center for kayaks, rowboats, canoes and sailboats. Closed Monday and Tuesday; limited hours in winter.

ÆOLIAN VENTURES ✉ *2072 West Captain Whidbey Inn Road, Coupeville* 📞 *360-678-4097, 800-366-4097* ✎ *www.svcuttysark.com* Lifelong sailor Captain John Colby Stone, who has sailed on several transoceanic sailing ship voyages—including the first joint Soviet-American sea trip from New York to Leningrad—takes charter groups out on his classic 52-foot wooden sailing ketch.

GATO VERDE ADVENTURE SAILING ✉ *Berth 3, 355 Harris Avenue, Bellingham* 📞 *360-220-3215* ✎ *www.gatoverde.com* Captain Todd Shuster takes groups of up to 12 people on day sails and sunset cruises, as well as full-service or skippered bare-boat cruises of one to six days through the Strait of Juan de Fuca for up to nine passengers in his 42-foot catamaran, the first plug-in diesel-electric charter boat on the West Coast.

SPORTFISHING

Catching-for reward when you head out on a fishing charter through Northern Puget Sound and the San Juan Islands. As a bonus, you're also likely to encounter seals, eagles and whales as you sail past islands wooded with red-bark madrone trees.

In winter, of course, the temperature on the water can get chilly and the water a bit choppy. All the charter fishing services listed here provide boats with heated, enclosed cabins to keep you comfortable. Charter fees include bait and tackle, but do not include a fishing license or food and drink.

Northern Puget Sound

With thousands of miles of tidal coastline, Puget Sound and the San Juan Islands once boasted some of the best sportfishing opportunities in North America. These days, the fish—especially salmon—are in great peril from various abuses. For the present, there are still five varieties of Pacific salmon (chinook, coho, chum, pink and sockeye), and anglers can also try for cod, flounder, halibut, ling, rockfish, sea perch, squid and sturgeon. Scuba divers often concentrate their efforts on harvesting crab, octopus, shrimp and squid, while shellfishers are rewarded with butter and razor clams. Clamming and fishing licenses are required and are available in sporting goods stores. For more information, contact **Washington's Department of Fish and Wildlife** (360-902-2700; 360-902-2943; www.wdfw.wa.gov/fishcorn.htm, fish regs@dfw.wa.gov.

RIP TIDE CHARTERS ⊠*Port of Bellingham, 1801 Roeder Avenue, Bellingham* ✆ *360-815-6568* ✐*www.rtcharters.com, captfrank@rtcharters.com* Captain Frank takes anglers out in his 24-foot sportfishing boat, using state-of-the-art electronics to locate salmon in season (February to mid-April for blackmouth salmon, July through October for other varieties). He also guides trips to catch Dungeness crab as well as halibut and other bottomfish.

ALL STAR FISHING CHARTERS ⊠*Port of Everett* ✆*425-252-4188, 800-214-1595* ✐*www.allstarfishing.com, gary@allstarfishing.com* All Star has a 28-foot fiberglass-bottom boat that can carry up to six people. Owner Gary Krein encourages "angler participation" on his full-day trips (two daily in summer, one in winter). The boat comes fully equipped with electronic fishfinding equipment that seeks out the salmon and bottomfish. Bait and tackle are included.

SEA HAWK SALMON CHARTERS ⊠*Skyland Marina, Anacortes* ✆*360-424-1350* ✐*www.seahawksalmoncharters.com* Mike Dunnigan is the skipper of these charters. He runs year-round, exclusive eight-hour charters for up to four people to fish for salmon, bottomfish and halibut. Bait and tackle are included. Closed in December.

CATCHMORE CHARTERS ✉4215 Mitchell Drive, Anacortes 360-293-7093 www.catchmorecharters.com Departing from Anacortes's Skyline Marina, this company's 27-foot *Trophyhunter II* is operated by a retired Washington Fish and Wildlife Department officer and his son, a top tournament competition champion. Besides taking sport anglers out to catch salmon and halibut, the pair offer naturalist tours in search of orcas, humpback, minke and gray whales and porpoises.

RIVER FISHING

Several rivers in the area—the Snohomish, Skykomish, Skagit and Sauk, for example—provide year-round catches, notably steelhead and all species of salmon except sockeye (it's not permitted to take this fish from rivers).

ALL RIVERS GUIDE SERVICE ☎425-736-8920 ✐www.allriversguide service.com, mark@allriversguideservice.com This company offers customized, seven- to nine-hour flyfishing trips in a 16-foot heated drift boat or a 20-foot jetsled. All bait and tackle are included, and the knowledgeable professional guides also offer instruction in fishing.

KAYAKING

For nonadventurers who want an outdoor experience that's a lot of fun but not extremely challenging, a guided water excursion in a sea kayak may be just the thing. No previous kayaking experience is necessary to join one of these groups for a paddling tour on the gentle waters of Chuckanut Bay, with its sandstone formations near Bellingham; of sea caves around Deception Pass State Park on Whidbey Island; or off San Juan Island, where you are likely to see whales, seals and other marine wildlife. Unless noted, the operators listed here generally offer a regular schedule of excursions from April–May to September–October. Cost for a sea kayak excursion ranges from $30 to $60. Most operators can also arrange overnight or longer trips.

Northern Puget Sound
MOONDANCE SEA KAYAKING ADVENTURES ✉Bellingham ☎360-738-7664 ✐www.moondancekayak.com Moondance leads half-day to five-day trips to nearby locations such as Chuckanut Bay, Cypress Island and Clark's Point (where you'll see a fossil of the entire trunk of a palm tree). A slightly longer trip to sea caves occasionally heads down to Deception Pass State Park, where the wave action is rougher.

Lopez Island
LOPEZ KAYAKS ✉2845 Fisherman Bay Road ☎360-468-2847 ✐www.lopez kayaks.com This group offers morning and afternoon sea-kayaking tours in double kayaks for eight people to MacKaye Harbor, which is also popular with seals. If you have experience, you can also rent a kayak for your own use without joining a tour. Closed November through April.

San Juan Island

Since the waters just off the west side of San Juan Island are in the main whale-migration corridor, your chances of seeing whales are good. If not, there's plenty of other wildlife to view, notably seals and bald eagles. (The highest density of bald-eagle nestings in the lower 48 states is in the San Juan Islands.) There are also kelp forests, jutting cliffs, sea caves and rocky outcroppings.

SEA QUEST KAYAK EXPEDITIONS ✉*Friday Harbor* 📞*360-378-5767, 888-589-4253* 🖱*www.sea-quest-kayak.com* A biologist or scientist accompanies the day excursions led by this outfitter for groups of four to twelve. There are also camping trips lasting from two to five days that go through primary orca viewing areas.

CRYSTAL SEAS KAYAKING ✉*Friday Harbor* 📞*360-378-4223, 877-732-7787* 🖱*www.crystalseas.com* Crystal Seas escorts up to ten people on morning or afternoon sunset excursions. You can also arrange custom camping trips from two to six days. Paddlers will see eagles, seals and whales.

Orcas Island

SHEARWATER SEA KAYAK TOURS ✉*P.O. Box 787, Eastsound, WA 98245* 📞*360-376-4699* 🖱*www.shearwaterkayaks.com, info@shearwaterkayaks.com* This company has been guiding small-group kayak tours for more than 25 years. They offer half-day excursions around Orcas Island and full-day tours to Sucia Island. Shearwater has also sold accessories and clothing since 1982, making it the oldest outfitter on the islands.

SCUBA DIVING

The protected waters of Puget Sound hold untold treasures for the diver: Craggy rock walls, ledges and caves of this sunken mountain range and enormous forests of bull kelp provide homes for a multitude of marine life. Giant Pacific octopus thrive in these waters, as do sea anemones and hundreds of species of fish.

"Within 15 minutes of Friday Harbor on San Juan Island, there are hundreds of great dive spots," says one local diver who grew up in the area. The west side of San Juan Island and the south side of Lopez Island are particular favorites, largely because the absence of silt means the water is cleaner and therefore clearer. There are also lots of ledges along these rocky coasts, which abound with exceptional wall-dive spots. Acres of bull kelp forests, with their teeming marine life, are also popular dive spots. But just as these waters hold great beauty, they can also be treacherous with tremendous tidal changes and strong currents.

Northern Puget Sound

WASHINGTON DIVERS, INC. ✉*903 North State Street, Bellingham* 📞*360-676-8029* 📞*360-647-5028* 🖱*www.washingtondivers.com* This group offers complete rental and diving services, including a full schedule of diving activities year-round, from one-day trips to two-week-long international excursions. A one-day dive charter to the San Juan Islands is the most popular trip. In the summer, extended daylight hours make it possible to make up to two dives during the six- to seven-hour trip. Scuba certification classes (open water) are also available.

Whidbey Island
WHIDBEY ISLAND DIVE CENTER ✉ *1020 Northeast 7th Avenue #1, Oak Harbor* ☎ *360-675-1112* 🖥 *www.whidbeydive.com, info@whidbeydive.com* Besides air fills, diving lessons and rental of wetsuits and other equipment, this dive center offers half- to full-day dive charters. One popular spot for experienced divers is under the bridge at Deception Pass State Park, where currents reach seven knots—"a diving rush." For the less experienced, Strawberry Island is an excellent spot to view marine life.

San Juan Island
UNDERWATER SPORTS INC. ✉ *205 East Casino Road #4, Everett* ☎ *425-355-3338* 🖥 *www.underwatersports.com* Check out this company for full-day chartered trips to the islands, night dives, rentals, open-water certification, classes and air fills. Closed Sunday and Monday.

WHALE WATCHING

From May to September you can often see the whales from shore when they range closest to the islands to feed on migrating salmon. The best shoreline viewing spots are **Lime Kiln Point** on San Juan Island or **Shark Reef Park** on Lopez Island. Sightings drop dramatically in the winter as the pods disperse from the core area in search of prey.

If you want to get a closer look, put on your parka and sunglasses, grab your binoculars and camera and climb aboard one of the **wildlife cruises** that ply the waters between the islands. Even if you don't see any orca during the trip, you will almost certainly spot other interesting forms of wildlife such as sleek, gray minke whales, Dall's porpoises (which look like miniature orca), splotchy brown harbor seals, bald eagles, great blue heron, cormorants or tufted puffin.

DEER HARBOR CHARTERS ✉ *P.O. Box 303, Deer Harbor, WA 98243* ☎ *360-376-5989, 800-544-5758* 🖥 *www.deerharborcharters.com* Deer Harbor offers four-hour whale-watching tours from April to October on a 36-foot boat that carries 20 people from Rosario Resort or on a 47-foot boat that carries 30 people from Deer Harbor Marina. Both boats have a naturalist guide.

ISLAND MARINER CRUISES ✉ *2621 South Harbor Loop, Bellingham* ☎ *360-734-8866, 877-734-8866* 📠 *360-734-8867* 🖥 *www.orcawatch.com, mariner@orcawatch.com* This company boasts a high success rate for spotting whales. It's no wonder: the naturalist has worked there for years and they use more spotting services—including a plane—than those on the island. Enjoy day-long nature and whale-watching expeditions with commentary on the history, flora and fauna of the San Juans as you cruise through the islands on a boat designed for whale watching that holds over 100 people. Whale-watching charters closed mid-September to mid-March.

WESTERN PRINCE WHALE & WILDLIFE TOURS ✉*Friday Harbor* ☎*360-378-5315, 800-757-6722* ⌖*www.orcawhalewatch.com* Western Prince has naturalist-accompanied wildlife tours on a half-day basis. Boats normally carry 30 people and the environmentally friendly *Western Prince II* is powered by biodiesel.

SAN JUAN BOAT TOURS INC. ✉*Friday Harbor* ☎*360-378-3499, 800-443-4552* ⌖*www.whaletour.com* You can contact this outfitter for a three-and-a-half-hour whale-sighting excursion aboard a 100-foot tour vessel.

Happy spotting!

RIDING STABLES

Northern Puget Sound
LANG'S PONY AND HORSE FARM ✉*21463 Little Mountain Road, Mt. Vernon* ☎*360-424-7630* ⌖*www.comeride.com* A year-round operation, Lang's takes up to 14 riders on a leisurely guided trail ride (half-hour to two hours) around the hilly and wooded ranch, which is about 30 miles south of Bellingham. The farm also offers a full moon ride, as well as summer camps and riding lessons. Call for reservations.

Whidbey Island
MADRONA RIDGE RANCH ✉*Madrona Way, Coupeville* ☎*360-678-4124* Put on jeans and a pair of sturdy leather shoes for a guided trail ride through the hilly, wooded Madrona Ridge Ranch. Please call ahead (evenings are best) to arrange a one-and-a-half-hour ride; groups are limited to up to two people at a time. Riding lessons are available for all ages, but the trail rides are for teens and adults only.

GOLF

Northern Puget Sound
DAKOTA CREEK ✉*3258 Haynie Road, Custer* ☎*360-366-3131, 888-465-3515* ⌖*www.dakotacreekgolf.com* This 18-hole course was named one of the most challenging by the Pacific Northwest Golf Association. Open to the public, the course, which is carved out of a mountain, is quiet, well maintained and hilly.

HOMESTEAD FARMS GOLF COURSE ✉*115 East Homestead Boulevard, Lynden* ☎*360-354-1196, 800-354-1196* ⌖*www.homesteadfarmsgolf.com* The 18th hole here is the Northwest's only par-five on an island green. The public course is flat, but has lots of water.

WALTER E. HALL MEMORIAL GOLF COURSE ✉*1226 West Casino Road, Everett* ☎*425-353-4653* ⌖*www.walterhallgolf.com* A good choice is this memorial golf course, an 18-hole public facility with well-kept grounds, a restaurant and cart rentals.

KAYAK POINT GOLF COURSE ✉*15711 Marine Drive, Stanwood* ☎*360-652-9676* The 18-hole course here has an 18-hole putting course, a driving range, a full-service restaurant and lounge, and cart, shoe and club rentals.

OVERLOOK GOLF COURSE ✉17523 State Route 9, Mt. Vernon ☎360-422-6444 A nine-hole public course with a view of Big Lake, Overlook offers club and cart rentals.

LAKE PADDEN MUNICIPAL GOLF COURSE ✉4882 Samish Way, Bellingham ☎360-738-7400 ⌕www.lakepaddengolf.com There's a hilly front nine at this course, located in Lake Padden Park. It's a tight, densely treed, 18-hole public course.

SUDDEN VALLEY GOLF AND COUNTRY CLUB ✉4 Club House Circle, Bellingham ☎360-734-6435 ⌕www.suddenvalleygolfclub.com Sudden Valley offers an 18-hole semiprivate course that sits on a lake. There are cart rentals, a driving range and a snack shop.

SEMIAHMOO GOLF AND COUNTRY CLUB ✉9565 Semiahmoo Parkway, Blaine ☎360-371-7015 ⌕semiahmoo.com The most expensive course (up to $70 greens fees) in the area is at this semiprivate country club. It's ranked as one of nation's best resort courses and was designated as a sectional qualifying course for the 1997 U.S. Open. The 18-hole, par-72 course was designed by Arnold Palmer; hole number 4 has a scenic view of Mt. Baker and the valley beyond.

AVALON GOLF CLUB ✉19345 Kelleher Road, Burlington ☎360-757-1900 ⌕www.avalonlinks.com This golf club has the hottest new links around the Sound. The 27-hole public course will keep you busy for a while. You can rent pull-carts, too.

San Juan Island

SAN JUAN GOLF AND COUNTRY CLUB ✉806 Golf Course Road, Friday Harbor ☎360-378-2254 ⌕www.sanjuangolf.com It's only nine holes, but this course "plays like 18." Private, but open to the public, the course is set on a wooded, rolling tract next to Griffin Bay. Cart rentals are available.

TENNIS

CLARK PARK ✉2400 Lombard Street, Everett Six lighted courts.

FAIRHAVEN PARK ✉107 Chuckanut Drive, Bellingham ☎360-676-6985 Two courts.

COUPEVILLE HIGH SCHOOL ✉501 South Main Street, Coupeville Four lighted courts.

OAK HARBOR CITY PARK ✉1501 City Beach Street, Whidbey Island Four courts.

ANACORTES HIGH SCHOOL FACILITY ✉2nd Street and J Avenue, Fidalgo Island Six courts.

FRIDAY HARBOR HIGH SCHOOL ✉Guard Street, San Juan Four courts.

ROCHE HARBOR RESORT ✉Roche Harbor Road, San Juan Two courts.

BIKING

For bicycling in the Bellingham area, the best map is "Bicycling in Bellingham and Whatcom County," which outlines trails according to traffic volume, surface status (gravel, paved, etc.) and hill difficulty; it also categorizes trails as City Ride, City Trail or Country Ride. The map is available in many bicycle stores and during the summer from the **Bellingham/Whatcom County Convention and Visitors Bureau** (904 Potter Street, Bellingham; 360-671-3990, 800-487-2032; www. bellingham.org).

If you plan to bike on the San Juan Islands, it's important to remember that the islands' narrow roads don't have special lanes or other provisions for cyclists. Lopez Island is probably the best bet for the occasional bicyclist: you'll be able to bike long, flat country roads, rather than the steeper, twisting roads of some of the other islands. You can rent a bike on the island or in Anacortes before ferrying over for the day.

The hardy cyclist might prefer a 20-mile hilly and winding route around San Juan Island or 16 miles of steep, twisting roads beginning at the ferry landing on Orcas Island.

For bike trails here and in other parts of the state, contact the **Washington Department of Transportation** (P.O. Box 47300, Olympia, WA 98504) to request a route map and informative brochure, or call the **Bicycle Hotline** (360-705-7277).

Northern Puget Sound
Bellingham offers several bike routes, some arduous, some easy, all highlighting the scenery and history of the area.

INTERURBAN TRAIL   This moderate, six-mile trail, which follows an old trolley route, begins at the Fairhaven Parkway and ends at Larrabee State Park.

LAKE PADDEN LOOP   The best of the trails is this fairly easy, 2.6-mile loop in Lake Padden Park. It connects to a series of trails on **Mt. Galbraith**, a local hot spot for mountain biking.

Whidbey Island
ISLAND COUNTY TOUR   Those looking for a long-distance ride will enjoy this 50-mile tour, which begins at Columbia Beach on Whidbey Island and continues on to Deception Pass at the northern tip of the island. This trip is moderately strenuous, with high traffic on a good portion of the ride, but the spectacular views of the Strait of Juan de Fuca and the Saratoga Passage are reward enough.

San Juan Island
SAN JUAN ISLAND LOOP   This slightly difficult, 30-mile loop leads along hilly, winding roads through Friday Harbor, Roche Harbor, San Juan Island National Historical Park and along the San Juan Channel.

Orcas Island

HORSESHOE ROUTE This is by far the most difficult island bike route, with 16 miles of steep, twisting roads beginning at the ferry landing in Orcas, continuing through Eastsound, then on to Olga. An alternative route for the very hardy starts in Olga, passes through Moran State Park and ends in Doe Bay, with a possible challenging 3.5-mile sidetrip up and back down Mt. Constitution.

Bike Rentals

THE BICYCLE CENTER ✉4707 Evergreen Way, Everett ☎425-252-1441 For mountain-bike sales and repairs in the Northern Puget Sound region, contact this company.

FAIRHAVEN BIKE & MOUNTAIN SPORTS ✉1108 11th Street, Bellingham ☎360-733-4433 Check out this shop for year-round mountain-bike rentals, sales and repairs in the Bellingham area.

SKAGIT CYCLE CENTER ✉1620 Commercial Avenue, Anacortes ☎360-588-8776 Located just off Route 20, the main drag into Anacortes, this shop rents bikes (and helmets) by the week. The center's location is ideal for cyclists heading to the San Juans ferry or just pedaling around nearby Skagit Valley.

LOPEZ BICYCLE WORKS ✉2847 Fisherman's Bay Road, Lopez Island ☎360-468-2847 ✎www.lopezbicycleworks.com This company rents, repairs and sells mountain bikes, touring bikes and hybrids and will let you drop off the bike at the ferry landing when you leave for the day. Closed October through April.

ISLAND BICYCLES ✉380 Argyle Avenue, Friday Harbor ☎360-378-4941 ✎www.islandbicycles.com For bike rentals on San Juan Island, contact this center, which offers hybrids and road bikes, as well as bike sales, repairs and friendly advice. Limited winter hours.

DOLPHIN BAY ✉Ferry Landing ☎360-376-4157 Rent, buy or repair mountain bikes and hybrids on Orcas Island at this shop, which also offers custom tours for 10 to 30 people.

WILDLIFE CYCLES ✉350 North Beach Road, Eastsound ☎360-376-4708 ✎www.wildlifecycles.com Mountain bikes, road bikes, tandems, bike trailers and trail-a-bikes can be found for sale or rent here. They also do repairs and offer off-road tours.

HIKING

All distances listed for hiking trails are one way unless otherwise noted.

Northern Puget Sound

LANGUS RIVERFRONT PARK NATURE TRAIL In Everett, hikers on this 2.5-mile trail are likely to spot red-tailed hawk or gray heron as they make their way through towering spruce, red cedar and dogwood trees along the banks of the Snohomish River, past Union Slough and on toward Spencer Island, a protected haven for nesting ducks.

PADILLA BAY NATIONAL ESTUARINE RESERVE ☎*360-428-1558*
The Puget Sound region is rich with hiking opportunities. Some of the best hikes in the area can be found at this reserve in the tiny community of Bay View (about six miles west of Burlington). Stop at the **Breazeale Interpretive Center** (360-428-1558) one mile north of the reserve's Shore Trail for exhibits about the local habitat and specific trail maps. The **Padilla Bay Shore Trail** (2.3 miles) is a bicycle/pedestrian path with views of the estuary, mudflat, sloughs and tidal marsh. Within the reserve is the **Upland Trail** full of indigenous plants. Binoculars and trail guides can be checked out at the interpretive center to aid your exploration of the forest and meadow along this trail (.8 mile).

THE INTERURBAN TRAIL This 6-mile Bellingham trail begins near the entrance to Larrabee State Park and hugs the crest above Chuckanut Drive overlooking the bay and the San Juan Islands. Chuckanut Drive passes the rose gardens of Fairhaven Park on its way into the revitalized Fairhaven District of the city.

SEHOME HILL ARBORETUM There are 5.9 miles of rolling trails through this lush arboretum, crowned by views of Mt. Baker and the San Juans from the observation tower at the summit.

LAKE PADDEN TRAIL

✉*To get there from I-5, take the Samish Way exit in Bellingham and drive south for about two miles to the park entrance.* ☎*360-676-6985* ⏐*www.cob.org/ parks.htm.* This 2.6-mile loop circles the glistening lake, taking you from the busy recreation facilities—picnic grounds, beaches, nonmotorized boat ramp, tennis courts and even a golf course—on the north shore to the peaceful south shore with its shady Douglas fir forest and rocky points. A 1000-foot-high ridge protects the lake from the noise of the nearby interstate highway. Other trails branch off and lead into the backcountry of the 1008-acre park.

TERRELL MARSH TRAIL In Birch Bay State Park in Blaine, this gently sloping trail (.5 mile) winds through a thickly wooded area of birch, maple, red cedar, hemlock and fir, home to pileated woodpeckers, bald eagle, ruffed grouse, blue heron, muskrats and squirrels, and on to Terrell Marsh, the halfway point on the loop, before passing back through the forest to the trailhead.

Whidbey Island
FORT EBEY STATE PARK The most picturesque hikes on Whidbey Island are found in and around this park. The **Ebey's Landing Loop Trail** (3.5 miles) has some steep sections on the bluff above the beach, but carry your camera anyway to capture the views of pastoral Ebey's Prairie in one direction and Mt. Rainier and the Olympic Mountains framed by wind-sculpted pines and fir in the other. Trimmed in wild roses, the trail swings around Perego's Lagoon and back along the driftwood-strewn beach. Be aware that the trail passes over some private

property. The **Partridge Point Trail** (3.5 miles) climbs through a mix of coastal wildflowers on a windswept bluff rising 150 feet above the water with wide views of Port Townsend, Admiralty Inlet, Protection Island and Discovery Bay. A fenced path at the southern end drops down the headland to the cobbly beach below.

DECEPTION PASS STATE PARK   There are numerous trails to choose from in Deception Pass State Park. Locals prefer **Rosario Head Trail** (.3 mile) on the Fidalgo Island side, stretching over the very steep promontory between Rosario Bay and Bowman Bay with sweeping views of San Juans, Rosario Strait and the Strait of Juan de Fuca. The **Lighthouse Point Trail** (1.5 miles), near Bowman Bay. On the Whidbey Island side of the bridge, climb the steep switchback on **Goose Rock Perimeter Trail** (3.5 miles) and you might see great blue heron on Cornet Bay, then follow the path down under the bridge next to the swirling waters of the pass and on to quiet North Beach. Heartier hikers might want to tackle the **Goose Rock Summit Trail** (.5 mile), with an altitude gain of some 450 feet for an unparalleled view of Deception Pass and the Cascades.

Fidalgo Island

WASHINGTON PARK LOOP ROAD   In Anacortes, your best bet is to head for this loop trail (3 miles), located on Fidalgo Head at the end of Sunset Avenue four miles west of downtown. Rewarding views on this easy, paved path with a few moderate slopes include incredible glimpses of the San Juan Islands, Burrows Pass and Burrows Island. You'll also find quiet, cool stretches through dense woods and access to beaches and romantic, hidden outcroppings suitable for a glass of champagne to toast the breathtaking sunsets.

Lopez Island

SHARK REEF PARK TRAIL   On Lopez, ideal hiking choices include this .5-mile mossy path that meanders through a fragrant forest area and along a rock promontory looking out over tidal pools, a large kelp bed, a jutting haul out spot for seals and across the channel to San Juan Island.

BEACH TRAIL   This Spencer Spit State Park trail (2 miles) travels down the spit and around the salt marsh lagoon alive with migratory birds; at the end of the spit is a reproduction of a historic log cabin built by early settlers, a fine spot for a picnic or brief rest stop with a nice view of the tiny islands offshore.

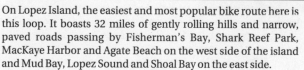

**LOPEZ ISLAND
PERIMETER LOOP** _____ hidden

On Lopez Island, the easiest and most popular bike route here is this loop. It boasts 32 miles of gently rolling hills and narrow, paved roads passing by Fisherman's Bay, Shark Reef Park, MacKaye Harbor and Agate Beach on the west side of the island and Mud Bay, Lopez Sound and Shoal Bay on the east side.

San Juan Island

SAN JUAN ISLAND NATIONAL HISTORICAL PARK   Two of the best hiking alternatives on San Juan are the established hiking trails of the San Juan Island National Historical Park. The **Lagoon Trail** (.5 mile) in American Camp is actually two trails intertwined, starting from a parking area above Old Town (referred to on maps as First) Lagoon and passing through a dense stand of Douglas fir connecting the lovely, protected cove beaches of Jakle's Lagoon and Third Lagoon. The highlight of the short but steep **Mt. Young Trail** (.75 mile) in English Camp are the plates identifying the many islands dotting the waters as far as the eye can see. If you want a closer view of the water, you can take the flat, easy **Bell Point Trail** (2 miles), also in the national park's English Camp, which runs along the edge of the coast.

Orcas Island

MORAN STATE PARK   Unless you plan to spend an extended period of time here, there's little chance of covering the many hiking trails that connect view spots, mountain lakes, waterfalls and campgrounds. For a taste of the scenic beauty, try the **Mountain Loop** (3.9 miles). It is fairly easy and takes in sights such as log cabins and a dam and footbridge at the south end of Mountain Lake.

TWIN LAKES TRAIL

✆ *360-376-2326* This hike (2 to 3.7 miles round-trip) is part of the extensive trail system that reaches out to every corner of 5252-acre Moran State Park, offering the best hiking in the San Juan Islands. From the boat launch at Mountain Lake, this trail follows a creek through old growth forest for two miles to the pair of lakes for which it is named and loops around both lakes in a figure eight. From there, a branch of the trail climbs by switchbacks to the top of 2027-foot Mt. Constitution for the best view possible of the San Juan Islands. Since this is not the shortest or easiest trail to the summit (which can also be reached by car), it is rarely crowded even on the busiest weekends.

CASCADE CREEK TRAIL   If you're a waterfall lover, take this trail (4.3 miles) from the south end of Mountain Lake past Cascade and Rustic falls and on to Cascade Lake.

TRANSPORTATION

Close to five million vehicles a year cross the U.S./Canada border at Blaine, Washington, making this the West Coast's busiest northern border station.

CAR

Route 5, also known as the Pacific Highway, parallels the Northern Puget Sound coastline all the way up to the Canadian border. **Route 20**

from Burlington takes you into Anacortes, the main jump-off point for ferry service to the San Juan Islands. **Route 16** leads from Tacoma across The Narrows and onto the Kitsap Peninsula where it connects to **Route 3** skirting the Sinclair Inlet and continuing north to Port Gamble.

AIR

Visitors flying into the Northern Puget Sound area usually arrive at either **Bellingham International Airport** (360-671-5674) or the much larger and busier **Seattle-Tacoma International Airport** (see Chapter Two for further information). Carriers serving the Bellingham airport include Allegiant Air, Horizon Airlines and San Juan Airlines.

Charter and regularly scheduled commuter flights are available into the tiny **Friday Harbor Airport** (360-378-4724) through Kenmore Air Express, Island Air and San Juan Airlines. Small commuter airports with limited scheduled service include **Anacortes Airport**, **Eastsound Airport** and **Lopez Airport**; all are served by San Juan Airlines.

FERRY

WASHINGTON STATE FERRIES ✆ 206-464-6400 🖥 www.wsdot.wa.gov/ ferries Part of the state highway system, these ferries provide transportation to the main islands of the San Juans—Lopez, Orcas, Shaw and Friday Harbor on San Juan—departing from the **Anacortes Ferry Terminal** (Ferry Terminal Road; 888-808-7977 in Washington). Schedules change several times per year, with added service in the summer to take care of the heavy influx of tourists. The system is burdened during peak summer months, so arrive at the terminal early and be prepared to wait patiently (sometimes three hours or more) in very long lines if you plan to take your car along; walk-on passengers seldom wait long. Passports are required for all ferry passengers arriving from the San Juan Islands, including U.S. citizens who have not left the country.

BUS

GREYHOUND BUS LINES ✆ 800-231-2222 🖥 www.greyhound.com Greyhound provides regular service into Bellingham, Everett and Mt. Vernon. Stations are in **Bellingham** (401 Harris Avenue in Fairhaven Station; 360-733-5251), in **Everett** (3201 Smith Avenue; 425-252-2143), and in **Mt. Vernon** (105 Kincaid Street, Suite 100; 360-336-5111).

AIRPORTER SHUTTLE/BELLAIR CHARTERS ✆ 360-380-8800, 866-235-5247 🖥 www.airporter.com This company provides express shuttle service between Bellingham, Mt. Vernon, Stanwood, Anacortes, Marysville, Oak Harbor and the SeaTac airport.

TRAIN

AMTRAK ✉ 3201 Smith Avenue, Everett ✆ 800-872-7245 🖥 www.amtrak.com Amtrak offers service into Everett on the Puget Sound shoreline via the "Empire Builder," which originates in Chicago and makes its final stop in Seattle before retracing its route. The "Amtrak Cascades" offers service to Bellingham, Mount Vernon and Everett en route between Vancouver, BC, and Eugene, OR. West Coast connections through Seattle on the "Coast Starlight" are also available.

CAR RENTALS

At the Bellingham International Airport, you'll find **Avis Rent A Car** (800-331-1212), **Budget Rent A Car** (800-527-0700), **Enterprise Rent-A-Car** (800-261-7331) and **Hertz Rent A Car** (800-654-3131).

A less expensive local rental agency is **U-Save Auto Rental** (360-293-8686) in Anacortes.

PUBLIC TRANSIT

WHATCOM TRANSPORTATION AUTHORITY (WTA) ✆ *360-676-7433* ✐ *www.ridewta.com* WTA provides public transit in Lynden, Bellingham, Blaine, Birch Bay, Ferndale and Gooseberry Point.

SKAGIT TRANSIT ✆ *360-757-4433* ✐ *www.skagittransit.org* This agency services the Mt. Vernon, Sedro Woolley, Anacortes and Burlington areas.

EVERETT TRANSIT ✆ *425-257-7777* In Everett you can get just about anywhere for 50 cents via this agency.

ISLAND TRANSIT ✆ *360-678-7771, 800-240-8747* ✐ *www.islandtransit.org* This transit service covers Whidbey Island, with scheduled stops at Deception Pass, Oak Harbor, Coupeville, the Keystone Ferry, Greenbank, Freeland, Langley and the Clinton Ferry.

In smaller towns like La Conner and Mt. Vernon and on most of the islands there are no public transportation systems set up; check the Yellow Pages for taxi service.

TAXIS

A cab company serving the Bellingham International Airport is **City Cab, Inc./Yellow Cab** (360-733-8294). For service from the Friday Harbor Airport contact **Bob's Taxi Service** (360-378-3550). **Triangle Taxi** (360-293-3979) serves the Anacortes Airport.

OLYMPIC PENINSULA & WASHINGTON COAST

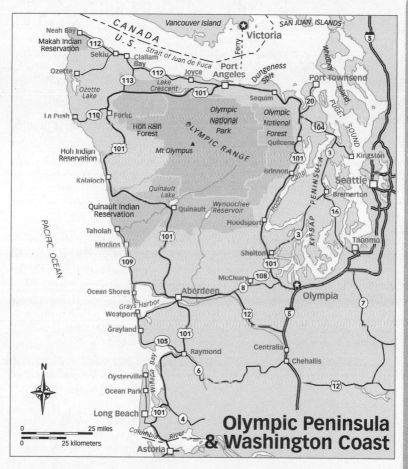

Olympic Peninsula & Washington Coast

One of the most spectacular sights for many Pacific Northwest visitors is sitting on the dock of the bay (Seattle's Elliott Bay, that is) watching the sun set behind the stark profile of the Olympic Mountains. The area is even more memorable looking from the inside out.

The Olympic Peninsula is a vast promontory bounded on the east by Puget Sound, the west by the Pacific Ocean and the north by the Strait of Juan de Fuca.

At the foot of the Olympic Mountains, this region often may be dry when it's pouring rain just a few miles south. With no major city—the largest town is Port Angeles, a community of only 19,000 people—it retains a feeling of country living on the edge of wilderness, which indeed it is. Remote it may be but the Olympic Peninsula is where much of the seattle Metropolitan area comes to play. Be sure to make reservations when possible at lodges, motels and campgrounds or arrive very early to get a spot, especially on weekends.

Olympic National Park, which dominates the peninsula, is a primeval place where eternal glaciers drop suddenly off sheer rock faces into nearly impenetrable rainforest, where America's largest herd of Roosevelt elk roams unseen by all but the most intrepid human eyes, where an impossibly rocky, protected coastline (at 73 miles, the longest wilderness beach in the lower 48) cradles primitive marine life forms as it has done for millions of years. No fewer than five Indian reservations speckle sections of a coast famed as much for its shipwrecks as for its salmon fishing.

South of the national park, the Washington coast extends down the Northwest's finest sand beaches and around two enormous river estuaries, to the mouth of the Columbia River and the state of Oregon. In this region, two towns have become major resort centers: Ocean Shores and Long Beach.

The Washington coast is known for its heavy rainfall, and justifiably so. Although the Olympics are not high by many standards—its tallest peaks are under 8000 feet—they catch huge amounts of precipitation blowing in from the Pacific Ocean. So much snow falls that more than 60 glaciers survive at elevations as low as 4500 feet. Even greater amounts fall on the windward slopes: 120 to 167 inches a year and more in the Forks area. Not only does this foster the rapid growth of mushrooms and slugs, but it has also led to the creation of North America's greatest rainforest in the soggy Hoh River valley. Yet a mere 40 miles away as the raven flies, Sequim—in the Olympic rain shadow—is a comparative desert, with only about 15 inches of rain per year.

The first residents of the peninsula and coast were tribes like the Makah, Ozette and Quileute, whose descendants still inhabit the area today. A seafaring people noted for their woodcarving, they lived in a series of longhouses facing the sea and are known to have inhabited this region for as long as 2500 years.

Their first contact with Europeans came in 1775, when they massacred a Spanish landing party. Three years later, the ubiquitous British captain James Cook sailed the coast and traded for sea otter furs with Vancouver Island natives; his report opened the gates to the maritime fur trade.

American entrepreneur John Jacob Astor established a fort at the mouth of the Columbia River in 1803, and two years later Meriwether Lewis and William Clark led a cross-country expedition that arrived at Cape Disappointment, on the Washington side of the Columbia, in the winter of 1805. White settlement was at first slow, but by the mid-19th century Port Townsend had established itself as Puget Sound's premier lumber-shipping port, and other communities sprang up soon after.

Olympic National Park was annexed to the national park system in 1938. But long before that, Washingtonians had discovered its natural wonders. A fledgling tourism industry grew, with lodges constructed at several strategic locations around the park, including lakes Crescent and Quinault, Sol Duc Hot Springs and Kalaloch, overlooking the Pacific. Coastal communities were also building a visitor infrastructure, and quiet beach resorts soon emerged.

Today, typical Olympic Peninsula visitors start their tour in Port Townsend, having traveled by ferry and car from Seattle or Whidbey Island, and use Route 101 as their artery of exploration. Port Townsend is considered the most authentic Victorian seacoast town in the United States north of San Francisco, and its plethora of well-preserved 19th-century buildings, many of them now bed and breakfasts, charms all visitors. Less than an hour's drive west, the seven-mile Dungeness Spit (a national wildlife refuge) is the largest natural sand hook in the United States and is famed for the delectable crabs that share its name. Port Angeles, in the center of the north coast, is home to the headquarters of Olympic National Park and is its primary gateway. The bustling international port town also has a direct ferry link to Victoria, Canada, across the Strait of Juan de Fuca.

Neah Bay, the northwesternmost community in the continental United States, is the home of the Makah Indian Museum and Cultural Center and an important marina for deep-sea fishing charters. Clallam Bay, to its east, and La Push, south down the coast, are other sportfishing centers. The logging town of Forks is the portal for visitors to the national park's Hoh Rainforest.

Route 101 emerges from the damp Olympic forests to slightly less moist Grays Harbor, with its twin lumber port towns of Aberdeen and Hoquiam. Though these towns combined have a population of over 25,000, they have limited appeal to travelers, who typically head over the north shore of Grays Harbor to the hotels of Ocean Shores, or down the south shore of the harbor to the quaint fishing village of Westport.

Serene Willapa Bay is another huge river estuary south of Grays Harbor. The resort strip of 28-mile-long Long Beach Peninsula, which provides a seaward dike for the bay, is older and less contrived than the Ocean Shores area. Wildlife refuges, oyster farms and cranberry bogs lend it a sort of 1950s Cape Cod ambience.

PORT TOWNSEND AREA

Before either Seattle or Tacoma were so much as a tug on a fisherman's line, Port Townsend was a thriving lumber port. Founded in 1851, it has retained its Victorian seacoast ambience better than any other community north of San Francisco. Much of the city has been designated a National Historic Landmark district, with more than 70 Victorian houses, buildings, forts, parks and monuments. Many of the handsomely gabled homes are open for tours and/or offer bed-and-breakfast accommodations.

SIGHTS

PORT TOWNSEND CHAMBER OF COMMERCE ⊠2437 East Sims Way, Port Townsend ☎360-385-2722, 888-365-6978 ⌨www.enjoypt.com, info@pt chamber.org The best way to see **Port Townsend** is on foot. When you drive into town on Route 20, you'll first want to stop at this visitors center for maps, brochures and event information. Then continue east on Route 20 as it becomes Water Street.

JEFFERSON COUNTY HISTORICAL SOCIETY MUSEUM ⊠540 Water Street, Port Townsend ☎360-385-1003 ☎360-385-1042 ⌨www.jchsmuseum. org, marsha@jchswa.org In Port Townsend's restored 1892 **City Hall** build-

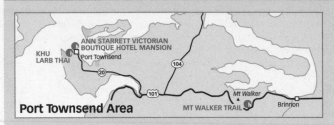

Port Townsend Area

KHU LARB THAI

PAGE 174

First Thai restaurant on the peninsula—piquant curries and creamy pad thai

ANN STARRETT VICTORIAN BOUTIQUE HOTEL MANSION

PAGE 173

Luxurious mansion-turned-hotel with frescoed ceilings and a free-hung spiral staircase

MT. WALKER TRAIL

PAGE 217

Ascending two-mile trail through a bright, multicolored rhododendron forest

ing, you'll find this museum, featuring Victorian antiques and artifacts. Closed weekdays in January and February. Admission.

Heading west on Water Street by foot, note the elegant stone and wood-frame buildings on either side of the street, most of them dating from the 1880s and 1890s.

ENOCH S. FOWLER BUILDING ✉*Corner of Polk and Washington streets, Port Townsend* From Water Street, turn right on Adams Street; halfway up the block on the right is this historical building, built in 1874, the oldest two-story stone structure in Washington. A former county courthouse, it now houses the weekly newspaper.

JAMES HOUSE ✉*1238 Washington Street, Port Townsend* ☎*360-385-1238, 800-385-1238* 📠*360-379-5551* ✐*www.jameshouse.com, info@jameshouse.com* Turn left at Washington Street and five blocks farther, on your left, you'll see this historical home, built in 1889. It has five chimneys and a commanding view of the harbor—and in 1973 became the Northwest's first bed and breakfast.

CAPTAIN ENOCH S. FOWLER HOME ✉*Franklin and Polk streets, Port Townsend; From Washington Street turn right up Harrison Street, then right again at Franklin Street and walk for two blocks* Built in 1860, this is the oldest surviving house in Port Townsend. It is typical of New England–style homes and has been registered as a National Historic Landmark.

ROTHSCHILD HOUSE ✉*Franklin and Taylor streets, Port Townsend* ✆*360-379-8076* ⌖*www.jchsmuseum.org* Two more blocks east, you will encounter this historic house, built in 1868 by an early Port Townsend merchant. Notable for its outstanding interior woodwork, it's maintained by the Jefferson County Historical Society for public tours. Closed October through April. Admission.

TRINITY METHODIST CHURCH ✉*609 Taylor Street, Port Townsend* ✆*360-385-0484* A block north of the Rothschild House, this church (1871) is the state's oldest standing Methodist church. Its small museum contains the Bible of the church's first minister.

ANN STARRETT VICTORIAN BOUTIQUE HOTEL MANSION

✉*744 Clay Street, Port Townsend* ✆*360-385-3205, 800-321-0644* ⌖*www.starrettmansion.com, info@starrettmansion.com* A block east of the Trinity Methodist Church is this 1889 mansion, now an inn. The Starrett offers public tours from noon until three during the months of July and August. Admission.

LUCINDA HASTINGS HOME ✉*Clay and Monroe streets, Port Townsend* At a cost of $14,000, this was the most expensive house ever built in Port Townsend when it was erected in 1889. Today, it houses several retail offices.

Turn right at the Hastings Home, and return down Monroe to Water Street and your starting point at City Hall. Get back in your car and drive north on Monroe Street. (The arterial staggers a half-block right at Roosevelt Street onto Jackson Street, then turns right onto Walnut Street.)

FORT WORDEN STATE PARK ✉*Port Townsend* ✆*360-344-4400* ⌖*www.parks.wa.gov/fortworden* All roads flow into W Street, the south boundary of **Fort Worden State Park Conference Center**. If the fort looks familiar, it could be because it was used in the filming of the Richard Gere–Debra Winger classic, *An Officer and a Gentleman*. Authorized in 1896, it includes officers' row and a refurbished **Commanding Officer's House** (limited hours from September through mid-May, admission), the **248th Coast Artillery Museum** (admission), gun emplacements, a concert pavilion, marine interpretive center and **Point Wilson Lighthouse**. Fort Worden offers stretches of beach that command impressive views of the Cascades and nearby islands.

PORT TOWNSEND MARINE SCIENCE CENTER ✉*Port Townsend* ✆*360-385-5582, 800-566-3932* 📠*360-385-7248* ⌖*www.ptmsc.org, info@ptmsc.org* On the dock at Fort Worden is this marine science center. Of special interest are its four large touch tanks, representing different intertidal habitats, where creatures like starfish, anemones and sea cucumbers can be handled by curious visitors. The adjoining natural history exhibit explores the region's geography over time. Daily guided walks as well as a birding boat trip around Protection Island National Wildlife Refuge are offered in the summer for a steep fee. Hours vary seasonally; call ahead. Admission.

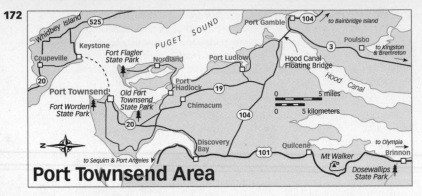

Port Townsend Area

HOOD CANAL FLOATING BRIDGE   Visitors driving to Port Townsend typically cross this one-and-a-half-mile floating bridge on Route 104 from the Kitsap Peninsula. Located 30 miles southeast of Port Townsend, it is the world's only floating bridge erected over tidal waters and one of the longest of its kind anywhere. Constructed in 1961, the bridge was washed away during a fierce storm in February 1979, but was rebuilt in 1982.

OLYMPIC MUSIC FESTIVAL   ✆360-732-4800   📠360-732-4803   ✐www. olympicmusicfestival.org, info@olympicmusicfestival.org   Chamber music doesn't come much more idyllic than this annual summer concert, held on a farm just south of Port Townsend between late June and early September. Founded by members of the Philadelphia String Quartet in 1984, the much-loved weekend Concerts in the Barn now attract more than 12,000 people a year. Concerts are held rain or shine on Saturday and Sunday.

QUILCENE   Traveling south from Port Townsend, Route 20 joins Route 101 at Discovery Bay. Twelve miles south of the junction is this town on the Hood Canal, a serpentine finger of Puget Sound. The town is especially noted for its oyster farming and processing and is the location of a state shellfish research laboratory (not open to the public).

MOUNT WALKER OBSERVATION POINT   This observation point—five miles south on Route 101, then another five miles on a gravel road that starts at Walker Pass—offers a spectacular view of the Hood Canal and surrounding area. On a clear day, you can see Seattle and the Space Needle.

LODGING

JAMES HOUSE _____

$$$ 10 ROOMS   ✉1238 Washington Street, Port Townsend
✆360-385-1238, 800-385-1238   📠360-379-5551   ✐www.jameshouse.com, info@jameshouse.com
Just a few steps from shops and restaurants at the foot of the bluff that stands behind lower downtown, it dates from 1889, though

it's only been a bed and breakfast since 1973. The house is unmistakable for its five chimneys; inside, the floors are all parquet. All rooms have private baths; some have fireplaces or garden views. There is a fireplace and a library, and a full breakfast is served. Save a few moments to enjoy the English gardens with an impressive view of the water. Two bungalow-style units, adjacent to the James House, are also available. Kids over 12 are welcome.

PALACE HOTEL

$$–$$$$ 15 ROOMS ✉1004 Water Street, Port Townsend
📞360-385-0773, 800-962-0741 📠360-385-0780 ✐www.palacehotelpt.com,
palace@olympus.net

For those less than enthralled with bed and breakfasts, this hotel provides historic accommodations in a former seafarers' bordello. Though nicely renovated, this is a bit rustic: After checking in at the main lobby you must climb a long flight of stairs (or two) to your room. Each guest chamber has antiques recalling the red-light flavor of the past.

ANN STARRETT VICTORIAN BOUTIQUE HOTEL MANSION

$$$–$$$$ 11 ROOMS ✉744 Clay Street, Port Townsend 📞360-385-3205,
800-321-0644 ✐www.starrettmansion.com, info@starrettmansion.com

This renowned boutique hotel, a National Historic Landmark built in 1889, is a classic mansion in Victorian style. High on a bluff overlooking downtown Port Townsend and Puget Sound, it combines diverse architectural elements—frescoed ceilings, a tree-hung spiral staircase, an eight-sided dome painted as a solar calendar, the requisite gables and dormer window—into a charming whole. The guest rooms all have private baths and are furnished with antiques, of course. Five-night minimum from November through Christmas.

THE TIDES INN

$$–$$$ 44 ROOMS ✉1807 Water Street, Port Townsend 📞360-385-0595,
800-822-8696 📠360-379-1115 ✐www.tides-inn.com, tidesinn@cablespeed.com

With so many heritage choices, few visitors actually opt for a motel stay. If you do, check out this inn, along the waterfront at the south end of town. Among the rooms are five efficiencies and 29 with hot tubs; most units have balconies overlooking the bay.

PILOT'S COTTAGE

$$ 2 ROOMS ✉327 Jackson Street, Port Townsend 📞360-379-0811
✐www.pilotscottage.com

Built in 1936 for use by pilots guiding ships through the Strait of Juan de Fuca, the two-bedroom, weathered-shingle cottage here exudes simple rustic charm and atmosphere from its quiet waterfront location overlooking Point Hudson Harbor. Amenities include a kitchen, living room and wood-burning stove. No smoking or pets. It's walking distance to downtown.

HI-OLYMPIC HOSTEL

$ 13 UNITS   ✉Fort Worden State Park, 272 Battery Way, Port Townsend   📞360-385-0655, 800-909-4776   🖳www.olympichostel.org, olympichostel@olympus.net

For students and backpackers, this hostel offers some of the least expensive accommodations on the Olympic Peninsula. Housed in a former World War II barracks building, it has dormitory beds and several private rooms for couples and families.

THE RESORT AT PORT LUDLOW

$$$$ 41 UNITS   ✉1 Heron Road, Port Ludlow   📞360-437-7000, 877-805-0868   📠360-437-7410   🖳www.portludlowresort.com, info@portludlowresort.com

South of town about 20 miles, this resort is one of the Northwest's premier family lodgings. It boasts a championship golf course, tennis courts, a marina, 15 miles of hiking and biking trails and 1500 acres of land. There are guest rooms with fireplaces, condominiums and one beach house. Other amenities include oversized jetted tubs and decks, and a restaurant with marvelous views of water and mountains.

DINING

CASTLE KEY RESTAURANT AND LOUNGE

$$$–$$$$ CONTINENTAL   ✉Manresa Castle, 7th and Sheridan streets, Port Townsend   📞360-379-1990   📠360-385-5883   🖳www.manresacastle.com, info@manresacastle.com

Located in an 1892 hilltop inn that overlooks the town and bay like a German castle on the Rhine River, Castle Key combines an elegant restaurant and an Edwardian pub. The menu offers regional and seasonal specialties, everything from jambalaya to butterflied tiger prawns. Sunday brunch is also served. Closed Monday and Tuesday.

FOUNTAIN CAFÉ

$$ SEAFOOD/PACIFIC NORTHWEST   ✉920 Washington Street, Port Townsend   📞360-385-1364

Ask locals where to eat, and chances are they'll recommend this café. You'll probably have to stand in line for a seat, but the wait will be worth it. Occupying the ground floor of a historic building, the Fountain serves outstanding seafood, including pan-fried oysters and fresh shrimp. Soups, pasta and desserts are homemade. The decor is eclectic and showcases young local artists.

KHU LARB THAI

$$ THAI   ✉225 Adams Street, Port Townsend   📞360-385-5023   🖳www.khularbthai.com, khularbthai45@msn.com

The first Thai restaurant on the Olympic Peninsula (opened in 1989), Khu Larb is still the best in Washington. Curries are rich, piquant and flavorful, and the pad thai tantalizes the taste buds. The restaurant has a number of Thai–Northwestern fusion dishes on its menu, such as pan-fried halibut steak seasoned with curry, lemongrass and kaffir lime. Closed Monday.

SALAL CAFE

$–$$ AMERICAN   ✉*634 Water Street, Port Townsend*   ☎*360-385-6532*

Breakfasts draw full houses at this café. Huge omelettes and various seafood and vegetarian recipes get *oohs* and *ahs*, as do the burgers and meat dishes. Lunch features gourmet home-style cooking, along with crêpes and sandwiches. No dinner.

SHANGHAI RESTAURANT

$–$$ CHINESE   ✉*265 Hudson Street, Point Hudson, Port Townsend* ☎*360-385-4810*   📠*360-385-0660*   ✐*www.ptshanghai.info*

Some say this restaurant serves the best Chinese food this side of Vancouver's Chinatown. Forget the view of the RV park across the street, and enjoy the spicy Szechuan and northern Chinese cuisine.

CHIMACUM CAFÉ

$–$$ AMERICAN   ✉*9253 Rhody Drive, Chimacum*   ☎*360-732-4631*

The Chimacum, nine miles south of Port Townsend, is a local institution. This is food like Grandma should have made—country-fried chicken dinners, baked ham and so forth, followed, of course, by homemade pies brimming with fresh fruit. Breakfast, lunch and dinner are served.

SHOPPING

Port Townsend offers the most interesting shopping on the peninsula with its array of galleries, antique and gift shops, bookstores, gourmet dining and all-purpose emporiums. Proprietors have paid particular attention to historical accuracy in restoring commercial buildings. Many of the shops feature the work of talented local painters, sculptors, weavers, potters, poets and writers.

PORT TOWNSEND ANTIQUE MALL ✉*Antique Mall, 802 Washington Street, Port Townsend* ☎*360-379-8069* If you're looking for antiques, try this antique mall or any of the many other shops along the 600 through 1200 blocks of Water or Washington streets.

NIGHTLIFE

LANZA'S RISTORANTE ✉*1020 Lawrence Street, Port Townsend* ☎*360-379-1900* Live jazz music accompanies dinner at Lanza's on the weekend. Closed Sunday and Monday.

BEACHES & PARKS

FORT WORDEN STATE PARK

✉*The entrance is located on W Street at Cherry Street, at the northern city limits of Port Townsend.*   ☎*360-344-4431*   📠*360-385-7248*   ✐*fwcamping@parks.wa.gov*

🚶 🚲 🚠 🛶 ⛵ 🏊 ♨ 🚤 ⛴ A 434-acre estate right in Port Townsend, this turn-of-the-20th-century fort includes restored Victorian officers houses, barracks, theater, parade grounds and artillery bunkers.

A beach and a boat launch are on Admiralty Inlet, at the head of Puget Sound. Try the dock or beach for salmon fishing. Restrooms, picnic areas, tennis courts and lodging are found here.

▲ There are 80 RV hookup sites ($37 to $38 per night). Primitive sites are also available ($21 per night). Reservations, by mail, by fax or via the internet, are strongly recommended year-round. Reservations: 200 Battery Way, Port Townsend, WA 98368.

KAH TAI LAGOON NATURE PARK
✉ *12th Street near Sims Way, Port Townsend*

🚶 🚲 This midtown park, which features 21 acres of wetlands and 40 acres of grasslands and woodlands, is a great place for birdwatching: More than 50 species have been identified here. There are two and a half miles of trails, a play area for kids, interpretive displays, restrooms and picnic areas.

OLD FORT TOWNSEND STATE PARK
✉ *Old Fort Townsend Road, two miles south of the town of Port Townsend off Route 20*
📞 *360-385-3595, 360-385-3595* 📠 *360-385-7248*

🚶 🚲 🎣 ⚓ Decommissioned in 1895 when American Indian attacks on Port Townsend (the town) were no longer a threat, the fort site has six and a half miles of trails and a beach on Port Townsend (the inlet). You can fish from the shore. You'll find restrooms and picnic areas. Closed October through April. Day-use fee, $7.

▲ There are 40 standard sites ($18 to $25 per night). Closed early November to mid-April.

FORT FLAGLER STATE PARK
✉ *Off Route 116, on the north tip of Marrowstone Island, eight miles northeast of Hadlock*
📞 *360-385-1259, 888-226-7688* 📠 *360-379-1746*

🚶 🚲 ⚓ 🎣 ⚓ ⚓ ⚓ ⚓ Fort buildings dating from 1898 are a major attraction here. In addition, the saltwater beach on Admiralty Inlet is popular for clamming, beachcombing and fishing for salmon, halibut, sole, crab and shellfish. There are also a boat launch, hiking trails, restrooms, picnic areas and lodging.

▲ There are 101 standard sites ($19 to $25 per night) and 12 RV hookup sites ($25 per night). No camping November through February. Reservations: 888-226-7688.

DOSEWALLIPS STATE PARK
✉ *Route 101, in Brinnon, 37 miles south of Port Townsend* 📞 *360-796-4415*
📠 *360-796-3242*

🚶 🚲 ⚓ ⚓ At the mouth of the Dosewallips River on the Hood Canal, a long, serpentine arm of Puget Sound, this 425-acre park is especially popular among clam diggers and oyster hunters during shellfish season. Five miles of scenic hiking trails also lace through the park, winding through forests of hemlock and Douglas fir. You'll find restrooms, showers and picnic areas.

▲ There are 100 standard sites ($19 per night) and 40 RV hookup sites ($26 per night). Reservations: 888-226-7688.

OLYMPIC
NATIONAL FOREST _____ idden

✉*Numerous access roads branch off Route 101, especially south of Sequim, and between Quilcene and Hoodsport, on the east side of the Olympic Peninsula.* 📞*360-956-2402* 📠*360-956-2330*

🏃🚴🎣 ⛵ 🚤 🛶 🚣 ⛵ ⌐ Surrounding Olympic National Park on its east, south and northwest sides, this national forest provides ample recreational opportunities, including good fishing for trout and, in some areas, for rock cod and salmon in the forest's many lakes and rivers. The Sol Duc River, within the Sol Duc River Valley here, is one of the few places where salmon run year-round. The forest includes five wilderness areas on the fringe of the park. There are restrooms and picnic areas. Dogs are allowed in the national forest, but not in Olympic National Park. Some areas of the park and some campgrounds close seasonally.

▲ There are 23 campgrounds throughout the forest. Camping costs range from free to $12 to $18 per night. Three cabins, sleeping four to six people, rent for $60 per night.

PORT ANGELES AREA

The northern gateway to Olympic National Park as well as a major terminal for ferries to British Columbia, the Port Angeles area is one of northwest Washington's main crossroads. Sequim on Route 101, 31 miles west of Port Townsend, and nearby Port Angeles are two of the peninsula's more intriguing towns.

SIGHTS

SEQUIM The town of Sequim (pronounced "Squim") is graced with a climate that's unusually dry and mild for the Northwest: it sits in the Olympic rain shadow. The mild weather has made Sequim a leading retirement area, resulting in the fastest growth in Washington. In 1990, the greater Sequim area had just 4000 residents; by 2000 it had 25,000, and today the population is 70,000.

OLYMPIC GAME FARM ✉*1423 Ward Road, Sequim* 📞*360-683-4295, 800-778-4295* 🖱*www.olygamefarm.com, info@gamefarm.com* A major attraction just north of town is this farm, whose animals—wolves, tigers, bears, buffalo and many others—are trained for film roles. Driving tours of the farm are available year-round; walking tours, including a studio barn, are offered from May through September. Admission.

MUSEUM AND ART CENTER _____ idden

✉*175 West Cedar Street, Sequim* 📞*360-683-8110* 🖱*www.macsequim.org, info@macsequim.org* In the Sequim–Dungeness Valley area, this museum preserves the native and pioneer farming heritage of Sequim and showcases the work of local artists, including Northwest American Indians. Past exhibits have included works by the Jamestown S'Klallam tribe, whose reservation is in town. Closed Sunday and Monday.

SEQUIM–DUNGENESS CHAMBER OF COMMERCE VISITORS CENTER ✉*1192 East Washington Street, Sequim* ☎*360-683-6197, 800-737-8462* 🖷*360-683-6349* 🖳*www.cityofsequim.com, info@cityofsequim.com* For visitor information, contact this helpful center. They can recommend great sights as well as help with lodging and dining needs.

North off Route 101, the Dungeness Valley is dotted with lavender, strawberry and raspberry fields. Weathered barns left over from the area's dairy farming days are still visible.

CEDARBROOK LAVENDER & HERB FARM ✉*1345 Sequim Avenue South, Sequim* ☎*360-683-7733, 800-470-8423* 🖳*www.cedarbrookherbfarm.com, marcella@cedarbrookherbfarm.com* Pay a visit to this sweeping farm, where 70 different varieties of lavender and 200 herbs and perennials fill the air with a marvelous (but indefinable!) aroma and inspire many a gourmet chef to go on a culinary buying spree. Closed in January.

DUNGENESS SPIT ———————————
Opposite the mouth of the Dungeness River is one of the Olympic Peninsula's most remarkable natural features: the Dungeness Spit, almost seven miles long and the largest natural sand hook in the U.S. The spit and the surrounding bay and estuary are teeming with wildlife, including seabirds, seals, fish and crabs. A short trail within the adjacent **Dungeness Recreation Area** provides access to this national wildlife refuge.

NEW DUNGENESS LIGHTHOUSE ☎*360-683-6638* 🖷*360-683-1251* 🖳*www.newdungenesslighthouse.com, lightkeepers@newdungenesslighthouse.com* At the end of the Dungeness Spit, this lighthouse rises 63 feet above the sea. Established in 1857, it is now on the National Register of Historic Places. Visitors who brave the five-and-a-half-mile walk out along the spit will be rewarded with an in-depth tour of the facilities.

CITY PIER ✉*Port Angeles* ☎*360-417-4557* Seventeen miles west of Sequim on Route 101 is the fishing and logging port of **Port Angeles**, the Olympic Peninsula's largest town. A major attraction here is the City Pier. East of the ferry terminal, it boasts an observation tower, promenade decks and a picnic area.

ARTHUR D. FEIRO MARINE LIFE CENTER ✉*315 North Lincoln Street, Port Angeles* ☎*360-417-6254* 🖳*www.olypen.com/feirolab, feirolab@olypen.com* Visitors can observe and even touch samples of local marine life at this center, which is found at the City Pier. Open weekends only in summer; limited hours the rest of the year. Admission.

OLYMPIC NATIONAL PARK VISITOR CENTER ✉*3002 Mt. Angeles Road, Port Angeles* ☎*360-565-3130* 🖳*www.nps.gov/olym* As the gateway to Olympic National Park, Port Angeles is home to national park headquarters.

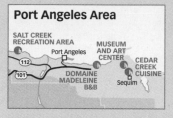

Port Angeles Area

SALT CREEK RECREATION AREA

PAGE 183

One-of-a-kind tidepool sanctuary with starfish, sea anemones, barnacles and mussels

DOMAINE MADELEINE BED AND BREAKFAST

PAGE 180

Romantic seaside inn surrounded by wildflowers offering panoramic ocean views

MUSEUM AND ART CENTER

PAGE 177

Gallery showcasing local history, including American Indian tools, jewelry, art and artifacts

CEDAR CREEK CUISINE

PAGE 181

Delightful restaurant set in a historic physician's office with Italian-inspired Northwest cuisine

At the visitor center, you'll find an excellent video and exhibits on the natural and human history of the park. Usually open daily in the summer, varying hours the rest of the year.

PORT ANGELES FINE ARTS CENTER ✉*Take Route 101 westbound to Race Street and the Olympic National Park Hurricane Ridge turnoff. Turn left (south) and proceed one mile towards Hurricane Ridge. Turn left (east) on Lauridsen Boulevard and proceed one-quarter mile to PAFAC parking adjacent to a domed water silo.* ☎*360-417-4590, 360-457-3532* ⌖*www.pafac.org, info@pafac.org* Nestled in the shadow of Olympic National Park, this award-winning center is located in a leafy five-acre sculpture park and hosts rotating multimedia exhibitions, lectures and concerts. Closed Monday and Tuesday.

MUSEUM AT THE CARNEGIE ✉*207 South Lincoln Street, Port Angeles* ☎*360-452-2662* ⌖*www.clallamhistoricalsociety.com, artifact@olypen.com* This museum houses a permanent exhibit about the history of Clallam County that includes period clothing and old photos. Displays in the lower level rotate annually. Closed Sunday through Tuesday.

For tourist information, contact the **Olympic Peninsula Visitor Bureau** (338 West 1st Street, Port Angeles; 360-452-8552, 800-942-4042; www.olympicpeninsula.org, info@olympicpeninsula.org).

LODGING

SEQUIM BAY RESORT

$–$$ 8 UNITS   ✉2634 West Sequim Bay Road, Sequim   ☎360-681-3853

☎360-681-3854   🖱www.sequimbayresort.com, sequimbayresort@yahoo.com

You'll feel good right down to your cockles—as well as your steamer clams and horse clams—after shellfishing on the saltwater beach outside this waterfront resort. The eight fully equipped housekeeping cottages here are suitable for vacationing families and shoreline lovers. There are guest laundry facilities, free wi-fi and 42 hookups for RVs. Two-night minimum stay required.

DOMAINE MADELEINE BED AND BREAKFAST

$$$$ 5 ROOMS   ✉146 Wildflower Lane, Sequim   ☎360-457-4174,

888-811-8376   ☎360-457-3037   🖱www.domainemadeleine.com,

romance@domainemadeleine.com

Situated on the water with beautiful gardens and spectacular views of the San Juan Islands, the Domaine Madeleine excels in both comfort and hospitality. There's the Renoir Suite, with a 14-foot-high basalt fireplace and impressionist art, and the Ming Room, with antiques, a jacuzzi and a large private balcony. All rooms have wi-fi access, fireplaces, feather beds and French perfumes; some boast jacuzzis. Relax in the cozy coffee nook or try your hand at the antique organ. The full gourmet breakfast is elegantly presented—don't miss it. Gay-friendly.

GROVELAND COTTAGE

$$ 4 ROOMS   ✉4861 Sequim-Dungeness Way, Dungeness

☎360-683-3565, 800-879-8859   ☎360-683-5181

🖱www.sequimvalley.com/groveland.mv, simone@olypen.com

Just a spit from the Spit—Dungeness, that is—is this charming cottage, by the coast north of Sequim. The early 20th-century building has rooms with art, antique decor and private baths; some boast jacuzzis and fireplaces. There is also a private cottage with a king-sized bed and private bath. The rooms may be simple, but service is not: Fresh coffee is served in the communal areas of the house before the hostess, Simone, serves her gourmet three-course breakfast. Wi-fi is available in all rooms. The overall accent is on comfort.

RED LION HOTEL

$$$$ 187 ROOMS   ✉221 North Lincoln Street, Port Angeles   ☎360-452-9215,

800-733-5466   ☎360-452-4734   🖱www.redlionportangeles.com,

portangelessales@redlion.com

Perhaps the nicest motel-style accommodation in these port communities is the Red Lion. A modern building that extends along the Strait of Juan de Fuca opposite the ferry dock, it offers rooms with private balconies overlooking the water. A strand of beach and swimming pool beckon bathers.

THE TUDOR INN

$$$ 5 ROOMS   ✉1108 South Oak Street, Port Angeles   ☏360-452-3138, 866-286-2224   📠360-457-9360   ⌨www.tudorinn.com, info@tudorinn.com

Victoria, across the strait on Vancouver Island, is said to be "more British than the British"—but the same slogan could almost apply to The Tudor Inn. The host serves a gourmet breakfast and afternoon refreshment in the restored Tudor-style home. Most of their antique collection is Old English, and the well-stocked library will steer you to books on a wide variety of subjects. All rooms have private baths; one has a gas fireplace and small balcony.

DINING

EL CAZADOR

$$ MEXICAN   ✉531 West Washington Street, Sequim   ☏360-683-4788
⌨www.el-cazador.com, info@el-cazador.com

This is a casual, family-run restaurant with festive murals. What sets it apart is its use of fresh seafood in traditional Mexican dishes that consistently win local "best of" awards. The burrito à la Veracruz—stuffed with shrimp, crab, carrots and bell peppers—is especially good.

CEDAR CREEK CUISINE

$$$ SEAFOOD/ITALIAN   ✉665 North 5th Avenue, Sequim
☏360-683-3983   ⌨www.cedarcreekcuisine.com

A delightful surprise in the bucolic Dungeness Valley is this delicious restaurant, which occupies a rustic two-story, 1896 country physician's home and office. Menus, inspired both by Italian cuisine and fresh local seafood, range from wild salmon, pan-roasted ling cod and prawns to osso bucco and steak florentine. Seafood *arabbiata* is a standout.

C'EST SI BON

$$$–$$$$ FRENCH   ✉23 Cedar Park Road, Port Angeles   ☏360-452-8888
⌨www.cestsibon-frenchcuisine.com

The undisputed winner in the northern Olympic Peninsula fine-dining sweepstakes is C'est Si Bon. The decor is modern and dramatic, with handsome oil paintings and full picture windows allowing panoramas of the Olympic Range. The cuisine, on the other hand, is classical French: quails stuffed with mushrooms, veal, pork and chicken, coquilles St. Jacques, filet mignon with Dungeness crab. There are French wines and desserts, too. Dinner only. Closed Monday.

BELLA ITALIA

$$ ITALIAN/PACIFIC NORTHWEST ✉118 East 1st Street, Port Angeles
📞360-457-5442 📞360-457-6112 🖱www.bellaitaliapa.com,
reservations@bellaitaliapa.com

A New England reader raved about the clam linguine at this charming Italian restaurant, and *Wine Spectator* magazine gave it an award of excellence. Indeed, this restaurant specializing in Olympic Coast cuisine is a destination in itself for many Puget Sound–area foodies. In addition to a variety of pasta, this intimate, candlelit eatery whips up Tuscan steak, cioppino and veal Marsala. It also has an extensive wine selection. Dinner only.

PORT ANGELES CRABHOUSE — hidden

$$–$$$ SEAFOOD ✉221 North Lincoln Street, Port Angeles
📞360-457-0424 📞360-452-4734 🖱www.pacrabhouse.com

Located next to the Red Lion Hotel, this restaurant offers sweeping waterfront views in a casually elegant dining room. Simple and straightforward seafood dishes such as cracked Dungeness crab and grilled salmon are the specialties.

FIRST STREET HAVEN

$ AMERICAN ✉107 East 1st Street, Port Angeles 📞360-457-0352 📞360-452-8502

Practically next door to the Port Angeles Crabhouse is the First Street Haven, one of the best places around for quick and tasty breakfasts and lunches. Have a homemade quiche and salad, along with baked goods and the house coffee, and you'll be set for the day. Breakfast and lunch only, but no lunch on Sunday.

NIGHTLIFE

You didn't come to this part of the state for its nightlife, and that's good. What little there is usually exists only on Friday and Saturday nights.

PORT ANGELES CRABHOUSE LOUNGE ✉Red Lion Hotel, 221 North Lincoln Street, Port Angeles 📞360-457-0424 This waterfront lounge in the Red Lion Hotel features daily drink specials. A huge plasma TV offers entertainment.

BEACHES & PARKS

SEQUIM BAY STATE PARK — hidden

✉Route 101, four miles east of Sequim 📞360-683-4235 📞360-681-5054

Shellfish (clams, oysters and crabs) as well as fishing for salmon and halibut are the main attractions at this park on Sequim Bay, sheltered from rough seas by two spits at its mouth and from heavy rains by the Olympic rain shadow. Hiking trails extend less than two miles, but they provide tremendous beauty through cedar and maple trees. There's a beach; you'll also find a baseball field, tennis courts, restrooms and picnic areas.

▲ There are 45 standard sites ($20 to $23 per night), 15 RV hookup sites ($28 per night) and 3 hike- or bike-in primitive sites ($15 per night). Reservations: 888-226-7688.

DUNGENESS RECREATION AREA

✉️*Located at the base of the Dungeness Spit, five miles west of Sequim on Route 101, then four miles north on Kitchen-Dick Road* 📞*360-683-5847* 📠*360-683-5847*

🚶🚴🐎🚐🛥️🎣 The Dungeness Spit is a national wildlife refuge, but a recreation area trail provides access. Marine birds, bald eagles and seals are among the impressive wildlife to be seen; the Dungeness crab is internationally famous as a fine food. There are restrooms, showers and picnic areas.

▲ There are 66 sites (no hookups); $18 per night. Closed October through January.

SALT CREEK RECREATION AREA ___ ⓗidden

✉️*Located three miles north from Joyce (or 15 miles west from Port Angeles) on Route 112, then another three miles north on Camp Hayden Road* 📞*360-928-3441* 📠*360-417-2395, www.clallam.net/countyparks, ccps@olypen.com*

🚶🚴🐎🚐🛥️🎣 One of the finest tidepool sanctuaries on the Olympic Peninsula is this three-mile stretch of rocky beach. Starfish, sea urchins, anemones, mussels, barnacles and other invertebrate life can be observed . . . but not removed. Anglers will find rockfish. Restrooms, picnic areas, playground and hiking trails are all here.

▲ There are 51 standard sites ($16 to $18 per night) and 39 RV sites ($22 to $24 per night).

OLYMPIC NATIONAL PARK

The Olympic Peninsula's main attraction—in fact, the reason most tourists come here at all—is Olympic National Park. Rugged, glaciated mountains dominate the 1442-square-mile park, with rushing rivers tumbling from their slopes. The rainier western slopes harbor an extraordinary rainforest, and a separate 57-mile-long coastal strip preserves remarkable tidepools and marvelous ocean scenery. The land was originally set aside to protect the largest unmanaged herd of rare Roosevelt elk in the country and was almost named Elk National Park. But other wildlife in the park includes deer, black bears, cougars, bobcats, a great many smaller mammals and scores of bird species. Besides the main part of the park, which encompasses the entire mountain wilderness in the center of the peninsula and can be entered from the north or west, Olympic National Park includes a separate Coastal Unit spanning 73 miles of Pacific headlands and beaches.

OLYMPIC NATIONAL PARK VISITOR CENTER ✆360-565-3130
⌐www.nps.gov/olym There is no lack of facilities throughout the park: picnic areas, hotels, restaurants and groceries. For general information on the park, call the visitor center.

HURRICANE RIDGE LODGE ✆360-565-3131 The most direct route into the park from Port Angeles is the Heart of the Hills/Hurricane Ridge Road. It climbs 5240 feet in just 17 miles to this lodge, where there are breathtaking views to 7965-foot Mt. Olympus, the highest peak in the Olympic Range, and other glacier-shrouded mountains. Summer visitors to Hurricane Ridge can dine in the day lodge, picnic, enjoy nature walks or take longer hikes. In winter, enjoy the small downhill ski area here and many cross-country trails.

An alternate, scenic route from Port Angeles to the park is to take Route 112, which starts near Port Angeles and runs to Neah Bay on the northwest tip of the Olympic Peninsula. From Port Angeles, follow Route 101 west for five miles, then turn off to the right on Route 112. For much of its length, this narrow two-lane highway runs within sight of the Strait of Juan de Fuca and partly traces the water's edge. Travel 46 miles to the sister communities of **Clallam Bay** and **Sekiu** (pronounced "C-Q"). These are prime sportfishing grounds for salmon and huge bottomfish, especially halibut. Check out the wonderful tidepools north of Clallam Bay at **Slip Point**. Just west of Sekiu, at the mouth of the Hoko River, visitors can view the remains of a 2500-year-old Makah Indian fishing village at the **Hoko Archaeological Site**.

NEAH BAY ✉18 miles north of Seiku This rather bleak little village has a few motels and a commercial fishing fleet, and visitors can book charter-fishing excursions from the harbor.

MAKAH CULTURAL AND RESEARCH CENTER **h**idden
✉1880 Bay View Avenue, Neah Bay ✆360-645-2711 ☏360-645-2656
⌐www.makah.com, makahmuseum@centurytel.net Neah Bay's touristic centerpiece is this cultural research center, which houses finds from the Ozette Dig at Cape Alava, about 20 miles down the Pacific coast, interpreted through the eyes of the Makah themselves. Few relics remain from the ancient culture of the Northwest Coast tribes because their wooden structures and implements rotted away quickly in the damp climate. Ozette, however, was buried 500 years ago by a mudslide that preserved it from the elements until archaeologists discovered it in the late 1960s. The artifacts exhibited in an atmospheric longhouse setting at the cultural center include baskets, log canoes, clothing, wood carvings and whaling harpoons. Closed Monday and Tuesday from September through May. Admission.

CAPE FLATTERY The winding, scenic coastal drive to the end of Route 112 climaxes at Cape Flattery, the northwesternmost corner of the contiguous United States. The road at times runs within feet of the

MAKAH CULTURAL AND RESEARCH CENTER

PAGE 184

Authentic handmade Northwest Indian jewelry, carvings and baskets displayed at the Makah Reservation

RIALTO BEACH

PAGE 187

Secluded, silver beach scattered with seashells and stacks of ocean-polished driftwood

RIVER INN B&B

PAGE 189

Rustic chalet nestled on the banks of Bogachiel River with views of elk, deer and river otters

HOH RAINFOREST

PAGE 187

Rare coniferous rainforest virtually untouched by man—one of the wettest spots in North America

water, providing spectacular blufftop views of the Strait of Juan de Fuca and Tatoosh Island—a great location for whale watching between March and May. A short trail leads to the shore with its windswept beaches, strewn with driftwood and shipwrecks. Beach hikers can find some of the last wilderness coast in Washington south of here.

LAKE OZETTE Returning from Neah Bay on Route 112, two miles before you reach Sekiu a paved secondary road turns off to the south (right) and goes 20 miles to Lake Ozette, the northernmost part of Olympic National Park's Coastal Unit. The largest of the park's three lakes, and one of the most hidden spots you can reach by road in the park, it is separated from the ocean by a strip of land just three miles wide. Several trails lead from here to the sea, including the Indian Village Trail, which leads to the Ozette Dig (no longer open) at Cape Alava, and the Ozette Loop Trail, which weaves past 56 petroglyphs that depict various aspects of historic Makah life. Backcountry permits are required for all overnight trips in the park.

MEMORIALS Much of the Olympic coastline remains undeveloped. Hikers can wander along the high-water mark or on primitive trails, some wood-planked and raised above the forest floor. Offshore reefs have taken many lives over the centuries since European exploration began, and two memorials to shipwreck victims are good destinations for intrepid hikers. Nine miles south of Ozette, the **Norwegian Memorial** remembers seamen who died in an early-20th-century ship-

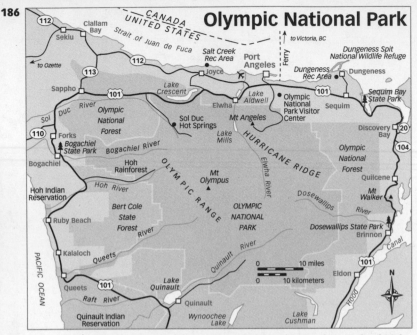

Olympic National Park

wreck. Six miles farther south, and about three miles north of Rialto Beach opposite La Push, the **Chilean Memorial** marks the grave of 20 South American sailors who died in a 1920 wreck.

LAKE CRESCENT   If you choose to take the more heavily traveled Route 101, 20 miles west of Port Angeles on Route 101 you'll come to Lake Crescent, one of three large lakes within park boundaries. Carved during the last Ice Age 10,000 years ago, it is nestled between steep forested hillsides. A unique subspecies of trout lures many anglers to its deep waters. There are several resorts, restaurants, campgrounds and picnic areas around the lake's shoreline. From National Park Service–administered **Lake Crescent Lodge** (416 Lake Crescent Road, Port Angeles; 360-928-3211, fax 360-928-3253; www.lakecresentlodge.com, lclodge@olypen.com), on the southeast shore, a three-quarter-mile trail leads up Barnes Creek to the beautiful **Marymere Falls**.

SOL DUC HOT SPRINGS   ☎ 866-476-5382 ☎ 360-327-3593 ✎ www.visitsolduc.com, info@visitsolduc.com   West of Lake Crescent, the Sol Duc River Road turns south to these hot springs, 12 miles off of Route 101. Long known to the Indians, the therapeutic mineral waters were discovered by a pioneer in 1880 and like everything else the white man touched, soon boasted an opulent resort. But the original burned to the ground in 1916 and today's refurbished resort, nestled in a valley of old-growth Douglas fir, is more rustic than elegant. The springs remain an attraction. Sol Duc is a major trailhead for backpacking trips into Olympic National Park; also located here is a ranger station. Closed November through mid-March.

SOL DUC FALLS

Often described as "thunderous," these falls are a beautiful contrast to the misty river of the same name. Shrouded by a thick evergreen forest, the trail leading to the cascades is equally enchanting.

FORKS

The main population center on the Olympic Coast, and the nearest to the Hoh Rainforest, is this lumber town. With over 3000 people, it is the largest town between Port Angeles and Hoquiam. (It's also Washington's rainiest town, with well over 100 inches a year.) Forks's economy recently found a new lease on life thanks to "vampire tourism"—fans who come to see the settings of Stephanie Meyer's phenomenally popular teen fantasy romances, the *Twilight* series, in which Forks is inhabited by high school vampires and the nearby Indian reservation by werewolves.

FORKS TIMBER MUSEUM ✉Route 101 South, Forks ☎360-374-9663 ☎360-374-9253 ⌨www.forkswa.com This museum is filled with exhibits of old-time logging equipment and historical photos, as well as pioneer and Indian artifacts. Interpretive trails, gardens and a logger memorial are next to the visitors center. Open April through October and by appointment in winter.

QUILEUTE INDIAN RESERVATION ☎360-374-6163 ☎360-374-6311 ⌨www.quileutenation.org On the coast 12 miles west of Forks is the 800-year-old American Indian fishing village of **La Push**, the center of this reservation. Sportfishing, camping and beach walking are popular year-round. An abandoned Coast Guard station and lighthouse here are used as a school for resident children.

RIALTO BEACH

A national park road eight miles west of Forks branches off La Push Road and follows the north shore of the Quileute River five miles to this beach, where spectacular piles of driftwood often accumulate. There are picnic areas and campgrounds here, and a trailhead for hikes north up the beach toward Cape Alava.

HOH RAINFOREST

This rainforest is 19 miles east of Route 101 via the Hoh River Road, 13 miles south of Forks. It's lauded as one of the only coniferous rainforests in the world. For national park information here, call the **Forks Ranger Station** (360-374-7566).

QUEETS RIVER ROAD   There's a less well-known rainforest at the end of this gravel, 19-mile river road, 14 miles off Route 101, 17 miles west of Quinault.

LAKE QUINAULT   On Route 101 at the southwestern corner of Olympic National Park this lake is the site of several resorts and campgrounds, including the venerable Lake Quinault Lodge. Water sports of all kinds are popular at this glacier-fed lake, surrounded by old-growth forest.

KALALOCH LODGE ✉️*Kalaloch Lodge: 157151 Route 101* 📞*360-962-2271, 866-525-2562* 📠*360-962-3391* ✎*www.visitkalaloch.com, info@visitkalaloch.com* The **Hoh Indian Reservation** is 25 miles south of Forks, off Route 101. Of more interest to most visitors is this lodge, 35 miles south of Forks on Route 101. A major national park facility, it affords spectacular ocean views at the southernmost end of the park's coastal strip.

OLYMPIC NATIONAL PARK COASTAL UNIT ——— **h**idden

This area includes some 3300 square miles of designated marine sanctuary both above and below water level. Although most of the 73-mile seacoast is unreachable by road, trails lead down to six diverse beaches from Route 101, including **Ozette**, **Kalaloch** and **Ruby**. Here you'll find broad, log-strewn expanses of sand, gravel stretches great for beachcombing and rocky tidepools teeming with tiny marine life.

LODGING

LAKE CRESCENT LODGE ——— **h**idden

$$–$$$ 37 UNITS   ✉️*416 Lake Crescent Road, 20 miles west of Port Angeles* 📞*360-928-3211* 📠*360-928-3253* ✎*www.lakecrescentlodge.com, lclodge@olypen.com*

Set on the south shore of gorgeous Lake Crescent, this 1916 lodge provides a variety of rooms and cottages with lake or mountain views. Units in the historic main building share bathrooms. Of the 17 cottages, four have fireplaces; if you don't opt for one of these, you can relax in front of the lobby's stone fireplace or in the sunroom. Amenities include an on-site restaurant and lounge, as well as rowboat rentals and wi-fi access. Pets are allowed to stay in the cottages with a daily charge. The main lodge in closed mid-October through April; the four fireplace cottages are open weekends only during this period (two-night minimum).

LOG CABIN RESORT

$$–$$$ 28 UNITS   ✉️*3183 East Beach Road, 21 miles west of Port Angeles* 📞*360-928-3325* 📠*360-928-2088* ✎*www.logcabinresort.net, reservations@logcabinresort.net*

This rustic resort is a historic landmark also on the shores of Lake Crescent along Route 101. Budget-watchers can stay in the cabins; more upscale are the lakeshore chalets and lodge guest rooms. There is also an

RV park with full hookups on Log Cabin Creek. The handsome log lodge has a restaurant and a gift shop; all manner of boats are rented at the marina. Closed October through April.

SOL DUC HOT SPRINGS RESORT

$$$–$$$$ 32 UNITS   ✉12076 Sol Duc Hot Springs Road, 40 miles west of Port Angeles 📞360-327-3583, 866-476-5382 📠360-327-3593 ✍www.visitsolduc.com, info@solduc.com

This historic property was originally built in 1910 around a series of hot sulphur pools 12 miles south of Route 101. The 32 cabins (11 with kitchens) were rebuilt in the mid-1980s and now have indoor plumbing. The River Suite is a three-bedroom house that sleeps ten. The best plunge, however, after a day of hiking or fishing, remains the water in three man-made mineral spring pools, kept between 98° and 104°F and cleaned nightly. There is also a full-size swimming pool. Camping sites and RV hookups are available. The resort is closed November to mid-March.

VAN RIPER'S RESORT

$–$$ 16 ROOMS   ✉280 Front Street, Sekiu 📞360-963-2334, 888-462-0803 📠360-963-2776 ✍www.vanriperresort.com

The hamlet of Sekiu flanks Route 112 on the protected shore of Clallam Bay, on the Strait of Juan de Fuca. This is the lone waterfront hotel here. Family owned and operated, it's a cozy getaway spot. More than half of the rooms have great views of the boats on the picturesque strait. There's also a campground and an RV park with full hookups available on a first-come, first-served basis.

THE CAPE MOTEL AND RV PARK

$ 10 UNITS   ✉1510 Bayview Avenue, Neah Bay 📞360-645-2250, 866-744-9944 📠360-645-2250

There are eight motel rooms and two cottages here; five have kitchens. Six months of the year, the RV park is open; restrooms are on-site and hookups are available.

RIVER INN B&B

$$ 2 UNITS   ✉2596 West Bogachiel Way, Forks 📞360-374-6526 📠360-374-6590 ✍www.jeffwoodwardsportfishing.com/river.htm, laura.riverinn@yahoo.com

Among several low-priced bed and breakfasts in Forks is this A-frame chalet on the banks of the Bogachiel River two-and-a-half miles from town. Both units include a private bath; one boasts a deck. You can fish from the shore or relax in the hot tub while keeping your eyes open for elk, deer and river otter. Full breakfast. Closed in September.

RAIN FOREST HOSTEL

$ 26 BEDS   ✉169312 Route 101 North, 23 miles south of Forks 📞360-374-2270 ✍www.rainforesthostel.com, go2hostel@centurytel.net

Forks also has a youth hostel, complete with the cosmopolitan atmosphere one would expect. Like other lodgings of its ilk, it offers dorm bunks and community bathrooms and a kitchen. The common room is a bonus with its fireplace and library. There is also one room for a couple and one room for a family as well as land for camping.

KALALOCH LODGE

$$$$ 57 UNITS   ✉157151 Route 101, 35 miles south of Forks   ☎360-962-2271, 866-525-2562   📠360-962-3391   ⌕www.visitkalaloch.com, info@visitkalaloch.com

This lodge is perched on a bluff high above the crashing surf. Accommodations here (which may disappoint some) include 10 lodge units, 10 motel units, 20 log cabins with kitchenettes (but no utensils provided) and 18 units atop the bluff, 7 of which are duplexes. The lodge has a dining room overlooking the Pacific Ocean, as well as a general store, gas station and gift shop.

LAKE QUINAULT LODGE

$$$ 64 UNITS   ✉345 South Shore Road, Quinault   ☎360-288-2900, 800-562-6672   📠360-288-2901   ⌕www.visitlakequinault.com, info@visitlakequinault.com

If you're planning a stay in the corner of Olympic National Park that includes beauteous Lake Quinault, consider this historic cedar-shingled lodge—especially if you can get a lakefront room. The huge building arcs around the shoreline, a totem-pole design on its massive chimney facing the water. Antiques and oversized leather furniture adorn the main lobby, constructed in the 1920s. There is also a sun porch, a dining room and a bar with panoramic mountain and lake views. You can rent boats in the summer, hike year-round or relax in the pool or sauna.

DINING

LOG CABIN RESORT

$$ AMERICAN   ✉3183 East Beach Road, 21 miles west of Port Angeles   ☎360-928-3325   📠360-928-2088   ⌕www.logcabinresort.net, logcabin@logcabinresort.net

The best choice for dining in the park is at this resort. Enjoy the view of beautiful Lake Crescent, where anglers dip their lines for the unique crescenti trout, a subspecies of rainbow trout. Dishes range from Cajun chicken quesadillas to clams and mussels sautéed in vermouth.

THE SPRINGS RESTAURANT

$$–$$$ PACIFIC NORTHWEST   ✉Sol Duc Hot Springs Resort,12076 Sol Duc Hot Springs Road   ☎360-327-3593, 866-476-5382   📠360-327-3593   ⌕www.visitsolduc.com, info@solduc.com

You'll find this restaurant at the Sol Duc Hot Springs Resort, just behind the hot sulphur springs. The food is solid Northwest fare, including some vegetarian dishes. Closed November to mid-March.

HURRICANE RIDGE VISITORS CENTER

$ AMERICAN   ✉Hurricane Ridge Road   ☎360-565-3131

A mile high in the Olympic Range, 17 miles south of Port Angeles, this visitors center frames glaciers in the picture windows upstairs from its coffee shop. Come for the view, but the standard American snacks served here aren't half-bad, either. Open January through May, weather permitting.

KALALOCH LODGE

$$–$$$ SEAFOOD   ✉157151 Route 101, 35 miles south of Forks   ☎360-962-2271,
866-525-2562 📠360-962-3391 🖥www.visitkalaloch.com

Sunsets from this lodge, high on a bluff overlooking the ocean in the national park's coastal strip, can make even the most ordinary food taste good. Fortunately, the fresh salmon and halibut and the Olympic-style crab cakes served here don't need the view for their rich flavor. Breakfast, lunch and dinner. Dinner reservations recommended.

THE ROOSEVELT DINING ROOM

$$$ SEAFOOD   ✉Lake Quinalt Lodge, 345 South Shore Road, Quinault
☎800-562-6672 📠360-288-2901 🖥www.visitlakequinault.com,
info@visitlakequinault.com

The Roosevelt at the park's Lake Quinault Lodge faces another gorgeous lake surrounded by lush cedar forests. As you've come to expect along this coast, the seafood is excellent. Breakfast, lunch and dinner year-round.

SMOKE HOUSE RESTAURANT

$$ AMERICAN   ✉193161 Route 101 North at La Push Road   ☎360-374-6258

Other than the national park lodges, pickings are slim in the restaurant department along this stretch of highway. A mile north of Forks, this restaurant serves standard American fare.

SHOPPING

MAKAH CULTURAL AND RESEARCH CENTER

✉1880 Bay View Avenue, Neah Bay ☎360-645-2711 🖥www.makah.com,
makahmuseum@centurytel.net For authentic Northwest Indian crafts, including jewelry, baskets and carvings, you won't do better than this gift shop at the Makah Cultural and Research Center on the Makah Indian Reservation at the end of Route 112.

BEACHES & PARKS

OLYMPIC NATIONAL PARK

✉Route 101 circles the park. The numerous access roads are well marked. ☎360-565-3000 ☎360-565-3015 (Port Angeles), 360-374-5877 (Forks), 360-327-3534 (Sol Duc)

This spectacular national park, 922,651 acres in area and ranging in elevation from sea level to nearly 8000 feet, contains everything from permanent alpine glaciers to America's lushest rainforest (the Hoh) to rocky tidepools rich in marine life. Wildlife includes deer in the mountains, elk in the rainforest, steelhead and salmon in the rivers and colorful birds everywhere. Three large lakes—Crescent (near Port Angeles), Ozette (on the coast) and Quinault (on the southwestern edge)—are especially nice destinations. There are restrooms, picnic areas, hotels, restaurants and groceries. A $15 vehicle pass lasts a week.

▲ There are 16 campgrounds, 10 of which are year round, weather permitting; $10 to $18 per night.

The Hoh Rainforest

No matter where you go on this earth, there's only one Hoh Rainforest. It's said to be one of the only coniferous rainforests in the world. Spared the logger's blade after a long-running battle between locals and conservationists, it's been undisturbed since time began. It's a natural wonder to be cherished.

Reached by traveling 13 miles south from Forks on Route 101, then 19 miles east on Hoh River Road, this is the wettest spot in the contiguous 48 states. In fact, wet isn't the word: even the air drips like a saturated sponge, producing over 30 inches of fog drip in the summer. The average annual precipitation due to rainfall is 145 inches, more than 100 inches of which fall between October and March. But temperatures at this elevation, between 500 and 1000 feet, rarely fall below 40° in winter or rise above 85° in summer. The legacy of this mild climate is dense, layered canopies of foliage.

The forest floor is as soft and thick as a shag carpet, cloaked with mosses, bracken ferns, huge fungi and seedlings. Hovering over the lush rug are vine maple, alder and black cottonwood, some hung with moss, stretching wiry branches to taste any slivers of sunlight that may steal through the canopy. Above them, Douglas fir, Sitka spruce, Western hemlock, Western red cedar and other gigantic conifers rise 200 to 300 feet, putting a lid on the forest. In all, over 300 plant species live here, not counting 70 epiphytes.

Some compare this environment to a cathedral. Indeed, the soft light is like sun filtered through stained glass, and the arching branches could pass for a vaulted apse. To others, it's simply mystical. The ancient coastal Indians would have agreed.

HOH RAINFOREST VISITOR CENTER ℘360-565-3130 ✎www.nps.gov/olym Though there are similar rainforests in Washington, the rainforest ecology is most conveniently studied at this visitor center and on the nature trails that surround it. The **Hoh River Trail** extends for 17.5 miles to the river's source in Blue Glacier, on the flank of Mt. Olympus, but the rainforest can be appreciated by most visitors on one of two loop hikes that are both about a mile long. About three-fourths of a mile in, you'll see enormous old-growth Douglas fir, spruce and hemlock, some over nine feet in girth and at least 500 years old. At about one mile, the trail drops down to Big Flat, the first of several grassy open areas. The winter grazing of Roosevelt elk, whose survival was a major reason for the creation of Olympic National Park, has opened up the forest floor. Keep your eyes open, too, for wildlife. Besides the elk, you may spot river otter or weasel. Black bears and cougars also inhabit these forests. Bald eagles and great blue heron feed on the salmon that spawn seasonally in the Hoh.

BOGACHIEL STATE PARK
✉Route 101, six miles south of Forks ℘360-374-6356
🚶 ⚓ Not far from the Hoh Rainforest, this eternally damp park sits on the Bogachiel River, famous for its salmon and steelhead runs. Hiking and hunting in the adjacent forest are popular activities, although this park is more of a campsite than a day-use area. Facilities include restrooms, showers and limited picnic areas.
▲ There are 36 standard sites ($17 per night), six RV hookup sites ($24 per night) and two primitive sites ($12 per night).

OCEAN SHORES–PACIFIC BEACH

A six-mile-long, 6000-acre peninsula, Ocean Shores was a cattle ranch when a group of investors bought it for $1 million in 1960. A decade later, its assessed value had risen to $35 million. Today, it would be hard to put a dollar figure on this strip of condominium-style hotels and second homes, many of them on a series of canals. The main tourist beach destination on the Grays Harbor County coastline, it's located along Route 115, three miles south of its junction with Route 109.

SIGHTS

OCEAN SHORES INTERPRETIVE CENTER ✉1033 Catala Avenue Southeast, Ocean Shores ✆360-289-4617 ✎360-289-0189 ⌨www.oceanshoresinterpretivecenter.com Folks come to **Ocean Shores** for oceanside rest and recreation, not for sightseeing. One of the few "attractions" is the interpretive center near the Ocean Shores Marina, which has exhibits describing the peninsula's geological formation and human development. Closed Monday through Friday from October through March.

QUINAULT INDIAN NATIONAL TRIBAL HEADQUARTERS ✉1214 Aalis Drive, Taholah ✆360-276-8215, 888-616-8211 ✎360-276-4191 ⌨www.quinaultindiannation.com The 22-mile beach that parallels Routes 115 and 109 north to Moclips is an attraction in its own right. Beyond Moclips, however, the coast gets more rugged. Eight miles past Moclips, this center on the Quinault Indian Reservation offers guided fishing trips on reservation land and tribal gifts in a small shop and museum.

LODGING

The nearest ocean beach area to the Seattle-Tacoma metropolitan area, Ocean Shores' condominiums and motels are frequently booked solid during the summer and on holiday weekends, even though prices can be high. At other times, it can be downright quiet . . . and inexpensive.

THE POLYNESIAN RESORT
$$$–$$$$ 69 ROOMS ✉615 Ocean Shores Boulevard Northwest, Ocean Shores ✆360-289-3361, 800-562-4836 ✎360-289-0294 ⌨www.thepolynesian.com, thepoly@techline.com
The Polynesian is as close to the water as you can get—a short quarter-mile trek across the dunes to the high-tide mark. The four-story building has guest rooms ranging from motel units to three-bedroom penthouse suites. It has a restaurant, lively lounge, indoor pool and spa, outdoor games area and indoor game room popular with families.

JUDITH ANN INN
$$$–$$$$ 10 UNITS ✉855 Ocean Shores Boulevard Northwest, Ocean Shores ✆360-289-0222, 888-826-6466 ⌨www.judithanninn.com, info@judithanninn.com
Each 900-square-foot suite in this big white inn is romantically deco-

rated with period replica furnishings and has a king-sized bed, a fully equipped kitchen, a gas fireplace and a private oceanview balcony, as well as wi-fi access. The most unusual feature in every suite is a two-person bowl-shaped jet tub in one corner of the living room, presumably for guests who like to converse and watch TV in the nude; there is also a conventional shower in the bathroom.

THE GREY GULL

$$–$$$ 37 UNITS   ✉*651 Ocean Shores Boulevard, Ocean Shores* ✆*360-289-3381,* *800-562-9712* 📠*360-289-3673* 🖥*www.thegreygull.com, greygull@thegreygull.com*

Units here are all studios or suites with fireplaces, wi-fi access, microwaves, VCRs and private decks or balconies. The Gull has an outdoor pool and jacuzzi guarded by a wind fence.

CAROLINE INN

$$ 4 UNITS   ✉*1341 Ocean Shores Boulevard, Ocean Shores* ✆*360-289-0450,* *800-303-4297* 📠*360-289-5149* 🖥*www.oceanshoreswashington.com*

This inn offers four bi-level townhouse suites with great views, just steps from the water. The decor follows a *Gone With the Wind* theme in soft rose colors. The rooms are furnished with sleigh beds and other antiques. Each suite offers all the comforts of home and then some: fireplaces, jacuzzis, complete kitchens and living areas.

PACIFIC SANDS MOTEL

$–$$ 9 UNITS   ✉*2687 State Route 109, Ocean City* ✆*360-289-3588* 🖥*www.pacific-sands.net, luismestas@earthlink.net*

At Ocean City, four miles north of Ocean Shores, this motel is one of the top economy choices on the coast. There are just nine units, but they're well kept; seven have kitchens and three have fireplaces. Pacific Sands also has a large house available for rent, with a kitchen, jacuzzi, piano and wood fireplace. The extensive grounds include a nice swimming pool, playground, picnic tables and direct beach access across a suspension bridge.

IRON SPRINGS RESORT

$$–$$$ 28 UNITS   ✉*3707 Route 109, Copalis Beach* ✆*360-276-4230* 📠*360-276-4378* 🖥*www.ironspringsresort.com, reservations@ironspringsresort.com*

At Iron Springs there are 28 units in 25 cottages built up a wooded hill and around a handsome cove at the mouth of Boon Creek. The beach here is popular for razor clamming, crabbing and surf fishing; the cottages are equally popular for their spaciousness and panoramic views. All have kitchens and most have fireplaces. There is an indoor pool and a playground.

OCEAN CREST RESORT

$$$ 45 ROOMS   ✉*Sunset Beach, 4651 South Route 109, Moclips* ✆*360-276-4465, 800-684-8439* 📠*360-276-4149* 🖥*www.oceancrestresort.com, info@oceancrestresort.com*

This may be the most memorable accommodation on this entire stretch of beach. It's built atop a bluff, so getting to the beach involves a 132-step descent down a staircase through a wooded ravine. But the views from the rooms' private balconies are remarkable, and all but the smallest rooms have fireplaces and refrigerators. There are exercise facilities with a swimming pool, jacuzzi and weight room open to all guests free of charge.

DINING

MARIAH'S

$–$$$ STEAK/SEAFOOD   ✉*615 Ocean Shores Boulevard, Ocean Shores* ✆*360-289-3315, 800-562-4836* 📠*360-289-0294* 🖱*www.thepolynesian.com, thepoly@techline.com*

Mariah's provides a spacious, relaxing cedar dining room with a domed ceiling and skylights. Offerings include fresh seafood, steaks, prime rib and pasta. Dinner only and Sunday breakfast buffet.

HOME PORT RESTAURANT

$$–$$$ STEAK/SEAFOOD   ✉*857 Point Brown Avenue opposite Shoal Street, Ocean Shores* ✆*360-289-2600* 📠*360-289-0558*

This restaurant is appointed like the private garden of a sea captain home from the waves. Steaks, seafood and pasta dominate the menu.

MIKE'S SEAFOOD

$–$$ SEAFOOD   ✉*830 Point Brown Avenue, Ocean Shores* ✆*360-289-0532*

No trip to the Washington coast would be complete without having at least one meal that includes seafood. Mike's is a casual eatery that can adequately oblige. Offering a fresh assortment of Pacific Northwest seafood, Mike's is particularly popular with the locals during the winter Dungeness crab season.

SAND CASTLE DRIVE-IN

$ AMERICAN   ✉*788 Point Brown Avenue, Ocean Shores* ✆*360-289-2777*

The Sand Castle is the in-spot for hamburgers, with interesting variations such as the oyster burger and the clam burger. Their menu also features other comfort food classics like hush puppies and deep-fried clams.

LAS MARACAS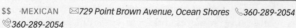

$$ MEXICAN   ✉*729 Point Brown Avenue, Ocean Shores* ✆*360-289-2054* 📠*360-289-2054*

A bit of Manzanillo on the Washington coast, Las Maracas feels like the tropics with its bright colors and profusion of plants. All the usual Mexican specialties are here, but the best bets are the fajitas, crab and prawn enchiladas and seafood *chiles relleños*.

GALWAY BAY IRISH RESTAURANT AND PUB

$$–$$$ IRISH   ✉*880 Point Brown Avenue Northeast, Ocean Shores* ✆*360-289-2300* 🖱*www.galwaybayirishpub.com, bgibbons@galwaybayirishpub.com*

Authentic Irish pub fare is dished up here, where you can ward off the coastal chill with Irish stew, beef sautéed in Guinness, and pasties. The pub decor is authentic, with wainscoted walls adorned with Irish prints and memorabilia. Breakfast, lunch and dinner.

OCEAN CREST RESORT

$$$–$$$$ SEAFOOD ✉4651 Sunset Beach, Route 109, Moclips
📞360-276-4465, 800-684-8439 🖰www.oceancrestresort.com,
info@oceancrestresort.com

For a gourmet Continental dinner in spectacular surroundings, check out this resort. Attentive service and superb meals with a focus on local seafood, amid an atmosphere of Northwest Indian tribal art, only add to the enjoyment of the main reason to dine here: the view from a bluff, through a wooded ravine, to Sunset Beach. Breakfast, lunch and dinner.

SHOPPING

While galleries exhibiting the works of local and regional artists can be found in most of Grays Harbor County's beach communities, the greatest concentration of them line the 700 and 800 blocks of Point Brown Avenue in Ocean Shores.

FUSIONS GALLERY ✉834 Point Brown Avenue Northeast, Ocean Shores 📞360-289-2811 🖰www.fusionsgallery.com, info@fusionsgallery.com A good place to start your gallery-hopping is at this spacious gallery, which shows the works of more than 75 Grays Harbor-area artists.

CAFFÉ AMICI ✉749 Point Brown Avenue, Ocean Shores 📞360-289-5600 🖰www.cafeamici.com If Fusions Gallery is the place to start your tour of Ocean Shores art galleries, this is the place to finish it up. The best reason for a stop here is to sip a steaming latte, hot chocolate or chai tea while viewing the paintings on the walls. Closed Monday and Tuesday.

NIGHTLIFE

MARIAH'S ✉615 Ocean Shores Boulevard, Ocean Shores 📞360-289-3315, 800-562-4836 🖰www.thepolynesian.com In Ocean Shores, at the Polynesian Hotel, Mariah's is a nice place to enjoy a nightcap.

GALWAY BAY IRISH RESTAURANT AND PUB ✉880 Point Brown Avenue Northeast, Ocean Shores 📞360-289-2300 🖰www.galwaybayirishpub.com Along with a convivial atmosphere nightly, Galway Bay hosts live music on Friday and Saturday nights and some Sunday nights.

BEACHES & PARKS

OCEAN CITY STATE PARK

✉Off Route 115 and Route 109 north of Ocean Shores; campground is two miles north of Ocean Shores on Route 115 📞360-289-3553 📞360-289-9405
🚶🚴🐎🎣♿🚿🚻⚓ This North Beach park, stretching for several miles along the Pacific coastline, offers a dozen access

points. There are clamming and surf fishing (in season), horse-back riding on the beach (but not on the dunes or soft sand), surf kayaking in summer, kite flying when the wind blows, birdwatching especially during migratory periods, and beachcombing year-round. Swimming is not recommended because of undertow and riptides. This flat, sandy beach is the same broad expanse that stretches 22 miles north to Pacific Beach. You can drive on some sections of the beach! You'll find restrooms and picnic areas.

▲ There are 149 standard sites ($19 per night) and 29 RV hookup sites ($26 per night). Reservations: 888-226-7688.

PACIFIC BEACH STATE PARK
✉ *Located along Route 109 in Pacific Beach* 📞 *360-276-4297* 📠 *360-276-4537*

🏃 🚣 ⚓ Broad, flat and sandy North Beach, extending 22 miles from Moclips (just north of Pacific Beach) to the north jetty of Grays Harbor at Ocean Shores, is the *raison d'être* of the entire park. Beachcombing, kite flying, jogging and surf-perchfishing (in season) and razor-clam digging are popular activities. Swimming is not recommended because of undertow and riptides. Facilities are limited to restrooms and picnic areas.

▲ There are 32 standard sites ($19 per night) and 32 RV hookup sites ($26 per night). Reservations: 888-226-7688.

GRAYS HARBOR AREA

Industrial towns are not often places of tourist interest. The twin cities of Aberdeen and Hoquiam, on the northeastern shore of the broad Grays Harbor estuary, are an exception. A historic seaport, a rich assortment of bird life and numerous handsome mansions built by old timber money make it worthwhile to pause in this corner of Washington.

Aberdeen has about 16,000 people, Hoquiam around 9000, and the metropolitan area includes some 33,000. Wood-products industries provide the economic base; in fact, more trees are harvested in Grays Harbor County than in any other county in the United States. Boat building and fisheries, both more important in past decades, remain key businesses.

SIGHTS

GRAYS HARBOR CHAMBER OF COMMERCE ✉ *506 Duffy Street at Route 101, Aberdeen* 📞 *360-532-1924, 800-321-1924* 📠 *360-533-7945* 🖥 *www.grays harbor.org, info@grays harbor.org* For information on the region, check with this visitor center. For details about local goings-on, pick up a copy of the *Coast & Rainforest Washington Visitors Guide*.

HOQUIAM'S CASTLE ✉ *515 Chenault Avenue, Hoquiam* 📞 *360-533-2005* 📠 *360-533-9814* 🖥 *www.hoquiamcastle.com, info@hoquiamcastle.com* If you're coming down Route 101 from the north during the summer, it's wise to follow the signs and make your first stop a guided tour of Hoquiam's. A stately, 20-room hillside mansion built in 1897 by a millionaire lumber baron, it has been fully restored with elegant antiques like Tiffany lamps, grandfather clocks and a 600-piece, cut-crystal chandelier. With

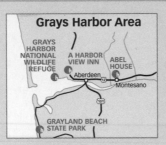

Grays Harbor Area

GRAYS HARBOR NATIONAL WILDLIFE REFUGE

PAGE 198

Scenic sanctuary for migratory birds with spectacular seasonal avian-watching

A HARBOR VIEW INN

PAGE 200

Historic four-story mansion with antique decor and private decks overlooking the harbor

ABEL HOUSE

PAGE 200

Stately 1908 B&B with impressive reading room and exquisite English garden

GRAYLAND BEACH STATE PARK

PAGE 204

Long, broad shoreline ideal for clam digging, beach combing, kite flying and other seaside explorations

its round turret and bright red color, the house is unmistakable. It is now a bed-and-breakfast inn. Open for tours by appointment. Admission.

POLSON MUSEUM ✉*1611 Riverside Avenue at Route 101, Hoquiam* ✆*360-533-5862* 📠*360-533-5862* 🖱*www.polsonmuseum.org, jbl@polsonmuseum.org* Built in the early 1920s by a pioneer timber family and furnished with pieces donated by Hoquiam and Grays Harbor County residents, the 26-room home represents the history of the area. It is surrounded by native trees and the Burton Ross Memorial Rose Gardens. Open Wednesday through Sunday from April through December; open weekends only from January through March. Admission.

GRAYS HARBOR NATIONAL WILDLIFE REFUGE _____

✆*360-753-9467* 📠*360-534-9302* A couple miles west of Hoquiam on Route 109, at Bowerman Basin on Grays Harbor, next to Bowerman Airfield, is this wildlife refuge, one of four major staging areas for migratory shorebirds in North America. Although this basin represents just two percent of the intertidal habitat of the estuary, fully half of the one million shorebirds that visit each spring make their stop here. The refuge is the last place to be flooded at high tide and the first to have its mudflats exposed, giving the avians extra feeding time. April and early May are the best times to visit, but smaller groups of migrants pass through from June through October. Thousands of birds, particularly dulin, stay here through the winter. An annual shorebird festival occurs the last weekend in April.

GRAYS HARBOR HISTORICAL SEAPORT

⊠*712 Hagara Street, Aberdeen* 📞*360-532-8611, 800-200-5239* 📠*360-533-9384* ⏚*www.historicalseaport.org* A major attraction in neighboring Aberdeen, just four miles east of Hoquiam on Route 101, is this historical seaport. Craftspersons at this working 18th-century shipyard have constructed a replica of the *Lady Washington*, the brigantine in which Captain Robert Gray sailed when he discovered Grays Harbor and the Columbia River in 1783. There are also two 18th-century longboat reproductions and a companion tall ship to the *Lady Washington*, the *Tall Chieftain*. Visitors can go for a sail on the *Lady Washington* when the ship isn't touring the West Coast. Call 24 hours ahead for schedules.

ABERDEEN MUSEUM OF HISTORY

⊠*111 East 3rd Street, Aberdeen* 📞*360-533-1976* ⏚*www.aberdeen-museum.org, museum@aberdeen-museum.org* A few blocks west of the seaport is this museum offering exhibits, dioramas and videos of regional history in a 1922 armory. Displays include several re-created early-20th-century buildings: a one-room school, a general store, a blacksmith's shop and more. Closed Monday.

WESTPORT MARITIME MUSEUM

⊠*2201 Westhaven Drive, Westport* 📞*360-268-0078* 📠*360-268-1288* ⏚*www.westportwa.com/museum, westport.maritime@comcast.net* Route 105 follows the south shore of Grays Harbor west from Aberdeen to the atmospheric fishing village of **Westport**, at the estuary's south head. Perhaps the most interesting of several small museums here is this maritime museum, housed in a Nantucket-style Coast Guard station commissioned in 1939 but decommissioned in the 1970s. Historic photos, artifacts and memorabilia help tell the story of a sailor's life. The museum also has exhibits of skeletons of marine mammals (including whales), a beachcombing exhibit and a children's discovery room. Closed Tuesday through Thursday from October through March. Admission.

LODGING

HOQUIAM'S CASTLE BED & BREAKFAST

$$$–$$$$ 4 ROOMS   ⊠*515 Chenault Avenue, Hoquiam* 📞*360-533-2005* 📠*306-533-9814* ⏚*www.hoquiamcastle.com, info@hoquiamcastle.com* There's considerable character at Hoquiam's, a three-story Victorian hillside mansion. Each of the guest rooms, all with private bath, are individually decorated with antiques. A full breakfast is served in the hand-carved oak dining room. Museum-quality period furnishings fill the house, which is open for tours by appointment.

OLYMPIC INN MOTEL

$$ 55 ROOMS   ⊠*616 West Heron Street, Aberdeen* 📞*360-533-4200, 800-562-8618* 📠*360-533-6223* The twin cities of Aberdeen and Hoquiam have a strip of look-alike motels along Route 101. Though it's hard to choose one above another, the Olympic Inn is notable for its modern, spacious rooms. Decor in the units is simple but pleasant.

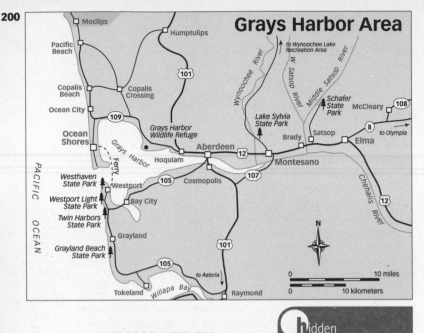

Grays Harbor Area

A HARBOR VIEW INN

$$$ 5 ROOMS ✉111 West 11th Street, Aberdeen ✆360-533-7996,
877-533-7996 🖉www.aharborview.com, info@aharborview.com

This historic four-story mansion, surveying Grays Harbor and
the Chehalis and Wiskah Rivers from its lofty hillside setting,
dates back to 1905, when a local doctor built it as a residence for
his family and serving staff. The present owners have modern-
ized it, so while the guest rooms are decorated in Victorian style,
they also feature such amenities as wi-fi and TVs with DVD play-
ers. Each room has a private bath and a view of the harbor. Com-
mon areas for guests' use include a living room, kitchen, dining
room and a sunroom where a complimentary breakfast is served
each morning.

ABEL HOUSE

$$ 4 ROOMS ✉117 Fleet Street South, Montesano ✆360-249-6002
📠360-249-6002 🖉www.abelhouse.com, info@abelhouse.com

East of Aberdeen in the county seat of Montesano is this stately
1908 home with four bedrooms, one with a private bath. There
are also a game room and reading room and an exquisite English
garden. A full breakfast and afternoon tea are included in the
room rate. Dinner (fee) made upon request.

THE MCCLEARY HOTEL

$ 2 ROOMS ✉42 Summit Road, McCleary ✆360-495-3678

Farther east—halfway from Montesano to Olympia, in fact, but still in Grays Harbor County—The McCleary maintains antique-laden rooms that seem to be especially popular with touring bicyclists.

201

CHÂTEAU WESTPORT

$$–$$$$ 108 UNITS ✉710 West Hancock Avenue, Westport ✆360-268-9101, 800-255-9101 📠360-268-1646 🖰www.chateauwestport.com, chateau@tss.net

In Westport, at the mouth of Grays Harbor, the largest motel is the Château Westport. Many of the units have balconies and fireplaces, and a third are efficiency studios with kitchenettes; all rooms have free wi-fi and some are pet-friendly. The upper floors of the four-story property, easily identified by its gray mansard roof, have excellent ocean views to enjoy with your complimentary continental breakfast. Dip into the indoor pool and hot tub.

THE ISLANDER RESORT

$–$$ 32 ROOMS ✉421 East Neddie Rose Drive, Westport ✆360-268-9166, 800-322-1740 📠360-268-0902 🖰www.westport-islander.com, info@westport-islander.com

For value-hunters, this resort offers simple but clean and spacious motel units. Forty-seven RV spaces are also available, some overlooking the harbor.

GRAYLAND MOTEL AND COTTAGES

$ 15 UNITS ✉2013 State Route 105, Grayland ✆360-267-2395, 800-292-0845 🖰www.westportwa.com/graylandmotel

You can catch a fish, clean it and cook it for dinner all without straying from the Grayland, located on the beach south of Westport. The grounds offer a fish- and clam-cleaning shed, children's play area, motel units and self-contained cottages with tiled kitchens, pine furnishings and small living/dining areas.

DINING

It's a comfort to know that Grays Harbor has a few memorable restaurants to go with its memorable accommodations.

BRIDGES RESTAURANT

$$–$$$ STEAK/SEAFOOD ✉112 North G Street, Aberdeen ✆360-532-6563 📠360-532-5490

Bridges is a handsome, garden-style restaurant with one dining room and two banquet rooms, one of which is actually a greenhouse. As the size of its parking lot attests, it's very popular locally, for its lounge as well as its cuisine. Local seafood, steaks, chicken and pasta highlight the menu. No lunch on Sunday.

BILLY'S BAR AND GRILL

$–$$ AMERICAN ✉322 East Heron Street, Aberdeen ✆360-533-7144 📠360-533-7508

For historic flavor with a slightly haunted aftertaste, you needn't look further than Billy's. Named for an early-20th-century ne'er-do-well notorious for mugging loggers and shanghaiing sailors, Billy's boasts an ornate century-old ceiling and a huge antique bar. This is the place to start the day with a hearty breakfast, or settle back with a burger and a beer and soak up the past.

HONG KONG RESTAURANT

$ CHINESE ✉*East 1st Street, Cosmopolis* ☎*360-533-7594*

The cuisine here is surprisingly authentic for a town so far removed from China. It has chop suey and egg foo yung, yes, but it also has egg flower soup, *moo goo gai pan* and other tastes from the old country. Closed Monday.

BEAR'S DEN

$ AMERICAN ✉*301 Simpson Avenue, McCleary* ☎*360-495-3822*

There aren't many restaurant choices in McCleary, but if you appreciate a good old-fashioned hamburger, head for this easy-going place. An authentic 1950s burger stand with drive-up service and a tiny inside dining area, the Den makes burgers to order with heated buns, homemade fries, quality beef and a variety of toppings. Some other specialties are fresh salads and soda fountain treats.

NIGHTLIFE

SIDNEY'S CASINO
✉*512 West Heron Street, Aberdeen* ☎*360-533-6635, 360-533-0296 (bar)* Folks in the Grays Harbor area show a predilection for Sidney's, which features a Harley bar.

BILLY'S BAR AND GRILL
✉*322 East Heron Street, Aberdeen* ☎*360-533-7144* Check out the Victorian bar at Billy's, which boasts free wi-fi if you want to bring your laptop.

BRIDGES RESTAURANT
✉*112 North G Street, Aberdeen* ☎*360-532-6563* The posh lounge at Bridges is also a happenin' spot for drinks.

BEACHES & PARKS

LAKE SYLVIA STATE PARK
✉*Off Route 12, via North 3rd Street, two miles north of Montesano* ☎*360-249-3621* ☎*360-249-5571*

Visitors can circumambulate this narrow, forest-enshrouded lake on a two-mile hiking trail. Also here are trout fishing (from a non-motorized boat or from shore), a swimming beach and boat rentals in season. There are restrooms, picnic areas and groceries. ▲ There are 35 standard sites ($18 per night). Closed early October to early April. Reservations: 888-226-7688.

SCHAFER STATE PARK
✉*West 1365 Schafer Park Road, 12 miles north of Elma, off Route 12 via Brady* ☎*360-482-3852* ☎*360-482-3852*

Once a family park for employees of the Schafer Logging Company, this tranquil 119-acre site on the East Fork of the Satsop River is still popular with families and offers two miles of beautiful hiking trails. This heavily forested park is also ideal for picnics and fishing. You can fish for cutthroat trout, salmon and steelhead in the river. Swimmers may find the water too cold. You'll find restrooms and picnic areas.

▲ There are 32 standard sites ($17 per night), 10 RV hookup sites ($24 per night) and two primitive sites ($12 per night). Closed in winter.

WYNOOCHEE LAKE RECREATION AREA
✉ *Off Route 12, about 35 miles north of Montesano on Wynoochee Valley Road. Take a left on Forest Service Road 22 and a right on Forest Service Road 2294.* ✆ *360-956-2402*

Originally an Army Corps of Engineers project, now run by Tacoma Power, this four-and-a-half-mile-long lake was created in 1972 by a water-supply and flood-control dam on the Wynoochee River. A ten-mile trail winds around the lake, past a beach and designated swimming area. Trout fishing, waterskiing, swimming (the water is cold, though), horseback riding and wildlife watching are also popular. Restrooms and picnic areas are the only facilities.

▲ There are 46 developed sites and 10 primitive sites ($10 to $12 per night) in the Coho campground. Closed October through April. Reservations: 888-226-7688.

WESTHAVEN & WESTPORT LIGHT STATE PARKS
✉ *Both parks are close to downtown Westport; Westhaven is about one and a half miles from downtown on East Yearout Drive; Westport Light is a half mile from downtown at the end of Ocean Avenue.* ✆ *360-268-9717* ✆ *360-268-0372*

Westhaven State Park, which occupies the southern headland at the mouth of Grays Harbor, is a great place for watching birds and wildlife, including harbor seals and whales during migratory periods. Surfing is excellent here (try the jetty) and there are yearly competitions. Surfers and swimmers should be very careful of riptides. Westhaven is adjacent to Westport Light State Park, from which you can see a historic lighthouse that's warned coastal ships of the entrance to Grays Harbor since 1897. There's a multi-use paved trail connecting the two parks that's open for hiking, bicycling, inline skating and other nonmotorized forms of transportation. You can fish for salmon, ocean perch, codfish and Dungeness crab from the shores of both parks or the jetty of Westhaven. There are restrooms and picnic areas.

TWIN HARBORS STATE PARK
✉ *Located along Route 105, three miles south of Westport and four miles north of Grayland* ✆ *360-268-9717* ✆ *360-268-0372*

The Washington coast's largest campground dominates this 172-acre park. It also includes the Shifting Sands Nature Trail with interpretive signs for dunes explorers. Beachcombing, kite flying and clamming are popular activities on the broad, sandy beach. There's fishing in the surf or from a boat (which you can charter at Westport) for cod, salmon, ocean perch and Dungeness crab, but swimming is not recommended because of riptides. You'll find restrooms and picnic areas.

▲ There are 250 standard sites ($19 per night) and 49 RV hookup sites ($26 per night). Reservations (May 15 to September 15): 888-226-7688.

GRAYLAND BEACH
STATE PARK

✉*925 Cranberry Road, off Route 105, Grayland* 📞*360-267-4301*
📠*360-267-0461* ✎*grayland.beach@parks.wa.gov*

🚶🏊 This 400-acre park has over 7500 feet of shoreline that is broad and flat and ideal for surf fishing, clam digging, beach-combing, kite flying and other seaside diversions. Swimming is discouraged due to riptides. You'll find restrooms, groceries and restaurants in Grayland.

▲ There are 100 RV hookup sites ($27 to $36 per night) and 16 yurts ($50 to $55 per night). Reservations: 888-226-7688.

LONG BEACH– WILLAPA BAY

This region is the largest "unpopulated" estuary in the continental United States. Its pristine condition makes it one of the world's best places for farming oysters. From Tokeland to Bay Center to Oysterville, tiny villages that derive their sole income from the shelled creatures display mountains of empty shells as evidence of their success. Begin your visit on Route 105 south from Westport, then head east along the northern shore of Willapa Bay.

SIGHTS

RAYMOND Thirty-three miles from Westport, Route 105 rejoins Route 101 at Raymond. This town of 3000, and its smaller sister community of **South Bend** four miles south on Route 101, are lumber ports on the lower Willapa River.

DENNIS COMPANY BUILDING ✉*5th Street and Blake Street, Raymond* You'll find murals—43 of them, to be exact—on walls from Ocean Shores to the Columbia River, Elma to Ilwaco. Chambers of commerce and other visitor information centers have guide pamphlets. But no mural is larger than the 85-foot-wide painting of an early logger on this company building.

PACIFIC COUNTY MUSEUM ✉*1008 West Robert Bush Drive, South Bend* 📞*360-875-5224* ✎*www.pacificcohistory.org, museum@willapabay.org* Attractions in South Bend include this museum, with pioneer artifacts from the turn of the 20th century.

PACIFIC COUNTY COURTHOUSE ✉*300 Memorial Drive off Route 101, South Bend* 📞*360-875-9334* Have a look at South Bend's 1910 courthouse, noted for its art-glass dome and historic foyer wall paintings.

LONG BEACH PENINSULA This peninsula, reached via Route 101 from South Bend (43 miles), features 28 miles of open sandy beaches, two lighthouses and a boardwalk above grassy dunes. Information is available from the **Long Beach Peninsula Visitor Bu-**

reau (3914 Pacific Highway at the intersection of Routes 101 and 103, Seaview; 360-642-2400, 800-451-2542, fax 360-642-3900; www.fun beach.com, ask@funbeach.com).

Route 103, which runs north–south up the 28-mile-long, two-mile-wide peninsula, is intersected by Route 101 at **Seaview**. The town of **Long Beach** is just a mile north of the junction.

BOARDWALK ⊠*South 10th Street to Bolstad Street, Long Beach* Long Beach's principal attraction is a half-mile-long wooden boardwalk, South 10th to Bolstad streets, elevated above the dunes, enabling folks to make an easy trek to the high-tide mark. The beach, incidentally, is open to driving on the hard upper sand, and to surf fishing, clamming (in season), beachcombing, kite flying and picnicking everywhere.

WORLD KITE MUSEUM AND HALL OF FAME

⊠*303 Sid Snyder Drive South off Route 103, Long Beach* ℰ*360-642-4020* ℰ*www.worldkitemuseum.com, info@worldkitemuseum.com* Kite flying is a big thing on the Washington coast, so it's no accident that this kite-centric museum is in Long Beach. The museum has rotating exhibits of kites from around the world—Japanese, Chinese, Thai and so on—with displays of stunt kites, advertising kites and more. Open daily May through September; closed Wednesday and Thursday from October to April. Admission.

PACIFIC COAST CRANBERRY RESEARCH FOUNDATION ⊠*2907 Pioneer Road, Long Beach* ℰ*360-642-5553* ℰ*www.cranberrymuseum.com, info@cranberrymuseum.com* In October and early November, the cranberry harvest takes precedence over all else on the peninsula. Most fields are owned by local farmers who sell much of their crop to Ocean Spray. This research foundation offers free self-guided tours of the cranberry bogs year-round. Go in October to see the harvest.

PACIFIC COAST CRANBERRY MUSEUM ⊠*2907 Pioneer Road, Long Beach* ℰ*360-642-5553* ℰ*www.cranberrymuseum.com, info@cranberrymuseum.com* This cranberry museum provides a historic view of the West Coast cranberry industry. Exhibits include hand tools, cranberry boxes, labels, pickers, sorters and separators. Open from April through mid-December; by appointment only the rest of the year.

OCEAN PARK Ten miles north of Long Beach is this commercial hub of the central and northern Long Beach Peninsula. Developed as a Methodist camp in 1883, it evolved into a small resort town.

OYSTERVILLE This town, another three miles north via Sandridge Road is older than Ocean Park. Founded in 1854, this National Historic District boasts the oldest continuously operating post office in Washington (since 1858) and 17 other designated historic sites. Get a walking tour pamphlet from the **Old Church** (Territory Road, Oysterville) beside the Village Green.

ILWACO South of Seaview just two miles on Route 103 is this town, spanning the isthmus between the Columbia River and the Pacific.

Long Beach–Willapa Bay

LEADBETTER POINT STATE PARK
PAGE 210

Northern tip of Long Beach Peninsula with seductively shifting dunes and mudflats, ponds and marshes

MOBY DICK HOTEL
PAGE 207

Nautical-themed inn with waterfront sauna and its own organic garden and oyster farm

CORRAL DRIVE IN
PAGE 209

Down-home diner with the Tsunami—at five pounds, supposedly the world's largest hamburger

WORLD KITE MUSEUM AND HALL OF FAME
PAGE 205

Eclectic museum with rotating exhibits of international kites, perfect for a windy Washington afternoon

COLUMBIA PACIFIC HERITAGE MUSEUM ✉115 Southeast Lake Street, Ilwaco ✆360-642-3446 ✍360-642-4615 ⌖www.columbiapacificheritagemuseum. org, cphm@willapabay.org Local history is featured at this impressive museum. A series of galleries depicts the development of southwestern Washington from early Indian culture to European voyages of discovery, from pioneer settlement to the early 20th century. Closed Sunday and Monday from Labor Day to Memorial Day. Admission.

FORT COLUMBIA STATE PARK ✉Route 101, Chinook ✆360-777-8221 About eight miles southeast, a short distance before Route 101 crosses the Columbia River to Astoria, Oregon, this state park is a highly recommended stop for history buffs. Two buildings at the site are museums: the **Fort Columbia Interpretive Center**, open Memorial Day through September, exhibits artifacts of early-20th-century military life in a former coastal artillery post, and the **Commanding Officer's House**, open in July and August only, which the Daughters of the American Revolution have restored to depict the everyday lifestyle of a military officer of the time.

LODGING

SHELBURNE COUNTRY INN
$$–$$$ 17 ROOMS   ✉4415 Pacific Way, Seaview ✆360-642-2442, 800-466-1896 ✍360-642-8904 ⌖www.theshelburneinn.com, innkeeper@theshelburneinn.com
Possibly the most delightful accommodation anywhere on the Washington coast is the Shelburne. The oldest continually operating hotel in

the state, it opened in 1896 and is still going strong. Guest rooms are furnished with Victorian antiques and fresh flowers. All have private baths and most have decks. A hearty country breakfast is served in the morning, as well as freshly baked cookies upon arrival.

THE HISTORIC SOU'WESTER LODGE, CABINS TCH! TCH! & RV PARK

$–$$$ 24 UNITS ✉Beach Access Road, 38th Place, Seaview ☎360-642-2542
🖥www.souwesterlodge.com, contactus@souwesterlodge.com

This is a place much beloved by youth hostelers who, well, grew up. Proprietors Leonard and Miriam Atkins have intentionally kept the accommodation simple and weathered. They advertise it as a B&(MYOD)B—"bed and (make your own damn) breakfast." Sleeping options include rooms in the historic lodge, cedar-shingled housekeeping cabins, a dozen-or-so vintage TCH! TCH! RVs and mobile homes ("Trailer Classics Hodgepodge"), and an area for RVs and tent campers. Almost every option includes kitchen facilities. The historic lodge draws an artistic clientele and often hosts cultural events such as poetry readings or evenings of chamber music and theater. It also is the closest lodging to the ocean in Seaview, separated from the water only by protected wetlands.

KLIPSAN BEACH COTTAGES

$$–$$$$ 10 UNITS ✉22617 Pacific Highway, Ocean Park ☎360-665-4888
📠360-665-3580 🖥www.klipsanbeachcottages.com,
call1947@klipsanbeachcottages.com

Numerous beachfront cabin communities speckle the shoreline of the Long Beach Peninsula north from the towns of Ilwaco and Seaview. One of the best is the Klipsan. Each of the ten cottages, in a lovely garden setting, has a kitchen and fireplace or wood-burning stove (with free firewood). There is also a two-bedroom and a three-bedroom unit. Closed in early January.

SHAKTI COVE

$–$$ 10 ROOMS ✉25301 Park Avenue, Ocean Park ☎360-665-4000
📠360-665-6000 🖥www.shakticove.com, info@shakticove.com

These woodframe accommodations are just five minutes from the water. Ten charming, rustic cottages have full kitchens and sleep up to four guests. The units are furnished with queen-sized beds, couches and feature eclectic decor. Pets are welcome. Gay-friendly. Two-night minimum stay on weekends March through October.

MOBY DICK HOTEL

$$ 10 ROOMS ✉25814 Sandridge Road, Nahcotta ☎360-665-4543,
800-673-6145 📠360-665-6887 🖥www.mobydickhotel.com,
mobydickhotel@willapabay.org

Willapa Bay oyster lovers frequent the beds near the north end of the Long Beach Peninsula, and this is where they'll find the

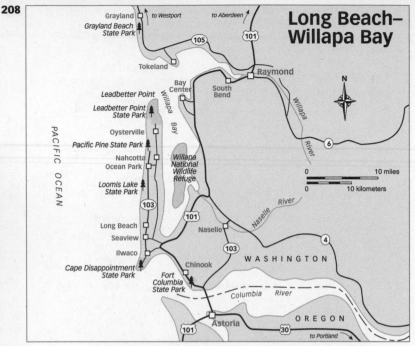

Long Beach–
Willapa Bay

Moby Dick. A bed-and-breakfast inn that first opened its doors in 1930, it maintains a country nautical atmosphere, with rambling grounds, its own organic vegetable garden and oyster farm. A fireplace, bayside pavilion sauna and piano beckon on rainy days. A 24-foot yurt with heated bamboo floor, skylight and circular space accommodates up to 30 people for retreats, meditations and workshops. Pets allowed for a fee.

DINING

TOKELAND HOTEL AND RESTAURANT

$$–$$$ AMERICAN   ✉ 100 Hotel Road, Tokeland   ☎ 360-267-7006   📠 360-267-7006
🖳 www.tokelandhotel.com, scott@tokelandhotel.com

Housed in the oldest hotel in Washington, the Tokeland pairs delicious local foods with panoramic views of Willapa Bay. Homecooked meals may include dishes ranging from pasta, salmon and crab Louie to steak and a nightly chicken special; breakfast involves blueberry pancakes, and crab and cheddar omelettes. Every Sunday the Tokeland offers a much sought-after cranberry pot roast.

DOCK OF THE BAY

$$ SEAFOOD   ✉ Bay Center Road at 2nd and Bridge streets, Bay Center
☎ 360-875-5130

For a unique dining experience, visit this restaurant on an off-the-beaten-track peninsula that juts into Willapa Bay 12 miles south of South Bend just off Route 101. Oysters, of course, are a specialty at this café/tavern; they even serve them for breakfast, along with other seafood omelettes. The fish market here also sells fresh crab and smoked salmon.

42ND STREET CAFÉ

$$$–$$$$ AMERICAN ✉*4201 Pacific Way, Seaview* ✆*360-642-2323*
📠*360-642-3439* ✐*www.42ndstreetcafe.com, blaine@42ndstreetcafe.com*

This café is fast making a reputation. Hand-cut ravioli sautéed in a cider glaze with apples and red onions, iron skillet–fried chicken, pot roast with vegetables and other down-home fare are prepared with a gourmet hand. The dining room is bright and casual with blue and green cloth napery, candles and fresh flowers; in the off season the chef plays her harp for guests on Sunday nights. Breakfast, lunch and dinner. Closed Wednesday seasonally; call ahead.

CORRAL DRIVE IN _____

$ AMERICAN ✉*North Pacific Highway and 95th Street North, Long Beach*
✆*360-642-2774*

The Corral claims its Tsunami is the world's largest hamburger—and who's to argue with a five-pounder on a 16-and-a-half-inch bun? Not only is it huge (the drive-in needs 24-hour notice—better have the whole family along), it's actually quite good. The place also has regular burgers, fries, milkshakes and such.

THE ARK RESTAURANT
AND BAKERY _____

$$–$$$ SEAFOOD ✉*3310 273rd Street and Sandridge Road, Nahcotta*
✆*360-665-4133* 📠*360-665-5043* ✐*www.arkrestaurant.com,*
dine@arkrestaurant.com

Mountains of oyster shells surround this restaurant, located near the north end of the Long Beach Peninsula on oyster-rich Willapa Bay. In fact, the casual, relaxed restaurant has its own oyster beds—as well as an herb and edible-flower garden and a busy bakery. Nearby are cranberry bogs and forests of wild mushrooms. All these go into the preparation of creative dishes like Scotch salmon, sturgeon Szechuan and oysters Italian, and the Ark oyster feed, a decades-old tradition. Dinner Tuesday through Sunday; Sunday brunch. Call for winter hours.

SHOPPING

MARSH'S FREE MUSEUM ✉*409 South Pacific Avenue, Long Beach* ✆*360-642-2188* 📠*360-642-8177* ✐*www.marshsfreemuseum.com, jake@marshsfreemuseum.com* There's wonderful bric-a-brac at Marsh's, from world-famous Jake the Alligator Man, an authentic shrunken head and freaks-of-nature stuffed animals to antique dishes and saltwater taffy.

ABOVE IT ALL KITES ✉*312 Pacific Boulevard South, Long Beach* ✆*360-642-3541* ✐*www.aboveitallkites.com* The souvenir most typical of beach recreation here, perhaps, would be a colorful kite, which you can get at this local shop.

WIEGARDT STUDIO GALLERY ✉*2607 Bay Avenue between Route 103 and Sandridge Road, Ocean Park* ✆*360-665-5976* 🖰*www.ericwiegardt.com* Noted watercolorist Eric Wiegardt displays his work at this gallery. Open Monday through Saturday in July and August, Friday and Saturday the rest of the year.

BEACHES & PARKS

LOOMIS LAKE STATE PARK

✉*Park Road off Route 103 (Pacific Way), four miles south of Ocean Park* ✆*360-642-3078* 📷*360-642-4216*

🚶🛶 Situated south of Klipsan Beach, this day-use park offers ocean beach access with good fishing from the shore and good clamming on the beach. Swimming is not recommended. Facilities include restrooms and picnic areas.

PACIFIC PINES STATE PARK

✉*At 274th Place off Park Avenue, a mile north of Ocean Park* ✆*360-642-3078* 📷*360-642-4216*

🚶🛶 This day-use park offers beach access for various activities, like beachcombing, kite flying, jogging, surf fishing and razor clam digging in season. The coastal dune environment bristles with foxglove, lupine and a variety of ferns; keep your eye out for hummingbirds, rabbits, deer and raccoons. There are restrooms and picnic areas. Closed November through March.

LEADBETTER POINT STATE PARK

✉*Stackpole Road, via Route 103 and Sandridge Road, three miles north of Oysterville* ✆*360-642-3078* 📷*360-642-4216*

🚶🚲🛶 Shifting dunes and mudflats, ponds and marshes, grasslands and forests make this northern tip of the Long Beach Peninsula an ideal place for those who like to observe nature. Originally named Low Point in 1788 and renamed Leadbetter Point in 1852, as many as 100 species of migratory birds stop over here. There are numerous hiking trails. Clamming is popular, as is surf fishing, but riptides discourage swimming. You'll find pit toilets, restrooms and picnic areas.

CAPE DISAPPOINTMENT STATE PARK

✉*Route 101, two miles southwest of Ilwaco* ✆*360-642-3078* 📷*360-642-4216*

🚶🚲⛺🚤🛶 The point where the Columbia River meets the Pacific Ocean has been a crossroads of history for two centuries. The Lewis and Clark expedition arrived at this dramatic headland in 1805 after 18 months on the trail. Two 19th-century lighthouses—at North Head on the Pacific and at Cape Disappointment on a Columbia sandbar—have limited the number of shipwrecks to a mere 200 through

1994. The fort was occupied from the Civil War through World War II. Today, the 1800-acre park contains the Lewis and Clark Interpretive Center (admission), numerous forest, beach and clifftop trails, a boat launch, a swimming beach, fishing (in the surf, from the jetty or from a boat), summer interpretive programs, lighthouse tours, restrooms, picnic areas and groceries.

▲ There are 152 standard sites ($22 per night), 83 RV hookup sites ($31 per night), and yurts and cabins ($60 per night). Reservations: 888-226-7688.

OUTDOOR ADVENTURES

SPORTFISHING

Despite charter operators' complaints that government restrictions hinder their operations, the Strait of Juan de Fuca is still one of the nation's great salmon grounds, with chinook, coho and other species running the waters during the summer months. From April to September, halibut is also big in these waters—literally: one local operator holds the state record, 288 pounds. Bottomfish like ling cod, true cod, red snapper and black bass round out the angling possibilities.

Olympic Coast
BIG SALMON FISHING RESORT ✉1251 Bay View Avenue (or Front Street), Neah Bay ✆360-645-2374, 866-787-1900 ✐www.bigsalmonresort.com When this resort isn't breaking state records for halibut (288 pounds), it runs half-day charters for salmon and bottomfish. The store also sells bait and rents tackle. Closed October to March.

OLSON'S RESORT & MARINA ✉Sekiu ✆360-963-2311 ✐www.olsons resort.com Olson's runs year-round charters out of Neah Bay and Sekiu for halibut, bottomfish and salmon (in season).

Grays Harbor Area
DEEP SEA CHARTERS ✉Across from Float 6, Westport ✆360-268-9300, 800-562-0151 ✐www.deepseacharters.biz This company operates eight boats for one-day bottomfish and overnight tuna charters.

ANGLER CHARTERS ✉2401 Westhaven Drive, Westport, across from Float 8 ✆360-268-1030, 800-422-0425 ✐www.anglercharters.net Contact this charter company for one-day trips for salmon, bottomfish and halibut.

Long Beach–Willapa Bay
SEABREEZE CHARTERS ✉185 Howerton Way Southeast, Ilwaco ✆360-642-2300, 800-204-9125 ✐www.seabreezecharters.net At the mouth of the Columbia River, Ilwaco is another center for deep-sea fishing. Salmon and sturgeon are caught near the river mouth, while tuna, rockfish, cod and sole are in deeper waters. Seabreeze arranges day charters, operating eight boats, most of which carry up to 16 people. Large engines cut down run times for deep-bottom trips.

OLYMPIC PENINSULA & WASHINGTON COAST OUTDOOR ACVENTURES

RIVER FISHING

It's not just the fish—salmon, steelhead, trout—that attract anglers to the mountain streams flowing from the Olympic Mountains. Spectacular scenery and glimpses of eagles, deer, elk and other wildlife sweeten the deal.

Port Angeles Area

An hour or two away are several destinations for river fishing: the Sol Duc, Bogachiel, Hoh, Queets and Calawah rivers.

Olympic National Park

QUINAULT INDIAN NATION DEPARTMENT OF NATURAL RESOURCES ✉ 1214 Aalis Drive, Taholah ✆ 360-276-8211 ext. 368, 888-616-8211 ⌨ www.quinaultindiannation.com The lower Quinault River is not "overpacked" with fishermen—yet—partly because nontribal people may not fish rivers on the reservation without a Quinault guide. Contact this department to receive information about available guides for drift boat or walk-in fishing.

THREE RIVERS RESORT & FISHING GUIDES ✉ 7764 La Push Road, Forks ✆ 360-374-5300 ⌨ www.forks-web.com/threerivers Three Rivers operates four 16-foot drift boats for two anglers on the Sol Duc, Bogachiel and Hoh rivers (another "quiet" spot). The eight-hour trips are for salmon and steelhead. Tackle, continental breakfast and lunch are provided.

SHELLFISHING

Folks who like to shellfish will be happy in Washington. There are clams (littleneck, butter, Manila and razor), scallops, oysters (Willapa Bay is famous for its oysters), mussels and crab (Dungeness Spit, north of Sequim, is the home of the renowned Dungeness crab). Then, of course, there's that Northwest oddity, the geoduck (say "gooey-duck"), whose huge foot cannot fit within its shell.

Before you start digging up clams or other shellfish, please remember that just like other forms of fishing, a license is required for this activity. You can pick one up at tackle shops and other locations that sell fishing licenses. Recreational harvesting of shellfish is permitted on public beaches, but you should double-check, because much of the state's tideland is privately owned. Generally, shellfishing is permitted year round; razor clams and oyster harvests are restricted by season and location. Call the **Washington State Department of Fish and Wildlife** (360-902-2464, 360-902-2700; wdfw.wa.gov) for information. You can also call the **Shellfish Rule Change Hotline** (866-880-5431; wdfw.wa.gov/fish) hotline. You must also check with the Health Department's **Recreational Marine Biotoxin Hotline** (800-562-5632; www.doh.wa.gov) to find out which waters are unhealthy for shellfish harvesting.

RIVER RUNNING

The Elwha River flows from the Olympic Mountains into the Strait of

Juan de Fuca. Along the way, there are some Class II whitewater rapids—not quite a thrill ride, but enough excitement for good family fun (it's the only commercially rafted whitewater on the peninsula). Besides that, there's plenty of wildlife to see—elk, osprey, bald eagles, deer, harlequin ducks—as well as a view of a glacier.

OLYMPIC RAFT AND KAYAK ✉ *123 Lake Aldwell Road, Port Angeles* ✆ *360-452-1443, 888-452-1443* ✇ *www.raftandkayak.com* This outfitter runs multiple trips daily, each lasting about two and a half hours. The trips down the Class II+ Elwha and Class II Hoh rivers are on rafts. Both beginning and experienced rafters can partake.

KAYAKING

Experienced or novice, kayakers who paddle around a mountain lake, through coastal marshlands or under sea cliffs will be rewarded with the opportunity to observe abundant wildlife in a wilderness setting. Companies offering guided tours generally operate during the warmer months (May through September). But think about this: Many kayakers swear the best time to paddle is in the rain.

Port Townsend Area

SPORT TOWNSEND ✉ *1044 Water Street, Port Townsend* ✆ *360-379-9711* ✇ *www.sporttownsend.com* Port Townsend is a sea-kayaking center; call this aptly named company, where you can buy backpacks and kayaks.

PT OUTDOORS ✉ *1017 Water Street* ✆ *360-379-3608, 888-754-8598* ✇ *www.ptoutdoors.com* For rentals, lessons and guided tours, contact this group. Closed in winter.

OLYMPIC OUTDOOR CENTER ✉ *18971 Front Street, Poulsbo* ✆ *360-697-6095, 800-592-5983* ✇ *www.olympicoutdoorcenter.com* This outdoor center offers private, sunset and overnight kayaking tours in the spring and summer. The center also rents kayaks and offers classes.

Port Angeles Area

SOUND BIKES AND KAYAKS ✉ *120 East Front Street, Port Angeles* ✆ *360-457-1240* ✇ *www.soundbikeskayaks.com* For kayak rentals and sales in Port Angeles, try this shop. Closed Sunday.

OLYMPIC RAFT AND KAYAK ✉ *123 Lake Aldwell Road, Port Angeles* ✆ *360-452-1443, 888-452-1443* ✇ *www.raftandkayak.com* You may have Lake Aldwell all to yourself, aside from the waterfowl nesting along its shores, when you join a two-hour guided tour of this clear blue lake. This company uses the more stable sea kayaks for these lake tours. The service also offers a four-hour trip in the saltwater Freshwater Bay just west of Port Angeles, which teems with bald eagles, otters and endangered marbled murrelets.

KITE FLYING

Several miles of wide, flat beach make the beaches at Ocean Shores and Long Beach ideal kite-flying spots. A nationally sanctioned kite-flying festival in June brings some of the sport's best fliers to Ocean Shores; the same month, competing stunt kites fill the sky over Long Beach. In August, Long Beach hosts the weeklong Washington State International Kite Festival, said to be the biggest kite festival in the country (about 100,000 people attend).

Kite Shops
OCEAN SHORES KITES ✉ *Shores Mall, 172 Chance a la Mer, Ocean Shores* 📞*360-289-4103* 📠*360-289-0517* 🖥*www.oceanshoreskites.com* Pick up a kite and some tips on how to fly it at this shop. Besides dozens of different kites, the store sells windsocks and other wind toys (frisbees, etc.).

Return of the Monster Slayers

Makah, the tribal name of Neah Bay's native people, means "generous food"—and no wonder! For 2000 years, the main protein in the Makah diet was the meat of the gray whale. Men of the tribe would chase one of the 35-ton leviathans in canoes, harpoon it, and kill it by stabbing it repeatedly with spears as it towed them through the open ocean. So vital was whaling to the Makah culture that in their 1855 treaty the U.S. government guaranteed their right to hunt whales forever—the only treaty ever made by the United States that contains such a guarantee. Thereafter, the tribe also sold whale oil to non-Indian settlers and became the wealthiest Indians in the Northwest. (They are now among the poorest.) They had to stop in the 1920s after the whales nearly disappeared from coastal waters due to industrial whaling.

In recent years, since the California gray whale population has recovered and the whales have been removed from the endangered species list, the Makah intend to hold new whale hunts on a limited scale, still in traditional hand-carved log canoes but using a specially designed rifle—hopefully a single carefully aimed shot at the same instant the harpoon is thrown—as a more humane alternative to spears. Meat from the whales would be divided among the 1800 tribal members, storing any excess in tribal freezers. Under the supervision of the National Marine Fisheries Service, the tribe is allowed to take up to 20 migrating adult whales without calves in a five-year period. After nearly five years of planning the hunt and practicing the use of the harpoon and rifle, and a year of ceremonial purification, tribal hunters killed their first whale in May 1999.

Makah whaling is the subject of one of the biggest animal rights controversies in the Northwest. Opponents interpret the language of the Makah treaty as allowing whaling only as long as non-Indians were also hunting whales, before the present international ban. They also fear that despite federal prohibitions the tribe might find the Japanese importers' $1 million offer for a single whale an irresistible temptation. Tribal leaders say whaling is a matter of cultural preservation, discipline and pride. They claim that many of the tribe's health problems may come from the loss of their traditional whale meat diet and point out that the indigenous Chukotki people of Russia's Pacific coast have been "harvesting" about 165 gray whales a year for the last 40 years, yet the whale population continues to grow. Escalating with each whale hunt, the dispute is unlikely to be resolved soon.

Snyder Drive, Long Beach ✆*360-642-4020* ⌘*www.worldkitemuseum.com* Check out the kite selection at this museum gift shop. Open Friday through Tuesday from October through April, daily the rest of the year.

WHALE WATCHING

California gray whales and humpbacks head back up to Alaskan waters between March and May. Orcas, or killer whales, are frequently seen in the waters of the Strait of Juan de Fuca, and we land-based mammals can't seem to get enough of the spectacle. Many fishing charter operators convert to whale-watching cruises during these months.

Two-hour cruises generally head offshore toward the whales' migration path, but occasionally the whales wander into Grays Harbor and the boats never get out to sea.

OCEAN CHARTERS ✉*Across from Float 14* ✆*360-268-9144, 800-562-0105* ⌘*www.oceanchartersinc.com* In Westport, contact these guides for whale-watching trips.

DEEP SEA CHARTERS ✉*Across from Float 6* ✆*360-268-9300, 800-562-0151* ⌘*www.deepseacharters.biz* In Grays Harbor, this crew offers more of the same from March to mid-October.

SKIING

HURRICANE RIDGE SKI AND SNOWBOARD AREA The only skiing on the Olympic Peninsula is within this area, 17 miles south of Port Angeles, in Olympic National Park. Here skiers will find a few downhill runs and several cross-country trails starting from the visitors center. There are two rope tows and a T-bar lift on site. The Hurricane Hill Road cross-country trail (1.5 miles one way) is probably the easiest of the area's six trails; the most challenging is the Hurricane Ridge Trail to Mt. Angeles, a steep three-mile route that's often icy. Rental equipment is also available. Open mid-December through March, weekends and weather permitting only. Contact the **Olympic National Park Visitor Center** (3002 Mt. Angeles Road, Port Angeles; 360-565-3130, for road conditions 360-565-3131; www.hurricaneridge.com).

RIDING STABLES

On the Olympic Peninsula, it's possible to saddle up for a guided mountain ride through forests of towering trees or a ride along the beach at sunset.

Ocean Shores–Pacific Beach

NAN-SEA STABLES ✉*255 State Route 115, Ocean Shores* ✆*360-289-0194* ✆*360-289-3918* ⌘*www.horseplanet.com, nansea@horseplanet.com* These guides teach natural horsemanship in Western or English style. A three-hour day camp in spring, summer and fall provides grooming, saddling, riding lessons and a trail ride that is great for kids and beginners, ages seven and up.

GOLF

Bay views, ocean views, mountain views—take your pick. They're part and parcel with the courses in this region, all of which rent power carts, push carts and clubs.

Port Townsend Area

DISCOVERY BAY GOLF CLUB ✉ *7401 Cape George Road, Port Townsend* ☎ *360-385-0704* ✍ *www.discobaygolf.com* The public 18-hole course here is set in the woods above Discovery Bay. It is a fairly flat course, although it can get a bit mushy after winter rains.

PORT TOWNSEND GOLF CLUB ✉ *1948 Blaine Street, Port Townsend* ☎ *360-385-4547* ✍ *www.porttownsendgolf.com* This public, double-teed, nine-hole course is considered the driest winter course in the area (it gets only 17 inches of rain), with rolling terrain, small greens and a driving range.

PORT LUDLOW GOLF COURSE ✉ *751 Highland Drive, Port Ludlow* ☎ *360-437-0272, 877-805-0868* ✍ *www.portludlowresort.com* *Golf Digest* has named this semiprivate 27-hole course designed by Robert Muir Graves one of the best in the country. Although housing flanks one section, the spectacular views of Ludlow Bay and abundant wildlife prompt comments like "Amazing" and "It's like golfing in a national park" from local duffers.

Port Angeles Area

SUNLAND GOLF AND COUNTRY CLUB ✉ *109 Hilltop Drive, Sequim* ☎ *360-683-6800* ✍ *www.sunlandgolf.com* Although this 18-hole private course goes through a housing development, it's well treed and fairly flat. Call for reciprocal play times.

DUNGENESS GOLF COURSE ✉ *1965 Woodcock Road, Sequim* ☎ *360-683-6344* This golf club offers a semiprivate, 18-hole course. The number-three hole, called "Old Crabbie," has ten contracts guarding the crab-shaped green.

Ocean Shores–Pacific Beach

OCEAN SHORES GOLF COURSE ✉ *500 Canal Drive Northeast at Albatross Street, Ocean Shores* ☎ *360-289-3357* The front nine holes of this municipal golf course have a links-like layout in the dunes; the back nine wanders into the trees.

Grays Harbor Area

OAKSRIDGE GOLF COURSE ✉ *1052 Monte–Elma Road, Elma* ☎ *360-482-3511* An old farming tract turned into a public 18-hole golf course in the early 1920s, this course is very flat. It's pretty wet in the winter, but drains fast. The front nine is long.

BIKING

Except along the southwestern shore areas, bicycling this part of Washington requires strength and stamina. There's spectacular beauty here, but there's also lots of rain and challenging terrain.

Port Townsend Area

FORT WORDEN STATE PARK   Recreational bicyclists will probably enjoy a ride through this beautiful state park, which overlooks the Strait of Juan de Fuca, in Port Townsend.

Olympic Coast

UPPER PENINSULA TOUR   A recommended road tour is this 85-mile ride from Sequim to Neah Bay. The 55-mile trip down Route 101 from Port Angeles to Forks is also recommended. A paved six-mile trail loops the Port Angeles waterfront. The trail is flat, mostly following the shoreline, with picnic tables and other stopping spots along the way. On a clear day, you can see across the strait to Victoria.

Ocean Shores–Pacific Beach

OCEAN SHORES LOOP   One of the area's gentlest biking opportunities is this 14-mile loop from North Beach Park. For a map, call the Ocean Shores Chamber of Commerce (360-289-2451; www.ocean shores.org).

Grays Harbor Area

ABERDEEN-RAYMOND-WESTPORT   Worthy of a long ride is this 69-mile loop on Routes 101 and 105. A new paved trail has been built in Westport along the beach. It runs for a mile and a half between two small state parks.

Long Beach–Willapa Bay

SEAVIEW-NASELLE   This 42-mile loop in Pacific County is popular.

Bike Rentals

PORT TOWNSEND CYCLERY   ✉ *252 Tyler Street, Port Townsend* ☎ *360-385-6470* ⌨ *www.ptcyclery.com* In Port Townsend, rent mountain bikes, tandems, running strollers, bike trailers and road bikes from this shop.

SOUND BIKES AND KAYAKS   ✉ *120 East Front Street, Port Angeles* ☎ *360-437-1240* ⌨ *www.soundbikeskayaks.com* This company rents hybrids and mountain bikes.

HIKING

All distances listed for hiking trails are one way unless otherwise noted.

Port Townsend Area

MT. WALKER TRAIL _____

This trail (2 miles) ascends the Olympics' easternmost peak (2804 feet) through a rhododendron forest. The view from the summit, across Hood Canal and the Kitsap Peninsula to Seattle and the Cascades, is unforgettable. The trailhead is one-fifth mile off Route 101 at Walker Pass, five miles south of Quilcene.

DUNGENESS SPIT TRAIL

This trail (5.5 miles) extends down the outside of the longest natural sandspit in the United States, and back the inside. The spit is a national wildlife refuge with a lighthouse at its seaward end. The trail begins and ends at the Dungeness Recreation Area.

Olympic National Park

OBSTRUCTION POINT TRAIL   Olympic National Park and adjacent areas of Olympic National Forest are rich in backpacking opportunities. Most trails follow rivers into the high country, with its peaks and alpine lakes. Obstruction Point Trail (7.4 miles) leads from the Deer Park Campground to Obstruction Point, following a 6500-foot ridgeline.

SPRUCE RAILROAD TRAIL   This easy trail (2 miles) begins near North Shore Picnic Area or the west side of Log Cabin Resort on Lake Crescent. It follows the railroad bed of the historic Spruce Railroad and offers spectacular views of glacial Lake Crescent and surrounding mountains. No elevation gain.

SEVEN LAKES BASIN LOOP

This loop (22.5 miles) has several trail options, starting and ending at Sol Duc Hot Springs.

CAPE ALAVA LOOP

Coastal areas of the Olympic Peninsula have hiking trails as well. This loop (9 miles) crosses from the Ozette Ranger Station to Cape Alava; follows the shoreline south to Sand Point, from which there is beach access to shipwreck memorials farther south; and returns northeast to the ranger station. Prehistoric petroglyphs and an ancient Indian village can be seen en route.

HOH RIVER TRAIL

One of the most unforgettable hikes is this river trail (17.5 miles), which wanders through lush, primeval rainforest teeming with deer from the Hoh Ranger Station to Glacier Meadows, at the base of the Blue Glacier on 7965-foot Mt. Olympus, the park's highest point.

Grays Harbor Area

WYNOOCHEE LAKE SHORE TRAIL   This trail (12 miles) circles the manmade reservoir in Olympic National Forest north of Montesano.

SHIFTING SANDS NATURE TRAIL   This nature trail (.5 mile) teaches visitors to Twin Harbors State Park, south of Westport, about plant and animal life in the seaside dunes.

Long Beach–Willapa Bay

Along the southwestern Washington coast there are few inland trails, but the long stretches of flat beach appeal to many walkers.

LEADBETTER POINT LOOP TRAIL *hidden*

A nice loop trail (2.5 miles) the Leadbetter Point trek weaves through the forests and dunes, and past the ponds, mudflats and marshes, of the wildlife sanctuary/state park at the northern tip of the Long Beach Peninsula. Accessible from Oysterville, it's of special interest to birdwatchers.

THE TRAIL OF THE ANCIENT CEDARS ✉ Milepost 24, Route 101 ✆ 360-484-3482 This trail (3.2 miles) goes through an important grove of old-growth red cedar, some as large as 11 feet wide and 150 feet tall, on Long Island, and be sure there is at least a six-foot tide. You must find your own boat access to Long Island. The Willapa Bay National Wildlife Refuge provides interpretive brochures at its headquarters.

TRANSPORTATION

CAR

Route 101 is the main artery of the Olympic Peninsula and Washington coastal region, virtually encircling the entire land mass. Branching off Route 5 in Olympia, at the foot of Puget Sound, it runs north to Discovery Bay, where **Route 20** turns off to Port Townsend; west through Port Angeles to Sappho; then zigzags to Astoria, Oregon, and points south. Remarkably, when you reach Aberdeen, 292 miles after you start traveling on 101, you're just 36 miles from where you started!

Traveling from Seattle, most Olympic Peninsula visitors take either the Seattle–Winslow ferry (to Route 305) or the Edmonds–Kingston ferry (to Route 104), joining 101 just south of Discovery Bay. From Tacoma, the practical route is **Route 16** across the Narrows Bridge. From the north, the Keystone ferry to Port Townsend has its eastern terminus midway down lanky Whidbey Island, off Route 20. Northbound travelers can reach the area either through Astoria, on Route 101, or via several routes that branch off Route 5 north of Portland.

AIR

WILLIAM R. FAIRCHILD INTERNATIONAL AIRPORT ✆ 360-417-3433 This international airport, near Port Angeles, links the northern Olympic Peninsula with Seattle and western Canada via Kenmore Air and Rite Bros. Aviation charter flights.

FERRY

WASHINGTON STATE FERRIES ☎206-464-6400, 888-808-7977 ✐www.wsdot.wa.gov/ferries The state ferries serve the Olympic Peninsula directly from Whidbey Island to Port Townsend and indirectly across Puget Sound (via the Kitsap Peninsula) from Seattle and Edmonds.

BLACK BALL TRANSPORT ☎360-457-4491 ✐www.ferrytovictoria.com Black Ball has daily service between Port Angeles and Victoria, B.C.

VICTORIA EXPRESS ☎360-452-8088 ✐www.victoriaexpress.com This agency provides foot-passenger service.

Some smaller cruise lines may make stops in Port Angeles.

CAR RENTALS

In Port Angeles, **Budget Car and Truck Rental** (800-527-0700) can be found in town.

PUBLIC TRANSIT

For local bus service in the northern Olympic Peninsula, including Port Angeles and Sequim, contact **Clallam Transit System** (360-452-4511, 800-858-3747; www.clallamtransit.com) in Port Angeles.

Port Townsend, Sequim and eastern Jefferson County are served by **Jefferson Transit** (360-385-4777, 800-371-0497; www.jeffersontransit. com).

The **Grays Harbor Transportation Authority** (360-532-2770, 800-562-9730; www.ghtransit.com) offers bus service to Aberdeen, Ocean Shores and the surrounding region.

Bus service between Raymond, Long Beach and Astoria, Oregon, is provided by the **Pacific Transit System**. (360-642-9418; www.pacific transit.org).

WASHINGTON CASCADES

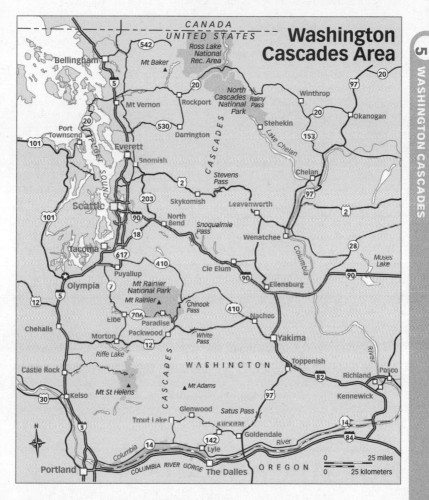

Perhaps without even realizing it, many Americans have a burning image of this region. For it was here, in the Cascade Range, that Mt. St. Helens blew its top in 1980. But the area has a lot more going for it than one hyperactive mountaintop. Indeed, think of the Cascades and Central Washington as one wild place for anyone who loves the outdoors.

The Cascade Range contains some of the most beautiful mountain scenery in the United States, much of it preserved by two major national parks, several national recreation areas and numerous wilderness areas that make this a major sports haven. There are also glaciers galore; 316 are in the North Cascades National Park Service Complex alone. Thousands of miles of trails and logging roads lace the Cascades, leading to mountaintop lookout towers, old gold mines, lakes, streams and gorgeous sights.

The hand of man has done little to alter the Cascades. When the North Cascades Highway (Route 20) was finally completed in 1972, it was with the understanding that it would be closed during the heavy snows, usually from November until April. Thus, most of the Cascades are still wild and remote, seen and experienced by humans but not transformed by them.

The range, about 700 miles long, begins at the Fraser River in southern British Columbia and extends southward through Washington and Oregon and into California just beyond Lassen Peak. The most dominant features of the Cascades are its 15 volcanoes. Washington lays claim to five, with Mt. Rainier the granddaddy at 14,411 feet. Most peaks are under 10,000 feet, and Harts Pass, the highest pass in the state, is only 6197 feet.

Although the range is not a comparatively high one, it served as an effective barrier to exploration and development until well into the 20th century. The pioneers who came over the Oregon Trail avoided it, choosing instead to go down the Columbia River to the Cowlitz River, travel up to present-day Toledo, then move overland to Puget Sound at Tumwater and Olympia.

Mining has always been part of the Cascades story. Although no major gold strikes have been found, several smaller ones have kept the interest alive, and there's probably never been a day since the mid-1870s when someone wasn't panning or sluicing in the mountains.

The range supports a wide variety of plants and wildlife because it has so many climatic zones. Naturalists have given names to eight distinct ones: Coastal Forest Zone, Silver Fir Zone, Sierran Mixed-Conifer Zone, Red Fir Zone, Subalpine Zone, Alpine Zone, Interior Fir Zone and Ponderosa Pine Zone. Each zone has its own community of plants, animals and birds.

Although most of the range is under the stewardship of the Forest Service, which by law has to practice multiple-use policies, most people think of the Cascades as their very own. It is used by mushroom hunters, hikers, runners, birdwatchers, anglers, hunters, photographers, painters, skiers, horse riders, loggers and miners. Whichever of these apply to you, enjoy.

NORTH CASCADES

Extending from the Canadian border south into the Mt. Baker–Snoqualmie National Forest, the North Cascades region has over 300 glaciers, valleys famous for their spring tulip fields and some of the best skiing in the Pacific Northwest. Backroads wind through old logging towns past mountain lakes to unspoiled wilderness areas. The North Cascades National Park Service Complex forms the core of this realm that includes Rainy and Washington passes, two of the Cascades' grandest viewpoints.

Beginning at the northernmost approach, **Route 542** enters the Cascades from Bellingham, a pleasant, two-lane, blacktop highway that is shared by loggers, skiers, anglers and hikers. Much of the route runs through dense forest beside fast streams and with only rare glimpses of the surrounding mountains. The road deadends a few miles beyond the Mt. Baker day-use lodge for skiers, at a lookout called Artist Point. In clear weather you will see 9127-foot **Mt. Shuksan**, one of the most beautiful peaks in the Cascades. It can't be seen from any other part of the range, but it probably appears on more calendars and postcards than its neighbor Mt. Baker or even Mt. Rainier.

MT. BAKER ✉*Mt. Baker Ranger District* ✆*360-856-5700* 🖂*360-856-1934* The ski slopes here usually open in November and run all the way into April, making for the longest ski season of any area in Washington. During summer the mountain is popular with day hikers and backpackers. Several hiking trails wind through high alpine meadows dotted with wildflowers in the Heather Meadows area.

Mt. Baker was named by George Vancouver in May 1792, in honor of Joseph Baker, a lieutenant on his ship. It was first climbed on August 17, 1868, by a party of four led by an experienced alpinist named Edmund T. Coleman. Although it is listed as an active volcano and occasionally steam is seen rising from it, Mt. Baker hasn't erupted since 1880.

ROUTE 20 This is one of America's premier scenic routes. It goes through the North Cascades National Park Service Complex and along the way provides hiking trails, roadside parks, boat launches and one of the more unusual tours in the Cascades. Because the highway is enclosed by the Ross Lake National Recreation Area, new development is virtually nonexistent, and the small company towns of Newhalem and Diablo look frozen in the pre–World War II days. When driving on Route 20, be forewarned: No gasoline is available between Marblemount and Mazama, a distance of more than 70 miles, and there are few places to buy groceries. Fill your tank and bring your lunch. Also, the highway at Milepost 134, just west of the Cascade Crest, is closed by mid-November due to heavy snows and doesn't open again until April.

SEATTLE CITY LIGHT SKAGIT TOURS ✆*206-684-3030* 🖂*206-233-1642* ⌨*www.skagittours.com, skagittours.reservations@seattle.gov* These tours offer a unique opportunity to experience the rugged wilderness. The two-and-a-half-hour Diablo Lake Adventure travels across Diablo Dam. It includes a scenic cruise (with dinner on Monday and Thursday in July and August) deep into the Skagit Gorge and across Diablo Lake. Often compared to the Swiss Alps, the North Cascades offer snow-capped mountain peaks, alpine valleys and glaciers. Reservations are recommended. Tours run seasonally May through September. Admission.

SKAGIT RIVER DAMS Three historic hydroelectric power plants and dams on the Skagit River generate 25 percent of Seattle's electricity. Diablo Dam was built a short distance downstream, creating the much smaller **Diablo Lake**. Stairstepped below Diablo is **Gorge Lake**, created by Gorge Dam. **Ross Lake**, a fjordlike lake between steep mountains,

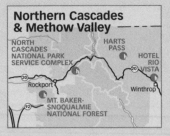

Northern Cascades & Methow Valley

NORTH CASCADES NATIONAL PARK SERVICE COMPLEX

PAGE 229

Nearly 700,000 acres of Washington's most rugged and remote forest, extending from Ross lake to the Canadian border

HARTS PASS

PAGE 230

Spectacular views from the summit of the state's highest point, 6197 feet up from the forested earth

HOTEL RIO VISTA

PAGE 232

Bright and airy rooms in a Western-inspired property overlooking the Methow River

MT. BAKER–SNOQUALMIE NATIONAL FOREST

PAGE 227

Trailside camping deep in a dormant volcano wilderness

was formed by Ross Dam. It is an international body of water because its backwaters cross the border into Canada, and when the timber was being cleared before the lake was formed, the work was done via a road in from British Columbia.

MOUNTAIN LOOP HIGHWAY   Another way to reach Route 20 is over what is locally known as the Mountain Loop Highway, a favorite weekend drive for years before Route 20 was completed across the mountains. The Mountain Loop begins in Granite Falls with Route 92, which goes along the South Fork of the Stillaguamish River past the one-store towns of Robe and Silverton. The road is crooked and slow driving because it follows the river route closely. It is always closed in the winter and sometimes landslides close it for much of the summer. Near the old mining town of Monte Cristo, the road turns north along the Sauk River and emerges in the logging town of Darrington. Here you can drive due north to catch Route 20 at Rockport or turn west on Route 530 and return to Route 5.

VIEWPOINTS   Route 20 plunges into the Cascades and goes over two passes—**Rainy Pass**, 4860 feet, and **Washington Pass**, 5477 feet—before descending into the Methow Valley. Stop at each viewpoint and turnout for stunning views of the region. One viewpoint above Ross Lake shows miles of the long, narrow lake, and another just beyond Washington Pass gives a grandstand view of the jagged mountains behind the pass.

LADY OF THE LAKE   ☎509-682-4584   ☎509-682-8206   ⌨www.ladyofthelake. com The only way to visit the resort town of **Stehekin**, at the tip of Lake Chelan, is by boat, plane or hiking. Most visitors take the trip up the lake on this tour-mail-supply boat for Stehekin and points between. The schedule allows you up to three hours in Stehekin, and you can buy lunch at the Stehekin landing. Bike and bus tours coordinated with the ferry schedule are available. Reservations suggested. Admission.

CHELAN AIRWAYS   ✉*1328 West Woodin Avenue (one mile west of Chelan on Route 97A)*   ☎*509-682-5555*   ⌨*www.chelanairways.com, sales@chelanairways.com* If you'd like to fly into Stehekin, contact this airline. The experienced floatplane pilots not only give passengers great views, they know every nook and cranny of the lake and all the stories that accompany them.

LODGING

GLACIER CREEK LODGE
$–$$$ 22 UNITS   ✉*10036 Mt. Baker Highway, Glacier*   ☎*360-599-2991,* *800-719-1414*   ⌨*www.glaciercreeklodge.com*
A rustic motor court, this lodge has nine motel-style units and thirteen blue-and-white cabins. The cabins are one or two bedrooms, with private bath, double bed, bedside table and tired furniture. The units are so small there's no room for a table. In addition to a hot tub, there is a large lobby where a continental breakfast is served.

BAKER LAKE LODGE
$–$$ 9 UNITS   ✉*46110 East Main Street, Concrete*   ☎*360-853-8341, 888-711-3033* ☎*425-462-3118*   ⌨*bakerlakerecpse@puget.com*
One of the larger lakeside resorts is 20 miles north of Concrete on Baker Lake Road. It is a mixture of RV sites and nine rustic cabins on the lake. Each unit includes a bathroom, shower and a refrigerator, but guests must bring their own cookware and utensils. Boating and fishing are popular; boat rentals are available. Closed early October to late May.

CASCADE MOUNTAIN LODGE
$$ 13 ROOMS   ✉*44628 Route 20, Concrete*   ☎*360-853-8870, 800-251-3054* ☎*360-853-7123*   ⌨*www.cascademountainlodge.com, cascadelodge@hotmail.com*
A country lodge with bed-and-breakfast ambience, this is a vintage Northwest cedar-shake hostelry with an adjoining restaurant and lounge. There are refurbished rooms, some with antique and hand-carved furnishings. All rooms come with modern comforts such as microwaves, refrigerators and TVs. Guests can have breakfast, lunch or dinner in the restaurant or on an adjoining outdoor patio adorned by a three-tiered fountain and dozens of hanging flower baskets.

STEHEKIN VALLEY RANCH
$$ 12 UNITS   ✉*P.O. Box 36, Stehekin, WA 98852*   ☎*509-682-4677, 800-536-0745* ⌨*www.stehekinvalleyranch.com, ranch@courtneycountry.com*
Rustic reigns in remote Stehekin. The most outdoorsy is this ranch, owned and operated by the Courtneys, the major family in the valley. The ranch is nine miles from town, up the Stehekin River Valley. Guests are housed in tent cabins with wooden walls and canvas-covered roofs. Showers and toilets are in the main building. Five newer cabins have private baths. All meals are included and served in the dining room,

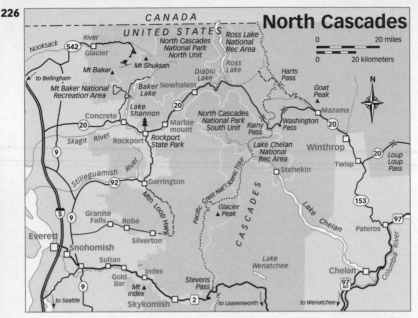

North Cascades

which has split logs for tables and seats. Horseback rides, river rafting and kayaking trips are offered. Closed October to mid-June.

SILVER BAY INN _____

$$$$ 4 UNITS ✉ 10 Silver Bay Road, Stehekin 📞 254-377-3912, 800-555-7781 📠 509-687-3142 🖉 www.silverbayinn.com, stehekin@silverbayinn.com

This is the fanciest Stehekin lodging, located at the head of Lake Chelan and the mouth of the Stehekin River, a short distance from the village. There is one efficiency unit with a kitchenette and private bath as well as three spacious, well-appointed cabins that will sleep four and are complete with kitchens, dishwashers and decks.

DINING

MILANO'S MARKET AND DELI

$ DELI ✉ 9990 Mt. Baker Highway, Glacier 📞 360-599-2863

A popular place along the Mt. Baker Highway is Milano's, a combination small restaurant and deli offering a hearty supply of soups, salads, fresh pasta dishes and homemade bread and desserts. This is a good place to have a picnic lunch made up. If the weather is right, the deck is open for outside dining.

THE EATERY RESTAURANT

$–$$ AMERICAN ✉ Route 20, Marblemount 📞 360-873-2250 📠 360-873-4077 🖉 www.northcascades.com

A big, airy place that doubles as a museum, this restaurant is decorated with family memorabilia dating back to the 1800s. The Eatery, located at the Skagit River Resort, specializes in downhome fare. Breakfast features biscuits and gravy, while lunch offers burgers and sandwiches and dinner means steaks, chops and fish. Don't miss the housemade pies and milkshakes.

CASCADE MOUNTAIN LODGE

$ AMERICAN   ✉ *44628 Route 20, Concrete*   ☎ *360-853-8771, 800-251-3054*   ✍ *www.cascademountainlodge.com*

On the western edge of Concrete, this lodge has established a local reputation for good, plain American food (steaks, chops, burgers) and delicious pie (made by a local woman especially for the restaurant). The interior is decorated with antique furnishings.

SHOPPING

CONCRETE SENIOR CENTER ✉ *45821 Railway Avenue, Concrete* If you're in Concrete on Saturday from mid-May through August, hit the **Saturday Market** in this center for arts and crafts and baked goods.

SAUK MOUNTAIN POTTERY ✉ *50303 Route 20, Concrete* ☎ *360-853-8689* Potter Stephen Murray is known for his wood-fired ceramic dinnerware that comes in a variety of lustrous glazes. He also works with stoneware and porcelain. Individual pieces are sold at his store east of Concrete.

NIGHTLIFE

The Cascades isn't the place to go for stellar nightlife. After a day traipsing around in the mountains, most people return to town tired and only want to eat and go to bed. Consequently, only the busiest areas even have live music.

PARKS

MT. BAKER SNOQUALMIE NATIONAL FOREST

hidden

✉ *Four east–west highways cross the national forest: Routes 90, 20, 2 and 410.* ☎ *425-783-6000, 800-627-0062* ✍ *425-744-3255*

🏃 🚵 🏇 🎿 ⛷ 🥾 🎣 🚣 🛶 🏞 This 1.7-million-acre forest begins at the Canadian border and goes south along the western slopes of the Cascades to Mt. Rainier National Park. It is dominated on the north by the inactive volcano, 10,778-foot Mt. Baker. Another inactive volcano, 10,568-foot Glacier Peak, lies in the middle of the forest. The Forest Service controls the land for the ski areas at Crystal Mountain, Mt. Baker, Stevens Pass and Snoqualmie Pass. Its best-known wilderness area is Alpine Lakes Wilderness, but it also includes the Glacier Peak, Noisy Diobsud, Boulder River, Henry M. Jackson, Clearwater, Norse Peak, Wild Sky and Mt. Baker Wilderness areas. Within the forest is excellent fishing for rainbow trout, salmon and steelhead in Baker Lake and many other streams and lakes. There are picnic areas, restrooms and showers. Parking permit, $5 per day or $30 for an annual pass.

▲ Camping is permitted (unless otherwise posted) along the highways, trails and the Pacific Crest Trail, as well as at established campsites. Most of the 40-plus campgrounds are primitive with vault toilets and vary from walk-in to drive-in sites (RV sites are available); $10 to $16 per night. Most sites are open from mid-May through September. Roughly 60 percent of sites are available for reservation: 877-444-6777.

ROCKPORT STATE PARK

✉*Route 20, one mile west of Rockport* ☎*360-853-8461* ✑*360-853-8461*

🚶 🚴 ♨ ⚓ There are picnic areas, restrooms, showers, good steelhead fishing spots and five miles of hiking trails in this 670-acre park along the Skagit River. The David Douglas Historical Marker, named for the noted horticulturalist who discovered the Douglas fir, is located in the park. This is a great place to view bald eagles in winter (open weekends only in winter).

▲ Heavy rains destabilized the old-growth forest of Douglas fir that has long been a popular place for camping. Unfortunately, the campground is closed indefinitely.

RASAR STATE PARK

✉*Off Route 20, about 12 miles northwest of Rockport* ☎*360-826-3942*

🚶 🚤 ⚓ This 169-acre park is located approximately 15 miles west of Rockport along the Skagit River and offers 4,000 feet of shoreline for boating, fishing, birdwatching and wildlife viewing. There are nearly four miles of hiking trails and a mile-long accessible trail through forests of Douglas fir, cedar, maple, spruce, alder and hemlock. Keep your eyes out for herons and eagles.

▲ There are 18 standard campsites ($17 per night), 20 campsites with hookups ($24 per night), two ADA-accessible campsites, eight walk-in sites, three primitive hiker/biker sites ($12 per night) and three Adirondack sleeping shelters ($23 per night). Reservations: 888-226-7688.

HOWARD MILLER STEELHEAD COUNTY PARK

✉*Located in the middle of Rockport at the junction of Routes 20 and 530*
☎*360-853-8808* ✑*360-853-7315*

🚶 🚴 🏕 ♨ ⚓ 🚤 ⚓ One of the most popular parks on the Skagit River for steelheaders and travelers alike, this county park covers 97 acres and has exhibits of a historic cabin, an old river ferry and dugout canoe. Anglers will find salmon and trout, and birders will enjoy bald-eagle watching from December to February. In fact, the greatest concentration of wintering bald eagles can be found near this park at the 7800-acre Skagit River Bald Eagle Natural Area between Marblemount and Rockport. Facilities include covered picnic areas, a playground, a clubhouse, restrooms, showers and a trailer dump.

▲ There are ten standard campsites ($16 per night), 54 RV sites (some with hookups, $22 to $24 per night) and two Adirondack sleeping shelters ($22 per night). Call the park for more information and reservations.

NORTH CASCADES NATIONAL PARK SERVICE COMPLEX — hidden

✉ *Only Route 20 goes through Ross Lake National Recreation Area, and in winter the road closes after the visitors center.* ☎ *360-854-7200* ✆ *360-856-1934* ✐ *noca_information@nps.gov*

🏃🏇🏕🚣🛶🚤�) Covering 684,313 acres in the north central part of the state, this park is divided into two units. The northern unit runs from the Canadian border to Ross Lake National Recreation Area. The southern unit continues on to the **Lake Chelan National Recreation Area.** Much of its eastern boundary is the summit of the Cascade Range, and the western boundary is the Mt. Baker–Snoqualmie National Forest. It is the most rugged and remote of the national parks in Washington and has the fewest roads. All visitor facilities and most roads in the northern portion are inside the **Ross Lake National Recreation Area.** On the southern end, the Lake Chelan National Recreation Area covers the heavy-use area on the north end of the lake, including the village of Stehekin. Try for steelhead and salmon in Ross Lake, rainbow and cutthroat trout in the Skagit River downstream from Newhalem and rainbow and eastern brook trout in high lakes. There are visitors centers in Newhalem and Stehekin, and rangers sometimes lead nature walks. Picnic areas, restrooms and nature walks are located here.

▲ There are over 350 campsites at four campgrounds. You can camp year-round at Goodell Creek, which has potable water in summer and vault toilets; $10 per night. Colonial Creek and Newhalem Creek campgrounds have potable water, flush toilets and dump stations; $12 per night. Gorge Lake sites are free, but you'll have to bring in your own drinking water. The adjacent Okanogan Forest has more sites, including the popular Lone Fir and Early Winters campgrounds. Backcountry camping is free, but requires a permit. Reservations: 877-444-6777.

METHOW VALLEY

The scenery changes quickly and dramatically once you have crossed Washington Pass into the Methow Valley. Located along Route 20 between Mazama and Pateros, this region includes the tourist center of Chelan, gateway to one of the state's most popular lake-resort areas.

SIGHTS

WINTHROP As you descend the east slope of the Cascades, the thick, fir forest gives way to smaller pine with almost no underbrush. The mountains become bare, and you can see for miles. And by the time you arrive in this little community, you will wonder if you are in Colorado or Wyoming because the small town is all falsefronts, saloon doors, hitching rails and wooden porches. Winthrop adopted a Wild

West theme years ago, and it has revitalized the sawmill town and surrounding area into one of the state's most popular destinations. Winthrop is named after Theodore Winthrop, a 19th-century Yale graduate and adventurer/traveler who wrote *The Canoe and the Saddle* and other novels about his excursions in the Pacific Northwest.

SHAFER MUSEUM ✉*One block up the hill off Route 20, Winthrop* ☎*509-996-2712* ⌨*www.shafermuseum.com, staff@shafermuseum.com* This museum is a collection of early 1900s buildings, including the cabin built by town founder Guy Waring in 1897. Exhibits include a stagecoach, antique automobiles and the largest collection of mining artifacts in the Pacific Northwest. Closed Tuesday and Wednesday, and from late September to late May.

HARTS PASS

There are several areas around Winthrop worth driving to, including this 6197-foot pass a short distance from town. This is the highest point to which you can drive in Washington and is only an hour's drive on a gravel Forest Service road. The views from the summit are spectacular.

Not long after driving south on Route 153, the last of the timbered mountains are left behind, and the Methow Valley flattens into a series of irrigated ranches with broad hayfields. The valley is gaining popularity with people from Puget Sound looking for more space, so houses are beginning to line the low hills on both sides.

COLUMBIA RIVER When you reach this notable river at Pateros, the landscape is one of basaltic cliffs on both sides. Instead of a fast-flowing river, there is a chain of lakes behind dams all the way past Wenatchee. Route 97 hugs the west side of the Columbia, then splits off onto 97A at Chelan Falls and swings away from the river to go through the resort town of Chelan, which sits at the end of Lake Chelan. The two highways meet again at Wenatchee.

LAKE CHELAN This lake is a remnant of the Ice Ages. Scoured out of the mountains by glaciers, it is one of the deepest lakes in the region, more than 1500 feet deep in at least one area, which places its bed at 400 feet below sea level. It is 50 miles long but quite narrow, and the mountains rising from its shores give it the appearance of a Norwegian fjord.

CHELAN A small town that has been given over almost entirely to tourism and apples, this place has some of the best orchards along the eastern slopes of the Cascades. If you take a drive northwest of town on Route 150 to Manson, you will see thousands of acres of apple orchards climbing up the sun-baked hills from the lake. Back in town, Woodin Avenue is the main drag and the lakefront is lined with resorts, but the small-town atmosphere remains intact, so a farmer can come to town and still buy a two-by-four or a cotter pin.

LAKE CHELAN HISTORICAL SOCIETY MUSEUM ✉*Woodin Avenue and Emerson Street, Chelan* ☎*509-682-5644* ⌨*www.chelanmuseum.com* American Indian artifacts and early farming equipment are on display here.

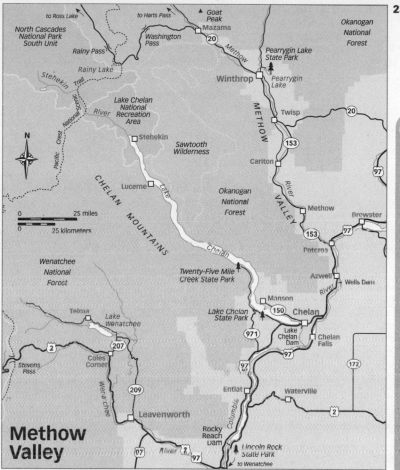

Methow Valley

One room depicts a miner's cabin, and another shows a typical country kitchen. Closed Saturday and Sunday October through April and Sunday from June through September.

LODGING

FREESTONE INN AT WILSON RANCH

$$$–$$$$ 27 UNITS   ✉31 Early Winters Drive, Mazama   ☎509-996-3906, 800-639-3809   📠509-996-3907   🖊www.freestoneinn.com, info@freestoneinn.com

If you want to get up close and personal with the North Cascades, head for this inn at Wilson Ranch. The 15 cabins sit across the highway from the Forest Service/National Park Service information center at the foot of the mountains. Varying in size and widely spaced, each cabin is heated with a propane fireplace; the bathrooms are heated. All cooking utensils are provided. In the inn, all 12 rooms have fireplaces, private porches or balconies, and lake views. The inn has one hot tub, the cabins have another. The Recreation Center offers cross-country ski rentals in the winter and mountain-bike rentals in the summer for adventurers who want to explore the Methow Valley Nordic Ski Trails—a 175-kilometer network of trails that intersect the property.

SUN MOUNTAIN LODGE
$$$–$$$$ 112 UNITS   ✉ *604 Patterson Lake Road, Winthrop* ☎ *509-996-2211,*
800- 72-0493 📠 *509-996-3133* 🖥 *www.sunmountainlodge.com,*
sunmtn@sunmountainlodge.com
Here you'll find the most elaborate place in the Methow Valley and one of the best resorts in the Pacific Northwest. Built at the 3000-foot level atop a small mountain, this low-rise, stone-and-timber resort gives a 360-degree view of the Cascades, Pasayten Wilderness, Okanogan Highlands and Methow Valley. The units are spread over three buildings atop the mountain and down the road in 16 rustic, cozy cabins. The resort has just about everything: several miles of hiking trails that become cross-country ski trails in the winter, two pools, two hot tubs, an exercise room, a full-service spa, saddle-and-pack horses, mountain-bike rentals, canoe and sailing on the lake, heli-skiing and tennis. It also has a great restaurant. Rooms feature bentwood furniture, a fireplace (only the suites have real-wood fireplaces), coffee, the thickest and softest towels and robes you can hope for and no television.

HOTEL RIO VISTA
$$–$$$ 30 UNITS   ✉ *285 Riverside Avenue, Winthrop* ☎ *509-996-3535,*
800-398-0911 🖥 *www.hotelriovista.com, info@hotelriovista.com*
This cozy hotel has a facade that looks like it was made out of matchsticks. The bright and airy rooms all overlook the Methow River and have mini-fridges and private decks. A hot tub and quaint riverside picnic area round out the amenities. Located on the south side of town, this lodging is within walking distance of downtown's eateries. It also runs a fully equipped Aspen loft cabin, ten miles west of town, which has a fireplace and sleeps six.

VIRGINIAN RESORT
$–$$ 45 UNITS   ✉ *808 North Cascades Highway, Winthrop* ☎ *509-996-2535,*
800-854-2834 📠 *509-999-2468*
On the south edge of Winthrop is this rustic resort. Located on the high bank of the Methow River, the riverfront rooms in this motel have balconies. There are also seven cabins, which are a bit more expensive, but several have wood stoves and room enough for four. Kitchens are equipped with microwaves. Also available is a three-bedroom cottage that has five beds and a full kitchen.

CAMPBELL'S RESORT
$$$$ 170 ROOMS   ✉ *104 West Woodin Avenue, Chelan* ☎ *509-682-2561,*
800-553-8225 📠 *509-682-2177* 🖥 *www.campbellsresort.com, info@campbellsresort.com*
The oldest and most reliable resort in Chelan is Campbell's, which has

been in business since 1901. It has two heated pools, two outdoor jacuzzis, a day spa, a good beach and boat moorage. The larger rooms
have kitchenettes and one king or two queen beds, and are decorated in
vibrant earth tones.

DARNELL'S LAKE RESORT

$$$$ 38 ROOMS   ✉ 901 Spader Bay Road, Chelan   ✆ 509-682-2015, 800-967-8149
📠 509-682-8736   ✑ www.darnellsresort.com, info@darnellsresort.com

One of the most complete resorts inside the Chelan city limits is
Darnell's, a few blocks southwest of the city center on Route 150. It has
a heated pool and hot tub, putting greens, lighted tennis courts, swimming beach, waterskiing, volleyball, badminton, wi-fi and game rooms.
The resort is divided into two three-story buildings. All units are suites
with balconies and lake views; some have two bedrooms. The penthouse suites have two fireplaces and private jacuzzi. Closed mid-
January through March.

APPLE INN MOTEL

$$ 41 ROOMS   ✉ 1002 East Woodin Avenue, Chelan   ✆ 509-682-4044, 800-276-3229
📠 509-682-3330   ✑ www.appleinnmotel.com, info@appleinnmotel.com

On the eastern edge of Chelan is this clean and comfortable motel with
white stucco walls and black wood trim. The rooms are small and clean;
some have kitchenettes, all have microwaves, coffeemakers, TVs and
wi-fi. The heated outdoor pool is open in the summer, and a hot tub is
open year-round.

DINING

SUN MOUNTAIN LODGE DINING ROOM

$$$$ PACIFIC NORTHWEST   ✉ Sun Mountain Lodge, Patterson Lake Road, Winthrop
✆ 509-996-2211, 800-572-0493   📠 509-996-3133   ✑ www.sunmountainlodge.com,
sunmtn@methow.com

The dramatic dining room here garners statewide attention. The room
is cantilevered with views down into the Methow Valley and Winthrop
1000 feet below. All seats here have a view. The menu features seafood
and creatively prepared grilled or roasted meats from local farms.

DUCK BRAND CANTINA

$$ INTERNATIONAL   ✉ 248 Riverside Avenue, Winthrop   ✆ 509-996-2192,
800-996-2192   📠 509-996-2001   ✑ www.methownet.com/duck, duckbrand@methow.com

One of Winthrop's trendiest restaurants is this oddly named cantina in
the hotel of the same name. The menu reflects an effort to please several palates, including Mexican, Continental and American. The restaurant is divided into two areas: a dining room filled with antiques and
old photographs and a deck overlooking Winthrop's sole street. Breakfast, lunch and dinner.

THREE FINGERED JACK'S SALOON AND RESTAURANT

$–$$ STEAK   ✉ 176 Riverside Avenue, Winthrop   ✆ 509-996-2411   📠 509-996-2411
✑ www.3fingeredjacks.com

Decorated in rustic Western style with wooden tables, hardwood floors
and elk heads mounted on the walls, this saloon and restaurant offers

fresh vegetables and meats, homemade soups, salads and desserts. The New York steaks are cut in-house in this family-run establishment. Vegetarians might try the pasta primavera.

CAMPBELL'S HOUSE CAFE

$$ AMERICAN ✉104 West Woodin Avenue, Chelan ☎509-682-2561, 800-553-8225 ☏509-682-2177 🖰www.campbellsresort.com, info@campbellsresort.com

Although Campbell's Resort is so large it overwhelms some people, it is hard to find a better place in the area for a good meal than the resort's café. The large room seats about 130 and is pleasantly decorated in early American furnishings with walls covered with an eclectic collection of prints, documents and paintings. The menu is large: prime rib, medallions of pork, Asian-style jumbo prawns, the catch of the day and a variety of pasta. In summer, open daily for all three meals; closed in winter.

J.R.'S BAR AND GRILL

$–$$ AMERICAN ✉116 East Woodin Avenue, Chelan ☎509-682-1031 🖰www.jrsbarandgrill.net

A few doors down from Campbell's on the lakefront is J.R.'s. It has two floors—with open-air seating on the top level—and specializes in lunches of sandwiches (some are purely vegetarian), soups and salads. Dinner offers a series of specials throughout the week, seafood, steak and several pastas.

SHOPPING

SUN MOUNTAIN LODGE ✉604 Patterson Lake Road, Winthrop ☎509-996-4716 Art by local artists is available in the gift shop here.

MAIN STREET GALLERY ✉208 East Woodin Avenue, Chelan ☎509-682-9262 🖰www.mainstreetgallerychelan.com Art is also a growth industry in the Chelan area. This eclectic gallery features watercolors, oils, pottery, glass and sculpture by local artists, as well as clothing and accessories.

CULINARY APPLE ✉109 East Woodin Avenue, Chelan ☎509-682-3618, 800-568-6062 🖰www.culinaryapple.com The apple is king in Chelan, and this mail-order store has more than 1500 apple gift items, packaged apples and other Northwest-produced foods.

NIGHTLIFE

RUBY THEATRE ✉135 East Woodin Avenue, Chelan ☎509-682-5016 🖰www.rubytheatre.com Not much happens in Chelan after dark, which may be fine if you're planning to wake up in time to catch the *Lady of the Lake* cruise in the morning. If you simply must go out, your best bet may be this small but historic pink theater that presents double-feature movies and weekend matinees.

MILL BAY CASINO ✉455 Wapato Lake Road, Manson ☎509-687-2102, 800-648-2946 🖰www.colvillecasinos.com Seven miles west of Chelan, the Colville Indian Reservation operates this casino, with blackjack, roulette, craps and slot machines.

PEARRYGIN LAKE STATE PARK

Bear Creek Road, four miles northeast of Winthrop 509-996-2370

This 696-acre park is popular for travelers in RVs because it is close to Winthrop and has a sandy beach on a small lake surrounded by mountains. Anglers will find rainbow trout off the fishing dock. Facilities include picnic areas, barbecue pits, restrooms and showers. Closed November through March.

There are 92 standard sites ($19 per night), two primitive sites ($14 per night) and 71 RV hookup sites ($26 per night). Reservations: 888-226-7688.

LAKE CHELAN STATE PARK

Route 971, nine miles west of Chelan 509-687-3710

This is a favorite park for youths yearning for sunshine, and in July and August the shoreline looks more like California than Washington with its broad, sandy beach (great swimming) and play area. Because it has docks and launching areas for skiers, it is equally popular with powerboaters and waterskiers. Anglers fish for rainbow trout, kokanee salmon, burbot, lake trout and bass as far away from the powerboats as possible. There are picnic tables, restrooms, a concession stand and showers.

There are 109 standard sites ($19 per night) and 35 RV hookup sites ($26 per night). Reservations highly recommended for summer: 888-226-7688.

TWENTY-FIVE MILE CREEK STATE PARK

Route 971, 20 miles up-lake from Chelan 509-687-3610

More remote than Lake Chelan State Park but popular with those more interested in mountain scenery than body scenery, this park is quiet, with the Chelan Mountains behind and the jagged peaks of the Sawtooth Wilderness across the lake. The small beach is mostly for wading, though boaters fish in the lake. There are picnic areas, restrooms, showers and moorage at the marina; a concession stand offers snacks, groceries and fishing supplies. Closed October through March.

There are 46 standard sites ($19 per night) and 21 RV hookup sites ($25 to $26 per night). Closed in winter. Reservations: 888-226-7688.

LINCOLN ROCK STATE PARK

Route 97/2, seven miles north of East Wenatchee 509-884-8702 509-886-1704

Named for a rock outcropping that resembles Abraham Lincoln's profile, this state park in the Columbia River canyon is a short distance north of Wenatchee. There is swimming, fishing for trout and salmon, and boating. Several species of wildlife reside in the park, including marmots, rabbits, deer, muskrats, nighthawks and swallows. Facilities include picnic shelters, restrooms, showers, volleyball courts, a playfield and play equipment for children. Closed mid-October to early March.

There are 27 standard sites ($19 per night) and 67 RV hookup sites ($25 to $26 per night). Reservations: 888-226-7688.

WENATCHEE AREA

Famous for its apple orchards, the sunny Wenatchee area is located in the heart of Washington. Popular with rafters and gold panners, this region is also home to one of the state's most picturesque gardens. In the past decade, the greater Wenatchee area has seen steady population growth, mainly telecommuters who work for Seattle companies via the internet. Today nearly 100,000 people live in metropolitan Wenatchee, and in the years leading up to the 2008 recession, real estate prices in Wenatchee rose more than almost any other community in the United States.

SIGHTS

You have a choice of two highways when leaving Chelan: You can continue along Route 97A, which cuts through the Cascade foothills back to the Columbia River and south to Wenatchee, or cross the Columbia at Chelan Falls, hardly more than a junction, and follow Route 97 south through the orchard town of Orondo to East Wenatchee.

ROCKY REACH DAM ✉️*Route 97A, 28 miles south of Chelan* 📞*509-663-7522* 📠*509-661-8149* 🖥️*www.chelanpud.org* Stop at this dam to visit the Fish Viewing Room where healthy numbers of migratory salmon, trout and steelhead swim past the windows. The dam also has a museum showing the natural and human history of the Columbia River, along with a Nez Perce Indian portrait collection and other rotating exhibits. Closed November to mid-March.

WENATCHEE The largest town in the region, this community is directed more toward orchards than tourists, although you will certainly feel welcome.

OHME GARDENS ✉️*3327 Ohme Road, Wenatchee* 📞*509-662-5785* 📠*509-662-6805* 🖥️*www.ohmegardens.com* On the northern edge of town, overlooking the Columbia River, Wenatchee and Rocky Reach Dam, are these alpine gardens. You will find nine acres of towering evergreens, tumbling waterfalls and verdant foliage developed by the Ohme family on the steep, rocky outcroppings at the edge of their property. Closed mid-October to mid-April. Admission.

WENATCHEE VALLEY MUSEUM & CULTURAL CENTER ✉️*127 South Mission Street, Wenatchee* 📞*509-888-6240* 📠*509-888-6256* 🖥️*www.wvmcc. org, info@wvmcc.org* Downtown, this museum has several permanent exhibits depicting life in Washington from the Ice Age to today, including a 1919 Wurlitzer theater pipe organ and an apple-packing shed featuring an apple wiper, sizing machine and a 1924 orchard truck. In the gift shop area is an original WPA mural by Peggy Strong depicting the change of the postal service from its pioneer days to a modern, organized unit. Closed Sunday and Monday. Admission.

CASHMERE PIONEER VILLAGE AND MUSEUM ✉️*600 Cotlets Way, Cashmere* 📞*509-782-3230* 📠*509-782-3219* 🖥️*www.cashmeremuseum.org, info@ cashmeremuseum.org* Ten miles west via Routes 2 and 97, **Cashmere**, so-named because it reminded a pioneer of Kashmir, India, has an early

Wenatchee–Leavenworth Area

ALL SEASONS RIVER INN
PAGE 242

Spacious suites with jacuzzis and fireplaces nestled along the wooded banks of the Wenatchee River

CAFÉ MOZART RESTAURANT
PAGE 242

Intimate, baroque-style dining room serving Central European favorites like *kaesespaetzle* and marzipan chocolate torte

OKANOGAN–WENATCHEE NATIONAL FORESTS
PAGE 240

Natural green wonderland with 200 campsites scattered across 4 million lake-dotted acres

TEQUILA'S
PAGE 238

Spicy, homemade Mexican favorites and fresh, tangy salsa in a lively diner

American theme to its downtown buildings. There are almost two dozen original structures from Chelan and Douglas counties assembled to recreate a pioneer village, including a blacksmith shop, school, gold mine and hotel. Closed Monday through Thursday from November to late December; closed late December through February. Admission.

From Cashmere, Routes 2 and 97 follow the swift Wenatchee River into the Cascades. Shortly before reaching Leavenworth, Route 97 turns south toward the Route 90 Corridor towns of Cle Elum and Ellensburg by going over 4101-foot **Blewett Pass**.

OLD BLEWETT PASS HIGHWAY   An alternative route, in the summer only, is to follow this old highway, which has been preserved by the Wenatchee National Forest. It comprises a series of switchbacks with sweeping views of the Cascades. No services are available until you reach Cle Elum and Ellensburg, other than a small grocery store at **Liberty**, a gold-mining town just off the highway that is making a comeback as people move into its modest cabins along the main street.

LODGING

COAST WENATCHEE CENTER HOTEL
$$$ 147 ROOMS   ✉ *201 North Wenatchee Avenue, Wenatchee*   ☎ *509-662-1234,*
800-716-6199   ✆ *509-662-0782*   ✐ *www.coasthotels.com*

Most hotels in Wenatchee are along North Wenatchee Avenue. This is the largest hotel in this part of the state; at nine stories it is one of the tallest buildings along the eastern edge of the Cascades. The rooms are

5 WASHINGTON CASCADES WENATCHEE AREA LODGING

newly remodeled and larger than those at most other hotels in town, and suites have desks, armoires and potted plants. A large lobby has a baby grand piano. There's a restaurant, an indoor-outdoor pool and jacuzzi and a fitness center.

SUPER 8

$–$$ 92 ROOMS ✉1401 North Miller Street, Wenatchee ☎509-662-3443, 800-800-8000 📠509-665-0715 🖅www.super8.com, super8@nwi.net

For a low-priced place, try this old standby. It has rooms on three floors decorated with subtly flowered bedspreads, unobtrusive furniture and wallhangings. There is an outdoor (seasonal) heated pool and hot tub. Continental breakfast included.

VILLAGE INN MOTEL

$ 21 ROOMS ✉229 Cottage Avenue, Cashmere ☎509-782-3522, 800-793-3522
📠509-782-8190 🖅www.cashmerevillageinn.com

This inn is conveniently located in the heart of town. The white-and-turquoise motel has simple rooms, six with refrigerators. A bit impersonal, but it's clean, quiet and reasonably priced.

DINING

VISCONTI'S RESTORANTE ITALIANO

$$–$$$ ITALIAN ✉1737 North Wenatchee Avenue, Wenatchee ☎509-662-5013
📠509-667-9543 🖅www.viscontis.com, wenatchee@viscontis.com

Want Italian? Try Visconti's. Both Southern and Northern Italian dishes are offered in a family-friendly atmosphere. Their wood-fired oven is used to "broil-roast" seafood and prime cuts of meat.

THE WINDMILL

$$–$$$$ STEAK ✉1501 North Wenatchee Avenue, Wenatchee ☎509-665-9529
📠509-662-5030 🖅www.thewindmillrestaurant.com,
greatsteaks@thewindmillrestaurant.com

This top-notch steakhouse is a down-to-earth place, with waitresses who have been there for years. A blackboard keeps a running total of the number of steaks sold there since 1962. Prime rib and lobster are now offered in addition to a wide selection of meat and seafood dishes. Fresh-baked pies round out the meals. Dinner only. Closed on Sunday from Labor Day to Memorial Day.

TEQUILA'S

$$ MEXICAN ✉800 North Wenatchee Avenue, Wenatchee
☎509-662-7239

As a reflection of Central Washington's growing Hispanic population, this restaurant is owned by former residents of Mexico. The refried beans are homemade, and the salsa is as tangy as you'd get in Guadalajara.

SHOPPING

PAK IT RITE ✉126 North Wenatchee Avenue, Wenatchee ☎509-663-1072, 800-666-2730 🖅www.pakitrite.com A wide range of Washington souvenirs and

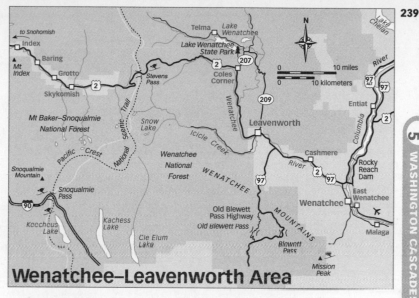

Wenatchee–Leavenworth Area

products, everything from jam to smoked salmon, can be found here. Closed Sunday.

VICTORIAN VILLAGE ✉611 South Mission Street, Wenatchee This is a small mall constructed in the best of the Victorian Carpenter Gothic style—round towers, falsefronts and steeples. You will find a hair salon, an equestrian shop and interestingly for a Victorian theme, a Mexican restaurant.

LIBERTY ORCHARDS ✉117 Mission Street, Cashmere ☎509-782-2191 ✐www.libertyorchards.com, service@libertyorchards.com Cashmere is the place to shop for a wide range of apple-based food products and gifts. Especially tempting is this shop, which has been making fruit confections since 1920. Known for their Aplets and Cotlets, fruit-and-nut concoctions sprinkled with powdered sugar, Liberty Orchards also sells a wide variety of apple-themed gifts. Tours of the candy factory are offered on weekdays from June through December.

WASHINGTON APPLE COUNTRY GIFT SHOP ✉5420 Woodring Canyon Road, Cashmere ☎866-459-9614 ✐www.washingtonapplecountry.com, info@washingtonapplecountry.com For cider or wine tastings and gifts with an apple theme, check out this gift shop, located at the Cashmere Cider Mill. Open Monday through Friday from May through October; limited hours through February.

NIGHTLIFE

Although Wenatchee is the largest town in the Cascades, the nightlife choice is slim. Your best bet may be the lounges in some of the chain motor inns, but don't expect much.

OKANOGAN-WENATCHEE NATIONAL FORESTS

✉ *The forest is crossed by Routes 12, 97/2 and 90*   ✆ *509-664-9200*
🖥 *509-644-9280*

🏃🚴🏇⛷🏂🛶🏊🛥🛶🚤 At 4 million acres, this is one of the largest national forests in the United States. It encompasses eight wilderness areas, hundreds of lakes, downhill-ski areas and more than 4000 miles of trails for hiking, riding and biking (including the Pacific Crest National Scenic Trail). Some of the most beautiful areas are the Enchantment Lakes Basin and Snow Lake, which overlaps into Mt. Baker-Snoqualmie National Forest. Salmon, steelhead, searun cutthroat trout, bull trout, bass, crappie, walleye and sturgeon are among the fish found in streams and lakes. There are picnic areas and restrooms.

▲ There are more than 120 campgrounds within the park offering more than 200 campsites; RVs accommodated in some campgrounds (no hookups); prices range from free to $18. For all campgrounds west of the Okanogan River, a Northwest Forest Pass (daily $5, annual $30) is required. The pass can be obtained at ranger stations on weekdays or at certain in-town businesses on weekends. Call the park headquarters for more information. Most campgrounds do not take reservations; the five that do can be reached at 877-444-6777.

LEAVENWORTH AREA

Think Bavarian! If you like cuckoo clocks, fancy woodwork, beer steins and alpenhorns, you'll love making a stop in Leavenworth.

SIGHTS

LEAVENWORTH   One of the major tourist spots in the Cascades, this community welcomes visitors with oompah bands, specialty stores and impressive alpine scenery. Almost everything here—architecture, hotels, restaurants, annual events—is centered around the Bavarian theme. Mountains are on three sides, and a river rushes through town. During most of the summer, free concerts and dancing exhibitions are given in the City Park, and outdoor art exhibits are held on weekends.

LEAVENWORTH NUTCRACKER MUSEUM

✉ *735 Front Street, Leavenworth*   ✆ *509-548-4573, 509-548-4708*   🖥 *509-548-2160*   🖱 *www.nutcrackermuseum.com, curator@nutcrackermuseum.com* The only museum in the country devoted exclusively to nutcrackers, this gallery displays artifacts from as early as the 14th century up to modern times. The collection consists of more than 5000 nutcrackers from around the world, including Italy, Germany, Turkey, the U.S. and India. You'll see the popular soldier nutcracker, as well as nutcrackers in the shape of dragons, dogs and rams. Moses, Abraham Lincoln, Bugs Bunny, Thomas Edison and Shakespeare have all been immortalized as, you guessed it, nutcrackers! Open 2 p.m. to 5 p.m. from May through October; open weekends only November through April. Admission.

TUMWATER CANYON   Just west of Leavenworth, Route 2 enters this canyon, which follows the Wenatchee River some 20 miles. It is marked by sheer canyon walls, plunging river rapids and deciduous trees along the riverbank that turn into brilliant colors in autumn.

STEVENS PASS   Route 2 continues through this popular ski area where the **Pacific Crest National Scenic Trail** (see "Hiking" at the end of this chapter) crosses the highway. Soon after crossing the summit and passing Skykomish, the **Skykomish River** parallels the highway. This is one of Western Washington's most popular whitewater rivers. Most trips originate in the small alpine village of **Index**, a short distance off the highway. The sheer-faced, 5979-foot **Mt. Index** looms behind the town. From there, the river rumbles down past the small towns of Gold Bar and Sultan, then flattens out onto the Puget Sound lowlands.

LODGING

HOTEL PENSION ANNA — hidden

$$$ 17 ROOMS   ✉926 Commercial Street, Leavenworth   ☎509-548-6273, 800-509-2662   📠509-548-4656   🖥www.pensionanna.com, info@pensionanna.com

This is one of the most pleasant spots to stay in Leavenworth. Rooms feature furniture and decor imported from Austria and Germany. Heavy wooden bed frames and cupboards are used throughout, along with featherbeds and down comforters. Four suites come with fireplace and jacuzzi, and all rooms have private baths. Breakfast is included.

ENZIAN INN

$$$ 105 ROOMS   ✉590 Route 2, Leavenworth   ☎509-548-5269, 800-223-8511   📠509-548-9319   🖥www.enzianinn.com, info@enzianinn.com

A Bavarian wood carver was imported to fashion the rails and ceiling beams of this inn, and the entire motel with its turret and chalet-styled roofs shows similar touches. The eight suites have king-size beds, spas and fireplaces. It has indoor and outdoor pools and hot tubs. During the winter, free cross-country ski equipment is available to guests; in summer, guests get a free round of putting at Enzian Falls Championship Putting Course. The complimentary buffet breakfast is served in the big solarium on the fourth floor.

LINDERHOF INN

$$ 33 UNITS   ✉690 Route 2, Leavenworth   ☎509-548-5283, 800-828-5680   📠509-548-6705   🖥www.linderhof.com, info@linderhof.com

For a change of pace, try renting one of the townhouses here. All 11 of them are divided into one- and two-bedroom units that sleep six and eight respectively. They have cathedral ceilings with balcony bedrooms and full kitchens with all appliances. There are 22 additional units, some with fireplaces and spas, all with handcrafted furniture. There is an outdoor pool and hot tub. Continental breakfast is included, and there's wireless internet throughout the property.

RUN OF THE RIVER INN & REFUGE

$$$$ 6 ROOMS   ✉ *9308 East Leavenworth Road, Leavenworth*   📞 *509-548-7171,* *800-288-6491* 📠 *509-548-7547* 🖱 *www.runoftheriver.com, info@runoftheriver.com*

More and more bed and breakfasts and inns are opening outside town. You'll find this B&B just a mile east of Icicle River from Route 2. The building is made of logs and has cathedral ceilings with pine walls and handmade log furniture. The rooms come with private baths and cable TV, as well as jacuzzis, river-rock fireplaces and private decks. A private lodge sleeps two. Stay here, kick back and just contemplate the beautiful setting. There are complimentary mountain bikes for exploring the surrounding trails and backroads and complimentary snowshoes in winter. Breakfasts are country-style. Nonsmoking; no children.

ALL SEASONS RIVER INN

$$$$ 6 UNITS   ✉ *8751 Icicle Road, Leavenworth*   📞 *509-548-1425,* *800-254-0555* 🖱 *www.allseasonsriverinn.com, info@allseasonsriverinn.com*

Located in a wooded setting on the banks of the Wenatchee River, this inn offers spacious rooms and suites overlooking the river, all with jacuzzis and most with fireplaces and private decks. The inn provides full breakfasts and bicycles for touring the nearby Icicle Loop. Nonsmoking; no children or pets.

DUTCH CUP MOTEL

$–$$ 20 UNITS   ✉ *819 Main Street, Sultan*   📞 *360-793-2215, 800-844-0488* 🖱 *www.dutchcup.com, dutchcup@mac.com*

Farther down the mountain you'll find this motel, which is popular with skiers. The two-story motel has environmentally friendly units with refrigerators, microwaves, wi-fi access and cable television. Small, quiet, supervised pets are welcome.

DINING

CAFÉ MOZART RESTAURANT

$$$$ GERMAN/FRENCH   ✉ *829 Front Street, Leavenworth* 📞 *509-548-0600* 🖱 *www.cafemozartrestaurant.com, mozart@crcwnet.com*

Café Mozart's wall sconces, gold chandeliers, floral carpeted floors and candlelit tables create an intimate baroque-style atmosphere in each of the four dining rooms. The German-born chef prepares Central European favorites such as *kaesespaetzle* and smoked half duck glazed with orange-raspberry confiture. You might also find grilled wild Alaskan salmon with toasted hazelnut butter. If you have room for dessert or if you stop by between meals, treat yourself to Mozart's chocolate torte (seven layers of rich marzipan wine crème covered with dark chocolate). Reservations recommended. Open daily for lunch and dinner from June through October; no lunch Monday through Thursday from November through May.

THE GINGERBREAD FACTORY

$ AMERICAN ✉828 Commercial Street, Leavenworth ☎509-548-6592, 800-296-7079 ✍www.gingerbreadfactory.com, sales@gingerbreadfactory.com

This festive place is a delight for children and parents alike, with decorated cookies and gingerbread houses. The café sells pastries, bagels, quiches, sandwiches, soups, salads, espresso and all sorts of gifts related to gingerbread. Lunch only; although coffee and pastries are available for breakfast. Closed Wednesday and another weekday in winter; call for hours.

INDEX CAFÉ

$ AMERICAN ✉49315 Route 2, Index ☎360-799-1133

This café offers breakfast and lunch to travelers heading up and down Route 2. Stop in for fish and chips, pot roast sandwiches and chicken with artichokes.

SHOPPING

A BOOK FOR ALL SEASONS ✉703 Route 2, Leavenworth ☎509-548-1451
Leavenworth has the best selection of specialty shops in the Cascades; about 80 are crammed into a two-block area. This shop offers a wide variety of books, cards and author readings.

NIGHTLIFE

ANDREAS KELLER GERMAN RESTAURANT ✉829 Front Street, Leavenworth ☎509-548-6000 ✍www.andreaskellerrestaurant.com This German restaurant offers live accordian music on weekends in winter and spring, nightly in summer and fall.

UNCLE ULI'S PUB ✉901 Front Street, Leavenworth ☎509-548-7262 For a variety of live music in the summer, try Uncle Uli's on weekends.

OLD POST OFFICE SALOON ✉213 9th Street, Leavenworth ☎509-548-7488 Leavenworth's major sports bar is this saloon, with TVs, pool tables and karaoke on Friday and Saturday nights.

PARKS

LAKE WENATCHEE
STATE PARK

hidden

✉Route 207, 18 miles northwest of Leavenworth and four miles off Route 2 ☎509-763-3101

🚶🚴🏇🐎🏕🏠🛶🚤⛵🚣🎣♨🚢🛥🔦 This glacier-fed lake is tucked away near Stevens Pass and is popular in summer for canoeing, kayaking, sailing, swimming and fishing (salmon, steelhead and trout) and in the winter for cross-country skiing. Dogsledders and snowshoers head to this park as well. The secluded, wooded campsites are great and half remain open through the winter. Picnic areas, restrooms and showers are found here, and in July and August there are interpretive programs on Saturdays.

▲ There are 155 standard sites ($19 per night) and about 42 RV hookup sites ($26 per night). Reservations: 888-226-7688.

ROUTE 90 CORRIDOR

This pristine area remains one of America's scenic icons. From snow-capped peaks to dramatic waterfalls, the corridor is one of the Northwest's hidden treasures. It extends from Snoqualmie across the Cascades to Ellensburg and the Kittitas Valley. Fasten your seat belts for a breathtaking ride past volcanic peaks, fir forests and rivers where you're likely to land tonight's dinner.

SIGHTS

The Cascades begin rising only a half-hour's drive east of Seattle.

SNOQUALMIE   This quiet town has an ornate, 1890 railroad depot that is the oldest continually operating train station in the state.

SNOQUALMIE VALLEY RAILROAD ⌧*38625 Southeast King Street, Snoqualmie* ☎*425-888-3030* 🖷*425-888-9311* ✐*www.trainmuseum.org; info@trainmuseum.org* Snoqualmie is also home to this railroad, which makes a five-mile trip through the Snoqualmie Valley on weekends (April through October) and runs a special Christmas train. The railroad is operated by the **Northwest Railway Museum** (located at the depot), a large building with an extensive train collection—worth visiting. Admission.

SNOQUALMIE FALLS   Near the Railway Museum is this thundering cataract with a small park, observation platform and trails leading to the river below the 270-foot falls.

NORTH BEND   This town has adopted an alpine theme for its downtown buildings, but it hasn't caught on with the vigor of Winthrop and Leavenworth. Not to be confused with the Oregon coastal town of the same name, this hamlet sits snugly in the shadow of the looming Mt. Si.

NORTH BEND RANGER DISTRICT FOREST SERVICE STATION ⌧*42404 Southeast North Bend Way, North Bend* ☎*425-888-1421* This ranger station offers maps, books and other outdoor-recreation information. Closed Sunday; also closed Saturday in off-season.

THE SUMMIT AT SNOQUALMIE PASS ⌧*1001 State Route 906, Snoqualmie Pass* ☎*425-434-7669* ✐*www.summitatsnoqualmie.com* Snoqualmie Pass has four major ski areas for downhill and snowboarding, and one cross-country ski area with more than 35 miles of groomed trails.

SNOQUALMIE PASS VISITOR CENTER ⌧*Exit 52 off Route 90 on State Route 906; on Snoqualmie Pass* ☎*425-434-6111* This visitor center offers maps and books. Open Thursday through Sunday. Closed Labor Day to Memorial Day.

CLE ELUM HISTORICAL TELEPHONE MUSEUM

✉️ *221 East 1st Street, Cle Elum* 📞 *509-674-5939* 🖱️ *www.nkcmuseums.org, nkchs@yahoo.com* In **Cle Elum**, an American Indian name meaning "swift water," you will find this unusual telephone museum, which commemorates and explains (through exhibits of ethnic costumes, old switchboards and railroad, logging and mining items) why Cle Elum was the last U.S. town to switch over from a manual long-distance switchboard. (Twenty-seven dialects were commonly heard during the town's early days as a mining center.) Open by appointment.

IRON HORSE STATE PARK   At the foot of 4th Street is the access point for this 113-mile-long state park, a section of the former railroad right of way with the rails and ties removed and the roadbed smoothed over for walking, jogging, cross-country skiing and biking. It is part of the **John Wayne Pioneer Trail** that will eventually run the width of the state.

ROSLYN

Three miles away from Cle Elum is this tiny town that was used as the set for TV's quirky *Northern Exposure*. It was formerly a coal-mining town with a large population of Italian, Croatian and Austrian immigrants who worked in the mines. There are separate cemeteries—23 in fact—for these nationalities.

ELLENSBURG   As you drive through the Kittitas Valley, notice that the prevailing wind off the Cascades gives trees a permanent lean toward the east. When you reach the town of Ellensburg, you're out of the Cascades and entering the arid climate that characterizes most of the eastern side of Washington. This community is perhaps best known for its rodeo each Labor Day weekend, and in keeping with the Western legacy, the Western Art Association has its headquarters there and holds an annual show and auction each May.

CLYMER MUSEUM OF ART ✉️ *416 North Pearl Street, Ellensburg* 📞 *509-962-6416* 📠 *509-962-6424* 🖱️ *www.clymermuseum.org, service@clymermuseum.org* This art museum displays work by the famous Western artist, John Ford Clymer, who lived in Ellensburg. Closed Sunday from January through April.

KITTITAS COUNTY HISTORICAL MUSEUM ✉️ *114 East 3rd Avenue, Ellensburg* 📞 *509-925-3778* 🖱️ *www.kchm.org, kchm@kchm.org* This historical museum displays American Indian and pioneer artifacts and has extensive rock, car and doll collections. Closed Sunday.

OLMSTEAD PLACE STATE PARK ✉️ *921 North Ferguson Road, Ellensburg* 📞 *509-925-1943* Four miles east of town is this state park, a working farm that uses pioneer equipment. The 217-acre farm and all its buildings were deeded to the state. Restrooms and picnic tables are available, and weekend tours are offered from Memorial Day to Labor Day.

246

HIDDEN LISTINGS

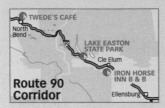

TWEDE'S CAFÉ
PAGE 247

Classic diner with gas lamps, wood paneling, "damn good coffee" and infamous cherry pie

LAKE EASTON STATE PARK
PAGE 249

Forested, lakeside campgrounds set in idyllic mountain foothills

IRON HORSE INN B&B
PAGE 247

Historic parkside house charmingly decorated in early-20th-century antiques with a railroad theme

LODGING

SALISH LODGE AND SPA AT SNOQUALMIE FALLS
$$$$ 89 UNITS ✉6501 Railroad Avenue Southeast, Snoqualmie ☎425-888-2556, 800-272-5474 📠425- 888-2420 ✑www.salishlodge.com, reservations@salishlodge.com

When I want to spend a pricey night in the lap of luxury, I can't think of a more dramatic setting to do it in than this clifftop lodge at Snoqualmie Falls, perched on the cliff overlooking the spectacular falls. Visitors might recognize it as the backdrop for the eerie David Lynch TV drama *Twin Peaks*. The rooms and suites are decorated in an upscale-country motif with down comforters, wicker furniture, woodburning fireplaces and jacuzzis. Only a few rooms have views of the falls, but the interiors are so well done that most visitors console themselves by watching the falls from the lounge or observation deck. There is also a full-service spa.

SUMMIT LODGE AT SNOQUALMIE PASS
$$$ 80 ROOMS ✉P.O. Box 163, Snoqualmie Pass, WA 98068 ☎425-434-6300, 800-557-7829 📠425-434-6396 ✑www.snoqualmiesummitlodge.com

About the only place to stay at Snoqualmie Summit is this lodge at Snoqualmie Pass. Outfitted for skiers, its rooms come with king-sized or two queen-sized beds, and it has a complimentary ski-storage area and coin-operated laundry. Tired guests also enjoy the indoor sauna, jacuzzi and heated outdoor pool. The large lobby is stocked with comfortable leather sofas set around the native-stone fireplace.

THE EDGEWICK INN
$$ 44 UNITS ✉14600 468th Avenue Southeast, North Bend ☎425-888-9000 📠425-888-9400 ✑www.edgewickinn.com

Located two miles east of town, this is a straightforward motel featuring clean and quiet units with queen-sized beds. There are also two suites with jacuzzis.

IRON HORSE INN B & B

$$–$$$ 11 UNITS   ✉*526 Marie Avenue, South Cle Elum*   ✆*509-674-5939,*
800-228-9246   🖵*www.ironhorseinnbb.com, maryp@ironhorseinnbb.com*

A former Milwaukee Railroad crew house and an establishment recognized in the National Historic Register, the Iron Horse is now one of the state's best inns. The rooms, three with shared baths, are named for former occupants. All are decorated in turn-of-the-20th-century antiques—with an emphasis, not surprisingly, on railroad trinkets and tools. Four remodeled cabooses sport queen-sized beds, refrigerators and sundecks with hot tubs. Two of the caboose cars and the deluxe honeymoon suite have jetted tubs; an outdoor hot tub serves everyone else. The Iron Horse is adjacent to the Iron Horse State Park Trail, where cross-country skiing, bicycling, horseback riding and walking are popular. Full breakfast is included in the rate.

TIMBERLODGE INN

$$ 36 UNITS   ✉*301 West 1st Street, Cle Elum*   ✆*509-674-5966, 800-584-1133*
📠*509-674-2737*   🖵*info@timberlodgeinn.com*

For more impersonal lodgings, the TimberLodge, on the western edge of town, has bright, clean rooms and one deluxe suite with fridge, microwave and wi-fi, far enough off the street to deaden the noise of the busy main drag. Amenities include a hot tub. There is a daily breakfast bar.

GUESTHOUSE ELLENSBURG

$$ 2 UNITS   ✉*606 North Main Street, Ellensburg*   ✆*509-962-3706*
🖵*www.guesthouseellensburg.com, info@guesthouseellensburg.com*

This restored Victorian home located near the Central Washington University campus in downtown Ellensburg has two guest suites furnished with antiques and private baths. Both rooms feature four-poster beds, flat screen TVs and CD players.

DINING

SALISH LODGE & SPA AT SNOQUALMIE FALLS

$$$$ PACIFIC NORTHWEST   ✉*6501 Railroad Avenue, Snoqualmie*   ✆*425-888-2556,*
800-272-5474   🖵*www.salishlodge.com, reservations@salishlodge.com*

The dining room here offers spectacular views over the falls and canyon below, and the food is first rate. The menu leans toward what has become known as Northwest cuisine: lots of seafood, fresh fruits and vegetables, and game. Try the truffle-crusted black cod with chanterelles and Brussels sprout leaves. The restaurant boasts the largest wine list in the state and a dessert list almost as long.

TWEDE'S CAFÉ

$ AMERICAN   ✉*137 West North Bend Way, North Bend*   ✆*425-831-5511*

Twede's, which served as the model for the diner in television's *Twin Peaks*, has faux gas lamps, wood paneling and neon

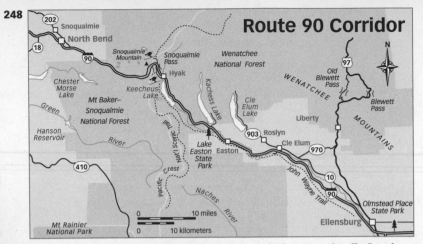

across the ceiling. Stay for a cup of "damn good coffee" and their infamous cherry pie.

MAMA VALLONE'S STEAK HOUSE

$$–$$$ STEAK/ITALIAN   ✉302 West 1st Street, Cle Elum   ✆509-674-5174
✎www.mamavallones.com

Cle Elum is better known for its inns and small hotels, but it has at least one good restaurant, Mama Vallone's, where you never have to wait for someone to replenish your water or bring more bread. A specialty is *bagna cauda*, a fondue-style mixture of olive oil, anchovy and garlic served with dipping strips of steak or seafood. Lunch served only in summer on weekends.

STARLIGHT LOUNGE

$$–$$$ AMERICAN   ✉402 North Pearl Street, Ellensburg   ✆509-962-6100

This lounge offers updates on comfort food such as pan-fried chicken, cinnamon-crusted pork chops and the classic martini. Weekend brunch, too.

THE VALLEY CAFÉ

$$ AMERICAN/PACIFIC NORTHWEST   ✉105 West 3rd Avenue, Ellensburg
✆509-925-3050 ✎www.valleycafe.org, valleycafe@fairpoint.net

The food at this café is American with a Northwest flair. Fish (frequently salmon) and chicken dominate the dinner menu at this Art Deco–style dining room. There are also lamb, steak, pasta and vegetarian options on the menu.

SHOPPING

Antique hunters will enjoy Ellensburg, which has at least half a dozen antique stores in a three-block area.

MAIN STREET MALL ANTIQUES   ✉309 North Main Street, Ellensburg
✆509-925-1762 ✎mainstreet@amerion.com Vintage furniture, clothing, textiles and miscellaneous items are showcased at this small but well-stocked

store in downtown Ellensburg. From Art Deco jewelry to 1950s hats, this shop has quality pieces for those seeking treasures from the past.

NIGHTLIFE

Cle Elum has almost nothing in nightlife other than taverns with jukeboxes.

THE CANARY LOUNGE ⊠*Suncadia Resort, 3600 Suncadia Trail, Cle Elum* ✆*509-649-6403* Swankier than a local bar, this fireside lounge features signature cocktails in a comfortable, upscale space with high ceilings. Closed November through March.

In Ellensburg between the rodeos there is little entertainment.

THE TAV ———————————— **h**idden

⊠*117 West 4th Avenue, Ellensburg* ✆*509-925-3939* Your best bet is to join the locals at this casual tavern where the beer flows freely and the burgers are cheap. A large TV and a jukebox add some entertainment, but it's the friendly staff and familiar small-town bar atmosphere that make this a good choice for a nightcap.

PARKS

LAKE EASTON STATE PARK ———————— **h**idden

⊠*Route 90, a mile west of Easton* ✆*509-656-2230*

🚶 🚴 🏕 🏊 🎣 🚤 🛶 On Route 90, near the summit at Snoqualmie Pass, this 516-acre lakeside park with forested trails is used as a base for skiers and snowmobilers in winter, as a lunch stop for travelers in spring and fall, and for hiking, swimming and trout fishing in the summer. Facilities include picnic areas, a swimming beach and restrooms.

▲ There are 95 standard sites ($19 per night) near the Yakima River and 45 RV hookup sites ($26 per night) near the lake. Reservations: 888-226-7688.

MT. RAINIER AREA

It is always a dramatic moment when Mt. Rainier suddenly appears ahead of you (in the Northwest it is often just called The Mountain). You could spend weeks in this area and only sample a small portion of its recreational possibilities. Whether you approach from the east or the west, the forest gets thicker and thicker and the roadside rivers get swifter and swifter. The national park is almost surrounded with national forest wilderness areas as buffer zones against clear-cut logging. Located southeast of Seattle, this peak is the site of the aptly named town of Paradise.

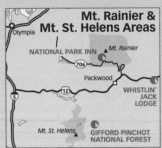

Mt. Rainier & Mt. St. Helens Areas

Olympia
NATIONAL PARK INN
706
Packwood
WHISTLIN' JACK LODGE
12
Mt. St. Helens
GIFFORD PINCHOT NATIONAL FOREST
Mt. Rainier

NATIONAL PARK INN
PAGE 253

Rustic lodging with a huge stone fireplace and rooms with stunning mountain views— stay *inside* the national park

WHISTLIN' JACK LODGE
PAGE 254

Surprisingly sophisticated atmosphere and seafood like fresh pan-fried rainbow trout or crab-stuffed artichoke hearts

GIFFORD PINCHOT NATIONAL FOREST
PAGE 259

Scenic trails winding through seven wilderness areas past spots like the Ice Cave, an ice-encrusted lava tube

SIGHTS

Mt. Rainier, the huge landmark mountain visible (on clear days) from everywhere in the Puget Sound area, makes for a spectacularly scenic all-day trip from Seattle. Heading south from the city on Route 5, take Exit 149, drive two miles to Kent, and turn south on Route 167, another wide, fast, divided highway. Go seven miles to Puyallup, turn off on Route 161, and suddenly you're off the freeway and on your way through the forests and farmlands of Pierce County.

NORTHWEST TREK WILDLIFE PARK ✉ *11610 Trek Drive East (off Route 161), Eatonville* ☏ *360-832-6117* 📠 *360-832-6118* 🖥 *www.nwtrek.org* About 17 miles south of Puyallup is this wildlife park. A free-roaming animal refuge owned by the Tacoma Metro Parks Department, it provides a rare opportunity to see native wildlife of the Pacific Northwest up close. The highlight is a 55-minute tram ride around a 435-acre expanse of forest and meadows inhabited by hundreds of large grazing animals, including bison, caribou, bighorn sheep, mountain goats, Roosevelt elk and a few elusive moose. Migratory sandhill cranes and geese also live in the park. There is often a wait of an hour or more for the tram ride. In the meantime, you can walk around the more conventionally zoolike area near the tour station and see predators such as wolves, bears, cougars, owls and eagles as well as smaller animals like beavers, raccoons and badgers that would be hard to spot in a free-roaming setting. There's also a network of paved and unpaved nature trails that can take an hour or more to explore fully, plus a hands-on discovery center for kids. If you're planning to visit Mt. Rainier, Northwest Trek is right on the way. Closed Monday through Thursday from November to mid-February. Admission.

MT. RAINIER SCENIC RAILROAD
⊠*P.O. Box 250, Mineral, WA 98355* ☎*360-492-5588, 888-783-2611* ⊘*www.mrsr.com, admin@mrsr.org* Ten miles south of the Northwest Trek Wildlife Park, Route 161 meets Route 7. The latter route boasts this scenic railroad with a steam-powered train that makes a 14-mile trip through the lush forest and across high bridges to Mineral Lake. It runs Thursday through Sunday from May through September; limited hours the rest of the year.

MT. RAINIER NATIONAL PARK
In Elbe, Route 7 meets Route 706, the well-marked road to this popular national park. Passing Alder Lake, it's about 15 miles to the park's Nisqually Entrance, where on sunny weekends you may have to wait in a long line to pay the $15-per-vehicle entrance fee. As you drive through lofty primeval forest at the base of the mountain, you'll see signs of a vast mudslide that occurred when the sleeping volcanic giant stirred and melted part of the glacier that caps its summit.

MT. RAINIER
☎*For park information, contact the National Park Service in the Long-mire Museum at 360-569-2211 ext. 3314* ⊘*www.nps.gov/mora* Once inside the park you may be almost overwhelmed by the scenery. "The Mountain" is so monstrous (14,410 feet) that it makes everything around it seem trivial. In fact, Mt. Rainier is the tallest mountain in the Northwest and has more glaciers—25—than any other mountain in the contiguous 48 states. The mountain is estimated to have last erupted between 1820 and 1894, and has been quiet since. However, steam vents on the summit are still active, and geologists warn another eruption is inevitable—someday. Mt. Rainier National Park has numerous visitor centers and interpretive exhibits along winding roads.

HENRY M. JACKSON MEMORIAL VISITOR CENTER
⊠*Paradise, WA* ☎*360-569-2211* About 15 miles into the park, a turnoff on the left takes you up to **Paradise**. In Paradise, head to this new visitor center, which has several exhibits and audiovisual shows. Paradise is one of the most beautiful places in the park, and the visitors center is one of the busiest. It has a cafeteria, gift shop and exhibits about climbing the mountain. Closed weekdays, except for holidays and from December 20 through January 4.

LONGMIRE MUSEUM
⊠*Longmire, WA* ☎*360-569-2211 ext. 3314* ⊘*www.nps.gov/mora* This museum emphasizes the natural history of the park with rock, flora and fauna exhibits as well as with exhibits on the human history of the area. Its old historic buildings have stood since the 1880s when the Longmire family lived there. The museum also has information for hikers, and next door at the National Park Inn you can rent cross-country skis or snowshoes.

OHANAPECOSH VISITOR CENTER
☎*360-569-6046* This visitor center, located down in the southeast corner near a grove of giant, ancient cedar trees, has history and nature exhibits. Closed mid-October through May.

SUNRISE VISITOR CENTER
☎*360-663-2425* Beyond the Paradise turnoff, Route 706 is closed in the winter but stunning in the summer as it traverses Backbone Ridge, offering panoramic views of the jagged Catamount Range to the southeast. In about 15 miles you'll join Route

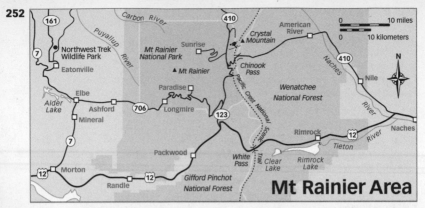

Mt Rainier Area

123 northbound. Another ten miles brings you to the summit of 4675-foot Cayuse Pass. Four miles farther on is the turnoff on the left that winds by switchbacks up the east slope of the mountain to this visitor venter, a 16-mile climb to the highest point in the park that you can reach by car. Another network of alpine hiking trails starts here, and it's usually much less crowded than Paradise. The visitor center has geological displays and at 6400 feet is the closest you can drive to the peak. Numerous trails fan out from the center for day hikes, but be aware that even into July, there is often snow on the trails.

MT. BAKER–SNOQUALMIE NATIONAL FOREST

When you descend from Sunrise, turn north (left) on Route 123 and you're on your way out of the park. The highway takes you 38 miles through this national forest to Enumclaw. Angle to the right on Route 164, drive 15 miles to Auburn, and hop onto divided four-lane Route 18 westbound. Three quick miles and you're back on Route 5, just 20 miles south of downtown Seattle.

OAK CREEK WILDLIFE RECREATION AREA   To the east of the mountain, at the intersection of Routes 410 and 12, you can watch elk and bighorn sheep being fed by game officials during the middle of winter at this wildlife recreation area, which is accessible only from Route 12.

LODGING

Two inns are located inside Mt. Rainier National Park, and several other places to stay are around the park in Ashford, Packwood, Elbe, Crystal Mountain, Morton and the White Pass area.

PARADISE INN

$$–$$$ 121 ROOMS   ⌧ *Paradise, WA 98398*   ✆ *360-569-2275*   ✆ *360-569-2770*
✐ *rainier.guestservices.com, mtrainierreservations@guestservices.com*

This popular inn was built in 1916. Nineteen miles into the park, this nonsmoking inn has a lobby that boasts exposed beams, peeled-log posts, wooden furniture, Indian-made rugs and two huge fireplaces. The views from outside are grand, but the rooms are ordinary.

NATIONAL PARK INN

$$–$$$ 25 ROOMS   ✉ *Longmire, WA 98397*   📞 *360-569-2275*
📠 *360-569-2770*   🖥 *ranier.guestservices.com*

This in-park hotel is located six miles from the Nisqually entrance. The inn offers much of the rustic charm of the Paradise Inn, yet is much smaller with only 25 rooms, 18 with private baths. Some rooms have views of the mountain. In keeping with the rustic theme, there are no telephones or televisions. The lobby has an enormous stone fireplace.

ALEXANDER'S COUNTRY INN & RESTAURANT

$$–$$$ 12 ROOMS   ✉ *37515 Route 706 East, Ashford*   📞 *360-569-2300,*
800-654-7615   📠 *360-569-2323*   🖥 *www.alexanderscountryinn.com,*
info@alexanderscountryinn.com

Equally popular with lovers of old inns is Alexander's. This inn was built in 1912 as a small hotel designed to look like a manor with turret rooms and grand entrance hall. It retains the Old World look while adding modern conveniences such as a hot tub in a backyard gazebo, a media room and a day spa. A full-course country breakfast is included, as is wine in the evening.

COWLITZ RIVER LODGE

$$ 32 ROOMS   ✉ *13069 Route 12, Packwood*   📞 *360-494-4444, 888-305-2185*
📠 *360-494-2075*   🖥 *www.escapetothemountains.com, cowlitz000@centurytel.com*

In Packwood on the southern flank of the national park is this lodge. It is notable for clean, brightly decorated rooms and views of the mountains, although not "The Mountain." It is set back from the busy Route 12 far enough for the logging trucks to be a distant hum rather than an immediate roar. An outdoor hot tub is available for guests.

CRYSTAL MOUNTAIN RESORT

$$$–$$$$ 97 UNITS   ✉ *Crystal Mountain Lodging, 33000 Crystal Mountain Boulevard, Crystal Mountain*   📞 *360-663-2558, 888-668-4368*   📠 *360-663-0145*
🖥 *www.crystalmountainlodging.com*

On the northeast boundary of the park is this year-round resort that is best known for its skiing. Visitors can choose from a number of places to stay, ranging from condominiums to inexpensive hotels, all of which are nonsmoking. Don't expect much charm because skiing, not hotel amenities, is the focus. Typical is **Silver Skis Lodge and Crystal Chalets**, which has a cluster of one- and two-bedroom units, some with fireplaces and views. All have kitchens and televisions and can sleep from four to eight people. They are decorated in the traditional rental-condo manner of wood furniture and durable fabrics.

THE WHITE PASS VILLAGE INN

$$–$$$ 50 UNITS   ✉ *48933 Route 12, Naches, WA 98937*   📞 *509-672-3131*
📠 *509-672-3133*   🖥 *www.whitepassvillageinn.com, info@whitepassvillageinn.com*

A bit farther east toward Yakima is this lodge in the White Pass ski area. The complex has 50 rental units designed for large groups, up to eight in many units, and they have a bit of variation in decor since all are privately owned. Some have fireplaces and sleeping lofts, while all have full kitchen facilities.

APPLE COUNTRY B&B

$–$$ 4 ROOMS   ✉*4561 Old Naches Highway, Naches*   ☎*509-965-0344,* *877-788-9963* ☎*509-965-1591* ✎*www.applecountryinnbb.com,* *apple@applecountryinnbb.com*

Peace and quiet are the overwhelming virtues of this B&B. With antique-furnished bedrooms in a 1911 house and a small cottage on a working farm, hard-working hostess Shirley Robert wants her guests to feel as serene as the setting suggests. Sit outside your antique-furnished rooms over looking the back yard and orchards beyond, sipping lemonade, and peace prevails.

DINING

Good restaurants are hard to find around Mt. Rainier but there are a few worth mentioning.

GATEWAY INN

$$ AMERICAN   ✉*38820 Route 706 East, Ashford*   ☎*360-569-2506*

Set on three wooded acres, which also include log cabins and an RV park, this inn offers a wood-paneled coffee shop– style restaurant serving breakfast, lunch and dinner. The standard road fare of burgers, steaks and omelettes is enhanced by local trout and freshly baked breads and fruit pies.

PETERS INN

$$ AMERICAN   ✉*13051 Route 12, Packwood*   ☎*360-494-4000*

One of the most popular restaurants between Mt. Rainier and Mt. St. Helens is this large, old-fashioned place where they serve burgers, steaks and some seafood. In busy seasons, they have a large salad bar. Pies and cinnamon rolls are made locally.

WHISTLIN' JACK LODGE

$$–$$$$ SEAFOOD/PACIFIC NORTHWEST   ✉*20800 State Route 410, Naches*   ☎*509-658-2433, 800-827-2299* ✎*www.whistlinjacklodge.com*

This is a rustic lodge 20 miles east of Mt. Rainier National Park that offers a sophisticated level of dining unusual in these parts. Pan-fried rainbow trout boned tableside and a signature appetizer of crab-stuffed artichoke hearts served with garlic toast points are among the specialties. Prime rib, lobster and desserts such as strawberry crème brûlée and wild blackberry pie round out the menu. Breakfasts are also exceptional, with items such as huckleberry coffee cake. The spacious dining area is set with white linen napery and the lounge features a huge fireplace built from local river rock. Picture windows overlook the Naches River.

PARKS

PARKS 255

MT. RAINIER NATIONAL PARK

✉*Entrances to the park are located on Route 410 on the northeast, Route 706 on the southwest and Route 123 on the southeast.* ✆ *360-569-2211 ext. 3314, 888-892-5462*

🚶 🚴 🐎 🎣 ⛺ ⛵ One of the most heavily used national parks in Washington, Mt. Rainier is everybody's favorite because the mountain can be approached from so many directions and the area around it is glorious no matter the time of year. The mountain is open for climbing for individuals or groups, and may be done under the leadership of **Rainier Mountaineering Inc.** (360-569-2227; www.rmiguides.com, info@rmiguides.com), or by direct registration with the climbing rangers, for experienced mountaineers. The park charges a climbing fee per person, per climb above 10,000 feet. Otherwise, you can hike the lower stretches of the mountain. The lower elevations are notable for the great views of vast meadows covered with wildflowers from July until August, and for dramatic fall colors in September and October. Numerous trails lead day hikers to viewpoints, and backpackers can register on a permit system for backcountry campsites. A backcountry fee may be charged for a reservation for overnight trips during the summer months. The park is open year-round with special areas set aside for winter sports at Paradise. Fishing is permitted in designated waters without a state license. Check with a ranger for regulations. You will find picnic areas, restrooms, four information centers, museums and self-guided nature trails. Day-use fee, $15 per vehicle (good for seven days).

▲ There are four car campgrounds, one walk-in campground, and one campground accessible only to high-clearance vehicles. Overnight hike-in backcountry areas are first-come, first-served, though you can reserve a spot ($20 reservation fee). RVs are allowed (no hookups). Fees range from free to $15 per night. Information about making reservations for two campgrounds during the summer months can be found at www.nps.gov/mora.

MT. ST. HELENS AREA

There are few certitudes in travel writing, but here's one: Don't miss Mt. St. Helens. At the southern end of the Washington Cascades an hour north of Portland, this peak might best be described as a cross between a geology lesson and a bombing range. East of this landmark is Gifford Pinchot National Forest and Mt. Adams Wilderness, the heart of a popular recreation area ideal for rafting and fishing.

On May 18, 1980, Mt. St. Helens, dormant for 123 years, blew some 1300 feet off its top and killed 57 persons, causing one of the largest natural disasters in recorded North American history.

Today, access to the volcano remains limited because the blast and resulting mudslides and floods erased the roads that formerly entered the area.

SIGHTS

MT. ST. HELENS VISITOR CENTER ✉*3029 Spirit Lake Highway, Castle Rock* ✆*360-274-0962* 📠*360-274-9285* A major sightseeing destination, this visitor center is on Route 504 at Silver Lake, five miles east of Route 5. The center is elaborate and includes a walk-in model of the inside of the volcano and other volcanoes in the Cascades. Two short films about the eruption play almost continuously. Closed Tuesday and Wednesday from January through March. Admission.

WINDY RIDGE This is the closest you can get to the volcano, and it is reached by driving south from Randle on a series of Forest Service roads. Hourly talks are given by rangers in the amphitheater there in summer. **Meta Lake Walk** is on the way to Windy Ridge, and rangers tell how wildlife survived the blast. A 30-minute talk is given in **Ape Cave** on the southern end of the monument. It includes a walk into the 1900-year-old lava tube that got its name from the first group of people who mapped and explored the cave, a boy scout group called St. Helens Apes.

GIFFORD PINCHOT NATIONAL FOREST HEADQUARTERS ✆*360-891-5001* 📠*360-891-5045* 🌐*www.fs.fed.us/gpnf* From Mt. St. Helens, continue south through Gifford Pinchot National Forest. You'll want to buy a copy of the national forest map at this main office, or from a ranger station before you begin to explore the area.

GIFFORD PINCHOT NATIONAL FOREST ————

✆*360-891-5000 (headquarters)* In this national forest, you can drive to the edge of the **Indian Heaven Wilderness Area** and hike through peaceful meadows and acres of huckleberry bushes, or continue east to the edge of the **Mt. Adams Wilderness Area** with views of that mountain reflected in lakes. There are other numerous hiking opportunities throughout the forest as well comprising 1200 miles of trails. Day and overnight permits are required to enter wilderness areas in the Gifford Pinchot National Forest. This whole area is known for wild huckleberries, and there are two seasons for them; in the lower elevations, they ripen in July and into August, then a week or two later the higher-elevation berries ripen.

The Day the Mountain Blew

At 8:32 a.m. on May 18, 1980, the growing bulge that had been forming in the past weeks pushed a small section of rock down the slope of Mt. St. Helens, and suddenly the mountain exploded with the force of 500 atomic bombs the size of the one dropped on Hiroshima. It powdered the mountainside and blew it into the atmosphere at about 500 miles per hour. Simultaneously, practically the whole north flank lurched down the mountain at about 200 miles per hour. By evening, ash had covered a quarter-million square miles in three states and the silhouette of Mt. St. Helens was left standing with a huge bite taken out of its north slope—1300 feet shorter than its 9677-foot stature the day before.

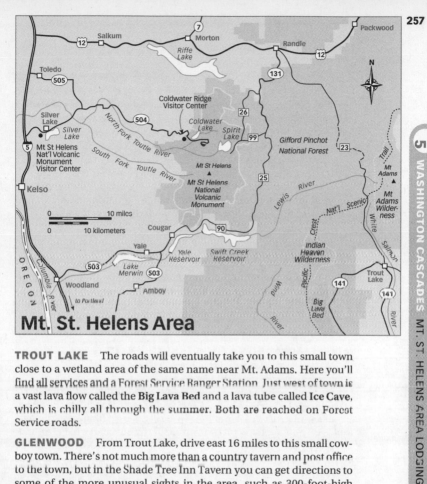

Mt. St. Helens Area

TROUT LAKE   The roads will eventually take you to this small town close to a wetland area of the same name near Mt. Adams. Here you'll find all services and a Forest Service Ranger Station. Just west of town is a vast lava flow called the **Big Lava Bed** and a lava tube called **Ice Cave**, which is chilly all through the summer. Both are reached on Forest Service roads.

GLENWOOD   From Trout Lake, drive east 16 miles to this small cowboy town. There's not much more than a country tavern and post office to the town, but in the Shade Tree Inn Tavern you can get directions to some of the more unusual sights in the area, such as 300-foot-high basalt columns and what is locally called "volcano pits," a series of small craters left behind by cinder cones.

From Glenwood, take the Glenwood-Goldendale Road to the junction with Route 142 and drive back southwest to Klickitat and the Columbia Gorge at Lyle. This takes you through the deep, winding Klickitat River Canyon with views of the river, a steelheaders' favorite. Mt. Adams often frames the scene.

LODGING

SEASONS MOTEL

$$ 49 ROOMS   ✉ *200 Westlake Avenue, Morton*   📞 *360-496-6835, 877-496-6835*
📠 *360-496-5127*   ✍ *www.whitepasstravel.com, reservations@whitepasstravel.com*
This motel, about halfway between Mt. Rainier and Mt. St. Helens, has

renovated rooms in a two-story, cream-colored building with burgundy trim at the intersection of Routes 12 and 7. All beds are queen-sized and wi-fi access is available in the rooms. A free continental breakfast is available.

THE SHEPHERD'S INN

$$ 5 ROOMS   ✉ *168 Autumn Heights Drive, Salkum* ☎ *360-985-2434,*
800-985-2434 🖰 *www.theshepherdsinn.com, shepherd@theshepherdsinn.com*

Located 17 miles west of Morton in the tiny town of Salkum, this inn is about 45 minutes away from Mt. Rainier and one hour away from Mt. St. Helens. The inn's rooms offer country Victorian furnishings and brass beds. If you have the urge to tickle the ivories, you may do so on the grand piano. There's also a double jacuzzi and free wi-fi. Full breakfast includes wild huckleberry crêpes.

THE FARM BED AND BREAKFAST

$$ 2 ROOMS   ✉ *490 Sunnyside Road, Trout Lake* ☎ *509-395-2488*
🖰 *www.thefarmbnb.com, innkeeper@thefarmbnb.com*

This quiet bed and breakfast is on six acres in Trout Lake, close to Mt. Adams. Two rooms decorated in antiques with cozy quilts are available in this three-story 1890 farmhouse. Surrounding the B&B are perennial gardens, a barn and a vegetable garden. Hosts Rosie and Dean Hostetter serve a full breakfast with fresh raspberries and strawberries in season.

MT. ADAMS LODGE AT THE FLYING L RANCH

$$–$$$ 14 UNITS   ✉ *25 Flying L Lane, Glenwood* ☎ *509-364-3488*
🖰 *www.mt-adams.com, flyingl@mt-adams.com*

On the southeastern edge of Mt. Adams is this outdoor-oriented lodge at the Flying L Ranch. Originally a working ranch, since 1960 the Flying L has been a guest ranch but now without horses. Hiking and photography are popular here. Bikes are available free of charge to get around the mostly flat roads in the area. In the winter, cross-country skiing and snowshoeing access is nearby. The main lodge has six rooms, five with private baths; a two-story guesthouse has five rooms with private baths, and three separate cabins sleep four to six. The main lodge has a large common kitchen where guests can prepare their own lunches and dinners.

DINING

WHEEL CAFÉ

$–$$ AMERICAN   ✉ *185 Main Street, Morton* ☎ *360-496-3240*

A longtime local fixture in downtown Morton is this café with all-pine paneling. Breakfast specialties include blueberry or strawberry pancakes, while dinner choices are a large salad bar, steaks, prime rib, burgers, fish and chips and house-made pies. There is also an adjoining bar area with dart boards, pool table and pull tabs.

PLAZA JALISCO

$$ MEXICAN   ✉ *200 Westlake Avenue, Morton* ☎ *360-496-6660*

Plaza Jalisco offers classic Mexican fare, with daily specials such as *pollo loco*. Clean, diner-style booths and huge windows make this a comfortable, casual eatery.

PARKS

MT. ST. HELENS NATIONAL VOLCANIC MONUMENT

From the west, Route 504 (Exit 49 from Route 5) leads to the Mt. St. Helens Visitor Center on the shores of Silver Lake, as well as the Coldwater Ridge Observatory (Milepost 43) and the Johnson Ridge Observatory (Milepost 52); Southside attractions are along Route 503 (Exit 21 from Route 5). The eastside blast area, including Windy Ridge, is located on Route 99, accessible from the north via Route 12 to Forest Road 25 and from the south via Route 503 to Forest Road 25. 360-449-7800 360-449-7801

The monument covers 110,000 acres and was created to preserve and interpret the area that was devastated by the 1980 eruption. Interpretive centers and overlooks along Route 504 show vast mud flows and the forests that were flattened by the blast. Access to the east side of the monument is limited to a few Forest Service roads, most of which are closed in the winter. Fishing is excellent for bass and trout in nearby Silver Lake and good for trout in lakes behind dams on the Lewis River, south of the monument. Facilities include interpretive centers, picnic areas, scenic overlooks and self-guided nature walks; viewpoints on the east side are closed during the winter.

▲ There are about 14 campgrounds in the monument's vicinity; most are run by the U.S. Forest Service. Reservations and fees vary by campground; check the Mt. St. Helen's website for full information.

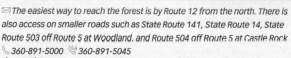

GIFFORD PINCHOT NATIONAL FOREST

hidden

The easiest way to reach the forest is by Route 12 from the north. There is also access on smaller roads such as State Route 141, State Route 14, State Route 503 off Route 5 at Woodland, and Route 504 off Route 5 at Castle Rock 360-891-5000 360-891-5045

This 1.37-million-acre forest covers most of the southern Cascades to the Columbia River, marked by the Mt. St. Helens Volcanic National Monument on the west and Mt. Adams on the east. Enclosing seven wilderness areas, the forest is well-accessed by a network of roads and trails used for a variety of recreational uses. Of particular interest are the **Big Lava Beds**, 14 miles west of Trout Lake, where unusual formations of basalt are found, and the **Ice Cave**, six miles southwest of Trout Lake, a lava tube where ice remains until late summer. Rivers and frequently stocked lakes offer excellent fishing. In late summer, huckleberry picking is very popular. You'll find picnic areas and restrooms. Parking fee, $5.

▲ There are 24 campgrounds ($12 to $90 per night), 21 primitive campgrounds (free to $10) and 10 horse camps (free to $12). Reservations: 877-444-6777, www.fs.fed.us/gpnf.

OUTDOOR ADVENTURES

FISHING

Winter steelhead, Dolly Varden, rainbow trout, eastern brook trout, walleye, sturgeon, catfish, bass, perch and crappie all can be caught in the interior and along the flanks of the Cascade Range. Fishing is typically done from the banks or on private boats, but most resorts on lakes and rivers have boats and fishing tackle for rent.

The other Cascade rivers, such as the Methow, Wenatchee, Yakima, Snake and Klickitat, drain into the Columbia River. All have good trout, walleye and steelhead fishing. The Klickitat River has an excellent summer steelhead run as does the Columbia. (During salmon runs, American Indians still fish with their traditional dip nets from the Fisher Hill Bridge near Klickitat.) As their numbers continue to dwindle, fewer and fewer salmon can be caught upstream from the Bonneville Lock and Dam, the first of 14 dams on the river.

You'll need a Washington State Fishing License to fish in most places, although not in all national parks. You can buy one at most bait shops.

North Cascades

Several rivers in the area—Skykomish, Snohomish, Sauk and Skagit for example—provide year-round catches, notably steelhead and all species of salmon except sockeye (it's not permitted to take this fish from rivers).

JOHN'S GUIDE SERVICE ✉Concrete ☎360-853-9801 ⬧www.johns-guide-service.com, johnsguidesvc@hotmail.com John's offers fishing trips for small groups throughout the North Cascades region.

RIVER RUNNING

"Mild to wild"—that's how one outfitter describes the range of whitewater-rafting experiences in the Cascades. From the easy Class I and II rapids on the Skagit, to the steady Class II and III staircase rapids on the Suiattle, to the Tieton's Class IV and the Skykomish's Class IV-plus rapids, whitewater-rafting trips are fun and popular throughout the Cascades. In the Wenatchee–Leavenworth area, the Wenatchee River, which has a relatively easy Class III rapid, makes a great trip for families with children. Depending on the river, outfitters generally operate April through October. From mid-December through January, the Skagit is the place for float trips to observe bald eagles, who migrate to the area to feed on salmon from the river. A caveat, though: One guide warns that classifications can be misleading, and inexperienced rafters may think they can handle rapids beyond their skill.

North Cascades

DOWNSTREAM RIVER RUNNERS ✉Seattle ☎206-910-7102 ⬧www.riverpeople.com, rafting@riverpeople.com This longtime outfitter rafts the Skagit, Sauk and Suiattle rivers in the North Cascades region, as well as several others elsewhere in the state. They do trips at all levels of difficulty (rivers range from Class I to Class V). Eagle-viewing trips are offered in December and January.

Wenatchee Area

ALL ADVENTURES RAFTING ✉️*BZ Corner* 📞*509-493-3926, 800-743-5628* 🖱️*www.alladventuresrafting.com, info@alladventuresrafting.com* Besides whitewater trips, this company offers eagle-viewing and scenic floats (accompanied by a naturalist) on rafts or inflatable kayaks on three rivers in Washington and one in Oregon. They can arrange rafting trips of all levels of experience, and for individuals using wheelchairs or with other special needs.

Leavenworth Area

ALPINE ADVENTURES' WILD AND SCENIC RIVER TOURS ✉️*221 Crost Avenue, Seattle* 📞*206-323-1220, 800-723-8386* 🖱️*www.alpineadventures. com* This tour company concentrates its operation on eleven rivers found within the Cascade Loop (the Route 2–Route 20 driving loop), including the Skykomish, Sauk, Nooksack, Wenatchee, Methow and Skagit. They also run trips on the Tieton River in September. Alpine's trips range from scenic floats to all classes of whitewater rafting, last from one hour to several days, and can accommodate from six to 200 people.

LEAVENWORTH OUTFITTERS ✉️*21312 Route 207, Leavenworth* 📞*509-548-0368* 🖱️*www.leavenworthoutfitters.com* Experienced guides from this outfitter lead rafting trips on the Wenatchee River. They arrange trips or provide gear for snow-shoeing, kayaking and cross-country skiing.

SKIING

It's all downhill from here: Yes, friends, we are going to take you skiing. Whether you are into slopes or cross-country, the best ski areas in Washington are stretched along the Cascades from Mt. Baker to Mt. Rainier. For skiing conditions call the Forest Service's Avalanche Center at 206-526-6677.

MT. BAKER ✉️*Route 542* 📞*360-734-6771, 360-671-0211 (snowline)* 📠*360-734-5332* 🖱️*www.mtbaker.us, snow@mtbaker.us* Beginning at the northernmost ski area and working south toward the Columbia River, this mountain is 56 miles east of Bellingham and has an elevation range of 3500 to 5090 feet. Receiving the highest amount of average snowfall of any ski area in North America, Mt. Baker's ski park has two options, one all natural, including their half pipe, and a six-acre manmade area. Seven lifts and two rope tows take you up to over 38 trails.

NORTH CASCADE HELI-SKIING ✉️*509-996-3272; 800-494-4354* 🖱️*www. heli-ski.com, info@heli-ski.com* The state's only helicopter skiing is North Cascade, which operates out of the Freestone Inn in Mazama.

STEVENS PASS 📞*206-812-4510* 🖱️*www.stevenspass.com, info@stevenspass. com* Some skiers prefer this area, located on Route 2 about 65 miles east of Everett, because it has an annual average snowfall of 450 inches. Closed late November through mid-April.

LEAVENWORTH
WINTER SPORTS CLUB

📞 509-548-5477 ✎ www.skileavenworth.com, info@skileavenworth.com One of the area's smaller mountains is at this sports club, a mile north of Leavenworth with a 400-foot vertical drop and a network of cross-country trails.

MISSION RIDGE ✉ On Mission Ridge Road, up Squilchuck Canyon 📞 509-663-6543, 509-663-3200 (snowline) ✎ www.missionridge.com, info@missionridge.com Probably the best powder snow at a large ski area is at this resort, 13 miles southwest of Wenatchee. Its base elevation is 4570 feet (the highest base area in the state of Washington), with a 2200-foot vertical rise and views of Mt. Rainier and the Columbia River. Closed Tuesday and Wednesday during non-holiday weeks.

THE SUMMIT AT SNOQUALMIE PASS 📞 425-434-7669 (general), 206-236-1600 (snow conditions), 800-695-7623 (road conditions), 206-236-7277 (information) ✎ www.summitatsnoqualmie.com The largest operation of all is this one, 47 miles east of Seattle. Four major ski areas are to be found in a space of two miles: **Alpental, Summit East, Summit West** and **Summit Central.** The average summit elevation is 4100 feet and the average base is 2900 feet. The Summit at Snoqualmie offers the largest night-skiing operation in the country, as well as a tubing center, a lodge and a Nordic center where you can cross-country ski, telemark and snowshoe.

CRYSTAL MOUNTAIN

📞 360-663-2265, 888-754-6199 ✎ www.skicrystal.com, comments@skicrystal. com Forty miles east of Enumclaw just off Route 410 and in the shadow of Mt. Rainier, this summit has an elevation of 7012 feet. Crystal has 2600 acres, including 300 acres of backcountry terrain and 1000 acres of lift-serviced terrain. The vertical drop is 3100 feet, and there are 50 trails, 11 percent of which are beginner, 54 percent of which are intermediate and 35 percent of which are advanced.

WHITE PASS

📞 509-672-3101, 509-672-3100 (snowline) ✎ www.skiwhitepass.com In the same general area, this pass is 20 miles east of Packwood on Route 12 southeast of Mt. Rainier. A family-oriented ski area, this place is rarely crowded. Six lifts serve 32 runs. Their 18-kilometer cross-country trail system is double tracked with a skating lane. Closed May through October.

METHOW VALLEY SPORT TRAILS ASSOCIATION ✉ P.O. Box 147, Winthrop, WA 98862 📞 509-996-3287 (office), 509-996-3860 (hotline) ✎ www. mvsta.com, info@mvsta.com Cross-country skiing is particularly popular on the eastern slopes of the mountains. Some of the best is in the Methow Valley, where more than 120 miles of groomed trails are available. This

association has a hotline for ski-touring information and a brochure showing the major trails.

ECHO VALLEY

hidden

✉*Seven miles northwest of Chelan on a dirt road off Route 150* ☎*509-687-3167 (weekends only)* ⌘*www.echovalley.org, info@echovalley.com* This area (with elevations of 3000 feet) offers downhill and cross-country skiing as well as rope tows, one lift, 14 miles of trails and a six-foot-wide skating lane for freestyle cross-country skating. A full-service rental shop stocks ski gear, and a school offers both downhill and cross-country lessons. In summer, there's a mountain-biking/hiking center.

LEAVENWORTH AREA   There are several ski trails maintained in this area, including the **Icicle River Trail** (7.5 kilometers), kid-friendly **Ski Hill** (5 kilometers) and **Leavenworth Golf Course** (8 kilometers). You can actually ski from your hotel in downtown Leavenworth to the golf course trails (2 kilometers).

LEAVENWORTH OUTFITTERS ✉*325 Division, Leavenworth* ☎*509-548-0368* ⌘*www.leavenworthoutfitters.com* This outfitter, located a half mile from five snow parks in the Lake Wenatchee area, offers cross-country ski lessons, and the store rents 120 pairs of cross-country skis and snowshoes.

GOLF

It seems that nearly every community in the foothills has a golf course. And the courses are as varied as the individual communities that host them.

Methow Valley

LAKE CHELAN GOLF COURSE ✉*1501 Golf Course Road, Chelan* ☎*509-682-8026, 800-246-5361* Along the eastern slopes of the North Cascades, in the Methow Valley, this public course is fairly challenging, with small elevated greens and a tenth-hole canyon to hit over. This 18-hole course is open March through November, weather permitting, and has golf lessons, a driving range and full-service restaurant and bar.

BEAR CREEK GOLF COURSE ✉*8-A Bear Creek Golf Course Road, Winthrop* ☎*509-996-2284* This public course has 18 holes and two sets of tees. Designed by Herman Court, the course is scenic with valleys, hills and mountains. Closed in winter.

Wenatchee Area

THREE LAKES GOLF COURSE ✉*2695 Golf Drive, Malaga* ☎*509-663-5448* ⌘*www.threelakesgolf.com* This is a pretty tough par-69, 18-hole public course, set on rolling terrain with a few water hazards. It includes a driving range, snack shop and restaurant. Closed in winter.

Leavenworth Area

LEAVENWORTH GOLF CLUB ✉*9101 Icicle Road, Leavenworth* ☎*509-548-7267* The Wenatchee River runs around this golf club, a semiprivate course that is closed to the public for a few hours each week. The spectacular mountain valley setting makes it worth the effort to get a tee time at this short, tight 18-hole course. The club, designed by members, is open April through October.

Route 90 Corridor

MT. SI GOLF COURSE ✉ *9010 Boalch Avenue Southeast, Snoqualmie* ✆ *425-391-4926* This 18-hole public course has breathtaking views of its namesake.

TALL CHIEF PUBLIC GOLF COURSE ✉ *1313 West Snoqualmie River Road South East, Fall City* ✆ *425-222-5911* Tall Chief has 12 easy holes.

CASCADE GOLF COURSE ✉ *14303 436th Avenue Southeast, North Bend* ✆ *425-888-0227* ✍ *www.cascadegolfcourse.com* Although it's relatively flat, this course, with good drainage, is probably the best winter set-up in the area. The public nine-hole course, designed by Emmett Jackson, has three sets of tees and easy access from Route 90.

SUN COUNTRY GOLF COURSE ✉ *841 St. Andrews Drive, Cle Elum* ✆ *509-674-2226* This public nine-hole course is equipped with RV spots for golfers who want to stay. Closed in winter.

ELLENSBURG GOLF CLUB ✉ *3231 Thorp Highway South, Ellensburg* ✆ *509-962-2984* This semiprivate golf club, designed by the Elks Club in the 1930s, has a nine-hole course available to the public. The Yakima River runs alongside it.

RIDING STABLES

Seen from atop a horse, the Cascades wilderness areas—deep mountain valleys, alpine meadows ablaze with wildflowers, heavily forested slopes and high peaks—take on new beauty. Besides guided rides, some outfitters also schedule pack trips that last overnight or longer. Always call ahead to make arrangements. Winter weather limits horseback riding to the warmer months, from mid-April through October.

North Cascades

STEHEKIN VALLEY RANCH ✉ *Stehekin* ✆ *800-536-0745* ✍ *www.stehekinoutfitters.com* For a 2.5-hour "nose-to-tail" guided ride—six riders maximum—through a pine forest to Coon Lake, which is in the North Cascades Wilderness Park, contact this ranch.

Methow Valley

SUN MOUNTAIN LODGE ✉ *Patterson Lake Road, Winthrop* ✆ *509-996-4735, 800-572-0493* ✍ *www.sunmountainlodge.com* Guided rides here are open to the public. The lodge's stable of 35 horses is one of the largest in the Cascades. The 90-minute ride is perfect for beginners; a four-hour trip through the aspen, pine and fir trees of the valley up to a lookout ridge is popular with more experienced riders. Private rides are also available, as are winter sleigh rides.

EAGLE CREEK RANCH ✉ *7951 Eagle Creek Road, Leavenworth, WA* ☎ *509-548-7798, 800-221-7433* ✎ *www.eaglecreek.ws, ranch@eaglecreek.ws* At this ranch, a guided ride into Wenatchee National Forest follows a trail through alpine meadows blooming with dozens of varieties of wildflowers before reaching a lookout peak for a spectacular view of the Cascades. The ranch also offers horse-drawn sleigh rides in the winter.

ICICLE OUTFITTERS AND GUIDES ✉ *P.O. Box 322, Leavenworth, WA 98826* ☎ *509-763-3647, 800-497-3912* ✎ *www.icicleoutfitters.com* Located in Lake Wenatchee State Park, this company has seasonal hourly guided rides, sleigh rides, day trips and summer pack trips that take two to ten people through timber past Nason Creek. Closed late September through May.

BIKING

For the most part, bicycling in the Cascades is not for the faint of heart or inexperienced. Besides that, unless you bring your own bike, it's hard to find bikes to rent. One exception is the Leavenworth area, where a relatively easy seven-mile loop will take you along the river and through town. You can pick up a free map at the **Leavenworth Chamber of Commerce** (940 Route 2, Leavenworth; 509-548-5807; www.leavenworth.org).

HIKING

The Cascades are a backpacker's paradise laced with thousands of miles of maintained trails. All distances listed are one way unless otherwise noted.

North Cascades

PACIFIC CREST NATIONAL SCENIC TRAIL

This trail (2650 miles) runs from its southern trailhead in Mexico to its northern terminus just north of Washington at the Canadian border. It is a hard hike in many places but can be broken into easier chunks, such as from Stevens Pass to Snoqualmie Pass. The natural beauty makes the trek worthwhile. Contact the **Outdoor Recreation Information Center** (REI building, 222 Yale Avenue North, Seattle; 206-470-4060) for further details. Closed Monday in winter.

HELIOTROPE RIDGE TRAIL

This 2.7-mile trail leads to a precipice where you can look down on Coleman Glacier. This popular hike has three hazardous stream crossings and can be accessed from Road 39 at Heliotrope Ridge, just east of the town of Glacier. Purchase a one-day trail parking pass ($5) before parking at the trailhead. Contact the **visitors center** (360-856-5700, 360-599-2714) for more information.

EAST BANK TRAIL

In Ross Lake Recreation Area, try the hike up Desolation Peak on this trail (19.3 miles from the highway). The views of the surrounding mountains and Ross Lake are spectacular, and might prove inspirational: Beat writer Jack Kerouac spent a summer at the lookout tower atop Desolation Peak.

CASCADE PASS TRAIL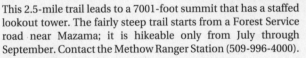

Perhaps the most historic route in the North Cascades is this 3.5-mile trail, the American Indians' route across the mountains for centuries. It is also a route from Marblemount to Stehekin (9 miles), if you want to really make a trip of it.

All along **Route 20** are signs for trailheads—all are worth exploring. The signs show the destination and distance of each trail.

IMAGE LAKE For a long trip—allow three or four days—this 16-mile lake trail is considered one of the most beautiful in the Central Cascades. The lake mirrors Glacier Peak, the most remote and inaccessible of the Washington volcanoes.

Methow Valley

GOAT PEAK TRAIL

This 2.5-mile trail leads to a 7001-foot summit that has a staffed lookout tower. The fairly steep trail starts from a Forest Service road near Mazama; it is hikeable only from July through September. Contact the Methow Ranger Station (509-996-4000).

Leavenworth Area

ICICLE GORGE TRAIL Winding 3.5 miles roundtrip, this trail is an interpretive loop a short distance west of Leavenworth.

ENCHANTMENT LAKES

The trek around these lakes (15 miles) is Washington's most beloved backpacking trip because the lakes are so otherworldly. They are approached from Icicle Creek near Leavenworth. The hike is a hard one, and permits ($5) must be obtained through the **Leavenworth Ranger Station** (509-548-6977).

Route 90 Corridor

IRON HORSE TRAIL STATE PARK The trail here (113 miles) is a former railroad right-of-way that is used by hikers, horse riders, cross-country skiers and bicyclists. No motorized vehicles are allowed on the trail, which goes from North Bend over Snoqualmie Pass to Vantage.

WONDERLAND TRAIL 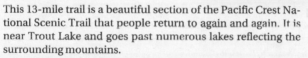 hidden

This beautiful trail (93 miles) goes entirely around Mt. Rainier and can be made in stages ranging from the 6.5-mile section between Longmire and Paradise to the 39-mile section from Carbon River to Longmire.

NORTHERN LOOP TRAIL Thirty-four miles roundtrip, this trail runs through the wilderness with frequent views of the mountain between Carbon River and Sunrise.

Mt. St. Helens Area

KLICKITAT TRAIL For 17 miles this trail takes you through a remote part of the Gifford Pinchot National Forest and is part of an old American Indian trail network. Closed November through May. For more information contact **Randle Ranger Station** (1 mile east of Randle on Route 12; 360-497-1100), or the **Klickitat Trail Conservancy** (www.klickitat-trail.org).

CONBOY LAKE NATIONAL WILDLIFE REFUGE Willard Springs Trail (3 miles roundtrip) winds through this national wildlife refuge just south of Glenwood. It skirts the lake, which is dry in summer, and passes back through Ponderosa pines.

INDIAN HEAVEN hidden

This 13-mile trail is a beautiful section of the Pacific Crest National Scenic Trail that people return to again and again. It is near Trout Lake and goes past numerous lakes reflecting the surrounding mountains.

TRANSPORTATION

CAR

Route 542 travels east from Bellingham through Glacier to dead-end at Mt. Baker Lodge. **Route 20**, also known as the North Cascades Highway, is one of the state's most popular highways and goes east from Route 5 at Burlington to the Methow Valley. **Route 2**, one of the last intercontinental, two-lane, blacktop highways, runs from Everett to Maine and is called the Stevens Pass Highway in Washington. From Seattle, **Route 90** goes over Snoqualmie Pass to Cle Elum and Ellensburg.

AIR

PANGBORN MEMORIAL AIRPORT ✉ *1 Pangborn Drive, East Wenatchee* 📞 *509-884-2494* 🖥 *www.pangborn airport.com* Only one airport serves this large area, and only one carrier, Alaskan Airlines/Horizon Air, offers scheduled service.

CHELAN AIRWAYS ☎ *509-682-5555* ✉ *www.chelanairways.com* The roadless Lake Chelan area is served by this airline, which makes scheduled and charter flights between Chelan and Stehekin.

FERRY

THE LADY OF THE LAKE ✉ *1418 West Woodin Avenue, Chelan* ☎ *509-682-4584* ✉ *www.ladyofthelake.com, info@ladyofthelake.com* This company provides daily transportation between Chelan, Manson, Fields Point, Prince Creek, Lucerne, Moore, Moore Point and Stehekin. You can also catch the smaller **Lady Express**, which has fewer stops but faster service and runs in the winter (except on Tuesday, Thursday and Saturday).

BUS

GREYHOUND BUS LINES ☎ *800-231-2222* ✉ *www.greyhound.com* Greyhound offers service to **Leavenworth** (limited stops, rotating) and **Wenatchee** (300 South Columbia Street; 509-662-2183) and a stop in **Cashmere** (102 Kitchenal Road; 509-782-5429).

LINK TRANSIT ☎ *509-662-1155* ✉ *www.linktransit.com* This transit company serves Ardenvoir, Cashmere, Chelan, Chelan Falls, Dryden, East Wenatchee, Entiat, Lake Wenatchee, Leavenworth, Malaga, Manson, Monitor, Orondo, Peshastin, Plain, Rock Island, Waterville and Wenatchee.

TRAIN

AMTRAK ☎ *800-872-7245* ✉ *www.amtrak.com* Amtrak offers service from Seattle, Portland and Spokane to Wenatchee via the "Empire Builder."

CAR RENTAL

At the Wenatchee airport are **Budget Rent A Car** (800-527-0700) and **Hertz Rent A Car** (800-654-3131). In Wenatchee is **John Clark Motors** (509-663-0587, 800-972-2298). Ellensburg has **Budget Rent A Car** (800-527-0700).

AERIAL TOURS

CHELAN AIRWAYS ✉ *1328 West Woodin Avenue (one mile west of Chelan on Route 97A)* ☎ *509-682-5555* 🖷 *509-682-5065 (call first)* ✉ *www.chelanairways.com, info@chelanairways.com* The best way to get to the remote resort town of Stehekin is also an incomparably scenic way to see Lake Chelan and its surroundings. Chelan Airways has been flying the lake for more than a half-century, and its experienced floatplane pilots are knowledgable tour guides. Round-trip passage is not too expensive, but it's worth a flight just to see the sights even if you don't stay "uplake." Closed November through March.

EAST OF THE CASCADES

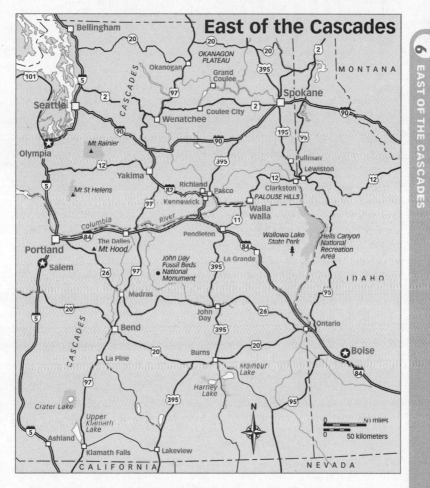

East of the Cascades

If state boundaries were determined by similar geography, customs and attitude, Washington and Oregon as we know them would simply not exist. Instead, they'd be split into two more states using the crest of the Cascades as the dividing line or would run vertically from California on the south to Canada on the north with one state taking either side of the mountain range.

Well, who ever said life was perfect? So what we have are two states whose eastern and western halves bear almost no resemblance to each other. From the Cascades west, the land is damp, the forests thick and the climate temperate. The eastern side of the range is almost exactly the opposite: Very little rain falls and most crops are irrigated by water from the Columbia Basin Project created by Grand Coulee Dam, or by water from deep wells. Here, the winters are cold and the summers are hot.

Even the people are as different as east and west. While those in the western halves tend to be liberal and innovative, the eastern residents are more conservative and content with the status quo. And since we're in a status-quo frame of mind now, we take you through both eastern Washington and Oregon in this chapter. Other chapters look at the western sides of the states. So buckle up!

In contrast, only bits and pieces of eastern Oregon are irrigated because it has not been blessed with any large rivers other than the Snake. It remains mostly arid, the northern reaches of the Great American Desert that runs north from Mexico through Arizona, California and Nevada. It is land more suitable for cattle grazing than growing crops, although in some valleys ranchers have drilled wells or dammed small streams to enable them to irrigate meadows. This kind of open and sparsely populated countryside doesn't appeal to all travelers, so you tend to see more recreational vehicles and truck stops than hotels and restaurants.

If urban amenities such as hotels, finer restaurants, theater and shopping centers are what you're after, head to Washington's larger cities—Spokane, Walla Walla, the Tri-Cities and Yakima. Elsewhere you'll find RV parks and inexpensive but clean motels. On the lakes and streams are rustic resorts, some with log cabins.

Away from the cities, hunting and fishing abound. Many streams and lakes are stocked regularly with trout, and a few sturgeon are still caught in the Snake and Columbia rivers. Deer, elk and an occasional black bear are popular quarry, as are waterfowl, pheasant, grouse and quail. Don't be startled while driving along a mountain road during hunting season if you spot someone in camouflage clothing carrying a rifle emerge from the forest.

Some of the most interesting geology in North America can be found in this region due to its tortured creation by volcanoes, lava flows through vast fissures and floods gigantic beyond imagining. Throughout the two states' eastern sides you will find vivid reminders of this creation process. In Oregon it is shown by hundreds if not thousands of dead volcanoes and cinder cones, the lava flows that have not yet been covered by windblown soil, the brilliantly colored volcanic ash deposits, and sheer canyons whose basalt walls were created by these lava flows. In Washington it is the dramatic Coulee Country along the Columbia River and the beautiful Palouse Country with its steep, rolling hills.

The forests are mainly pine with very little underbrush. Along some parts of the eastern slope of the Cascades you will find larch, the only species of coniferous trees that are deciduous. They are brilliantly colored in the fall and stand out as vividly as sumac and maples in the dark green forest.

One stretch of landscape of unusual origin is the Channeled Scablands south and west of Spokane, which was created by floods from a lake formed at the end of the Ice Age in the valley around Missoula, Montana.

In Oregon you will find the painted hills of the John Day Fossil Beds National Monument, the dramatic canyons of the Owyhee River and the vast Alvord Desert, barren of vegetation and flat as an airport. In both states east of the mountains is another treasure: peace and quiet. There are lonesome roads undulating off into the distance, small rivers stocked with trout, open pine forests, vast lakes made by man, working cowboys and mornings so tranquil you can hear a door slam.

As is true elsewhere in America, the general rule is the smaller the town, the friendlier the people, so don't be surprised if folks stop to talk about anything or nothing in particular. Also, nearly everything is less expensive than along the coast.

Traveling these remote areas, you will have a continual sense of discovery as you visit places barely large enough to get themselves onto state maps. And you will find small towns that don't bother opening tourist bureaus but have a clean motel, a good café, friendly people to talk to and a small city park for your picnic.

Compared with the rest of the country, the Northwest's history is both recent and benign. The Northwest is so new that East Coast visitors look askance when they find that the major cities weren't founded until the latter part of the last century. Very little recorded history goes back before 1800; the Lewis and Clark Expedition of 1804–1806 was the first overland crossing between the original 13 states and the Pacific Coast, and they were the first to describe the lower Snake River.

While the Indian wars had less bloodshed than in other parts of the West, one campaign has become almost legendary for the skill with which the Nez Perce tribe eluded the white army, and for the "humane" manner in which the war was fought. This was the running battle of 1877, when Chief Joseph led his band of a few warriors and a lot of women, children and elderly people on a brilliant retreat from their ancestral home in the Wallowa Valley 1400 miles across Idaho and Montana, only to be captured a few miles south of their goal, the Canadian border.

A few remnants of the pioneer years still remain standing in eastern Oregon and Washington. Here and there you'll see the remains of a cabin with the tall tripod of a windmill where a homesteader tried but failed to "prove up" the land given him by the Homestead Act. You'll also see remains of ghost towns (although some have been rediscovered and are peopled again). Most of these towns were built at or near mines and abandoned when the mines began coughing up only rocks and sand.

For your own exploration of this fascinating region, this chapter is divided into six sections:

The Okanogan Highlands, often called the Okanogan Country or simply the Okanogan, has boundaries that are fairly easy to determine: Route 97 to the west, the Canadian border to the north, the Columbia River on the east and the Colville Indian Reservation on the south.

Grand Coulee Area includes all the Columbia River system from where it swings west at the southern end of the Colville Indian Reservation and follows past Grand Coulee Dam south to the Vantage–Wanapum Dam area, where the Columbia enters the Hanford Nuclear Reservation.

The Spokane Area covers the only true metropolitan center east of the Cascades.

Southeastern Washington encompasses the famed Palouse Hills between Spokane and Pullman; the Snake River town of Clarkston; Walla Walla; the Tri-Cities of Pasco, Kennewick and Richland; and Yakima and the agricultural and wine-producing valley of the same name.

Northeastern Oregon covers the Pendleton and La Grande areas, the Blue Mountains, the beautiful Enterprise and Joseph area on the edge of the Eagle Cap Wilderness, and across the Wallowa Mountains to the few entrances to Hells Canyon on the Snake River. The centerpiece of this region is the Wallowas, a broad valley in the Enterprise and Joseph area where Wallowa Lake, one of the most beautiful in America, reflects the mountains of the Eagle Cap Wilderness.

Southeastern Oregon is the largest area covered and the least populated. It includes the cowboy country of the vast high desert that occupies most of the region, as well as the lava wasteland near La Pine and the multicolored John Day Fossil Beds National Monument.

OKANOGAN HIGHLANDS

One of the pleasures of touring the Okanogan Country is simply driving down country roads to see where they lead. A number of ghost towns, some no more than a decaying log cabin today, dot the map.

Most visitors enter the Okanogan Country from Route 97, the north–south corridor that runs up the Columbia River Valley to Bridgeport, then follows the Okanogan River Valley north toward Canada. This is desertlike country, with irrigated orchards on either side of the highway and open range climbing back up the mountains.

SIGHTS

OMAK VISITOR INFORMATION CENTER ✉ *401 Omak Avenue, Omak* ☎ *509-826-4218, 800-225-6625* 📠 *509-826-6201* 🖥 *www.omakchamber.com/omakvic.html, omakvic@northcascades.net* First, contact this visitor center for brochures and maps. They'll have information about local events too, such as their annual rodeo held in August. Closed weekends in winter.

OKANOGAN COUNTY HISTORICAL MUSEUM ✉ *1410 2nd Avenue North, Okanogan* ☎ *509-422-4272* 🖥 *ochs@ncidata.com* This museum, also headquarters for the county historical society, has a collection of pioneer farm and ranch implements and historical photos. This is also a good place to start your travels because members of the volunteer staff have lived in the region for many years and know where everything is, including skeletons in the county's closets. Open from Memorial Day to Labor Day. Admission.

RUBY ———————————

✉ *Salmon Creek Road, 10 to 15 miles northwest of Omak* Northwest of Omak is a region that was a silver mining area in the 1880s. Here, adventurers will find this remote short-lived town site. Named for either the type of silver prospectors hoped to find there or for a prospector's girlfriend or prostitute, the site has no structures left, only foundations and wagon roads.

NIGHTHAWK West of Oroville is this former ghost town. The paved county road, which heads west from Route 97 near the Canadian border, curves along the Similkameen River Valley, then swings south into a valley between the mountains of the Pasayten Wilderness of the North Cascades National Park and a series of steep ridges to the east. This area

Okanogan Highlands & Grand Coulee Area

HIDDEN HILLS COUNTRY INN

Old West–style bed and breakfast surrounded by fields of wildflowers and pine forests

COLVILLE TRIBAL MUSEUM, GALLERY AND GIFT SHOP

Handcrafted beaded jewelry and other North Coast Indian artwork in a tribal gallery dedicated to native history

SIAM PALACE

Warm, inviting local Chinese and Thai dining room with delicious curries and traditional favorites

GINGKO PETRIFIED FOREST STATE PARK

Nearly 8000 miles of lava-preserved trees on the shore of the Columbia River Gorge

is dotted with old mines, some still worked from time to time, but most of the land along the valley floor and stretching up the hillsides a few hundred feet has been turned into orchards or expanses of alfalfa with grazing cattle. Nighthawk now has two permanent residences, but mostly consists of a historic old store, post office, hotel and pink house from the few-year boom when prospectors found precious metals here in the 1890s.

LOOMIS   This mining town farther south on the loop drive is no longer a ghost town. The highway passes Palmer Lake and Spectacle Lake, both of which have public beaches, before rejoining Route 97.

MOLSON _____

One of the most interesting drives is to this ghost town 15 miles east of Oroville off Route 97 near the Canadian border. Molson was founded when a nearby mine was attracting hundreds of prospectors and workers. Owing to a land-claim mix-up, a farmer took over the whole town, so a new one had to be built and it was named New Molson. The two towns, less than a mile apart, fought over everything except education for their children. They built a school halfway between the towns, and it became Center Molson. Today **Old Molson** is an outdoor museum with one historic building, two homesteads, sheds, early 1900s machinery, a steam engine and more.

CENTER MOLSON SCHOOL BUILDING ✆ *509-485-3292* This school building has three stories of artifacts and a tea room. Open Memorial Day weekend to Labor Day weekend. Call for information (ask for Mary Louise Lowe).

ROUTE 20 This route is one of Washington's best highways for leisurely rural driving, especially as it traverses the Okanogan Country on its way to the Idaho border. It comes in from the Cascades to Omak-Okanogan, joins Route 97 north to Tonasket, swings east across the heart of the highlands through Wauconda and Republic, crosses the Columbia River at Kettle Falls and continues on to Tiger, where it follows the Pend Oreille River south to the Idaho border at Newport. There it disappears. The highway follows the path of least resistance beside streams and along valleys where ranches stretch off across rolling hills that disappear in pine forests.

REPUBLIC Heading east from Tonasket, the first notable town you'll come to is this one, created by a gold rush in the late 1890s. It still hosts one last operative gold mine, the Kinross Gold mine, a short distance outside town.

**STONEROSE
INTERPRETIVE CENTER**
✆ *509-775-2295* 🖥 *www.stonerosefossil.org, srfossils@rcabletv.com* This center lets visitors dig for fossils on a hillside on the edge of Republic. The site is named for family rose fossils found there. Closed November through April; closed Monday and Tuesday from May through October. Admission to the fossil dig site.

ST. PAUL'S MISSION ✉ *Route 395, Kettle Falls* If you continue eastward, you'll reach this historical site where Route 395 crosses the Columbia River. It was built as a chapel for American Indians in 1845 and operated until the 1870s. A modest museum is also here.

KELLER HERITAGE CENTER MUSEUM AND PARK ✉ *700 North Wynne Street, Colville* ✆ *509-684-5968* 🖥 *www.stevenscountyhistoricalsociety.org, schs@ultraplix.com* In **Colville**, ten miles east of Kettle Falls, several buildings make up this complex. There is a museum, a fire lookout tower, Colville's first schoolhouse, a trapper's cabin, a blacksmith shop, mine, a farmstead cabin, a machine shop, a sawmill and the 1910 home of the pioneer Keller family complete with original furniture. Open to the public May through September and by appointment the rest of the year. Admission to museum.

LODGING

OKANOGAN INN

$$ 77 UNITS ✉ *1 Appleway Street and Route 97, Okanogan* ✆ *509-422-6431, 877-422-7070* 📠 *509-422-4214* 🖥 *www.okanoganinn.com, reservations@okanoganinn.com*
The most modern motel in Okanogan is this inn. It has 77 rooms (in-

Okanogan Highlands

cluding four suites with full kitchens), an unpretentious dining room, lounge and a seasonally heated swimming pool. Pet-friendly.

PONDEROSA MOTOR LODGE

$ 25 ROOMS ✉ 1034 South 2nd Avenue, Okanogan ☎ 509-422-0400, 800-732-6702
📠 509-422-4206 🖳 www.ponderosamotorlodge.com, pond@communitynet.org

A cheap downtown Okanogan motel is this clean one-story lodge of basic design with a pool. Two-bedroom suites with kitchens are available. Pet-friendly.

RODEWAY INN & SUITES

$ 61 ROOMS ✉ 122 North Main Street, Omak ☎ 509-826-0400, 877-424-6423
📠 509-826-5635 🖳 www.rodewayinn.com

The Rodeway has standard motel-style rooms with refrigerators and microwaves; some include whirlpool tubs and fireplaces. A heated outdoor pool is available for guests, and a hot buffet breakfast is served each morning.

BONAPARTE LAKE RESORT

$ 10 UNITS ✉ 615 Bonaparte Lake Road, Tonasket ☎ 509-486-2828
📠 509-486-1987 🖳 www.bonaparte-lake-resort.com

This resort, 26 miles from both Republic and Tonasket, has airy and clean log cabins along the lake shore. Three have bathrooms and kitchens; the "Penthouse" also comes with linens. There are public showers and a bathroom. RV and tent sites are also available. A general store and lakeside café round out the amenities.

HIDDEN HILLS COUNTRY INN

$$ 8 ROOMS ✉ 104 Hidden Hills Lane, Tonasket ☎ 509-486-1895,
800-468-1890 📠 509-486-8264 🖳 www.hiddenhillsresort.com,
information@hiddenhillsresort.com

For a trip back to the Old West, head to this rustic-style bed and breakfast surrounded by fields of wildflowers and pine trees. The

276

guest rooms, most of which offer mountain views, have a turn-of-the-20th-century feel with floral wallpaper, pedestal sinks, brass beds and gleaming woodwork. Free wi-fi access is available throughout the inn. Full breakfast.

K DIAMOND K RANCH

$$$ 16 ROOMS   ✉15661 Route 21 South, Republic   ☎509-775-3536, 888-345-5355
📠509-775-3536   🖥www.kdiamondk.com, kdiamond@kdiamondk.com

Farther east of Tonasket, near Republic, this ranch offers total immersion in ranch living: sleeping in a group lodge, riding lessons, eating with the ranch owners, relaxing with campfire sing-alongs and hayrides. Guests can also hike, bike, fish, explore old mines and pan for gold. A working ranch, the K Diamond K is open year-round.

DOMINION MOUNTAIN RETREAT

$$ 1 UNIT   ✉694 Mosby Road, Colville   ☎509-684-6878
🖥www.dominionmountainretreat.com, lwaters@plix.com

This Craftsman-style bungalow is in the foothills of Old Dominion Mountain, six and a half miles from Colville. The loft cabin can sleep up to four people (a fifth on the window seat) and has a fully equipped kitchen stocked with breakfast foods, a propane heating stove, private tiled bath, two decks (one of them rooftop), a covered porch and free wi-fi. Hot tub shared with owner. Access by four-wheel drive only in winter. Fresh cookies on arrival. No credit cards. Reservations required.

DINING

SUN VALLEY RESTAURANT AND LOUNGE

$–$$$ AMERICAN   ✉Okanogan Inn, 1 Appleway Street and Route 97, Okanogan
☎509-422-2070   📠509-422-4214   🖥www.okanoganinn.com

Basic, standard fare is pretty much the order of the day here. For starters, there is the Sun Valley, which serves adequate, straightforward lunches and dinners and farmer-sized breakfasts.

BREADLINE CAFE

$$ AMERICAN   ✉102 South Ash Street, Omak   ☎509-826-5836
🖥www.breadlinecafe.com; info@breadlinecafe.com

The choices are few in Omak, but this antique-decorated café and bakery rates high. Lunch features big sandwiches on fresh-baked, whole-grain breads and dinner includes shrimp Creole, jambalaya, pepper steak, portobello and eggplant marinara over pasta and beef burgundy crêpes. Closed Sunday and Monday.

NORTH COUNTRY PUB

$–$$ AMERICAN   ✉15 South Main, Omak   ☎509-826-4271

There's nothing fancy here—burgers, steaks, tacos and barbecue—but it's solid, filling food. The lunch specials are usually pretty good, and if you're there on a Thursday night, the steak special is a bargain.

HIDDEN HILLS COUNTRY INN

$$$$ STEAK   ✉104 Hidden Hills Lane, Tonasket   ☎509-486-1895   📠509-486-8264
🖥www.hiddenhillsresort.com, information@hiddenhillsresort.com

One of the few deluxe dining choices in the region is provided by this country inn. The contemporary hotel has created a dining room built to resemble an 1890s mansion. The large room overlooks a pond and is handsomely decorated with cherry and maple furnishings, China cabinets and fringed lamps. The menu offers just one multicourse dinner selection that changes every night. Steaks and chicken breast are among the possibilities. Reservations required.

WAUCONDA STORE & CAFE

$$ AMERICAN   ✉2360 Route 20, Wauconda, east of Tonasket   📞509-486-4010

One of the more interesting places to stop for a snack or down-home American meal is this store, the only one in Wauconda. A breakfast and lunch counter to the left of the door is between the cash register and a large dining room overlooking a valley and low mountains beyond. The food is hearty and uncomplicated, and the portions are generous. Limited hours on Sunday.

F.B.'S DINER

$ DINER   ✉1518 Main Street, Oroville   📞509-476-4100

Downtown Oroville sports a few restaurants, including this classic joint specializing in burgers, steaks and barbecued ribs, with a few pasta dishes on the side. Breakfast is served daily.

SHOPPING

MUSTARD SEED GALLERY & GIFTS ✉21 North Main Street, Omak 📞509-826-2463 Omak's Main Street provides a few good browsing spots such as this gift shop, which features handmade Polish pottery, plus crafts, jewelry and collectibles. Closed Saturday through Monday.

DETROS WESTERN STORE ✉107 Main Street, Riverside 📞509-826-2200 Western wear of all kinds plus handcrafted silver jewelry, Pendleton blankets and saddles are stock and trade at this Western shop, a few miles north of Omak in Riverside. Closed Saturday.

PRINCE'S CENTER ✉1000 23rd Avenue, Oroville 📞509-476-3651 You don't have many retail options in the small town of Oroville. However, this center may be all you need (or find). Half of Prince's is devoted to groceries; the other side carries general merchandise—everything from footwear and apparel to toys and garden tools.

NIGHTLIFE

Most nightlife in this cowboy and fruit-picking area is limited to taverns, a few of which have live bands on weekends.

SHORTHORN TAVERN ✉3 North Main Street, Omak 📞509-826-0338 Big-screen TVs, pool, darts, karaoke on Wednesday and beer on tap are provided by the Shorthorn in downtown Omak.

PARKS

CONCONULLY STATE PARK

✉Located 22 miles north of Omak on Conconully-Okanogan Highway 📞509-826-7408

🏃 🚴 🛶 🏕 🎣 ⛵ 🚤 🎵 Strung along the edge of the town of the same name, this site is popular with boaters, swimmers, families and anglers seeking kokonee, large- and smallmouth bass, rainbow trout, German brown trout and Eastern brook trout. For hikers, there is a nature trail. Other facilities here include picnic areas, restrooms, a children's play area and a wading pool. Day use fee, $5.

▲ There are 82 standard sites ($17 per night). Closed weekdays in winter except holidays or by appointment.

OSOYOOS LAKE STATE VETERAN'S MEMORIAL PARK
✉Route 97, on the northern end of Oroville ✆509-476-3321

This lakeshore park is one quarter mile north of Oroville and stretches along the southern end of Osoyoos Lake. It has some of the few trees in the area for shade while picnicking and camping and is the most popular state park in the area. It is heavily used by Canadians and Americans alike since it is almost on the Canadian border. For nature lovers, the lake is a prime nesting area for Canadian geese; for anglers, this is a year-round spot for bass, kokanee and salmon. Facilities are limited to picnic areas and restrooms. Closed weekdays (except holidays) in winter.

▲ There are 86 standard sites ($19 per night) that accommodate RVs (no hookups). Reservations: 888-226-7688.

CURLEW LAKE STATE PARK
✉Route 21, ten miles north of Republic ✆509-775-3592

This 123-acre setting is on the southeastern shore of a lake in a pine forest with several islands. Remnants of homesteaders' cabins can be seen near the park, and a large variety of animals, including chipmunks, squirrels and deer, lives in the area. Several species of birds also can be seen. The park is bordered on the south by Colville National Forest. Picnic area and restrooms are the facilities here. Closed November to April.

▲ There are 57 standard sites ($17 per night), 25 RV hookup sites ($24 per night), and 2 primitive sites ($12 per night). First-come, first-served.

GRAND COULEE AREA

The centerpiece of the Grand Coulee Area, not surprisingly, is Grand Coulee Dam with its spectacular laser light shows during the summer months. The sheer mass of the dam is almost overwhelming and for decades was the largest concrete structure in the world.

Also of interest are the many lakes created by the dam that have become some of the Northwest's most popular recreation areas. The backwaters of the dam itself, named in honor of President Franklin D. Roosevelt, reach far north nearly to the Canadian border and east into the Spokane River system. A chain of lakes and some smaller dams were built to hold irrigation water for distribution south and east of the dam. These include Banks Lake and the Potholes Reservoir, known as the Winchester Wasteway. Don't be put off by the name—wasteway refers to the water that has been used for irrigation and has seeped along bedrock to emerge again ready for reuse. These lakes continue south to the Crab Creek Valley before re-entering the Columbia River below Vantage.

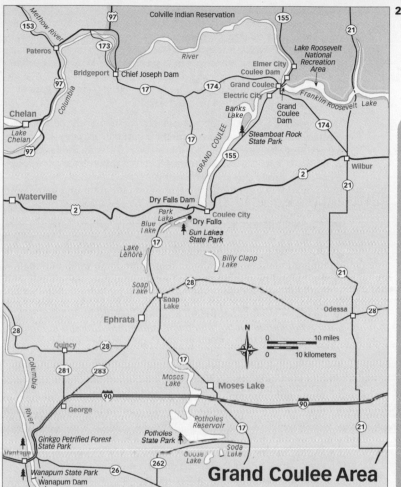

Grand Coulee Area

Before venturing ahead, be aware that this area is frequently baffling to visitors because of the similarity of place names. The towns of Coulee Dam and Grand Coulee are at the site of Grand Coulee Dam itself, while Coulee City is 30 miles away at the southern end of Banks Lake. In the same area are still two more small towns with names that often get confused: Elmer City and Electric City. Keep a map on hand to avoid confusion.

SIGHTS

GRAND COULEE DAM This major dam was built in the 1930s and memorialized by the songs of Woody Guthrie. The area that became known as the Columbia Basin was so barren before the dam that locals liked to say you had to prime yourself to spit and that jackrabbits cross-ing the basin had to carry canteens. The dam was the largest concrete pour in the world for many decades after its completion at the begin-ning of World War II. It stands 550 feet above bedrock, as tall as a 46-story building, and at 5223 feet is nearly a mile long. While its 12 million cubic yards of concrete may be difficult to imagine, the Bureau of Re-clamation points out that this is enough to build a standard six-foot-wide sidewalk around the world at the equator.

In addition to powering the hydroelectric system with the 151-mile-long Lake Roosevelt, the dam serves the additional purpose of irrigating more than 500,000 acres. Water is pumped 280 feet up the canyon wall to fill Banks Lake's reservoir, from which the water is moved through canals and pipes to the area's farmland.

You may think of Washington as a rainy place, but without Grand Coulee Dam and the string of smaller dams that came along later to turn the Columbia and Snake rivers into a series of lakes, eastern Wash-ington would be barren. Instead, in this part of the state one of the most common scenes is an irrigation sprinkler going about its business of turning the sand into a rich soil that grows wheat, wine grapes, fruit, soybeans, barley, oats, rape, grass seed, corn, alfalfa, potatoes, peas and a host of other crops.

GRAND COULEE CHAMBER OF COMMERCE ☎ *509-633-9265* ⌨ *www.grandcouleedam.org, chamber@grandcouleedam.org* Visitors are welcome at the dam and can go on guided tours. One of the most popular events is the nightly **laser show**, a free, 40-minute demonstration that uses the spillway of the dam for its screen. It is shown nightly from Memorial Day through September. More information is available through the chamber of commerce.

COLVILLE TRIBAL MUSEUM, GALLERY AND GIFT SHOP ⓗidden
✉ *512 Mead Way, Coulee Dam* ☎ *509-633-0751* ⌨ *webmaster@colvilletribes. com* Check out this gallery for displays of authentic village and fishing scenes, coins and metals dating from the 1800s and many ancient artifacts. The gift shop sells local beadwork and other artwork by tribal members. Closed Sunday and from October through April.

BANKS LAKE The best way to appreciate the stark beauty of the Grand Coulee Area is to drive south from the dam on Route 155 along this lake. The artificial lake is used for all water sports, and its color and character change dramatically with the time of day and weather.

DRY FALLS DAM At Coulee City you come to this dam, which holds Banks Lake water and sends it on south into a system of canals. Pinto Ridge Road heads due south from Coulee City and passes **Sum-mer Lake**, a favorite picnic spot. The falls are created by the irrigation water from Banks Lake.

The main route out of Coulee City is across Dry Falls Dam, then south on Route 17 past Dry Falls and Sun Lakes State Park, along a series of smaller lakes in the coulees—Park Lake, Blue Lake, Lake Lenore (where you can see the form of a small rhinoceros that was trapped in a prehistoric lava flow) and finally to Soap Lake.

SOAP LAKE   This lake was so named because the water used to foam before the ground water rose. The water is rich in minerals—sodium, chloride, carbonate, sulfate, bicarbonate and plenty of others—and matches the contents of water in the Baden Baden Spa in Germany. It has attracted a number of motels that pump water for use in the rooms or into spas where people go to soak themselves seeking comfort for a variety of skin, muscle and bone afflictions.

MOSES LAKE   South of Soap Lake the coulees flatten out, and the landscape away from the Columbia River becomes the gently rolling wheat-growing region. Moses Lake in the center of the Columbia Basin, is better known as a hub for farmers of the basin than as a tourist destination. The lake for which the town is named joins the Potholes Reservoir to the south.

LODGING

COLUMBIA RIVER INN

$$ 32 ROOMS   ✉10 Lincoln Avenue, Coulee Dam   📞509-633-2100, 800-633-6421
📠509-633-2633   🖃www.columbiariverinn.com, info@columbiariverinn.com

Right across the street from Grand Coulee Dam, this inn provides great views. Most rooms have a view of the spillway, and nightly laser light shows are across the street in the summer. The motel has 32 rooms, a sauna, an exercise facility, an outdoor pool and a hot tub. Two rooms have jacuzzis.

COULEE HOUSE MOTEL

$$–$$$ 61 ROOMS   ✉110 Roosevelt Way, Coulee Dam   📞509-633-1101,
800-715-7767   📠509-633-1416   🖃www.couleehouse.com, info@couleehouse.com

This motel, which is up a hill, provides a top-notch view. It has clean, standard motel-style rooms, and a swimming pool and hot tub. Free internet is available.

ALA COZY

$ 14 UNITS   ✉9988 Route 2 East, Coulee City   📞509-632-5703, 877-678-2918
📠509-632-5383   🖃alacozymotel.com, info@alacozymotel.com

Several budget-priced motels and resorts are located near Banks Lake and Lake Roosevelt. A mile and a half from the marina at the end of Banks Lake, this inn offers motel-style units with private bathrooms and refrigerators. There's a pool on the premises.

NOTARAS LODGE

$–$$ 15 ROOMS   ✉236 East Main Street, Soap Lake   📞509-246-0462
📠509-246-1054   🖃www.notaraslodge.com, notaras@notaraslodge.com

In Soap Lake, this lodge is the best-known and one of the most modern motels in town. The four-building complex plus restaurant has 15 rooms, 7 of which have jacuzzis. The rooms boast unusual decor, with names like the "Old Mexico" room—with a red roof, stucco walls and wrought-iron balcony—and the "Bunkhouse," complete with a wooden pack horse saddle and a 1900 cistern pump that turns the water on for the copper kettle sink. The accommodations are spacious and equipped with microwave ovens, refrigerators and coffee makers. Massages, whirlpool therapy and mineral baths in Soap Lake water are available.

Moses Lake is one of the most popular RV destinations in the central part of the state because several lakes are in the immediate vicinity, and hot, sunny weather is almost guaranteed.

BEST WESTERN LAKEFRONT HOTEL

$$ 157 UNITS ✉3000 West Marina Drive, Moses Lake ☎509-765-9211, 800-937-8376 📠509-766-0493 🌐www.bestwestern.com, char@bwlakefronthotel.com

Several motels are also along the Route 90 corridor and the lake, including this Best Western, which has fully renovated units, some on Moses Lake. In addition to boating and waterskiing right off the dock, the motel has a heated pool, a sauna, and a restaurant and lounge.

LAKESHORE RESORT MOTEL

$ 33 UNITS ✉3206 West Lakeshore Court, Moses Lake ☎509-765-9201 📠509-765-1800 🌐www.lakeshoreresortmotel.com, hapnravi@yahoo.com

The Lakeshore is also on the lake, where a marina and waterskiing are available. The motel has 24 units, nine housekeeping cabins and a heated pool.

DINING

MELODY RESTAURANT & LOUNGE

$–$$ AMERICAN ✉512 River Drive, Coulee Dam ☎509-633-1151 📠509-633-2925

A well-known eatery in this region is the Melody, which offers views of the Grand Coulee Dam and its summer laser light show. The menu features standard American fare, seafood and pasta. Breakfast, lunch and dinner.

SIAM PALACE

$ CHINESE/AMERICAN ✉213 Main Street, Grand Coulee ☎509-633-2921

If you want Asian food, this is the place to go. Thai, Chinese and American dishes are served, including a variety of curries and traditional favorites. No lunch on Saturday. Closed Sunday and Monday.

MICHAEL'S ON THE LAKE

$$–$$$ STEAK/AMERICAN ✉910 West Broadway, Moses Lake ☎509-765-1611 📠509-766-2804 🌐www.michaelsonthelake.com, michaels@michaelsonthelake.com

A light-filled, contemporary restaurant built of native stone, Michael's offers both indoor and outdoor dining. A spacious deck overlooks Moses Lake. Prime rib, hamburgers and seafood specials round out the menu; try the new vodka-tomato pasta with Italian sausage. Home-style desserts like cobblers are especially popular here.

COLVILLE TRIBAL MUSEUM, GALLERY AND GIFT SHOP

hidden

✉512 Mead Way, Coulee Dam ☎509-633-0751 This gallery and gift shop sells local beadwork and other items crafted by the tribal members. Closed Sunday and from October through April.

NIGHTLIFE

MOSES LAKE ✉Located 49 miles south of Coulee City ☎509-765-7888, 800-992-6234 There are a series of free concerts here, all beginning at 8 p.m., on most Saturdays from July to September, in a 5000-person-capacity outdoor amphitheater on the lakeshore. Nationally known musicians perform at this venue.

PARKS

LAKE ROOSEVELT NATIONAL RECREATION AREA

✉The lake can be accessed from Grand Coulee and Davenport in the south and Kettle Falls to the north. ☎509-633 9441, 800-824-4916 (for lake levels) ✉509-633-9332

This area stretches 151 miles along the entire length of Lake Roosevelt, including parts of the Spokane and Kettle rivers. Owing to the arid climate, the lake has miles and miles of sandy beaches and outcroppings of dramatic rocks. Only when you get close to the Spokane River do trees begin appearing along the shoreline. It is a particular favorite for waterskiers. Sailing and windsurfing are also popular activities. More than 30 species of fish are found here, including walleye, rainbow trout, sturgeon, yellow perch and kokanee, the land-locked salmon. There are only picnic areas.

▲ There are 27 campgrounds with over 600 sites; $10 per night from May through September, $5 per night from October to April.

STEAMBOAT ROCK STATE PARK

✉Route 155, 12 miles south of Grand Coulee ☎509-633-1304 ✉509-633-1294

This is one of Washington's most popular state parks and thus is one of the many parks where camping-space reservations are a necessity. The park is on the shores of Banks Lake at the foot of the butte by the same name. The ship-shaped butte rises 800 feet above the lake and has a good trail to the 640-acre flat top. Fishing for bass, walleye, trout, crappie, kokanee and perch is good year-round, and it's a popular place to ice fish. You'll find picnic tables, playground equipment, a bathhouse and a seasonal snack bar.

▲ There are 26 standard sites ($19 per night), 100 RV hookup sites ($26 per night) and 12 primitive boat-in sites ($14 per night). Reservations: 888-226-7688.

SUN LAKES STATE PARK

✉Route 17, seven miles southwest of Coulee City

This park is located on the floor of the coulee that was scoured out when the Columbia River's normal course was blocked by ice and debris at the end of the Ice Age. The river, three and a half miles wide, flowed over nearby 400-foot-high Dry Falls, which was the original name of the state park but was changed because of the lakes and recreation. It is now home to boating, riding, hiking and golfing. Picnic areas and restrooms are here. Included in the park is 76-person Camp Delaney, an environmental learning center.

▲ There are 152 sites and 39 with RV hookups; $19 to $26 per night. Note: A private concessionaire (**Sun Lakes Park Resort**, 34228 Park Lake Road Northeast, Coulee City, WA 99115; 509-632-5291; www.sun lakesparkresort.com) operates a portion of the park and offers 50 cabins ($93 to $103 per night for three to four people, $149 to $189 for lake views), 10 mobile homes ($119 to $149 per night for up to six people) and 112 full hookups ($23 to $36 per night). There's a general store, a snack bar, a heated swimming pool, boat rentals and marina, laundry, an 18-hole mini-golf course and a nine-hole golf course.

POTHOLES STATE PARK

✉ *Route 262, 17 miles southwest of Moses Lake*   ☏ *509-346-2759*   ℱ *509-346-1732*

🏃 🚣 🛥 ⌿ The potholes were created by floods following large lava flows during the Pleistocene era. Now the dunes stand above the water level and are used for campsites, bird blinds and picnic areas. The area supports a large population of waterfowl and other birds, including blue herons, white pelicans, sand-hill cranes, hawks and eagles. A lawn and shade trees, tables and stoves are beside the lake. Rainbow trout, bass, perch, crappie, bluegill and walleye are found in the park. There are restrooms and showers.

▲ There are 60 RV hookup sites ($27 per night) and 61 primitive sites ($14 per night). Reservations: 888-226-7688.

GINKGO PETRIFIED FOREST STATE PARK

✉ *Located on the edge of Vantage, a tiny town on Route 90 where it crosses the Columbia River*   ☏ *509-856-2700*   ℱ *509-856-2294*

🏃 More than 30 species of fossilized trees have been identified in this area of barren hillsides and lava flows, making it one of the largest fossil forests in the world. The park has an interpretive center overlooking the Columbia River with a wide selection of petrified wood and also has a three-mile interpretive hiking trail. No camping, fishing or swimming are permitted at Ginkgo, but you can head four and a half miles south on the Columbia River to **Wanapum State Park** for swimming and camping. Fishing is popular and boat ramps are available. There are picnic areas and restrooms.

▲ Wanapum has 50 RV hookup sites ($26 per night). Open weekends only in winter. Reservations: 888-226-7688.

SPOKANE

The northeastern corner of Washington is an area of pine forests, sparkling lakes, sprawling wheat farms and urban pleasures in a rural setting. Spokane is where the Midas-rich miners from Idaho came to live in the late 19th century, so the city has an abundance of historic homes, museums, bed and breakfasts and inns, and one of the most beautiful city park systems in the West.

SIGHTS

SPOKANE CONVENTION AND VISITORS BUREAU ⊠*201 West Main Avenue* ☎*509-747-3230, 888-776-5263* ⏎*www.visitspokane.com* The best way to become acquainted with Spokane is to take the self-guided "City Drive Tour" outlined in a brochure that is available at the visitors bureau. The tour takes you along Cliff Drive where many of the finest old homes stand and through one of the city's largest parks. The tour continues past **Coeur d'Alene Park**, off 2nd Avenue, and the stately **Patsy Clark Mansion** at 2nd Avenue and Hemlock Street. Another useful brochure is the self-guided tour of historic architecture in downtown Spokane, also available at the visitors bureau.

MANITO PARK ⏎*www.manitopark.org* This 90-acre park features five gardens, including the Japanese Garden built by Spokane's sister city in Japan and the **Duncan Formal Gardens** (Grand Avenue between 17th and 25th avenues), whose lush scenery looks like something out of a movie set in 18th-century Europe.

NORTHWEST MUSEUM OF ARTS & CULTURE ⊠*2316 West 1st Avenue* ☎*509-456-3931* ✉*509-363-5303* ⏎*www.northwestmuseum.org, themac@ northwestmuseum.org* This museum showcases a major collection of regional history and fine art. Closed Monday. Admission.

JOHN A. FINCH ARBORETUM ⊠*3404 West Woodland Boulevard, off Sunset Boulevard* ☎*509-363-5455* ✉*509-363-5454* Along with a rhododendron grove and patches of lilacs, this arboretum features an extensive collection of deciduous and evergreen trees from all over the world.

RIVERFRONT PARK ⊠*507 North Howard Street* ☎*509-625-6600, 800-336-7275* ✉*509-625-6630* ⏎*www.spokaneriverfrontpark.com, helloriverfrontpark@spokanecity.org* The city is most proud of its Riverfront Park, located in the heart of downtown and known for the natural beauty of its waterfall and island. A glorious addition to Spokane built for the 1974 World's Fair, the park has the restored 1909 Looff Carrousel and various other rides and food concessions, plus an IMAX Theater (admission). The Spokane Falls Skyride offers aerial views of the waterfall. It also has footpaths, natural amphitheaters, lawns and hills, and always the roar of the waterfall for a backdrop. Admission.

SPOKANE COUNTY COURTHOUSE ⊠*Broadway just off Monroe Avenue* A must see is this château-style courthouse across the river from downtown. Oddly enough, it was designed in the 1890s by a young man whose only formal training in architecture came from a correspondence course. It is a magnificent conglomeration of towers and turrets, sculpture, iron and brickwork in the French Renaissance manner.

ARBOR CREST WINE CELLARS ⊠*4705 North Fruit Hill Road* ☎*509-927-9463* ✉*509-927-0574* ⏎*www.arborcrest.com, info@arborcrest.com* Spokane has several wineries with sales and tasting rooms. On a bluff overlooking

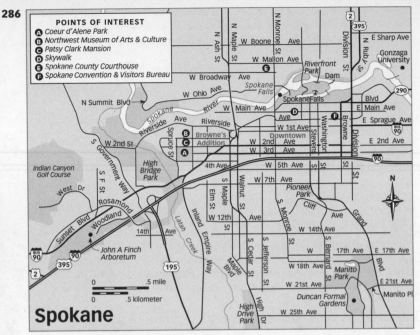

POINTS OF INTEREST
- Ⓐ Coeur d'Alene Park
- Ⓑ Northwest Museum of Arts & Culture
- Ⓒ Patsy Clark Mansion
- Ⓓ Skywalk
- Ⓔ Spokane County Courthouse
- Ⓕ Spokane Convention & Visitors Bureau

Spokane

the Spokane River, Arbor Crest is a family-owned winery in a building designated as a National Historic Site.

LATAH CREEK WINE CELLARS ✉ 13030 East Indiana Avenue ✆ 509-926-0164 📠 509-926-0710 🔗 www.latahcreek.com, info@latahcreek.com Latah Creek has a Spanish-style building with a large courtyard and a tasting room decorated with oak.

LODGING

Spokane has some pleasant hotels that don't carry big-city rates like those found in Seattle and Portland. You won't find deluxe or luxury accommodations here, but the down-home hospitality of the hotel staffs more than makes up for it.

DOUBLETREE HOTEL SPOKANE CITY CENTER

$$–$$$ 375 ROOMS ✉ 322 North Spokane Falls Court ✆ 509-455-9600, 800-222-8733 📠 509-455-6285 🔗 www.doubletree.com
This hotel was built for Spokane's 1974 World's Fair and has the best location, right along the Spokane River and on Riverfront Park. The lobby is impressive, and most rooms have good views of the river, park or downtown. It also has two restaurants.

SPOKANE HOUSE TRAVELODGE

$–$$ 60 ROOMS ✉ 4301 West Sunset Highway ✆ 509-838-1471, 800-550-7635 📠 509-838-1705
The Spokane House is a favorite of many who visit this area frequently. Built on a hill west of town, it is roughly halfway between the airport and downtown, is quiet and affords good views of the city's growing skyline.

DAVENPORT HOTEL

$$$$ 611 ROOMS   ✉10 South Post Street   ☎509-455-8888, 800-899-1482
📠509-624-4455   🖮www.thedavenporthotel.com, info@thedavenporthotel.com

Housed in a restored building in downtown Spokane, this is the region's classiest place to stay. The 1914 building has 283 rooms outfitted with hand-carved mahogany furniture and suites with whirlpool tubs; all units boast free wi-fi. Be sure to check out the Hall of the Doges, a ballroom decorated in Venetian palatial style, and the stained-glass ceiling of the Peacock Room. Amenities include a spa and health club, as well as a restaurant, café and lounge. The Davenport Tower is an extension of the hotel just across the street with an additional 328 rooms and its own restaurant.

E. J. ROBERTS MANSION

$$–$$$ 23 ROOMS   ✉West 1923 1st Avenue   ☎509-456-8839,
866-456-8839   🖮www.ejrobertsmansion.com

Built in 1889 as a personal residence for the Roberts family, this mansion is now a bed and breakfast furnished with period antiques. There are four beautifully decorated guest rooms with private baths and vintage fixtures. The Marian Room is softly decorated in velvet and brocade, includes a queen-sized bed and is washed with sunset light. A library, a parlor, a sunroom and a billiard room are also available. Full breakfast is served in the large dining room. You can also rent the Secret Garden Cottage complete with full kitchen facilities, just 30 feet from the mansion.

DINING

THE ONION

$$ AMERICAN   ✉302 West Riverside Street   ☎509-747-3852   📠509-624-3903

This is a favorite lunch and dinner spot, which occupies a vintage downtown building. The Onion has a 1904 mahogany bar, 1890s prints and brass accents. A wide menu of appetizers and entrées includes onion rings, deep-fried mozzarella, burgers, caesar and taco salads, vegetable stir-fries and baby back ribs.

PALM COURT GRILL

$$$–$$$$ NORTHWEST/STEAK/SEAFOOD   ✉10 South Post Street   ☎509-789-6848,
800-899-1482   📠509-624-4455   🖮www.thedavenporthotel.com,
info@thedavenporthotel.com

Located in the opulent Davenport Hotel, the Palm Court serves up a winning mixture of big-city elegance and small-town informality. Lunches and dinners are unabashedly gourmet, featuring artfully arranged plates. Dishes include crab cakes with yellow cherry tomato vinaigrette, salmon with huckleberry sauce and papaya salad, and fresh pappardelle pasta. Breakfasts and the celebrated champagne Sunday brunch are more traditional, but with a twist: omelettes made with crab and avocado, french toast made with baguettes, and fresh pastries. Reservations recommended.

SHOPPING

SKYWALK   In the downtown core, this series of weatherproof bridges that connects 15 blocks on the second level makes downtown shopping pleasant year-round. It leads to the major downtown department stores such as **Nordstrom** (Lincoln Street and Main Avenue; 509-455-6111) and **Macy's** (Wall Street and Main Avenue; 509-626-6015), several specialty shops, restaurants and art galleries.

SHOPPING CENTERS   With more and more Canadians driving just over a hundred miles to Spokane, where nearly all goods are less expensive, the city has had a surge of discount stores, from national chain stores to the West Coast warehouse stores. Shopping centers have sprung up on the north and northeast edges of town. Covered shopping areas include **Northtown Mall** (Division Street and Wellesley Avenue), **Franklin Park Mall** (Division Street and Rowan Avenue) and **University City** (Sprague Avenue and University Street).

FLOUR MILL   ✉ *621 West Mallon Avenue* ✆ *509-755-7551* ✑ *www.spokaneflour mill.com*   This is one of the more charming places to shop. It was built as a flour mill but was turned into a specialty shopping center in 1974 with more than a dozen shops, including gift stores, cafés and restaurants.

NIGHTLIFE

DEMPSEY'S BRASS RAIL   ✉ *West 909 1st Street* ✆ *509-747-5362*   Dempsey's is a popular gay and lesbian nightspot with a dancefloor and drag shows. Cover on Friday and Saturday.

SPOKANE JAZZ ORCHESTRA   ✉ *P.O. Box 174, Spokane, WA 99210* ✆ *509-838-2671* ✇ *509-747-3739* ✑ *www.spokanejazz.com, sales@spokanejazz.com*   The oldest continually performing professional community jazz orchestra in the country, this group performs big band–style concerts as well as Latin, jazz, blues and more throughout the year at various venues around town.

SPOKANE SYMPHONY ORCHESTRA   ✉ *Ticket office, 818 West Riverside Avenue, Suite 100* ✆ *509-326-3136* ✇ *509-326-3921* ✑ *www.spokanesymphony. org*   The symphony performs more than 60 orchestral concerts per year, including 10 concert classic performances, six superpops shows and three pairs of chamber orchestra concerts.

SPOKANE CIVIC THEATRE   ✉ *1020 North Howard Street* ✆ *509-325-1413, 800-446-9576 (box office)* ✑ *www.spokanecivictheatre.com*   This theatre presents musicals, comedies and dramas from late September through June.

PARKS

RIVERSIDE STATE PARK

✉ *Located six miles northwest of Spokane at 9711 West Charles Road, Nine Mile Falls* ✆ *509-465-5064* ✇ *509-465-5571* ✑ *www.riversidestatepark.org, riverside@parks.wa.gov*

🚶 🚴 ⛷ 🚗 🚤 ⚓   On the edge of Spokane, this 10,000-acre park includes nearly eight miles of Spokane River shoreline (perfect for rainbow trout fishing), odd basaltic rock formations in the river and Indian petroglyphs. It houses the Spokane House interpretive center (open weekends from Memorial Day to Labor Day), which tells the history of the oldest trading post in Washington. Canoes and kayaks are available for rent. Facilities include a 600-acre off-road vehicle park, picnic areas with shelters, restrooms, hot showers and horse trails; wheelchair accessible.

⚑ There are two campgrounds with tent and RV sites ranging from $19 to $30. Reservations: 888-226-7688.

MT. SPOKANE STATE PARK

✉ Located at the end of Route 206, 30 miles northeast of Spokane   ☎ 509-238-4258
✎ 509-238-4078

🚶🚴🐎🏍🏕 This 5883-foot mountain is used as much or more in the winter as it is in summer, but warm-weather visitors find its views spectacular. Idaho, Montana, Canada and much of Washington can be seen from its summit. It is especially pretty during the spring when its slopes are blanketed with flowers and in the fall when the fields are brown and the leaves have turned. For those into winter sports, there are skiing (downhill and cross-country) and snowmobiling. During warm weather, the park has some of the best mountain biking in Washington. There are picnic areas and restrooms.

⚑ There are 12 standard sites ($17 per night). All sites are first-come, first-served. Closed in winter.

TURNBULL NATIONAL WILDLIFE REFUGE

✉ Cheney Plaza Highway, five miles south of Cheney   ☎ 509-235-4723   ✎ 509-235-4703

🚶🚴🏕 One of the most popular natural places for day trips in the Spokane area, the refuge was established in 1937 primarily for waterfowl. It has several lakes and wooded areas and a marked, self-guided auto-tour route. You will also find hiking trails, cross-country skiing areas and restrooms. Day-use fee March through October.

SOUTHEASTERN WASHINGTON

The drive from Spokane south into Oregon is one of unusual beauty, especially early or late in the day, or in the spring and fall. The entire region between the wooded hills around Spokane to the Blue Mountains is known as the Palouse Country. Here the barren hills are low but steep, and wheat is grown on nearly every acre. In fact, it is acknowledged as the best wheat-growing land in the world.

SIGHTS

KAMIAK BUTTE COUNTY PARK ✉ 18 miles east of Colfax and 15 miles north of Pullman just off Route 27 Proceeding south from Spokane along Route 195, you'll find that the two best places to view the Palouse Hills are **Steptoe Butte State Park** (see "Parks" below) and this county park. Kamiak Butte stands 3360 feet high and offers bird's-eye views of the

PALOUSE FALLS STATE PARK/ LYONS FERRY STATE PARK

PAGE 300

Two-part woodland area with both perfect picnic spots and dramatic waterfall overlooks

EMERALD OF SIAM

PAGE 298

Authentic Thai delicacies such as coconut milk soup and deep-fried fish with ginger in a family-owned restaurant

PURPLE HOUSE B&B

PAGE 296

Charming lavender-colored 1882 Queen Anne mansion with manicured lawns and antique-furnished rooms

FIELD SPRING STATE PARK

PAGE 299

Forested campground on the slope of the Blue Mountains—a wilderness hideaway

Palouse Hills. The park has picnic areas, a hiking trail and, unlike Steptoe Butte, a fringe of trees on its crest and over 100 kinds of vegetation, including the Douglas fir more common to the damp, coastal climate.

PULLMAN   This town is almost entirely a product of Washington State University, although a few agricultural businesses operate on the edge of town. Continuing south from this campus town, Route 195 gains elevation through the small farming communities of Colton and Uniontown, then crosses over into the edge of Idaho just in time to disappear into Route 95 and then take a dizzying plunge down the steep Lewiston Hill, where you drop 2000 feet in a very short time over a twisting highway. The old highway with its hairpin turns is still passable and is exciting driving if your brakes and nerves are in good condition.

SNAKE RIVER   Clarkston, Washington, and Lewiston, Idaho, are separated by the Snake River, which flows almost due north through Hells Canyon before taking a sudden westward turn where Idaho's Clearwater River enters in Lewiston. Boat operators will take you up to the Snake River—you can't drive there. Most of the Snake River boat operators are headquartered in these two towns. For more information, contact the **Clarkston Chamber of Commerce** (502 Bridge Street, Clarkston; 509-758-7712, 800-933-2128, fax 509-751-8767; www.clarkston chamber.org, info@clarkstonchamber.org).

The population has followed the Snake on its way west to join with the Columbia, but it is a tamed river now, a series of slackwater pools in deep canyons behind a series of dams: Lower Granite, Little Goose, Lower Monumental and Ice Harbor. The main highway doesn't follow the Snake River because of the deep canyon it carved, so from Clarkston you follow Route 12 west through the farming communities of Pomeroy and Dayton to Walla Walla, then on to the Tri-Cities area around Richland, where the Snake enters the Columbia River.

DAYTON HISTORIC DEPOT ✉*222 East Commercial Street, Dayton* ☎*509-382-2026* ✍*www.daytonhistoricdepot.org, info@daytonhistoricdepot.org* **Dayton** is an agricultural town with over 117 buildings listed on the National Register of Historic Places. Most impressive is this beautiful 1881 historic depot, a classic Victorian building, which has been turned into a historical museum with rotating exhibits. Closed Sunday through Tuesday.

WALLA WALLA This quaint area looks much like a New England town that was packed up and moved to the rolling hills of Eastern Washington, weeping willows, oak and maple trees included. Best known for its colleges, Whitman and Walla Walla College, the town with a double name has many ivy-covered buildings, quiet streets lined with old frame houses, enormous shade trees and, rather incongruously amid this Norman Rockwellian beauty, the state penitentiary.

WALLA WALLA CHAMBER OF COMMERCE ✉*29 East Sumach Street, Walla Walla* ☎*509-525-0850* ☏*509-522-2038* ✍*www.wwvchamber.com, info@wwvchamber.com* To see more of the city by foot, stop by the chamber of commerce for four different historic walking trail guides, including the *Historic Homes Trail Guide.*

WHITMAN MISSION NATIONAL HISTORIC SITE ✉*Route 12, seven miles west of Walla Walla* ☎*509-529-2761* ☏*509-522-6355* ✍*www.nps.gov/whmi* One of the Northwest's worst tragedies occurred here because of a basic misunderstanding of American Indian values by an American missionary, Marcus Whitman. He and his wife, Narcissa, founded a mission among the Cayuse Indians in 1836 to convert the Cayuse to Christianity. As traffic increased on the Oregon Trail, the mission became an important stop for weary travelers. Eleven years later the Cayuse felt betrayed by Whitman because his religion hadn't protected them from a measles epidemic that killed half the tribe. On November 29, 1847, the Cayuse killed both Whitmans and 11 others and ransomed 50 to the Hudson's Bay Company. The site is now run by the National Park Service and there's a visitors center, a memorial monument, a millpond and walking paths to sites where various buildings once stood. None of the original buildings remain. Admission.

COLUMBIA RIVER This spectacular river runs free for about 60 miles through the Hanford Reservation, but when it swings through Richland, Pasco and Kennewick it becomes Lake Wallula, thanks to McNary Dam. Several city parks with picnic and boating facilities are along the river, such as **Columbia Park** (off Route 240, between Edison and Columbia Center Boulevard, Kennewick).

TRI-CITIES The contiguous towns of Richland, Pasco and Kennewick, with a collective population of 160,000, are known as the Tri-Cities. The cities were once best known for the nuclear-power plant and research center at the nearby Hanford Reservation where the components for the first atomic bombs were assembled. From the 1960s to the 1980s, the main employer in the area was the Hanford site, whose nuclear reactors produced 75,000 pounds of weapons-grade plutonium a day—and countless tons of nuclear waste. When environmental scientists discovered that leakage from buried waste had made the Columbia the most radioactive river on earth, Washington state government forced the U.S. Department of Energy to shut the site down, temporarily devastating the local economy and driving residential prices absurdly low. Today, the Tri-Cities have bounced back, as the nuclear waste cleanup effort—the largest in U.S. history—employs more people than the plutonium factory ever did. A nearby nuclear-related visitors center tells the whole story.

COLUMBIA RIVER EXHIBITION OF HISTORY, SCIENCE AND TECHNOLOGY ✉95 Lee Boulevard, Richland ✆509-943-9000, 877-789-9935 ✆509-943-1770 ⌂www.crehst.org, gwen@crehst.org This information center features exhibits and historical displays that focus on people's interaction with the environment, such as hydroelectric power, nuclear energy and environmental restoration. Admission.

YAKIMA VALLEY From the Tri-Cities, the population follows the Yakima River, which flows into the Columbia at the Tri-Cities. The Yakima Valley is the state's richest in terms of agriculture: Yakima County ranks first nationally in the number of fruit trees, first in the production of apples, mint and hops and fifth in the value of all fruits grown. It is also the wine center of the state: Some 40 wineries have been built between Walla Walla and Yakima, and they have helped create a visitor industry that has encouraged the growth of country inns and bed and breakfasts. Brochures listing the wineries and locations are available in visitors centers and many convenience stores, and once you're off Route 82, signs mark routes to the wineries.

L'ECOLE N° 41 ✉41 Lowden School Road, Lowden ✆509-525-0940 ✆509-525-2775 ⌂www.lecole.com, info@lecole.com This bucolic, family-owned winery got its name from the 1915 schoolhouse near Walla Walla in which it was built. The tasting room is in a restored classroom with the original chalkboard and light fixtures. Be sure to browse the library and enjoy a book by the fireplace before hitting the gift shop. Fee.

KIONA VINEYARDS ✉44612 North Sunset Road, Benton City ✆509-588-6716 ✆509-588-3219 ⌂www.kionawine.com, kiona1wine@aol.com The most homey of the wineries is probably Kiona. It is a second-generation family operation, with a tasting room, winery and vineyard at a former family home. The winery was one of the originals to produce lemberger.

COLUMBIA CREST WINERY ✉Route 221, Paterson ✆509-875-2061, 800-309-9463 ✆425-415-3657 ⌂www.columbia-crest.com Built on a hillside overlooking the Columbia River, this dramatic winery produces more than a million gallons of wine annually and has a reflecting pool, fountain and courtyard, a luxurious lobby and tasting-and-sales room.

PONTIN DEL ROZA ✉35502 North Hinzerling Road, Prosser ☎509-786-4449 ⌂www.pontindelroza.com, pontindelroza@mac.com This vineyard came into being because the Pontin family's Italian heritage included a love of wine. They decided to add wine grapes to the crops they had been growing on their Prosser farm for two decades and produce both reds and whites.

HOGUE CELLARS ✉2800 Lee Road, Prosser ☎509-786-4557 ext. 208, 800-565-9779 ☏509-786-4580 ⌂www.hoguecellars.com, info@hoguecellars.com Founded in 1982 with a planting of riesling grapes, this winery located in the Columbia Valley is known for grapes with intense fruit flavor and natural acidity.

TEFFT CELLARS ✉1320 Independence Road, Outlook ☎509-837-7651, 888-549-7244 ☏509-839-7337 ⌂www.tefftcellars.com Joel Tefft focuses on limited bottlings of fine handcrafted wines at his vineyard outside Sunnyside. Aside from cabernet sauvignon and lush, velvety merlot, the Teffts make unique, light, dry sparkling wines and ports, a rarity in Washington.

FORT SIMCOE STATE PARK ⌂Located at the end of Fort Simcoe Road, about 35 miles south of Yakima ☎509-874-2372 ☏509-874-2351 This state park is probably the best-preserved frontier army post in the West and was one of the few forts where no shots were fired in anger. It was used in the late 1850s during the conflict with the local American Indian people. There's a museum/interpretive center (closed Monday and Tuesday from April to September; closed October through March). Five of the original buildings are still standing, including the commanding officer's home. The park is closed weekdays from October through March.

YAKAMA NATION CULTURAL HERITAGE CENTER ⌂Route 97, 100 Spiel-yi Loop, Toppenish ☎509-865-2800 ☏509-865-5749 ⌂www.yakama museum. com, heather@yakama.com The life-sized diorama here fires my imagination. It's of the Yakama catching salmon by hand at Celilo Falls. Imagining is all one can do, since the falls vanished when The Dalles Dam was constructed and the Yakama turned to growing asparagus and hops. The history of the tribe is told in dioramas and writings by and about the tribe preserved in a large library. The center also has a theater for films and concerts and a restaurant that serves traditional dishes. Admission (to museum).

CENTRAL WASHINGTON AGRICULTURAL MUSEUM ✉4508 Main Street, Union Gap ☎509-457-8735, 509-248-0432 ⌂www.centralwaagmuseum. org A large collection of early farm machinery, including a working sawmill, a blacksmith shop, a steam engine and more than 3000 antique hand tools, are on display at this museum. Closed Sunday and Monday in summer, Monday and Wednesday in winter.

YAKIMA VALLEY MUSEUM ✉2105 Tieton Drive, Yakima ☎509-248-0747 ☏509-453-4890 ⌂www.yakimavalleymuseum.org, info@yakimavalleymuseum.org This museum has a comprehensive collection of horse-drawn vehicles, a recreation of the office of the late Supreme Court Justice William O. Douglas and a unique collection of neon signs. There is also an interactive children's museum and an operating ice cream soda fountain. Closed Monday from November to March. Admission.

294

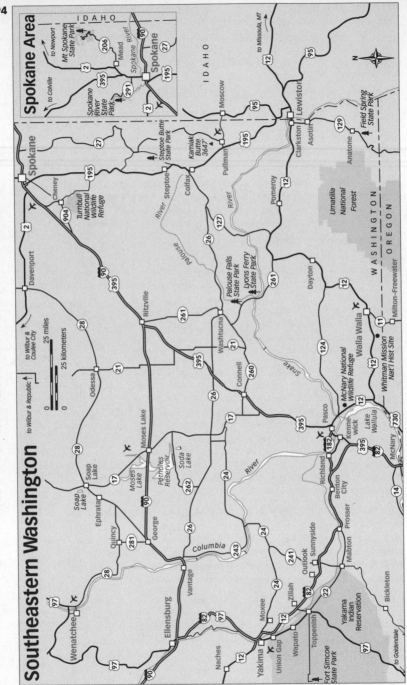

Southeastern Washington

MABTON-BICKLETON ROAD ___ hidden

The main road leading from the Yakima Valley to the beautiful Columbia River Gorge (see Chapter Seven) is Route 97, which runs south from Toppenish, crosses Satus Pass (3107 feet) and reaches the Gorge just past Goldendale. An alternate route from the Yakima Valley down to the Columbia River is this road, which heads south from the small town of Mabton through the even smaller Bickleton. An unincorporated town with a scattering of Victorian houses and falsefront store buildings, Bickleton's claim to fame is hundreds of houses for (are you ready for this?) bluebirds. Maintained by residents, the houses are on fence posts along the highway and country lanes and literally all over town. The one in front of the community church is a miniature copy of the church itself.

ALDER CREEK PIONEER ASSOCIATION CAROUSEL MUSEUM
✉ Market Street, Bickleton ⌂ www.bickleton.org Opened in 2007, this historical museum celebrates East Klickitat County's past. Displays include an exhibit about the area's wheat farming, collections of barbed wire and bit and spurs, a turn-of-the-century medical office, and American Indian artifacts accompanied by old photographs and petroglyphs. The focal point is the rare 1905, 24-horse Herschel Spillman Carousel, which has been used since 1929 in Bickleton's Pioneer Picnic and Rodeo—the state's oldest rodeo. Closed Monday through Wednesday. Admission.

BONAIR WINERY ✉ 500 South Bonair Road South, Zillah ☎ 509-829-6027 509-829-6410 ⌂ www.bonairwine.com, shirley@bonairwine.com The Puryear family, Gail and Shirley, call their winery a "hobby that got out of hand." The winery not only offers a versatile range of wines, including fine chardonnays, cabernets and ports. The setting, on a curve of land inside one of the valley's main irrigation canals, is inviting. Bonair also boasts a new chateau-style welcome center to add to guests' experience.

SAGELANDS VINEYARDS ✉ 71 Gangl Road, Wapato ☎ 509-877-2112, 800-967-8115 509-877-3377 ⌂ www.sagelandsvineyard.com, sagelands.info@sagelandsvineyard.com Located in a French-country building set on a rolling hillside above the Yakima River is this lovely vineyard. The tasting room features a stone fireplace and cathedral ceilings.

WHITE HERON CELLARS ✉ 10035 Stuhlmiller Road, Quincy ☎ 509-797-9463 ⌂ www.whiteheronwine.com, info@whiteheronwine.com Featuring syrah and bordeaux varieties, White Heron emphasizes a natural winemaking process, leaving as much of the ecosystem undisturbed as possible. It also features a concert venue showcasing jazz and blues with a spectacular view. Closed Tuesday and Wednesday.

LODGING

It's difficult to find anything other than your basic, cookie-cutter motel in southeastern Washington, although Yakima shows some imagination.

HILLTOP INN

$$–$$$ 59 ROOMS   ✉928 Northwest Olson Street at Davis Way, Pullman
📞509-332-0928, 800-527-1133 📠509-334-5275 🖱www.hotelonthehill.com,
hilltopinn@pullman.com

The best view from the dozen or so motels in the area is at the Hilltop. In-room DVD players and free wi-fi provide entertainment. There is a pool, hot tub and fitness center on-site.

QUALITY INN PARADISE CREEK

$$–$$$ 66 ROOMS   ✉1400 Southeast Bishop Boulevard, Pullman 📞509-332-0500,
800-669-3212 📠509-334-4271

Near both the campus and the airport, this inn boasts a convenient location. Rooms are standard, but an on-site heated pool, sauna and hot tub provide welcome amenities.

PURPLE HOUSE B&B _____ ⓗidden

$$ 4 ROOMS   ✉415 East Clay Street, Dayton 📞509-382-3159,
800-486-2574 📠509-382-3159 🖱www.purplehousebnb.com,
info@purplehousebnb.com

The Purple House is an unexpected pleasure. This elegant inn, on the National Register of Historic Places, is housed in an 1882 Queen Anne mansion that was built by a pioneer physician. Two upstairs bedrooms share a bath; the master suite downstairs has a private bath. All rooms are furnished in period antiques; there's a library and heated outdoor pool. A separate carriage house has full amenities and a private bath. The full breakfast is cooked to order. Small pets are welcome.

BUDGET INN

$ 58 ROOMS   ✉305 North 2nd Avenue, Walla Walla 📞509-529-4410, 888-529-4161
📠509-525-5777 🖱www.wallawallabudgetinn.com

Within easy walking distance of downtown is this standard hotel. Rooms include microwaves and refrigerators, and there is a seasonal outdoor pool.

CLOVER ISLAND INN

$$ 151 ROOMS   ✉435 Clover Island Drive, Kennewick 📞509-586-0541,
866-586-0542 🖱www.cloverislandinn.com, cloverisland.inn@verizon.net

The Tri-Cities area has several fair-sized motels, many with meeting rooms. One of the largest is the Clover Island, built on an island in the Columbia River. Half of the rooms have views of the river. The complex has a pool, hot tub, restaurant and lounge.

RED LION YAKIMA CENTER HOTEL

$$ 153 ROOMS   ✉607 East Yakima Avenue, Yakima 📞509-248-5900, 800-733-5466
📠509-575-8975 🖱www.redlion.com, yakimactrsales@redlion.com

Yakima does a lively convention business, and one of the best places to stay is next door to the convention center at this Red Lion. The hotel has large, comfortable rooms with colorful furnishings and spacious bathrooms, two heated pools, a dining room and a lounge.

PATIT CREEK RESTAURANT

$$$ FRENCH ✉725 East Dayton Avenue, Dayton ☎509-382-2625

If you're good at what you do, so goes the saying, the world will beat a path to your door. This could be the slogan for Patit Creek. It has been in business since 1978 and has built a national reputation for excellent dishes in what is most accurately described as French country cuisine. Meat is the specialty—beef and lamb. Most of the food is grown locally, some by the staff, and since some of the luxurious plants inside and around the outside are herbs, they may one day season your food. No lunch Saturday through Tuesday. Closed Sunday through Tuesday.

MERCHANTS DELICATESSEN & BAKERY

$–$$ DELI ✉21 Main Street East, Walla Walla ☎509-525-0900 509-522-3065
www.merchantsdeli.com

If you're feeling nostalgic for New York delis, Merchants will help. It has a wide choice of foods and a sidewalk café ideal for Walla Walla's mostly sunny weather.

Washington Wine

For a long time, Washington's liquor laws were so restrictive that it was illegal to bring wine into the state; you had to buy it from the state-run stores. The best Washington wine in those days was made by an Italian immigrant, Angelo Pellegrini, who taught Shakespeare at the University of Washington and made wine in his basement—illegally. That has changed completely. Over 580 wineries are spread across the state, most in Eastern Washington, and many of those in the Puget Sound region own vineyards in Eastern Washington or buy their grapes there.

WASHINGTON WINE COMMISSION ✉1000 2nd Avenue, Suite 1700, Seattle ☎206-667-9463 206-583-0573 www.washingtonwine.org The soil and climate are excellent for wine grapes, and the Washington Wine Commission likes to remind us that Eastern Washington is on the same latitude as some of France's great winegrowing regions.

Washington has four viticultural regions: Columbia Valley, which extends southward from the Okanogan Country into Oregon and east to Idaho; Yakima Valley, which runs from the foothills of the Cascades east to the Kiona Hills near Richland and is bisected by Interstate 82, making it the most convenient for visits; the Walla Walla Valley region, which straddles the Oregon–Washington border, taking in some vineyards in the Milton-Freewater area; and the Puget Sound region, which covers areas from Olympia in the south to Bellingham in the north, and includes various Puget Sound and San Juan Islands in between.

In keeping with the French adage that the best grape vines "like to be in sight of the water but don't want to get their feet wet," some of the best vineyards in Eastern Washington are on south-facing slopes above the Columbia, Yakima and Snake rivers, where they get as much as 16 hours of sunlight a day and fresh irrigation water on well-drained soil. As with all wine-producing areas, many wineries have been built in palatial settings.

Cheers!

THE CEDARS

$$–$$$ AMERICAN ✉355 Clover Island Drive, Kennewick ☎509-582-2143
🖷509-582-2144 ✐www.cedarsrest.com

This is one of the Tri-Cities' most striking restaurants. It is cantilevered over the Columbia River with boat-docking facilities. The specialties are steaks, seafood and prime rib. Favorites include the *biergarten* steak and the daily fresh fish specials. Dinner only.

EMERALD OF SIAM

$$ THAI ✉1314 Jadwin Avenue, Richland ☎509-946-9328
✐www.emeraldofsiam.com

This aptly named gem of a restaurant serves authentic Thai food such as silky coconut milk soup and savory cashew chicken in a former drugstore decorated with original Thai paintings. A buffet is served at lunch on weekdays and dinner on Friday and Saturday, or you may order from the menu. Closed Sunday.

THE BLUE GOOSE

$$–$$$ TUSCAN/AMERICAN ✉306 7th Street, Prosser ☎509-786-1774
🖷509-786-7557 ✐www.bluegoose-restaurant.com

Prosser is a farm town, pure and simple. So what better place for fine, gourmet country cuisine? At The Blue Goose, local wine and produce form the basis for a Tuscan/American menu that ranges from veal marsala to chicken-fried steak (well, it is a country restaurant). The wine list features more than 50 local wines, some of them superb vintages, at prices you'll never see in any urban restaurant. Closed Sunday and Monday.

BIRCHFIELD MANOR

$$$$ FRENCH/NORTHWEST ✉2018 Birchfield Road, Yakima ☎509-452-1960,
800-375-3420 🖷509-452-2334 ✐www.birchfieldmanor.com,
reservations@birchfiledmanor.com

Over the years, Birchfield Manor has won more magazine awards than any other Washington restaurant outside the Puget Sound region. The owners restored an old farmhouse and filled it with antiques, then opened the restaurant with a menu of seven entrées, including fresh salmon in puff pastry, filet mignon, rack of lamb, and shrimp and prawn cakes. Local fruit and vegetables are used, and the fixed menu includes an appetizer, a salad and a homemade chocolate treat. Closed Sunday through Wednesday except for large groups.

SHOPPING

NORTH FRONT STREET HISTORICAL DISTRICT Yakima offers several intriguing shopping areas. One is this historical district, where the city's oldest buildings, some of them made of rough-hewn local rock, now house an assortment of boutiques, restaurants and brew pubs.

YESTERDAY'S VILLAGE ✉15 West Yakima Avenue, Yakima ☎509-457-4981 Yesterday's is a collection of shops in the former Fruit Exchange

Building. The remodeled building houses some 75 shops that sell antiques, glassware, collectibles, furniture and jewelry.

NIGHTLIFE

Yakima has one of the widest selections of nightlife in southeastern Washington, ranging from cultural events to country-and-western taverns.

YAKIMA SYMPHONY ORCHESTRA ⊠*32 North 3rd Street, Suite 333, Yakima* ✆*509-248-1414* ✐*www.yakimasymphony.org* Yakima has frequent concerts put on by their locally celebrated orchestra. Season runs October through April.

YAKIMA SQUARE AND ROUND DANCE CENTER ⊠*207 East Charron Road, Moxee* ✆*509-452-6438* **Square dancing** is very popular in the Yakima Valley, and numerous clubs welcome travelers to their dances. Dances are held Thursday and Saturday nights at this local dance center.

PARKS

STEPTOE BUTTE STATE PARK
⊠*Off Route 195, roughly 50 miles south of Spokane* ✆*509-646-9218* ✇*509-646-9288* ✐*cpt.central@parks.wa.gov*

🏃 This park consists of the butte, a picnic area and primitive toilets at the base and summit. The reason for the park's existence is the butte itself, which rises to an elevation of 3612 feet out of the rolling Palouse Hills with panoramic views that are popular with photographers. The butte is actually the top of a granite mountain that stands above the lava flows that covered all the other peaks. The word "steptoe" has entered the international geological vocabulary to represent any similar remnant of an earlier geological feature standing out from the newer feature. There are seven picnic sites at the foot of the butte; no water.

FIELD SPRING STATE PARK
⊠*Route 129, four miles south of Anatone* ✆*509-256-3332*

🏃 🚴 ⛷ This secluded 792-acre wilderness park is in forested land on the eastern slope of the Blue Mountains. Part of the park sits atop Puffer Butte, a 4500-foot mountain that overlooks the Grand Ronde River Canyon. For hikers, there are a one-mile trail to the summit of Puffer Butte and ten miles of hiking paths. Winter brings cross-country skiing, snowshoeing and tubing. There are restrooms and showers.

⛺ There are 20 standard sites ($17 per night) and two primitive sites ($12 per night). There are two teepees for eight people each ($20 per night).

FORT WALLA WALLA PARK AND MUSEUM
⊠*The southeast side of Walla Walla on Dalles Military Road at Myra* ✆*509-527-4527*

🏃 🚴 This collection of 17 pioneer buildings is located on a 208-acre former Army fort and cemetery containing victims from both sides of the first conflicts during the Indian Wars. It also has five large exhibit halls housing one of the largest collections of horse-drawn farm equipment in the Northwest (admission; closed November through March; 755 Myra Road, Walla Walla; 509-525-7703; www.fortwallawalla museum.org, info@fortwallawallamuseum.org). There are also nature and bicycle trails in the park. Other facilities include picnic areas, a skate park and BMX track, a golf course, restrooms, play equipment and volleyball courts.

PALOUSE FALLS STATE PARK/ LYONS FERRY STATE PARK — hidden

✉ Route 261, 23 miles southeast of Washtucna, Lyon's Ferry ☎ 509-646-9218

🚶‍♂️🚤🎣🛶⛵🛷 This two-part, remote park is out in the rugged Channeled Scablands. The Lyons Ferry section consists of a pleasant, grassy area with boat ramps at the confluence of the Snake and Palouse rivers. About seven to eight miles up the Palouse River is the Palouse Falls section, with a dramatic picnic area and viewpoint overlooking the thundering 198-foot-tall Palouse Falls. There are picnic areas and restrooms; a wheelchair-accessible hiking trail there and at Lyons Ferry, as well as a boat launch ramp, concessionaire, hiking areas and a restaurant, are nearby.

⛺ Palouse Falls has 10 primitive sites ($12 per night); Lyons Ferry has 50 standard sites ($17 per night) and two primitive sites ($12 per night). Both close in winter.

MCNARY NATIONAL WILDLIFE REFUGE

✉ 500 East Maple Street, southeast of Pasco just off Route 395 on the Snake River ☎ 509-547-4942 ☎ 509-544-9047

🚶‍♂️🛷 This is one of the major resting areas in the Pacific Flyway for migratory waterfowl, especially Canada geese, American widgeon, mallards, pintails and white pelicans. The population peaks in November, and the few summer migratory birds, such as the pelicans and long-billed curlews, arrive in the spring and summer. The refuge covers over 15,000 acres that stretch along the confluence of the Snake River down-

The Oldest Man in Washington

The Tri-Cities area was the site of the 1996 discovery of the controversial Kennewick Man, one of the oldest human skeletons ever found in North America, radiocarbon-dated to between 8400 and 9200 years old. Because the skull was much different from those of modern American Indians, the find was first thought to suggest the presence of Caucasians in archaic America but is now believed to be "proto-Mongolian," with possible genetic links both to Russian Europeans and to native peoples' Asian ancestors. The Colville, Yakima, Umatilla and Nez Perce tribes each claim Kennewick Man as an ancestor, demanding reburial rights under the Native American Graves Protection Act. The ancient bones were locked up at the University of Washington's Burke Museum until 2005, when a court cleared the way for scientists to study the skeleton. Preliminary findings suggest that he was indeed American Indian, about 45 years old, 5 feet 9 inches, and may have been a hunter when the climate was cooler and wetter.

stream into the mouth of the Walla Walla River. Hunters look for waterfowl and upland birds, while anglers cast a rod for largemouth black bass, catfish and crappie. Self-guided wildlife trail through the marsh and croplands.

NORTHEASTERN OREGON

For the most part, northeastern Oregon remains the parched land so inhospitable to settlers nearly two centuries ago. Nowadays, towns are still few and far between, leaving plenty of room for viewing the wagon ruts left by the original pioneers. Also a part of the northeastern Oregon experience are the vividly colored earthscapes at the John Day Fossil Beds National Monument and the whitewater rafting opportunities in the Snake River along the Idaho border. Capping it off in the state's northeastern corner is a surprisingly lush area surrounding the Wallowa Mountains that reminds many visitors of the Swiss Alps.

SIGHTS

ROUTE 129 Only in the late 1980s was the highway completely paved between the Snake River Canyon and the Wallowas in Oregon. But now you can take one of the prettiest mountain drives in the Northwest by following this highway south from Clarkston in the southeastern corner of Washington through Anatone, then down into the Grande Ronde River valley over probably the most crooked highway in the Northwest. Be sure your brakes (and fortitude) are in good condition.

WALLOWA RIVER VALLEY At the Oregon–Washington border, Route 129 heading south from Clarkston, Washington, changes to Route 3 and runs along high ridges and through ponderosa-pine forests until it enters the Wallowa River Valley. This valley is postcard-perfect with the jagged Wallowa Mountains providing an ideal backdrop to the broad valley with the lush farms and ranches, rail fences, ranch buildings and the small, winding Wallowa River. Once you've seen it you'll understand why it is becoming a haven for artists and writers.

ENTERPRISE AND JOSEPH The twin towns of Enterprise and Joseph can be used as a base for exploratory trips around Wallowa Lake and backpacking into the Eagle Cap Wilderness. Joseph is named after the revered Chief Joseph, head of the Nez Perce tribe last century. It is well worth exploring for its array of art galleries and for an introduction to the history of the region.

WALLOWA COUNTY MUSEUM ✉*110 South Main Street, Joseph* ✆*541-432-6095* Stop by this museum to see exhibits depicting the worlds of the white pioneers and the Nez Perce Indians. The building, dating from 1888 and serving at various times as a newspaper office, hospital, meeting hall and bank, is of interest itself. Closed from the third weekend in September to Memorial Day.

HAT POINT From Joseph, a gravel road takes you another 25 miles to this nearly 7000-foot-high viewpoint of one of the most rugged stretches of Hells Canyon.

WILSON RANCHES RETREAT

PAGE 305

Historic family B&B with Western-style rooms and generous ranch breakfasts

GHOST TOWNS

PAGE 302

More than half a dozen falsefront mining towns with abandoned windmills and fire stations—a trip back in time

WALLOWA LAKE STATE PARK

PAGE 307

Waterfront forested area with wilderness hiking trails through pine and spruce groves

OREGON TRAIL The last miles of this well-known trail, which began in St. Joseph, Missouri, run along the same general route taken by Route 84 from the city of Ontario northwest through Baker City, La Grande, Pendleton and along the Columbia River until hitting the rapids in the Cascades. Several sites have been set aside that show ruts made by the wagons along the trail. You can see them at Vail, west of Ontario, and along the route near Baker City in Burnt River Canyon, Gold Hill, Durkee, Pleasant Valley and Baker Valley.

NATIONAL HISTORIC OREGON TRAIL INTERPRETIVE CENTER ✉*Top of Flagstaff Hill on Route 86 east of Baker City* ✆*541-523-1843* ✆*541-523-1834* ✎*oregontrail.blm.gov* Don't miss this interpretive center, which looks rather like a prairie schooner from a distance. A permanent collection of artifacts can be found along the trail, and there is a theater for stage productions and outdoor exhibits showing a wagon-train encampment and mine operation. Admission.

GHOST TOWNS _____

You'll want to visit a number of local ghost towns, all visible records of the boom-and-bust nature of the mining industry—with broken windmills, abandoned shacks and fireplaces surrounded by ashes from burned houses that bear witness to failed homesteads. Some of these towns are making a comeback. Neighboring Baker City are such falsefronted old-timers as

Greenhorn, Sumpter, Granite, Whitney, Bourne, Sparta and Cornucopia, which have colorful remains of the original towns and mining equipment standing among the summer homes that have taken root. Most of these towns are along Route 7 or on Forest Service roads leading off it.

JOHN DAY AND CANYON CITY   Route 7 leads from Baker City southwest to Route 26, which you can stay on heading west to John Day and Canyon City, twin towns that look very much like the Old West. In fact, twice a year the main street of John Day is closed to vehicular traffic so that a local rancher can drive his cattle through town to and from their summer range.

KAM WAH CHUNG & CO. MUSEUM   ✉Ing Hay Way, John Day ☎541-575-2800 The best-known museum in these parts was a store owned for decades by two Chinese immigrants, Ing Hay and Lung On. Next to the city park in the center of John Day, this museum began as a trading post on the military road that ran through the area. Then the Chinese laborers in the mines bought the building for a community center, general store and an herbal doctor's office. A National Historic Landmark, the museum underwent a major restoration in 2008 and has thousands of artifacts related to the building's history and more than a thousand herbs, some from China and others from the immediate area. Closed November through April.

JOHN DAY FOSSIL BEDS NATIONAL MONUMENT   ✉32651 Route 19, Kimberly ☎541-987-2333 📠541-987-2336 🖥www.nps.gov/joda, joda_interpretation@nps.gov This national memorial is a three-part monument that attracts serious and amateur photographers from all over the world, who attempt to capture the vivid colors of the volcanic-ash deposits and the fossils of plants and animals.

The fascinating fossils and fantastic scenery of John Day Fossil Beds National Monument are a long way from any populated area—and that's part of what makes a trip here special. This scenic drive is hard to complete in a single day, so plan to spend the night at a motel in John Day or Mitchell. From Portland, drive 108 fast miles east on Route 84 and turn south on Route 97 at Biggs, on the Columbia River just below John Day Dam. (Just about everything in this part of the state is named John Day, after an early explorer for John Jacob Astor's fur-trading company. Robbed by Indians and left afoot in this vast wasteland, Day eventually made it back to his base camp on the coast but never regained his sanity.)

MORE GHOST TOWNS   Driving 57 miles south on two-lane Route 97 will bring you to the semi-ghost town of **Shaniko** (page 439), where well-preserved wooden buildings and old wagons create an open-air museum. Another eight miles bring you to the equally unpopulated ranch town of **Antelope**, which was overwhelmed in the 1980s when cult leader Bhagwan Shree Rajneesh and 500 followers established an ashram here (to the horror of the locals), and voted to change the town's name to Rajneesh. (Later, the guru left the country due to IRS trouble, his followers moved away, and the 90 remaining residents changed the name back.)

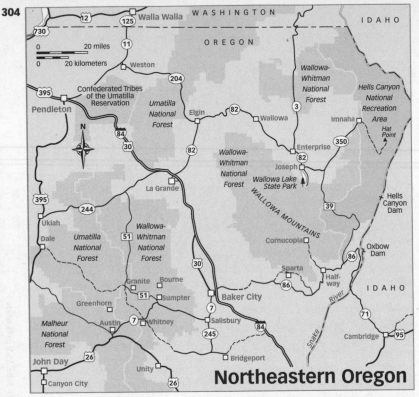

Northeastern Oregon

CLARNO UNIT   At Antelope, turn east on Route 218. A 22-mile drive through drab brown hills leads to this unit of John Day Fossil Beds. The least colorful of the national monument's several units, it has a hillside trail among the petrified logs of a prehistoric forest and exhibits of fossilized seeds and nuts. Twenty more miles east lead to the tiny town of **Fossil**, where a homespun local museum displays not only fossils but also such oddities as an antique poker table and a two-headed calf.

SHEEP ROCK UNIT   Sixty-five miles south of Fossil on Route 19, the highlight of this John Day Fossil Beds unit is the **Basin Trail**, a colorful hike through blue and green painted desert with replica skeletons of prehistoric rhinoceroses and saber-tooth cats in the spots where the originals were found. The nearby visitors center has historical displays and a lab full of paleontologists at work.

PAINTED HILLS UNIT   Turn west (left) on Route 26 and drive 32 miles, then take the well-marked three-mile access road to this unit in national monument. Though the fossilized leaves found here may be of interest mainly to paleobotanists, the hike through the brilliant yellow, white and scarlet landscape is unforgettable. From here, the shortest route back to civilization is to continue west on Route 26, a distance of 194 miles back to Portland, traversing the south slope of Mt. Hood along the way.

RED LION HOTEL

$$–$$$ 169 ROOMS ✉304 Southeast Nye Avenue, Pendleton ☎541-276-6111, 800-733-5466 📠541-278-2413 🖥www.redlion.com, pendletonsales@redlion.com

One of the best hotels in Pendleton is the Red Lion Hotel, just off Route 84 on a hill above the city. Rooms here have picture windows and balconies overlooking the wheat fields rolling off to the north and west. The hotel has a formal dining room with a window wall, a coffee shop, a lounge and a pool.

WALLOWA LAKE LODGE

$$$–$$$$ 30 UNITS ✉60060 Wallowa Lake Highway, Joseph ☎541-432-9821 📠541-432-4885 🖥www.wallowalake.com, information@wallowalake.com

Most of the hotels in the Enterprise–Joseph area are in the moderate category. The lone exception is this lodge under continual renovation that dates back to the 1920s. It is located on the lakeshore with adjoining cabins (with kitchens) and rooms that are simply but pleasantly decorated.

CHANDLER'S INN

$$ 5 UNITS ✉700 South Main Street, Joseph ☎541-432-9765 🖥www.josephbedandbreakfast.com, cbbti700@eoni.com

An alpine look was adopted by builders of the Chandler's Inn, which has five simply furnished units. Three rooms at the top of a log staircase have private baths and the two downstairs share one and a half baths off of a common sitting room and game room.

WILDERNESS INN

$–$$ 29 ROOMS ✉301 West North Street, Enterprise ☎541-426-4535

This is a basic motel: clean and uncomplicated. Some rooms feature kitchenettes; all boast free wi-fi. Pet-friendly.

COUNTRY INN

$ 14 ROOMS ✉402 West North Street, Enterprise ☎541-426-4986, 877-426-4986 🖥www.neoregon.net/countryinn

Accomodations range from one-bedroom units to family suites; some include kitchens. All units are decorated in simple country style.

WILSON RANCHES RETREAT

$$ 7 ROOMS ✉16555 Butte Creek Road, Fossil ☎541-763-2227, 866-763-2227 🖥www.wilsonranchesretreat.com, npwilson@wilsonranchesretreat.com

Though only three miles from the block-long main street of Fossil (pop. 469), this historic ranch offers the same air of solitude established by the original homesteaders more than 100 years ago. Individually decorated in Western motifs featuring family heirlooms, the rooms range from a no-frills unit with twin beds and a bath down the hall to a suite with king, queen and double beds, a private bath, a red brick fireplace, TV with video player and an outdoor entrance. There's an outdoor deck for relaxing and watching the birds or the sunset. A generous ranch breakfast is served family-style in the dining room.

GEISER GRAND HOTEL

$–$$ 30 ROOMS   ✉1996 Main Street, Baker City   📞541- 523-1889, 888-434-7374
📠541-523-1800   ✍www.geisergrand.com, info@geisergrand.com

Heading south, you'll find the landmark Geiser Grand, which was built by the Geiser family in 1889, during Baker City's gold-rush era. The current owners have painstakingly restored the grand staircase and the wrought-iron-and-mahogany balustrade, as well as the crystal chandeliers and ten-foot-high windows. I can attest to the haunted reputation of this hotel. While staying in the ornate Cupola Suite, I was kept awake all night by the sound of running bathwater in my bathroom, partying noises in a nonexistent upstairs room and the sensation of someone getting into bed with me. I was later told that working girls once occupied this room when the hotel was a brothel.

BEST WESTERN JOHN DAY INN

$$ 39 UNITS   ✉315 Main Street, John Day   📞541-575-1700, 800-243-2628
📠541-575-1558   ✍www.bestwestern.com

The selection is thin in the area of John Day Fossil Beds National Monument. A comfortable option is this Best Western, located near a handful of shops and restaurants. The hotel boasts a fitness center, a pool and free wi-fi. Pet-friendly.

LITTLE PINE INN

$ 13 ROOMS   ✉250 East Main Street, John Day   📞541-575-2100
✍littlepineinn@centurytel.net

Rooms here include microwaves, refrigerators and free wi-fi. The decor is standard, but the price is right.

DINING

RAPHAEL'S RESTAURANT & CATERING

$$$ AMERICAN   ✉233 Southeast 4th Street, Pendleton   📞541-276-8500,
888-944-2433   ✍www.raphaelsrestaurant.com

Red meat is almost required eating in cowboy towns, but in Pendleton you can find a wider variety at Raphael's, a restaurant and cocktail lounge that displays the work of local American Indian artists. The menu has beef (of course), but entrées may include crab, lobster or wild game. Closed Sunday and Monday.

VALI'S ALPINE DELICATESSEN AND RESTAURANT

$$ GERMAN/HUNGARIAN   ✉59811 Wallowa Lake Highway, Joseph   📞541-432-5691
✍vali@uci.net

Good food is making inroads in the Wallowa Valley, and one of the first notable eateries was Vali's. German-Hungarian dishes such as goulash, chicken paprikas and wienerschnitzel are served, but for the nonadventurous there is also plain old American fare. The decor is also German-Hungarian. Open for continental breakfast (on Saturday and Sunday) and dinner only. Closed Monday and Tuesday between Memorial Day and Labor Day.

ARMCHAIR BOOKS ✉ *39 Southwest Dorion Street, Pendleton* ☎ *541-276-7323*
Offering a fine selection of books on regional history and travel is this local shop. Closed Sunday.

COLLECTORS GALLERY ✉ *223 Southeast Court Street, Pendleton* ☎ *541-276-6697* This gallery highlights books of local interest and is a good source for Umatilla Indian artwork. Closed Sunday.

Baker City has become an antiques mecca. You'll find items dating back to the pioneer years of the town, including oak furniture bought at estate sales, glass, rock collections, kitchen utensils and tools.

MEMORY HOUSE ANTIQUES ✉ *1780 Main Street, Baker City* ☎ *541-523-6227* Memory House specializes in Depression glass and furniture. Closed Sunday and Monday in winter, Sunday in summer.

NIGHTLIFE

CRABBY'S UNDERGROUND SALOON AND DANCE HALL
✉ *220 Southwest 1st Street, Pendleton* ☎ *541-276-8118* Live music is hard to come by except on special occasions, such as rodeos and patriotic holidays. An exception is in Pendleton. Crabby's has deejay music on Thursday, Friday and Saturday night. It's located in a basement beneath several small shops, and in addition to the music and dancefloor has poker and pool tables. Closed Sunday.

PARKS

**WALLOWA LAKE
STATE PARK** _____ **h**idden

✉ *Located at the southern end of Wallowa Lake on Route 82* ☎ *541-432-4185*
🚶🐎⛵🎣🥾🚐⛴️⚓ On the southern end of the lake with large playground areas surrounded by trees, this park stretches from the lakeshore well back into the pine and spruce timber. Hiking trails thread the woodland areas. Good rainbow trout fishing can be found north of the park. There are day-use areas, a marina, a boat dock and a concessionaire.

▲ There are 89 tent sites ($13 to $17 per night) and 121 RV hookup sites ($17 to $21 per night), two yurts ($29 per night) and one cabin ($58 to $80 per night).

HELLS CANYON NATIONAL RECREATION AREA
✉ *You can reach the area two ways: by taking Route 86 from Baker City through Halfway to Forest Service Road 39; or by heading east on Route 350 from the town of Joseph south to Forest Service Road 39.* ☎ *541-426-5546* 🖳 *www.fs.fed.us/hellscanyon.com*
🚶🐎⛵🚤⚓ This 652,488-acre monument was well known to early American Indians and white settlers alike, as evidenced by 8000-year-old petroglyphs, artifacts from Chief Joseph's Nez Perce, remnants of

1860s gold mines and 1890s homesteads. Today it protects the Snake River Gorge, a canyon that has an average depth of 6000 feet, the deepest river gorge in the world. It is one of the most popular whitewater-rafting trips in the United States. Rafts can be launched from Hells Canyon Dam in Oregon and Pittsburg Landing on the Idaho side of the river. The Snake River is very swift, and swimming is allowed only in certain spots. There's fishing access from 18 sites; smallmouth bass, catfish and crappie are best. There is also sturgeon (catch-and-release only). Facilities include day-use picnic areas, scenic overlooks, a visitors center (closed Saturday and Sunday from Labor Day to Memorial Day) and restrooms. Higher elevations in the park are closed in winter.

▲ There are numerous campgrounds. Indian Crossing (14 tent sites, $6 to $10 per night) is the starting point for some of the area's horseback riding and hiking trails, making it an ideal place to set up camp. Ollokot Campground (12 campsites, $8 to $10 per night) is also popular. Both campgrounds are only open in summer. There is also primitive camping along the river for rafters and backpackers.

SOUTHEASTERN OREGON

If you thought northeastern Oregon seemed lonely, you probably haven't yet experienced southeastern Oregon. To travel in this part of the state you need a sturdy, reliable car, a cooler for cold drinks and snacks, and it might not be a bad idea to take along camping equipment because hotels/motels are few and far between.

Harney County is the largest county in the United States, larger in fact than many northeastern states, but this part of the country is really wide open. Harney is the largest of the three counties in southeastern Oregon at 10,228 square miles and has the smallest population, just over 7500. One town, Wagontire on Route 395, has a population that hovers around seven. Some say it depends on how many children are home for the holidays.

Few roads run through this area: Route 395 from California and Route 95 from Nevada are the main north–south corridors. Route 20 goes across the center from Idaho to the Cascades, and Route 140 runs across the bottom from northern Nevada through Lakeview to Klamath Falls. In Malheur County you will find evidence of its diverse culture as Basque shepherds, Mexican cowboys and laborers, Japanese-American laborers and various Europeans came through and left their marks.

In Harney County are wildlife refuges around Malheur Lake and Steens Mountain. The only real population center is Burns. Crane, a tiny town southeast of Burns on Route 78, has the only public boarding school in the country.

SIGHTS

ABERT RIM   At 30 miles, this is the largest exposed fault in North America, located northeast of Lakeview on Route 395. The massive fault

Southeastern Oregon

Bend

FOUR RIVERS CULTURAL CENTER

Burns

LOST FOREST

HOTEL DIAMOND

HART MOUNTAIN NATIONAL ANTELOPE REFUGE

Lakeview

CALIFORNIA NEVADA

FOUR RIVERS CULTURAL CENTER

PAGE 312

Well-stocked museum and gift shop boasting handmade native artwork and pieces from the region's richly diverse heritage

LOST FOREST

PAGE 309

Idyllic ponderosa-pine groves thriving amidst shifting golden sand dunes

HOTEL DIAMOND

PAGE 310

Rustic 1898 family-owned property with wood-trimmed rooms and country-style furnishings

HART MOUNTAIN NATIONAL ANTELOPE REFUGE

PAGE 312

Expansive yet secluded wild animal refuge laced with graded roads, great for exploring

juts up into the desert sky like a continuous cliff on the east side of Route 395, while on the west side of the highway is the talcum white wasteland around **Lake Abert.**

HOLE IN THE GROUND   Northwest of Lakeview just off Route 31 on county roads in Christmas Valley is this 700-foot-deep crack caused by an earthquake.

FORT ROCK   In the same area as Hole in the Ground, this is the remnant of a volcano crater and ocean shoreline that looks like one side of a destroyed fort. Indian sandals found there were carbon-dated and found to be 10,000 years old.

LOST FOREST

About 25 miles northeast of Christmas Valley is this 9000-acre ponderosa-pine forest that has managed to survive in the middle of the harsh desert. The forest is surrounded by shifting sand dunes, which are popular with the all-terrain-vehicle set.

LAKE OWYHEE   Oregon's longest lake, this manmade body of water has miles of striking desert topography along its shores. It is reached by taking Route 201 south from Nyssa to the small town of Owyhee, then a county road that dead-ends at the lake. Farther down in the desert where the Owyhee River still runs free is some of the state's best whitewater for river runners.

LODGING

DAYS INN PONDEROSA MOTEL

$ 52 ROOMS ✉*577 West Monroe Street, Burns* ☎*541-573-2047*
🖰*www.daysinn.com*

Down in the desert, Burns has four or five motels, including the Days Inn. It has ordinary but clean rooms and a swimming pool.

SILVER SPUR MOTEL

$ 28 ROOMS ✉*789 North Broadway Avenue, Burns* ☎*541-573-2077, 800-400-2077*
📠*541-573-3921* 🖰*www.silverspurmotel.net, silverspurmotel@yahoo.com*

Cozy and simple guest rooms with cable television, wi-fi, microwaves, refrigerators and coffee makers are the standard here. Pine furnishings, floral linens and wallpaper create a more pleasant, homey feel than the average motel. Guests have free access to a nearby health club. There is also a golf course nearby.

HOTEL DIAMOND

$-$$ 8 ROOMS ✉*10 Main Street, Diamond* ☎*541-493-1898*
🖰*www.central-oregon.com/hoteldiamond*

This hotel is located 54 miles southeast of Burns. Built in 1898 as a hotel, the wood structure serves as a point of departure for Malheur National Wildlife Refuge, Diamond Craters and the Pete French Round Barn Historical site. The hotel has five small, wood-trimmed rooms with shared baths and three rooms with private baths. Continental breakfast included. Closed November to April.

FRENCHGLEN HOTEL

$ 13 ROOMS ✉*39184 Route 205, Frenchglen* ☎*541-493-2825, 800-551-6949*
📠*541-493-2828* 🖰*fghotel@centurytel.net*

There are just a few places to stay in the area around Steens Mountain, Alvord Desert and Malheur and Harney lakes, so reservations are strongly recommended. A historic place is this 1924 classic ranch house with screened porch. Frenchglen has eight rooms decorated with rustic pine and patchwork quilts and has two shared baths. A newly built addition provides five more rooms, all with private baths. Breakfast, lunch and a family-style dinner are available. Closed November to mid-March.

HUNTER'S HOT
SPRINGS RESORT

$-$$ 19 ROOMS ✉*18088 Route 395 North, Lakeview* ☎*541-947-4142,*
800-858-8266 📠*541-947-2800* 🖰*www.huntersresort.com,*
huntersresort@aol.com

Two miles north of Lakeview is Hunter's, which has Oregon's only geyser. Named Old Perpetual, it shoots water and steam 60

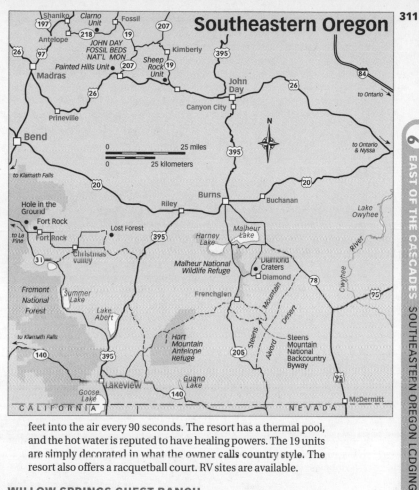

Southeastern Oregon

feet into the air every 90 seconds. The resort has a thermal pool, and the hot water is reputed to have healing powers. The 19 units are simply decorated in what the owner calls country style. The resort also offers a racquetball court. RV sites are available.

WILLOW SPRINGS GUEST RANCH

$$$ 4 UNITS   ✉34064 Clover Flat Road, Lakeview   ☎541-947-5499
🖳www.willowspringsguestranch.com, Info@willowspringsguestranch.com

For a real cowpoke experience, head to this 2500-acre working cattle ranch in Lakeview. Guests can enjoy a comfortable overnight bed-and-breakfast experience or saddle up with the ranch hands and learn something about the ranching lifestyle. Activities include horseback riding, bicycling, hiking and campfire cookouts. Rustic Western cabins are duplex style and include a queen bed, private bath, pedestal fireplace, art by famous Western artists such as Frederic Remington, and a long covered porch with rockers. There is a wood-fired hot tub. The ranch generates all its electricity from wind and solar power and generators (lanterns are provided for night owls). No pets or children under 12. Closed October to early May.

DINING

BROADWAY DELICATESSEN CO.

$ DELI ✉530 North Broadway, Burns ✆541-573-7020

For a casual lunch or picnic fixings, a good bet is this bright, cheerful deli inside a historic quarried-rock storefront. The menu features made-to-order sandwiches on a choice of seven breads, pasta and potato salads, tossed green salads, a full espresso bar and daily soup specials. There are also house-made cheesecakes, bread pudding and other tempting desserts. Breakfast and lunch only.

SHOPPING

FOUR RIVERS CULTURAL CENTER

✉676 Southwest 5th Avenue, Ontario ✆541-889-8191 ⬦www.4rcc.com

Unless you're a rock hound, souvenir shopping is likely to prove challenging in these parts. Perhaps your best bet is this gift shop, where you'll find artworks and handmade gift items from the four cultures represented in the museum, as well as a large selection of adults' and children's books on Western history, American Indian and Japanese cultures, Japanese gardening and koi ponds.

PARKS

MALHEUR NATIONAL WILDLIFE REFUGE

✉Located 30 miles southeast of Burns on Route 205, then 6 miles on Princeton-Narrows Road ✆541-493-2612 ⬦www.fws.gov/malheur

At 187,000 acres, Malheur covers an interesting and diverse wildlife population and geological features. Malheur Lake is a major resting area for migratory birds on the Pacific Flyway. Fishing is permitted at Krumbo Reservoir. Malheur Field Station (541-493-2629) has dormitory and family housing and meals available.

HART MOUNTAIN NATIONAL ANTELOPE REFUGE

✉Located 65 miles northeast of Lakeview on county roads off Routes 395 and 140 ✆541-947-3315 ⬦sheldon-hart@fws.gov

This 275,000-acre refuge 65 miles northeast of Lakeview protects a large population of antelope, bighorn sheep, mule deer, coyotes, a variety of smaller animals and a bird population. Hart Mountain, the centerpiece of the refuge, rises to 8065 feet and has deep gorges, ridges and cliffs on the west side. The east side of the mountain climbs more gradually. For rock hounds, collections are limited to seven pounds per person. Fishing is permitted in Rock and Guano creeks and Warner Pond depending on conditions. Restrooms and a visitors center are the only facilities.

▲ Hot Springs Campground has 30 primitive sites (no fee).

OUTDOOR ADVENTURES

FISHING

Although eastern Washington is not, as one local guide puts it, "blue ribbon" fishing territory for most of the year, the region has its moments: come August, some big salmon show up in the Klickitat River; September starts the steelhead run in the Snake River; and trout in June and July make the Yakima River the most popular flyfishing stream in the Northwest. Some outfitters can also arrange hunting trips for game like elk, deer and bighorn sheep.

Grand Coulee Area

COULEE PLAYLAND RESORT ✉ *P.O. Box 457, Electric City, WA 99123* 📞 *509-633-2671* 🌐 *www.couleeplayland.com* For information on fishing in Banks and Roosevelt lakes, contact this resort.

Spokane Area

DOUBLE SPEY OUTFITTING ✉ *West 11254 Meadowview Lane, Nine Mile Falls* 📞 *509-466-4635* 🌐 *deanriver@aol.com* G. L. Britton of Double Spey Outfitting has been flyfishing since he was a boy; he now guides visiting anglers for half-day walk-and-wade flyfishing trips for trout on the Spokane during August and September, and full-day steelhead trips on a driftboat on the Snake and Grande Rhonde rivers in October and November. The rest of the year, Britton will take you out to one of the local lakes for a full day of fishing that's more "teach-you" than "trophy." Flies, rods and leaders are provided.

Southeastern Washington

RBF EXCURSIONS ✉ *P.O. Box 271, Klickitat, WA 98628* 📞 *541-993-1351* 🌐 *www.rbf-excursions.com, rbfexcursions@hotmail.com* If you'd "rather be fishing," then call Dan Little at this company to arrange a day of flyfishing for steelhead or guided summer salmon and steelhead trips to the Klickitat River, about 65 miles away; for part of the year, Dan guides winter steelhead trips on Olympic Peninsula Rainforest rivers as well.

BEAMER'S HELLS CANYON TOURS ✉ *1451 Bridge Street, Clarkston* 📞 *509-758-4800, 800-522-6966* 📠 *509-758-3643* 🌐 *www.hellscanyontours.com, jill@bhct. net* Fishing excursions on the Snake River between the Idaho/Washington border are offered by Beamer's. Spring and summer half-day to three-days trips on a fishing sled seek bass, trout and sturgeon; in fall, it's steelhead. Bait and tackle provided.

SNAKE RIVER ADVENTURES ✉ *4832 Hells Gate Road, Lewiston, ID* 📞 *208-746 6276, 800-262-8874* 📠 *208-746-9906* 🌐 *www.snakeriveradventures.com, info@ lewistondsl.com* Snake River provides day tours as well as single or multi-day guided trips for steelhead, sturgeon, bass and trout on the Snake, Salmon and Clearwater rivers.

In September on the Tieton River, in southeastern Washington, water is released from the dam that controls the flow, creating Class III and some Class IV rapids and drawing ever-increasing crowds of rafters. It may not be a "hidden" spot, but it's still a thrill. Whitewater thrills come on the Snake River in Northeastern Oregon, where it cuts through walls of black basalt, forming Hells Canyon, the deepest gorge in the country. Spring is the best time to hit good whitewater, but be forewarned: classifications are arbitrary and the hard classes aren't necessarily the best. Watch water levels more closely than class.

Southeastern Washington

CHINOOK EXPEDITIONS ✉ P.O. Box 256, Index, WA 98256 ☎ 360-793-3451, 800-241-3451 ✎ www.chinookexpeditions.com, sturnbull@earthlink.net This company has been leading guided trips and wildlife-watching tours since 1974. Rivers rafted include the Skagit, Snohomish, Skykomish, Wenatchee and Methow rivers. Guide Shane Turnbull says all trips are very interpretive. All river and camping gear is included.

RIVERS, INC. ✉ P.O. Box 2092, Kirkland, WA 98083 ☎ 425-822-5296 Full-day guided trips on paddle rafts down the Wenatchee, Methow, Suiattle and Tieton rivers are offered here during the summer.

IDAHO AFLOAT ✉ P.O. Box 542, Grangeville, ID 83530 ☎ 208-983-2414, 800-700-2414 ✎ www.idahoafloat.com This group leads one- to six-day rafting trips down Class II to Class IV rivers.

SNAKE DANCER EXCURSIONS ✉ 1550 Port Drive, Suite B, Clarkston ☎ 509-758-8927, 800-234-1941 ☏ 509-758-8925 ✎ www.snakedancerexcursions.com, sdexcursions@qwestoffice.net Snake Dancer provides full- and half-day jet boat tours up the Snake River and through Hells Canyon, with stops at various historical sites, including Kirkwood Ranch. Trips cover 85 sets of rapids that rate as high as Class V. Food and drinks are provided.

O.A.R.S. DORIES ✉ P.O. Box 67, 2687 South Route 49, Angels Camp, CA 95222 ☎ 209-736-4677, 800-346-6277 ☏ 209-736-2902 ✎ www.oars.com, info@oars.com Another popular location for rafting is the Snake River between the Washington and Idaho border. Contact these experts for guided tours on rafts, dories and inflatable kayaks on Class III and Class IV rivers. Trips on the Snake River last three to five days; Salmon River expeditions are four to seventeen days.

Northeastern Oregon

OREGON RIVER EXPERIENCES ✉ 18074 South Boone Court, Beavercreek ☎ 503-632-6836, 800-827-1358 ✎ www.oregonriver.com Some of the most challenging whitewater rapids anywhere can be found on the Owyhee River in southeastern Oregon's Malheur County. This outfitter will brave the rapids with you. They offer river rafting trips on the Owyhee from April through May.

OREGON WHITEWATER ADVENTURES ✉ 39620 Deerhorn Road, Springfield ☎ 541-746-5422, 800-820-7238 ✎ www.oregonwhitewater.com Oregon Whitewater offers four- or five-day trips on the Owyhee.

For a list of other outfitters licensed to operate raft or float trips in Hells Canyon, write or call this visitors center.

HORSEBACK RIDING

WALLOWA MOUNTAINS VISITOR CENTER ✉88401 Route 82, Enterprise, OR 97828 📞541-426-5546 🖙541-426-5522 🖗www.fs.fed.us/hellscanyon Several outfitters are licensed to lead overnight horse pack trips into the Hells Canyon National Recreation Area and Eagle Cap Wilderness. A few offer day rides and llama pack trips. For a list, contact park headquarters.

GOLF

Mountain valleys and high desert vistas give golfers satisfying course options, and greens fees that are lower than in urban areas sweeten the deal. Winter weather closes many courses for two to five months.

Okanogan Highlands

OROVILLE GOLF CLUB ✉3468-A Nighthawk Road, two miles west of Oroville 📞509-476-2390 🖙509-476-2408 Hilly terrain makes a cart rental highly recommended at this nine-hole course. The scenic public course runs beside a river. Closed Thursday afternoon.

OKANOGAN VALLEY GOLF CLUB ✉105 Danker Cutoff, off the Okanogan–Conconully Route 📞509-826-6937 🖙509-826-4043 🖗www.okanoganvalleygolf.com Between Omak and Okanogan is this scenic golf club. The nine-hole public course is surrounded by hills on one side and orchards on the other. Closed November through mid-March.

Grand Coulee Area

BANKS LAKE GOLF AND COUNTRY CLUB ✉19849 Lundolph Road Northeast, one mile south of Electric City 📞509-633-0163 This club offers 18 holes for golf enthusiasts. The public course is next to Banks Lake, and offers a few canyons and wide fairways. Closed in winter.

Spokane Area

INDIAN CANYON GOLF COURSE ✉4304 West Drive 📞509-747-5353 🖙509-747-0622 If you've seen San Francisco's Lincoln Park Municipal Golf Course, with its view across the city skyline, this Spokane course will seem familiar. Set on a hillside that undulates downward toward Spokane, the public 18-hole course is well known throughout the region. Closed in winter.

Southeastern Washington

SUNTIDES GOLF COURSE ✉231 Pence Road, Yakima 📞509-966-9065 🖙509-966-2742 🖗www.suntidesgolf.com In Yakima, the public, 18-hole Suntides course is fairly flat, so it's very walkable, making it popular with seniors and junior golfers. There's water on 13 of the holes. You'll find a restaurant on the premises.

APPLE TREE GOLF COURSE ✉8804 Occidental Road, Yakima ✆509-966-5877 The 17th hole at this public golf course is called Apple Island. It is shaped like an apple and surrounded by water (this is apple country, after all).

SUN WILLOWS GOLF COURSE ✉2535 North 20th Avenue, Pasco ✆509-545-3440 ✆509-545-6758 ◁www.sunwillowgolfcourse.com Sun Willows offers a public, 18-hole course that's very playable for all handicaps. It's fairly flat, but has several lakes. Carts are available for rent.

CANYON LAKES GOLF COURSE ✉3700 West Canyon Lakes Drive, Kennewick ✆509-582-3736 ✆509-585-0914 ◁www.canyonlakesgolfcourse.com A canyon runs through this 18-hole, public course, which makes for plenty of interesting shots. Rated one of the top ten courses in the Northwest, Canyon Lakes also has a champion putting course and full practice facilities.

Northeastern Oregon

ECHO HILLS GOLF COURSE ✉400 Gold Course Road, Echo; Take the Echo exit off Route 84 ✆541-376-8244 Courses are scarce in eastern Oregon simply because there aren't that many people around. The nine-hole course here is par 36 and rather challenging, with hills and gullies. It's 23 miles northwest of Pendleton.

PENDLETON COUNTRY CLUB ✉69772 Route 395 South, Pendleton ✆541-443-4653 ◁www.pendletoncc.com For 18 holes, try the fairly flat but attractive course at this country club.

BAKER CITY GOLF COURSE ✉2801 Indiana Avenue ✆541-523-2358 South of Pendleton, the public, 18-hole Baker City course is fairly easy.

ALPINE MEADOWS ✉66098 Golf Course Road, Enterprise ✆541-426-3246 Near Hells Canyon is the laidback, nine-hole Alpine Meadows. The par-36 course is surrounded by beautiful mountains.

JOHN DAY GOLF ✉27631 Golf Club Road, John Day ✆541-575-0170 John Day Golf is a challenging nine-hole course with hills and a sand-trap.

SKIING

Ski areas in this part of the state, particularly the southeast part, are a little farther away from the hustle and bustle of the larger, more popular spots elsewhere. The full-service resorts all offer equipment rentals for downhill skiing, cross-country skiing and snowboarding. In addition, lessons are available for all levels.

Okanogan Highlands

Downhill and cross-country skiing are both popular in this region, particularly the latter because there is so much open country and powdery snow. Cross-country trails are maintained at most downhill areas, but any country road, most golf courses and parks may be used by skiers.

LOUP LOUP SKI AREA ___ hidden

⊠*Route 20, between Twisp and Okanogan* ☎*509-826-2720* 🖷*509-826-5469*
🖳*www.skitheloup.com, info@skitheloup.com* This area has a 1240-foot
vertical drop for downhill skiing and snowboarding. Its four lifts
serve over a dozen runs. There is a small half-pipe for snowboarders, and 25 kilometers of groomed trails for cross-country
skiers. Closed Monday, Tuesday and Thursday, and April to
mid-December.

SITZMARK SKI LODGE ___ hidden

⊠*Located 20 miles northeast of Tonasket on Havillan Road* ☎*509-485-3323*
🖳*www.skisitzmark.org* Sitzmark has a base elevation of 4950 feet
and a modest 650-foot drop. There is a chair lift, a rope tow and
runs for snowboarders. The majority of runs are intermediate (60
percent). Closed Monday, Tuesday, Wednesday and Friday,
mid-March to mid-December.

49° NORTH ⊠*Located ten miles east of Chewelah* ☎*509-935-6649, 866 376 4949*
🖳*www.ski49n.com* This family-friendly resort has six chairlifts on 1900
feet as well as a snowboard park and 380 miles of groomed trails. Closed
Wednesday and Thursday and mid-April to mid-November.

Southeastern Washington

SKI BLUEWOOD ___ hidden

⊠*262 East Main Street* ☎*509-382-4725* 🖷*590-382-4726* 🖳*www.bluewood.
com, info@bluewood.com* Twenty-two miles southeast of Dayton at
the end of a Forest Service road, this resort has 1125 vertical feet
of downhill skiing. There are two triple-chair lifts and one surface lift, as well as a snowboard terrain park. Closed Monday and
Tuesday, and from mid-April to mid-November.

BIKING

For the most part, automobile traffic is sparse in these regions, so bicyclists have little trouble finding long stretches of road that are practically deserted, and scenically beautiful. But they're also challenging
and attract avid cross-country bicyclists, especially along Routes 3 and
86 in the Wallowa National Forest near Hells Canyon. Recreational bicyclists, however, have a couple of options.

CENTENNIAL TRAIL Along the bank of the Spokane River, this
paved trail extends from Riverside State Park to the Washington–Idaho
state line (37 miles) and continues on to Coeur d'Alene, Idaho, 25 miles
farther. The trail is a relatively flat, easy ride with a few hills in the park
(and nobody says you have to go the full distance; you might just want
to go as far as Plante's Ferry Park, where you'll find some interesting
basalt rock formations in the water).

RIVERSIDE STATE PARK   Just west of Spokane is this forested state park, which has several gravel trails for mountain biking. Mt. Spokane, which rises some 5800 feet, is another recommended destination.

YAKIMA VALLEY VISITORS AND CONVENTION BUREAU
✉ *10 North 8th Street* ☎ *509-575-6062, 800-221-0751* 🖳 *www.visityakima.com* In the Yakima area, besides an easy five-mile multi-use route along the **Yakima Greenway**, which meanders along the river, there are several possible routes through the local wine country. This visitors bureau has information and maps.

SNAKE RIVER BIKEWAY   For six miles, this bikeway runs between Clarkston and Asotin along both the Clearwater and Snake rivers. Access it from Beachview Park at the corner of Beachview and Chestnut in Clarkston.

PALOUSE   A great option is the 24-mile tour beginning and ending in this town. It leads south on Route 27 to Clear Creek Road to Route 272 back to Palouse.

In some cities, you'll find some bicycle routes that double as hiking trails (see "Hiking," below).

Bike Rentals & Tours
NORTH DIVISION BICYCLE SHOP ✉ *10503 North Division Street, Spokane* ☎ *509-467-2453, 888-222-2453* 🖳 *www.northdivision.com* There are three bike shops along Spokane's main street. Rent or repair a mountain bike or buy equipment at this shop.

SPOKE 'N SPORT ✉ *212 North Division Street, Spokane* ☎ *509-838-8842* This store rents and sells mountain bikes, racks and trailers. There's also a full-service bike shop.

VALLEY CYCLING AND FITNESS ✉ *1802 West Nob Hill Boulevard, Yakima* ☎ *509-453-6699* 🖳 *www.valleycyclingandfitness.com* Mountain-bike sales and repairs are available through this outfitter.

MOUNT ADAMS CYCLING ✉ *P.O. Box 745, Yakima, WA 98907* 🖳 *www. mountadamscycling.org* For a variety of scheduled rides in the Yakima area, check out this shop.

HIKING

All distances listed for hiking trails are one way unless otherwise noted.

Okanogan Highlands
RANGER STATION ✉ *1240 South 2nd Avenue* ☎ *509-826-3275* 🖳 *509-826-3789* Backpackers and day hikers alike enjoy this area because the weather is often clear and dry. A number of established hiking trails are shown on Forest Service maps and in free brochures given out at the ranger station in Okanogan.

A good walk for a family with small children is the one-mile trail leading from Bonaparte Campground just north of the one-store town of Wauconda to the viewpoint overlooking the lake.

BIG TREE TRAIL This is an easy 1-mile loop from Lost Lake Campground, which is only a short distance north of Bonaparte. It goes through a signed botanical area.

KETTLE CREST TRAIL

☎509-684-7000 One of the most ambitious highlands hikes is the southern segment of this trail (15 miles). The trek begins at the summit of Sherman Pass on Route 20 and winds southward past Sherman Peak and four other major mountains, the highest peak measuring 7135 feet. The trail is through mostly open terrain, and you'll have great views of the mountains and Columbia River Valley.

Grand Coulee Area

COMMUNITY TRAIL A system of paths and trails connects the four towns clustered around Grand Coulee Dam. The Bureau of Reclamation built a paved route about two miles long called the Community Trail, which connects Coulee Dam and Grand Coulee. An informal system of unpaved paths connects these two towns to Elmer City and Electric City.

DOWN RIVER TRAIL

☎509-633-9503 A new walking/biking trail is this one that continues for 6.5 miles. It runs north along the Columbia River from Grand Coulee, beginning in the Coulee Dam Shopping Center. Some access points are accessible for wheelchairs.

BUNCHGRASS PRAIRIE NATURE TRAIL ☎509-633-9441 This nature trail (.5-mile roundtrip) begins in the Spring Canyon Campground, which is three miles up Lake Roosevelt by water and two miles from Grand Coulee. This loop trail starts in the campground and goes through one of the few remaining bunchgrass environments here.

Southeastern Washington

COWICHE CANYON

Starting five miles from Yakima, this is a 3-mile trek. The trail is actually an old railroad bed that ran through the steep canyon. The canyon has unusual rock formations, and you can expect to see some wildlife.

NOEL PATHWAY This 4.6-mile trail is inside the city limits of Yakima and follows the Yakima River. The pathway is used by bicyclists, as well.

TRANSPORTATION

CAR

Eastern Washington and Oregon is served by a network of roads that range from interstates to logging roads that have been paved by the Forest Service. **Route 97** serves as the north–south dividing line between the Cascade Mountains and the arid, rolling hills that undulate to the eastern boundaries of the states.

Route 90 runs through the center of the Washington, from Spokane southwest through Moses Lake, George and across the Columbia River at Vantage, where the highway turns almost due west for its final run to Puget Sound.

Route 5 bisects Portland, Oregon, and provides access from the north via Vancouver, Washington. This highway is also the main line from points south like the Willamette Valley and California.

Route 82 begins near Hermiston, Oregon, crosses the Columbia River to the Tri-Cities (Richland, Kennewick and Pasco) and runs on up the Yakima Valley to join Route 90 at Ellensburg. **Route 84** runs almost the entire length of the Columbia River Gorge in Oregon before swinging southeast at Hermiston and connecting Pendleton, La Grande and Baker City with Ontario on the Idaho border.

Other major highways are **Route 395**, starting south of Lakeview, Oregon, and continuing into Washington at the Tri-Cities to Ritzville. It joins with Route 90 at Ritzville only to emerge again at Spokane, where it continues north into British Columbia. Smaller but important highways include **Route 12** between Clarkston and Walla Walla, and **Route 195** running between Spokane and the Clarkston–Lewiston area.

Perhaps the most beautiful of all the highways in Washington is **Route 20**, which starts at Whidbey Island and continues to the North Cascades, through the Methow Valley, then straight through the Okanogan Highlands to Kettle Falls, where it merges with Route 395. It becomes Route 20 again at Colville, and continues southeast to Newport on the Idaho border.

AIR

SPOKANE INTERNATIONAL AIRPORT *www.spokaneairports.net*
This is by far the busiest airport in Eastern Washington with ten airlines serving the area: Alaska Airlines, Delta Airlines, ExpressJet, Frontier Airlines, Horizon Air, Northwest Airlines, Skywest Airlines, Southwest Airlines, United Airlines, United Express and US Airways.

Other airports with scheduled service in Washington are **Moses Lake**, **Pullman**, **Wenatchee**, **Yakima**, the **Tri-Cities** and **Walla Walla**. Most of these smaller cities are served by either Horizon Air or United Express, or both. In addition, Delta Airlines and US Airways serve the Tri-Cities.

GREYHOUND BUS LINES ☎*800-231-2222* ⌕*www.greyhound.com* This nationwide bus company serves the Spokane Terminal (221 West 1st Avenue, 509-624-5251) and the Yakima Depot (602 East Yakima Avenue, 509-457-5131).

NORTHWESTERN TRAILWAYS ☎*509-838-5262* Contact this transportation agency for bus service from the Spokane Terminal (221 West 1st Avenue).

ALPHA OMEGA TOURS AND CHARTERS ✉*419 North Jefferson Street* ☎*509-299-5545, 800-351-1060* ⌕*www.alphaomegatoursandcharters.com* Operating from Medical Lake (just southwest of Spokane) is Alpha Omega Tours and Charters.

TRAIN

AMTRAK ☎*800-872-7245* ⌕*www.amtrak.com* Washington is one of the few states to have two Amtrak routes. Both start in Spokane. The first route runs from Spokane due west with stops in Ephrata, Wenatchee, Everett and Edmonds before arriving in Seattle. The other route runs southwest from Spokane to the Columbia River Gorge with stops in Pasco, Bingen and Vancouver, and ultimately goes to Portland, Oregon.

CAR RENTALS

Car-rental agencies in Spokane include the following: **Budget Car and Truck Rental** (800-527-0700) and **Thrifty Car Rental** (800-367-2277).

Agencies in the Tri-Cities include **Avis Rent A Car** (800-331-1212), **Budget Rent A Car** (800-527-0700) and **Hertz Rent A Car** (800-654-3131). Walla Walla is served by **Budget Rent A Car** (800-527-0700).

PUBLIC TRANSIT

The Tri-Cities area has **Ben Franklin Transit** (509-735-5100; www.bft.org). **Valley Transit** serves Walla Walla and College Place (509-525-9140; www.valleytransit.com). Pullman has **Pullman Transit** (509-332-6535; www.pullmantransit.com). Yakima has **Yakima Transit** (509-575-6175).

TAXIS

Major taxi companies in the area are **Valley Cab** (509-535-7007) and **Spokane Cab** (509-568-8000).

PORTLAND & THE COLUMBIA RIVER GORGE

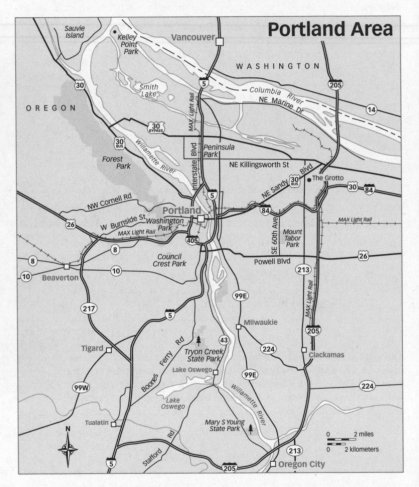

Portland Area

Sauvie Island
Kelley Point Park
Vancouver
WASHINGTON
Columbia River
NE Marine Dr
OREGON
Smith Lake
Willamette River
Forest Park
Interstate Blvd
MAX Light Rail
Peninsula Park
NE Killingsworth St
The Grotto
NW Cornell Rd
Portland
W Burnside St
Washington Park
MAX Light Rail
Council Crest Park
Powell Blvd
Mount Tabor Park
SE 60th Ave
NE Sandy Blvd
MAX Light Rail
Beaverton
Tigard
Boones Ferry Rd
Tryon Creek State Park
Lake Oswego
Lake Oswego
Milwaukie
Clackamas
Willamette River
Mary S Young State Park
Tualatin
Stafford Rd
MAX Light Rail
Oregon City

0   2 miles
0   2 kilometers

But for the flip of a coin, Portland could have been called Boston. Our story begins with two pioneers, Asa Lovejoy of Massachusetts and Francis Pettygrove of Maine, hitting the Oregon Trail in search of the American Dream. On a fall 1843 canoe journey up the Willamette River from Fort Vancouver to Oregon City, Tennessee drifter William Overton (traveling with Lovejoy) thought the land was perfect for a settlement. Lacking the 25-cent filing fee, he split the claim with Lovejoy in return for the money. Overton soon grew tired of working the land, and sold his **323** half to Francis W. Pettygrove.

Soon, Lovejoy found himself partners with Pettygrove at "The Clearing," what native guides called the area. Lovejoy wanted to call the new town Boston, but Pettygrove preferred to appropriate the name of Maine's Portland. True gentlemen, they settled the matter with a coin toss at Oregon City's Francis Ermatinger House.

Pettygrove won, but it was years before Portland began to rival Oregon City, the immigrant hub at the end of the overland trail. Even today, with a metropolitan population of more than 2 million, many visitors wonder how this city emerged as Oregon's centerpiece. Unlike the largest cities of the Pacific Northwest or California, it is not located on a major coast or sound. Although it is midway between the equator and the North Pole, Portland is not central to the geography of its own state. Yet from the arts and winter recreation to architecture and vineyards, this city is an admirable metropolis, one that merits inclusion on any Northwest itinerary.

The community boasts a rich cultural life, has a popular National Basketball Association franchise, is blessed with some of the prettiest urban streets in the Northwest, is a veritable haven for antique lovers, runners, cyclists and garden aficionados and has an impressive array of jazz clubs, bistros and offbeat museums.

And yet the legacy of "The Clearing" is very much intact as the city remains intimately connected to the great outdoors. Near the entrance to the fabled Columbia River Gorge, Portland is just 65 miles from the nearest glacier and 110 miles from the ocean. Riverfront greenspace, the 5000-acre Forest Park and the wonderful wetlands of Sauvie Island all demonstrate why this city has been named "best" on the Green Index, a study of pollution, public health and environmental policy.

When the weather turns very wet, as it does in the winter months, residents head for the powder-packed slopes of Mt. Hood or start gearing up for a bit of steelheading on the nearby coastal rivers. Winter is also the height of the cultural season, enjoyed at the Portland Center for the Performing Arts and dozens of other venues around town.

Portland's emergence as a major city owes much to emigrant New England ship captains who decided, in the mid-19th century, that the town's deep riverfront harbor was preferable to the shallows of Oregon City. Easy ocean access via the Columbia made the new port a convenient link to the emerging agrarian economy of the Willamette Valley, as well as the region's up-and-coming lumber mills. Like San Francisco, Portland flourished as an international shipping hub and as a gateway for the 1852 gold rush that began in the Jacksonville region.

As the Northwest's leading port and economic center, the town soon attracted the state's new gentry, the lumber barons, shipping titans, traders, mercantilists and agribusiness pioneers. They drew heavily on the architectural legacy of the Northeast and Europe, erecting Cape Cod–style homes, Victorian mansions, villas and French Renaissance–style mini-châteaus complete with Italian marble and virgin-redwood interiors.

A city that started out in life as a kind of New England–style village crafted out of native fir was made over with brick office blocks sporting cast-iron facades. Florentine, Italianate, gothic, even Baroque architecture began to emerge along the main drags. City fathers worked hard to upgrade the town's agrarian image, often with mixed results.

PORTLAND & THE COLUMBIA RIVER GORGE

To unify the community, planners added a 25-block-long promenade through the heart of town. Lined with churches, office blocks, apartments and homes, these "Park Blocks" offered a grassy median ideal for contemplating the passing scene. Like a Parisian boulevard, this was the place where one might come for an hour and stay for the day. Brass water fountains, known as Benson Bubblers and left on 24 hours a day, brought the pure waters of the Cascades to street level.

While the city's New England quality made Bostonians feel right at home, Portland also attracted a significant Chinese community that labored long and hard on railroad lines and in salmon factories. Badly persecuted, they were just one of many victims of intolerance in this city that became a Ku Klux Klan center. Blacks, Jews and Catholics were also victimized at various times. But as Portland grew, this deplorable bigotry was replaced by a new egalitarianism. The city's intellectual life flourished thanks to the arrival of several major universities and prestigious liberal arts colleges.

As Portland modernized, it developed into a manufacturing center famous for everything from swimsuits to footwear. But as the city flourished as a center for high-tech industry, it did not forget its roots. Visitors eager to discover the Northwest still flock here and to the Columbia River Gorge in pursuit of outdoor activities from windsurfing to birding. An ideal home base, this city has also drawn many famous artists, musicians and writers from larger, more congested and expensive communities like New York and Los Angeles.

Although much of Portland's best is within easy walking distance of downtown, the city's outer reaches are also well worth your time. The touchstones of great urban centers—science museums, zoos, children's museums and craft centers—are all found here. Amid its multiple museums and theater companies, as well as countless other amenities, Portland also offers many pleasant surprises such as a strong used book–seller community, the sole extinct volcano within the limits of a continental U.S. city and the world's smallest park.

Careful restoration of the downtown core and historic old town, a beautiful riverfront area and thriving nightlife make Portland a winner. Neighborhoods such as Nob Hill, Hawthorne and Sellwood all invite leisurely exploration. And when it comes to parks you can choose from more than 80 spanning 37,000 acres.

In this chapter we have divided the city into three geographic regions. The Central Portland region encompasses downtown, the Skidmore Old Town District and the Yamhill Historic District. Portland West covers the balance of the city and metropolitan region west of the Willamette River. Portland East explores the metro area east of the Willamette River including Lloyd Center, Burnside, Sellwood and southerly destinations like Oregon City.

Because of its proximity to Portland, we have included the Columbia River Gorge region in this chapter. Even if you only have a couple of hours to cruise up to Multnomah Falls, by all means go. The Columbia River Gorge National Recreation Area is 292,500 acres in size and includes 80 miles of the most scenic part of the Columbia River Gorge corridor. It extends beyond Hood River and White Salmon, as far as The Dalles. The main historic drive ends at Multnomah Falls, but the other side of Cascade Locks takes visitors to the Rowena Plateau past orchards to The Dalles. This area includes part of the journey west for many Oregon pioneers; imagine how it felt for them to glide through this verdant, waterfall-lined canyon after 2000 miles of hardscrabble, blazing desert and treacherous mountain passes.

CENTRAL PORTLAND

The urban renaissance is clearly a success in Portland. A walkable city with perpetually flowing drinking fountains, this riverfront town is a place where commerce, history, classic architecture and the arts flourish side by side. Even when the weather is foul, Portland is an inviting place.

Downtown Portland *does* have its sleek towers, but it also contains plenty of low-lying delights as well. It's easy to tell that the city has spent a lot of time and money on parks and public art projects—Portland, after all, is the city whose mayor dreamed up the "Expose Yourself to Art" campaign in the 1970s (and that was mayor Bud Clark himself clad in an open trench coat on the famous poster).

A city that focuses so much on user-friendly public spaces certainly is welcoming to visitors. Whether you're taking a slow stroll along Park Avenue or shopping the markets of Portland's Chinatown (once the West Coast's largest Chinese community), Central Portland will impress you as much more than just the place where the populace clocks in from 9 to 5.

SIGHTS

TRAVEL PORTLAND INFORMATION CENTER ✉*1000 Southwest Broadway Avenue, Suite 2300* ✆*503-275-9750, 800-962-3500* ✐*www.travelportland. com, info@travelportland.com* A good place to orient yourself is at this center where you can pick up helpful maps and brochures. Closed Sunday.

PIONEER COURTHOUSE SQUARE ✉*Bounded by Southwest Yamhill, Southwest Morrison and Southwest Broadway* ✆*503-223-1613* ✆*503-222-7425* ✐*www. pioneercourthousesquare.org* This is a popular gathering point. A waterfall and more than 71,000 red bricks inscribed with the names of local residents who donated money for the square's construction are all here. Named for adjacent **Pioneer Courthouse**, the oldest public building in Oregon (completed in 1873), which you may want to explore, the square offers a variety of special events, including concerts and, at Christmastime, a ceremonial Christmas tree lighting. The **Visitor Information Center** (701 Southwest 6th Avenue; 503-275-8355, 877-678-5263) is a great place to pick up maps and brochures for a walking tour of the area.

OREGON HISTORICAL SOCIETY ✉*1200 Southwest Park Avenue* ✆*503-222-1741* ✆*503-221-2035* ✐*www.ohs.org, orhist@ohs.org* Head west on Yamhill Street for one block then south on Park Avenue to this museum, the place to learn the story of the region's American Indians, the arrival of the Europeans and the westward migration. Permanent exhibits include a maritime gallery, a Northwest art gallery and a comprehensive Oregon history exhibit. You'll also find a museum store and research library. Closed Monday. Admission.

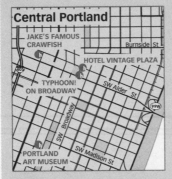

JAKE'S FAMOUS CRAWFISH

PAGE 333

Landmark 19th-century, mahogany-paneled dining room with a seafood menu that stretches for miles

HOTEL VINTAGE PLAZA

PAGE 331

Swank resting spot with a ten-story atrium, nightly wine tastings and deluxe rooms named for local wineries

TYPHOON! ON BROADWAY

PAGE 332

Popular spot for reinvented Thai delights like shrimp in hot chili garlic sauce and pineapple fried rice

PORTLAND ART MUSEUM

PAGE 326

Diverse galleries and a large collection of American Indian pieces like masks and pre-Colombian box drums

FIRST CONGREGATIONAL UNITED CHURCH OF CHRIST

✉ *1126 Southwest Park Avenue* ✆ *503-228-7219* ✇ *503-228-6522* ✐ *www.uccportland. org* Adjacent to the Oregon Historical Society is this church, dating from 1895. The Venetian gothic–style basalt structure, modeled on Boston's Old South Church and crowned by a 175-foot tower, is at its best in the fall. Elms shade the street in front of the church, making this one of the prettiest corners in Portland.

PORTLAND ART MUSEUM

✉ *1219 Southwest Park Avenue* ✆ *503-226-2811* ✇ *503-226-4842* ✐ *www. portlandartmuseum.org, info@pam.org* Directly across the street from the First Congregational Church is this art museum, known for its collection of Asian and European art as well as 20th-century American sculpture. There is also a vast collection of American Indian art and artifacts showcasing excellent tribal masks and wood sculptures. The pre-Columbian pieces, box drums, potlatch dishes and cones are all notable. Don't miss the skylit sculpture courtyard. The Silver gallery has more than 100 rare objects on display. Closed Monday. Admission.

THE OLD CHURCH ✉1422 Southwest 11th Avenue ✆503-222-2031 ✎503-222-2981 ✐www.oldchurch.org, staff@oldchurch.org From the Portland Art Museum, head east to 11th Avenue and then turn south to find this church. Built in 1883, the gothic classic is one of the city's oldest and best-loved buildings. Noon concerts are held Wednesday. Closed weekends.

PORTLAND BUILDING ✉1120 Southwest 5th Avenue ✆503-823-4000 ✎503-823-3050 From the Old Church, head east on Columbia Street to Southwest 5th Avenue. Take 5th Avenue north to this postmodern business hub that opened in 1982. Above the entrance is *Portlandia*, the world's second-largest hammered-bronze sculpture. Designed by Michael Graves, this whimsical skyscraper represents the Northwest with an American Indian motif, making extensive use of turquoise and earth tones.

METROPOLITAN CENTER FOR PUBLIC ART ✉1120 Southwest 5th Avenue ✆503-823-5111 ✎503-823-5432 ✐www.racc.org, info@racc.org On the Portland Building's second floor is this public art center. Here you'll find a portion of the *Portlandia* mold and renderings of the building, as well as pieces from the *Visual Chronicle of Portland*, a continually evolving series of works on paper meant to represent how the city views itself. The center is unstaffed—it's more an exhibition space than a museum—but it has assembled a walking-tour book that will lead you to over 80 public art treasures located throughout the city. This booklet is available at the information desk on the first floor of the Portland Building. Closed Saturday and Sunday.

PORTLAND POLICE HISTORICAL MUSEUM ✉Room 1682, 1111 Southwest 2nd Avenue ✆503-823-0019 ✐www.portlandpolicemuseum.com From the Portland Building, walk east on Main Street to Justice Center and learn about the history of local law enforcement at the Portland Police Historical Museum. Included in the permanent exhibits are a display about the nation's first female detective as well as a display about the nation's original crime-fighting mascot, McGruff the Crime Dog. Closed Saturday through Monday.

IRA KELLER MEMORIAL FOUNTAIN ✉Clay Street between 3rd and 4th avenues Located across from the Civic Auditorium is this fountain situated in a pretty little park. It's a lovely spot to rest your weary feet.

RIVERPLACE Farther south of the memorial fountain, past the Hawthorne Bridge on Harbor Way, you'll come to the sloped-roof buildings of this popular shopping, hotel, restaurant and nightclub complex on the water. A promenade overlooks the Willamette River and the marina's many plush yachts.

SALMON SPRINGS FOUNTAIN ✉Salmon Street at Front Avenue North of RiverPlace is this synchronized fountain that is a favorite meeting place. Kids and dogs love to play in its cool water on hot days.

MILL ENDS PARK Located in the median at Southwest Front Avenue and Taylor Street is this petite park. Just two feet wide, it is the smallest official city park in the world, according to the *Guinness Book of World Records*.

Central Portland

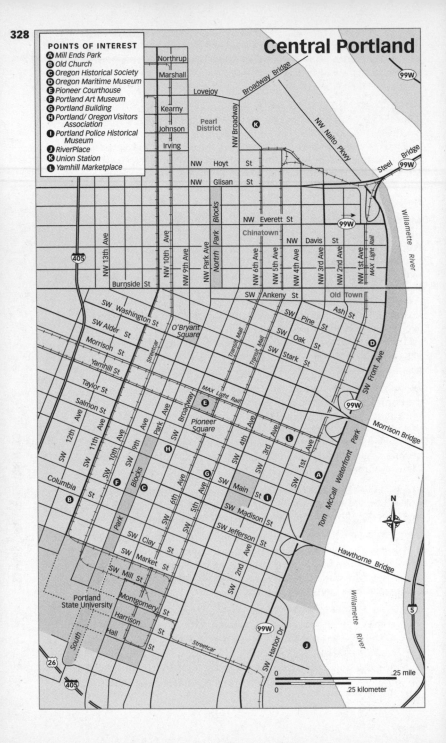

POINTS OF INTEREST
- **A** Mill Ends Park
- **B** Old Church
- **C** Oregon Historical Society
- **D** Oregon Maritime Museum
- **E** Pioneer Courthouse
- **F** Portland Art Museum
- **G** Portland Building
- **H** Portland/ Oregon Visitors Association
- **I** Portland Police Historical Museum
- **J** RiverPlace
- **K** Union Station
- **L** Yamhill Marketplace

TOM McCALL WATERFRONT PARK ✉*Front Avenue* From Mill Ends Park, proceed northward to this waterfront park, which is notable for being the green river frontage that in the 1970s replaced a busy, ugly stretch of freeway blocking the Willamette. You'll get a great view of Portland's skyline here.

OREGON NIKKEI LEGACY CENTER

✉*121 Northwest 2nd Avenue* 📞*503-224-1458* 🖥*www.oregonnikkei.org*
Occupying a historic former hotel in the heart of what was once Portland's *Nihonmachi*, or Japantown, this museum and research center traces the history of Japanese settlement in the city from the 1880s until 1942, when the U.S. government relocated all Japanese-Americans from the Pacific Coast to internment camps in the Midwest and Southwest. Most never returned to the Portland area. Historical documents, photographs and family mementos recall not only the shameful history of discriminatory laws in the 1920s and internment during World War II, but also Nikkei community accomplishments, including one of the largest amateur baseball leagues in the Pacific Northwest.

YAMHILL HISTORIC DISTRICT Bounded by the Willamette River, Southwest 2nd Avenue, and Morrison and Taylor streets is this historic district. This area, on the National Register of Historic Places, boasts 19th-century cast-iron architecture favoring the Italianate style. Walk west on Yamhill to the shops and cafés of **Yamhill Marketplace**.

OREGON MARITIME MUSEUM ✉*River Wall, between Morrison and Burnside bridges at the foot of Pine Street* 📞*503-224-7724* 📠*503-224-7767* 🖥*www.oregon maritimemuseum.org, info@oregonmaritimemuseum.org* Here's your chance to learn Northwestern maritime history and see models of early ships, historical photographs and interpretive displays, all aboard the steam sternwheeler *Portland*. Closed Monday and Tuesday. Admission.

STERNWHEELER ROSE 📞*503-286-7673* 📠*503-286-9661* 🖥*www.stern wheelerrose.com, staff@sternwheelerrose.com* To fully experience the Portland waterfront, consider boarding an excursion boat. This one departs from the Oregon Museum of Science and Industry and offers scenic Willamette River cruises.

PORTLAND SPIRIT 📞*503-224-3900, 800-224-3901* 📠*503-231-9089* 🖥*www.portlandspirit.com* This is Portland's cruise ship, which has year-round lunch, brunch and dinner cruises. It leaves from Salmon Street Springs Fountain in Tom McCall Waterfront Park.

PORTLAND SATURDAY MARKET ✉*108 West Burnside Street* 📞*503-222-6072* 📠*503-222-0254* 🖥*www.saturdaymarket.org, info@saturdaymarket.org* This open-air market, held on weekends from late February to Christmas Eve, offers a wonderful slice of local life. Ankeny Park and the district beneath the Burnside Bridge is a great place to shop for arts and crafts, sample savory specialties served up by vendors and enjoy performances by musicians, street performers and clowns. A permanent store showcases arts and crafts during the week.

SKIDMORE/OLD TOWN   This area between Front and 3rd streets both north and south of Burnside Street boomed in the later 19th century when the harbor was bustling. The look of the buildings from that era derives from Florentine civic palaces: broad, strong, imposing facades constructed of brick and cast iron. Eventually this became the rowdy part of town where sailors caroused, and polite society began to keep away as the buildings fell into disrepair. But interest has grown in the waterfront over the past 30 years, and historic commercial buildings and warehouses have been reborn as trendy shops, galleries, restaurants and nightclubs.

CHINATOWN   Not as large as it was at the turn of the 20th century, this area is still packed with Chinese restaurants and markets. The ornate entry gate to Chinatown at the corner of Burnside Street and 4th Avenue looks a bit out of place among the neighboring adult bookstores.

PORTLAND CLASSICAL CHINESE GARDEN ___ ⓗidden
✉*Corner of Northwest 3rd Avenue and Northwest Everett Street* ☎*503-228-8131* ⊜*503-228-7844* ⌨*www.portlandchinesegarden.org, web@portland chinesegarden.org* A walled oasis of plants, ponds, stone sculptures and pavilions, this garden is linked by winding pathways. The traditional teahouse here provides a serene setting for a light snack after strolling the premises. Admission.

UNION STATION ✉*800 Northwest 6th Avenue* ☎*503-273-4866* You'll want to check out this spot, Portland's marble-walled Amtrak Station.

LODGING

Lodgings in tightly packed downtown Portland are concentrated in large, historic hotels similar to those you'll find in cosmopolitan eastern cities like New York or Boston. As a result of the hustle for space, the majority of quality hotels in Central Portland are priced in the deluxe or ultra-deluxe range. If you're looking to save money, you may want to stay outside the downtown area (see "Lodging" in the "Portland East" and "Portland West" sections below).

THE BENSON HOTEL
$$$–$$$$ 287 UNITS   ✉*309 Southwest Broadway* ☎*503-228-2000, 888-523-6766* ⊜*503-471-3920* ⌨*www.bensonhotel.com, reservations@bensonhotel.com*
A grand hotel and a registered historic landmark, The Benson offers casual fireside elegance in the lobby and comfortably large guest rooms and suites with understated gray decor, oak furniture, armoires and Early American prints. Like a good English club, the walnut-paneled lobby court contains easy chairs, comfortable sofas and a mirrored bar. Marbled halls, chandeliers, brass fixtures, a grand staircase and grandfather clock add an elegant touch. The stamped-tin ceiling, a common architectural feature in the late 19th and early 20th centuries, is one of the finest we've seen. Amenities include a health club and two restaurants.

HOTEL LUCIA

$$$ 127 ROOMS   ✉*400 Southwest Broadway*   ✆*503-225-1717, 877-225-1717*
📠*503-225-1919*   ✍*www.hotellucia.com, info@hotellucia.com*

A good value is this hotel, conveniently located next to shops, cafés and clubs. Contemporary in feel, the cozy guest rooms have mostly king- or queen-sized beds covered with down comforters and plush bathrooms for guests' use. A lounge, restaurant, fitness center and business center round out the amenities.

HOTEL VINTAGE PLAZA

$$$$ 107 ROOMS   ✉*422 Southwest Broadway*   ✆*503-228-1212,*
800-263-2305   📠*503-228-3598*   ✍*www.vintageplaza.com,*
reservations@vintageplaza.com

Boutique hotels are one of the fastest-growing trends in the lodging industry and Portland has one of its own. A remake of the historic Wells Building, this hotel features a ten-story atrium. Each of the guest rooms and expansive suites is named for a local winery. Rooms with burgundy and green color schemes come with cherry-wood armoires, neoclassical furniture, columned headboards, black-granite nightstands and Empire-style column bedside lamps. On the top floor are some "Starlight" rooms, with light-sand beach motifs and one-way solarium windows for stargazers. Local fine wines can be sampled at the complimentary tasting held each evening in front of the lobby fireplace.

THE HEATHMAN HOTEL

$$$–$$$$ 150 ROOMS   ✉*1001 Southwest Broadway at Salmon Street*
✆*503-241-4100, 800-551-0011*   📠*503-790-7110*
✍*www.heathmanhotel.com, info@heathmanhotel.com*

When the inevitable Portland rain begins to fall, I like to sneak off to the library at this hotel, where many of the books are signed by authors who've stayed here. Later I'll mosey down to the lounge for an evening of soft jazz or have dinner in the lively restaurant. These are just the everyday delights offered by this landmark hotel. How far does The Heathman go to make its guests happy? When Luciano Pavarotti wanted to sleep in after a late arrival, the hotel manager asked a contractor across the street to postpone the start of noisy construction from 7 to 10 a.m. They agreed and the tenor slept soundly.

RIVERPLACE HOTEL

$$$$ 84 UNITS   ✉*1510 Southwest Harbor Way*   ✆*503-228-3233,*
800-227-1333   📠*503-295-6161*   ✍*www.riverplacehotel.com,*
reservations@riverplacehotel.com

Enjoying one of the best locations in town, the RiverPlace offers rooms, suites and condos, many with views of the Willamette. In the midst of the Esplanade area featuring bookstores, antique shops and restaurants, this establishment is a short walk from the downtown business district. Wing-back chairs, teak tables, writing desks and earth-toned decor make the rooms inviting; deluxe suites boast fireplaces. A sauna, whirlpool, 24-hour room service and a business center are all available.

HOTEL DELUXE

$$–$$$ 130 UNITS   ✉*729 Southwest 15th Avenue*   ☎*503-219-2094, 866-986-8085*
📠*503-219-2095*   🖳*www.hoteldeluxeportland.com, sales@hoteldeluxeportland.com*

This Art Deco–style establishment built in 1912 has a mirrored lobby, leaded skylights and a chandelier. The eclectic rooms here come with down bedding, oak furniture, contemporary couches and flat-screen TVs. There is also a classy dining room with marble pillars supporting the embossed gold-leaf ceiling.

DINING

TYPHOON! ON BROADWAY

hidden

$$ THAI   ✉*Hotel Lucia, 410 Southwest Broadway*   ☎*503-224-8285*
📠*503-224-3468*   🖳*www.typhoonrestaurants.com,*
broadway@typhoonrestaurants.com

Thai native Bo Kline re-invents the complex flavors of her home country at this downtown restaurant crowded with satisfied diners. Artfully presented dishes include superwild shrimp in hot chili garlic sauce, pineapple fried rice and ginger beef stir-fry. If you have room for dessert, there's homemade coconut ice cream or espresso crème brûlée.

SAUCEBOX

hidden

$$$ PAN-ASIAN/PACIFIC ISLAND   ✉*214 Southwest Broadway*
☎*503-241-3393*   📠*503-243-3251*   🖳*www.saucebox.com, info@saucebox.com*

The interior of this restaurant is mesmerizing, with glowing lanterns, a gleaming bar and striking original artwork. The food is equally stunning, a pan-Asian and Pacific Islands–inspired menu featuring Tahitian-style tuna ceviche, Korean-style baby back ribs and seared *ahi*. The bar is known for its expansive repertoire of fabulous drinks—try a coconut-lime Rickey, a ginger cosmopolitan or wild ginseng martini. Dinner only. Closed Sunday and Monday.

THE HEATHMAN RESTAURANT

$$$–$$$$ FRENCH/PACIFIC NORTHWEST   ✉*1001 Southwest Broadway at Salmon
Street*   ☎*503-790-7752*   📠*503-790-7105*   🖳*www.heathmanrestaurantandbar.com*

A favorite in Portland is The Heathman. The award-winning menu, which changes seasonally, transforms traditional French dishes with Northwest ingredients, seafood and game meats. Some specialties include grilled lightly smoked salmon, seared ahi tuna wrapped in prosciutto, and roast rack of lamb. This spacious dining room and adjacent brass and marble bar is a great place to watch the passing scene on Broadway. The walls are graced with a classy collection of contemporary art. The Heathman also has an extensive breakfast menu.

PAZZO RISTORANTE

$$–$$$ ITALIAN   ✉627 Southwest Washington Street   ☎503-228-1515
📠503-228-5935   🖳www.pazzoristorante.com, pazzoristorante@pazzo.com

The brick pizza oven, trattoria ambience, dark-wood booths and gleaming bar make this dining room a valuable member of the Portland restaurant scene. Dip a little of the fresh-baked bread in the special-press extra virgin olive oil, hoist a glass of the red and survey the Northern Italian menu. Brick oven–baked pizza, housemade pastas, line-caught fish and organic, local beef are some of the popular entrées.

ALEXIS RESTAURANT

$$ GREEK   ✉215 West Burnside Street   ☎503-224-8577   📠503-224-9354
🖳www.alexisfoods.com, restaurant@alexisfoods.com

Pass the retsina and toast the Alexis. This family-style taverna brings the Aegean to the Columbia in the time-honored manner. Belly dancing on the weekend, wallhangings and long tables upstairs with checkered blue-and-white tablecloths add to the ambience. Lamb souvlaki, moussaka, charbrolled shrimp and vegetarian specialties are all on the menu. Be sure to try the dolmas and share an order of hummus and homemade pita. No lunch on Saturday. Closed Sunday.

JAKE'S FAMOUS CRAWFISH

$$–$$$ SEAFOOD   ✉401 Southwest 12th Avenue   ☎503-226-1419,
888-344-6861   📠503-220-1856

This mahogany-paneled, late 19th-century landmark has a grand bar, big tables and a seafood menu that seems to stretch from here to Seattle. Inevitably packed, the restaurant offers tasty chowder, smoked and fresh salmon, halibut, oysters and a good bouillabaisse. For the non-seafood lover, they also offer pasta and steak dishes.

MCCORMICK & SCHMICK'S HARBORSIDE AT THE MARINA

$$–$$$ SEAFOOD   ✉0309 Southwest Montgomery Street   ☎503-220-1865,
888-344-6861   📠503-220-1855   🖳www.mccormickandschmicks.com

With a vast menu of Northwest cuisine, the Harborside is a kind of culinary United Nations. Window tables on the river and paneled booths on the upper levels provide great views of the harbor traffic. Excellent seafood salads, pasta dishes, stir frys, steaks, hamburgers and pizza are served.

WILF'S RESTAURANT AND BAR

$$$–$$$$ PACIFIC NORTHWEST   ✉800 Northwest 6th Avenue   ☎503-223-0070
📠503-223-1386   🖳www.wilfsrestaurant.com, wilfsrestaurant@aol.com

With fresh flowers and big red chairs, Wilf's is one of the most elaborate dining rooms in Portland. In this elegant setting along the tracks you can enjoy a menu emphasizing organic and sustainably produced ingredients in dishes like Northwest salmon filet with an apricot glaze, veal lafayette or rack of lamb. Since they specialize in tableside cooking, entrées such as steak Diane and prawns flambé, and desserts like bananas Foster or crêpes Suzette are works of performance and culinary art. No lunch on Saturday; no dinner on Monday. Closed Sunday.

OLD TOWN PIZZA

$ PIZZERIA ⊠226 Northwest Davis Street ✆503-222-9999
🖉www.oldtownpizza.com

The setting alone justifies a trip. Built in 1880, this landmark building with stained glass, wicker furniture, enough antiques to furnish a store and old root beer advertising signs make this two-level establishment a genuine period piece. On the menu, over two dozen pizza toppings from feta cheese to roasted garlic give you plenty of options. Focaccia, antipasti, lasagna and salads are also available.

OBI

$$ JAPANESE ⊠101 Northwest 2nd Avenue ✆503-226-3826

This is the place for sushi, *yakisoba*, shrimp tempura, salmon teriyaki and dozens of other Japanese specialties. The dark dining room has modest plastic tables and displays silk-screen art, watercolors and traditional costumes. No lunch Saturday. Closed Sunday.

SHOPPING

OREGON HISTORICAL SOCIETY MUSEUM STORE

⊠Corner of Southwest Broadway and Madison ✆503-306-5230 📠503-221-2035 🖉www.ohs.org, museumstore@ohs.org This museum store has an outstanding collection of local and regional history titles and a beautiful selection of North Coast Indian art. Featuring wooden masks and handcrafted jewelry, this admirable shop is definitely worth a look. Souvenir books, guides, children's literature and historical toys as well as regional gifts are all found in abundance.

RICH'S CIGAR STORE ⊠820 Southwest Alder Street ✆503-228-1700, 800-669-1527 🖉www.richscigar.com Classic newsstands are rare these days. Fortunately, Rich's, dating to the late 1800s, continues this grand tradition. Browse for your favorite magazine (Rich's carries over 2500 periodicals) or out-of-town newspaper in this beautiful wood-paneled shop.

POWELL'S CITY OF BOOKS ⊠1005 West Burnside Street ✆503-228-4651, 800-878-7323 🖉www.powells.com, help@powells.com Bigger than many libraries, Powell's is only one of Portland's many fine bookstores. What makes it unique is its size—it would be hard to dispute its claim of being the world's largest bookstore. With over a million new and used titles, this Goliath encourages customers to pick up a large map, indexed into hundreds of categories ranging from abortion to Zen. Somewhere in

between you're likely to find the title you want. Powell's also hosts guest readings by well-known authors.

2ND AVENUE RECORDS ✉400 Southwest 2nd Avenue ☎503-222-3783 Whether you're on the lookout for hard-to-find vintage vinyl or the newest indie releases, look no farther than this shop. Punk music is well-represented here, as is metal, hip hop, electronica, ska, reggae and rock. The sheer volume of merchandise can be daunting, but the knowledgeable sales staff can point you in the right direction. There's also a wide selection of T-shirts, buttons, patches and stickers.

ATTIC GALLERY ✉206 Southwest 1st Avenue ☎503-228-7830 ⌨www.attic gallery.com The Attic features paintings, sculpture, prints and ceramics by major Northwest artists. Closed Sunday.

PIONEER PLACE ✉700 Southwest 5th Avenue ☎503-228-5800 ⌨www.pioneer place.com This mall boasts 80 stores spread across a three-block area.

THE PORTLAND PENDLETON SHOP ✉900 Southwest 5th Avenue ☎503-242-0037, 800-760-4844 ⌨www.pendleton-usa.com One of the region's best-known apparel makers offers its line here. Skirts, shirts, slacks, jackets and blankets are sold at this popular store. While its reputation was built on woolens, it also sells high-quality apparel in silk, rayon and other fabrics.

ELIZABETH LEACH GALLERY ✉417 Northwest 9th Avenue ☎503-224-0521 ⌨www.elizabethleach.com This gallery presents an array of regional and national painters, sculptors, photographers and print makers. Closed Sunday and Monday.

PORTLAND SATURDAY MARKET ✉Southwest Naito Boulevard underneath the Burnside Bridge ☎503-222-6072 ☎503-222-0254 ⌨www.portlandsaturday market.com, info@saturdaymarket.org Nearly 300 artisans display handcrafted glass, jewelry, hats, clothing, furniture, rugs, music boxes, and folk and fine art at this open-air market. There's also live entertainment and a plethora of exotic food stands. Open Saturday and Sunday only. Closed January and February.

NIGHTLIFE

PORTLAND CENTER FOR THE PERFORMING ARTS ✉1111 Southwest Broadway ☎503-248-4335 ⌨www.pcpa.com The city's cultural hub is this performing arts center. Included are the Arlene Schnitzer Concert Hall and the Newmark and Winningstad theaters. The center (which houses the world's largest electronic organ) is home to the **Oregon Symphony Orchestra** (503-228-1353, 800-228-7343; www.or symphony.org), the **Keller Auditorium** (222 Southwest Clay Street; 503-248-4335) and **Portland Center Stage** (128 Northwest 11th Avenue; 503-445-3700; www.pcs.org).

ARTISTS REPERTORY THEATER ✉1516 Southwest Morrison Street ☎503-241-1278 (box office) ⌨www.artistsrep.org This is the place for off-Broadway productions with a focus on current contemporary playwrights and modern-day issues.

KELLER AUDITORIUM ⊠*222 Southwest Clay Street* ☎*503-248-4335* Both the **Oregon Ballet Theatre** (503-222-5538; www.obt.org) and **Portland Opera** (503-241-1802; www.portlandopera.org) perform here.

THE HEATHMAN LOBBY LOUNGE ⊠*1001 Southwest Broadway at Salmon Street* ☎*503-241-4100, 800-551-0011* ⌂*www.heathmanhotel.com* At the Heathman, musicians like Johnny Martin play jazz on the Steinway.

SILVERADO ⊠*318 Southwest 3rd Avenue* ☎*503-224-4493* ⌂*www.silverado pdx.com* With male strippers six nights a week, neon bar signs and a swinging dancefloor, this gay-friendly venue has plenty of action. In addition, you'll encounter deejay music, a long bar and dining room. Cover Friday and Saturday.

THE PILSNER ROOM ⊠*0309 Southwest Montgomery Street* ☎*503-220-1865* An upscale bar attached to a microbrewery, this place serves fish-and-chips, hamburgers and the like.

SCANDAL'S RESTAURANT AND LOUNGE ⊠*1125 Southwest Stark Street* ☎*503-227-5887* ⌂*www.scandalspdx.com* Billiards, darts and beer on tap create a relaxed atmosphere at Scandal's, which has a loyal gay following.

DARCELLE XV ⊠*208 Northwest 3rd Avenue* ☎*503-222-5338* ⌂*www.darcelle xv.com* Female impersonators perform Wednesday through Saturday nights at this small theater where dinner is available by reservation. Closed Sunday and Monday. Cover.

EMBERS ON THE AVENUE ⊠*110 Northwest Broadway* ☎*503-222-3082* ⌂*www.emberspdx.net* This gay-friendly venue features drag shows Wednesday through Saturday. The rear of this brick building houses Portland's largest dancefloor, hosting a mixed crowd of gay and straight partygoers. With neon-lit walls, two bars and deejay music, this room is always jumping. Cover Friday and Saturday.

JIMMY MAK'S BAR & GRILL ⊠*221 Northwest 10th Avenue* ☎*503-295-6542* ⌂*www.jimmymaks.com* Regarded as one of the top places in the world for jazz music, Jimmy Mak's features soulful live acts almost every night. Intimate and often crowded, you can ensure a comfortable seat by arriving early for dinner. A basement lounge with two pool tables and a full bar provides a casual alternative to the main stage. Closed Sunday.

PORTLAND EAST

Just across the Willamette from the frenzied downtown core are some of Portland's most inviting neighborhoods. The city planners have emphasized good public transportation throughout the entire metropolitan area, keeping the neighborhoods east of the river unified with the downtown core. But only here can you glimpse Portland's lower-key charms: a shopping area devoted exclusively to antiques, a city park featuring an extinct volcano and a religious retreat doubling as a peaceful garden. Portland East is also home to a rare heirloom—a classic old-time amusement park.

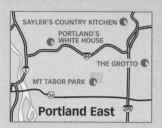

SAYLER'S COUNTRY KITCHEN

PAGE 341

As American as apple pie: Down the 72-ounce steak with all its side dishes and your dinner's free!

PORTLAND'S WHITE HOUSE

PAGE 339

Rooms with four-poster beds, clawfoot tubs and oak floors in a stunning estate fit for the first family

THE GROTTO

PAGE 339

Peaceful ponds, tranquil shrines and expansive mountain views—a Catholic sanctuary with a touch of Zen

MT. TABOR PARK

PAGE 343

Extensive, forested trails winding up an extinct volcano for smashing views of Portland's skyline

This section of Portland also includes such suburbs as Oregon City and Milwaukie, the former of which once welcomed settlers who had made the arduous trek overland on the Oregon Trail. Today, Portland East is a network of streets and parks designed, like much of Portland, for maximum use by its residents.

SIGHTS

OREGON CONVENTION CENTER ✉777 Northeast Martin Luther King Jr. Boulevard ☎503-235-7575, 800-791-2250 ≋503-235-7417 ✑www.oregoncc.org, ask@oregoncc.org Cross the Willamette via MAX Light Rail and disembark at this beautiful plaza, landscaped with terraced planters. Stroll over for a look at the 18-acre campus of the center crowned by a matching pair of glass-and-steel spires soaring 250 feet above the hall. The center's interior contains art, dragon boats, a bronze pendulum and inspirational quotes about the state. Everywhere you go, even in the restrooms, you'll find talented artists and craftspeople have left their decorative touch.

OREGON MUSEUM OF SCIENCE AND INDUSTRY (OMSI) ✉1945 Southeast Water Avenue ☎503-797-4000, 800-955-6674 ✑www.omsi.edu A mile south of the convention center, this museum is a 220,000-square-foot science education center. Four exhibition halls offer displays on the physical, earth, life and information sciences, while another has traveling exhibits. In addition, you'll find an OMNIMAX theater and the Harry C. Kendall Planetarium presenting astronomy and laser light shows (additional admission). Special exhibits focus on biotechnology,

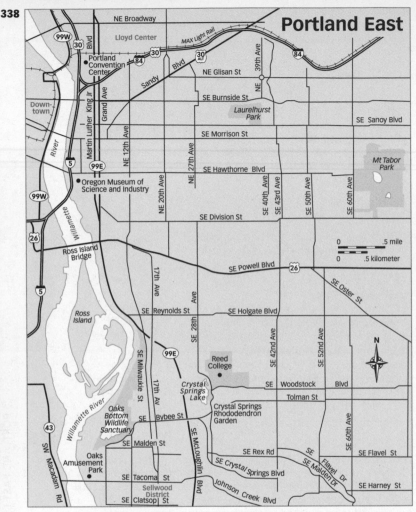

Portland East

computers, engineering for kids, communications and chemistry. Closed Monday (unless it's a Portland public schools holiday). Admission.

HAWTHORNE BOULEVARD AND SELLWOOD   To the south of OMSI are two popular Portland shopping districts. Hawthorne Boulevard from 30th to 40th avenues has become one of the city's more intriguing commercial districts. A great place to browse, shop and eat, this district is known for its used bookstores and offbeat boutiques. Another popular neighborhood is Sellwood, an antique center extending along 13th Avenue from Clatsop to Malden streets.

OAKS AMUSEMENT PARK   ✉ *7805 Southeast Oaks Park Way, east end of the Sellwood Bridge* 📞 *503-233-5777* 📠 *503-236-9143* 🖅 *www.oakspark.com* While cities across the land have scrapped these period pieces, Portland has held on to this old school–style amusement park, located just west of the Sellwood district. In addition to vintage thrill rides, you can enjoy roller skating to the strains of the last Wurlitzer organ playing at a rink in the United States. This pretty park is next to the **Oaks Bottom Wildlife Sanctuary**, a major Portland marsh habitat. Rides are closed mid-October to mid-March.

REED COLLEGE ✉3203 Southeast Woodstock Boulevard ☎503-771-1112 ☏503-777-7769 ✐www.reed.edu One of the nation's most progressive liberal arts institutions, this college has a wooded, 98-acre campus cloaked in ivy. Reed's gothic buildings and old dorms are close to Crystal Springs Rhododendron Garden at 28th Avenue and Woodstock Boulevard (see "Parks" below for more information). Pick up a visitors guide in Eliot Hall or the Greywood Community Service Building.

THE GROTTO _____ **h**idden

✉8840 Northeast Skidmore Street (parking at Northeast 85th Avenue and Sandy Boulevard) ☎503-254-7371 ☏503-254-7948 ✐www.thegrotto.org, gifts@thegrotto.org No visit to the city's east side is complete without a stop here. Near the Portland airport, this 62-acre Catholic sanctuary and garden is a peaceful refuge that seems to have as much in common with a Zen retreat as it does with the Vatican. Beautiful ponds and shrines, paths leading through flower gardens and expansive views of the mountains and the Columbia River make The Grotto a local favorite. In December, the grounds are illuminated by 200,000 lights during the Festival of Lights. Choral performances, a petting zoo and refreshments round out the festival experience. Admission for festival

LODGING

THE LION AND THE ROSE VICTORIAN BED AND BREAKFAST _____ **h**idden

$$–$$$ 6 ROOMS ✉1810 Northeast 15th Avenue ☎503-287-9245, 800-955-1647 ☏503-287-9247 ✐www.lionrose.com, innkeeper@lionrose.com In northeast Portland's Irvington District, this historical Queen Anne–style mansion has rooms furnished in period antiques. The decor is warm with rich shades of plum and ivy green, and natural light makes the rooms bright and airy. Amenities range from jacuzzi and clawfoot tubs to wrought-iron and four-poster beds. Enjoy tea in the outdoor gazebo and English gardens.

PORTLAND'S WHITE HOUSE _____ **h**idden

$$–$$$ 8 ROOMS ✉1914 Northeast 22nd Avenue ☎503-287-7131, 800-272-7131 ☏503-249-1641 ✐www.portlandswhitehouse.com, web@portlandswhitehouse.com Hail to the chief! Portland's White House strongly resembles the other White House in Washington, D.C. The stately Greek

columns, circular driveway and crystal chandeliers would all make the first family feel right at home. The difference here is that you don't have to stand in line for a tour, and there are no Secret Service agents to hustle you along. Originally built as a lumber baron's summer home, this White House features hand-painted murals of garden scenes and oak-inlaid floors. Canopy and four-poster beds, clawfoot tubs and leaded glass adorn the eight rooms. Three additional rooms in an adjacent carriage house have feather beds and stained glass. The price of a room includes a full gourmet breakfast.

HOSTELLING INTERNATIONAL—PORTLAND HAWTHORNE
$ 6 UNITS   ✉3031 Southeast Hawthorne Boulevard   ✆503-236-3380, 866-447-3031   ☏503-236-7940   ✎www.portlandhostel.org, hip@portlandhostel.org

In the Hawthorne neighborhood, this hostel offers co-ed as well as single-sex dorm accommodations, a family room and a couples room. This older home also has a self-serve kitchen and all-you-can-eat pancakes in the morning. Internet kiosks and free internet connections for laptops are available. Check-in begins at noon. Quiet time starts at 10 p.m. Complimentary bread and pastries are included. Reservations recommended.

DINING

DINGO'S MEXICAN GRILL _____ h idden
$ MEXICAN   ✉4612 Southeast Hawthorne Boulevard   ✆503-233-3996   ☏503-233-0778   ✎www.dingosonline.com

Inventive Mexican food and an extensive cocktail menu distinguish Dingo's from your run-of-the-mill burrito place. Entrées include lime chicken enchiladas, rock shrimp tacos and ahi burritos. Happy hour (3 p.m. to 6 p.m.) features $3-a-plate specials. Thursday is Girl's Night Out, popular with local lesbians.

TABOR HILL CAFÉ
$ AMERICAN   ✉3766 Southeast Hawthorne Boulevard   ✆503-230-1231

One of Portland's better breakfasts is found at this café in the Hawthorne neighborhood. The small, red-brick establishment with eclectic decor features modern art, gray carpet and red tables. The seasonal fruit pancake (that's singular, not plural) is large enough to blanket your entire plate. Other choices are chicken omelettes and a fresh fruit cup. Lunch specialties include avocado-and-bacon sandwich, burgers, marinated chicken breast and blackened-snapper salad. They serve breakfast, lunch and dinner, so there's plenty to choose from.

BREAD AND INK CAFÉ
$$ AMERICAN   ✉3610 Southeast Hawthorne Boulevard   ✆503-239-4756   ✎www.breadandinkcafe.com

It's not easy to find a hearty Sunday brunch these days, but we did it here. The coffee is strong, the lox is fresh and the children are kept content with crayons and paper. In addition to bagels and cream cheese, challah and a variety of omelettes, you'll enjoy the family-style atmosphere. Set in an elegant commercial building adorned with terra cotta, this weekly happening is a Portland original. The restaurant is also famous for its burgers and uses as many local ingredients and natural meats as possible. Breakfast, lunch and dinner. Closed Wednesday.

SAYLER'S COUNTRY KITCHEN _____ h idden

$$ STEAKHOUSE ✉10519 Southeast Stark Street ☎503-252-4171
☎503-257-0088 ✐www.saylers.com

Yes, there really is such a thing as a free dinner. Sayler's has been offering it since 1946. The only catch is that you have to eat the 72-ounce top sirloin steak, along with a salad, french bread, ten fries or a baked potato, two carrot sticks, two celery sticks, two olives, a beverage and a scoop of ice cream—within one hour, and they'll pick up the tab. More than 500 customers have won the bet over the years. If you're not quite that hungry, other beef entrees range from a six-ounce filet mignon to a 40-ounce porterhouse. There's also an array of seafood options, including Dungeness crab Louie, an Oregon Bay shrimp cocktail and twin lobster tails.

PAPA HAYDN

$$ AMERICAN/FRENCH ✉5829 Southeast Milwaukie Avenue ☎503-232-9440
☎503-236-5815 ✐www.papahaydn.com, east@papahaydn.com

Located in the Sellwood district known for its antique stores, this is a cozy restaurant where watercolors grace the lemon-colored walls and walnut furniture accommodates guests who don't come to count calories. Weekend brunch features french toast brioche rolled in hazelnuts or an aged white cheddar omelette. Dinner entrées include woodgrilled steak with bleu cheese butter and organic chicken with bacon and bucatini pasta. A full bar, an extensive wine list and espresso drinks are found here along with one of the longest dessert menus in the Pacific Northwest.

SHOPPING

OREGON MOUNTAIN COMMUNITY ✉2975 Northeast Sandy Boulevard ☎503-227-1038, 800-538-3604 ✐www.e-omc.com This is the ultimate shop for recreational equipment and supplies. In addition to a full line of outdoor wear, there's skiing, backpacking and climbing gear.

ARTICHOKE MUSIC ✉3130 Southeast Hawthorne Boulevard ☎503-232-8845 ☎503-232-3476 ✐www.artichokemusic.com Along Hawthorne Boulevard are many small, independent shops with interesting selections. Stop by Artichoke for acoustic and folk instruments, guitar sheet music and lesson books. On a weekend you can catch live acoustic music or join the song circle; on Fridays check out the highly acclaimed variety revue. Closed Monday.

MURDER BY THE BOOK ✉3210 Southeast Hawthorne Boulevard ☎503-232-9995 ☎503-232-2554 ✐www.mbtb.com, books@mbtb.com Death can be proud here. Mystery addicts will get their fix here and also become acquainted with many well-known Northwest authors. In addition to new and used books, you can buy accessories, games and puzzles.

MOVIE MADNESS & MIKE'S MUSEUM OF MOTION PICTURE HISTORY

✉ *4320 Southeast Belmont* ☎ *503-234-4363* ✐ *www.moviemadnessvideo.com* This independent video rental shop boasts one of the most extensive libraries of classic, alternative and art house films anywhere, but the reason for out-of-town film buffs to pay it a visit is the movie memorabilia museum amassed by owner Mike Clark, a former Hollywood film editor. His collection of more than 100 screen artifacts includes a dress worn by Diane Keaton in *Godfather II*, the runaway baby carriage from *The Untouchables* and the knife from Hitchcock's original *Psycho*.

NIGHTLIFE

BAGHDAD THEATER AND PUB ✉ *3702 Southeast Hawthorne Boulevard* ☎ *503-236-9234, 503-249-7474 (movie line)* ✐ *www.mcmenamins.com, baghdad@mcmenamins.com* This Moorish-style theater has fairy-tale decor with painted walls and a fountain in the lobby. Every other row of theater seating has been removed to accommodate tables where patrons can order food and drinks and enjoy second-run films. Customers under 21 years of age are welcome for the Saturday and Sunday matinees only when accompanied by a parent.

DO JUMP! EXTREMELY PHYSICAL THEATER ✉ *1515 Southeast 37th Avenue* ☎ *503-231-1232* ☏ *503-231-2937* ✐ *www.dojump.org, dojump@dojump.org* The **Echo Theater** is the home of this "extremely physical" performance troupe. Shows include acrobatic and trapeze acts. Visiting dance troupes also use the theater's stage.

CHAMBER MUSIC NORTHWEST ☎ *503-223-3202 (general), 503-294-6400 (tickets)* ☏ *503-294-1690* ✐ *www.cmnw.org, info@cmnw.org* One of the city's finest classical programs is this chamber ensemble. Nationally known groups perform year-round in the beautiful settings at Kaul Auditorium at Reed College, with a five-week festival in June and July.

EGYPTIAN CLUB ✉ *3701 Southeast Division Street* ☎ *503-236-8689* ✐ *www.eroompdx.com, egybobbi@aol.com* This 9000-square-foot club, located in a former milk plant, features three different rooms. There's a dancefloor in the Tomb and a retro bar room with pool tables and video games. A third bar, the Room, features open-mic night and karaoke. Every Monday and Wednesday nights there are poker tournaments in the Tomb. The crowd is primarily lesbian. Cover Friday and Saturday.

WILLAMETTE WEEK ✐ *www.wweek.com* For a listing of current shows and popular venues in the area, pick up a copy of this free alternative newspaper available at groceries and newsstands.

KELLEY POINT PARK

✉ *Located in northernmost Portland at the intersection of Lomband Street and North Marine Drive* ☎ *503-823-7529, V/TDD 503-823-2223* ☒ *503-823-6007*

🚶 🚤 At the confluence of the Willamette and Columbia rivers, this forested site is popular for biking and hiking. The park, largely undeveloped, is busy during the summer months but wide open the rest of the year. There are picnic tables and restrooms.

PENINSULA PARK

✉ *North Albina Street and Portland Boulevard* ☎ *503-823-7529* ☒ *503-823-6007*

🌹 This 16-acre park features beautiful sunken rose gardens highlighted with fountains and a charming gazebo. Extensive recreational facilities, a formal rose garden and a small pond make Peninsula popular with families. Facilities include picnic tables, a basketball court, horseshoe pits, a pool, a soccer field, tennis courts and restrooms.

POWELL BUTTE NATURE PARK

✉ *16160 Southeast Powell Boulevard at Northeast 162nd Avenue* ☎ *503-823-7529* ☒ *503 823 6007*

🚶 🚴 🐎 This rustic, 600-acre park centers around a 630-foot-high volcanic mound that offers great views of the city and the Cascades. If you can, circle this volcanic butte via a two-mile loop route at day's end and take advantage of the sunset. Facilities are limited to restrooms and picnic tables.

LAURELHURST PARK

✉ *Southeast 39th Avenue and Stark Street* ☎ *503-823-7529* ☒ *503-823-6007*

Bordered by rhododendron, a pretty lake is the heart of this 27-acre park in a historic residential district. Along the way you're likely to spot geese, ducks, swans and turtles. Forested with fir and oak, the park also features glens, gardens and contemporary sculpture. You'll find restrooms, picnic tables, a playground, a soccer field and tennis, volleyball and basketball courts.

MT. TABOR PARK

✉ *Southeast Salmon Street and 60th Avenue* ☎ *503-823-7529* ☒ *503-823-6007*

🚶 🚴 One of two extinct volcanoes within the limits of an American city, Mt. Tabor was discovered during excavations in 1912. While the cinder cone is the park's star attraction, it also offers an extensive network of trails for hiking and jogging. This forested setting affords smashing views of the city. There are picnic tables, restrooms, horseshoe pits, a playground, tennis courts, basketball courts, a volleyball court and an amphitheater.

344

LEACH BOTANICAL GARDEN

✉ *6704 Southeast 122nd Avenue*   ✆ *503-823-9503*   🖷 *503-823-9504*
🖱 *www.leachgarden.org, info@leachgarden.org*

These 15 acres are home to over 2000 flowers and plants, including many native species. Johnson Creek meanders through the original Leach Property. You can explore the grounds of this one-time estate on your own or via a guided tour. You'll find a manor house, stone cabin and carriage house, a library, a gift shop and plant table, restrooms and self-guiding brochures. Closed Monday.

CRYSTAL SPRINGS
RHODODENDRON GARDEN

✉ *6015 Southeast 28th Avenue north of Woodstock Boulevard*
✆ *503-771-8386*

Boasting almost ten acres of flora and fauna, this park is at its best in April and May. The colorful panorama of more than 2000 rhododendron and azalea is enhanced by three waterfalls and two bridges spanning a creek that flows into Crystal Springs Lake. Ducks and other waterfowl are found year-round at this refuge near Reed College. Call ahead to arrange a guided tour. There are restrooms. Admission during the summer months.

CLACKAMETTE PARK

✉ *Take Exit 9 from Route 205 toward Oregon City and Gladstone. Go west on Clackamette two-tenths of a mile.*   ✆ *503-496-1201*   🖷 *503-656-7488*

🚤 A haven for ducks and geese, Clackamette's 22 acres border the Willamette River in the Oregon City area. It's also a prime spot to see blue herons nesting on Goat Island. Restrooms are available.

🅰 There are 35 RV hookup sites; $18 to $22 per night, ten-day maximum stay. No reservations taken.

PORTLAND WEST

From vineyards to Japanese gardens, Portland's west side has many of the city's best parks, major museums and wildlife preserves. Charming Victorians line many streets and the city's fabled Pittock Mansion reminds visitors of Portland's glamorous past. Washington Park, the city's beloved green oasis, presides over Portland West in much the same way that Central Park does in New York. Most of the other worthwhile attractions here also involve the outdoors: just half an hour from downtown, you can enjoy wilderness areas or cycle along placid sloughs, in addition to other delights.

Heading south from downtown along the western side of the Willamette, you'll pass residential 'burbs like Tigard and Beaverton before encountering the vineyards that comprise Oregon's wine country. The

3D CENTER OF ART AND PHOTOGRAPHY

PAGE 348

Victorian stereopticons, 1950s View-Masters and modern 3D movies at a one-of-a-kind museum

MIO SUSHI

PAGE 352

Local favorite with first-rate maki rolls like the Oregon, with avocado, crab, asparagus and salmon

JAPANESE GARDEN SOCIETY OF OREGON

PAGE 346

Tranquil paths winding through five gardens amid waterfalls, koi ponds and bridges

original settlers believed the Willamette Valley to have some of the best soil in the world, and the area just beyond the city limits does maintain a rural flavor. But Portland's populace has also worked hard not to overdevelop all of its own land, and this section of the city definitely benefits as a result. Still, the area closest to downtown does maintain a cosmopolitan air.

SIGHTS

NOB HILL We begin our tour in this neighborhood, one of the trendiest areas in Portland. The district was given its name by a 19th-century San Franciscan who saw a similarity to his old neighborhood. At the **Visitor Information Center** downtown (Pioneer Courthouse Square, 701 Southwest 6th Avenue; 503-275-8355, 877-678-5263), you can pick up the walking guide to this district focused around Northwest 23rd Avenue, north of Burnside Street. Home of many of the city's finest restaurants, bookstores and antique and art shops, Nob Hill also has noteworthy early-20th-century Victorian and Georgian homes, as well as churches and commercial buildings. Among them are the **Charles F. Adams House** (2363 Northwest Flanders Street) and the **Ayer-Shea House** (1809 Northwest Johnson Street).

WASHINGTON PARK ✉Southwest Park Place, two blocks west of Vista Avenue ☎503-823-7529 ☎503-823-6007 The treelined Nob Hill district is also convenient to this 130-acre refuge created by the Olmsted brothers, from the family of landscape architects who gave the world Central Park in New York and Golden Gate Park in San Francisco. Home to several gardens and the zoo, this park is one of Portland's most worthy destinations.

INTERNATIONAL ROSE TEST GARDEN

✉ *400 Southwest Kingston Avenue* ☎ *503-823-3636 (direct), 503-823-3635 (Washington Park information)* ☎ *503-823-1667* ◈ *www.rosegardenstore.org* Consisting of three terraces, this four-and-a-half-acre gem has over 8700 bushes, enough to make this park a true mecca for rose aficionados worldwide. When the roses are in bloom (from late June to early September) it's hard to find a better vantage point for the city. In addition to the test area, visitors are welcome to see the Shakespearean Garden and Gold Medal Award Garden.

JAPANESE GARDEN SOCIETY OF OREGON

✉ *611 Southwest Kingston Avenue* ☎ *503-223-1321* ☎ *503-223-8303* ◈ *www. japanesegarden.com* Directly west of the Rose Garden is this Japanese garden. Five traditional gardens spread across five and a half acres make this tranquil spot a great place for a quiet walk. The Flat Garden is a sea of raked sand. The Sand and Stone Garden is abstract and inspired by Zen Buddhism. The Tea Garden contains a Japanese teahouse, while the Natural Garden is filled with foliage growing in its natural state. Don't miss the Strolling Pond Garden with its Heavenly Falls, koi pools and beautiful moon bridge. There's also a pavilion overlooking Mt. Hood, Oregon's answer to Mt. Fuji. Admission.

OREGON ZOO ✉ *4001 Southwest Canyon Road* ☎ *503-226-1561* ◈ *www.oregon zoo.org* From the Japanese Garden, follow Kingston Avenue until you see signs leading to this 64-acre zoo. Also accessible by a steam train from the Japanese and International Rose Test gardens during the summer months, the zoo features an African rainforest as well as a savannah roamed by giraffes, zebras, rhinos, lions and hippos. Stellar Cove is a marine environment with sea lions, sea otters, a kelp forest and a coastal tide pool display. Other points of interest are the zoo's Humboldt penguins, Arctic polar bears and orangutans. The staff is proud of the fact that it has one of the world's most successful Asian elephant–breeding programs. Don't miss the small Lilah Callen Holden Elephant Museum, hidden behind the elephant enclosure, where you'll learn about the centuries-old working relationships and spiritual connections between humans and elephants. You'll also find an extensive collection of Pacific Northwest animals, including beavers and otters. Admission.

PORTLAND CHILDREN'S MUSEUM ✉ *4015 Southwest Canyon Road* ☎ *503-223-6500* ☎ *503-223-6600* ◈ *www.portlandcm.org* This museum is a must for families with small children. Fun-filled exhibits here include a pint-sized grocery complete with a bar-code scanner and a medical center where kids can "operate" on parents and friends. Closed Monday from September through February. Admission.

WORLD FORESTRY DISCOVERY MUSEUM ✉ *4033 Southwest Canyon Road* ☎ *503-228-1367* ☎ *503-228-4608* ◈ *www.worldforestry.org, mail@world*

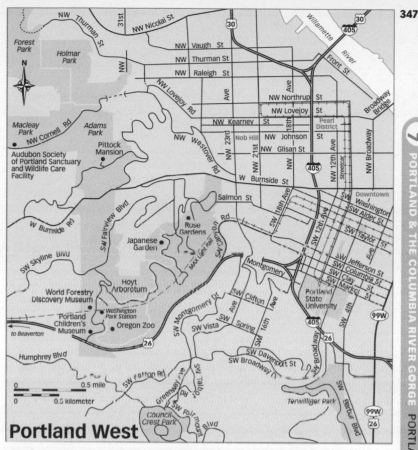

Portland West

forestry.org Here's your chance to learn about tree nomenclature, logging history and subterranean forest life. The center has a pro-logging slant but does offer a useful perspective on the state's lumber industry. Admission.

HOYT ARBORETUM ✉*4000 Southwest Fairview Boulevard* ☎*503-865-8733* ✆*503-823-4213* ✑*www.hoytarboretum.org, info@hoytarboretum.org* One way to tell the trees from the forest is to visit this 185-acre arboretum. You'll have a chance to see over 1100 varieties of shrubs and trees, including one of the nation's largest collection of conifers.

PITTOCK MANSION ✉*3229 Northwest Pittock Drive* ☎*503-823-3623* ✆*503-823-3619* ✑*www.pittockmansion.com, emarcum@pittockmansion.org* North of Washington Park is this favorite Oregon house. Built by *Oregonian* publisher Henry Pittock and his wife Georgiana, this 16,000-square-foot, château-style residence features an Edwardian dining room, French Renaissance drawing room, Turkish smoking room and Jacobean library. Chandeliers, Italian marquetry, friezes on the doorways, a carved-stone fireplace and bronze grillwork make this 1914 home a treasure. The finest craftspeople of the day used native Northwest materials to make this house Portland's early-20th-century masterpiece. The 46-acre estate, landscaped with roses, azaleas, rhododendrons and cherry trees, has a great view of the city and the mountains. Closed in January. Admission.

3D CENTER OF ART AND PHOTOGRAPHY

 hidden

✉ *1928 Northwest Lovejoy Street* ✆ *503-227-6667* ✑ *www.3dcenter.us* This one-of-a-kind storefront gallery and museum contains more than a century's worth of three-dimensional visual arts, from Victorian-era stereopticons and 1950s View Masters to holograms, 3-D movies, lenticular prints and other optical-illusion technologies. In addition, works by a different 3-D artist are shown for sale each month.

AUDUBON SOCIETY OF PORTLAND SANCTUARY AND WILDLIFE CARE CENTER ✉ *5151 Northwest Cornell Road* ✆ *503-292-6855*
✆ *503-292-1021* ✑ *www.audubonportland.org, general@audubonportland.org* A 150-acre facility this refuge helps rehabilitate over 3500 injured native animals and birds each year. Visitors can watch the staff handle animals through an observation window and can also view up close a few of the center's permanent creatures: a red-tailed hawk, a peregrine falcon and a northern spotted owl. Naturalist guides often lead tours through the flora and fauna of the sanctuary, and miles of hiking trails here link up with Forest Park.

FOREST PARK ✉ *Northwest 29th Avenue and Upshur Street to Newberry Road*
✆ *503-797-1850* To experience one of the country's biggest wilderness parks, continue on Skyline Boulevard along the Tualatin Mountains. Overlooking the Willamette River, this park extends west for eight miles. If you turn right at Germantown Road and head north, you can drive through the park's idyllic woodlands.

HOWELL TERRITORY PARK ✉ *13901 Northwest Howell Park Road* ✆ *503-797-1850* From Forest Park, continue west to the Sauvie Island Bridge. Cross the bridge and proceed one mile to this bucolic, 120-acre public park with the historical James F. Bybee House. On the grounds of the homestead is the **Agricultural Museum** displaying pioneer equipment, shops and hands-on exhibits. In addition you'll want to explore the **Pioneer Orchard**, containing over 120 varieties of apple trees, as well as pears and plums.

OAK KNOLL WINERY ✉ *29700 Southwest Burkhalter Road, Hillsboro* ✆ *503-648-8198, 800-625-5665* ✆ *503-648-3377* ✑ *www.oakknollwinery.com, info@oakknoll winery.com* Washington County west of Portland has a number of excellent wineries. This one, known for pinot noir and pinot gris, produces more than a dozen wines. The small vineyard has a white-tiled tasting room with a country feel and a charming picnic area.

WILLAMETTE SHORE TROLLEY ✉311 North State Street, Lake Oswego
📞503-697-7436 💻www.oerhs.org/wst Traveling south, this trolley offers a
90-minute, 12-mile roundtrip scenic tour along the Willamette River
that takes you through two parks, stately mansions and a tunnel. Your
trip aboard a vintage trolley runs along a section of the Jefferson Street
Line built in the late 19th century.

OREGON CITY Following the Willamette River south of Mary S.
Young Park, you'll come to this city, which still looks the way it did during the rush of Western expansion in the mid-1800s. Just a half-hour
south of Portland, it was built along the 40-foot-high Willamette River
waterfalls, and it is one of the best places in the Pacific Northwest to understand and appreciate manifest destiny. For this was the destination
that launched the migration of over 300,000 Americans to a blank slate
known as the promised land.

WILLAMETTE FALLS The center of human endeavor for more
than 10,000 years, this was an important place long before the first
white immigrants arrived. But once they did show up, things moved
quickly. In 1010, just five years after the British took control of the
Northwest region from the Astorians, the Americans and British agreed
to jointly occupy Oregon Country. In 1829, Dr. John McLoughlin, the
shrewd operator of the Hudson's Bay Company base at Fort Vancouver, built three homes at the Willamette Falls. Although the American
Indians responded by burning these buildings, McLoughlin forged
ahead with a new sawmill and flour mill.

American settlers began trickling in, and by 1841 the first wagon trains
started to arrive. Pouring in by boat and by land, the pioneers soon
spread across the Willamette Valley in search of farmsteads. Thankfully,
you don't have to retrace the entire trail to learn of this riveting history.
Just head to Oregon City's museums, homes, farms and cemeteries.

**END OF THE OREGON TRAIL INTERPRETIVE CENTER AND
HISTORIC SITE** ✉1726 Washington Street, Oregon City 📞503-657-9336
📞503-557-8590 💻www.endoftheoregontrail.org The place to begin your visit
is at this interpretive center. The center offers guided shows featuring
living history presentations, a multimedia presentation, a hands-on
area and exhibits displaying notable artifacts, photographs and maps.
You'll gain a well-rounded perspective on immigrant history. You can
also pick up helpful walking and driving tour guides to the community.
Closed Sunday and Monday, except in summer. Admission.

MCLOUGHLIN HOUSE ✉713 Center Street, Oregon City 📞503-656-5146
💻www.mcloughlinhouse.org Among the major Oregon City highlights is
this historical homestead, where the Hudson's Bay Company leader
and "Father of Oregon" retired. Although his employer was British,
John McLoughlin generously aided the new settlers and helped lay the
groundwork for Americanization. Regular 45-minute tours show off
this 1846 home, which was a social hub in pioneer days. Highlights include a Chilkat Indian ceremonial robe, banjo-shaped clock, Hudson's
Bay Company sideboard and lots of original McLoughlin family and

Fort Vancouver furnishings. The home is closed on Monday and Tuesday and during the month of January. Incidentally, you can learn the rest of the McLoughlin story by visiting Fort Vancouver across the Columbia River from Portland.

FRANCES ERMATINGER HOUSE ✉ *6th and John Adams streets, Oregon City* Step into this Federal-style residence showcasing antiques and memorabilia for another peek into this area's past. Admission.

STEVENS-CRAWFORD HERITAGE HOUSE ✉ *603 6th Street, Oregon City* ✆ *503-655-2866* A historically preserved turn-of-the-20th-century site, this house has a small collection of American Indian artifacts. Closed Sunday through Tuesday, and the month of January. Call ahead for hours. Admission.

ROSE FARM MUSEUM ✉ *536 Holmes Lane, Oregon City* ✆ *503-656-5146* Well worth your time is this museum (also known as the William Holmes House), one of the state's oldest residences. The first territorial governor was inaugurated at this home surrounded by rose plantings in 1849. A two-tiered piazza and second-story ballroom are highlights of this restored residence, now on the National Register of Historic Places. Open Saturday from early July to early September and by appointment the rest of the year. Admission.

CLACKAMAS COUNTY HISTORICAL SOCIETY MUSEUM OF THE OREGON TERRITORY ✉ *211 Tumwater Drive, Oregon City* ✆ *503-655-5574* 🖥 *503-655-0035* 🌐 *www.historicoregoncity.org* This museum explores the history of Clackamas County with exhibits covering geology, traders and trappers, immigration, government and religion. Closed Sunday and Monday. Admission.

OREGON CITY MUNICIPAL ELEVATOR ✉ *300 7th Street (at Main Street), Oregon City* ✆ *503-657-0891* Founded in 1916, this ride was designed to make it easy for residents to journey from the riverfront to the upper part of town. One of only four municipal elevators in the world, the 90-foot ride is a great way to enjoy views of Willamette Falls, particularly at sunset.

LODGING

PARK LANE SUITES _____ **h**idden

$$$$ 44 UNITS ✉ *809 Southwest King Avenue* ✆ *503-226-6288, 800-532-9543* 🖥 *503-274-0038* 🌐 *www.parklanesuites.com, info@parklanesuites.com* Within walking distance of the popular shops and restaurants in the Nob Hill district, this five-story motel building is tucked into a residential neighborhood. Nondescript from the outside, the inn has attractive carpeted suites with cherry wood furniture, fully equipped kitchenettes and custom Park Lane beds. The upper-story rooms have great views of downtown Portland, Mt. Hood and Mt. St. Helens.

HERON HAUS

$$–$$$ 4 ROOMS ✉2545 Northwest Westover Road ✆503-274-1846
✆503-248-4055 ✑www.heronhaus.com, pam@heronhaus.com

After a busy afternoon perusing Nob Hill's trendy boutiques, I doubly appreciate the quiet, secluded garden here. What's more, this beautifully renovated English Tudor provides pleasant views of the city, the Cascades, Mt. Hood and Mt. St. Helens. The blend of country casual and contemporary furniture, oak-parquet flooring, mahogany library, sun room and patio make the establishment a delight. Fireplaces, private baths and quilts add to the comfort of the six spacious rooms. A homemade breakfast served every morning includes delicious french toast and fresh fruit.

SHILO INN HOTEL

$$ 142 ROOMS ✉9900 Southwest Canyon Road, Beaverton ✆503-297-2551,
800-222-2244 ✆503-297-7708 ✑www.shiloinns.com

Just south of Portland in Beaverton, the Shilo is a good choice for families and long-stay visitors. Each of the resort's rooms features a queen- or king-sized bed, private bath and free high-speed internet access. There's an on-site sports bar, 24-hour fitness center, seasonal outdoor pool, picture-perfect gazebo, as well as a pond with geyser fountains in the courtyard.

BEST WESTERN RIVERSHORE HOTEL

$$ 114 ROOMS ✉1900 Clackamette Drive, Oregon City ✆503-655-7141,
800-443-7777 ✆503-655-1927 ✑www.rivershorehotel.com, info@rivershorehotel.com

In Oregon City, south of Portland and on the banks of the Willamette, this Best Western is pretty much the only remaining lodging option. Each of the rooms has a balcony with a view and a queen- or king-sized bed—clean and comfortable, but nothing to write home about. There is, however, an indoor spa and an outdoor heated pool.

DINING

BRAZIL GRILL

$$$$ BRAZILIAN ✉1201 Southwest 12th Avenue ✆503-222-0002
✑www.brazilgrillrestaurant.com

When you're dining at this festive grill, you won't be ordering off a menu. Instead you will be greeted by a "gaucho" (in this case, a roaming server) who will handcarve and present bacon-wrapped chicken, parmesan spareribs, chili-lime pork loin and other delectably carniverous entrées. While meat is their mainstay, it's the roasted cinnamon pineapple that keeps the locals coming back. Along with your prix fixe meal comes an all-you-can-eat salad bar. Dinner only.

BLUEHOUR

$$$$ CONTINENTAL/MEDITERRANEAN ✉250 Northwest 13th Avenue
✆503-226-3394 ✆503-221-3005 ✑www.bluehouronline.com, info@bluehouronline.com

Inventive Continental/Mediterranean cuisine and a chic, postmodern setting draw a well-dressed crowd to this restaurant. Suspended draperies divide the converted warehouse space (with 20-foot floor-to-ceiling windows) into more intimate spaces. Savory starters may include salmon *tartare* and bacon-wrapped scallops; main dishes might feature crispy duck confit with flageolet beans or roasted suckling pig with polenta. Finish the meal off on a sweet note with chocolate truffle cake. Diners without reservations can drop by the casual café/bar. Sunday brunch.

WILDWOOD RESTAURANT AND BAR

$$$ PACIFIC NORTHWEST ✉1221 Northwest 21st Street ☎503-248-9663 🖷503-222-5153 ⬧www.wildwoodrestaurant.com, wildwood@wildwoodrestaurant.com
Wildwood draws from local Northwest ingredients to create a distinctive Oregon flavor just as it displays regional artwork to enhance its decor. You'll find such dishes as beet, endive, pistachio and feta salad; pan-roasted Muscovy duck confit with roasted parsnips, grilled persimmons, satsuma mandarins and toasted pistachios. The menu changes weekly to accommodate seasonal produce; a chalkboard details specialty cocktail drinks. No lunch on Sunday.

MIO SUSHI _____ ⓗidden

$-$$ SUSHI/JAPANESE ✉2271 Northwest Johnson Street ☎503-221-1469 🖷503-827-4932 ⬧www.miosushi.com, contact@miosushi.com
If sushi is what you crave, join the locals here. You may have to huddle outside with the crowd that's arrived before you, but your tastebuds will thank you for your patience. The *maki* rolls are superb and include unique options like the Oregon roll, a succulent combo of avocado, fresh crab, asparagus and salmon. Non-fishy fare such as noodles and teriyaki is also available. Closed Sunday.

SHOPPING

PULLIAM DEFFENBAUGH GALLERY ✉929 Northwest Flanders Street

☎503-228-6665 ⬧www.pulliamdeffenbaugh.com This gallery specializes in contemporary Northwest art but includes work from other regions as well. Closed Sunday and Monday.

LAURA RUSSO GALLERY ✉805 Northwest 21st Avenue ☎503-226-2754

⬧www.laurarusso.com An excellent place to look for fine local art is at this gallery. Paintings, original prints, drawings, watercolors and sculptures in a variety of media are all shown here. Closed Sunday and Monday.

MUSEUM OF CONTEMPORARY CRAFT ✉724 Northwest Davis Street

☎503-223-2654 🖷503-223-0190 ⬧www.museumofcontemporarycraft.org, info@museumofcontemporarycraft.org We were impressed by the breadth of the offerings at this nonprofit organization showcasing everything from ceramic pins and medallions to metal sculpture. Highlighting crafts of the five disciplines (clay, glass, wood, fiber and metal), this eclectic gallery is a great place to shop for a gift. Closed Monday.

NIGHTLIFE

PORTLAND BAROQUE ORCHESTRA ✉First Baptist Church, 909 Southwest 11th Avenue; Kaul Auditorium at Reed College ☎503-222-6000 🖷503-226-6635

✐*www.pbo.org* Classical music buffs will enjoy this baroque orchestra. Make it a point to hear this group if they're performing during your visit (October through April).

MCMENAMINS MISSION THEATER ✉*1624 Northwest Glisan Street* ☏*503-223-4527, 503-249-7474 (movie showtimes)* ✐*mcmenamins.com, mission@ mcmenamins.com* This is a historic movie theater that now doubles as a pub, with seating at tables and couches where you can dine and watch second-run films.

PARKS

MACLEAY PARK

✉*Take Lovejoy Street west to Northwest Cornell Road and continue to the park.* ☏*503-823-2223* ✇*503-823-6007*

🏃 This natural 104-acre park offers several excellent trails, a pond, creek and viewing windows overlooking a bird-feeding area. In addition, Pittock Mansion provides stunning views of the city and Mt. St. Helens. There's a good chance you'll spot deer and other wildlife on your walk. Hiking trails lead down to Lower Macleay Park, which is a gateway to 5000-acre Forest Park. The Portland Audubon Society's headquarters, bookstore and wildlife care center are adjacent to the park. Facilities include restrooms and a playground.

COUNCIL CREST PARK

✉*Southwest Council Crest Drive near Fairmount Boulevard* ☏*503-823-2223* ✇*503-823-6007*

🏃 Atop a Tualatin Mountain peak, this forested 43-acre park is a great way to see the Cascades and the Coast Range. Make your way through stands of fir and maple via Marquam Hill Trail. There's also a sculptured fountain of a mother and child. Facilities include picnic tables.

SAUVIE ISLAND WILDLIFE AREA

hidden

✉*Take Route 30 west from Portland toward Astoria. Four miles past St. John's Bridge, take the Sauvie Bridge turnoff to the island.* ☏*503-621-3488* ✇*503-621-3025* ✐*www.sauvieisland.org, info@sauvieisland.org*

🏃 ⛵ 🚣 🏊 🎣 This 12,000-acre haven ten miles northwest of Portland is an ideal place to spot great blue heron, bald eagles, sandhill cranes (during March and April migration) and 230 other bird species. Featuring a sandy beach on the Columbia, the refuge is also home to 37 mammal species, including black-tailed deer. Small craft explore the sloughs while oceangoing freighters cruise by on the Columbia. For fishing, try for catfish, perch and crappie from slough and pond banks. The trails that lead through orchards and gardens here are ideal for leisurely exploration on foot. There are portable toilets and bird observation platforms. Some areas are open year-round; other areas are closed from October to mid-April. Day-use only; you must obtain a parking permit ($3.50 per day/$11 annually), available at the Cracker Barrel and the Redder Beach RV Park on the island.

ELK ROCK GARDEN

✉ *11800 Southwest Military Lane* ☎ *503-636-5613, 800-452-2562*
📠 *503-636-5616* 🖥 *www.diocese-oregon.org/theclose*

Ever since 1957 this refuge, also known as the Garden of the Bishop's Close, has been a favorite of Portland's garden societies. And why not? A terraced 13-acre estate overlooking the Willamette River and Elk Rock Island, the garden is also home to the Episcopal Diocese of Oregon's main office. Formal gardens and native plants, including 77 magnolia varieties, make this a spot for Zen-like contemplation. Also here are lily ponds, a rock garden and a small spring. Self-guided tour information is available from the visitors center.

TRYON CREEK STATE NATURAL AREA

✉ *Located six miles southwest of downtown Portland. Take the Terwilliger exit off Route 5 and follow signs to the park.* ☎ *503-636-9886, 800-551-6949* 📠 *503-636-5318*

🚶 🚲 🐎 Set in a shallow, steep-walled canyon, this 645-acre suburban park is a hot spot for hiking, biking and horseback riding. Tryon is forested with fir, alder and maple and also has a grassy meadow. Look for beaver and pileated woodpeckers. There's a trillium festival in the spring. Facilities here are restrooms, an observation area and a nature center.

MARY S. YOUNG PARK

✉ *Located nine miles south of Portland on Route 43* ☎ *503-557-4700* 📠 *503-656-4106*
🖥 *www.ci.west-linn.or.us*

🚶 🚲 ⛵ A popular day-use area forested in fir, maple, cottonwood and oak, the park sits on the Willamette River. With 133 acres, this leisurely spot is perfect for fishing from the riverbank, riding or walking. There are restrooms and picnic tables.

THE COLUMBIA RIVER GORGE

All visitors to Portland owe it to themselves to see the Columbia River Gorge. The spectacular scenery includes one of the Northwest's most important historical sites, Fort Vancouver. Heaven for windsurfers, kayakers, waterfall lovers, hikers and history buffs, this is the ultimate Portland day trip. Of course, if you love it as much as we did, you'll probably want to spend the night.

There are also many different visitors centers and museums in Columbia River Gorge National Recreation Area because it is managed cooperatively by a board made up of representatives from the states of Washington and Oregon and each of the counties in which it falls, as well as the U.S. Forest Service.

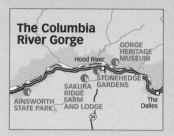

AINSWORTH STATE PARK

PAGE 368

Serene forest getaway where miles of hiking trails extend away from civilization into the lush wilderness

SAKURA RIDGE FARM AND LODGE

PAGE 363

Cozy rooms with views of majestic Mt. Hood on an organic farm with cherries and heirloom tomatoes

STONEHEDGE GARDENS

PAGE 365

Tucked-away, antique-filled restaurant with fresh Northwest seafood dishes like sambuca shrimp

GORGE HERITAGE MUSEUM

PAGE 359

Small-town gallery full of American Indian artifacts like tools, arrow points and beadwork

SIGHTS

FORT VANCOUVER Although it's only half an hour from downtown Portland and the logical starting point for touring the Columbia Gorge region, many visitors to the region miss this historic fort. What a pity. Located across the Columbia River from Portland, on the Washington side, this National Historic Site is a cornerstone of Pacific Northwest history. Organized by the Hudson Bay Company in 1825, the fort was originally a British fur-trading post and focal point for the commercial development of an area extending from British Columbia to Oregon and from Montana west to the Hawaiian Islands.

FORT VANCOUVER NATIONAL HISTORIC SITE ✉ *612 East Reserve Street, Vancouver, WA* ✆ *360-816-6230* ✆ *360-816-6363* ✍ *www.nps.gov/fova* Ten structures have been reconstructed on their original fort locations. Collectively known as Fort Vancouver National Historic Site, they give a feel for life during the arrival of the first white settlers. One of the best ways to start your tour is at the visitors center with the introductory video.

The **Fur Warehouse** interprets how furs were collected and prepared for shipment to England. Also worth a visit are the **Blacksmith Shop**, **Bake House**, **Kitchen**, **Wash House**, **Palisade**, **Bastion**, **Jail** and a **Carpenter Workshop**. At the **Indian Trade Shop and Dispensary**, you'll

Columbia River Gorge

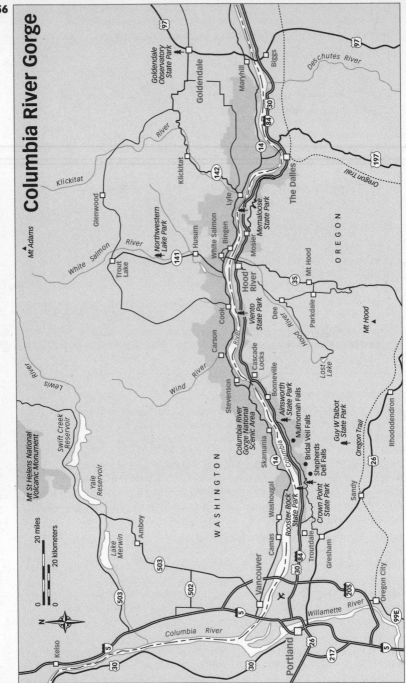

learn how American Indians skillfully bartered their collected furs for British-made goods. Because most of the items were imported, there was a two-year hiatus between ordering goods and receiving them. Fort Vancouver: Admission.

OFFICERS ROW   Near the fort, you'll see 21 grand homes built for American Army leaders who served here during the latter half of the 19th and the early 20th centuries. These charming Victorians are the focus of a rehabilitation program combining interpretive and commercial use. Among the residences you can tour is the **Grant House** (360-906-1101), built for and frequented by Ulysses S. Grant; the building currently houses a restaurant serving classic Northwestern food. The **George C. Marshall House** (360-693-3103), an imposing Queen Anne structure, also offers tours every day. Call for weekend hours; tours are available Saturday and Sunday except during weddings or other event rentals.

PEARSON FIELD & AIR MUSEUM

✉1115 East 5th Street, Vancouver, WA ☎360-694-7026 ✆360-694-0824 ✐www.pearsonairmuseum.org Next to Fort Vancouver is this military museum. The field, opened in 1905, is the oldest operating airfield in the United States. Exhibits feature a display on the world's first nonstop transpolar flight (Moscow to Vancouver) in 1937—the Soviet aviators were greeted by General George Marshall, who hosted them at his residence—as well as the last remaining artifact from the *Hindenburg*. The airpark exhibit features flyable vintage aircraft, an aviation theater, a hands on activity room, the nation's oldest wooden hangar and the world's first bomber. Closed Sunday to Tuesday. Admission.

CLARK COUNTY HISTORICAL MUSEUM ✉1511 Main Street, Vancouver, WA ☎360-993-5679 ✆360-993-5683 ✐www.cchmuseum.org, cchm@pacifier.com Originally constructed in 1909 as a Carnegie Library, this museum has a better than good regional collection—from the American Indian artifacts and handicrafts to the historical doctor's office and general store. Closed Sunday and Monday. Admission.

GREATER VANCOUVER CHAMBER OF COMMERCE ✉1101 Broadway, Suite 100, Vancouver, WA ☎360-694-2588 ✆360-693-8279 ✐www.vancouverusa.com, yourchamber@vancouverusa.com To see more of Vancouver, stop by this chamber of commerce and pick up the handy downtown walking tour brochure. Closed Saturday and Sunday.

HISTORIC COLUMBIA RIVER HIGHWAY   Returning to the Oregon side of the river, take Route 84 east up the Gorge to this historic highway. This magnificent scenic route parallels Route 84, skirting the foot of sheer cliffs of the Columbia River Gorge with its wonderland of waterfalls, side canyons and verdant forest. The road was built by concrete tycoon Sam Hill, creator of the Maryhill Museum of Art, in 1916 as an attempt to convince Oregon legislatures to let him extend a highway up the length of the Columbia River. It was the first rural paved road in the Pacific Northwest.

VISTA HOUSE At the mouth of the Gorge, a road turns off to the right and winds up to this house in Crown Point State Park. This octagonal structure, perched 733 feet above the river, has an information desk, a gift shop, an espresso bar and an awesome view.

WATERFALLS Among the major waterfalls that plunge into the Gorge alongside the highway are **Latourelle Falls** (249 feet) in Guy W. Talbot State Park, **Shepherd's Dell Falls** (two tiers, 50 and 60 feet) in Sheppards Dell State Park, **Bridal Veil Falls** (two tiers, 100 and 60 feet) and **Wahkeena Falls** (242 feet), where a mile-long trail leads to **Fairy Falls**, a magical 30-foot fan-shaped fall.

MULTNOMAH FALLS The most popular tourist attraction in Oregon, this cascade plunges 620 feet, making it the second-tallest waterfall in the United States. Walk up the paved trail to the observation bridge between the upper and lower falls, where you'll get a misty view of the entire falls. In 1995, a 400-ton rock the size of a Greyhound bus fell from the top of the falls to the upper pool as a result of the ongoing erosion that originally formed the gorge. It caused about 20 minor injuries from flying debris, reminding us that the amazing geology here is still transforming on a grand scale.

STILL MORE FALLS Two and a half miles beyond Multnomah Falls is **Horsetail Falls** (176 feet). Nearby, a trail leads almost two miles through the lush greenery of Oneonta Gorge to **Triple Falls**, a 135-foot segmented fall. The historic highway rejoins the interstate at Ainsworth State Park—unbelievably a mere 18 miles from where it began.

BRADFORD ISLAND VISITORS CENTER ✉*Route 84, Exit 40, three miles west of Cascade Locks, OR* ☎*541-374-8820* 📠*541-374-4516* The taming of the Columbia River to provide low-cost power is one of the most controversial issues associated with the river. You'll get the pro side of the picture at **Bonneville Lock and Dam**, which includes this visitors center. You can also witness salmon swimming up underwater fish ladders. Extensive interpretive displays and an informational film provide an overview of the dam's operation and history.

FORT CASCADES NATIONAL HISTORIC SITE
☎*503-230-1221* On the Washington side of the Gorge, you can learn how the dam operates, enjoy underwater views of fish ladders and visit this historic site. To get there, cross the Columbia River at Cascade Locks, Oregon, using the **Bridge of the Gods** (named after an Indian legend) and head west two miles on Route 14. The 59-acre historic site includes a one-mile self-guided trail featuring the sites of the old Portage Railroad, a one-time Chinook Indian village, a pre–Civil War military fort and a nature preserve. A quiet nine-mile segment of the historic highway continues east of Hood River, between Mosier and The Dalles, winding onto the Rowena Plateau. Views include channeled scabland terraces, fruit orchards, and the **Tom McCall Preserve**, a beautiful and little-known nature re-

serve run by The Nature Conservancy that protects many of the hundreds of unique Columbia River Gorge wildflower species.

CASCADE LOCKS MUSEUM ✉ *Marine Park, 1 Northwest Portage Road, Cascade Locks, OR* ☎ *541-374-8535* Retrace your route across the Bridge of the Gods to the Oregon side and stop at this museum to see exhibits on American Indians, the first Columbia River locks, the portage road, logging and fishwheels. Water-powered, these rotating devices scooped so many salmon from the river that they were banned by the state in 1926. Closed October through April.

COLUMBIA GORGE ☎ *503-224-3900, 800-224-3901* ✆ *503-231-9089* ⌨ *www.sternwheeler.com, sales@sternwheeler.com* This sternwheeler is docked in Cascade Locks year-round. The multidecked old paddlewheel steamboat leads daytime sightseeing excursions and weekend brunch and dinner cruises through the Gorge.

COLUMBIA GORGE INTERPRETIVE CENTER ✉ *990 Southwest Rock Creek Drive, Stevenson, WA* ☎ *509-427-8211, 800-991-2338* ✆ *509-427-7429* ⌨ *www.columbiagorge.org, info@columbiagorge.org* On the Washington side of the bridge in Stevenson is this spacious interpretive center, where the focus is on the cultural and natural history of the Gorge. Located on an 18-acre site overlooking the river, the center includes a 37-foot-high replica of a 19th-century fishwheel, a restored Corliss Steam Engine, two theaters (one with a self-activated video re-creating the cataclysmic formation of the Gorge) and several exhibits drawn from the oral histories of local American Indians and pioneer settlers. The world's largest rosary collection is also housed here. Admission.

CARSON MINERAL HOT SPRINGS RESORT ✉ *372 St. Martin's Spring Road, Carson, WA* ☎ *509-427-8292, 800-607-3678* ✆ *509-427-7242* ⌨ *www.carsonhotspringsresort.com, carsonhs@hotmail.com* Farther east on Route 14 is this hot springs resort. On the Wind River, the resort is well-known by weary travelers for its mineral baths and massages, and can provide a restful stop for those who have been hiking all day on its beautiful hiking trails; there's also an 18-hole golf course. From here you can drive east along Route 14 to Route 141, which leads north along the White Salmon River Valley to Trout Lake, then return to Route 14 and the town of White Salmon.

GORGE HERITAGE MUSEUM
✉ *202 East Humboldt Street, Bingen, WA* ☎ *509-493-3228* ⌨ *ghm@gorge.net*
Just east of White Salmon in the small town of Bingen, Washington, is this museum, where you can view historic photographs and American Indian artifacts, including tools, arrow points and beadwork. Closed Monday through Wednesday, and October through May.

HOOD RIVER Your next stop should be on the Oregon side at this main river, which has become a windsurfing capital thanks to the strong breezes here. Stop at the **Hood River County Visitors Center** (720 East Port Marina Drive, Hood River, OR; 541-386-2000, 800-336-

3530, fax 541-386-2057; www.hoodriver.org, hrccc@hoodriver.org) for information on this scenic hub. Closed weekends from mid-October to mid-April.

HOOD RIVER COUNTY HISTORICAL MUSEUM ✉*300 East Port Marina Park, Hood River, OR* ✆*541-386-6772* ✆*541-386-6772* ✐*www.co.hood-river.or.us* This historical museum features exhibits on American Indian culture, the westward migration, pioneer farming, logging and the Columbia River. Also found here is a collection of period furniture and early 20th-century artifacts. Closed November through March.

HOOD RIVER SATURDAY MARKET ✉*5th Street and Cascade Avenue, across from the Full Sail Brewing Company* ✆*541-387-8349* ✐*www.communitygorge.net/saturdaymarket, hrsm@gorge.net* If you're in town between May and September, visit this Saturday market, which features local foods, crafts and artwork.

MT. HOOD RAILROAD ✉*110 Railroad Avenue, Hood River, OR* ✆*541-386-3556, 800-872-4661* ✐*www.mthoodrr.com, mthoodrr@gorge.net* You'll enjoy panoramic views of the Cascades from the restored coaches of this scenic railroad. Two- and four-hour journeys link the Gorge with Mt. Hood along a route pioneered in 1906. The trains climb up the Hood River Valley through steep canyons, orchards and forests. Special events are offered throughout the high season. The railroad runs April through October, with selected holiday trips between Thanksgiving and Christmas.

LOST LAKE — hidden

One of the prettiest drives in Oregon is the 20-mile trip from Hood River to this lake (elevation 3140 feet). At the lake you'll have a stunning angle on Mt. Hood—have your camera ready—and can rent a canoe or paddleboat (motorized boats are banned on the lake). In addition to fishing for rainbow trout, visitors like to walk the three-mile Lakeshore Trail that circles the lake. To reach the idyllic retreat, take Route 281 south to Dee and then follow the signs west to the lake. Do keep an eye out for logging trucks en route.

NORTHWESTERN LAKE ✉*Head west from White Salmon on Route 14 to Route 141. Continue north five miles to the park.* A little Washington gem on the White Salmon River north of the Columbia, this lake is an ideal destination for a day trip where you can swim, fish, hike or just loaf. There are also summer cabins nearby for those who want to stay longer.

THE DALLES Although many visitors miss it, we strongly recommend a visit to this city, on the Oregon side of the Gorge. The end of the Oregon Trail, where immigrants boarded vessels to float down the Columbia (the Barlow Trail later made it possible to complete the overland journey), this city has a superb old-town walking tour. Pick up a copy of the route map at **The Dalles Area Chamber of Commerce** (404 West 2nd Street, The Dalles, OR; 541-296-2231, 800-255-3385, fax 541-296-1688; www.thedalleschamber.com, tdacc@gorge.net). Closed weekends.

Highlights on this walk include the state's oldest bookstore, **Klindt's** (315 East 2nd Street), and the circa-1863 **Waldron Brothers Drugstore** nearby.

FORT DALLES MUSEUM ✉*500 15th Street at Garrison Street, The Dalles, OR* ☎*541-296-4547* 📠*541-296-4547* ✐*fortdallesmuseum@netcnct.net* Only two fort buildings, the Surgeon's Quarters and the Garden Cottage, remain today, but this museum does preserve an excellent collection of pioneer artifacts, rifles, quilts and historic photographs. Closed December through February. Call for hours otherwise. Admission.

COLUMBIA GORGE DISCOVERY CENTER AND WASCO COUNTY HISTORICAL MUSEUM ✉*5000 Discovery Drive, The Dalles* ☎*541-296-8600* 📠*541-298-8660* ✐*www.gorgediscovery.org* Don't miss this attractive, 48,000-square-foot discovery center. It is the official Columbia River Gorge National Scenic Area interpretive center and has exhibits on the natural and cultural history of the gorge, as well as artifacts from local collectors in its airy, modern structure.

THE DALLES DAM ✉*From the Columbia Gorge Discovery Center, take Route 30 east to Route 197 north. Cross the freeway to Bret Clodfelter Way and follow signs to the dam.* Before this dam was built, these waters served as the Gorge's best-known American Indian fishing grounds. Wherever you go along this part of the Columbia River, in coffee shops and hotel lobbies, phone company offices and visitors centers, you're likely to see classic photographs of American Indians dipping their nets into the river at heavenly Celilo Falls. To get the full picture, leaf through the scrapbook of Celilo Falls fishing pictures at the Fort Dalles Museum. One hopeful sign, though. If you look carefully below The Dalles Dam, you may see contemporary Indian dipnet subsistence fishermen fishing from platforms. Treaties have upheld the right of Indian fishers to half the annual take of fish along the river for subsistence and cultural use only.

CELILO FALLS MARKER If you continue on Route 84 east of The Dalles for 12 miles, you'll come to this small marker, which indicates where bounteous fishing waters prospered before being destroyed by The Dalles Dam in the late 1950s.

MARYHILL MUSEUM OF ART

✉*35 Maryhill Museum Drive, Goldendale, WA* ☎*509-773-3733* 📠*509-773-6138* ✐*www.maryhillmuseum.org, maryhill@maryhillmuseum.org* A few miles farther east, on the Washington side, is one of the most isolated (and reportedly haunted) museums in America. It was designed in 1914 as the mansion residence of eccentric millionaire Sam Hill, and was supposed to oversee a Quaker agricultural town. But the plan for a new town flopped and the house on the hill eventually became a museum. This eclectic assemblage was dedicated in 1926 by Queen Marie of Romania, which helps explain the presence of treasures from that nation's royal collection. Also here are Russian icons, a large collection of Rodin sculptures, Charles M. Russell's *Indian Buffalo Hunt*, French decorative arts, a good display of American Indian handicrafts and artifacts (including strange, ancient carved lava heads found in the Columbia Valley) and contemporary Pacific Northwest art, as well as one of the world's great chess collections. The museum also includes the world's only collection of post–World War II fashion mannequins. Views of the Columbia Gorge are spectacular, as are the sunsets. Closed mid-November to mid-March. Admission.

STONEHENGE

Three miles east of the Maryhill Museum of Art is this surprising site, which is Sam Hill's full-sized concrete replica of the original Stonehenge, erected as a memorial to local soldiers who died in World War I.

LODGING

HOOD RIVER BED AND BREAKFAST ASSOCIATION ☎541-386-6767 ⌖www.gorgelodging.com With rooms often in short supply during the summer windsurfing season, visitors who arrive in the Hood River area without reservations may want to call this association's room-finder hotline for information on what is available at local inns.

SKAMANIA LODGE
$$$$ 254 ROOMS ✉ 1131 Skamania Lodge Way, Stevenson, WA ☎509-427-7700, 800-221-7117 ⌕509-427-2547 ⌖www.skamania.com

Located just above the Columbia Gorge Interpretive Center in Stevenson, Washington, is this modern resort built in the tradition of the grand mountain lodges of the late 18th century. Guests can congregate in the wood-paneled Gorge Room with its deep sofas and three-story river-rock fireplace. Public areas and the guest rooms are handsomely decorated with mission-style furniture, petroglyph rubbings and American Indian–inspired rugs. The grounds include an 18-hole golf course, fitness center, whirlpools, swimming pool and more.

BRIDGE OF THE GODS MOTEL
$–$$ 16 ROOMS ✉630 WaNaPa Street, Cascade Locks, OR ☎541-374-8628 ⌖www.bridgeofgodsmotel.com, info@bridgeofgods.com

In Cascade Locks, 20 miles west of Hood River, this motel provides affordable rustic rooms. All units have queen-sized beds; 11 of them offer kitchenettes. There's also an RV park on-site.

INN OF THE
WHITE SALMON
$$–$$$ 15 ROOMS ✉172 West Jewett Boulevard, White Salmon, WA ☎509-493-2335, 800-972-5226 ⌖www.innofthewhitesalmon.com, innkeeper@innofthewhitesalmon.com

This lovely bed and breakfast has countrified rooms featuring brass beds and antiques. One of the rooms is a spacious hostel-style affair with eight beds. Breakfast is a feast of breads, cheeses, egg dishes and fruit. Across the Columbia from Hood River, this inn also boasts a comfortable parlor.

HOOD RIVER HOTEL

$–$$$ 41 ROOMS   ✉102 Oak Avenue, Hood River, OR   ☏541-386-1900, 800-386-1859 ✆541-386-6090 ✐www.hoodriverhotel.com, hrhotel@gorge.net

This chandeliered hotel is a restored brick landmark with both rooms and suites. Brightly painted rooms are appointed with oak furniture, four-poster beds, casablanca fans, wing chairs and antiques. Some offer views of the Columbia River. Comfortable sitting areas and a cheery restaurant are part of the charm. Kitchenette suites are available. Pet-friendly.

OAK STREET HOTEL

$$ 9 ROOMS   ✉610 Oak Street, Hood River, OR   ☏541 386 3845, 866-386-3845 ✆541-387-8696 ✐www.oakstreethotel.com, reservations@oakstreethotel.com

Situated in a restored 1909 historic downtown home, this charming hotel offers nine guest rooms (one of which is a suite). Queen-sized beds with intricate iron frames and handcrafted furnishings enliven the rooms, all of which have a private bath. There's a comfortable lounge downstairs with a fireplace.

VAGABOND LODGE

$–$$ 42 UNITS   ✉4070 Westcliff Drive, Hood River, OR   ☏541-386-2992, 877-386-2992 ✆541-386-3317 ✐www.vagabondlodge.com, info@vagabondlodge.com

Beautifully located overlooking the Columbia, the Vagabond offers spacious, carpeted rooms and suites—some opening right onto the riverfront. All feature contemporary furniture, double or queen-sized beds, microwaves, refrigerators, wi-fi access and a secluded garden setting. Some suites have fireplaces, whirlpools and full kitchens. For the price, it's hard to beat this motel west of town.

INN AT THE GORGE BED & BREAKFAST

$$–$$$ 5 UNITS   ✉1113 Eugene Street, Hood River, OR   ☏541-386-4429 ✆541-386-4429 ✐www.innatthegorge.com, stay@innatthegorge.com

Located just five blocks from downtown Hood River is this 1908 bed and breakfast. Three suites and two bedrooms have antique furnishings and private baths. Enjoy the surrounding gardens, nap in the hammock beneath the cedar tree or just laze the day away on the wraparound porch. Full breakfast included.

SAKURA RIDGE FARM AND LODGE

$$$–$$$$ 5 ROOMS   ✉5601 York Hill Drive, Hood River, OR ☏541-386-2633, 877-472-5872 ✆320-386-2633 ✐www.sakuraridge.com, info@sakuraridge.com

At the end of a gravel dead-end road that climbs to a ridgeline above the Hood River Golf and Country Club, this bed and break-fast is set in a working orchard where the owners grow organic cherries, pears, berries and heirloom tomatoes. The location commands spectacular views of fir-clad foothills rising to the majesty of Mt. Hood. The individualized decor blends rustic and ultra-modern, with king-sized beds in most rooms. Each guest room has a private bath and a view of either Mt. Hood or the orchards and the Columbia Valley; several have outdoor decks or patios, and one features a fireplace. Room rates include a full, farm-fresh breakfast. Closed November through February.

COLUMBIA WINDRIDER INN

$ 4 ROOMS   ✉200 West 4th Street, The Dalles, OR   ☎541-296-2607
🖥www.windriderinn.com, chuck@windriderinn.com

The Windrider is operated by an avid Columbia Gorge sailor and wind-surfer who likes to play host to other sailboard afficionados. Situated on a quiet residential street, this historic 1921 home has maple wood floors and four large guest rooms, each with private bath, air conditioning, complimentary wi-fi and a queen- or king-sized bed. Facilities include a swimming pool, a hot tub and a recreation room.

COUSINS COUNTRY INN

$$ 93 ROOMS   ✉2114 West 6th Street, The Dalles, OR   ☎541-298-5161, 800-848-9378   📠541-298-6411   🖥www.cousinscountryinn.com, info@cousinscountryinn.com

For contemporary motel accommodations, try this inn. The fully car-peted rooms have oak tables, cable TV with HBO and queen-sized beds; some have kitchenettes. Guests receive free use of the nearby health club. There's a pool on the premises, as well as Cousins, the only restaurant we know that has a John Deere tractor in the middle of the dining room.

DINING

MULTNOMAH FALLS LODGE

$$–$$$ AMERICAN   ✉Off Route 84, Bridal Veil, WA   ☎503-695-2376
📠503-695-2338   🖥www.multnomahfallslodge.com, info@multnomahfallslodge.com

After a visit to Multnomah Falls it makes sense to dine at this name-sake restaurant. The smoked-salmon-and-cheese platter and gener-ous salads are recommended. The European-style lodge building with a big stone fireplace, scenic paintings of the surroundings and lovely views will add to your enjoyment of the Gorge. Buffet champagne brunch on Sunday.

CASCADE ROOM

$$$–$$$$ PACIFIC NORTHWEST   ✉Skamania Lodge, 1131 Skamania Lodge Way, Stevenson, WA   ☎509-427-7700, 800-221-7117   📠509-427-2547
🖥www.skamania.com

In Stevenson, Washington, this restaurant has a grand dining room with massive wooden ceiling beams and superb views of the Gorge. The specialties are Northwest-inspired dishes prepared in a wood-burning oven, like cider-brined pork chops or big eye tuna with oven-roasted tomatoes, not to mention a Sunday champagne brunch.

THE LOGS

$–$$ AMERICAN   ✉1258 Route 141, White Salmon, WA   ☎509-493-1402

✍thelogs@earthlink.net

About 20 minutes north of the Gorge, and well worth the trip, is this eatery, one of the Gorge's most intriguing restaurants. You'll be impressed by the roasted chicken, hickory-smoked ribs, giant fries and huckleberry pie served in this log-cabin setting. The battered and deep-fried chicken gizzards and cheese sticks are a big hit with the regular clientele, who include locals, rafters, skiers and devotees of the rich mud pie. In business for six decades, this is the place where city slickers will come face to face with their first jackalope, safely mounted on the wall.

STONEHEDGE GARDENS

$$–$$$ SEAFOOD/PACIFIC NORTHWEST   ✉3405 Cascade Avenue, Hood River, OR   ☎541-386-3940 ✍www.hoodriverrestaurants.com, stonehedge@gorge.net

Tucked away in the woods on the Oregon side is this antique-filled restaurant preparing Northwest dining at its finest. Set in a beautiful garden, this paneled dining room has a tiny mahogany bar and a roaring fireplace. Among the dishes are salmon with lemon-thyme beurre blanc and sambuca shrimp. Light entrées, such as a seafood platter, are also recommended. Dinner only. Closed Monday in winter.

CORNERSTONE CUISINE

$$–$$$ AMERICAN   ✉In the Hood River Hotel, 102 Oak Street, Hood River, OR ☎541-386-1900, 800-386-1859 ☎541-386-6090 ✍www.hoodriverhotel.com, hrhotel@gorge.net

Cornerstone has breezy indoor and sidewalk seating in the center of this resort town. The heart of the dining room is a handcrafted bar with an etched-glass mirror. Entrées include almond-crusted salmon, seafood paella and roasted rosemary chicken breast.

SIMON'S RESTAURANT

$$$–$$$$ PACIFIC NORTHWEST   ✉Columbia Gorge Hotel, 4000 Westcliff Drive, Hood River, OR ☎541-387-5428, 800-345-1921 ☎541-387-5414 ✍www.columbiagorgehotel.com, cghotel@gorge.net

An elegant dining room overlooking the Gorge, Simon's is a romantic place to dine on roast pork tenderloin, fresh Oregon salmon, rack of lamb or Dungeness crab with lobster sauce and risotto. Done in an Early American design with oak furniture and candlelit tables, this establishment is well known for its lavish farm breakfast.

BALDWIN SALOON

$$–$$$ SEAFOOD   ✉205 Court Street, The Dalles, OR ☎541-296-5666 ✍www.baldwinsaloon.com

Located in one of the most historic buildings in The Dalles, this saloon was built in 1876 and has an 18-foot-long mahogany back bar and turn-of-the-20th-century oil paintings on the brick walls. The restaurant is known for its seafood and oyster dishes (baked and on the half-shell) and also serves sandwiches, burgers, soups and desserts. Closed Sunday.

SHOPPING

FORT VANCOUVER GIFT SHOP ✉*1501 East Evergreen Boulevard, Vancouver, WA* ☎*360-992-1824* This shop is the place to go for books, maps and pamphlets on Pacific Northwest history. We recommend picking up a copy of *Outpost* by Dorothy Morris.

PEARSON AIR MUSEUM ✉*1115 East 5th Street, Vancouver, WA* ☎*360-694-7026* ✆*360-694-0824* ✎*www.pearsonairmuseum.org* Aviation buffs will want to stop by the gift shop here. The shop has an ace collection of memorabilia and souvenirs for adults and juniors alike. Closed Sunday through Tuesday.

PENDLETON WOOLEN MILLS AND OUTLET STORE ✉*2 17th Street, Washougal, WA* ☎*360-760-4844* This outlet store offers big savings on irregulars. Tours of the mill, in operation since 1912, are available, but call first for schedule information.

WAUCOMA BOOKSTORE ✉*212 Oak Street, Hood River, OR* ☎*541-386-5353* A good place to find books on the region is this bookstore, which is also well stocked with fiction, children's books, cards, magazines, children's toys and handcrafted pottery.

COLUMBIA ART GALLERY ✉*Columbia Art Center, 215 Cascade Avenue, Hood River, OR* ☎*541-387-8877* ✎*www.columbiaartgallery.org* This gallery represents over 150 artists, primarily from the Columbia Gorge region. Featured are the works of photographers, printmakers, potters, glassblowers, jewelers, weavers, sculptors and painters.

THE GIFT HOUSE ✉*204 Oak Street, Hood River, OR* ☎*541-386-9234* ✎*www. hoodrivergifthouse.com* Locally made jams, jellies, wine and other food products make terrific presents for the folks back home. This shop carries a variety of home-grown products, including both wine and jams.

THE WINE SELLERS ✉*514 State Street, Hood River, OR* ☎*541-386-4647* ✎*www.wine-sellers.com* Pick up a fine Oregon white or red at this neighborhood shop. Closed Sunday.

RASMUSSEN FARMS ✉*3020 Thomsen Road off Route 35 south of Hood River, OR* ☎*541-386-4622, 800-548-2243* ✆*541-386-4702* ✎*www.rasmussenfarms.com, info@rasmussenfarms.com* This company sells strawberries, Hood River apples, Comice pears and cherries when they're in season. Apples, cherries and pears can be shipped as gift packs.

On the Washington side of the Gorge, Stevenson's small, walkable downtown has some distinctive art galleries and gift shops.

KLINDT'S ✉*315 East 2nd Street, The Dalles, OR* ☎*541-296-3355* The Dalles is home to Oregon's oldest bookstore, Klindt's, which dates from 1870 and still has an old-time ambience with high ceilings and glass-topped counters. Books on the Pacific Northwest, both new and used, are a specialty, as are rare and out-of-print books.

NORTH BANK BAR & GRILL ✉ *106 West 6th Street, Vancouver, WA* ☎ *360-695-3862* A popular gay and lesbian nightspot in Vancouver, Washington, is the North Bank, which has a dancefloor and outdoor patio. Cover for cabaret shows.

POWER STATION PUB AND THEATER ✉ *2126 Southwest Halsey Street, Troutdale, OR* ☎ *503-492-4686, 800-669-8610* ✎ *www.mcmenamins.com, power@mcmenamins.com* The Power Station is located in the former Multnomah County poor farm. The theater presents second-run movies in the farm's former power plant. The pub serves a full menu in the converted laundry building. Also on the premises is the **Edgefield Brewery** and a working winery and distillery.

SKAMANIA LODGE ✉ *1131 Skamania Lodge Way, Stevenson, WA* ☎ *509-427-2527* 🖷 *509-427-2547* There's occasional live music here. If it's not a music night, settle in near the speakers before a woodburning fireplace in summer.

BUNGALOW BAR & GRILL ✉ *812 Wind River Highway, Carson, WA* ☎ *509-427-4523* Bungalow has televised sports, two pool tables and dart boards.

FULL SAIL BREWING COMPANY ✉ *506 Columbia Avenue, Hood River, OR* ☎ *541-386-2247, 888-244-2337* ✎ *www.fullsailbrewing.com* This brewery offers tastings of their very popular handcrafted beers, as well as a pub-style menu and deck seating with fine views of the Columbia.

PARKS

ROOSTER ROCK STATE PARK
✉ *Located in Oregon 22 miles east of Portland on Route 84 at Exit 25* ☎ *503-695-2261, 800-551-6949* 🖷 *503-695-2226*

Offering more than three miles of sandy Columbia River frontage, this 872-acre park is near the Gorge's west end. The rock, named for a towering promontory, is near a camping site chosen by Lewis and Clark in 1805. Well-known for swimming and beginner windsurfing, Rooster Rock also has excellent hiking trails, a small lake and a forested bluff. Anglers can fish for salmon. There are picnic tables and restrooms. Day-use fee, $3, or $25 for an annual pass.

VIENTO STATE PARK
✉ *Route 84 Exit 56, eight miles west of Hood River in Oregon* ☎ *541-374-8811, 800-551-6949*

Originally a rest stop on the old Columbia River Highway, this 247-acre park includes a riverfront and Viento Creek forest section. Dramatic views of the Columbia River make this a popular camping and picnicking facility. It can get very windy, and be aware that trains pass through the gorge at night. Facilities include picnic tables, barbecue pits, showers and restrooms. Closed November through mid-April. Day-use fee, $3.

▲ There are 18 tent sites ($10 to $14 per night) and 56 RV hookup sites ($12 to $16 per night).

AINSWORTH STATE PARK

✉Route 30, the Columbia River Scenic Highway, 37 miles east of Portland on the Oregon side ☎503-695-2301, 800-551-6949 ⌨503-695-2226

🏃 Ranking high among the treasures of the Columbia River Scenic Highway is this 156-acre park. Near the bottom of St. Peter's Dome, the forested park has a gorgeous hiking trail that connects with a network extending throughout the region. A serene getaway, the only sound of civilization you're likely to hear is that of passing trains. There are picnic tables, showers and restrooms. Closed November through March.

▲ There are 45 RV hookup sites; $12 to $16 per night. There are also six walk-in sites; $10 to $14 per night.

MEMALOOSE STATE PARK

✉Off Route 84, 11 miles west of The Dalles in Oregon. Take the Memaloose Rest Stop exit, then make a right into the park. Westbound access only. ☎541-478-3008 ⌨541-478-2369

The park is named for an offshore Columbia River island that was an American Indian burial ground. "Memaloose" is a Chinook word linked to the sacred burial ritual. This 336-acre site spreads out along a two-mile stretch of riverfront and is forested with pine, oak and fir. Much of the park is steep and rocky. It can also be very windy. There are horseshoes, a playground, interpretive programs in summer, showers and restrooms. Closed November through mid-March.

▲ There are 66 tent sites ($12 to $16 per night) and 44 RV hookup sites ($16 to $20 per night). Reservations: 800-452-5687.

BEACON ROCK STATE PARK

✉Off Route 14 ☎509-427-8265

🏃 🚴 🐎 ⚓ Located next to Beacon Rock, a volcanic landmark on the Washington side of the river named by Lewis and Clark, this park has several lovely trails, including one that goes up 800-foot-high Beacon Rock itself. There is also fishing on the river and a 53-table picnic site.

▲ The attractive forested campground built in the 1930s by the Civilian Conservation Corps has 28 first-come, first-served private tent sites with restrooms and two showers; a group site at Hamilton Mountain Trailhead may be reserved (888-266-7688) for groups of up to 200 for tent and/or RV camping.

OUTDOOR ADVENTURES

ROLLERSKATING & ICE SKATING

Skating may not be big-thrills adventure, but it sure is fun. In Portland, rollerskating even takes on an old-fashioned aura when you've got an amusement-park organ playing the music. Skaters are welcome to use any hard surface in the city's parks. **Portland Parks Department** (503-823-2223; www.portlandparks.org).

Portland East

OAKS AMUSEMENT PARK ✉7805 Southeast Oaks Park Way, Portland ☎503-233-5777 ⌖www.oakspark.com Rollerblade or rollerskate to the strains of the mighty Wurlitzer at this early 20th-century park on the east bank of the Willamette. Skate rentals are available.

SKATEWORLD ✉4395 Southeast Witch Hazel Road, Hillsboro ☎503-640-1333 You can rent skates, including inlines here. Public skating sessions are held Tuesday through Sunday.

Portland West

WATERFRONT PARK ✉Front Street, from Southwest Harrison Street to Northwest Glisan Street City ordinance prohibits skaters (and skateboarders) from most city center streets. One happy exception is the esplanade in Waterfront Park. When the weather is particularly pleasant, the concrete pathway (it's about ten feet wide) can get congested with cyclists, runners, skaters, skateboarders and strollers. But the mood is always congenial.

Portland East

LLOYD CENTER ICE RINK ✉953 Lloyd Center shopping mall, between Northeast Multnomah and Halsey streets and Northeast 9th and 15th avenues, Portland ☎503-288-6073 ⌖www.lloydcenterice.com At this ice rink, the music is recorded but the fun is genuine. Skate rentals are available here, too. Closed one week in May.

Portland West

VALLEY ICE ARENA ✉9250 Southwest Beaverton-Hillsdale Highway, Beaverton ☎503-297-2521 ⌖www.valleyicearena.com This arena hosts several public skating sessions a day. Skate rental is included in admission fee. Call for times.

WINDSURFING

Between the high cliff walls of the Columbia Gorge, east of Portland, winds on the river can hit 60 knots, so it's no wonder this is one of the world's best windsurfing areas, with Hood River its capital. According to a local expert, "Once you learn the tricks and let the wind do the work for you, it's not as hard as it looks." And if you don't mind cool temperatures (50°F and lower) in winter, you can windsurf year-round.

Columbia River Gorge

BIG WINDS ✉207 Front Street, Hood River, OR ☎541-386-6086, 888-509-4210 ⌖www.bigwinds.com This company offers rentals and instruction for children and adults, and a full-service retail shop. Kitesurfing equipment is also available.

DOUG'S SPORTS ✉*101 Oak Street, Hood River, OR* ☎*541-386-5787, 800-211-8207* ⏚*www.dougsports.com* If you're experienced and want to rent equipment, contact Doug's.

HOOD RIVER WATERPLAY ✉*Port Marina Park, Hood River, OR* ☎*541-386-9463, 800-963-7873* ⏚*www.hoodriverwaterplay.com* Contact this group for lessons and equipment. They also have a beginner beach area in front of the Hood River Inn.

SWISS SWELL ✉*13 Oak Street, Hood River, OR* ☎*541-490-9626* ⏚*www.swiss-swell.com* This company offers lessons in the Hood River area.

FISHING

Imagine catching a 350-pound sturgeon, even if you've never fished before. You can haul in these babies, which can come in at seven to ten feet and weigh upward of 300 pounds, year-round, right out of the Columbia. Walleye is another year-round favorite found in the Willamette; Tillamook Bay, about 65 miles west on the coast, is well known for trophy-size fall chinook salmon.

Portland
PAGE'S NORTHWEST GUIDE SERVICE ✉*Portland* ☎*503-760-3373, 866-760-3370* ⏚*www.fishingoregon.net* Page's can set up a one-day Tillamook Bay fishing trip on a 25-foot, all-weather boat, or arrange an outing on the Willamette, Clackamas, Columbia or Sandy rivers.

Portland East
DON SCHNEIDER'S REEL ADVENTURES ✉*57206 East Marmot Road, Sandy* ☎*503-622-5372,   877-544-7335* ⏚*www.donsreeladventures.com* Don Schneider's specializes in full-day fishing trips on the Columbia River but also provides trips on the Sandy and Willamette. Schneider can custom-tailor an outing in a drift boat.

Columbia River Gorge
THE GORGE FLY SHOP ✉*201 Oak Street, Hood River, OR* ☎*541-386-6977* ⏚*www.gorgeflyshop.com* The art of flyfishing abounds on rivers in the Gorge region. This fly shop arranges flyfishing excursions to such popular destinations as Deschutes. All levels of lessons are available.

RIVER RUNNING

About 90 minutes from downtown Portland is a whitewater thrill ride—the White Salmon River, just north of the Columbia, in Washington. Designated a Wild and Scenic River, it moves "fast and furious" through the forest canyon. Southeast of Portland is the Clackamas, another popular whitewater river, with some Class III and IV rapids. It's about an hour away. Most whitewater-rafting trips are done in paddleboats (*you* paddle!), holding six to eight people, plus a guide. The passive adventurer who'd like to photograph the gorgeous mountain scenery instead of paddle should ask about oar-powered raft trips.

RIVER DRIFTERS ✉️ *405 Deschutes Avenue, Maupin* 📞 *800-972-0430* 🖱️ *www.riverdrifters.com* About 35 miles southeast of Portland, the Clackamas River is the best bet for a one-day whitewater adventure. From March through October, the Clackamas River runs with some Class III and IV rapids (the water is too low the rest of the year). This outfitter, one of the only ones operating in the spring on the Clackamas, can arrange a complete full-day trip on several rivers, including the Deschutes and White Salmon rivers. They also offer a whitewater and wine trip on the White Salmon, stopping for lunch or dinner at a local winery.

GOLF

Portland East

EASTMORELAND GOLF COURSE ✉️ *2425 Southeast Bybee Boulevard, Portland* 📞 *503-775-2900* 🖱️ *www.eastmorelandgolfcourse.com* This is an 18-hole regulation course rated by *Golf Digest* as one of the country's most affordable places to play.

GLENDOVEER GOLF COURSE ✉️ *14015 Northeast Glisan Street, Portland* 📞 *503-253-7507* 🖱️ *www.golfglendoveer.com* The two 18-hole courses here are lined with fir trees. There's also a driving range.

THE CEDARS ON SALMON CREEK ✉️ *15001 Northeast 181st Street, Brush Prairie, WA* 📞 *360-687-4233* 🖱️ *www.golfcedars.com* Across the state border you can tee off on this par-72, 18-hole course.

Portland West

MERIWETHER NATIONAL GOLF CLUB ✉️ *5200 Southwest Rood Bridge Road, Hillsboro* 📞 *503-648-4143* 🖱️ *www.meriwethergolfclub.com* Just 30 minutes from downtown Portland, the four nine-hole greens here are good walking courses.

KING CITY GOLF CLUB ✉️ *15355 Southwest Royalty Parkway, Tigard* 📞 *503-639-7986* This is a challenging, nine-hole, semiprivate course that, says a local golf pro, is "harder than it looks."

Columbia River Gorge

HOOD RIVER GOLF AND COUNTRY CLUB ✉️ *1850 Country Club Road, Hood River, OR* 📞 *541-386-3009* 🖱️ *www.hoodrivergolf.com* This country club has 18 holes, full mountain views, pear orchards and a driving range.

INDIAN CREEK GOLF COURSE ✉️ *3605 Brookside Drive, Hood River, OR* 📞 *541-386-7770, 866-386-7770* 🖱️ *www.indiancreekgolf.com* Indian Creek, with its gentle rolling hills, is a dry, year-round 18-hole course.

TENNIS

PORTLAND TENNIS CENTER ✉️ *324 Northeast 12th Street* 📞 *503-823-3189* Four indoor courts (hourly per-person charge) and eight lighted outdoor courts (free).

BIKING

To say that the Portland area is bicycle friendly is like saying New York has a lot of tall buildings—so what else is new? There are 260 miles of bike lanes in the metropolitan area (plus 83 miles of multi-use lanes), and city buses all have bike racks. *Bicycling* magazine has picked Portland as the country's top bicycle city. Morning, afternoon or entire-day bicycling in the area presents a variety of options, from a mountain-bike ride in a city park to a long-distance excursion along the Columbia River.

Visitors interested in bicycling in the Portland metropolitan area will find the going easier by first contacting one or more of these resources.

PORTLAND BICYCLE PROGRAM OFFICE ⊠*1120 Southwest 5th Avenue, Room 800* ✆*503-823-2925* ✆*503-823-7576* This city office publishes a small map of the city's bikeway system; an accompanying brochure explains how to take your bike along on a bus. The map and brochure are free and available at the program's office and in some bike shops.

BIKE THERE! The best resource is this detailed bicycle map and safety guide for the metropolitan area. Bike and multi-use lanes are color coded to a use-suitability scale (off-street, low-traffic, etc.). *Bike There!* is put out by Metro (an elected regional government). You can pick one up at Powell's Bookstore, most bike shops or at Metro headquarters at 600 Northeast Grand Street in Portland.

THE BIKE GALLERY ⊠*12345 Southwest Canyon Road, Beaverton* ✆*503-641-2580* ⌂*www.bikegallery.com* Just as the riders using them come in a variety of shapes and sizes, bike routes in the area are of varying lengths and distances. Beginners and intermediate riders would do well to contact this company, which sponsors weekend group rides that are open to the public. Two rides are usually offered: a road ride one day, a mountain ride the next.

City riders will find the northeast and southeast portions of the city more suitable. The terrain is relatively flat, and marked bike routes follow low- or medium-traffic streets.

Portland East
SPRINGWATER CORRIDOR This path follows an old railroad route along the southern flank of the city. The 16-mile trail extends from Southeast McLoughlin Boulevard east through Powell Butte Nature Park and Gresham to the city of Boring in Clackamas County. Most of this multi-use trail is unpaved.

Portland West
SAUVIE ISLAND An excellent cycling getaway in the area is this island, located ten miles northwest of Portland. Light traffic makes it a pleasure to pedal through this wildlife sanctuary. You can drive or take a Tri-Met bus to the island.

FOREST PARK Mountain bikers will like this park, which comprises 5000 acres west of downtown. The park has some rather hilly terrain, perfect for mountain biking, and one multi-use trail, Leif Erickson, is especially popular.

VINEYARDS More experienced riders, of course, have the option of longer rides, perhaps west to the vineyards around Hillsboro. The Bike Gallery in Beaverton is a good source for information on suggested routes, distances and length of trips.

Columbia River Gorge
East of Portland, the Columbia River Gorge along Route 84 is prime cycling territory, particularly along any portion of the 62-mile route from Portland to Hood River. The old Columbia River Highway, which parallels Route 84, is less trafficked, calmer, scenic and a wonderful way to experience the Gorge. The Dalles Riverfront Trail, a paved bike trail, extends from the west part of The Dalles to Dalles Dam.

Bike Rentals
DISCOVER BICYCLES ✉ *116 Oak Street, Hood River, OR* ✆ *541-386-4820* ✐ *www.discoverbicycles.com* This store rents and sells mountain and road bikes and can provide information about guided bike tours.

HIKING

A hiker's paradise, the Portland region has beautiful riverfront walks, urban trails and wilderness loops perfect for a brief interlude or an all-day excursion. Trail information is available from the Portland Oregon Information Center or the Bureau of Parks and Recreation (1120 Southwest 5th Avenue; 503-823-2223, fax 503-823-6007). All distances listed for hiking trails are one way unless otherwise noted.

Central Portland
TOM MCCALL WATERFRONT PARK Named for a former governor, this park offers a 2-mile-long path along the Willamette River. It is an ideal way to get an overview of the downtown area.

Portland East
SPRINGWATER CORRIDOR This trail (16.5 miles) begins at Tideman-Johnson Park and heads to Gresham and south to Boring, shadowing Johnson Creek. A multipurpose trek, it is a converted railway line that's part of the Rails to Trails project.

MT. TABOR PERIMETER LOOP You don't have to go all the way to Mt. St. Helens to hike a volcano. Just take this loop trail (2.7 miles). Your hike on Southeast 60th Avenue, Southeast Yamhill Street, Southeast 71st Avenue and Southeast Harrison Drive (which becomes Southeast Lincoln Street) provides a pleasant overview of this landmark.

Portland West
SAUVIE ISLAND This island is ideal for short or long strolls. One of

our favorite walks in the region is the hike from parking lot #5 in Crane Unit around **Willow Hole to Domeyer Lake** (1.5 miles). Another good bet is the hike from Walton Beach along the Columbia to **Warrior Rock Lighthouse** (3 miles).

FOREST PARK   With more than 5000 acres, this park offers over 50 miles of connecting trails. Many of the routes are spurs off **Wildwood Trail** (27 miles), the primary route traversing this vast urban refuge. Depending on your time and mood, hike as much of this trail as you want, connecting easily to other convenient routes. Your starting point for Wildwood is Hoyt Arboretum's Vietnam Memorial.

MARQUAM NATURE TRAIL   If you're feeling more ambitious, try this trail (5 miles), leading from Hines Park to Washington Park via Terwilliger Boulevard and Council Crest Park.

CONIFER TOUR AND OAK TOUR   Two mile-long walks will add to your enjoyment of Hoyt Arboretum. The Conifer Tour leads through a forest thick with spruce, fir and redwood. Also well worth your time is the Oak Tour.

Columbia River Gorge

LATOURELL FALLS TRAIL   This 2.2-mile trail, on the Columbia River Highway, located three miles east of Crown Point, is a moderately difficult walk leading along a streambed to the base of the upper falls. To extend this walk another mile, take a loop trail beginning at the top of lower Latourell Falls and returning to the highway at Talbot Park.

#415 ANGELS REST TRAIL   Near the Bridal Veil exit off Route 84 is this easy hike (4.5 miles) leading to an overlook. This route can be extended another 15 miles to Bonneville Dam by taking the **#400 Gorge Trail**, an amazing path that passes many of the Gorge's stunning cascades, including Multnomah Falls, Triple Falls and Horsetail Falls.

#440 EAGLE CREEK TRAIL   Eagle Creek Campground at Exit 41 on Route 84 is the jumpoff point for this easy trail to Punch Bowl Falls (2 miles) or Tunnel Falls (6 miles), where a manmade tunnel passes behind the cascading water. You can continue to follow the wildflower-riddled path (part of the Pacific Crest Trail) through the Columbia Wilderness, up to Wahtum Lake (13 miles). Four campsites provide rest between Eagle Creek and the lake.

BEACON ROCK TRAIL   On the Washington side of the river west of Bonneville Dam is this one-mile trail leading to the top of the 800-foot monolith noted by Lewis and Clark. Ascended by a series of switchbacks guarded by railings, this trail offers numerous views of the Gorge.

DOG MOUNTAIN TRAIL   East of Home Valley, Oregon, on Route 14 is this trail (6 miles), a difficult climb up 2900 feet for impressive views of Mt. Hood, Mt. St. Helens and Mt. Adams. During May and June, the surrounding hills are covered with wildflowers, making this an extraordinary time to hike the trail.

TRANSPORTATION

CAR

Most visitors to Portland arrive on one of three primary highways. **Route 5** bisects the city and provides access from the north via Vancouver, Washington. This same highway also is the main line from points south like the Willamette Valley and California. From points east, **Route 84** along the Columbia River is the preferred way to enter Portland. From the west, **Route 26** is a major highway into town. Secondary routes include **Route 30** from the west and **Route 99** from the south. For road conditions, call 503-222-6721.

AIR

PORTLAND INTERNATIONAL AIRPORT *www.flypdx.com* Located ten miles northeast of downtown, this major airport is served by Air Canada Jazz, Alaska Airlines, American Airlines, Big Sky Airlines, Continental Airlines, Delta Air Lines, Frontier Airlines, Hawaiian Airlines, Horizon Air, JetBlue Airlines, Lufthansa, Mexicana, Northwest Airlines, Southwest Airlines, United Airlines and US Airways.

LIMOUSINES DOT COM *866-546-6726* *www.limos.com* If you want to ride in style, contact this company.

BUS

GREYHOUND BUS LINES *503-243-2361, 800-231-2222* *www.greyhound.com* Greyhound offers bus service to Portland from across the nation. The main downtown terminal is at 550 Northwest 6th Avenue.

GREEN TORTOISE *494 Broadway, San Francisco, CA 94133* *415-956-7500, 800-867-8647* *www.greentortoise.com* This New Age company offers a fleet of funky buses. Each is equipped with sleeping platforms allowing travelers to rest as they cross the country. The buses stop at interesting sightseeing points en route. The Green Tortoise, an endangered species from the '60s, travels to and from the East Coast, Portland, Seattle, Los Angeles and elsewhere. It provides a mode of transportation as well as an experience in group living.

TRAIN

AMTRAK *800 Northwest 6th Avenue* *800-872-7245* *www.amtrak.com* Amtrak provides service from Washington and California via the "Coast Starlight." There is also a northerly connection to Spokane on the "Empire Builder."

RENTAL CARS

At the Portland International Airport try **Avis Rent A Car** (503-249-4950), **Budget Rent A Car** (503-249-6331), **Dollar Rent A Car** (503-249-4792), **Enterprise Rent A Car** (503-252-1500), **Hertz Rent A Car** (503-249-5727).

PUBLIC TRANSIT

TRI-MET BUSES/MAX LIGHT RAIL ☎ *503-238-7433* ✍ *www.tri-met.org*
This agency serves the Portland region. Buses blanket the city, while the MAX blue line extends east from downtown to the Gateway transit center and then on to Gresham. The red line provides direct service from downtown to the airport. There is free bus service downtown and in the Lloyd District in the "Fareless Square" region spanning 300 blocks.

TAXIS

Broadway Cab (503-227-1234), **Radio Cab** (503-227-1212) and **Yellow Cab** (503-253-2277) all provide convenient local service. In Hood River, call **Hood River Taxi and Transportation** (541-386-2255).

OREGON COAST

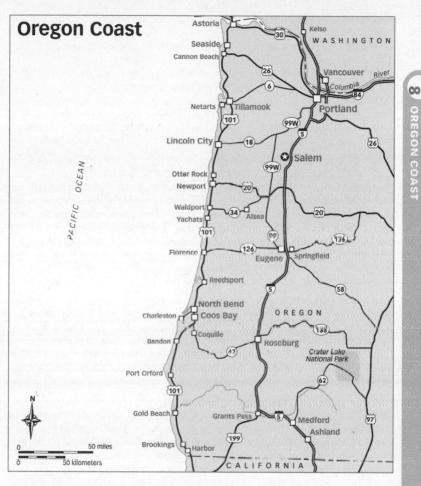

Oregon Coast

Astoria
Kelso
WASHINGTON
Seaside
Cannon Beach
30
26
Vancouver River
6
Columbia
84
Netarts Tillamook
Portland
101
99W
Lincoln City
18
5
26
PACIFIC OCEAN
99W
Salem
Otter Rock
Newport
20
Waldport
34
Alsea
20
Yachats
101
126
Florence
126
Eugene
Springfield
Reedsport
5
58
North Bend
Charleston
Coos Bay
OREGON
138
Coquille
Bandon
42
Roseburg
Crater Lake
National Park
Port Orford
101
62
N
Gold Beach
Grants Pass
5
Medford
97
199
Ashland
Brookings
Harbor
0   50 miles
0   50 kilometers
CALIFORNIA

As you take in the wonders of the Oregon Coast, do it with respect, for in a very real sense you are stepping into a paradise borrowed. In 1805, when Lewis and Clark arrived at the mouth of the Columbia River, only about 10,000 American Indians in such coast tribes as the Tillamook and Yaquina called this home. With roughly three square miles per inhabitant, these tribes were undisputed masters of their realm. The American Indians traveled almost entirely by water, were intensely spiritual and had, for the most part, a modest and self-sufficient lifestyle. Working hard during the spring and summer months, they harvested enough from the sea and forests to relax during the winter.

But their world began to change, indeed it was doomed, when distant entre-preneurs set sights on the region's vast resources. These men believed that the

Northwest did not belong to its native populace but was instead destined to be claimed by a new master race of settlers thousands of miles away. Among them was John Jacob Astor, the richest man in America. Eager to monopolize the lucrative fur trade in the uncharted Northwest, he dispatched the ship *Tonquin* from New York in the fall of 1810. Then, in the spring of 1811, just about the time the *Tonquin* was sailing across the Columbia River Bar, a second overland group sponsored by Astor left St. Louis. They began by following the river route pioneered by Lewis and Clark but then forged a new trail across the Rockies, eventually reaching the Snake River, where they were turned back by impenetrable rapids. By early 1812, when the party limped into Astoria, the little settlement created by men from the *Tonquin*, it was clear that their patron's great vision remained distant. For one thing, most of the *Tonquin* group had headed north to Vancouver Island, where dictatorial captain Jonathan Thorn spurned the American Indians, triggering a massacre that destroyed almost everyone aboard. In a final insane act of revenge, a surviving crew member lured the American Indians back on the ship, went below and lit the ship's magazine, killing everyone aboard.

In September 1812, not long after they received news of this tragedy, the Astorians left behind at the little Columbia River settlement were visited by a party from the rival North West Fur Company. These newcomers announced that a British warship was en route to seize Fort Astoria. To make matters worse, they declared that the British had just won the War of 1812. Cut off from the news that would have exposed this lie, the Astorians decided to sell off their pelts and the first American settlement west of the Mississippi for pennies on the dollar. Then they began the long journey home.

While the British took over the fur trade, Americans began heading west on the Oregon Trail, inspired by the dream of Manifest Destiny, which would unite the continent "from sea to shining sea." In 1846, the Oregon Country was returned to the Americans and new settlers gradually returned to the coast. Astoria and other settlements along the coast emerged as fishing, farming and logging centers. The arrival of the railroads spawned the development of resort towns like Newport and Seaside. Boardwalks, modeled after those found on the East Coast, soon sprang up to serve the growing clientele.

The coast may have been the magnet, but it didn't take the new arrivals long to discover that the lofty headlands, picturesque estuaries, rocky points, sand dunes and tidepools were only part of the attraction. Back behind the coastal rhododendron fields were rivers that offered legendary steelhead fishing. Sunny valleys forested with fir, spruce, hemlock and cedar were perfect for camping. Stands of weird carnivorous plants, plunging waterfalls, myrtle groves and pristine lakes were all part of the draw. And the Indians, decimated by white man's diseases, were subjugated by the new settlers and ultimately forced onto reservations.

Having pushed the natives conveniently out of the way, the pioneers soon began reaping nature's bounty from the coastal region. Coos Bay became a major wood-processing center, and commercial fishing dominated the economies of communities like Port Orford. In other towns, such as Tillamook, the dairy trade flourished. And, of course, farming also began to emerge in the sunnier valleys east of the coast.

Today, thanks in part to a comprehensive network of state parks, the coast is equally appealing to motorists, bikers and hikers. While it's hard to improve on this landscape, humans have done their best to complement nature's handiwork. **379** From bed and breakfasts heavy on chintz and lace to bargain oceanfront motels furnished from garage sales, accommodations serve every taste. Everywhere you turn, another executive chef weary of big-city life seems to be opening a pasta joint or a pita stand. Theater, classical music, jazz, pottery and sculpture galleries have all found a home in towns ranging from North Bend to Cannon Beach. A major aquarium in Newport, a world-class maritime museum in Astoria, a printing museum in Coos Bay, an antiquarian curio shop in Florence—these are just a few of the special places that are likely to capture your attention.

If you must go down to the sea again, and you must, rest assured that this coast offers the space all of us need. True, some of the northern beaches draw a crowd on weekends and holidays. But traffic is lighter on the South Coast, where beach-combing can be a solitary experience. With vast national recreation areas, national forests and sloughs, it's easy to get lost in the region. Often foggy, the Oregon coast is hit by frequent storms in the winter months. But this rugged weather is offset by mild periods in the summer or early fall. Even when the coast itself is socked in, inland valleys just a few miles away can be warm and sunny. The contrast continues: Temperatures along the coast seldom fall below freezing, but the adjacent coastal peaks are frequently snowbound in the winter months. And while the surf is bracing, lakes adjacent to the coast feature warmer waters ideal for swimming and waterskiing.

To fully experience the coast, you're well advised to see it border to border, from Astoria to Brookings. But many travelers prefer to focus on one or two areas. If you're history minded, Astoria is a must. For pure scenic grandeur and small-town charm, it's hard to beat the Tillamook–Three Capes area. Another winner in this category is the Otter Rock community north of Newport. Windy Port Orford is a very special place, scenic, uncrowded and ideal for steelheading.

Groups with diverse interests such as surf fishing, arcade games and shopping for folk art will want to consider well-rounded resort towns like Lincoln City, Seaside and Newport. They offer sporting life, cultural attractions and all the cotton candy you can eat. These towns are also convenient to rural gems when you're ready to make a great escape.

One of the most alluring communities on the coast is Florence. A delightful historic district, some of Oregon's finest dunes, a good restaurant scene and easy access to the Willamette Valley make this community a popular getaway. In the same category is Bandon, a charming port with a commercial district that will delight the shoppers in your group. Those who are eager to take a jet boat to the wilderness will doubtless find themselves in Gold Beach, a major fishing center. And Brookings is the gateway to one of our favorites, the Chetco River country.

The Bay Area, Coos Bay/North Bend/Charleston, is an ideal choice for clamming on the tidal flats. The parks, sloughs and country roads south of the area will keep you busy for days. And there is an impressive variety of museums, including one of the state's finest art institutions.

When it comes to a trendy resort atmosphere with tasteful shopping malls, sign ordinances, café au lait, classical music, French cuisine and gallery openings, Cannon Beach is the coast's class act. Every day the tourist tide from the east washes in patrons of the arts and Oregon varietals. This town may set the record for mer-chant-punsters operating shops with names like "Sometimes a Great Lotion."

There are many other destinations that don't appear on any map. In fact, the best of the Oregon Coast may not be its incorporated cities or parklands. Think instead of rocky points home only to sea lions. Eddies so beautiful you don't care if you catch anything. Offshore haystacks that don't even have names. Dunes that form the perfect backdrop for a day of kite flying. Points that seem to have been created solely for the purpose of sunset watching.

All these possibilities may seem overwhelming, but we believe the following pages will put your mind at ease. An embarrassment of riches, the Oregon Coast is more byway than highway. As you explore the capes and coves, visit the sea lion caves and sea-cut caverns, you're likely to make numerous finds of your own.

Those hidden places we're always talking about will tempt you to linger for hours, maybe even days. And however long you stay, give pause to remember that another people once lived here.

NORTH COAST

Oregon's North Coast is one of the most heavily traveled tourist routes in the Pacific Northwest. From June to early October, you can expect to have plenty of company. While most travelers hug the shoreline, some of the best sightseeing is actually found a few miles inland. Less crowded and often sunnier, these hidden spots reward those willing to veer off Route 101.

A special tip for those who prefer to drive during off-peak times: Around 5 p.m. most of the logging trucks are berthed and the RVs are bedded down for the night. In the summer consider allocating a good part of your day for sightseeing. Then, at 5 p.m., when many of the museums and attractions close, take a couple of daylight hours to proceed to your next destination. Not only is the traffic lighter, the sunsets are remarkable. Plus, you'll be able to dine fashionably late.

SIGHTS

ASTORIA Why not follow the path of Lewis and Clark by taking Route 30 west from Portland along the Columbia River to this town, the first American settlement established west of the Rockies? Set on a hillside overlooking the Columbia River, Astoria is one of the Pacific Northwest's most historic cities, founded in 1812 by John Jacob Astor as a fur-trading post. Grand Victorians, steep streets and skies that belong to the gulls and shorebirds make this river town a must. Head to the **Astoria–Warrenton Area Chamber of Commerce** (111 West Marine Drive, Astoria; 503-325-6311, 800-875-6807, fax 503-325-9767; www.oldoregon.com, old oregon@ charterinternet.com) to pick up a helpful map and background.

UPPERTOWN FIREFIGHTERS MUSEUM ✉ *30th Street and Marine Drive, Astoria* ☎ *503-325-2203* ◌ *www.cumtux.org, cchs@cumtux.org* This is a museum for kids of all ages. The vintage collection, housed in a 1920s firehouse, includes a classic 1878 horse-drawn ladder wagon, antique

Radio Free Astoria

About 20 miles west of Portland you can tune in **KMUN** (91.9 or 89.5 FM), one of the finest public-broadcasting stations in the Northwest. A kind of Radio Free Astoria, this listener-sponsored station features local kids reading their favorite fiction, opera buffs airing Bellini, and river pilots doing classical and variety shows.

motorized pumpers and firefighting memorabilia. Closed Sunday through Tuesday.

COLUMBIA RIVER MARITIME MUSEUM ✉ *1792 Marine Drive, Astoria* ✆ *503-325-2323* ✇ *503-325-2331* ⌨ *www.crmm.org* One of the nation's finest seafaring collections, this 44,200-square-foot building tells the story of the Northwest's mightiest river, discovered in 1792 by Captain Robert Gray and navigated by Lewis and Clark in 1805 on the final leg of their 4000-mile journey from St. Louis. Besides documenting shipwrecks, the museum offers exhibits on American Indian history, the Northwest fur trade, navigation and marine safety, fishing, canneries, whaling, sailing and steam and motor vessels. Interactive exhibits include a Coast Guard rescue mission, fishing on the Columbia River and taking the helm in a tugboat Wheelhouse. And that's not all. Docked outside is the Columbia, the last of numerous lightships that provided navigational aid along the Pacific Coast. Admission.

FLAVEL HOUSE ✉ *441 8th Street, Astoria* ✆ *503-325-2203* ⌨ *www.cumtux.org, cchs@cumtux.org* Among the many Astoria Victorians on the National Register of Historic Places is this 1885 Queen Anne with Italianate columns and Eastlake-style woodwork around the doors and windows. Featuring six fireplaces, a library and a music parlor, this home is one of the most visited residences on the Oregon coast. Admission.

HERITAGE MUSEUM ✉ *16th and Exchange streets, Astoria* ✆ *503-325-2203* ⌨ *www.cumtux.org, cchs@cumtux.org* Built in 1904, this museum, located in Astoria's former city hall, has exhibits that feature the early pioneers, American Indians, immigrants and local industries of Clatsop County. A "vice and virtue" exhibit explores the county's colorful past. Admission. Closed Sunday and Monday.

FORT ASTORIA ✉ *15th and Exchange streets, Astoria* This small blockhouse replica was the home base for the Astorians when they settled here in the early 19th century.

COXCOMB HILL For a good overview of the area, follow the signs up 16th Street to this hill. Pictorial friezes wrapping around the 125-foot-high Astoria column, built in 1926, cover the region's heritage from its American Indian past to modern times. Unless you're prone to vertigo, climb the circular stairway to the top for a panoramic view of Astoria.

FORT STEVENS HISTORIC AREA AND MILITARY MUSEUM ✉ *Fort Stevens State Park, Hammond* ✆ *503-861-2000* ✇ *503-861-0879* ⌨ *www.visitfortstevens.com, foofs@teleport.com* About eight miles west of Astoria in the town of Hammond is this historic fort. On June 21, 1942, the fort became the first American continental military installation shelled since

North Coast

SHIP INN, Astoria
SADDLE MOUNTAIN STATE NATURAL AREA
TILLAMOOK HEAD TRAIL
SEAROSE BED & BREAKFAST, Tillamook

SHIP INN

PAGE 391

Generous plates of fresh-caught halibut and cod and huge bowls of hot seafood chowder in a waterfront dining room

SADDLE MOUNTAIN STATE NATURAL AREA

PAGE 396

Forested campground off the beaten path with easy coastal access and plenty of peace and quiet

TILLAMOOK HEAD TRAIL

PAGE 383

Seven-mile coastal hike through Ecola State Park with spectacular views leading to rocky Indian Beach tidepools

SEAROSE BED & BREAKFAST

PAGE 391

Quiet, oceanside inn with two simple, country-inspired rooms just minutes from the beach

the War of 1812. Nine shots fired by a Japanese submarine hit the fort. Fortunately, none caused any damage. (Three months later, the same pilot also dropped a few ineffective bombs near Brookings on the southern Oregon coast.) While visiting, you can tour the fort in a two-and-a-half-ton Army truck or take an underground tour of Battery Mishler (fee; May through September). Don't miss the wreck of the *Peter Iredale*, now a rusty skeleton easily reached by following signs inside the park. Parking fee.

LEWIS AND CLARK NATIONAL HISTORICAL PARK AT FORT CLATSOP ✉*Five miles south of Astoria off of Route 101* ☎*503-861-2471* ☏*503-861-2585* 🖥*www.nps.gov/lewi* During the rainy winter of 1805–1806, the 33-member Lewis and Clark party built a fort and lived at this site for three months before returning east. Named in honor of the Clatsop tribe, this reconstructed fort has introductory movie presentations and interpretive displays. In the summer, buckskin-clad rangers armed with flintlock rifles offer muzzle-loading demonstrations or show how Lewis and Clark's team made candles, did woodworking and sewed hides. There are trails upon which visitors can wander. Admission.

SEASIDE Oregon's answer to Coney Island, this town is the kind of place to go when you long for saltwater taffy and game arcades, boardwalks and volleyball. Just head down Broadway to find the carnival atmosphere. By the time you reach the beach you'll feel a restless urge to start building sandcastles. The oldest and one of the most popular resorts on the coast, it is easy to visit with a little help from the **Seaside Visitors Bureau** (7 North Roosevelt Drive, Seaside; 503-738-3097, 888-306-2326, fax 503-717-8299; www.seasideor.com, visit@seaside-oregon.com).

PROM   The two-mile boardwalk known as the Prom offers a historical look at Seaside. Along the way are Victorian-style homes, Arts and Crafts–style bungalows, Colonial revivals and English-style cottages. Another highlight is the Prom "Turnaround," marking the end of the Lewis and Clark Trail. At the south end is a reproduction of the cairn where the Lewis and Clark expedition boiled seawater during the winter of 1806 to make salt. More than three and a half bushels were produced for the return trip.

SEASIDE MUSEUM ✉ *570 Necanicum Drive, Seaside* ☎ *503-738-7065* 🖳 *www.seasidemuseum.org, smhs@seasurf.net* Inside this museum are American Indian artifacts (some dating back 2000 years), turn-of-the-20th-century photos of boardwalk hotels and bathhouses, a linotype printing press and antique fire-fighting equipment. Admission includes a tour of the historic Butterfield Cottage.

SEASIDE AQUARIUM ✉ *200 North Promenade, Seaside* ☎ *503-738-6211* 🖳 *www.seasideaquarium.com, aquarium@seasideaquarium.com* At this aquarium you can see marine mammals and feed local harbor seals. Kids love the hands-on interaction at the touch tank. Call for winter hours. Admission.

CAMP 18 LOGGING MUSEUM ✉ *42362 Route 26, Elsie* ☎ *503-755-1818,* 800-874-1810 ☎ *503-755-2815* 🖳 *www.camp18restaurant.com* Eighteen miles east of Seaside on Route 26 is this historical museum. Steam donkeys, cranes, train cabooses and other vintage equipment are among the exhibits. (There's a restaurant on the premises.)

JEWELL MEADOWS WILDLIFE AREA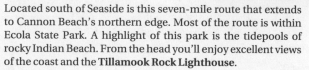
✉ *Route 202* ☎ *503-755-2264* 🖳 *503-755-0706* Follow Route 26 east to Jewell Junction and continue north on Fishawk Falls Highway toward Jewell. Just north of town is this wildlife area. Run by the Oregon Department of Fish and Wildlife, the sanctuary is a good place to spot raptors, red-tailed hawks, songbirds and, in spring, bald eagles and Roosevelt elk.

TILLAMOOK HEAD TRAIL
Located south of Seaside is this seven-mile route that extends to Cannon Beach's northern edge. Most of the route is within Ecola State Park. A highlight of this park is the tidepools of rocky Indian Beach. From the head you'll enjoy excellent views of the coast and the **Tillamook Rock Lighthouse**.

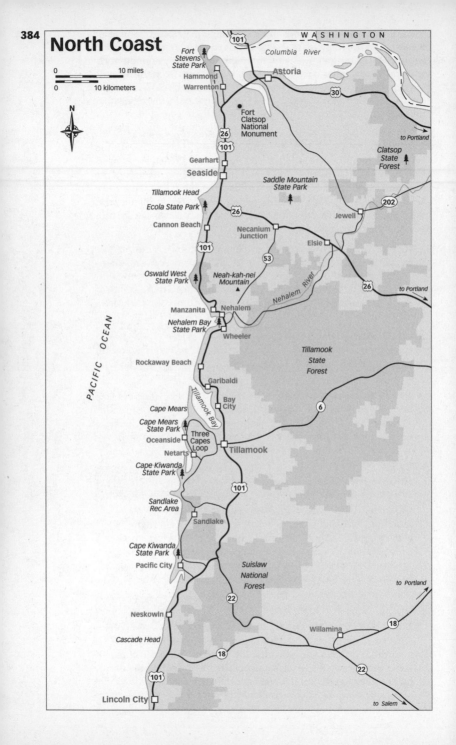

North Coast

0   10 miles
0   10 kilometers

N

WASHINGTON

Columbia River

101

Fort Stevens State Park

Hammond
Warrenton

Astoria

30

to Portland

Fort Clatsop National Monument

Clatsop State Forest

26
101

Gearhart

Seaside

Saddle Mountain State Park

Tillamook Head

Ecola State Park

Cannon Beach

26

Necanium Junction

Jewell

202

101

53

Elsie

Oswald West State Park

Neah-kah-nei Mountain

Nehalem River

26

to Portland

Manzanita

Nehalem

Nehalem Bay State Park

Wheeler

PACIFIC OCEAN

Rockaway Beach

Tillamook State Forest

Garibaldi

Bay City

Tillamook Bay

6

Cape Mears

Cape Mears State Park

Oceanside

Three Capes Loop

Tillamook

Netarts

Cape Kiwanda State Park

Sandlake Rec Area

Sandlake

Suislaw National Forest

Cape Kiwanda State Park

Pacific City

101

22

to Portland

Neskowin

Willamina

18

Cascade Head

18

22

101

to Salem

Lincoln City

HAYSTACK ROCK **Cannon Beach**, one of the most popular villages on the North Coast, is an artists' colony and home of this photogenic rock. Rising 235 feet ("the third-largest coastal monolith in the world") and accessible at low tide, this geologic wonder is a marine and bird sanctuary, and a good place to explore tidepools and look for puffins. With its resorts and condos, boutiques and small malls, Cannon Beach (it's named for a cannon that drifted ashore after a shipwreck) can be a busy place, especially in summer when the population increases fourfold. Gallery shows, the Stormy Weather Festival (early November's artist showcase), sandcastle contests and concerts in the park add to the fun.

OSWALD WEST STATE PARK This state park offers a series of beautiful viewpoints and picturesque forest hikes. Western red cedar, Douglas fir and spruce trees dominate the landscape and the shore is a half mile out.

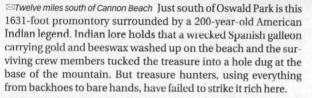

NEAH-KAH-NIE MOUNTAIN

✉ *Twelve miles south of Cannon Beach* Just south of Oswald Park is this 1631-foot promontory surrounded by a 200-year-old American Indian legend. Indian lore holds that a wrecked Spanish galleon carrying gold and beeswax washed up on the beach and the surviving crew members tucked the treasure into a hole dug at the base of the mountain. But treasure hunters, using everything from backhoes to bare hands, have failed to strike it rich here.

NEHALEM BAY A lovely spot on the North Coast is this bay, separated from the ocean by a sandspit. The Nehalem River, a waterway filled with Chinook salmon, empties into the bay, making it one of the best fishing spots in the Pacific Northwest. You'll see boats crowding the bay during the prime fall fishing months.

MANZANITA Along Nehalem Bay are three small resort towns. This is the northernmost, which sits amidst trees at the foot of Neah-kah-nie Mountain. Many residents of Portland and Seattle make Manzanita a weekend retreat. In fact, more than 60 percent of the homes here are owned by people who are not residents year-round. A five-block-long strip of gift shops, restaurants and motels make this the bay's center for provisions.

NEHALEM The historic Nehalem waterfront, located right where the river meets the bay, was an American Indian community before being replaced by canneries, lumber mills and dairy farms. Today, despite disastrous flooding in 1966, Nehalem continues to thrive, sporting an increasing number of clothing, gift and specialty shops.

WHEELER This is an increasingly popular town situated on the southern side of Nehalem Bay on a hill sloping down to the Pacific. Boutiques are beginning to sprout up in Wheeler, which is also the site of the **Nehalem Bay Visitors Center** (327 Nehalem Boulevard, Wheeler; 503-368-5100, 877-368-5100; www.nehalembaychamber.com, nehalem@

nehalemtel.net). You can pick up information about Wheeler, Manzanita and the entire Nehalem Bay area here. Closed weekdays from November through April.

TILLAMOOK CHEESE ✉*4175 North Route 101, Tillamook* 📞*503-815-1300, 800-542-7290* 📠*503-815-1305* ✐*www.tillamookcheese.com* Heading south, Route 101 follows the curving shoreline around Tillamook Bay. On your way into **Tillamook** you'll probably want to stop to sample the familiar orange cheddar here. A self-guided tour makes it easy to see the Pacific Northwest's largest cheese factory, Tillamook County Creamery Association. You may be surprised to learn how old your Tillamook cheese is. Medium cheddar is aged for 60 days, sharp cheddar for nine months and extra sharp for nearly a year and a half! An observation room offers a bird's-eye view of the packaging process. Free cheese samples.

TILLAMOOK CHAMBER OF COMMERCE ✉*3705 North Route 101, Tillamook* 📞*503-842-7525* 📠*503-842-7526* ✐*www.tillamookchamber.org, tillchamber@oregoncoast.com* Next, stop by this chamber of commerce to pick up helpful background information about the area. Closed weekends.

TILLAMOOK COUNTY PIONEER MUSEUM ✉*2106 2nd Street, Tillamook* 📞*503-842-4553* 📠*503-842-4553* ✐*www.tcpm.org, clb@tcpm.org* Unlike many museums that display only a small portion of their holdings, this museum is packed with 35,000 antiques, artifacts, dioramas, mounted animals, gems and gemstones and other items connected with the coast's pioneer life and natural history. Highlights include Tillamook basketry, pioneer implements, antique-clock section and fire-lookout cabin. You'll also learn that the giant hangars south of town berthed blimps that patrolled the West Coast for the Navy during World War II. Closed Monday. Admission.

TILLAMOOK AIR MUSEUM ✉*6030 Hangar Road, Tillamook* 📞*503-842-1130* 📠*503-842-3054* ✐*www.tillamookair.com, info@tillamookair.com* If you'd like to explore the world of dirigibles, head to this museum, housed in a former blimp hangar that dates from 1943. It's the largest wooden clear-span structure in the world. The museum's collection features photographs, artifacts and 30 vintage World War II and modern airplanes. Admission.

SIUSLAW NATIONAL FOREST
From Tillamook, Route 101 runs inland for 26 miles, much of it through this commanding national forest, before returning to the seashore six miles north of Neskowin.

THREE CAPES LOOP West of Tillamook is this 35-mile drive, one of the most picturesque on the Oregon Coast. The three capes are Cape Meares, Cape Lookout and Cape Kiwanda, each of which contains a state park of the same name (see "Beaches & Parks" for more information). The route starts in central Tillamook. From Route 101, take Bay Ocean Road west, and when you reach the fork in the road, bear right along the coast.

Let There Be Light

No matter where you are on the Oregon Coast, a powerful beacon may be sweeping the high seas and shoreline. Nine of these classic sentinels built since 1857 still stand. Five continue to operate as unmanned Coast Guard stations, and three inactive lighthouses are restored and open to the public. Those not open to the public attract visitors who come to admire the architecture.

TILLAMOOK ROCK LIGHTHOUSE   Opened in 1881 and the state's only lighthouse that is actually offshore, this beacon was built over a course of more than 500 days, often in rough weather. Though not open to the public, the lighthouse is still worth a look from a distance. It has been added to the National Register of Historic Places.

CAPE MEARES   ✉ *Off Route 101, ten miles west of Tillamook*   ✆ *503-842-2244 (tours)*   ✑ *www.capemeareslighthouse.org* One of the best lighthouses, located at Cape Meares, five miles south of Tillamook Bay, is a dormant beam that was built in 1890. Open daily from April through October for a self-guided look-see, the lighthouse is part of Cape Meares State Scenic Viewpoint.

YAQUINA BAY LIGHTHOUSE   Off Route 101, just north of Yaquina Bay Bridge, is this lighthouse, built in 1871. Authentically restored with 19th-century furniture, Yaquina Bay features an interpretive exhibit.

YAQUINA HEAD LIGHTHOUSE   ✉ *Four miles north of Yaquina Bay*   ✑ *www.yaquinalights.org* Newport's lighthouse (at 93 feet, it's the tallest in the state) was constructed in 1873. The automated light flashes every 14 seconds and is supplemented by a powerful radio beacon. Admission.

HECETA HEAD LIGHTHOUSE   ✉ *Off Route 101, 13 miles north of Florence*   ✑ *www.hecetalighthouse.com* One of the most photographed spots is this lighthouse, the brightest beacon on the coast. Built in 1894, it is a national historic landmark that is still in operation.

UMPQUA LIGHTHOUSE   ✉ *Off Route 101, six miles south of Reedsport*   ✆ *541-271-4631* Built in 1857, this lighthouse was the coast's first. Destroyed in an 1861 flood, it was replaced in 1894. The 65-foot tower emits a distinctive automated red-and-white flash and is adjacent to Umpqua Lighthouse State Park. Tours are offered from May through September.

CAPE ARAGO LIGHTHOUSE   ✉ *Next to Sunset Bay State Park off Route 101* This 1866 lighthouse is on a rocky island at the Coos Bay entrance. The unmanned Coast Guard beacon has been deactivated but the structure still stands.

COQUILLE RIVER LIGHTHOUSE   ✉ *At the south end of Bullards Beach State Park, a mile north of Bandon* The 1896 lighthouse here was the last lighthouse built on the Oregon Coast. It serves as a public observatory with interpretive displays on the Coquille River region.

CAPE BLANCO LIGHTHOUSE   ✉ *Nine miles north of Port Orford off Route 101* In service since 1870, this is the westernmost navigational beacon in Oregon. It is also Oregon's oldest continuously operated light. This 320,000-candlepower light is near Cape Blanco State Park. Open Tuesday through Sunday from April through October for guided tours.

BAY OCEAN PARK   As you follow Bay Ocean Road along the southern edge of Tillamook Bay, you'll come to one of this region's most fascinating ghost towns. Designed to become a pre-casino Atlantic City of the West, this 1912 subdivision eventually grew to 59 homes. But between 1932 and 1949 the sea cut a half-mile swath across the spit, turning it into an island. Over the next 20 years the ocean eroded the Bay Ocean landscape and one by one homes were swept into the sea. Finally, in 1959, the last five remaining houses were moved. Today only a sign marks the site.

CAPE MEARES   The Three Capes Loop continues past this lake, a haven for waterfowl and shorebirds, before continuing to **Cape Meares State Scenic Viewpoint**. While here you'll want to visit the **Octopus Tree**, a legendary Sitka spruce with six trunks extending horizontally for up to 30 feet before making a skyward turn. With just two more limbs this could have been the world's largest Hanukkah menorah. You can also take the short trail to the century-old Cape Meares lighthouse, surrounded by wild roses in the warm months.

THREE ARCH ROCKS   If you continue south to Oceanside, you'll arrive at this wildlife refuge, home of Oregon's largest seabird colony. Half a mile offshore, these islands harbor 200,000 common murres as well as tufted puffins, pigeon guillemots, storm petrels, cormorants and gulls. You might spot a noisy sea-lion colony perched on the rocks below.

CAPE LOOKOUT STATE PARK _____
Nature trails and coast walks delight visitors at this state park. With 2000 acres of forested headlands abutting sandy dunes, Cape Lookout has some of the best walking trails on the coast.

SAND LAKE RECREATION AREA   Dune buffs will enjoy visiting this recreation area seven miles south of Cape Lookout State Park. These 1000 acres of dunes attract the ATV crowd, who zoom up and over the dunes ceaselessly.

PACIFIC CITY   On Cape Kiwanda, this community is famous for its dory fleet launched into the surf from the Cape Kiwanda beach.

The Three Capes Loop returns to Route 101 two miles east of Pacific City, two miles south of Cloverdale, and eight miles north of Neskowin.

MUNSON CREEK FALLS _____
Seven miles south of town via Route 101, take the turnoff to this 319-foot-high waterfall, easily reached via a half-mile trail. The horsetail falls is the highest in the Coast Range, and is a perfect spot for picnicking. The creek gorge is lovely.

RESEARCH FACILITIES   South of Neskowin, Cascade Head Road leads to the **Cascade Head Scenic Research Area** and the **Cascade Head Experimental Forest**. These two areas, run as research facilities by the U.S. Forest Service, are full of colorful wildflowers and birds. The moderately difficult six-mile-long Cascade Head Trail follows the coast and provides plenty of opportunities to whale watch. Because these are special research areas, be sure to stay on the trails and not disturb any flora or fauna.

NESKOWIN GHOST FOREST

✉ *Route 1, Neskowin* Just north of Cascade Head, near the forested sea stack called Proposal Rock, this "forest" of more than 100 tree stumps can sometimes be seen rising out of the water offshore. They look a lot like pilings from some vast, ruined pier, but in fact the stumps are remnants of a 2000-year-old primeval forest. Scientists theorize that an earthquake, tsunami or some other natural disaster suddenly lowered the ground level by 25 or 30 feet, burying the giant trees in sand or mud and preserving them from the oxygen that would have caused them to rot away. Mysteriously, the "ghost forest" appears and disappears. When especially severe winter storms erode the beach sand away, the stumps stand exposed for months or even years. At other times, they are entirely covered by sand. Severe storms during the winter of 2008 exposed them once again, so the ghost forest now stands clearly visible several feet above the high tide mark.

LODGING

ROSEBRIAR INN B&B

$$–$$$ 12 ROOMS   ✉ *636 14th Street, Astoria*   ☎ *503-325-7427, 800-487-0224*   ☏ *503-325-6937*   ✎ *www.rosebriar.net, rbinn@pacifier.com*

This neoclassical revival with fir wainscoting, leaded glass, traditional American furnishings and a formal dining room offers rooms in a renovated former convent. The rooms have wing-back chairs and mahogany furniture; some have fireplaces. One unit is located in a separate carriage house with a kitchenette and jacuzzi. The Captain's Suite has a great view of Astoria and the Columbia River. A gourmet breakfast is included.

CREST MOTEL

$–$$ 40 UNITS   ✉ *6366 Lieft Erickson Drive, Astoria*   ☎ *503-325-3141, 800-421-3141*   ☏ *503-325-3141*   ✎ *www.astoriacrestmotel.com, frontdesk@astoriacrestmotel.com*

East of town, this motel sits on a grassy hilltop overlooking the Columbia River. This trim and tidy establishment has modernized units with watercolor prints and writing desks, a jacuzzi and laundry facilities. Try for one of the quieter rear rooms.

BEST WESTERN LINCOLN INN OF ASTORIA

$$–$$$ 75 ROOMS   ✉ *555 Hamburg Avenue, Astoria*   ☎ *503-325-2205, 800-621-0641*   ☏ *503-325-5550*   ✎ *38156@hotel.bestwestern.com*

On the Columbia River is this local Best Western. The units are spacious and comfortable, and most rooms have Columbia River or Young Bay views. The indoor pool, sauna and spa are open for guests' use; laundry facilities are a plus. Convenient to Astoria's historic district, this is an ideal spot to watch river traffic or fish. A full hot breakfast buffet is included, and freshly baked cookies are offered nightly. Pet-friendly.

HILLCREST INN

$$ 26 UNITS ✉118 North Columbia Street, Seaside ✆503-738-6273, 800-270-7659
📠503-717-0266 🌐www.seasidehillcrest.com, hillcrest@email.com

Attractive, pine-shaded units in a quiet garden setting close to shops, restaurants and nightlife are found here. Choose between studios and one- and two-bedroom units with kitchens. Eclectic furniture ranges from foldout sofas to wicker living-room sets. Some units have fireplaces, decks and spas. Barbecue facilities and picnic tables are provided for guest use. Adjacent to the inn is a six-bedroom beachhouse that sleeps up to 16 people; it rents weekly in the summer and requires a two-night minimum in the off-season.

OCEAN FRONT MOTEL

$ 35 UNITS ✉50 1st Avenue, Seaside ✆503-738-5661, 866-808-5661
📠503-738-3084 🌐www.oceanfrontor.com

This motel has one- and two-room units on the beach. The carpeted rooms have wooden bedframes, refrigerators and picture windows ideal for sunset watching. Kitchenettes are also available. Number 13, a one-bedroom cottage, is a bargain for the budget-minded.

SEASHORE INN ON THE BEACH

$$$ 54 ROOMS ✉60 North Promenade, Seaside ✆503-738-6368, 888-738-6368
📠503-738-8314 🌐www.seashoreinnor.com, info@seashoreinnor.com

Located right on the beach, this three-story inn has spacious guest rooms with comfortable furniture, vanities, an enclosed pool, sauna and whirlpool. Within walking distance of Seaside's most popular attractions, it overlooks volleyball courts and the surf. Continental breakfast and free wi-fi available

MCBEE MOTEL COTTAGES

$$–$$$ 10 UNITS ✉888 South Hemlock Street, Cannon Beach ✆503-436-1392, 800-238-4107 🌐www.mcbeecottages.com, cbhl@oregoncoastlodging.com

A mix of sleeping rooms and one-bedroom units, the completely non-smoking cottages here are conveniently located on the south side of town, only one block from the beach. Most of the units in this older, motel-style complex offer kitchenettes and fireplaces and are pet-friendly.

WHEELER VILLAGE INN

$ 6 UNITS ✉2nd and Gregory streets, Wheeler ✆503-368-5734
🌐otoole@nehalemtel.net

Set on a hill with commanding views of Nehalem Bay, the motel rooms here are small, clean and brightly painted. All rooms have carpets and kitchenettes. Pull up a chair and enjoy the sunsets or relax outside in the landscaped garden. All rentals are long term with a one-month minimum stay.

WHEELER ON THE BAY LODGE AND MARINA

$–$$ 12 UNITS ✉580 Marine Drive, Wheeler ✆503-368-5858, 800-469-3204
📠503-368-4204 🌐www.wheeleronthebay.com, wheelerlodge@nehalemtel.net

On Nehalem Bay, this lodge certainly is on the bay; it even has its own private docks. Motel-style units and suites, some with private decks, spas and kitchenettes, are furnished with fireplaces and VCRs. The lodge runs an on-site video store as well as kayak and canoe rentals and private bay cruises. Rooms range from Victorian-style to Art Deco; all are carpeted. It's convenient to fishing, crabbing, sailboarding, hiking and birdwatching.

OCEAN ROGUE INN

$$ 9 UNITS ✉19130 Alder Street, Rockaway Beach ☎503-355-2093
🖱www.oceanrogueinn.com, info@oceanrogueinn.com

Eclectic is surely the word for this inn, which features units overlooking Twin Rocks, a pair of giant rocks rising from the surf facing Rockaway Beach. One-, two- and three-bedroom units have full kitchens and ocean views and two more basic units offer beds, TVs, microwaves and refrigerators. Three units have gas fireplaces. Lawn furniture, a horseshoe pit, volleyball, barbecues, a fire pit, a play structure, and clam rakes and buckets make this family-oriented establishment appealing.

SEAROSE BED & BREAKFAST _____ ⓗidden

$$$ 2 ROOMS ✉1685 Maxwell Mountain Road, Oceanside
☎503-842-6126 🖱www.searosebandb.com, judy@searosebandb.com

This small oceanview inn offers a quiet, soothing stay just three minutes from the beach. The rooms have queen-sized beds and private baths with clawfoot tubs and antique brass fixtures; one has a private deck overlooking the sea. From the dining room you can sometimes spot whales, sea lions or sea birds while enjoying your full complimentary breakfast.

TERIMORE MOTEL

$-$$ 26 UNITS ✉5105 Crab Avenue, Netarts ☎503-842-4623, 800-635-1821
☎503-842-3743 🖱www.oregoncoast.com/terimore, terimore@oregoncoast.com

On the Three Capes Scenic Loop, this motel has units ranging from sleeping rooms to cottages. Located on the beach, these clean, modernized units are comfortably furnished. Some have lofts, sitting areas, kitchens and fireplaces. A quiet retreat, it's ideal for fishing, crabbing, clamming, whale watching and agate collecting.

DINING

SHIP INN _____ ⓗidden

$$-$$$ SEAFOOD ✉One 2nd Street, Astoria ☎503-325-0033

For fish and chips, you'll have a hard time beating this local haunt. Huge portions of cod and halibut are served in the waterfront dining room along with chowder, generous salads and desserts. The full bar is one of the town's most crowded gathering places. Live music is featured Friday nights. Nautical decor gives diners the feeling they're out on the bounding main.

CAFÉ UNIONTOWN

$$–$$$$ PACIFIC NORTHWEST   ✉218 West Marine Drive, Astoria   📞503-325-8708
✍cafeuniontown@charterinternet.com

An elegant, paneled setting with a mirrored bar, white tablecloths and a river view make this restaurant *the* place to go to enjoy rib-eye steak with shiitake mushrooms, almond baked halibut, cioppino, steaks and pasta dishes. Located under the bridge in the historic Uniontown district, this is also a relaxing spot for a drink after a hard day of sightseeing. Dinner only.

CREEKSIDE PIZZERIA

$$ ITALIAN   ✉2490 North Route 101, Seaside   📞503-738-7763
✍www.shopseaside.com/creekside

This pizzeria overlooks a river that's home to gulls and ducks. Locals swarm this Italian eatery for its famous twice-baked Sicilian crust pizza. Kids have a blast in the covered play area. Closed Monday.

PIG 'N PANCAKE

$$ AMERICAN   ✉323 Broadway, Seaside   📞503-738-7243   📠503-738-7014
✍www.pignpancake.com, comment@pignpancake.com

This local institution, open since 1961, can seat over 200 patrons at booths and tables to feast upon Swedish pancakes, crêpes suzettes and strawberry waffles. Lunch and dinner entrées include patty melts, garden sandwiches, seafood and steaks.

DOOGER'S
SEAFOOD AND GRILL _____

$$–$$$ SEAFOOD   ✉505 Broadway, Seaside   📞503-738-3773
✍www.cannon-beach.net/doogers

Convenient to the city's popular attractions, Dooger's serves crab legs, prawns, fish and chips, pasta dishes, burgers and steaks. The carpeted dining room sports oak furniture. Dessert specialties include marionberry cobbler.

LAZY SUSAN CAFÉ

$–$$ AMERICAN   ✉126 North Hemlock Street, Cannon Beach   📞503-436-2816
✍www.lazy-susan-cafe.com

Start your day with an omelette or oatmeal waffles at this place, a cut above your average café. Try their seafood salad or seafood stew for lunch or dinner. The paneled dining room with bright blue tablecloths and watercolor prints on the walls make the Lazy Susan a local favorite. Breakfast and lunch are served year-round, dinner only in the summer. Closed Tuesday.

PIZZA A FETTA

$–$$ ITALIAN   ✉Village Center, 231 North Hemlock Street, Cannon Beach
📞503-436-0333, 877-436-0003   📠503-738-7104   ✍www.pizza-a-fetta.com,
james@pizza-e-fetta.com

With both take-out and in-house dining, this pizza joint is a good choice for a slice or an entire pie. In addition to regular toppings, you can order sun-dried tomatoes, artichoke hearts, pancetta, bacon or fruits. Cheeses include Oregon blue, French feta, fontina and Montrachet chèvre.

BISTRO
RESTAURANT AND BAR _____ ⓗidden

$$ SEAFOOD   ✉263 North Hemlock Street, Cannon Beach
☎503-436-2661

Set in a small house, this intimate dining room serves specialties such as sautéed oysters in a lemon-butter sauce, a hearty seafood stew and fresh seafood dishes nightly. Dishes change seasonally. From November through April, call for weekday hours; open on weekends year-round.

ARTSPACE

$$ PACIFIC NORTHWEST   ✉9120 5th Street, Bay City   ☎503-377-2782
📠503-377-2010

Many museums have cafés in the basement or out on the patio. But this fine restaurant in an elegant gallery setting is a rare find. You'll walk past contemporary paintings, prints, sculpture and jewelry by outstanding Northwest artists on the way to the dining area. Warm gold walls, a deep olive ceiling, and fun natural-paper tablecloths to draw on all add up to a cozy setting for homemade breads, soups and specialties like oysters Italia. Sunday brunch includes treats such as vegetarian eggs Benedict, eggs florentine and quiche. Closed Thursday through Saturday. Call for winter hours.

LA CASA MEDELLO _____ ⓗidden

$-$$ MEXICAN   ✉1160 North Route 101, Tillamook   ☎503-842-5768

Set in a shingled Craftsman house, this is the right place to go when you want south-of-the-border fare on the North Coast. The dark-wood interior featuring beautiful built-in cabinetry and casablanca fans is brightened by floral arrangements and plants. You can dine family-style at the big tables offering specialties like *chiles rellenos*, Spanish rice salad, homemade tamales and generous burritos. If you're hungry, try *la casa* fajita tostada with steak or chicken breast.

ROSEANNA'S CAFÉ

$$-$$$ PACIFIC NORTHWEST   ✉1490 Pacific Street, Oceanside   ☎503-842-7351
🖱www.roseannascafe.com

Nautical decor, pink walls and valances, ocean views and an oak counter make Roseanna's an inviting spot to enjoy Willapa Bay oysters, daily fish specials, vegetable penne, burgers, steaks and their famous gorgonzola-pear pasta. This board-and-batten building is packed on the weekend with a loyal clientele that likes to toast those delicious moments when the sun finally burns through the fog.

SHOPPING

M AND N WORKWEAR ✉248 West Marine Drive, Astoria ☎503-325-7610, 877-272-5100 📠503-325-7610 🖱www.mnworkwear.com, neilc@mnworkwear.com This is where you can find flannel shirts, jeans, outerwear and casual menswear. Located beneath the bridge in the old Finnish Hall, this establishment is popular with fishermen, lumberjacks, farmers and tourists in the midst of shopping-mall deprogramming. Located in Astoria's historic Uniontown district, this is not a place for quiche eaters.

LET IT RAIN ✉ *1124 Commercial Street, Astoria* ☎ *800-998-0773* ✐ *www.let-it-rain.com, sales@let-it-rain.com* Caught in a downpour? Duck into this shop, where you can find any imaginable accessory, from rain boots to waterproof purses, to keep you dry. Be sure to check out their gallery of fine art and unique umbrellas.

WINE SHACK _____ idden

✉ *124 Hemlock Street, Cannon Beach* ☎ *503-436-1100, 800-787-1765* ✐ *www.beachwine.com, info@beachwine.com* This funky little shack, with cozy wood-paneled walls and a stained glass chandelier offers a fine selection of rare, international and local wines. Every Saturday afternoon you can stop in for a sip during its wine tasting.

ARTSPACE ✉ *9120 5th Street, Bay City* ☎ *503-377-2782* 🖷 *503-377-2010* This is my idea of a coastal gallery. Contemporary Northwest sculpture and painting, jewelry and arts and crafts are all found in this intriguing showplace. WPA art from the '30s, '40s and '50s is also on display. There's a restaurant on the premises.

RAINY DAY BOOKS ✉ *2015 2nd Street, Tillamook* ☎ *503-842-7766* ✐ *rdb@gorge.net* Rainy Day focuses on new and used titles and has an excellent section on the Pacific Northwest as well as a large selection of greeting cards. This is also a good place to pick up inexpensive paperbacks that come in handy when you want to relax by the fireplace. Closed Sunday.

BLUE HERON FRENCH CHEESE COMPANY ✉ *2001 Blue Heron Drive, Tillamook* ☎ *503-842-8281, 800-275-0639* 🖷 *503-842-8530* ✐ *www.blueheron oregon.com, blueheron@oregoncoast.com* This jam-packed shop is stocked with gift baskets full of local goodies such as cheese (made on-site), wine and salami. They also feature signature stemware and clothing.

NIGHTLIFE

GIRTLE'S _____ idden

✉ *311 Broadway Street, Seaside* ☎ *503-738-8417* ✐ *www.girtles.com* This live music venue, one of the few on the Oregon Coast, presents their house rock band on Friday and Saturday nights. Every other night is devoted to karaoke. Cover on Friday and Saturday.

BISTRO RESTAURANT AND BAR ✉ *263 North Hemlock Street, Cannon Beach* ☎ *503-436-2661* In Cannon Beach, this bistro has a guitarist on the weekends. Take a seat at the bar or order drinks and dessert at one of the adjacent tables. This romantic setting is the ideal way to wind up the evening. Call for winter hours.

COASTER THEATRE PLAYHOUSE ✉ *108 North Hemlock Street, Cannon Beach* ☎ *503-436-1242* 📠 *503-436-9653* 🖥 *www.coastertheatre.com, info@coaster theatre.com* For musicals and jazz piano, Broadway shows, murder mysteries, revivals, classical concerts, comedies and melodramas, check out the Coaster. Closed in January.

BEACHES & PARKS

OREGON PACIFIC COAST PASSPORT ☎ *800-551-6949* This $35 annual park passport covers entry, vehicle parking and day-use fees at all 17 state and federal park sites along the Oregon Coast, including the Yaquina Head Lighthouse, the Cape Lookout State Park headlands and the Shore Acres gardens. The passport is available by calling the State Park Information Center listed above and at a number of visitors centers and ranger stations throughout Oregon. A $10 five-day pass is available as well for shorter visits.

FORT STEVENS STATE PARK
✉ *Take Pacific Drive west from Hammond* ☎ *503-861-1671* 📠 *503-861-9890*
🚶 🚴 ⛵ 🎣 🏊 🚤 🚣 This 3762-acre state park embraces a Civil War–era fort that defended the coast during World War II. The site of a rare coastal attack by a Japanese submarine in 1942, the park includes shallow lakes, dunes, sand flats and a pine forest. The paved bike trails are also good for skating. Of special interest are the oceanfront remains of a wrecked British ship, the *Peter Iredale*. A museum and guided tours offer historical perspective on the region. Fish the surf for perch. The razor clamming is excellent. There are picnic tables, showers, restrooms and a gift shop. Day-use fee, $3.

▲ There are 19 tent sites ($13 to $18 per night), 174 hookup sites ($18 to $22 per night) and 15 yurts ($30 per night). Hiker-biker sites ($4 per night) are available by request. Reservations: 800-452-5687.

ECOLA STATE PARK _____ ⓗidden
✉ *Off Route 101, two miles north of Cannon Beach* ☎ *503-436-2844*
🚶 🚴 ⛵ 🎣 🏊 Forested with Sitka spruce and western hemlock, this 1303-acre park includes Ecola Point and the steep shoreline leading to Tillamook Head. The name Ecola comes from the Chinook word for whale, which was hunted in the waters offshore. You may see deer and elk during your visit. You can fish for perch. At Indian Beach, you can take the Clatsop Loop Trail, an interpretive hike that lets you explore the same place as Lewis and Clark. You'll find barbecue pits, picnic tables, group picnic shelter (available by reservation at 800-551-6949) and restrooms. Day-use fee, $3.

▲ There are three primitive Adirondack-style shelters located at the summit of the Clatsop Loop Trail; no fee.

SADDLE MOUNTAIN STATE NATURAL AREA

✉ *Off Route 26, eight miles northeast of Necanicum Junction* 📞 *503-368-5943* 📠 *503-368-5090*

🚶 A 3283-foot twin peak is the heart of this natural heritage site that features unusual plants and flowers. You can hike to the top, but it's a cold, challenging trek. The reward is well worth it, though: a uniquely beautiful landscape. Saddle Mountain was originally called Swallahoost for a chief who, after being murdered, was said to have returned to life as an eagle. From the mountaintop you can see both the Columbia River's mouth and the Pacific Coast. Douglas fir, spruce, hemlock and alder shade the 2911-acre park. There are picnic tables and restrooms. Closed in winter from November to March, or until the snow melts.

🏕 There are 10 primitive sites ($5 to $9 per night); closed November through March.

OSWALD WEST STATE PARK

✉ *Off Route 101, ten miles south of Cannon Beach* 📞 *503-368-3575, 800-551-6949*

🚶 🎣 🚴 ⛵ 🛶 With four miles of Pacific shoreline, this 2484-acre park provides great views of Nehalem Bay, as you walk only a half-mile from old growth forest to beach. Douglas fir, spruce and western red cedar dominate the rainforest in this park bounded on the south by legendary Neah-kah-nie Mountain. You'll want to visit the picturesque creeks, coves and scenic Arch Cape. Fishing is good at the beach for cod, perch and bass. You'll find picnic tables and restrooms.

🏕 There are 30 primitive sites accessible by foot with wheelbarrows for walk-in campers; $10 to $14 per night. Closed all of 2009 for research.

NEHALEM BAY STATE PARK

✉ *Off Route 101, three miles south of Manzanita Junction* 📞 *503-368-5943, 800-551-6949*

🚶 🚴 🐎 ⛷ 🛥 🛶 Encompassing a three-mile-long sandspit at Nehalem Bay's mouth, this 889-acre park is a popular recreational area. The open, windswept landscape is ideal for kite flying. Nehalem Bay State Park is also a favorite for horseback riding, cycling and walking. There's good crabbing in the bay and, depending on the season, good fishing for steelhead, cutthroat trout, perch and chinook salmon. Facilities include picnic tables, restrooms, showers and an on-site airport. Day-use fee, $3.

🏕 There are 265 RV hookup sites ($16 to $20 per night), 18 yurts ($27 per night), 17 horse camp sites ($12 to $16 per night) and hiker-biker sites ($4 per person per night). Reservations: 800-452-5687.

CAPE MEARES STATE SCENIC VIEWPOINT

✉ *Off Route 101, ten miles west of Tillamook* 📞 *503-842-3182, 800-551-6949* 🌐 *www.capemeareslighthouse.org*

🚶 Named for an 18th-century British naval officer and trader, this 94-acre park and adjacent wildlife refuge encompass a spruce-hemlock forest and memorable ocean headlands. While the historic lighthouse (closed November through March) no longer shines, the cape remains a landmark for tourists, who come to see the offshore national wildlife refuge and birds, including bald eagles and peregrine falcons. It is a prime location for spotting migrating whales. When you're here, look for the Octopus Tree, an exotic Sitka spruce that was once a meeting point for Tillamook American Indian medicine men. There are picnic tables and restrooms.

CAPE LOOKOUT STATE PARK

✉ *Off Route 101, 11 miles southwest of Tillamook* ☎ *503-842-4981 (reservation information), 503-842-3182 (ranger station)*

🚶 🚲 ⛱ With two miles of forested headlands, a rainforest, beaches and sand dunes on Netarts Bay, it's hard to resist this 2000-acre gem. It is also one of the highlights of the Three Capes Loop. There's excellent crabbing in Netarts Bay. You'll find picnic tables, restrooms and showers. Day-use fee, $3.

⛺ There are 173 tent sites ($12 to $16 per night), 38 RV hookup sites ($16 to $20 per night), 13 yurts ($27 per night), three deluxe log cabins ($45 to $66 per night) and a hiker-biker camp ($4 per person per night). Reservations: 800-452-5687.

CAPE KIWANDA
STATE NATURAL AREA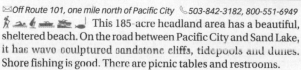

✉ *Off Route 101, one mile north of Pacific City* ☎ *503-842-3182, 800-551-6949*

🚶 ⛵ 🎣 🚤 🏊 ⛱ This 185-acre headland area has a beautiful, sheltered beach. On the road between Pacific City and Sand Lake, it has wave-sculptured sandstone cliffs, tidepools and dunes. Shore fishing is good. There are picnic tables and restrooms.

CENTRAL COAST

Proceeding down the coast you'll appreciate an impressive state-park system protecting coastal beaches and bluffs, rivers and estuaries, wildlife refuges and forested promontories. With the Pacific to the west and the Siuslaw National Forest to the east, this section of the coast is sparsely populated but has more than its share of state parks and beaches. Anglers and hikers have plenty of options here, with many of the best spots only about 90 minutes away from Salem or Eugene.

SIGHTS

LINCOLN CITY One of the largest communities on the coast, this city stretches along the shore for roughly ten miles. This region offers many fine parks, lakes and restaurants, and seven miles of clean, sandy (not rocky) beaches. Stop by the **Lincoln City Visitors and Convention Bureau** (801 Southwest Route 101, Suite 401, Lincoln City; 541-996-1274, 800-452-2151, fax 541-994-2408; www.oregoncoast.org, info@oregon coast.org) for helpful details on beachcombing, shopping for crafts and recreational activities.

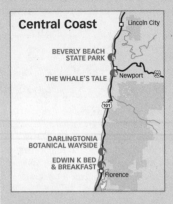

Central Coast

BEVERLY BEACH STATE PARK
THE WHALE'S TALE — Newport — 20
101
DARLINGTONIA BOTANICAL WAYSIDE
EDWIN K BED & BREAKFAST — Florence

Lincoln City

BEVERLY BEACH STATE PARK

PAGE 409

Picturesque, windswept seaboard spanning 130 acres from Otter Rock to the Yaquina Head Lighthouse

THE WHALE'S TALE

PAGE 407

Nautically themed, dark-wood café offering straight-from-the-sea fresh crab and fish

DARLINGTONIA BOTANICAL WAYSIDE

PAGE 402

Small state reserve, home to lush rhododendron gardens and rare, orchid-like cobra lilies

EDWIN K BED AND BREAKFAST

PAGE 406

Stately 1914 Craftsman-style inn with elegant, antique-furnished rooms and a deluxe, five-course breakfast

DEVIL'S LAKE

Many visitors flock to this popular water sports and fishing area. But few of them realize that **D River**, located at the lake's mouth, is reputedly the world's shortest river, just under 120 feet long at low tide. This is also a terrific place to fly a kite.

MEDICINE ROCK

When it's foggy on the coast, it makes sense to head inland where the sun is often shining. One way to do this is to take Route 229 inland along the Siletz River. Six miles beyond the town of Kernville you'll come to this pioneer landmark. Indian legend held that presents left here would assure good fortune.

SILETZ   Proceed south to this town, named for one of the coast's better-known American Indian tribes. In 1856, at the end of the Rogue River Wars, the American Army created the Siletz Indian Agency, which became home for 2000 American Indians. Within a year, unspeakable conditions diminished their numbers to 600. The agency closed for good in 1925, and today the Siletz tribe gathers each August for its annual powwow featuring dancing and a salmon bake.

TOLEDO You'll want to visit the popular galleries and antique shops here. This small town operated one of the world's largest spruce mills during World War II.

NEWPORT From Toledo, follow Route 20 west to this harbor town with an array of tourist attractions. Newport is a busy place, especially during the summer. Like Seaside, it is filled with souvenir shops, salt-water taffy stores and enough T-shirt shops to outfit the city of Portland. There are also fine museums, galleries and other sightseeing possibilities. Begin your visit to this popular vacation town with a stop at the **Greater Newport Chamber of Commerce** (555 Southwest Coast Highway, Newport; 541-265-8801, 800-262-7844, fax 541-265-5589; www.newportchamber.org). Closed weekends from October through May.

LINCOLN COUNTY HISTORICAL SOCIETY ✉545 Southwest 9th Street, Newport ☎541-265-7509 📠541-265-3992 🌐www.oregoncoast.history.museum, coasthistory@newportnet.com A short walk from the chamber are the Burrows House and Log Cabin Museum, which make up this local historical society. You'll see Siletz basketry, maritime memorabilia, farming, logging and pioneer displays, Victorian-era household furnishings and clothing, and many historic photographs. Closed Monday.

UNDERSEA GARDENS ✉250 Southwest Bay Boulevard, Newport ☎541-265-2206 📠541-265-8195 🌐www.marinersquare.com The most popular tourist area in Newport is **Bay Boulevard**, where canneries, restaurants, shops and attractions like this one peacefully coexist. Located on Yaquina Bay, this waterfront extravaganza gives you a chance to view more than 5000 species, including octopus, eel, salmon and starfish. Scuba divers perform daily for the crowds in this bayfront setting. Hours change seasonally from October through May; call ahead. Admission.

OSU MARK O. HATFIELD MARINE SCIENCE CENTER ✉2030 Southeast Marine Science Drive, Newport ☎541-867-0100 📠541-867-0138 This is the coast's premier aquarium, featuring a quarter-mile-long, wheelchair-accessible estuary nature trail. The center features hands-on displays, aquariums and exhibits interpreting the research being conducted at the center. Guided tours are available (fee). Closed Tuesday and Wednesday from Labor Day to Memorial Day.

OREGON COAST AQUARIUM ✉2820 Southeast Ferry Slip Road, Newport ☎541-867-3474 📠541-867-6846 🌐www.aquarium.org, info@aquarium.org This aquarium has indoor and outdoor exhibits showcasing seabirds, marine mammals, crustaceans and fish in a re-created natural environment. Children love the interactive exhibits and the touch tank. A 200-foot underwater tunnel has you completely surrounded by sharks, halibut and other sea creatures. Admission.

YAQUINA BAY LIGHTHOUSE ✉Newport Follow the signs west to visit this lighthouse beacon, the only wooden lighthouse still standing in Oregon, at Yaquina Bay State Park.

NYE BEACH ✉Newport If you continue north on Mark Street, you'll come to this neighborhood in Newport's historic beach district. It's more than a century old, but many of the early-day hotels, cabins and beach houses still survive.

Central Coast

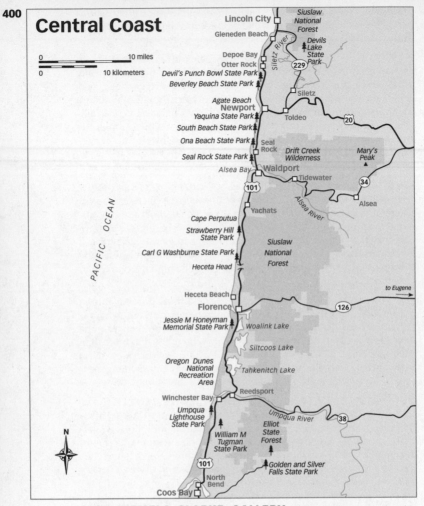

0 _____ 10 miles
0 _____ 10 kilometers

Lincoln City
Siuslaw National Forest
Gleneden Beach
Siletz River
Devils Lake State Park
229
Depoe Bay
Otter Rock
Devil's Punch Bowl State Park
Beverley Beach State Park
Siletz
Agate Beach
Newport
Yaquina State Park
Toldeo
20
South Beach State Park
Ona Beach State Park
Seal Rock
Drift Creek Wilderness
Mary's Peak
Seal Rock State Park
Alsea Bay
Waldport
Tidewater
34
101
Alsea River
Alsea
Yachats
Cape Perpetua
Strawberry Hill State Park
Siuslaw National Forest
Carl G Washburne State Park
Heceta Head
to Eugene
Heceta Beach
Florence
126
Jessie M Honeyman Memorial State Park
Woalink Lake
Siltcoos Lake
Oregon Dunes National Recreation Area
Tahkenitch Lake
Winchester Bay
Reedsport
Umpqua River
Umpqua Lighthouse State Park
Elliot State Forest
38
William M Tugman State Park
N
101
Golden and Silver Falls State Park
North Bend
Coos Bay
PACIFIC OCEAN

CLOE–NIEMELA–CLARKE GALLERY ✉ *839 Northwest Beach Drive, Newport* ☎ *541-265-5133* ✎ *www.yaquinaart.org, yaquinaart@yahoo.com* Near Nye Beach you'll find this gallery, where you can familiarize yourself with paintings, sculpture, pottery, handicrafts and photography by members of the Yaquina Art Association.

idden

AGATE BEACH _____
✉*Newport* Drive north on Route 101 to this great spot for rockhounds. Moonstones, jasper and tiger eyes are all found here.

DEVIL'S PUNCH BOWL STATE NATURAL AREA ✉*Outside of Otter Rock* If you continue north on Route 101 from Newport, you'll come to the Otter Crest Loop, which will bring you to this park, named for a collapsed cavern flushed by high tides. It is a great place for a picnic.

DEPOE BAY North of Cape Foulweather, named by Captain James Cook in 1778, is this bay, home to the smallest harbor in the world. The six-acre port is fun to explore on foot thanks to its seafood restaurants and shops.

SPOUTING HORN ✉*Depoe Bay* You may want to head across Route 101 to the coast to one of the best whale-watching spots in Oregon. A location for the movie *One Flew Over the Cuckoo's Nest*, Depoe Bay is also famous for this natural wonder, where the surf surges above the oceanfront cliffs in stormy weather.

SEAL ROCK STATE PARK

Return to Newport on Route 101 and continue southward ten miles to this state park, which has some of the best tidepools in the area and is a great place to watch the barking pinnipeds and hunt for agates.

WALDPORT Farther south from Newport on Route 101 is this town and **Alsea Bay**, one of the best clamming spots on the coast. The bay is easily accessed from numerous parks. The town is a relatively peaceful alternative to the coast's busy tourist hubs.

KOZY KOVE RESORT

✉*9464 Alsea Highway, Tidewater* ☎*541-528-3251* ✆*541-528-3837* Pick up Route 34 east along the Alsea River for nine miles to this resort. You can launch your boat here and explore this tributary bounded by the Siuslaw National Forest. You'll find a campground and a great fishing spot. This section of the Alsea can be a sunny alternative to the foggy coast.

ALSEA FALLS _____

For a picturesque, albeit windy, drive, travel east 39 miles on Route 34 to the village of Alsea and follow the signs to this waterfall. The area around the 35-foot cascade makes a good spot for a picnic, and there's also three and a half miles of hiking trails through old-growth forest and Douglas firs. Along the way you may catch a glimpse of woodpeckers, beavers and white-tailed deer.

YACHATS Return to Waldport and continue southward on Route 101 to this community (pronounced "Ya-hots"), a classy village with fine restaurants, inns and shops.

LITTLE LOG CHURCH AND MUSEUM ✉*Located at 3rd and Pontiac streets, Yachats* ☎*541-547-3976* Surrounded by a charming garden, this tiny house of worship and museum has a handful of white pews for congregants warmed by a pioneer stove. Closed Thursday.

CAPE PERPETUA   To the south is this town, discovered by Captain James Cook in 1778. The whole 2700-acre **Cape Perpetua Scenic Area** has miles of trails ideal for beachcombing and exploring old-growth forests and tidepools. The **Cape Perpetua Visitors Center** (2400 Route 101 South, Cape Perpetua; 541-547-3289) is a good place to learn about the region's original inhabitants, the Alsi. Known for their woodworking, canoes and decorative, watertight basketry, the Alsi hunted in the Coast Range hills.

STRAWBERRY HILL STATE PARK

✉ *Off Route 101 near mile post 169*   The white blossoms of wild strawberries at this park create a floral panorama in the spring months. This park is also a popular spot for seals that sunbathe on the shoreline's basalt rocks. A short path of steps will take you quite close to the seals. The tidepools shelter sea stars, anemones and bright-purple spin sea urchins. However, the pools are a protected reserve, so removal of anything is strictly forbidden. Down the road another two miles is the distinctive **Ziggurat** (95330 Route 101, Yachats; 541-547-3925), a four-story pyramid-shaped holistic center and bed and breakfast.

SEA LION CAVES   ✉ *91560 Route 101, 11 miles north of Florence* ☎ *541-547-3111* 📠 *541-547-3545* ✐ *www.sealioncaves.com, info@sealioncaves.com*   It's pinniped heaven here, just south of Heceta Head Lighthouse. Ride the elevator down to the two-story-high cave to see the resident stellar sea lions enjoying a life of leisure. The outside ledges are a rookery where these marine mammals breed and give birth in the spring and early summer. The bulls vigilantly protect their harem's territory. An overlook adjacent to the entrance is a great whale-watching spot. Admission.

DARLINGTONIA BOTANICAL WAYSIDE

As you continue on toward Florence, about six miles north of the city is this pretty place with a short path that takes you to see the bog where Darlingtonia, serpent-shaped plants also known as cobra lilies, trap insects with a sticky substance and devour them. They are in full bloom from May to mid-June.

FLORENCE   With the help of a chamber walking-tour guide, explore this community's old town. A small artists' colony with a gazebo park overlooking the Siuslaw waterfront, Florence has a popular historic district centered around Bay Street. Here you can browse or sip an espresso.

CHAMBER OF COMMERCE   ✉ *290 Route 101, Florence* ☎ *541-997-3128* 📠 *541-997-4101* ✐ *www.florencechamber.com, florence@oregonfast.net*   The chamber of commerce will quickly orient you to this Siuslaw River community. Grab a walking-tour guide here too. Closed Sunday.

OREGON DUNES NATIONAL RECREATION AREA _____ **h**idden

Florence is also the northern gateway to this recreation area. Forty miles of sandy beaches and forested bluffs laced by streams flowing down from the mountains make this area a favorite Oregon vacation spot. Woodlands and freshwater lakes provide a nice contrast to the windswept beaches. Numerous parks offer access to the dunes. Among them is **Oregon Dunes Overlook** (541-271-3611; fax 541-271-6019), ten miles south of Florence. Fee.

SIUSLAW PIONEER MUSEUM ✉278 Maple Street, Florence ✆541-997-7884 ✐spmfrontdesk@oregonfast.net To gain perspective on the region's American Indian and pioneer history, visit this museum, a former school built in 1905. Closed Monday and the month of January. Admission.

DEAN CREEK ELK VIEWING AREA Near Reedsport on Route 38 about four miles east of Route 101 is this elk viewing area. The herd of Roosevelt elk make for an unusual photo opportunity.

LODGING

INN AT SPANISH HEAD
$$$–$$$$ 120 UNITS ✉4009 Southwest Route 101, Lincoln City ✆541-996-2161, 800-452-8127 ✆541-996-4089 ✐www.spanishhead.com, info@spanishhead.com
Located right on the beach, this inn has rooms and suites with floor-to-ceiling windows and kitchens or kitchenettes. Many have balconies and each unit is uniquely decorated. A heated pool, spa, recreation room, lounge and restaurant add to the resort atmosphere. Wi-fi access is available.

SALISHAN SPA & GOLF RESORT
$$$$ 205 UNITS ✉7760 North Route 101, Gleneden Beach ✆541-764-2371, 800-452-2300 ✆541-764-3681 ✐www.salishan.com, reservations@salishan.com
In a forested setting above Siletz Bay, this lodge accommodates guests in two- and three-story, hillside buildings. All units feature gas fireplaces, balconies and upscale mountain-lodge decor. Golf, tennis, a fitness center, a library and an art gallery are just some of the amenities at this four-star resort.

TROLLERS LODGE
$–$$ 15 UNITS ✉355 Southwest Route 101, Depoe Bay ✆541-765-2287, 800-472-9335 ✐www.trollerslodge.com, trollers@newportnet.com
One of the area's best deals is this lodge set on an oceanview bluff. The establishment has clean rooms and suites with eclectic furniture, picture windows, TV and VCR, and kitchenettes; suites have full kitchens. Picnic tables and benches are the ideal spots for watching the residential whale pod and migrating whales in season. The location is good for deep-sea fishing trips. Wi-fi is available. Pets are welcome for an additional charge.

HARBOR LIGHTS INN

$$–$$$ 13 UNITS ✉235 Southeast Bay View Avenue, Depoe Bay ☎541-765-2322, 800-228-0448 🖥www.theharborlightsinn.com, innkeeper@theharborlightsinn.com

Modeled after a 19th-century New England–style inn, this cozy place overlooks the nation's smallest harbor. The inn's rooms and suites have balconies or patios overlooking the picturesque harbor; some have bathtubs with whirlpool jets and fireplaces. There is also a parlor with comfortable sofas, and a library with a fireplace. One room is pet-friendly. Full breakfast is included.

ALPINE CHALETS _____ hidden

$$–$$$ 11 UNITS ✉Otter Crest Loop, Otter Rock ☎541-765-2572, 800-825-5768 📠541-765-2394 🖥www.oregonalpinechalets.com, info@oregonalpinechalets.com

Don't be surprised if you find a couple sitting on an oceanview bench outside here. They are probably coming back to remember a honeymoon spent at this oceanfront retreat adjacent to Devil's Punchbowl State Park. Blessed with its own private park and beach access, each two- and three-bedroom A-frame chalet here has a large, paneled sitting area furnished with contemporary foldout sofas. All units are fully carpeted and come with kitchens and casablanca fans. Pet-friendly.

THE INN AT OTTER CREST

$$$–$$$$ 144 UNITS ✉301 Otter Crest Drive, Otter Rock ☎541-765-2111, 800-505-5735 📠541-765-2047 🖥www.innatottercrest.com, havefun@innatottercrest.com

This secluded inn offers one- and two-bedroom suites with fireplaces, fully equipped kitchens and decks. The semiprivate cove boasts great tidepools; you can look for seals and, in season, migrating gray whales. Set in a fir forest, with duck ponds and wild rhododendron, the inn also sports a playground, a workout room, a pool, a hot tub and a sauna. There's also a restaurant and lounge on the premises.

SYLVIA BEACH HOTEL

$$–$$$ 20 ROOMS ✉267 Northwest Cliff Street, Newport ☎541-265-5428, 888-795-8422 🖥www.sylviabeachhotel.com

This four-story hotel is named for the proprietor of Shakespeare and Co. and first publisher of James Joyce's *Ulysses*. Her Paris bookstore and coffeehouse was a home away from home for writers like Joyce, Ernest Hemingway, T. S. Eliot and Samuel Beckett. Each room is themed after an author. Our favorites are the ornate Oscar Wilde room featuring garish Victorian wallpaper (while dying in a Paris hotel room his last words were: "Either this wallpaper goes or I do"), the Dr. Seuss room (*The Cat in the Hat* is front and center), the Mark Twain room (fireplace, deck, clawfoot tub) and the Emily Dickinson room (marble dresser, green carpet, beautiful antique desk). While Henry Miller (*Tropic of Cancer*) didn't get his own quarters, this man of letters is appropriately commemorated in the basement restrooms. Incidentally, we'd love to see the owners add a James Joyce room in the years ahead. The hotel is completely nonsmoking and two friendly house cats reside there. Breakfast is included.

SUMMER WIND BUDGET MOTEL

$ 33 ROOMS ✉728 North Coast Highway, Newport ☎541-265-8076
☏541-265-9475

Summer Wind offers fully carpeted rooms—seven with kitchenettes, all with woodframe beds, sofas, pine coffee tables and stall showers. One of many Route 101 strip motels serving the Newport crowd, it's set back from the highway, and the rear rooms are relatively quiet.

CLIFF HOUSE

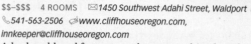

$$–$$$ 4 ROOMS ✉1450 Southwest Adahi Street, Waldport
☎541-563-2506 🌐www.cliffhouseoregon.com,
innkeeper@cliffhouseoregon.com

A bed and breakfast set on the ocean, this place features a big fireplace in the living room and a gazebo in the front yard. Convenient to ten miles of walking beach, the inn also offers a jacuzzi and an on-call masseuse. Some of the four theme-decorated rooms have chandeliers and wall-to-wall carpeting. Full gourmet breakfast included. Reservations highly recommended. Gay-friendly.

THE OREGON HOUSE

$$–$$$ 12 UNITS ✉94288 Route 101, Yachats ☎541-547-3329
☏541-547-3754 🌐www.oregonhouse.com, office@oregonhouse.com

Romantic, secluded accommodations on three-and-a-half forested acres above the ocean can be found at this inn and retreat center. Cottages, guest rooms, suites and townhouse units housed within five buildings across the grounds, include kitchens, fireplaces and marble bathrooms. One of the most charming is Oak Cabin, which has red-and-white-checked curtains, a red fireplace, a hot tub and a brass-and-iron bed. The grounds include a private beach, trails and a creek. Gay-friendly.

YACHATS INN

$$$ 35 UNITS ✉331 South Coast Highway, Yachats ☎541-547-3456, 888-270-3456
☏541-547-4331 🌐www.yachatsinn.com, gcninfo@yachatsinn.com

Here you'll find pleasant motel accommodations, several of which are suites, some with a rustic knotty-pine look and superb ocean views. Especially nice are the upstairs units, which include a glassed-in sunporch, great for watching a winter storm roll in. There is an indoor swimming pool and a lounge with stone fireplace, books, games, puzzles and free coffee. Some suites feature decks or patios. Gay-friendly.

SEE VUE

$$–$$$ 11 UNITS ✉95590 Route 101, Yachats ☎541-547-3227, 866-547-3237
🌐www.seevue.com, seevue@seevue.com

On a 60-foot cliff overlooking the Pacific, six and a half miles south of Yachats, this inn offers individually named and themed units. All have plants and antiques, and some offer kitchens and fireplaces. Weekend reservations recommended well in advance. Pets are welcome. Closed weekdays in January. Gay-friendly.

EDWIN K BED AND BREAKFAST

$$$ 6 ROOMS ✉ *1155 Bay Street, Florence* ☎ *541-997-8360,*
800-833-9465 ☎ *541-997-2423* 🖥 *www.edwink.com, info@edwink.com*

Turn up the Vivaldi and step right in to this circa-1914 bed and breakfast, where the rooms are named for six seasons (including Autumn and Indian Summer). Furnished with oak armoires, chandeliers and wool area carpets, this elegant home has a back-yard waterfall and Siuslaw River views. A deluxe five-course meal is included for breakfast; tea, sherry and cookies are served each evening. A separate apartment suite is also available for families or couples seeking more space and privacy.

RIVER HOUSE INN

$$ 40 UNITS ✉ *1202 Bay Street, Florence* ☎ *541-997-3933, 888-824-2750*
☎ *541-902-2312* 🖥 *www.riverhouseflorence.com, riverhouse@harborside.com*

On the Siuslaw River, the River House is a one-block walk from this popular town's historic shopping district. Many of the units have decks overlooking the river traffic and drawbridge. Rooms feature oak furniture and queens and kings with floral-print bedspreads. Some rooms have jacuzzis and overlook the waterfront.

DRIFTWOOD SHORES RESORT & CONFERENCE CENTER

$$–$$$ 125 UNITS ✉ *88416 1st Avenue, Florence* ☎ *541-997-8263, 800-422-5091*
☎ *541-997-5853* 🖥 *www.driftwoodshores.com, reservations@driftwoodshores.com*

If you're interested in cetaceans, consider checking in to this resort. An estimated 21,000 whales migrate south past this inn each winter and return northward in the spring. Overlooking Heceta Beach, the establishment has rooms and kitchenette suites featuring nautical prints, stone fireplaces, picture windows, decks and contemporary furniture. An indoor pool, hot tub and restaurant are located on the premises.

DINING

SUN ROOM

$$–$$$ AMERICAN ✉ *Salishan Resort, 7760 Route 101, Gleneden Beach*
☎ *541-764-2371, 800-452-2300* ☎ *541-764-3681* 🖥 *www.salishanspa.com,*
reservations@salishan.com

This casual restaurant features views of the resort's driving range and putting course. The lodge-style restaurant offers pasta dishes, pan-seared salmon and a Dungeness crab melt, along with a variety of salads and sandwiches. Breakfast, lunch and dinner.

DINING ROOM

$$$$ AMERICAN ✉ *Salishan Resort, 7760 Route 101, Gleneden Beach*
☎ *541-764-2371* ☎ *541-764-3681* 🖥 *www.salishanspa.com, reservations@salishan.com*

For a step above in price, try Salishan's romantic, tri-level gourmet restaurant. Seasonal specialties may include pan-seared duckling, ham-wrapped sturgeon chop and Chinook salmon.

ROGUE ALES PUBLIC HOUSE

$–$$ AMERICAN ✉748 Southwest Bay Boulevard, Newport ✆541-265-3188
📠541-265-7528 🖰www.rogue.com

Popcorn shrimp with ale sauce, a pizza crust made with stout, bangers with beer mustard, oysters with ale sauce—do we detect a trend here? This brewery serves these specialties with its golden ales, stouts, lagers, award-winning Old Crustacean barley wine and gold medal–winning Rogue Smoke (there are 35 brews available on tap) in a wood-paneled lounge. Tiffany-style lamps illuminate the booths, and the walls are decorated with classic advertising signs and pieces of the pub's history. The game room in the rear is good for a round of pool, or try your hand at blackjack in the card room.

GINO'S SEAFOOD AND DELI

$ SEAFOOD ✉808 Southwest Bay Boulevard, Newport ✆541-265-2424

Gino's offers crab and deli sandwiches, chowder and fish and chips. You can dine alfresco on picnic tables. Also a good bet for picnic fare. No dinner.

THE WHALE'S TALE _____ h̲idden

$$–$$$ SEAFOOD/AMERICAN ✉452 Southwest Bay Boulevard, Newport
✆541-265-8660

This restaurant is renowned for excellent breakfasts, vegetarian lasagna, cioppino, hamburgers and seafood poorboys. The dark-wood café has an open-beam ceiling, inlaid mahogany and oak tables and Tiffany-style lamps. A kayak frame, harpoon, whale's vertebrae and tail suspended from the ceiling complete the nautical decor. Closed Tuesday and Wednesday.

CANYON WAY BOOKSTORE AND RESTAURANT

$–$$ AMERICAN ✉1216 Southwest Canyon Way, Newport ✆541-265-8319

Canyon Way serves up a host of delectables in a contemporary setting. Choose between a main room with wood tables that has inlaid tiles, a garden room with view of the bayfront and, best of all, in the summer a handsome, enclosed brick patio with tables in a garden setting (lunch only). Dinner entrées change but may feature beef, seafood and chicken. Closed Sunday.

YUZEN JAPANESE CUISINE

$$–$$$$ JAPANESE ✉10111 Northwest Route 101, Seal Rock ✆541-563-4766
🖰takaya@yuzen.com

If you're looking for a sushi bar, try Yuzen. Set in a former rathskeller with leaded glass windows and Tiffany-style lamps, the restaurant has been redecorated with red paper lanterns, paper screens and a wooden sushi bar. The menu includes tempura, sukiyaki, *katsu don*, bento dinners and sashimi. Closed Monday.

TRAVELER'S COVE GOURMET CAFÉ AND IMPORT SHOP

$–$$ SEAFOOD/MEXICAN ✉1362 Bay Street, Florence ✆541-997-6845

In Florence, this café provides a perfect lunch-and-shop stop. The open-air deck overlooks the Siuslaw River, and the kitchen turns out light seafood fare such as "crabby" caesar salad, Boston clam chowder and hot shrimp sandwiches. Be sure to try the garlic-pepper fries. They also offer a variety of Mexican entrées.

SHOPPING

OREGON SURF SHOP ✉3001 Southwest Route 101, Lincoln City ✆541-996-3957, 877-339-5672 ✆541-996-3957 ✑www.oregonsurfshop.com There are good beachwear and swimwear departments at this surf shop, which also sells and rents surfboards, boogieboards, skimboards, wetsuits and kayaks for fun in and out of the water.

CATCH THE WIND ✉130 Southeast Route 101, Lincoln City ✆541-994-9500 ✑www.catchthewind.com, catchthewindkites@yahoo.com Forget your kite? For stunt, quad-line, box, delta, cellular, dragon and diamond kites try this aptly named shop. A full line of accessories, repairs and free advice are also available from the resident experts.

MICHAEL GIBBONS GALLERY ✉140 Northeast Alder Street, Toledo ✆541-336-2797 ✆541-336-2797 ✑www.michaelgibbons.net, michaelgibbonsart@charter.net The town of Toledo is home to one of the best galleries along the coast. Located in the old vicarage of the city's Episcopal church, this gallery is both home and workspace for noted landscape painter Michael Gibbons. Closed Monday through Wednesday.

INSCAPES GALLERY ✉818 Southwest Bay Boulevard, Newport ✆541-265-6843, 800-359-1419 ✑www.inscapesgallery.com Inscapes shows the work of over 400 artists: beautiful wooden sculptures, myrtlewood bowls and jewelry boxes. Also here are graphite sculptures, jewelry, ceramics, pottery and classic handcrafted board games.

OCEANIC ARTS ✉444 Southwest Bay Boulevard, Newport ✆541-265-5963 ✆541-265-3946 There are innovative fountains as well as limited-edition prints, pottery, jewelry and decorative basketry here.

MYSTIC WOODS WILDLIFE DESIGNS ✉05890 Mercer Creek Drive, Florence ✆541-997-9262 ✑www.mysticwoods.net, woodwiz@charter.net Check out the original chainsaw wood carvings by artist Timothy Robins at his shop, Mystic Woods. He specializes in caricature statues and bear carvings, but you'll also find intricately carved benches and nautical pieces.

NIGHTLIFE

SALISHAN LODGE ✉7760 Route 101, Gleneden Beach ✆541-764-3605 ✆541-764-3681 To enjoy rock and jazz you can dance to, try the second-story lounge here on Thursday, Friday and Saturday. When you're tired of the dancefloor, take a table by the fireplace or at the bar. There is also a deck that overlooks the golf course. Contemporary painting completes the decorating scheme.

NEWPORT PERFORMING ARTS CENTER ✉777 West Olive Street, Newport ✆541-265-2787, 888-701-7123 ✑www.coastarts.org, occa@coastarts.org Concerts, dance programs and theatrical events in the Alice Silverman Theater and the Studio Theater are presented at this center. Both local groups and touring companies perform. The box office is closed on the weekend.

ROOKIE'S SPORTS BAR ✉️ *Best Western Agate Beach Inn, 3019 North Coast Highway, Newport* 📞 *541-265-9411* 📠 *541-265-5342* 🖱️ *www.agatebeachinn.com/rest bar.html* At Rookie's large-screen televisions project every sporting event imaginable. There's a pool table, sports memorabilia, darts and a relaxing view.

BEACHES & PARKS

DEVIL'S LAKE STATE RECREATION AREA

✉️*The West Devil's Lake section is at 1450 Northeast 6th Drive off Route 101. The day-use section is located two miles east of Route 101 on East Devil's Lake Road.* 📞*541-994-2002*

🚶🚴🏊🛶🏖️🎣🛥️🚤⛵ Is there really a devil in the deep blue sea? That's what American Indian legend says right here in Lincoln City. Find out for yourself by visiting this 109-acre spot offering day-use and overnight facilities. The camping area is protected with a shore-pine windbreak. A day-use area is available at East Devil's Lake down the road. Fish for bass and trout. Facilities include picnic tables, restrooms, showers and a boat moorage. An interpreter conducts kayak nature tours.

⛺ There are 54 tent sites ($13 to $17 per night), 28 RV hookup sites ($17 to $23 per night) in the Devil's Lake section, and ten yurts ($29 per night). Hiker-biker sites ($4 per person per night) are available. Reservations: 800-452-5687.

DEVIL'S PUNCH BOWL STATE NATURAL AREA

✉️*Off Route 101, eight miles north of Newport* 📞*800-551-6949*

🚶 Don't miss this one. The forested, eight-acre park is named for a sea-washed cavern where breakers crash against the rocks with great special effects. Besides the thundering plumes, the adjacent beach has impressive tidepools. There are picnic table and restrooms in the Marine Gardens area.

BEVERLY BEACH STATE PARK hidden

✉️*Route 101, seven miles north of Newport* 📞*541-265-9278*

🚶⛵ Numerous coastal creeks make ideal hiking and camping areas. Among them is Spencer Creek, part of this 130-acre refuge. The windswept beach is reached via a highway underpass. Some of Oregon's best surf fishing is found here. You'll find picnic tables, restrooms and showers.

⛺ There are 128 tent sites ($13 to $18 per night), 128 RV hookup sites ($18 to $22 per night) and 21 yurts ($30 per night). Hiker-biker sites ($4 per person per night) are also available. Reservations: 800-452-5687.

SOUTH BEACH STATE PARK

✉️*Route 101, two miles south of Newport* 📞*541-867-4715*

🚶🚴🏄🏖️🏊🎣🛶🛥️🚤⛵ South of Newport's Yaquina Bay Bridge, this 434-acre park includes a sandy beach and a forest with pine and spruce. Extremely popular in the summer months, the park includes rolling terrain and a portion of Yaquina Bay's south-jetty entrance. There is a paved bicycle trail. For anglers, try for striped perch in the south jetty area. Explore the Beaver Creek area on a guided kayak tour (541-867-6590). Boat ramps at the marina make it possible to boat in the bay. Facilities include picnic tables, restrooms and showers.

▲ There are 228 RV hookup sites ($18 to $22 per night), 27 yurts ($30 per night), a hiker-biker camp ($4 per person per night) and group tent sites ($44 to $66 per night). There is one pet-friendly yurt available. Reservations: 800-452-5687.

ONA BEACH STATE PARK ___ hidden

✉ *Route 101, eight miles south of Newport* ☎ *800-551-6949*

🚶 🚴 🛶 🚤 ⛵ Beaver Creek winds through this forested, parklike setting to the ocean. Picturesque bridges, broad lawns and an idyllic shoreline are the draws of this 220-acre gem. Good fishing can be found in the river for perch or trout in season, and from the shore. Kayak tours are available for a fee (541-867-6590). There are picnic tables and restrooms.

CARL G. WASHBURNE MEMORIAL STATE PARK ___ hidden

✉ *Route 101, 14 miles north of Florence* ☎ *541-547-3416*

🚶 🚴 ⛵ Five miles of sandy beach with forested, rolling terrain make this park yet another coastal gem. Elk are often sighted at 1238-acre Washburne Park. The south end of the park connects to Devil's Elbow State Park's Cape Creek drainage. There are six miles of hiking trails, including the spectacular Lighthouse Trail, which leads along dramatic coastline to the Heceta Head Lighthouse. Nearby fishing is excellent: There's perch, tuna, bass and snapper in the sea, and several streams offer trout, salmon and steelhead. Clamming is also good. There are picnic tables, restrooms and showers.

▲ There are seven walk-in tent sites ($13 to $17 per night), 58 RV hookup sites ($17 to $22 per night), two yurts ($29 per night) and a hiker-biker camp ($4 per person per night).

SIUSLAW NATIONAL FOREST

✉ *Route 101 passes through the Siuslaw in Tillamook, Lincoln and Lane counties*
☎ *541-750-7000* 🌐 *541-750-7234*

🚶 🚴 🏇 🏕 🛶 🚤 ⛵ With two sections on the coast, this 630,000-acre region has more seacoast, 54 miles, than any other national forest in the continental United States. The terrain includes the Coast Range, Mt. Hebo and Mary's Peak. Oceanfront areas include the Cascade Head Scenic Area, Oregon Dunes National Recreation Area, Sand Lake Recreation Area and the Cape Perpetua Interpretive Center. While hiking some of the forest's 125 miles of trails, you may see deer, elk, otter, beaver, fox and bobcat. Northeast of Waldport, several trails lead into the old-growth forests at Cape Perpetua Scenic Area. Furthermore, there's boating and horseback riding. Incidentally, Siuslaw is taken from a Yakona Indian word meaning "far away waters." More than 200 species of fish, including salmon, perch and trout can be caught in local streams and along the coast. Facilities include picnic areas, restrooms, showers and horseback corrals.

▲ There are 40 campgrounds, one with full hookups; $15 to $25 per night. Two of the best known are the Blackberry Campground between Corvallis and the coast on Route 34 (32 tent/RV sites at $15 per night; no hookups) and the Tillicum Beach site on the coast near Waldport (59 tent/RV hookup sites at $20 to $25 per night). The former is situated on the Alsea River near a boat landing and hiking trails; the latter is right beside a nice beach.

JESSIE M. HONEYMAN MEMORIAL STATE PARK

✉Route 101, three miles south of Florence ✆541-997-3641, 800-585-6949

🚶🚴🛶⛵🎣🛶🛶🚤🛶⛵ This park is richly endowed with 500-foot-high sand dunes, forested lakes, rhododendron and huckleberry. Bisected by Route 101, 505-acre Honeyman is ideal for water sports, dune walks and camping. As far as we know, it has the only bathhouse on the National Register of Historic Places. A stone-and-log structure at Cleawox Lake, the unit now serves as a store and boat rental. Anglers may find bass or crappie, but rainbow trout is the main catch at Cleawox and Woahink Lake. Boating and waterskiing are allowed at Woahink. From October through April, off-road vehicles are allowed access to the dunes from the H-loop only. Picnic tables, restrooms, showers, a playground, a store (Memorial Day to Labor Day only) and boat rentals are available here. Day-use fee, $3.

▲ There are 187 tent sites ($13 to $17 per night), 168 RV hookup sites ($17 to $22 per night), 10 yurts ($29 per night), 6 group tent areas ($43 to $65 per night) and a hiker-biker camp ($4 per person per night). Reservations: 800-452-5687.

UMPQUA LIGHTHOUSE STATE PARK

✉Off Route 101, six miles south of Reedsport ✆541-271-4118,
541-271-4631 (lighthouse)

🚶🛶🛶🚤🛶 South of Winchester Bay, this park offers beautiful sand dunes and a popular hiking trail. Forested with spruce, western hemlock and shore pine, the 320-acre park is at its peak when the rhododendron bloom. Lake Marie provides calm water for canoeing or fishing. Trout is the most common catch. Great views of the Umpqua River are available from the highway. The lighthouse (which belongs to neighboring Douglas County Park) was built to signal the river's entrance; catch a tour any day of the week during the summer. You'll find picnic tables, restrooms and showers.

▲ Camping options include 24 tent sites ($12 to $16 per night), 20 RV hookup sites ($16 to $20 per night), 8 yurts ($27 to $66 per night) and 2 cabins ($35 per night). Reservations: 800-452-5687.

WILLIAM M. TUGMAN STATE PARK

✉Route 101, eight miles south of Reedsport ✆541-759-3604

🚶🛶🛶🛶🚤🛶 This 800-acre park includes Eel Lake, cleaned of logging debris and turned into a popular recreational area. An excellent day-use area, Tugman is ideal for swimming and boating. Fishing will get you either a largemouth bass or a variety of other fish, including crappie and rainbow trout. Restrooms and showers are available.

▲ There are 94 RV hookup sites ($12 to $16 per night), 16 yurts ($27 per

8 OREGON COAST CENTRAL COAST BEACHES & PARKS

night) and a hiker-biker camp ($4 per person per night). Reservations: 800-452-5687.

GOLDEN AND SILVER FALLS STATE NATURAL AREA

⊠ *Off Route 101, 24 miles northeast of Coos Bay*   ☎ *800-551-6949*

🚶🛶 ⤴ A pair of 100-foot-high waterfalls, old-growth forest including myrtlewood trees, and beautiful trails make this 157-acre park an excellent choice for a picnic. Cutthroat trout is a common catch here, as are crawdads. There are picnic tables, fire pits and restrooms. Bring your own water.

SOUTH COAST

The quietest part of the Oregon coastline, Oregon's South Coast offers miles of uncrowded beaches, beautiful dunes and excellent lakes for fishing or waterskiing. The smaller towns make an excellent base for the traveler who appreciates fine restaurants, museums, festivals and shopping. The Rogue and Chetco rivers offer rugged detours from the coast, ideal for the angler or rafter.

SIGHTS

COOS BAY/NORTH BEND/CHARLESTON BAY AREA   This is the coast's largest metropolitan area, a college town, fishing center and former logging center. Historic residential and commercial buildings, a grand harbor and a wide variety of outdoor adventure options lend character to this area.

COOS BAY VISITOR CENTER ⊠ *50 Central Avenue, Coos Bay*   ☎ *541-269-0215, 800-824-8486*   ✆ *541-269-2861*   ⌂ *www.oregonsadventurecoast.com* This visitor center is the ideal place to orient yourself. Pick up a self-guided walking tour, which includes 22 local landmarks. The route includes Victorian homes, Greek Classic commercial buildings and the Myrtle Arms Apartments, a rare Oregon building done in the Mission/Pueblo style. Closed Sunday.

COOS ART MUSEUM ⊠ *235 Anderson Avenue, Coos Bay*   ☎ *541-267-3901*   ✆ *541-267-4877*   ⌂ *www.coosart.org, info@coosart.org* One of our favorite galleries in the Pacific Northwest is at this museum, where 20th-century American graphic art and Northwest paintings, sculpture and prints form the heart of the collection. Special exhibits feature local and nationally known artists as well as occasional traveling international exhibitions. Of particular interest is the **Prefontaine Memorial Room**, a collection honoring the life and times of Steve Prefontaine, the distance runner who died in a 1975 car accident at the age of 24. During his short life Prefontaine set 11 United States indoor and outdoor records including several that still stand. Every year, a running event commemorates the memory of this Coos Bay native. Closed Sunday and Monday. Admission.

COOS HISTORICAL MARITIME MUSEUM ✉1220 Sherman Avenue, North Bend ☎541-756-6320 ⏴www.cooshistory.org, cmuseum@verizon.net Worth a visit is this museum, where the diverse history of this ocean-dependent region is examined. Pioneer logging and mining and maritime equipment, along with American Indian artifacts and a photo collage of local history, are on display here. Closed Sunday and Monday. Admission.

WATER SPORT SITES A popular recreational region, the Bay Area offers watersports and fishing at **Tenmile Lakes**. The **Charleston Boat Basin** is ideal for sportfishing, clamming, crabbing, birdwatching and boating.

SHORE ACRES STATE PARK ✉89814 Cape Arago Highway, Coos Bay ☎541-888-3732 ◉541-888-5650 ⏴www.shoreacres.net, shoreacres@state.or.us From Charleston, continue south four miles to this beautiful state park. Although the mansion of lumberman Louis Simpson burned down years ago, the grand, seven-acre botanical garden, including a 100-foot lily pond, is preserved. Admission.

CAPE ARAGO STATE PARK ✉End of Cape Arago Highway From Shore Acres, head south to this state park, your best bet for local tidepools and seal watching. The road into the park is closed to vehicle traffic, but you can still walk in, feet willing.

SOUTH SLOUGH NATIONAL ESTUARINE RESEARCH RESERVE ✉Charleston ☎541-888-5558 ◉541-888-5559 ⏴www.southsloughestuary.org Return toward Charleston and head south on Seven Devil's Road to this splendid nature reserve. An extension of the Coos Bay Estuary, it is a drowned river mouth where saltwater tides and freshwater streams create a rich estuarine environment. Even if you only have time to stop at the Interpretive Center, don't miss South Slough. Easily explored on foot, thanks to a network of trails and wooden walkways, the tideflats, salt marshes and open water of the estuary and forest communities are a living ecology textbook. A major resting spot for birds like the great blue heron, the slough can also be navigated by canoe. Open year-round, but the interpretive center is closed on Sunday and Monday from Labor Day to Memorial Day.

INLAND RIVER ROUTE Back at Charleston and Coos Bay, pick up Routes 42 and 33 between Coos Bay and Gold Beach, which are popularly known as the Inland River Route. Following the Coquille River south through the town of the same name, this route is the hidden Oregon of your dreams. You'll see farms, pastureland, orchards, birdlife and towering stands of fir. Twenty-three miles beyond the Route 101 turnoff is **Hoffman Memorial Wayside**, the first of two protected groves of the distinctive myrtlewood tree. Turning right onto Route 33 here, you'll come to the other grove in a few miles at **Coquille Myrtle Grove State Park** and soon enter **Siskiyou National Forest**. After traversing the east slope of 4075-foot **Iron Mountain**, you'll follow the **Rogue River** from the coastal mountains to the ocean, returning to Route 101 at Gold Beach. Allow at least half a day to drive this winding 123-mile route.

KUM-YON'S
PAGE 420

Crispy tempura, fresh sushi and spicy Mongolian beef in an eclectic, pan-Asian restaurant full of Chinese fans and Korean ornaments

SHRADER OLD GROWTH TRAIL
PAGE 433

One-mile, subtly sloping loop path through virgin Douglas fir forest dotted with colorful rhododendrons

CHETCO RIVER INN BED AND BREAKFAST
PAGE 420

Secluded, eco-friendly retreat set on 40 wooded acres with romantic gardens, tranquil streams and forested hiking trails

ALFRED A. LOEB STATE PARK
PAGE 417

Serene, 320-acre reserve on the Chetco River boasting redwood and myrtle groves and warm picnic spots

BANDON This is one of those popular resort towns that seems to have everything. From myrtlewood and cranberry bogs to salmon bakes, it's hard to be bored in Bandon. Swing by the **Bandon Chamber of Commerce** (300 Southeast 2nd Street, Bandon; 541-347-9616, fax 541-347-7006; www.bandon.com, bandoncc@mycomspan.com) for brochures and information.

BANDON DRIFTWOOD MUSEUM

✉ 1st and Baltimore streets, Bandon ✆ 541-347-3719 Bandon's **Old Town** is an engaging neighborhood where you can shop for cranberry treats and pottery or visit one of the local art galleries. Located in an old general store is this museum featuring driftwood sculptures that are well worth a look.

TUPPER ROCK One of the town highlights used to be this rock, a site sacred to the Coquille tribe and returned to them in 1990. Unfortunately, most of the blue-colored rock was removed many years ago to build the town jetty, and what was left of it now lies buried underneath a new rest home operated by the Coquille.

BEACH LOOP ROAD   South of town, this road leads past Bandon's scenic trio—Table Rock, Elephant Rock and legendary Face Rock. One of Oregon's most photographed spots, the offshore seastacks make an ideal backdrop at sunset.

WEST COAST GAME PARK SAFARI   ✉ *46914 Route 101, seven miles south of Bandon* ☎ *541-347-3106* ✎ *www.gameparksafari.com, support@gamepark safari.com* Located seven miles south of Bandon, this park gives visitors a chance to see more than 75 species, including lions, tigers, snow leopards, bison, zebras and elk. On their walk through the park, children can pet cubs, pups and kits in the company of attendants. Many endangered species are found at this wooded, 23-acre site. Winter hours vary; call ahead. Admission.

PORT ORFORD   This first townsite on the Oregon Coast and westernmost town in the continental United States is a major commercial and sportfishing center. Windsurfers flock to local Floras and Garrison lakes. The Sixes and Elk rivers are popular salmon and steelhead fishing spots. Harbor seals and sea lions breed on offshore rocks near this area, which is known as the "Thousand Island Coast."

HUMBUG MOUNTAIN STATE PARK   ☎ *541-332-6774* Six miles south of Port Orford is this state park, where hiking trails offer majestic views of the South Coast.

PREHISTORIC GARDENS   ✉ *36848 Route 101 between Port Orford and Gold Beach; Six miles south of Humbug Mountain State Park* ☎ *541-332-4463* Filled with life-size replicas of dinosaurs and other prehistoric species, this touristy menagerie includes the parrot-beaked *Psittacosaurus*, an ancestral form of the horn-faced dinosaur. Closed Monday through Thursday in winter; call for changing hours the rest of the year. Admission.

GOLD BEACH   At this town, a settlement at the mouth of the Rogue River, you'll find yourself on the edge of one of the coast's great wilderness areas. Here you can arrange an ocean-fishing trip or a jet boat ride up the wild and scenic Rogue River. Along the way, you may see deer, bald eagle, bear or otter. Accessible only by water, some of the rustic Rogue lodges are perfect for an overnight getaway. It's also possible to drive along the Rogue to Agness. For more details about this waterfront town, check with the **Gold Beach Visitor Center** (94080 Shirley Lane, Gold Beach; 541-247-7526, 800-525-2334, fax 541-247-0187; www.goldbeach.org, visit@goldbeach.org). Closed Sunday and Monday in winter.

SAMUEL H. BOARDMAN STATE SCENIC CORRIDOR   Fifteen miles south of Gold Beach is this scenic corridor, where you'll begin a 12-mile stretch that includes Arch Rock Point, Natural Bridges Cove, House Rock and Rainbow Rock. Many visitors and locals agree this is the prettiest stretch on the Oregon coastline.

BROOKINGS   Just when you thought it would never end, the Oregon Coast comes to a screeching halt. The end of the line is this Chetco River

South Coast

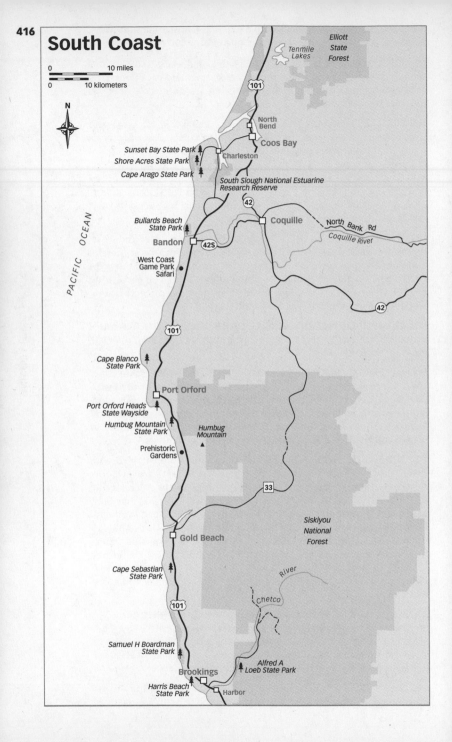

port town that produces nearly 90 percent of the Easter lilies grown in America. They are complemented by exotic lilies and daffodils raised commercially in the area. **North Bank Chetco River Road** provides easy access to the fishing holes upstream.

ALFRED A. LOEB STATE PARK hidden

One of the most worthwhile destinations is this park ten miles northeast of Brookings. Redwood and myrtlewood groves are your reward. You can loop back to Brookings on South Bank Road. En route consider turning off on **Forest Service Road 1205** (Bombsite Trail) and take the trail to one of only two continental United States locations bombed by a Japanese pilot during World War II. The other location, bombed by the same raider, is farther up the Oregon coast at Fort Stevens. The raider, who used a plane built aboard an offshore submarine, returned years later to give the city a samurai sword as a peace offering.

BROOKINGS/HARBOR CHAMBER OF COMMERCE ✉16330 Lower Harbor Road, Brookings ☎541-469-3181, 800-535-9469 ☏541-469-4094 ✎www. brookingsor.com, chamber@brookingsor.com
The chamber of commerce can provide additional information on visiting this region. Closed Sunday.

CHETCO VALLEY HISTORICAL SOCIETY MUSEUM ✉15461 Museum Road, Brookings ☎541-469-6651
Shortly before reaching the California line, you'll see the Blake House, site of this museum and the oldest standing house in the region. Visitors can check out a turn-of-the-20th-century kitchen, antique sewing machines, Lincoln rocker, patchwork quilts dating back to 1844 and American Indian artifacts. Once a trading post and way station, the old home is filled with period furniture. A new attachment contains old logging equipment and details the area's settlement days. You'll also see the world's largest Monterey cypress, which is found on the grounds. Closed weekdays in winter; closed Sunday through Tuesday the rest of the year.

LODGING

COOS BAY MANOR hidden

$$ 5 ROOMS ✉955 South 5th Street, Coos Bay ☎541-269-1224, 800-269-1224 ✎www.coosbaymanor.com, cbmanor@charter.net

A historic 1912 Colonial-style house, this bed and breakfast has five rooms (four with private baths) themed in Victorian, regal and country styles. Also here are a Colonial room with four-poster or twin beds and a garden room furnished with white wicker furniture. A rhododendron garden, redwoods and a delicious breakfast add to the fun. The ten-minute walk to downtown Coos Bay and the boardwalk is a bonus.

CAPTAIN JOHN'S MOTEL

$–$$ 44 ROOMS   ✉63360 Kingfisher Drive, Charleston   ☎541-888-4041
📠541-888-6563   🖰www.captainjohnsmotel.com, info@captainjohnsmotel.com

If you're eager to crab or clam, consider unpretentious Captain John's. On the small boat basin, this establishment is within walking distance of fishing and charter boats. Special facilities are available to cook and clean crabs. Forty-four newly renovated rooms and kitchenettes are fully carpeted and feature contemporary motel furniture. Other accommodations include a two-bedroom apartment.

SEA STAR GUEST HOUSE

$–$$ 6 UNITS   ✉375 1st Street, Bandon   ☎541-347-9632, 888-732-7871
🖰www.seastarbandon.com, seastarbandon@q.com

One block from Bandon's old-town district, the Sea Star offers modern, carpeted units with brass or step-up beds, quilts and harbor views. These include rooms and suites with living rooms and lofts. There is a well-furnished two-bedroom penthouse with bright wood features.

SEA STAR YOUTH HOSTEL

$ 4 ROOMS   ✉375 2nd Street, Bandon   ☎541-347-9632
🖰www.seastarbandon.com, seastaroregon@earthlink.com

There are two private rooms and two semi-private rooms (with shared bath) at this waterfront property. The larger private room features cable TV, a refrigerator and a microwave—great for a couple or family. No curfew.

BANDON BEACH MOTEL

$$ 22 UNITS   ✉1090 Portland Avenue Southwest, Bandon   ☎541-347-9451,
866-945-0133   🖰www.bandonbeachmotel.com, bandonbeachmotel@yahoo.com

You can hear the foghorn from this motel where every room looks out on the ocean. Units range from single rooms with balconies to two-bedroom suites with two fireplaces. Nautical decor, wood paneling and vanities add to the appeal. There's also a pool and spa. Small pets are welcome in some rooms.

BEST WESTERN INN AT FACE ROCK

$$$–$$$$ 74 UNITS   ✉3225 Beach Loop Drive, Bandon   ☎541-347-9441,
800-638-3092   📠541-347-2532   🖰www.facerock.net, info@innatfacerock.net

American Indian legend tells us that Ewauna, the willful daughter of Chief Siskiyou, wandered too far out into the surf and was snatched up by Seatka, the evil spirit of the sea. Today, Bandon visitors learn that images of all the protagonists in this tragedy have been frozen in stone at Face Rock. That may be one of the reasons the proprietors caution guests to be wary of the local surf. Adjacent to a public golf course, this resort—including 20 suites with fireplaces, kitchenettes and balconies—also has ocean views. Wallhangings and decks make the king- and queen-bedded rooms appealing. A restaurant, pool, spa and exercise room are other amenities.

CASTAWAY-BY-THE-SEA MOTEL

$$ 13 UNITS   ✉545 West 5th Street, Port Orford   ☎541-332-4502   📠541-332-9303
🖰www.castawaybythesea.com, stay@castawaybythesea.com

The Castaway offers rooms and suites overlooking one of the South Coast's most picturesque, albeit windblown, beaches. Kitchenettes, glassed-in decks, contemporary upholstered furniture, wall-to-wall carpeting, wi-fi and easy access to fishing make this 13-unit motel a popular place.

HOME BY THE SEA

$$ 2 ROOMS ✉444 Jackson Street, Port Orford ☎541-332-2855, 877-332-2855 🖳www.homebythesea.com, reservations@homebythesea.com

Breathtaking views of the coast are found at this bed and breakfast. Ceramic tile floors, myrtlewood beds with quilted spreads, a leather loveseat, a rocking chair, oriental carpets and stained glass add to the charm of these units. The two rooms include private baths and mini-refrigerators; each room in this bed and breakfast comes with binoculars perfect for whale watching through the picture windows. Laundry and wi-fi are available.

JOT'S RESORT

$$–$$$$ 150 UNITS ✉94360 Wedderburn Loop, Gold Beach ☎541-247-6676, 800-367-5687 📠541-247-6716 🖳www.jotsresort.com, information@jotsresort.com

If you're an adventurer eager to deep-sea fish, raft the Rogue, boat, cycle or hike the coastal mountains, consider this resort. Jot's has attractive, contemporary rooms, suites and condos with wall-to-wall carpeting, oak furniture, vanities and decks featuring river views. Family units are available with two bedrooms, a kitchenette, and living and dining rooms. Crabbing and clamming are great here. There's a jacuzzi, sauna and two pools, an indoor and outdoor.

TU TU' TUN LODGE

$$$$ 20 UNITS ✉96550 North Bank Rogue River Road, Gold Beach ☎800-864-6357 📠541-247-0672 🖳www.tututun.com, lodge@tututun.com

On the Rogue River, Tu Tu' Tun can be a sunny alternative to the cloudy coast. Seven miles upriver from Gold Beach, this lodge offers rooms with 12-foot-window walls, refrigerators, lounge chairs and decks or patios overlooking the water. Several have fireplaces and outdoor soaking tubs. There are also two houses for rent and two suites with kitchen facilities. Amenities include hiking trails, horseshoes and a library and game tables. Outside you'll find a four-hole putt course and kayaks.

SOUTH COAST INN BED & BREAKFAST

$$$ 4 ROOMS ✉516 Redwood Street, Brookings ☎541-469-5557, 800-525-9273 📠541-469-6615 🖳www.southcoastinn.com, innkeeper@southcoastinn.com

Located in a Craftsman-style home designed in 1917 by Bernard Maybeck, this inn boasts four individually decorated rooms. Especially choice is the Victorian Rose Room, which has a large picture window framing the Pacific, a high-rise four-poster bed, and an old-fashioned clawfoot tub in the bathroom. A fully furnished apartment with a deck and sleeper sofa is also available to rent. A full breakfast is included (continental breakfast only in the cottage).

BEST WESTERN BEACHFRONT INN

$$$–$$$$ 102 UNITS ✉16008 Boat Basin Road, Brookings ☎541-469-7779, 800-468-4081 📠541-469-0283 🖳info@beachfrontinn.com

The units here, all with ocean views and some with kitchenettes, offer a quiet resting place. Furnished with contemporary oak dressers and tables, the king- and queen-bedded units come with microwaves, refrigerators, sofas and decks and also boast free wi-fi. Suites and some rooms have ocean-view jacuzzis. Inn amenities include a heated pool, an outdoor spa, sundeck and meeting rooms.

CHETCO RIVER INN BED AND BREAKFAST

$$$ 6 UNITS ✉*21202 High Prairie Road, Brookings, 17.5 miles east of Brookings on the Chetco River* &541-251-0087 *www.chetcoriverinn.com, chetcoriverinn@hughes.net*

A one-lane road leads you to this bed and breakfast, a get-away-from-it-all establishment on 40 wooded acres. An ideal retreat for fishing, swimming, hiking through myrtle groves or loafing on the riverbank, this contemporary solar-, propane- and battery-powered home is furnished with antiques and eclectic furniture. The inn has down comforters and large brass beds, casablanca fans and, by advance request, dinner. The cooking is innovative, and portions are generous. All five rooms have private baths. A private cottage is also available. Special discounts are offered for anglers who agree to catch and release their fish.

DINING

EL SOL

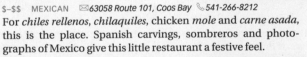

$-$$ MEXICAN ✉*63058 Route 101, Coos Bay* &541-266-8212

For *chiles rellenos*, *chilaquiles*, chicken *mole* and *carne asada*, this is the place. Spanish carvings, sombreros and photographs of Mexico give this little restaurant a festive feel.

KUM-YON'S

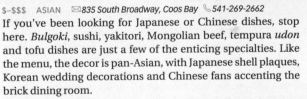

$-$$$ ASIAN ✉*835 South Broadway, Coos Bay* &541-269-2662

If you've been looking for Japanese or Chinese dishes, stop here. *Bulgoki*, sushi, yakitori, Mongolian beef, tempura *udon* and tofu dishes are just a few of the enticing specialties. Like the menu, the decor is pan-Asian, with Japanese shell plaques, Korean wedding decorations and Chinese fans accenting the brick dining room.

PORTSIDE RESTAURANT AND LOUNGE

$$-$$$ SEAFOOD ✉*Charleston Bay Boat Basin, 63383 Kingfisher Road, Charleston* &541-888-5544 ✆541-888-9206 *www.portsidebythebay.com*

To get a big laugh at this waterfront restaurant, just ask if the fish is fresh. Grilled sole, deep-fried scallops, steamed clams, salmon and Coquille St. Jacques are among the specialties, as well as Maine lobster and Dungeness crab. I also recommend the cucumber boat, a salad with shrimp, crab and smoked salmon served with cucumber dressing and garlic toast. The contemporary dining room features photos of the fishing industry.

WHEELHOUSE SEAFOOD GRILL AND LOUNGE

$$$ SEAFOOD ✉1st and Chicago streets, Bandon ✆541-347-9331

The Wheelhouse serves fresh seafood, pasta and steak in an upstairs lounge that overlooks the water. A lighter lunch menu offers tasty burgers and sandwiches.

PAULA'S BISTRO

$$–$$$ AMERICAN ✉236 Route 101, Port Orford ✆541-332-9378 ✆541-751-1999

Paula's, where the dimly lit bar and knotty pine–paneled dining room are decorated with local art for sale, provides an interesting mixture of artsy bohemian culture. You'll find pasta, steak, seafood and chowder on the menu; the kitchen accepts special requests from guests who want something not found on the menu. A piano is available for your use. Dinner only. Closed Sunday and Monday.

NOR'WESTER SEAFOOD RESTAURANT

$$$ $$$$ SEAFOOD ✉10 Harbor Way, Gold Beach ✆541-247-2333

For waterfront dining, try this restaurant with cedar woodwork, local artwork on the walls and a large fireplace. Sample the fresh fish, steaks, pasta or chicken. Dinner only. Closed December and January.

OCEANSIDE DINER ————— ⓗidden

3 AMERICAN/SEAFOOD ✉16403 Lower Harbor Road, Brookings ✆541-469-7971 ✆541-469-7971

When the natives get restless for 4 a.m. breakfasts, fish and chips, burgers, clam chowder or shrimp cocktail, they head for this delicious seafood spot. The modest establishment seats customers at pine tables in the nautically themed dining room featuring fishing photos.

O'HOLLERAN'S RESTAURANT AND LOUNGE

$$$ AMERICAN/SEAFOOD ✉1210 Chetco Avenue, Brookings ✆541-469-9907

A culinary time warp on the coast, O'Holleran's serves well-prepared middle-of-the-road entrées in a modest dining room with wood tables and pictures on the wall. You'll find few bells or whistles on the traditional menu featuring steaks, prime rib and seafood. Dinner only.

SHOPPING

BANDON PACIFIC SEAFOOD ✉250 Southwest 1st Street, Bandon ✆541-347-4454 ✆541-347-4313 If you're looking for smoked salmon, smoked albacore, crab or shrimp, head for this prime spot. Closed Monday.

ZUMWALT'S MYRTLEWOOD ✉Route 101, six miles south of Bandon ✆541-347-3654 ✎www.zumwaltsmyrtlewood.com Zumwalt's is the place to see the owner creating dinnerware, vases, sculptures, clocks and other popular souvenirs.

JERRY'S ROGUE RIVER MUSEUM AND GIFT SHOP ✉29980 *Harbor Way, Gold Beach* ✆541-247-4571, 800-451-3645 ✎*www.roguejets.com* Jerry's offers a broad selection of locally made arts and crafts. There is also an extensive collection of artifacts, photos and natural-history exhibits on the Rogue River area.

THE GREAT AMERICAN SMOKEHOUSE AND SEAFOOD COMPANY

✉*15657 South Route 101, Brookings* ✆*800-828-3474* ✎*www.smokehouse-salmon.com* This "Great American" company produces gift packs with such delicacies as smoked salmon jerky, hand-packed tuna, sweet hot mustard and wild blackberry jam.

NIGHTLIFE

ON BROADWAY THESPIANS ✉*226 South Broadway, Coos Bay* ✆*541-269-2501* ✎*www.onbroadwaytheater.com* These thespians present contemporary drama, mysteries and musical theater in three different venues, one of which is an intimate 90-seat auditorium.

PORTSIDE LOUNGE ✉*63383 Kingfisher Road, Charleston* ✆*541-888-5544* 🖷*541-888-9206* ✎*www.portsidebythebay.com, dine@portsidebythebay.com* For great sunsets, harbor views and music Friday through Sunday nights, try this lounge.

LLOYD'S ✉*119 2nd Street, Bandon* There's rock-and-roll bands on weekends year-round here, and the large dancefloor is a great spot to let loose.

LORD BENNETT'S

✉*1695 Beach Loop Drive, Bandon* ✆*541-347-3663* 🖷*541-347-3062* ✎*www.lordbennetts.com* Spectacular views are the real draw here, but Lord Bennett's, with an antique-filled lounge, also provides an elegant location for a nightcap. Winter hours vary; call ahead.

RASCALS LOUNGE ✉*Lower Harbor Road, Brookings* ✆*541-469-5503* 🖷*541-469-7281* Rascals is a dimly lit room with café seating and a full bar. Check out their bargain lottery games and struggle against the odds.

BEACHES & PARKS

SUNSET BAY STATE PARK
✉*Off Route 101, 12 miles southwest of Coos Bay* ✆*541-888-4902* 🖷*541-888-5650*
A splendid park on dramatic headlands, Sunset is forested with spruce and hemlock. Highlights include Big Creek, a popular stream flowing into the bay. As the name implies, this is the place to be when the sun sets. Swimming, canoeing, boating, clamming and crabbing are also popular activities in the surrounding area. Picnic tables, restrooms and showers are the facilities here.

▲ There are 66 tent sites ($12 to $16 per night), 63 RV hookup sites ($16 to $20 per night), eight yurts ($27 per night) and a hiker-biker camp ($4 per person per night). Reservations: 800-452-5687.

SHORE ACRES STATE PARK

✉*Off Route 101, 13 miles southwest of Coos Bay* ☎*541-888-3732*
🖰*www.shoreacres.net, shoreacres@state.or.us*

Let's skip the superlatives and get to the point: Visit Shore Acres State Park. This 745-acre estate was once the site of a timber baron's mansion. Although the house burned down, the formal garden remains a showcase. Planted with azaleas, rhododendrons, irises, dahlias and roses, Shore Acres also offers trails on the forested bluffs. There are picnic tables, restrooms, an observation shelter and a gift shop. Between Thanksgiving and New Year's, check out the nightly Holiday Lights display. Day-use fee, $3.

BULLARDS BEACH STATE PARK — hidden

✉*Off Route 101, two miles north of Bandon* ☎*541-347-2209, 800-551-6949*

🚶 🚴 🐎 ⛵ 🛶 🚤 ⚓ 🎣 All good things come to an end, even the Coquille River. Fortunately, this 1383-acre park makes it possible to enjoy the tail end of the stream as it flows into the estuary and the Pacific opposite the city of Bandon. The Coquille River lighthouse is located in the park (open May through October). A great recreation area, the park has fine dunes, beaches and forested lowlands. It's also ideal for crabbing and clamming. Fish for steelhead, silver and chinook salmon. Facilities include picnic tables, restrooms and showers.

▲ There are 185 RV hookup sites ($16 to $20 per night), 13 yurts ($27 per night), 8 primitive horse camp sites ($12 to $16 per night) and a hiker-biker camp ($4 per person per night). Reservations: 800-452-5687.

CAPE BLANCO STATE PARK

✉*Off Route 101, nine miles north of Port Orford* ☎*541-332-2973*

🚶 🚴 🐎 🎣 Settled by an Irish dairy farmer, these dramatic, pastured headlands include the westernmost lighthouse in Oregon. A windswept, 1856-acre retreat, Cape Blanco welcomes visitors to the Hughes House, built by a pioneer family in 1898. Both the lighthouse and the Hughes House are open April through October (fee). There's good surf fishing. You'll find picnic tables, restrooms and showers.

▲ There are 53 RV hookup sites ($12 to $16 per night), four log cabins ($35 per night), eight primitive horse-camp sites ($10 to $14 per night) and a hiker-biker camp ($4 per person per night). Call to reserve cabins and horse-camp sites: 800-452-5687.

PORT ORFORD HEADS STATE PARK

✉*Off Route 101, Port Orford* ☎*800-551-6949*

🚶 🎣 You'll love this windblown and unforgettable 126-acre wayside. It encompasses the ocean bluff as well as Nellies Cove. The park protects marine gardens and prehistoric archaeological landmarks. A former 1934 Coast Guard Station now houses a free museum that is open Thursday through Monday from April through October. There are picnic tables and restrooms.

HUMBUG MOUNTAIN STATE PARK

✉ *Off Route 101, six miles south of Port Orford* ☎ *541-332-6774*

A 1756-foot peak forested with fir, spruce, alder and cedar, Humbug is one of the coast's finest parks. Hiking trails, viewpoints, Brush Creek and ocean frontage make the sanctuary a great retreat. If you're feeling ambitious, why not take the three-mile hike up the wildflower-lined trail to the summit? You'll find picnic tables, restrooms and showers.

▲ There are 62 tent sites ($10 to $14 per night), 32 RV hookup sites ($12 to $16 per night) and a hiker-biker camp ($4 per person per night).

CAPE SEBASTIAN STATE SCENIC CORRIDOR

✉ *Off Route 101, seven miles south of Gold Beach* ☎ *800-551-6949*

This narrow park includes several miles of exceptional coastline. The centerpiece of the 1224-acre place is the cape, carpeted with wildflowers and rhododendron in the spring. Views are magnificent from the two parking vistas 200 feet above sea level and whale watching is excellent. A spectacular one-and-a-half-mile trail leads to the tip of the Cape. Old-growth Douglas fir and Sitka spruce form a handsome backdrop. There is no drinking water here. Not recommended for long RVs or vehicles towing trailers.

HARRIS BEACH STATE PARK

✉ *1655 North Route 101, Brookings* ☎ *541-469-2021*

Named for Scottish pioneer George Harris, this one-time sheep and cattle ranch is the southernmost state camping facility on the coast. The 172-acre park offers sandy beaches and great sunsets. The shoreline is punctuated with dramatic, surf-sculptured rocks, which make kayaking and surfing challenging. There's good fishing for salmon, perch and rockfish. There are picnic tables, restrooms and showers.

▲ There are 63 tent sites ($13 to $17 per night), 86 RV hookup sites ($17 to $22 per night), six yurts ($29 per night) and a hiker-biker camp ($4 per person per night). Reservations: 800-452-5687.

ALFRED A. LOEB STATE PARK

✉ *Located ten miles northeast of Brookings along the Chetco River* ☎ *541-469-2021*

On the Chetco River, this park can be a warm place when the coast is not. A one-mile trail leads to Loeb's redwood grove. There's also a myrtle grove here. A popular fishing region, particularly during the steelhead season, the Chetco is one of Oregon's special havens. With 320 acres, the park provides easy access to a prime stretch of this river canyon. Picnic tables, firepits and restrooms round out the facilities.

▲ There are 48 RV hookup sites ($12 to $16 per night) and three log cabins ($35 per night). Call to reserve a cabin: 800-452-5687.

OUTDOOR ADVENTURES

SPORTFISHING

From mid-May or June through September or mid-October, charter companies and outfitters up and down the coast regularly run ocean fishing trips: from a half day of bottomfishing to longer reef-fishing outings. Tackle is usually provided, but a fishing license is required (you can purchase it through charter operators). And don't forget to bring lunch.

North Coast Area

CHARLTON DEEP SEA ✉470 Northeast Skipanon Drive, Warrenton ✆503-338-0569 ⌨www.charltondeepsea.com This service accommodates up to 15 people, May through September, on trips for tuna, salmon, sturgeon and halibut.

GARIBALDI CHARTERS ✉Route 101, Garibaldi ✆503-322-0007, 800-900-4665 ⌨www.garibaldicharters.com Garibaldi runs an annual trip each May for halibut; it's so popular, however, it's booked a year in advance. They offer several other trips, so you should have no trouble getting a spot on the salmon, light-tackle or deep-reef bottomfish trips.

Central Coast Area

NEWPORT TRADEWINDS ✉653 Southwest Bay Boulevard, Newport ✆541-265-2101, 800-676-7819 ⌨www.newporttradewinds.com The oldest charter fishing company in the area, this crew has been running trips for halibut, salmon, tuna, bottomfish and crab since 1949.

DEPOE BAY TRADEWINDS ✉Depoe Bay ✆541-765-2345, 800-445-8730 ⌨www.tradewindscharters.com This service runs fishing trips year-round for tuna, halibut, salmon and clams, as well as bottomfish like sea bass and red snapper. They also offer crabbing trips.

DOCKSIDE CHARTERS ✉Depoe Bay ✆541-765-2545, 800-733-8915 ⌨www.docksidedepoebay.com You can arrange a guided fishing trip with this charter company for salmon, halibut and tuna; some trips are combined with crabbing.

South Coast Area

BETTY KAY CHARTERS ✉7788 Albacore Street ✆541-888-9021, 800-752-6303 ⌨www.bettykaycharters.com In Charleston, Betty Kay has year-round half- and full-day bottomfishing trips, as well as seasonal runs for tuna and halibut.

FISHING

You can rent a small boat and row out into a bay, such as Yaquina or Nehalem, for year-round recreational crabbing (always call first for tide information), as well as seasonal catches of perch, flounder, bass and salmon. Near Coos Bay, Ten Mile Lake is stocked with trout, crappie and catfish. Well known for salmon, Oregon's coastal waters are also fished for ling cod, cabazon (a big, ugly bottom fish), sea bass, red snapper, albacore and halibut.

North Coast Area

JETTY FISHERY ✉ *Route 101 at Nehalem Bay, Rockaway Beach* ☏ *503-368-5746* ⌨ *www.jettyfishery.com, jettyfishery@coastwipi.com* This company rents 16-foot aluminum Klamath boats. August through November, a run of salmon moves through the bay to spawn in the Nehalem River. Crabbing is good year-round. Crab-cooking and fish-cleaning facilities are provided.

Central Coast Area

NEWPORT MARINA CHARTER AND STORE ✉ *2122 Southeast Marine Science Drive, South Beach* ☏ *541-867-4470* ⌨ *www.nmscharters.com* Here you can rent 14-foot aluminum fishing boats and equipment for fishing and crabbing year-round.

MCKINLEY'S MARINA ✉ *Route 34* ☏ *541-563-4656* In Waldport, try McKinley's, which rents small boats that seat up to four. Boat rentals include bait.

WESTLAKE RESORT ✉ *4785 Laurel Avenue, Westlake* ☏ *541-997-3722* ⌨ *www.westlakeresort.com* Near the Florence area try this resort, where you can rent 15-foot boats and try for perch, crappie and catfish.

WHALE WATCHING

The Oregon Coast provides a front-row seat to one of nature's magnificent shows: the annual migrations of the California gray whales. Although the southbound leg of the mammals' trip peaks in late December, it continues until February. Then, with calves in tow, the mammals begin the northbound journey in March. It continues through May. This is an excellent time to take a whale-watching tour: during this leg of the trip, the whales travel more slowly and closer to shore.

Central Coast Area

Depoe Bay calls itself the whale-watching capital of the Oregon Coast. Several California gray whales have taken up summer residence along the Central Coast—one, at least, has returned to Depoe Bay since the 1970s and has been christened "Spot." The mammals are probably attracted to the bay because of a unique environment that provides plenty for the whales to feed on.

OREGON PARKS AND RECREATION DEPARTMENT WHALE-WATCHING CENTER ✉ *119 Southwest Route 101, Depoe Bay* ☏ *541 765 3407* ⌨ *www.whalespoken.org* This whale-watching center has 200 volunteers who position themselves at 28 overlooks along the Oregon Coast and offer tips to whale watchers. Trained by researchers at Mark O. Hatfield Marine Science Center in Newport, the volunteers are mines of information about the gray whale's behavior and life cycle. Closed Monday and Tuesday from September through May.

DOCKSIDE CHARTERS ✉ *Depoe Bay* ✆ *541-765-2545, 800-733-8915* ✍ *www.docksidedepoebay.com* Daily whale-watching tours are run through this charter service. Once the boat reaches the migration route—usually about a mile or two offshore—it will stop and drift for a while so visitors can watch the whales feed. Owner Jim Tade will also take up to six people out in inflatable Zodiac boats for up-close looks at the mammals.

DEPOE BAY TRADEWINDS ✉ *Depoe Bay* ✆ *541-765-2345, 800-445-8730* ✍ *www.tradewindscharters.com* Contact this company for daily one-hour whale-watching trips year-round.

NEWPORT TRADEWINDS ✉ *653 Southwest Bay Boulevard, Newport* ✆ *541-265-2101, 800-676-7819* ✍ *www.newporttradewinds.com* This group offers two-hour whale-watching trips all through the year.

SURFING

If you go surfing, keep in mind that you will be sharing the waves with cold water–loving great white sharks, so stick to common surfing areas. Surfing in Oregon hasn't reached the crescendo of activity that it has in California. Nevertheless, there are local contingents of surfers up and down the coast. Ecola State Park, Indian Beach and Oswald West State Park are recommended North Coast surfing spots, and good for all skill levels. Along the Central Coast, Otter Rock, south of Newport, is good place for beginners. But only a few shops rent surfboards, wetsuits and various other "board" sports equipment.

North Coast Area

CLEANLINE SURF SHOP ✉ *725 1st Avenue, Seaside* ✆ *503-738-7888, 888-546-6176* 🖷 *503-738-9793* ✍ *www.cleanlinesurf.com* This surf shop in Seaside started out in 1980, renting wetsuits to diehard surfers ready to brave the cold winter waters. Now it rents just about everything, including wetsuits, surfboards and snowboards.

Beastly Behavior

Once you have spotted a whale, keep your eyes peeled for it to rise above the surface. Gray whales often "spyhop," thrusting their heads out of the water and balancing with their eyes exposed. Experts believe this is done to look around above the surface and possibly to orient themselves with reference to the shore or the sun. The most spectacular whale behavior, from a landlubber's viewpoint, is "breaching"—leaping completely out of the water, rolling sideways and falling slowly backward to land with an enormous splash. The reason for this is unknown. It could be to knock off barnacles or to signal other whales. It might be a courtship ritual, or then again, it might just be the giant beast's playful way of expressing the joy of life.

Central Coast Area

SAFARI TOWN SURF SHOP ✉*3026 Northeast Route 101, Lincoln City* ☎*541-996-6335* Safari Town rents wetsuits, surfboards, bodyboards and skimboards. The shop is about a half-hour's drive north of Otter Rock.

OREGON SURF SHOP ✉*3001 Southwest Route 101, Lincoln City* ☎*541-996-3957, 877-339-5672* ☎*541-996-3957* ⌕*www.oregonsurfshop.com* Surfboards, boogieboards, skimboards, kayaks and wet suits can be rented or purchased from this shop.

WINDSURFING & KAYAKING

Kayaking is popular on Coffenberry Lake at Fort Stevens State Park in Astoria. And in Langlois, on the South Coast, there's a windsurfing bed-and-breakfast inn, where you can take lessons after your continental breakfast.

FLORAS LAKE HOUSE ✉*92870 Boice Cope Road, Langlois* ☎*541-348-2573* ⌕*www.floraslake.com, reservations@floraslake.com* A sandspit separates the freshwater, spring-fed Floras Lake from the ocean. At this bed and breakfast that sits just off the lake, the owners also operate a windsurfing school (equipment and wetsuit included for beginners). Mornings are best for lessons (steady northwest winds blow during the afternoon) on the lake, which is shallow and warm. Closed mid-September through March; call for hours after Labor Day.

RIDING STABLES

Look no further than the Oregon Coast for impressive scenic backdrops to half-day guided rides through coastal mountain pine forest, open rides along beach dunes or mountain trail rides near the mouth of the Rogue River.

North Coast Area

NORTHWEST EQUINE OUTFITTERS ✉*Nehalem Bay State Park* ☎*503-801-7433* ⌕*www.horserental.us, ride@occybercafe.com* Based out of Nehalem Bay State Park, this outfitter offers early-morning and sunset rides along the coast, as well as half- and full-day rides. Customized trips can be arranged. Open daily Memorial Day to Labor Day; by appointment only the rest of the year.

Central Coast Area

C&M STABLES ✉*90241 Route 101, Florence* ☎*541-997-7540* ⌕*www.oregonhorsebackriding.com* C&M has guided rides through the dunes and along the beach or the mountains. Long (half-day) rides through the beaches and dunes can also be arranged.

South Coast Area

BANDON BEACH RIDING STABLES ✉*54629 Beach Loop Drive, Bandon* ☎*541-347-3423* This company specializes in open rides along the beach, and operates year-round. Maximum group of 16 people.

When rainfall along the coast can measure 60, 70, even 80 inches a year, good drainage is important for a golf course. The courses listed here all report good drainage, making them playable year-round. You can rent clubs and carts at the courses listed below.

North Coast Area

HIGHLANDS GOLF COURSE ✉33260 Highlands Lane, Gearhart ✆503-738-5248 🖰www.discountdansgolf.com For a round of nine holes, try the public course here, run by Discount Dan. It's a fun but challenging course, with ocean views from some holes.

GEARHART GOLF LINKS ✉1157 North Marion Street, Gearhart ✆503-738-3538 🖰www.gearheartgolflinks.com At the 18-hole course here, ocean views are obscured by a condominium complex, but the terrain is relatively flat, making this public green quite walkable.

Central Coast Area

CHINOOK WINDS GOLF RESORT ✉3245 Northeast 50th Street, Lincoln City ✆541-994-8442 This resort has a hilly, moderately challenging 18-hole course.

SALISHAN GOLF LINKS ✉Gleneden Beach ✆541-764-3632 🖰www.salishan.com Try the 18-hole course at the Salishan Resort.

AGATE BEACH GOLF COURSE ✉4100 North Coast Highway (Route 101), Newport ✆541-265-7331 🖰www.agatebeachgolf.net This scenic nine-hole, privately owned but publicly accessible course is fairly flat and walkable, with ocean views from some holes. The 3002-yard-long course has a driving range.

SAND PINES GOLF LINKS ✉1201 35th Street ✆541-997-1940, 800-917-4653 🖰www.sandpines.com In Florence, Sand Pines has an 18-hole course built on sand dunes, which provide excellent drainage and spectacular scenery.

OCEAN DUNES GOLF LINKS ✉3345 Munsel Lake Road ✆541-997-3232 🖰www.oceandunesgolf.com There's a "wee bit o' Scotland" in Florence at this 18-hole, public course, an older, well-known, "true" links course, with high slope and difficulty ratings.

CRESTVIEW HILLS GOLF COURSE ✉1680 Crestline Drive, Waldport ✆541-563-3020, 888-538-4463 🖰www.crestviewhillsgolf.com This nine-hole golf course is flat and walkable, complete with a pro shop and a driving range.

South Coast Area

SUNSET BAY GOLF COURSE ✉11001 Cape Arago Highway, Coos Bay ✆541-888-9301 🖰www.sunsetbaygolf.com The John Zahler–designed, nine-hole course here is adjacent to Sunset Bay. It's public and is "about the only course in the area playable in the winter," according to a local pro.

BANDON FACE ROCK GOLF COURSE ✉3235 Beach Loop Road, Bandon ✆541-347-3818 Lessons are offered during the summer at this nine-hole executive course.

CEDAR BEND GOLF COURSE ✉34391 Cedar Valley Road, Gold Beach ✆541-247-6911 ⌖www.cedarbendgolf.com About 12 miles north of Gold Beach, this nine-hole, public golf course is set in a valley with a creek winding through it. Alder, hemlock and fir trees add to the scenic beauty.

TENNIS

GOODSPEED PARK ✉3rd Street and Goodspeed Place, Tillamook ✆503-842-7525 Two courts.

BANDON HIGH SCHOOL ✉11th and Franklin streets, Bandon ✆541-347-9616 Two courts.

BUFFINGTON PARK ✉14th and Arizona streets, Port Orford ✆541-332-8055 One court.

CANNON BEACH ✉2nd and Spruce streets, Cannon Beach ✆503-436-2623 Two lighted courts.

ROLLING DUNES PARK ✉Siano Loop and 35th Street, Florence ✆541-997-3436 One court.

BIKING

OREGON COAST BIKE ROUTE hidden
Route 101 is the state's most popular biking trail. Every year, thousands of travelers do the coast, taking advantage of many side roads, hiker-bike camps and facilities that cater to the cycling crowd. Even to nonbicyclists, the 370-mile Oregon Coast Bike Route is well known. There are numerous sections that take in scenic and quiet county and city streets that have low volume traffic and slow traffic speeds. There are also backcountry sites set up for cyclists. It should be noted that Oregon Coast Bike Route is really for experienced cyclists. Besides the length of the trip (the journey takes about six or eight days), the route rises and falls 16,000 feet along the way.

OREGON DEPARTMENT OF TRANSPORTATION BIKEWAY PROGRAM ✉355 Capitol Street Northeast, Room 222, Salem, OR 97301 ✆503-986-3556 ⌨503-986-3749 ⌖www.oregon.gov If you're thinking about making the Oregon Coast ride, get hold of the **Oregon Coast Bike Route Map**. It's free and published by the Oregon Department of Transportation. The department also publishes the **Oregon Bicycling Guide** that maps out bike routes throughout the state and provides information on various route conditions.

North Coast Area

FORT STEVENS STATE PARK An eight-mile paved route passes through this park's historic section, then leads into a wooded area before crossing to parallel the ocean and looping back into the park. In Seaside you can ride along the two-mile boardwalk or head back into the Lewis and Clark area for rides along paved roads and some old logging roads.

Central Coast Area

OCEAN VIEW DRIVE   In Newport, this is an excellent, four-mile alternative to Route 101. This route leads past the Agate Beach area and takes you through the historic Nye Beach community, one of Newport's earliest resorts. You'll wind up at Yaquina Bay State Park, home of the community's signature lighthouse.

South Coast Area

NORTH BANK ROAD   Off Route 101 north of Bandon, this road winds for 16 miles along the Coquille River. This flat, scenic route is lightly trafficked (but watch out for logging trucks), lush and unforgettable. Then head south on Route 42 to Coquille and pick up South Route 42 back to Bandon. The roundtrip is 52 miles.

Bike Rentals

PROM BIKE AND HOBBY SHOP ⊠*622 12th Avenue, Seaside* ☎*503-738-8251* In Seaside, this shop is just three blocks from the beach. They rent three-speed cruisers, mountain bikes, kids' bikes, tandems, beach cruisers and even tricycles. Or you might try a surrey, rollerskates or in-line skates. Closed Tuesday and Wednesday.

MIKE'S BIKE SHOP ⊠*248 North Spruce Street, Cannon Beach* ☎*503-436-1266, 800-492-1266* A few miles south, Mike's rents "fun-cycles"—big three-wheelers—for riding on the fairly level wide beach at low tide. Otherwise, you can rent mountain bikes to ride on nearby logging trails (they're private, however) or up to Ecola State Park, about a mile away. You may also rent beach cruisers. Closed Tuesday and Wednesday during the winter.

THE BIKE SHOP ⊠*223 Northwest Nye Street, Newport* ☎*541-265-2481, 800-446-9243* Stop here for mountain, road and tandem bike rentals, as well as equipment and repairs. Closed Sunday.

BICYLES 101 _____ *hidden*
⊠*1537 8th Street, Florence* ☎*541-997-5717* ✆*541-997-5717* In Florence, check out this shop that rents mountain bikes and cruisers. Closed Sunday.

HIKING

The Oregon Coast abounds with beautiful hiking opportunities within state parks and national forests. All distances listed for hiking trails are one way unless otherwise noted.

North Coast Area

FORT STEVENS STATE PARK   This state park has several easy trails, including the two trail, 1.8-mile stroll from Battery Russell to the wreck of the *Peter Iredale*.

432

SADDLE MOUNTAIN TRAIL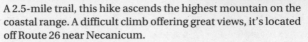

A 2.5-mile trail, this hike ascends the highest mountain on the coastal range. A difficult climb offering great views, it's located off Route 26 near Necanicum.

TILLAMOOK HEAD TRAIL   Beginning south of the town of Seaside, this 7-mile trail ascends to 1200 feet on the route to Escola State Park's Indian Beach. This is believed to be the route followed by Lewis and Clark when they journeyed to Ecola Creek.

KINGS MOUNTAIN TRAIL   Inland from Tillamook on Route 6 is this moderate-to-difficult trail (2.5 miles). The route takes you through the area of the famed Tillamook Burn, a series of 1933, 1939, 1945 and 1951 fires that took out enough lumber to build over one million homes. While the area, now the Tillamook State Forest, is covered with younger timber, some evidence of the old burn can still be seen.

NEAH-KAH-NIE MOUNTAIN TRAIL   This trail (4 miles) is a challenging climb that begins 2.6 miles south of Oswald West State Park's Short Sands parking area. Great views of the coast.

Central Coast Area

SIUSLAW NATIONAL FOREST   In this national forest east of Pacific City, the **Pioneer Indian Trail** (8 miles) is highly recommended. The moderately difficult trail runs from Itebo Lake to South Lake through a fir forest and a meadow that has a wide array of wildflowers in the summer.

HATFIELD MARINE SCIENCE CENTER ⊠ *2030 South Marine Science Drive, Newport* ✆ *541-867-0100* The **Estuary Trail** (.25 mile) at this science center is a great introduction to local marine life. The posted route is wheelchair accessible.

CAPTAIN COOK'S TRAIL

This trail (.6 mile) leads from the Cape Perpetua visitors center below Route 101 past American Indian shell middens to coastal tidepools. At high tide you'll see the spouting horn across Cook's Chasm.

CUMMINS CREEK LOOP

A bit more challenging is this 10-mile trail up Cook's Ridge to Cummins Creek Trail and back down to the visitors center. Enjoy the old-growth forests and meadows.

BLUEBILL TRAIL   At the southern end of the Oregon Dunes National Recreation Area, this trail (1 mile roundtrip), two and a half miles off Route 101 near Horsefall Beach Road, offers an easy and beautiful loop hike around the marshy area once known as Bluebill Lake. It includes an extensive boardwalk system.

South Coast Area

ESTUARY STUDY TRAIL   At South Slough National Estuarine Research Reserve south of Coos Bay (1.5 miles) is this trail, one of the finest hikes on the Oregon Coast. Leading down through a coastal forest, you'll see a pioneer log landing, use a boardwalk to cross a skunk-cabbage bog and visit a salt marsh.

SHRADER
OLD GROWTH TRAIL

Off Jerry's Flat Road, east of Gold Beach, is this pleasant 1.5-mile loop where you'll see rhododendron, cedar, streams and riparian areas. The marked route identifies coastal species along the way.

LOWER ROGUE RIVER TRAIL   To really get away from it all, hike this river trail (12.2 miles) south from Agness. You'll pass American Indian landmarks, see picturesque bridges and spot wildlife as you hike this wild and scenic canyon.

BANDON TO FOURMILE CREEK   This 8.5-mile trek is one of the coast's most scenic walks. Begin at Bandon Harbor and head south past the Bandon Needles, dunes, ponds and lakes to the creek. Of course, you can abbreviate this hike at any point. One easy possibility is to head south on Beach Loop Drive to the point where it swings east toward Route 101. Park here and take the short .2-mile walk through the woods and up over the dune to Bradley Lake, a good swimming hole.

REDWOOD TRAIL

North of Alfred A. Loeb State Park, ten miles east of Brookings, this 1-mile trail is a beautiful streamside walk leading past rhododendron, myrtlewood and towering redwoods.

TRANSPORTATION

CAR

From Northern California or Washington, the coast is easily reached via **Route 101**. Within Oregon, many roads link Portland and the Willamette Valley to resort destinations. **Routes 30** and **26** provide easy access to the North Coast communities of Astoria and Seaside, while **Route 6** connects with Tillamook. **Route 18** leads to Lincoln City, and **Routes 20** and **34** connect with the Central Coast region in the vicinity of Newport and Waldport. **Route 126** is the way to Florence. **Route 38** heads to Reedsport. To reach Bandon and the South Coast, take **Route 42**.

AIR

Horizon Air flies to **North Bend Municipal Airport** (www.coosbay northbendairport.com). The **Portland International Airport** (503-460-4234, 877-739-4636) and **Eugene Airport** (541-682-5430), described in other chapters, also provide gateways to the coast.

BUS

GREYHOUND BUS LINES ☎800-231-2222 ✐www.greyhound.com Greyhound serves many coast destinations. There is a stop in **Florence**, along with stops in **Newport** (956 Southwest 10th Street, 541-265-2253).

CAR RENTALS

HERTZ RENT A CAR ☎800-654-3131 Hertz has a location at North Bend Municipal Airport, as well as one at 1492 Duane Street in Astoria.

PUBLIC TRANSIT

LINCOLN COUNTY TRANSIT ☎541-265-4900; co.lincoln.or.us/transit In Otis, Lincoln City, Newport, Waldport, Yachats, Toledo and Siletz, local service is provided by this transit agency. The same company provides service from Siletz and Yachats to Newport, and from Newport to Lincoln City.

VALLEY RETRIEVER BUS LINES ☎541-265-2253 Connections can be made from Bend, Corvallis, Newport, Salem and Albany through this company.

TAXIS

For service in Seaside, try **Seaside Yellow Cab** (503-738-5252). On the South Coast, there's **Yellow Cab** (541-267-3111), which operates in Coos Bay/North Bend.

OREGON CASCADES

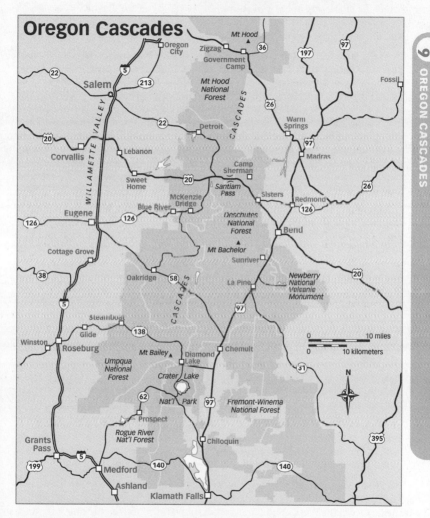

Oregon Cascades

Some questions are impossible to answer. Here's one that came to mind while we traveled the highways and byways of the Oregon Cascades, swimming in crystal-clear pools, basking at alpine resorts, fishing pristine streams, dining on fresh salmon and cooling off beneath the spray of yet another waterfall: Why isn't this heavenly space positively jammed with people who want to get away from it all?

Except for a handful of places, such as Mt. Hood on a Saturday afternoon, Route 97 in the vicinity of Bend or Crater Lake's Rim Drive, it's often hard to find a crowd in this seemingly inexhaustible resort area. Sure, there's a fair number of timber rigs out on major routes. And the No Vacancy sign does pop up a good deal at popular resorts during the summer and weekends. But who cares when you can head down the road half a mile and check into a glorious streamside campground where the tab is rock-bottom and there's no extra charge for the nocturnal view of the Milky Way? The fact is that mile for mile, the Oregon Cascades offer some of the best wilderness and recreational opportunities in the Pacific Northwest.

To really get a feel for the area, you need a week or longer. But even if you only have time to buzz up to Mt. Hood for an afternoon, this is the best place we know to gain perspective on the volcanic history of the Pacific Northwest. A chain of peaks topped by 11,235-foot Mt. Hood, the Cascades have an average elevation of about 5000 feet. Heavily forested, these mountains are also the headwaters for many important rivers such as the Rogue, the Umpqua and the McKenzie. Klamath Falls is the principal southern gateway to the region, and Bend and Redmond provide easy access from the east. Within the mountains are a number of charming towns and villages such as Sisters, McKenzie Bridge and Camp Sherman. While the summer months can be mild and sunny, winter snowfalls blanket the western slopes with 300 to 500 inches of snow.

For some perspective on the Cascades, take a look at the area's good old days. Begin with the evolution of one of the Northwest's signature attractions, Crater Lake. Looking at this placid sea, it's hard to imagine what this region looked like 60 million years ago during the late Cretaceous period. As Lowell Williams has written: "At that time the Coast Ranges of Oregon . . . were submerged and the waves of the Pacific lapped against the foothills of the Sierra Nevada and the Blue Mountains of Oregon. Where the Cascade peaks now rise in lofty grandeur, water teemed with shellfish . . . giant marine lizards swam in the seas, and winged reptiles sailed above in search of prey."

Later, in the Eocene and Oligocene periods, roughly 25 million to 60 million years ago, the Crater Lake region became a low plain. Throughout this period and the late Miocene, volcanoes erupted. Finally, about one million to two million years ago, in the last great Ice Age, the Cascades were formed. The largest of these peaks became 12,000-foot Mt. Mazama. About 7000 years ago, this promontory literally blew its top, leaving behind the caldera that is now Crater Lake.

The American Indians, who viewed this area as a sacred and treacherous place, went out of their way to avoid Crater Lake. It was only after the white man arrived in the 19th century that it became a tourist attraction and eventually a national park. Today the lake is considered a unique national treasure.

Because they provided a tremendous challenge to settlers heading toward the Pacific Ocean on the Oregon Trail, the Cascades also gained an important place in the history of the West. Landmarks surrounding Mt. Hood tell the dramatic story of pioneers who blazed time-saving new routes to the promised land across this precipitous terrain. Of course, their arrival permanently altered American Indian life. Inevitably, efforts to colonize the Indians and turn them into farmers and Christians met with resistance. American Indian leader Captain Jack led perhaps the most famous tribal rebellion against the miseries of reservation life in the 1872–73 Modoc War. This fighting raged in an area that is now part of the Lava

Beds National Monument across the border in California. Captain Jack and his **437** fellow renegades were ultimately hanged at Fort Klamath.

While logging became the Cascades' leading industry, tourism emerged in the late 19th century. Summer resorts, typically primitive cabins built at the water's edge, were popular with the fishing crowd. Later, the arrival of resort lodges like the Timberline on the slopes of Mt. Hood drew a significant winter trade. But even as Oregon's best-known mountain range evolved into a major resort area, it was able to retain carefully guarded secrets. Little-known fishing spots, obscure trails, waterfalls absent from the maps—this high country became Oregon's private treasure.

Today, Oregon, one of the nation's most environmentally conscious states, is trying to find peaceful coexistence between the logging industry and environmentalists. The continuing "spotted owl" controversy has led to logging restrictions in the past over the fight to save old-growth forests for future generations. But with political changes, the battle lives on.

In 2003 President George Bush signed the Healthy Forest Restoration Act, which allowed vast areas of forests to be logged as a fire prevention measure. The Act was in response to the massive 2002 Biscuit fire that devoured 500,000 acres of Oregon and California forests. Though by 2006 it was determined that the Act cost the federal government $2 million that had not yet been used to restore the logged trees or habitats, and despite appeals from environmentalist groups that haven't let up since the Act's inception, Bush included more funding for the plan in the 2007 fiscal budget.

You'll be able to take a firsthand look at the subject in question on some of our recommended walks through old-growth preserves. Because logging has traditionally been such an important component of the local economy, many residents worry that further restrictions will threaten their livelihood.

Walking into the Cascades backcountry, you can easily spend hours on a road or trail with only yourself for company. This solitude is the area's greatest drawing card. Appreciate the fact that the only lines you'll have to bother with most of the time are the kind with a hook on the end.

NORTHERN CASCADES

Given their proximity to the state's major urban centers such as Portland and Eugene, the Northern Cascades are a popular destination, particularly on weekends and during the summer months. Most of the highlights, in fact, can be reached within a couple of hours. And thanks to dependable snowpack throughout the warmer months, it is possible—for instance—to spend the morning skiing on Mt. Hood and devote the afternoon to swimming in the warm waters of nearby Cascade Lake. Pioneer history, American Indian culture and scenic wonders are just a few more of the Cascades' treasures. And if you're looking for uncrowded, out-of-the-way places, relax. Those hidden spots are easily located, often just a mile or two off the most popular routes.

SIGHTS

BARLOW TRAIL   Our visit to the **Mt. Hood** region begins on Route 26. Portions of this road parallel the time-saving trail first blazed in 1845 by pioneer Samuel Barlow. The following year he and a partner turned this discovery into a $5 toll road at the end of the Oregon Trail, the final tab for entry to the end of the rainbow. Today a series of small monuments commemorates the trail. At Tollgate campground, a quarter-mile east of Rhododendron on the south side of Route 26, you'll want to visit a reproduction of the historic Barlow Tollgate.

LAUREL HILL CHUTE   If you continue five miles east of Rhododendron, you come to this marker. You can take the short, steep hike to the infamous "chute" where wagon trains descended the perilous grade to Zigzag River Valley.

RIVERS   Two of the region's most popular fishing streams, the **Salmon River** and the **Sandy River** are convenient to old-growth forests, waterfalls and hiking trails.

LOLO PASS ROAD   Continuing east from Salmon and Sandy rivers, you'll reach Zigzag and this backcountry route on the west side of Mt. Hood. It leads to Lost Lake, a great escape (see Chapter Seven for more on the lake).

TIMBERLINE LODGE   ⊠Timberline Ski Area ☎503-272-3311, 800-547-1406 ☏503-622-0710 ✐www.timberlinelodge.com, info@timberlinelodge.com After returning to Route 26, drive east to Government Camp and head uphill to this Mt. Hood lodge, one of the Northwest's most important arts and crafts–style architectural landmarks. Massive is the word for this skiing hub framed with giant timber beams and warmed by a two-level, octagon-shaped stone fireplace. In the summer you can hike the wildflower trails surrounding the lodge or take a guided tour of the monumental building. Be sure to check out the lower-level display on the lodge's fascinating history and current restoration.

WATERFALLS   The Mt. Hood area offers some of the loveliest falls. Head east to Route 35 to the entrance of the Mt. Hood Meadows ski area. You'll see a sign marking the .2-mile trail to **Umbrella Falls**. Although these falls drop only about 60 feet, the verdant setting and fields of wildflowers make this an excellent choice, especially for families with small children. In early summer, the falls trail is reached via a hike through fields of wildflowers. Return to Route 35 and continue 1.4 miles east to **Switchback Falls**. At its peak, in the late spring, North Fork Iron Creeks drops 200 feet.

TRILLIUM LAKE   ⊠Two miles east of Government Camp Turn south on Route 26 to this picturesque lake, a popular fishing, swimming and non-motorized boating spot created by the damming of Mud Creek. It is an ideal place for a picnic lunch and wildlife viewing.

MT. HOOD NATIONAL FOREST–ZIGZAG DISTRICT RANGER STATION   ⊠70220 East Route 26, Zigzag ⊠503-622-3191 The visitors center for the 105-mile Mt. Hood National Scenic Byway was closed in 2008. A new, larger information center, now in the planning stage but not yet fully funded, will be located on the Mt. Hood National Forest boundary at Zigzag on Route 26, midway between Sandy and Government Camp. Meanwhile, all visitor information on the Mount Hood National Scenic Byway is available at this district ranger station, along with the daily or annual Northwest Forest Pass, which is not needed for motorists driving the scenic byway but is required for all hiking trails along the route.

PIONEER WOMEN'S GRAVE   Returning to Route 26, pick up Route 35 over Barlow Pass. East of the junction of these two highways, you'll pass this stone cairn. It commemorates the heroism of all the women who bravely crossed the Oregon Trail. Continue another one and three quarters miles to Forest Road 3530 and the **Barlow Road Sign**. Handcarved by the Civilian Conservation Corps, this marker is a short walk from the wagon ruts left behind by the pioneers.

CLOUD CAP INN   ⊠*Located 10.5 miles north of Route 35, Mt. Hood* Half a century after the pioneers arrived, tourism began to put down roots on this Cascades Peak. Overnight guests were accommodated at this turn-of-the-20th-century inn, the first structure built on Mt. Hood. Although it no longer accepts the public, the shingled inn is on the National Register of Historic Places. Today, it serves as a base for a mountain-climbing-and-rescue organization and provides views of Mt. Hood's north side. It is accessible in late summer and early fall via a washboard dirt road.

WARM SPRINGS   Return south to Route 26 and continue southeast to one of the Pacific Northwest's most intriguing American Indian reservations. Near the lodge entrance an interpretive display offers background on the Confederated Tribes of Warm Springs. American Indian dance performances and a traditional salmon bake are held at the lodge each Saturday in the summer months. Tribe members skewer Columbia River salmon on cedar sticks and cook it over alderwood coals. The hot springs pool is also highly recommended.

KAH-NEE-TA HIGH DESERT RESORT AND CASINO   ⊠*124 Southwest Yamhill Street, Warm Springs* ☎*541-553-1112, 800-554-4786* ⊜*541-553-1071* ⊲*www.kahneeta.com* This arrow-shaped casino-hotel is a great base for visiting the Warm Springs reservation.

SHANIKO   An interesting side trip along Route 97 about 41 miles northeast of Madras is this ghost town, which was once the bustling terminus of the Columbia Southern Railroad and an important shipping center for cattle, sheep and gold at the turn of the 20th century. Tour the 1901 schoolhouse and the city hall, which once accommodated the jail and firehouse, and imagine the streets filled with boys in buckskin and girls in bonnets.

RICHARDSON'S ROCK RANCH   ⊠*6683 Northeast Haycreek Road; 11 miles north of Madras on Route 97, at Milepost 81 turn right and continue southeast three miles.* ☎*541-475-2680, 800-433-2680* ⊜*541-475-4299* ⊲*www.richardsonrockranch.com, richardsonranch@bendnet.com* Richardson's could also be called the world's largest pick-and-pay thunder-egg farm. Formed as gas bubbles in rhyolite flows and filled with silica, these colorful stones range from the size of a seed to 1760 pounds. You can pick up, chisel or dig your

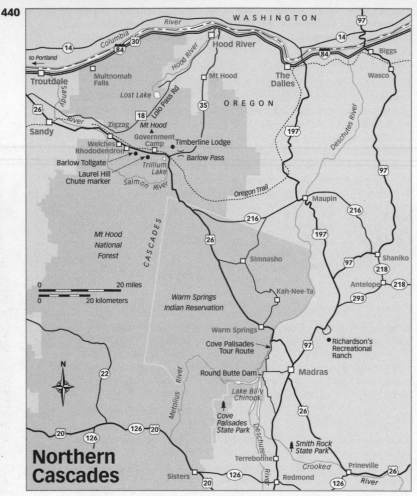

WASHINGTON

Columbia River

to Portland

14

84

30

Hood River

84

14

Biggs

97

Troutdale

Multnomah
Falls

Mt Hood

The
Dalles

Wasco

OREGON

Lost Lake

35

197

Sandy

26

Sandy River

18

Zigzag

Mt Hood

Government
Camp

Timberline Lodge

Deschutes River

97

Welches
Rhododendron

Barlow Tollgate

Laurel Hill
Chute marker

Barlow Pass

Trillium
Lake

Salmon River

Oregon Trail

Maupin

216

197

197

216

C A S C A D E S

Mt Hood
National
Forest

26

Simnasho

97

Shaniko

218

0   20 miles

0   20 kilometers

Warm Springs
Indian Reservation

Kah-Nee-Ta

Antelope

293

218

N

22

Metolius River

Warm Springs

Cove Palisades
Tour Route

Round Butte Dam

97

Madras

Richardson's
Recreational
Ranch

Lake Billy
Chinook

26

20

126

20

126

Cove
Palisades
State Park

Deschutes River

Smith Rock
State Park

**Northern
Cascades**

Sisters

Terrebonne

Crooked

Prineville

20

126

Redmond

River

26

126

thunder eggs out of 12 beds spread across this 4000-acre rock ranch.
Make sure to arrive before 3 p.m. if you want to dig. Closed mid-
November to mid-April, depending on the weather.

COVE PALISADES TOUR ROUTE   This 31-mile route off Route 97
is a worthwhile excursion. Just southwest of Madras, the route circles
Lake Billy Chinook, a popular place for recreational water sports. Three
major rivers, the Deschutes, Crooked and Metolius, have cut canyons
through this Oregon plain and merged at Lake Billy Chinook behind
Round Butte Dam. Be sure to visit the observatory viewpoint on the
lake's Metolius River arm.

COVE PALISADES STATE PARK   Adjoining Lake Billy Chinook is
this state park, a mostly arid landscape interrupted by towering volcanic cones. Pick up a brochure that details opportunities for camping,

hiking and a variety of water sports at the **Madras-Jefferson County Chamber of Commerce** (274 Southwest 4th Street, Madras; 541-475-2350, 800-967-3564, fax 541-475-4341; www.madraschamber.com, office@madraschamber.com).

SMITH ROCK STATE PARK ☎800-551-6949 A favorite of world-class rock climbers is this state park. Don't worry if you forgot to bring your spikes and pitons. You can still enjoy the Cascades scenery from your vantage point along the Crooked River Gorge. The 651-acre park also offers miles of hiking trails. Day-use fee.

LODGING

OREGON CASCADES NORTHERN CASCADES LODGING

TIMBERLINE LODGE

$$$–$$$$ 70 UNITS   ✉Timberline   ☎503-272-3311, 800-547-1406   📠503-622-0710   🖉www.timberlinelodge.com, reservations@timberlinelodge.com

When it comes to architecture, history, location and ambience, few hotels in the Cascades match this place. A veritable museum of Northwest arts and crafts, the lodge was built in 1937 by the Works Progress Administration on the slopes of Mt. Hood. All of the 60 guest rooms and 10 chalet dorm rooms (with bunk beds) have handwoven draperies, bedspreads and rugs featuring a variety of themes; there are iron and oak beds, writing desks, WPA watercolors and views of the valley and mountain. While the rooms are small, there is nothing modest about the public areas, which feature a two-level, octagon-shaped stone fireplace and banisters. It's perfectly situated for skiing, hiking or climbing. In winter, sit inside and watch skiers glide by on snowbanks that reach halfway up the massive windows.

HUCKLEBERRY INN

$$ $$$ 16 UNITS   ✉Route 26 at Government Camp Business Loop, Government Camp   ☎503-272-3325   📠503-272-3031   🖉www.huckleberry-inn.com

This inn offers accommodations in varying price ranges. The units are spare and woodsy, and are popular with hikers scaling Mt. Hood. Standard rooms sleep one to six people, while larger rooms with spiral staircases leading up to sleeping lofts accommodate up to ten. Budget dorm rooms are sometimes available as well. The inn's 24-hour restaurant is also worth checking out for its wide selection of dishes using locally grown huckleberries.

KAH-NEE-TA HIGH DESERT RESORT AND CASINO

$$–$$$ 189 UNITS   ✉124 Southwest Yamhill Street, Warm Springs   ☎541-553-1112, 800-554-4786   📠541-553-1071   🖉www.kahneeta.com, reservations@kahneeta.com

In the mid-1960s the federal government built the Dalles Dam on the Columbia River, submerging the ancestral fishing grounds of local Indians. The Confederated Tribes of Warm Springs used their compensation to pay for this resort. Located in the midst of the 600,000-acre reservation, it offers visitors a variety of lodging choices. There are 139 rooms at the lodge, 30 guest rooms at the village, an RV park, and tepees with cement floors. Set in a red-rock canyon about an hour southeast of Mt. Hood, this resort offers kayaking, golfing, horseback riding, swimming pools, tennis, a water slide, bike rentals and gambling in a casino.

DINING

CASCADE DINING ROOM

$$$$ PACIFIC NORTHWEST ✉*Timberline Lodge, Timberline* ☎*503-272-3104*
🖨*503-272-3145* 🖱*www.timberlinelodge.com, info@timberlinelodge.com*

If you pass on dining at the Timberline Lodge, you'll be missing one of the best meals in the Pacific Northwest. Liveried waiters and waitresses preside over this Arts-and-Crafts-style establishment with a stone fireplace and views of the Cascade Mountains. On a frosty morning there's no better place to down fresh salmon hash or apple oat cakes. Dinner entrées include rack of lamb, wild salmon, roast duckling and vegetarian specialties.

ICE AXE GRILL

$$ AMERICAN ✉*87304 East Government Camp Loop, Government Camp*
☎*503-272-3172* 🖨*503-272-3283* 🖱*www.iceaxegrill.com, pubinfo@mthoodbrewing.com*

Convenient to the Timberline area is this grill, home of the Mt. Hood Brewing Company and Brew Pub. Located in a three-story, stone-and-wood building, this establishment features a flyfishing motif with knotty-pine paneling, a red-quarry tile floor and a 43-foot-long copper bar. Through the large windows you can see the beer-brewing kettles. (Brewery tours are available on a limited basis.) The family-style menu offers gourmet pizza, pasta, steaks, salads and hamburgers.

CHINOOK ROOM

$$–$$$ AMERICAN ✉*124 Southwest Yamhill Street, Warm Springs* ☎*541-553-1112*
🖨*541-553-1071* 🖱*www.kahneeta.com*

At the Kah-Nee-Ta High Desert Resort, try this informal spot for a hearty buffet that may include anything from barbecued ribs to the lodge's famous Indian fry bread. The Juniper Room (only open in summer) has specialties like venison steak, prawns, halibut, steamed clams blended in a seafood pot and birds in clay, a specialty that is cooked for three hours.

SHOPPING

KAH-NEE-TA HIGH DESERT RESORT AND CASINO ✉*124 Yamhill Street, Warm Springs* ☎*541-553-1112, 800-554-4786* 🖨*541-553-1071* 🖱*www.kahneeta.com* When it comes to shopping for American Indian arts and crafts, why not go to the source? At the Kah-Nee-Ta , both the lodge and village have gift shops offering beautiful basketry, handicrafts, blankets and jewelry. Many are made right on the reservation.

WY'EAST STORE ✉*Timberline* ☎*503-272-3311 ext. 763* 🖨*503-272-3145* For limited-edition prints, posters, books, cards and other high-country souvenirs, visit this shop adjacent to Timberline Lodge. A cross between a gift shop and a mountain outfitter, this is also a good place to find sportswear that will make you even more stylish on your way down the slopes.

RICHARDSON'S ROCK RANCH GIFT SHOP ✉*6683 Northeast Haycreek Road; Located 11 miles north of Madras on Route 97, at Milepost 81 turn right and continue southeast three miles.* ☎*541-475-2680* 🖨*541-475-4299* 🖱*www.richardsonrockranch.com, richardsonranch@bendnet.com* Richardson's has a wide variety

of polished spheres, as well as rocks from around the world. Choose from agates, jasper, marble, petrified wood, Moroccan fossils, novelty items and jewelry.

NIGHTLIFE

CHARLIE'S MOUNTAIN VIEW ✉*Government Camp Loop off Route 26, Government Camp* ✆*503-272-3333* ⌨*www.charliesmountainview.com, charliesmountain@gmail.com* On Saturday, live bands play a variety of music at Charlie's. This rustic mountain lodge offers booth, table and whiskey barrel seating. The walls and ceilings are appointed with old-time skis, boots, snowshoes, ski bibs and other high-country memorabilia.

APPALOOSA LOUNGE ✉*Kah-Nee-Ta High Desert Resort, 124 Southwest Yamhill Street, Warm Springs* ✆*541-553-1112, 800-831-0100* 🖷*541-553-1071* ⌨*www.kahneeta.com* You can dance to live bands, enjoy stand-up comedy or try karaoke here. It's also fun to enjoy the music outside on the adjacent deck or to watch a game on the nine-foot-wide projector screen. When the stars are out this is a particularly romantic setting.

PARKS

MT. HOOD NATIONAL FOREST
✉*Access is via Routes 84, 30, 35, 224 and 26* ✆*503-668-1700* 🖷*503-668-1794* ⌨*www.fs.fed.us/r6/mthood, www.mthood.info*

🚶🚵🏇🚣⛷🏕🚤⛵🛶 This one-million-acre national forest is named for the 11,239-foot Cascades peak that dazzles newcomers and natives alike. Extending from the Columbia River Gorge south to the Willamette National Forest boundary, the resort region includes four major wilderness and roadless areas. Popular destinations include the Olallie scenic area, known for its beautiful lakes and wildflowers, and the Mt. Hood Loop, a 150-mile scenic drive circling Oregon's highest peak. Along the way, you'll see mountain meadows, waterfalls, scenic streams, major ski areas and the magical Columbia River Gorge. More than 4500 miles of rivers and streams and more than 160 lakes and reservoirs will delight anglers seeking trout, salmon or steelhead. Some trails are wheelchair accessible. Restrooms are available. The forest headquarters is located outside the forest in Sandy and there are ranger stations scattered throughout the park. Trailhead fee, $6 per vehicle for some trails, available at the visitors center. Some sites and trailheads within the park require a specific National Forest Recreation Day Pass. Call 800-270-7504 for more information.

🏕 Permitted in 106 campgrounds; $16 to $18 per night; RV sites without hookups are available. Three of the best sites for tent/RV camping are on Timothy Lake: the Gone Creek (50 sites), Hoodview (43 sites) and Oak Fork (46 sites). Or try Trillium Lake, with 57 tent/RV sites close to boating and fishing. No hookups are available at any of the sites. Reservations: 877-444-6777 ($9 reservation fee).

COVE PALISADES STATE PARK
✉*Off Route 97, 15 miles southwest of Madras* ✆*541-546-3412* 🖷*541-546-2220*

🚶🎣⛵🏕🚤🛶 Located at the junction of the Crooked, Deschutes and Metolius rivers, this 4129-acre park encompasses two arms of Lake

Billy Chinook. The cove is set beneath towering palisades and located on benchland punctuated by volcanic cones. Rich in petroglyphs and American Indian history, this region is a geological showcase. Fishing is excellent for smallmouth bass, trout and kokanee. Ten miles of hiking trails offer excellent panoramic views and opportunities to see wildlife. There is also a picnic area, restrooms, a marina, a playground, nature trails and concessions. Day-use fee, $3.

▲ There are 92 tent sites ($17 to $20 per night), 173 RV hookup sites ($21 to $24 per night) and three cabins ($48 to $70 per night). Reservations: 503-731-3411, 800-452-5687.

CENTRAL CASCADES

One of Oregon's top recreational areas, the Central Cascades include some of the state's finest museums and interpretive centers. A year-round getaway for hiking, fishing, climbing and skiing, this area is also famous for its volcanic scenery, mountain lakes and rafting. Within the national forests are some of the West's leading wilderness areas and great opportunities for wildlife viewing. The region is an ideal family resort and also boasts one of the best scenic drives in the Northwest, the Cascades Loop Highway.

Although none of the peaks have the name recognition of Mt. Hood, the Central Cascades are by no means inferior mountains. A trio known collectively as the Three Sisters rises above 10,000 feet, while relatively diminutive Mt. Bachelor (a mere 9065 feet) provides some of the Northwest's best alpine skiing. The topography is so daunting, in fact, that not many roads cross the Central Cascades, although a few open up in the summer to provide access to the area's voluminous mountain lakes and rivers. Still, plenty of destinations can be reached year-round, and there are enough outdoor activities to keep you busy for weeks.

SIGHTS

SISTERS A good way to begin your visit is by heading west from Redmond 20 miles on Route 126 to this town. Gateway to some of the Cascades' most memorable scenery, this small town has a Wild West–style main street that delights tourists driving between the Willamette Valley and the Bend area. Stop by the **Sisters Chamber of Commerce** (291 East Main Avenue; 541-549-0251, 866-549-0252, fax 541-549-4253; www.sisterschamber.com, info@ sisterschamber.com) to find out more information.

After pausing to shop, dine or provision, head west nine miles on Route 20 and then turn north to the Metolius River Recreation Area. Here you can enjoy flyfishing and, in the winter, cross-country skiing.

BLACK BUTTE RANCH ✉*12940 Hawksbeard; Route 20, eight miles west of Sisters* ☎*541-595-6211, 866-901-2961* ☏*541-595-2077* ⌨*www.blackbutteranch.com, info@blackbutteranch.com* Near Sisters is this ranch, a resort area (see "Lodging" below) named for a towering volcanic cone.

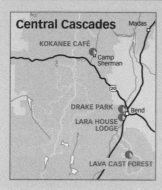

KOKANEE CAFÉ

PAGE 455

Upscale, wild-caught seafood like sesame crab fritters or Northwest salmon in a red current glaze

DRAKE PARK

PAGE 459

Verdant forested stretch along the Deschutes River, perfect for a peaceful stroll or family picnic

LARA HOUSE LODGE

PAGE 453

1910 Craftsman house with inviting rooms and a gourmet breakfast served on the sun porch

LAVA CAST FOREST

PAGE 448

Unique 6000-year-old landscape resulting from lava sweeping across a pine forest, leaving a mold of each tree

LAKES To the west off Route 20, **Blue Lake** is a resort destination as well, with easy access to the scenic treasures of the Mt. Washington Wilderness to the south. Continue west on Route 20 to Route 22 and **Detroit Lake**, a recreational area ideal for waterskiing.

SHADY COVE BRIDGE

This area is also home to this unusual, three-span, wooden-truss structure. The bridge, hand-cut and hand-assembled using hundreds of small interlocking pieces, links French Creek Road with Little North Santiam drainage.

BREITENBUSH HOT SPRINGS RETREAT AND CONFERENCE CENTER ✉53000 Breitenbush Road, Detroit ☎503-854-3320 ☏503-854-3819 ✐www.breitenbush.com, office@breitenbush.com From Detroit Lake, take Forest Road 46 northeast ten miles to this New Age wilderness resort. Before the arrival of the white man, American Indians conducted rituals and ceremonies here. Now, yoga, guided forest hikes, meditation, hot-springs pools, steam saunas and massage therapy are all part of the fun. The artesian hot springs boast 30 minerals said to have curative powers.

CLEAR LAKE Return to Route 22 and head southeast. Along this route is this major volcanic landmark, the source of the McKenzie

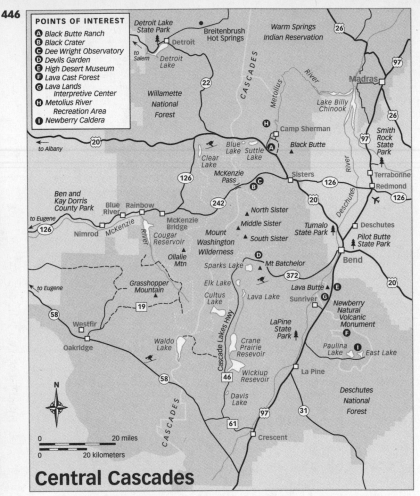

POINTS OF INTEREST
- Ⓐ *Black Butte Ranch*
- Ⓑ *Black Crater*
- Ⓒ *Dee Wright Observatory*
- Ⓓ *Devils Garden*
- Ⓔ *High Desert Museum*
- Ⓕ *Lava Cast Forest*
- Ⓖ *Lava Lands Interpretive Center*
- Ⓗ *Metolius River Recreation Area*
- Ⓘ *Newberry Caldera*

Central Cascades

River. Created when lava blocked a canyon, the lake lives up to its name in every respect.

WATERFALLS Continue south on Route 126 to **Sahalie Falls**, a wheelchair-accessible spot where the McKenzie River cascades 100 feet over lava cliffs. A short drive south is **Koosah Falls**, which plunges more than 80 feet. In the fall this waterfall divides into several sections. A trail takes you down the river canyon to enjoy the view from a series of overlooks. Continue another 5.2 miles south to a road that heads to the McKenzie River Trailhead. After hiking upriver for 2 miles you'll discover that **Tamolitch Falls** have now run dry. Although the river has been diverted to a reservoir at this point, it remains a scenic spot. Thanks to local springs, the river begins anew at this location.

MCKENZIE BRIDGE Southeast on Route 126 another 17.6 miles is this hamlet, gateway to many scenic highlights of the Central Cascades.

The town proper consists of little more than the Log Cabin Inn and a small market.

AUFDERHEIDE NATIONAL SCENIC BYWAY   Head east to the **McKenzie River Ranger District and Cascade Center** (541-822-3381) and pick up this byway's audio tape (summer only). Following old logging roads, the byway winds through the Three Sisters Wilderness, passing mid-sized peaks like Olallie Mountain (5708 feet) and Grasshopper Mountain (5651 feet). The byway parallels the south fork of the McKenzie River for much of the way.

OAKRIDGE PIONEER MUSEUM   ✉*76433 Pine Street, Oakridge* ✆*541-782-2402* ✐*www.oakridgemuseum.com* Before returning north to the McKenzie Bridge area, take a look around the Oakridge area. We liked this museum, located south of Westfir on Route 58. Even if you're not into chainsaws—one of the Northwest's best collections is found here—you'll enjoy seeing the antique logging implements, grocery displays, American Indian artifacts and vintage crockery. Parked just down the street are an antique logging truck, fire truck and caboose. The museum is open Saturday from 1 to 4 p.m., Tuesday and Thursday from 10 a.m. to noon, and with advance notice.

WALDO LAKE _____ **hidden**

✉*Route 58* Twenty miles east of Oakridge is this pristine lake. Clean enough to qualify as distilled water, the six-mile-long lake has astonishing visibility. Out on the water you can see down 100 feet to the bottom. While there are facilities, the lake, one of Oregon's largest, also has wilderness on the west and north shores.

DEE WRIGHT OBSERVATORY   Heading north to the McKenzie Bridge area again, pick up Route 126 east to Route 242 (a narrow route not recommended for long motor homes) up McKenzie Pass to this observatory, where a half-mile paved trail leads through one of the Cascades' largest lava fields. From the observatory you can see 11 mountain peaks. Also worth a visit nearby is **Black Crater**, a volcanic summit close to North Sister Mountain.

BEND   Continue east to Sisters and pick up Route 20 east to this modest city. One of Oregon's fastest-growing resort communities and a sunny alternative to the more drizzly parts of the Northwest, this town has become a year-round recreational center.

BEND CHAMBER OF COMMERCE   ✉*777 Northwest Wall Street, Suite 200, Bend* ✆*541-382-3221, 800-905-2363* ✉*541-385-9929* ✐*www.bendchamber.org, info@bendchamber.org* As you drive into town, be sure to stop at the Bend Chamber of Commerce. This is the best place to orient yourself. Closed weekends.

DRAKE PARK   In the center of Bend, this park on Riverside Boulevard shouldn't be missed. On the Des Chutes River, this urban sanctuary features picturesque **Mirror Pond**. Put out a blanket on the lawn, have a picnic, feed the ducks and study your own reflection.

DESCHUTES HISTORICAL MUSEUM ✉*129 Northwest Idaho Avenue, Bend* ☎*541-389-1813* 📠*541-317-9345* 🖥*www.deschuteshistory.org, info@deschutes history.org* Although strip development along Route 97 is changing Bend's small-town character, the past is well preserved at this historical museum. Located in the Reid School building on the south end of downtown, the museum features exhibits on American Indian history, early-day trappers and explorers, pioneer trails and the lumber industry. Closed Sunday and Monday. Admission.

HIGH DESERT MUSEUM ✉*59800 South Route 97, three miles south of Bend* ☎*541-382-4754* 📠*541-382-5256* 🖥*www.highdesertmuseum.org, info@highdesert museum.org* One of the finest collections in the Pacific Northwest, the indoor galleries here are complemented by 20 acres of nature trails and outdoor exhibits. Permanent exhibits share the contemporary reservation experience of the Columbia Plateau Indians, as well as the natural history and settlement. A nice display here is a dawn-to-dusk "walk through time" that showcases the history of the West. The Brook and Collins galleries feature regional art, culture and history exhibits. Visitors head outdoors to view the river otter pool and a birds of prey show. Admission.

NEWBERRY VOLCANO The region's largest geologic feature is this 500-square-mile volcano, created by eruption from thousands of volcanos over the past half-million years in the area just south of Bend. **Paulina and East lakes**, two popular resort areas for anglers, are found in the 20-square-mile **Newberry Caldera**. Within the crater is 100-foot-high **Paulina Creek Falls**, an easy walk from Paulina Creek Falls picnic ground. Accessible only in summer. Also worth a visit is the crater's shiny, black obsidian flow.

NEWBERRY NATIONAL VOLCANIC MONUMENT ___ h**idden**

Continue south on Route 97 to this volcanic monument, one of Oregon's geologic showcases and the product of more than 500,000 years of volcanic eruptions. Part of the Deschutes National Forest, the monument encompasses numerous volcanic landmarks.

LAVA CAST FOREST ___ h**idden**

Much of the best sightseeing in the monument is found on the east side of Route 97. Two worthy spots in this fascinating region are **Lava River Cave** and this preserved forest. The former, a lava tube, is great for spelunkers (fee). Flashlight in hand, you can walk a mile down this eerie tunnel (Oregon's longest uncollapsed lava tube), but bring warm clothing since it stays around 40° in the tube; it's closed in winter because of hibernating bats. The latter, explored via a mile-long, self-guided trail, is a unique piece of Oregon scenery. This unusual landscape was shaped when lava swept across a stand of pine 6000 years ago, creating molds of each tree.

LAVA LANDS INTERPRETIVE CENTER ✉*58201 South Route 97* ☎*541-593-2421 (in summer), 541-383-5300 (national forest)* At this interpretive center, you'll find exhibits, dioramas, videos and interpretive staff who can suggest a variety of nature trails that lead through the lava flow. Closed September 15 through May. Admission.

LAVA BUTTE Within this ten-square-mile lava flow are highlights like this 6650-year-old butte, which changed the course of the Deschutes River. Reached by a paved road from the interpretive center, the butte offers a 360-degree view of the Cascades, the Lava Lands and the high desert to the east. You'll have to hike the final 100 yards to the summit. After enjoying the vista, you can continue west four miles from the interpretive center (follow the signs saying "Deschutes River Views") to reach **Benham Falls**, a popular picnic spot next to the Deschutes. To reach the falls, continue on the trail another quarter of a mile.

CASCADE LAKES HIGHWAY This 87-mile highway leads to some of the most idyllic resort regions in the area. Todd, Sparks, Devils, Elk, Hosmer, Lava, Cultus and Davis lakes are a few of the popular spots for fishing, boating, swimming and camping. For those eager to head for the outback, there's easy access to high-country lakes, streams and creeks in the Three Sisters Wilderness.

MORE WATERFALLS ✉*Cascade Lakes Highway* Century Drive, the beginning of the Cascade Lakes Highway west of Bend, provides easy access to **Lava Island Falls** on the Deschutes River. Take this road to Route 41 and drive south for .4 mile. Go left on Route 620 for .8 mile to reach the falls. If you take Route 41 south from Century Drive 3 miles and pick up Route 100 for .9 mile you'll reach **Dillon Falls**.

MT. BACHELOR ✉*Cascade Lakes Highway* Nearby is central Oregon's premier ski area (see "Outdoor Adventures" below). Near the mountain, **Tumalo Falls** drops nearly 100 feet in an area burned by a 1979 fire.

TODD LAKE ✉*Cascade Lakes Highway* Following Route 46 west from Bend, after 23 miles you'll pass the turnoff to the Mt. Bachelor Ski Area. Another two miles brings you to an unpaved road that turns off to the right and leads about a quarter-mile to this lake. Though close to the highway, it has a wonderful sense of seclusion in a glacial valley filled with wildflowers. There's a fishermen's trail around the 60-foot-deep lake and a primitive campground.

SPARKS LAKE ✉*Cascade Lakes Highway* About two miles past the Todd Lake turnoff, this lake has one of the prettiest views on this route, reflecting the snowcaps of the Three Sisters in its placid water. Although motorboats are allowed, the 10-mph speed limit and shallow water areas discourage them. The lake is ideal for canoeing and flyfishing.

DEVILS GARDEN ⓗidden
✉*Cascade Lakes Highway* Scenic highlights in this region include spots like this beautiful meadow where you can spot pictographs left behind by Warm Springs Indians. A piece of vol-

canic rock from this area—the Devils Hill Flow—was flown to the moon by Apollo astronaut James Irwin, who as an astronaut candidate trained in the area. The flow is located on Cascade Lakes Highway, between Devils and Sparks lakes.

Gorges in the Mist

The land of falling waters, the Pacific Northwest is the place to go for plunging rivers. Thousands of waterfalls are found here, often convenient to major highways or trails. Reached via fern canyons, paths through old-growth forests and along pristine streams, waterfall hunting is great sport, even on a rainy day. And part of the fun is getting misted or sprayed by the raging waters.

In the Cascades, these falls are at their peak in late spring or early summer. But even if you come later in the summer or fall, there will still be plenty to see: deep, plunging streams, tiered falls that split into roaring ribbons before converging in swirling pools, horsetails that drop at a 90-degree angle while retaining contact with bedrock. And, of course, you can count on frequently spotting the distinctive waterfall that gives this region its name—the Cascades that drop down in a series of steps.

In the Umpqua River Valley, Route 138, nicknamed "The Highway of Waterfalls," provides access to 11 falls within a 50-mile stretch. Among them is **Susan Creek Falls**, located via a trail 7.5 miles east of Idleyld Park. You'll hike 1 mile north of the highway to reach the falls. Drive Steamboat Road northeast from Steamboat 4.2 miles to reach **Steamboat Falls**. Located at a forest-service campground, this small waterfall is circumvented by fish that use an adjacent ladder. Near mile marker 42 about 3 miles southeast of Steamboat are **Jack Creek** and tiered **Jack Falls**. These three falls are particularly rewarding for photo buffs.

Also popular are **Toketee Falls**. To see this 90-foot drop, take Route 138 to the Toketee Lake turnoff. Continue north .3 mile to the trail leading west .6 mile to the falls. East of Toketee Lake is Lemolo Lake, a popular resort destination. From here, Thorn Prairie Road leads to Lemolo Falls Road. Hike the Lemolo Falls Trail 1 mile west to this cataract.

Off Route 62, the main highway from Medford to Crater Lake, is one of the Cascades' grander waterfalls, 175-foot **Mill Creek Falls**. Accessible by Mill Creek Road, this scenic spot is an easy .3-mile hike from the Mill Creek Falls Scenic Area trailhead on the south side of Prospect. Also accessible on this hike are **Barr Creek Falls**, **Prospect Falls**, **Pearsoney Falls** and **Lower Red Blanket Falls**.

Within Crater Lake National Park, **Annie Falls** is off Route 62, 4.7 miles north of the park's southern entrance. Because this falls is located in an unstable canyon-rim area, visitors should approach it with extreme caution. Also in the park, close to Applegate Peak, is **Vidae Falls**.

To get a complete rundown on these watery delights, check with local park or ranger offices. Or pick up a copy of the definitive guide to this subject, *A Waterfall Lover's Guide to the Pacific Northwest* (The Mountaineers).

DEVILS LAKE ✉Cascade Lakes Highway Four miles from Sparks Lake, this glacier-fed body of water is one of the few lakes that can be seen from the highway and one of the high points of this drive. The crystalline turquoise water and 10-foot-deep white pumice bottom make it easy to see the trout that swim below, though catching them may be a challenge. There's a small campground, a hiking trail, and a trailhead for longer trails into the Three Sisters Wilderness.

HOSMER LAKE ✉Cascade Lakes Highway Five miles beyond Devils Lake is the turnoff to this popular catch-and-release fishing lake that supports a landlocked salmon population. The tiny islands in the north part of the lake are home to otters and minks. Reeds and marshes make it hard to walk close to the water's edge, but hikers in the surrounding wildflower meadows and conifer forests may spot elk, deer and porcupines.

CRANE PRAIRIE RESERVOIR ✉Cascade Lakes Highway About 20 miles beyond the Hosmer Lake turnoff, this manmade reservoir is one of the most popular destinations on the east slope of the Cascades for recreational motorboating. It's also a major habitat for ospreys, and visitors can watch as these big "fish eagles" dive at high speed to snag fish with their talons.

The Cascade Lakes Highway passes two other large manmade lakes, **Wickiup Reservoir** and **Davis Lake**, before returning to Route 97 at Crescent, midway between Bend (46 miles) and Crater Lake (51 miles). If you're planning to return to Bend, shortcut roads return due east to Route 97 from both Crane Prairie and Wickiup reservoirs.

LODGING

SISTERS MOTOR LODGE

$$–$$$ 11 UNITS ✉511 West Cascade Avenue, Sisters ☎541-549-2551
☎541-549-9399 ⌖www.sistersmotorlodge.com, info@sistersmotorlodge.com

This lodge offers comfortable bed-and-breakfast-style accommodations with funky, antique-decorated rooms. Four of the rooms have kitchenettes; two-bedroom units are available. A patio area with a fire-pit is available for a backyard barbecue.

BLACK BUTTE RANCH

$$$–$$$$ 120 UNITS ✉12940 Hawksbeard; Route 20, eight miles west of Sisters
☎541-595-6211, 866-901-2961 ☎541-595-2077 ⌖www.blackbutteranch.com,
info@blackbutteranch.com

When it comes to lodging, you really can get just about anything you want here. This 1830-acre resort offers more than 120 condos, cabins and private homes. Chalet-style accommodations nestled in the pines have paneled walls and ceilings, decks, fireplaces and, in some condos, fully equipped kitchens and outdoor hot tubs. Choose between two golf courses, five swimming pools, 18 miles of bike and jogging trails and 23 tennis courts. There's canoeing in a spring-fed lake, as well as skiing, hiking, fishing, boating and horseback riding.

LONG HOLLOW RANCH _____ hidden

$$$ 6 ROOMS ✉71105 Holmes Road, Sisters ☎541-923-1901,
877-923-1901 ☜www.lhranch.com, lhranch@communitybroadband.com

Situated in the high desert 13 miles from the town of Sisters, this authentic working ranch raises cattle and a string of riding horses and grows hay in the broad fields that surround the ranch buildings. While the original homestead cabin built in the 1880s is still standing and serves as a gift shop, the main ranch house and guest cottage date back to the early 20th century. The refurbished guest rooms have a historic Old West feel. Most have queen-sized beds and all have private baths, as well as modern amenities such as air-conditioning and wireless internet access. No smoking, hard liquor or pets. Closed December through February.

METOLIUS RIVER LODGES

$$–$$$ 13 UNITS ✉Five and a half miles north of Route 20, Camp Sherman
☎541-595-6290, 800-595-6290 ☜www.metoliusriverlodges.com,
cabins@metoliusriverlodges.com

These lodges in Camp Sherman include 13 cabins with one, two or three bedrooms. Located about 15.5 miles northwest of Sisters, this wooded retreat is in an area ideal for mountain biking, cross-country skiing, flyfishing and water sports. The wood-paneled units have carpeting, fireplaces, kitchens, barbecues and rustic cabin furniture.

LAKE CREEK LODGE

$$$–$$$$ 20 UNITS ✉13375 Southwest Forest Service Road #1419, Camp Sherman,
four miles north of Route 20 ☎541-595-6331, 800-797-6331 ☏541-595-1016
☜www.lakecreeklodge.com, stay@lakecreeklodge.com

A small lake created by a dammed stream is just one of the attractions at this lodge. Two- or three-bedroom knotty pine–paneled cabins feature early American furniture, full kitchens; some have fireplaces. Near the Metolius River, this 40-acre resort has tennis courts, a heated swimming pool, bike and hiking trails. In the summer they serve meals family style and offer special activities for children.

BREITENBUSH HOT SPRINGS RETREAT
AND CONFERENCE CENTER

$–$$ 30 UNITS ✉Forest Road 46, Milepost 10, Detroit ☎503-854-3314,
503-854-3320 (day-of reservations) ☏503-854-3819 ☜www.breitenbush.com,
office@breitenbush.com

As far as luxurious New Age facilities go, this secluded property has it all. Located in the western Cascades, this retreat provides everything from massage therapy to yoga to a spiritual/self-help workshop. Guests bring their own bedding and are housed in spartan, cedar-shake cabins paneled with fir; platform tents and campsites are available in summer. Geothermal heat and electricity from hydropower provide energy self-sufficiency. Guests can choose between hot tubs, *au naturel* hot springs overlooking the river and mountains and a hot natural-steam sauna complete with a cold-water tub. Vegetarian meals are included. Reservations required.

MCKENZIE RIVERSIDE COTTAGES

$$–$$$ 10 UNITS   ✉54466 McKenzie River Drive, Blue River   ☎541-822-3715,
800-823-3715   📠541-822-0346   🖳www.mckenzieriversidecottages.com,
mcrivercottages@aol.com

Roomy units complete with fireplaces, decks and kitchenettes are the standard here. The cottages make an ideal fishing retreat—you can cast for trout from your porch! For larger gatherings, there are two three-bedroom suites complete with kitchens and decks that can easily sleep 16 people.

THE RIVERHOUSE

$$$–$$$$ 220 UNITS   ✉3075 North Business 97, Bend   ☎541-389-3111,
866-453-4480   📠541-389-0870   🖳www.riverhouse.com, marketing@riverhouse.com

This is one of over a dozen motels on Bend's main drag. There are one- and two-bedroom suites featuring contemporary furniture, floral-print bedspreads and sitting areas. In the evening you can relax in front of the fireplace or have a drink on your deck overlooking the Deschutes River. Deluxe-priced suites include kitchen facilities. An 18-hole golf course, jogging trail, two pools, two saunas and three whirlpools make this a good place to relax.

ECONOLODGE

$ 59 ROOMS   ✉437 Northeast 3rd Street, Bend   ☎541-382-2211, 877-424-6423
📠541-385-0989   🖳www.econolodge.com

In the heart of Bend is this place, featuring uniform motel rooms, all with free wi-fi. If you've got a four-legged friend with you, this lodge will happily make accommodations (fee). Continental breakfast served.

DESCHUTES MOTEL

$$ 30 ROOMS   ✉1515 Northeast 3rd Street, Bend   ☎541-395-2626, 877-899-6608
🖳www.deschutesmotel.com, carol@deschutesmotel.com

Single and double rooms are available at this family-owned and -operated motel. All units include refrigerators, air conditioning and TV. A shaded yard is available for barbecues or simply relaxing.

LARA HOUSE LODGE _____ ⓗidden

$$$–$$$$ 6 ROOMS   ✉640 Northwest Congress Street, Bend
☎541-388-4064, 800-766-4064   📠541-388-4064   🖳www.larahouse.com,
larahousebandb@bendbroadband.com

Located across from Drake Park, Lara House hosts guests in six rooms, all with private baths. You can take your full breakfast on the sun porch. Wine and hors d'oeuvres are served in the afternoon. This 1910 Craftsman also has a comfortable living room and a candlelit front porch.

BEND RIVERSIDE MOTEL

$$–$$$ 100 UNITS   ✉1565 Northwest Wall Street, Bend   ☎541-389-2363,
800-284-2363   📠541-312-3900   🖳www.bendriversidemotel.com, bendrivers@aol.com

This motel offers rooms, studios and suites with river views. The studios and suites have fireplaces, kitchen facilities, sauna and hot tubs. Convenient to downtown in a secluded setting.

SUNRIVER RESORT

$$$$ 700 UNITS   ✉*17600 Center Drive, Sunriver; Route 97, 15 miles south of Bend*   📞*800-801-8765*   📠*541-593-5458*   🖱*www.sunriver-resort.com,* *info@sunriver-resort.com*

At this 3300-acre resort, you can choose between 300 rooms and suites featuring pine furniture, fireplaces, wall-to-wall carpets and decks with views of the Cascades. About 400 condos and homes are also available. All guests can take advantage of the pools, tennis courts, bicycles, canoes, skiing, golf, horseback riding and spa and fitness facilities.

THE SEVENTH MOUNTAIN RESORT

$$–$$$$ 170 UNITS   *18575 Southwest Century Drive, five miles west of Bend*   📞*541-382-8711, 800-452-6810*   📠*541-382-3517*   🖱*www.seventhmountain.com,* *info@seventhmountain.com*

In the wooded Cascades foothills, Seventh Mountain may be the only resort in Oregon with its own skating rink and outdoor pool open in the winter. The units have kings, queens and Murphy beds, knotty-pine paneling, fireplaces and contemporary prints. Convenient to Mt. Bachelor, the inn is ideally located for horseback riding, whitewater rafting and mountain biking.

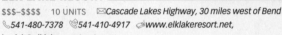

ELK LAKE RESORT

$$$–$$$$ 10 UNITS   ✉*Cascade Lakes Highway, 30 miles west of Bend*   📞*541-480-7378*   📠*541-410-4917*   🖱*www.elklakeresort.net,* *jwalsh@elklakeresort.net*

Built around a circa-1923 lodge, this resort is a forested retreat ideal for fishing, canoeing, kayaking and loafing. The knotty-pine cabins, with two or three bedrooms, kitchens and small decks, are near wilderness hiking and Nordic skiing. For the adventurous, the resort is accessible only by cross-country skiing, snowcat and snowmobile in the winter months. Pet-friendly.

DINING

ALI'S

$ DELI   ✉*161 East Cascade Avenue, Town Square, Sisters*   📞*541-549-2547*

In Sisters, this café provides a convenient solution for those who can't decide between a sandwich or a salad. Generous sandwiches served on an open-faced bagel or wrapped in pita bread include curry chicken, dill tuna and lemon-ginger chicken. A wide variety of vegetarian sandwiches and smoked turkey sandwiches are offered, as well as soups, pasta salads, bagels and ice cream. Lunch only.

PAPANDREA'S

$$–$$$ ITALIAN/AMERICAN   ✉*442 East Hood Street, Sisters*   📞*541-549-6081*   📠*541-549-7407*   🖱*www.papandreaspizza.com*

One of the most popular pizza parlors in these parts is this place. The modest board-and-batten establishment has indoor seating and patio service on picnic tables covered with green tablecloths. Antique farm implements decorate the dining room. All dough and sauces are home-made, and the tomatoes are fresh.

LODGE RESTAURANT AT BLACK BUTTE RANCH

$$$ AMERICAN ✉12940 Hawksbeard; Route 20, eight miles west of Sisters ☎541-595-1260 📠541-595-2077 🖱www.blackbutteranch.com, info@blackbutteranch.com

For dining in a contemporary setting, consider the Lodge Restaurant. This split-level establishment has cathedral ceilings, picture windows and early American furniture. While enjoying the panoramic Cascades view, you can order prime rib, roast duck, oysters, halibut filet, pasta primavera with chicken or vegetables. Closed Monday through Wednesday in winter.

KOKANEE CAFÉ _____ (h)idden

$$$-$$$$ PACIFIC NORTHWEST/SEAFOOD ✉25545 Forest Service Road, Camp Sherman ☎541-595-6420 🖱www.kokaneecafe.com

Located in a shingled lodge-style building adjacent to the Metolius River, this café is recommended for Pacific Northwest cuisine, especially the fresh wild-caught seafood dishes. Start with the sesame crab fritters with rose-scented orange and carrot salad or sample the wild Northwest salmon in a red currant glaze. Organic meats and produce round out the menu. The desserts are exceptional. Worth a special trip. Dinner only. Closed January to April. Call for hours and reservations.

ERNESTO'S ITALIAN RESTAURANT

$$ ITALIAN ✉1203 Northeast 3rd Street, Bend ☎541-389-7274 📠541-389-1686

In a café-style dining room set in an old church, this family-run restaurant serves up rich, homemade lasagna, veal parmigiana and calzone.

PINE TAVERN

$$-$$$ AMERICAN ✉967 Northwest Brooks Street, at the foot of Northwest Oregon Street, Bend ☎541-382-5581 📠541-382-5583 🖱www.pinetavern.com, pinetavern@pinetavern.com

A Bend tradition since 1936 and one of my state-wide top spots, this tavern has an enviable location overlooking Mirror Pond. Built around late 18th-century ponderosa pines, the restaurant prides itself on home-cooked dishes like chicken marsala, fresh salmon and their specialty, Oregon County prime rib using grain-fed beef. Don't miss the sourdough scones with honey butter. Seafood specials are offered each evening; there's also a children's menu. No lunch on Sunday.

DESCHUTES BREWERY AND PUBLIC HOUSE

$$-$$$ AMERICAN ✉1044 Northwest Bond Street, Bend ☎541-382-9242 📠541-385-8095 🖱www.deschutesbrewery.com, info@deschutesbrewery.com

For some different fare, head for Deschutes Brewery. This microbrewery, known for its Mirror Pond Pale Ale and Black Butte Porter, homemade root beer and ginger ale, serves upscale pub fare like a pastrami Reuben, buffalo wings and elk burgers.

MARCELLO'S
CUCINA ITALIANA

$$–$$$ ITALIAN   ✉*Beaver Drive and North Ponderosa Road, Sunriver*
 📞*541-593-8300* 📠*541-593-5965*

Located in a chalet-style building, Marcello's packs locals into its carpeted brick dining room nightly. Their reward is pasta, veal and chicken specialties, as well as calzones, seafood and, of course, a dozen varieties of pizza. Dinner only.

THE MEADOWS

$$$–$$$$ PACIFIC NORTHWEST/SEAFOOD   ✉*Sunriver Resort, Sunriver*
 📞*541-593-3740* 📠*541-593-4678* ✍*www.sunriver-resort.com, info@sunriver-resort.com*

For dining with a view of the Cascades, this is a good choice. The restaurant serves fresh seafood and Northwestern cuisine such as glazed wild salmon with cranberry relish and cassoulet with braised elk, cannellini beans and duck confit. In summer you can dine on the outdoor deck with its panoramic view.

MERCHANT TRADER CAFÉ

$–$$ AMERICAN   ✉*Sunriver Resort, Sunriver* 📞*541-593-3790* 📠*541-593-4678*
✍*www.sunriver-resort.com, info@sunriver-resort.com*

At Sunriver Resort is this more casual café with outdoor patio seating. Breakfast includes homemade scones and granola. Baby back ribs, sandwiches, wraps and gourmet salads are offered for lunch and dinner.

ELK LAKE RESORT ____

$$–$$$ AMERICAN   ✉*Cascade Lakes Highway, 30 miles west of Bend*
 📞*541-480-7378* ✍*www.elklakeresort.net, jwalsh@elklakeresort.net*

If you're looking for a hearty breakfast or coffee-shop lunch fare, try the counter at this rustic resort. The dining area is a great place for bacon and eggs, pancakes or french toast. Burgers, salads and sandwiches fill the lunch menu. Although table service is available, take a stool for the maximum waterfront view. Dinner specials nightly. Limited hours Monday and Tuesday.

SHOPPING

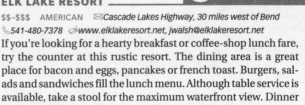

BLUE SPRUCE GALLERY &
POTTERY STUDIO ____

✉*20591 Dorchester East, Bend* 📞*866-382-0197* ✍*www.bluesprucepottery.com* Stop by the Blue Spruce Gallery, which carries a beautiful collection of pottery, ceramic vases, custom-made lamps and dinnerware, paintings and decorative art. Closed Sunday.

SILVER SAGE TRADING ✉*59800 South Route 97, Bend* 📞*541-382-4754* 📠*541-382-5256* ✍*www.highdesertmuseum.org* This gift shop at the High Desert Museum is a great place to browse for American Indian basketry, nature books, handmade jewelry, beadwork, cultural items, cards and photos. It also offers birdfeeders, mobiles and wildflower seeds.

DESCHUTES GALLERY ✉521 Northwest Colorado Avenue, Bend ☎888-981-8200 ⏏www.deschutesgallery.com Northwest American Indian and Inuit art pieces are on display here, including masks, boxes, bowls, blankets, jewelry and dolls, as well as prints and paintings.

NIGHTLIFE

RIVERHOUSE ✉3075 North Business 97, Bend ☎541-389-8810 ⊠541-389-0870 ⏏www.riverhouse.com For live Top 40 and classic rock music nightly, head to this contemporary lounge. It has a roomy dancefloor, full bar and spacious deck overlooking the Deschutes. In warm weather you can enjoy dining and drinks on the deck.

CASCADES THEATRICAL COMPANY ✉148 Northwest Greenwood, Bend ☎541-389-0803 ⏏www.cascadestheatrical.org, ctcinfo@cascadestheatrical.org This company has presented musicals, dramas, comedies and Broadway hits since 1978. This theater produces six shows from early September to late June.

PARKS

DETROIT LAKE STATE PARK
✉Route 22, two miles west of Detroit ☎503-854-3406

This 104-acre park is a popular day-use and overnight facility on the shore of one of the busier Cascade Lakes. A forested spot on the north shore of Detroit Reservoir, the park is divided into two units. The smaller Mongold is for day-use picnicking, boat launching and swimming. To the east is the Detroit Lake State Park campground, with a boat launch and boat slips. You can fish for rainbow trout and kokanee salmon. There are restrooms, showers, a visitors center and picnic areas. Closed November through mid-March. Day-use fee, $3.

▲ There are 133 tent sites ($12 to $16 per night), 178 RV hookup sites ($16 to $20 per night). Reservations: 800-452-5687.

WILLAMETTE NATIONAL FOREST _____ (h)idden

✉Access via Routes 22, 20, 126, 242 and 58 ☎541-225-6300
⏏www.fs.fcd.us/r6/willamette

This 1.6-million-acre region (larger than the state of Connecticut!) covers from 10,495-foot Mt. Jefferson to the Calapooya Mountains northeast of Roseburg. Diverse terrain ranges from volcanic moonscapes to wooded slopes and cascading rivers. The National Forest recently annexed Opal Creek Wilderness; more than 400,000 acres of wilderness encompass seven major Cascade peaks. Home to more than 300 animal species, including deer, cougar, grouse and Roosevelt elk, this forest also boasts more than 600 varieties of rhododendron. There are over 1600 miles of hiking trails here, and mountain bikers cluster near the town of Oakridge to ride the foothills. In the winter months, heavy snowfall blankets the popular Nordic and alpine skiing areas at Willamette Pass and Hoodoo Ski Bowl. More than 1500 miles of rivers and streams, as well as 375 lakes (including one of the world's purest bodies of water, Waldo Lake), offer countless opportunities for fishing. You'll find picnic tables, interpretive centers and restrooms. Trailhead parking fee, $5. Specific wilderness permits are required to enter any of the forest's wilderness areas in addition to the Northwest Forest Pass that is required to enter the forest itself. Check the forest service website (above) for details.

⚤ Permitted at over 60 campgrounds; free to $18 per night; RV sites available at most campgrounds. Some of the most popular sites are the Hoover Campground at Detroit Reservoir, and the Paradise and McKenzie Bridge campgrounds near the town of McKenzie Bridge along Route 126. One of the more secluded sites (Homestead Campground) can be accessed by Forest Service Road 19 near Blue River. For details, access the National Forest website. Reservations: 877-444-6777; www.reserveusa.com.

BEN AND KAY DORRIS COUNTY PARK

✉️*Route 126, 31 miles east of Springfield* 📞*541-682-2000* 📠*541-682-2009*
🖥️*www.lanecounty.org/parks, laneparks@co.lane.or.us*

🚶🚤⛵🛶 A picturesque, 92-acre park at the head of Martin Rapids blending river frontage with an old orchard, this park is shaded by Douglas fir and big-leaf maple that add color to the region in the fall months. While a mile of river frontage is the park's leading attraction, the "Rock House," an outcropping that provided shelter for pioneers traveling the historic wagon road, is also worth a visit. This is one of Oregon's better places to catch trout. Facilities include picnic areas and pit toilets.

SMITH ROCK STATE PARK

✉️*Northeast Crooked River Drive, east of Route 97, nine miles northeast of Redmond*
📞*800-551-6949*

🚶🛶 Along steep Crooked River Canyon, this day-use park is popular with climbers since there are thousands of different climbs, many that are bolted routes. They enjoy scaling striated Smith Rock, a formation rising several hundred feet above the tributary's north bank. Named for John Smith, a 19th-century pioneer, the park features decent fishing for rainbows and smallmouth bass. There are picnic areas and restrooms. The forest on the south bank suffered a fire in 1996, but the area has been replanted and is recovering. However, open fires are prohibited throughout the park. Day-use fee, $3.

⚤ Permitted in the Bivouac Area for primitive hike-in camping. Space limited by parking; $4 per person per night.

TUMALO STATE PARK idden

✉️*Located five miles northwest of Bend on O. B. Riley Road off Route 20*
📞*541-382-3586, 800-551-6949*

🚶🚴🛶⛵ Convenient to the Bend area in Deschutes River Canyon, it is forested with juniper, ponderosa pine, willow and poplar. This 333-acre park has handsome basalt bluffs above the canyon. There's fair trout fishing, too. Facilities include a picnic area, restrooms, showers and nature trails. Day-use fee, $3.

⚠ There are 54 tent sites ($13 to $17 per night), 23 RV hookup sites ($17 to $22 per night) and seven yurts ($29 per night). Reservations: 800-452-5687.

DRAKE PARK idden

✉ *777 Northwest Riverside Boulevard; Take Franklin Avenue west from Route 97 into downtown Bend where it becomes Riverside Boulevard. Continue west to the park.* ☎ *541-388-5435* 📠 *541-388-3163*

🚶 This verdant, 13-acre park is along the Deschutes River and includes a riverfront strollway and footbridge across the river. Beloved by the local populace, the park is home to most of Bend's community events. Stroll alongside the river and be serenaded by geese and ducks. Adjacent to downtown Bend, it includes picturesque Mirror Pond, actually just a part of the river that was widened and made into a peaceful place to sit beside. You'll find picnic areas and a playground (across the bridge at Harmon Park).

PILOT BUTTE STATE PARK

✉ *Greenwood Avenue (Route 20), Bend* ☎ *800-551-6949*

🚶 🚵 A cinder cone that served as a landmark for Oregon pioneers is the heart of this 100-acre urban park. The 511-foot-high volcanic dome is located on the east side of Bend and is a very popular climb (it takes only about 15 minutes to scale). Ascend the spiral road to the top of this pine-covered butte to enjoy great views of the Cascades from Mt. St. Helens to the Three Sisters. In the winter, car access is not available. Bring your own water.

LAPINE STATE PARK

✉ *Located west of Route 97 on State Rec Road, 27 miles southwest of Bend* ☎ *541-536-2071, 800-551-6949* 📠 *541-536-2143*

🚶 🏊 🚣 ⛷ This rolling Deschutes River Valley park is shaded by pine and old-growth forest. In fact, Oregon's largest ponderosa pine tree is within the park, boasting 162 feet in height and more than 500 years in age. Expect to spot mule deer as you explore this uncrowded 2333-acre getaway. It's ideal for kayaking or canoeing, and a good base for visiting the surrounding volcanic landmarks including Newberry Crater. Small motorized boats can launch from here but can only go downstream. Anglers can fly cast for rainbow and brown trout. There are restrooms, showers and picnic areas.

⚠ There are 128 RV hookup sites ($13 to $17 per night), rustic cabins ($39 per night) and five deluxe cabins ($49 to $70 per night). Reservations: 800-452-5687.

DESCHUTES NATIONAL FOREST  idden

✉ *Access via Routes 126, 242, 58, 97, 31, 20 and 46* ☎ *541-383-5300*
📠 *541-383-5531* 🌐 *www.fs.fed.us/r6/centraloregon*

🚶 🚴 🏕 🏊 🚣 ⛷ Named for the popular river that descends the east slope of the Cascades, this 1.6-million-acre forest embraces Mt. Bachelor, the Three Sisters Wilderness, the Cascade

Lakes region and Newberry National Volcanic Monument. Many popular resorts and five wilderness areas are found in the Deschutes forests, meadows and high country. Climbing from 3000 to 10,358 feet, the forest is dominated by lodgepole and ponderosa pine. You can explore the Three Sisters Wilderness via the South Sisters Climbing Trail from the Cascade Lakes Highway at Devils Lake Campground. The forest is known for its raftable rivers, spelunking and skiing. There are innumerable places to ski cross-country, including Dutchman Flat, Edison Butte and the Skyliner/Meissner area. Bend is the most convenient jump-off point. More than 240 miles of streams and 158 lakes and reservoirs make for ideal fishing. There are picnic tables, interpretive centers, marinas and restrooms.

▲ There are over 100 campgrounds for tents and RVs throughout the national forest; $5 to $17 per night; call for details. The best camping is found off the Cascade Lake Highway near one of the many lakes in the area. Paulina Lake in the Newberry National Volcanic Monument has 69 tent/RV sites ($10 to $12; no hookups). South of Elk Lake, the Hosmer campground has two campgrounds with lots of room for tent camping ($5; no hookups).

SOUTHERN CASCADES

Blessed with several major wilderness areas that are great for viewing wildlife or birdwatching, the Southern Cascades are also the home of Oregon's only national park, Crater Lake. In addition to being drop-dead gorgeous—its chilly waters are an extraordinarily piercing shade of blue—the lake offers many recreational possibilities, from Nordic skiing to snowshoeing to hiking. The Southern Cascades also include a real sleeper, the Klamath Lake area.

SIGHTS

CRATER LAKE One of the world's most famous mountain lakes, tucked inside the caldera of a collapsed volcano, Crater Lake is known for its shimmering vistas and dark, cold depths.

RIM DRIVE While the crystal-clear waters are the prime attraction at Crater Lake, the 1000- to 2000-foot-high rim walls create an excellent cutaway view of the remains of Mt. Mazama. The best way to see this geologic wonder is to take this 33-mile road circling the lake. With more than 20 turnouts, it provides a thorough overview of the mountain-rimmed, deep-blue lake. Vertical lava flow patterns add to the majesty of the volcanic scenery. Allow at least two hours for this trip around the 20-square-mile, 1194-foot-deep lake. The road is closed from mid-October to late June. You'll want to begin your tour at the **Rim Village Visitor Center** (541-594-3100; www. nps.gov/crla), which is open June through September.

SINNOTT MEMORIAL OVERLOOK A short walk below Rim Village Visitors Center is this overlook. There's a small museum on this

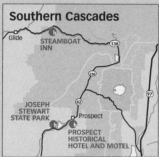

Southern Cascades

STEAMBOAT INN

PAGE 466

Outstandingly fresh seafood served family-style on gleaming wood tables beside the glowing fireplace

JOSEPH STEWART STATE PARK

PAGE 469

Lush green area tucked in the Rogue River Canyon, with ideal spots to spend the night under the stars

PROSPECT HISTORICAL HOTEL AND MOTEL

PAGE 465

1890 inn full of antiques and memories of former guests like Jack London and Teddy Roosevelt

rock ledge where rangers present interpretative geology talks during the summer months.

DISCOVERY POINT   Drive clockwise around the lake to this point, where in 1853 explorer John Wesley Hillman became the first white man to spot this treasure.

VIEWPOINTS   About three miles past Discovery Point is a turnout ideal for seeing one of the park's major volcanoes, **Union Peak**. Continue another seven-tenths of a mile to **Wizard Island Overlook**. It's named for the small Crater Lake island that is actually the top of a small volcano. Rim Drive's highest viewpoint is **Cloudcap**. This is a great spot to see how part of Mt. Mazama was sliced away by the caldera's collapse. Also of special interest is **Pumice Castle**, an orange and pink landmark sculpted by the elements into a fortress-like formation.

CRATER LAKE BOAT TOURS   ☎541-594-2255 The only access to the lakeshore is found at **Cleetwood Cove Trail**. This steep route takes you down to Cleetwood Boat Landing, where you can tour the lake by boat (admission). On the two-hour tour you'll be able to explore **Wizard Island**, a 700-foot-high cinder cone and see remnants of an older volcano called the **Phantom Ship**.

STEEL INFORMATION CENTER   ☎541-594-3100 (main visitor center), 541-594-2211 (national park) Although America's deepest (1943 feet) lake is the centerpiece of this national park, other attractions are well worth your time. Southeast of Rim Village you'll find this information center (open year-round), where you can see a 20-minute video on the lake, as well as interpretive exhibits.

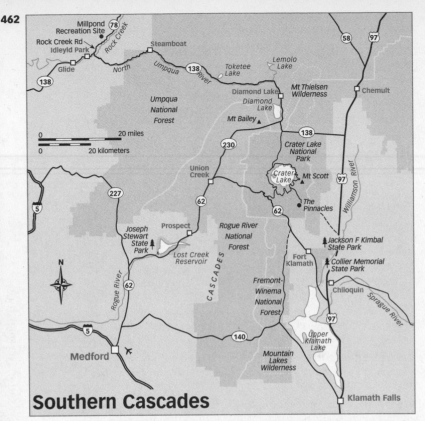

Southern Cascades

THE PINNACLES   We also recommend visiting this area on the park's east side. Pumice and ash left behind by the Mt. Mazama collapse were gradually eroded by rain and snow. These formations evolved into rock pinnacles, further eroded by the elements into weird, hoodoo shapes.

ROGUE RIVER GORGE   Sixteen miles west of Crater Lake National Park in the vicinity of Union Creek is this mighty river. It's channeled into a beautiful little canyon easily accessed on foot. In the same area, a mile west of Union Creek, is **Natural Bridge** where the Rogue flows into a lava tube for a short distance before reappearing. The bridge is well worth a visit and an easy walk.

Klamath Lake Region

Although not in the mountains, its proximity to the high country makes the area around Upper Klamath Lake a favorite of travelers coming or going to them.

UPPER KLAMATH LAKE TOUR ROUTE   One of the best ways to explore the Klamath Lake area is via this route. Several state parks, botanical areas, nature sites, canoe trails and waterfowl observation points make this tour a winner. Take Route 97 south to Chiloquin and then turn north on Route 62 to Fort Klamath. (If you're coming direct from Crater Lake simply take Route 62 south.)

463

UPPER KLAMATH LAKE This is the centerpiece of your tour. At nearly 64,000 acres, it is one of the state's largest lakes, extending south more than 25 miles to the town of Klamath Falls. The shallow waters here are prime fishing territory and a major wildlife refuge. One of the best birdwatching areas in the Pacific Northwest, these wetlands and marsh are also home to otter, beaver and muskrat.

SENATOR BALDWIN HOTEL MUSEUM ⊠*31 Main Street, Klamath Falls* ☎*541-883-4207, in the winter 541-883-4208* In Klamath Falls, this museum has been restored to its early-20th-century heyday. A guided tour shows off the four-story building's architectural gems and historic memorabilia. The building is not wheelchair accessible. Closed Monday and from October through May. Special tours can be made in the winter by request. Admission.

KLAMATH COUNTY MUSEUM ⊠*1451 Main Street, Klamath Falls* ☎*541-883-4208* ✆*541-883-5170* At this county museum, flora and fauna and American Indian and pioneer history are on display, including a large collection of historic photos. Closed Sunday and Monday. Admission.

FAVELL MUSEUM ⊠*125 West Main Street, Klamath Falls* ☎*541-882-9996* ✆*541-850-0125* 🖳*www.favellmuseum.org, favellmuseum@favellmuseum.org* This contemporary building features American Indian and Western art and artifacts and a vast collection of miniature firearms. You won't have trouble finding arrowheads because more than 60,000 are on display. Closed Sunday. Admission.

LODGING

CULTUS LAKE RESORT
$-$$ 23 UNITS   ⊠*Located 45 miles southwest of Bend off Cascade Lakes Highway* ☎*800-616-3230* 🖳*www.cultuslakeresort.com*
For cabins in a wooded setting, head for this resort. Spacious, pine-paneled (unfurnished) units equipped with brick fireplaces, alcove kitchens and drop-beam ceilings are set in a forest glen. The lake is great for sailing, fishing, waterskiing and kayaking. There's also a beach for sunbathing and swimming. Be advised: some readers have had rude service from management. Units are rented by the week. Closed October to mid-May.

DAWSON HOUSE LODGE idden
$$ 8 UNITS   ⊠*Route 97 at 1st Street, Chemult* ☎*541-365-2232,*
888-281-8375 ✆*541-365-4451* 🖳*www.dawsonhouse.net,*
dawsonhouse@hotmail.com
Twenty-five miles from Crater Lake in the small highway-side town of Chemult is this 1929 train station boarding house that has been converted into a rustic yet cozy inn. Choose from five upstairs hotel rooms (all with private bathrooms), furnished with antiques, including one double unit featuring log-framed

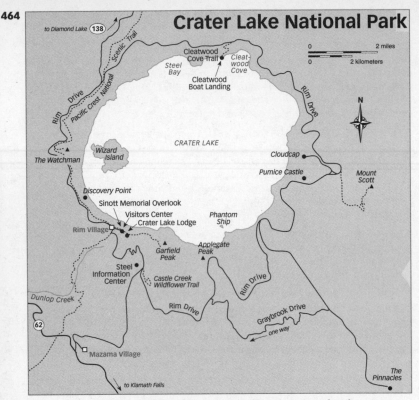

Crater Lake National Park

to Diamond Lake (138)

Scenic Trail

Rim Drive

Pacific Crest National

Steel Bay

Cleatwood Cove Trail

Cleatwood Cove

Cleatwood Boat Landing

0   2 miles
0   2 kilometers

Rim Drive

N

CRATER LAKE

The Watchman

Wizard Island

Cloudcap

Pumice Castle

Mount Scott

Discovery Point

Sinott Memorial Overlook

Visitors Center

Crater Lake Lodge

Phantom Ship

Rim Village

Garfield Peak

Applegate Peak

Steel Information Center

Castle Creek Wildflower Trail

Rim Drive

Graybrook Drive

one way

Dunlop Creek

62

Rim Drive

Mazama Village

to Klamath Falls

The Pinnacles

four-poster beds. The inn also offers three motel-style rooms, which do not include the Continental breakfast that awaits in the fireplace-warmed lobby each morning.

STEAMBOAT INN

$$$–$$$$ 20 UNITS   ✉42705 North Umpqua Highway, Steamboat
☎541-498-2230, 800-840-8825   🖷541-498-2411   🖊www.thesteamboatinn.com, steamboatinn@hughes.net

Zane Grey loved the north Umpqua River, and today a 31-mile stretch has been limited to "flyfishing only." In the heart of the river region 18 miles east of Idleyld Park is this waterfront inn. An eclectic mix of streamside cabins, hideaway cottages, river suites and ranch-style homes, the inn serves meals family-style in the main lodge. Some of the units are pine paneled; others offer river views, mini-kitchens, fireplaces, soaking tubs, quilted comforters and paintings by leading Northwest artists. Massage therapists are available for in-room service. Closed in January and February.

CRATER LAKE LODGE

$$$–$$$$ 71 UNITS   ✉Crater Lake National Park   ☎541-830-8700   🖷541-830-8514
🖊www.craterlakelodges.com

This lodge is a magnificent wood and stone structure built between 1909 and 1924 on the rim overlooking Crater Lake. The lodge has 71 rooms including a few lofts, all with natural-wood furnishings and many with views of the lake. Other superb views can be enjoyed from the lodge's Great Hall, which features a massive stone fireplace, historic photographs and floor-to-ceiling windows framed in rustic wood bark. Closed mid-October to mid-May.

THE CABINS AT MAZAMA VILLAGE

$$ 40 UNITS   ✉*Crater Lake National Park, Route 62*   ☎*541-830-8700*
📠*541-830-8514*   💻*www.craterlakelodges.com*

Forty modern units are available from June to October here. Board-and-batten exteriors, paneled interiors and wall-to-wall carpeting make these gray-toned accommodations rather appealing.

DIAMOND LAKE RESORT

$$–$$$$ 90 UNITS   ✉*350 Resort Drive, Diamond Lake; Five miles north of the Crater Lake entrance on Route 138*   ☎*541-793-3333, 800-733-7593*   📠*541-793-3309*
💻*www.diamondlake.net, info@diamondlake.net*

This resort is the largest hostelry in the Crater Lake region. The complex includes 38 motel rooms, 10 studios and 41 cabins, all a short walk from the busy waterfront. Expect hardwood-paneled rooms with fireplaces, Franklin stoves and marine views. The studios and cabins come with kitchen facilities and, in some cases, private decks. An 11.5-mile biking trail circles the lake, and there are boat and bike rentals and hiking trails as well. The resort also has a café and a restaurant. While some find Diamond Lake too crowded for their tastes, it is convenient to many beautiful wilderness areas.

PROSPECT HISTORICAL HOTEL AND MOTEL

$$–$$$ 24 UNITS   ✉*391 Mill Creek Drive, Prospect*   ☎*541-560-3664,*
800-944-6490   📠*541-560-3825*   💻*www.prospecthotel.com,*
info@prospecthotel.com

If you like the ambience of a historic inn but prefer the comfort of motel-style units, the Prospect may be just the place. Located just a quarter mile off Route 62 and 28 miles from the south entrance to Crater Lake National Park, the white frame 1890 hotel has ten cozy rooms decorated with antiques, historical photos, quilts, vanities and access to a pleasant front porch. Once a stagecoach inn, it's now a National Historic Site. Famous former guests include Jack London, Teddy Roosevelt and Zane Grey. There are also 14 motel rooms, some with kitchenettes.

ROCKY POINT RESORT

$$ 9 UNITS   ✉*28121 Rocky Point Road, Klamath Falls*   ☎*541-356-2287*
📠*541-356-2222*   💻*www.rockypointoregon.com, rvoregon@aol.com*

Motel-style units and cabins convenient to Upper Klamath Lake's Pelican Bay are found at this waterfront resort. Set in a fir forest frequented by deer, this is a good place to photograph bald eagles, osprey and white pelican colonies. The five paneled rooms are clean and comfortable, and the four cabins offer kitchen facilities. Camping (33 RV hookups, five tent sites), canoe and kayak rentals, moorage, fishing tackle and gift shop are all available on the premises. Closed November to April.

MAVERICK MOTEL

$ 50 ROOMS ✉1220 Main Street, Klamath Falls ☎541-882-6688, 800-404-6690
📠541-885-4095 🖳www.maverickhotel.com

For inexpensive lodging try the Maverick. Carpeted guest rooms are furnished with simple, standard furniture. There's laundry facilities and a continental breakfast.

DINING

WHEEL CAFE

$–$$ AMERICAN ✉Route 97, Chemult ☎541-365-2284 📠541-365-2202
🖂wagonwheel@presys.com

With American Indian and pioneer decor, a menu featuring specialties like the buckaroo breakfast, and a parking lot filled with diesel rigs, station wagons and motorcycles, it's obvious that this café cultivates an eclectic clientele. Take a seat at the counter and order turkey, swiss cheese, bacon and tomato on a sourdough roll or a chef's salad.

STEAMBOAT INN

$$$$ SEAFOOD/AMERICAN ✉42705 North Umpqua Highway, Steamboat
☎541-498-2230, 800-840-8825 📠541-498-2411
🖳www.thesteamboatinn.com, steamboatinn@hughes.net

You'll have a hard time beating the Steamboat. After enjoying hors d'oeuvres, wine and champagne in the library, guests head inside to the lodge where dinner is served family-style on gleaming wood tables illuminated by the glow of the fireplace. Appetizers are followed by an entrée, side dishes, homemade bread and dessert. One set dinner menu is served nightly. Entrées may include beef, fish, lamb or pork. The Steamboat is famous for its gourmet fisherman's dinner because given the inn's riverside location, the seafood is fresh as can be. Breakfasts (seasonal) here are also memorable. Don't miss the fruit rollups, an inn tradition. Dinner by reservation only. Closed January and February.

MUNCHIES

$ MEXICAN/AMERICAN ✉20142 Route 138, Glide ☎541-496-3112

For Mexican food, hamburgers, sandwiches and homemade soups, try this laid-back eatery. A full-service restaurant, they also serve fresh-baked pie.

PROSPECT HISTORIC HOTEL AND MOTEL RESTAURANT

$$$ PACIFIC NORTHWEST ✉391 Mill Creek Drive, Prospect ☎541-560-3664,
800-944-6490 📠541-560-3825 🖳www.prospecthotel.com, info@prospecthotel.com

An early American setting makes this restaurant a comfortable dining spot. A fixed-price dinner includes salad, antipasto, bread, choice of an entrée (including prime rib or lemon-dill roasted salmon) and dessert. There's also a selection of Northwest wines and beers to complement your meal. The ambience is elegant. Dinner only. Closed November through April; limited hours during winter holidays.

ROCKY POINT RESORT

$$–$$$ AMERICAN   ✉28121 Rocky Point Road, Klamath Falls   ☎541-356-2287   📠541-356-2222   🖰www.rockypointoregon.com, rvoregon@aol.com

With its beautiful setting overlooking Klamath Lake, rustic Rocky Point is best known for its steaks and seafood. Closed Monday and Tuesday during the summer; call for spring and fall hours.

SHOPPING

FAVELL MUSEUM GIFT SHOP ✉125 West Main Street, Klamath Falls   ☎541-882-9996   📠541-850-0125   🖰www.favellmuseum.org, favellmuseum@favell museum.org An excellent collection of limited-edition prints, American Indian and Western art, American Indian jewelry and arrowheads is found at this museum gift shop. Exhibited in an attractive, two-story shop, this store features many one-of-a-kind pieces on consignment from local and well-known artists, as well as a multitude of "made in Oregon" products like jams, syrups and candies.

OREGON TRAIL OUTFITTERS ✉5728 South 6th Street, Klamath Falls   ☎541-883-1369, 800-511-1369   📠541-883-8881   🖰www.oregontrailoutfitter.com, info@ oregontrailoutfitter.com For knives, cutlery, beads and beading supplies, American Indian earrings, moccasins, buckskins and leather goods, visit this board-and-batten building. It is extremely popular with visitors searching for a piece of the Old West. Closed Sunday.

NIGHTLIFE

ROSS RAGLAND THEATER ✉210 North 7th Street, Klamath Falls   ☎541-884-5483   📠541-884-8574   🖰www.rrtheater.org, rrt@rrtheater.org This theater hosts touring theater companies, country-and-western bands, jazz and blues and classical performers. The year-round calendar also includes special children's shows and, in the summer, locally produced musicals.

THE LINKVILLE PLAYHOUSE

✉201 Main Street, Klamath Falls   ☎541-884-6782, 541-882-2586 (tickets) Linkville offers a variety of plays and musicals from August through June. The local productions feature classics such as *A Funny Thing Happened on the Way to the Forum.*

PARKS

UMPQUA NATIONAL FOREST

✉Access via Routes 138, 1, 62 and 230   ☎541-672-6601   📠541-957-3495   🖰www.fs.fed.us/r6/umpqua

🚶🚴🏇🏕🏊⛵⛴🛶⛷ Named for the Umpqua Indians, this forest spans almost a million acres and embraces three wilderness areas, numerous waterfalls and 530 miles of high-country trails. Among the Umpqua landmarks are the world's tallest sugar pine, bedrock gorges and volcanic-rock formations. Within the Umpqua are volcanic ridges, pine benches, alpine forests and meadows laced by snow-fed streams. Major destinations include the scenic Umpqua River and Diamond, Lemolo and Toketee lakes. Most lakes allow swimming; only Lemolo Lake allows waterskiing. The forest is also convenient to Crater Lake. Kayaking and rafting are popular on the North Umpqua River. Mt. Bailey near Diamond Lake has downhill skiing, while the areas around Diamond and Lemolo lakes offer good cross-country trails. Hundreds of miles of streams and numerous lakes make this a great spot for angling, especially in the North Umpqua River. There are picnic tables, history programs, pack stations and restrooms. Trailhead parking fee, $5.

▲ There are 57 campgrounds in the forest; $6 to $8 per night; RV sites without hookups are available. The Diamond Lake area is probably the most developed for camping, with three campgrounds around the lakeshore. Even better for those who want to be away from drive-in sites is the Twin Lakes campground (43 miles east of Glide), a walk-in (or bike-in) campground 10 miles from Route 138. You'll be camping in a primitive site under the stars amidst cold, clear high mountain lakes.

MILLPOND RECREATION SITE

✉ *From the town of Idleyld Park take Route 138 east to Route 78 (Rock Creek Road) and head north five miles* 📞 *541-440-4930* 📠 *541-440-4948*

⚓ With half a mile of frontage on Rock Creek, this serene campground is a beautiful getaway near the community of Idleyld Park. It has a picturesque swimming hole and towering, moss-covered trees, and is the small Oregon park at its finest. You'll find picnic areas, a pavilion, a group campground, a softball field and restrooms. Closed mid-October to early May.

▲ There are 12 tent/RV sites (no hookups); $10 per night. The group campground includes 11 sites for $130 per night.

CRATER LAKE NATIONAL PARK

✉ *Route 62, 54 miles northwest of Klamath Falls* 📞 *541-539-3000* 📠 *541-539-3010* 🌐 *www.nps.gov/crla*

🚶 🚴 ⛺ ♪ One of the unique geologic features of the Pacific Northwest, Crater Lake is irresistible. The 183,224-acre park offers 100 miles of hiking and cross-country skiing trails, a fascinating boat tour of this volcanic lake and opportunities for biking, fishing and backpacking. For anglers there's nothing to get excited about, though there are rainbow trout and kokanee salmon off Wizard Island. There are picnic areas, restaurants, lodging, exhibits and ranger-guided boat tours and snowshoe ecology walks (Saturday and Sunday). Entrance fee (good for seven days), $10 per vehicle, $5 walk-in.

▲ There are 213 tent/RV sites at Mazama Campground; $18 to $20 per night (without electrical hookups) or $23 per night (with electrical hookups). There are 16 tent sites at Lost Creek; $10 per night, no hookups. Backcountry camping by permit only. Campgrounds and lodging are closed in winter.

✉*Routes 97, 395, 31 and 140 all provide easy access* 📞*541-947-2151* 📠*541-947-6399*
🖥*www.fs.fed.us/r6/frewin*

The Fremont-Winema National Forests lie on the eastern slopes of the Cascade Mountain Range in south central Oregon and expand east to "Oregon's Outback" and the Warner Mountains. The 203-million-acre forests are famous for their fishing and waterfowl habitat, expansive views, dramatic cliffs and solitude. Although the forest elevation ranges from roughly 4100 to 9200 feet, much of the eastern portion of this semiarid region is high-plateau country. The Fremont-Winema are forested with pine and fir and have four designated wilderness areas, including the Mountain Lakes Wilderness Area. More than 200 bird species have been identified on this Pacific Flyway. In addition, antelope, elk, deer, bear, coyote, bobcat, beaver, otters and many other species live here. Dozens of lakes and rivers like the Sycan, Sprague and Williamson offer good opportunities to catch trout and mullet. Rock hounds can be happy here. You'll find picnic tables and restrooms. The Northwest Forest Pass is required to enter the forest; check the website above for details.

▲ Camping is permitted anywhere in the forest and there are 11 developed campgrounds with tent/RV sites; free to $13 per night.

JACKSON F. KIMBALL STATE PARK

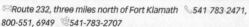

✉*Route 232, three miles north of Fort Klamath* 📞*541-783-2471,*
800-551, 6949 📠*541-783-2707*

This 19-acre Oregon state park is a scenic, forested spot on the headwaters of the Wood River. It's ideal for those seeking a quiet getaway. There's good flyfishing for rainbow and brown trout. There is a picnic area. Closed November through March.

▲ There are ten primitive sites; $5 to $9 per night.

COLLIER MEMORIAL STATE PARK

✉*Route 97, 35 miles north of Klamath Falls* 📞*541-783-2471* 📠*541-783-2707*
🖥*www.oregonstatepark.gov*

Set in a ponderosa-pine forest at the junction of Spring Creek and Williamson River, this 655-acre park is a perfect place to spend the day or the night. The park is also a logging heritage site, filled with important mementos and lumberjack equipment. There's good trout fishing in the streams. You'll find picnic tables, showers, restrooms, a laundry facility, a playground and a museum.

▲ There are 18 tent sites ($15 per night) and 50 RV hookup sites ($17 per night). Closed November through March. Reservations: 800-452-5687.

JOSEPH STEWART STATE PARK

✉*Route 62, 35 miles northeast of Medford* 📞*541-560-3334* 📠*541-560-3855*

A lush lawn leads down to Lost Creek Reservoir, making this park on the road to Crater Lake particularly inviting on a warm day. With 910 acres, there's room to spare for day and overnight use. Take a seat on a blanket beneath one of the pine groves and watch the waterskiers. Or toss in a line and wait for the big ones to nibble. With more than a mile of waterfront, this Rogue River Canyon park is a great place to take the kids. There's excellent fishing for bass, rainbow, brook or brown trout. Facilities include a picnic area, restrooms, showers and a marina.

▲ There are 50 tent sites ($10 to $14 per night) and 151 RV hookup sites ($12 to $16 per night). Closed November through February.

OUTDOOR ADVENTURES

FISHING

The Cascades are famous for rivers and lakes brimming with trout, salmon, bass and steelhead. Now that more and more people are trying to fish these waters, "We've got a shrinking resource," as one guide says; that's why you'll find him and others encouraging a catch-and-release policy for all fish caught. The point is that you can still wade out into the Deschutes to flyfish for wild trout or pull steelhead out of the Umpqua from aboard a drift boat and have the kind of experience immortalized in the fiction of Zane Grey.

Northern Cascades Area

WY'EAST EXPEDITIONS ✉*Mt. Hood* ☎*541-352-6457* ✐*www.wyeast expeditions.com* Whether you're an experienced fisher or a beginner, this group can arrange day-long flyfishing trips along the Deschutes, McKenzie or John Day rivers for fall steelhead or, in the spring, wild rainbow trout. Overnight trips let you get out into areas that are a bit more remote.

GORGE FLY SHOP ✉*201 Oak Street* ☎*541-386-6977* ✐*www.gorgeflyshop. com* If you need gear, contact this fly shop in Hood River. Besides renting gear and obtaining information, you can set up a guided trip on the Deschutes River, the John Day River, and other prime fishing spots in the area.

MICHAEL MCLUCAS ✉*Oasis Resort* ☎*541-395-2611* ✐*www.deschutes riveroasis.com* In Maupin, this local expert has been a fishing guide for over 25 years. He or his partner Mike Malefyt can take you out on the Deschutes for trout or steelhead fishing trips.

Central Cascades Area

FLY FISHER'S PLACE ✉*151 West Main Street, Sisters* ☎*541-549-3474* ✐*www.theflyfishersplace.com* Although there's no commercial use permitted on the Metolius River (that is, no guided trips), it's a very popular flyfishing spot. This company can rent or sell you gear or arrange a guided trip on the McKenzie, the Deschutes or, near Prineville, on the Crooked River, where you can catch wild trout.

HIGH DESERT DRIFTERS, GUIDES, & OUTFITTERS ✉*1710 Northeast Hollow Tree Lane, Bend* ☎*541-389-0607, 800-685-3474* ✐*www.theflyfishers*

place.com High Desert Drifters specializes in flyfishing float trips for rainbow trout and steelhead on the Deschutes for either one day or several days.

SUNRIVER FLY SHOP ✉*56805 Venture Lane, Sunriver* ✆*541-593-8814* ⌨*www.sunriverflyshop.com* This guide service offers fishing classes if you want to learn more. Some of its popular trips are to the Davis, Hosmer and Crane Prairie lakes, where you will catch a variety of trout between April and November.

HELFRICH RIVER OUTFITTERS ✉*42091 McKenzie Highway, Springfield* ✆*541-896-3017, 800-507-9889* ⌨*www.helfrichoutfitter.com* Guided expeditions are also available through these outfitters, who specialize in flyfishing trips on the McKenzie and Rogue rivers. Trips are led by a third-generation guide.

Southern Cascades Area

NORTH RIVER GUIDE SERVICE ✉*P.O. Box 575, Glide, OR 97443* ✆*541-496-0309 (main), 541-784-6714 (direct)* ✆*541-496-0309* Guide Bill Conner primarily fishes the Umpqua, specializing in drift boat trips for two people per boat. Up to four couples may go at a time. Conner also leads flyfishing trips.

WHITEWATER RAFTING

The fun and excitement of a day of whitewater rafting is hard to beat, even with a crowd. Guided full-day trips usually include a riverside lunch stop along the way.

Central Cascades Area

A. HELFRICH OUTFITTERS ✉*1950 Yolanda Street, Springfield* ✆*541-726-5039, 800-328-7688* ⌨*www.mckenzierafting.com* This group (not to be confused with their cousins who run the fly-fishing trips) leads full- and half-day rafting on the McKenzie River.

RAPID RIVER RAFTERS ✉*500 Southwest Bond Street, Bend* ✆*541-382-1514, 800-962-3327* ⌨*www.rapidriverrafters.com* For a 17-mile run through Class III and IV rapids on the Deschutes, Rapid River puts in at Maupin, about 89 miles north. There are also whitewater trips down the McKenzie, North Santiam and Owyhee rivers (Class III).

SUN COUNTRY TOURS ✉*531 Southwest 13th Street, Bend* ✆*541-382-6277, 800-770-2161* ⌨*www.suncountrytours.com* Sun Country rafts only on the Class III rapids; they run the Upper and Lower Deschutes, Upper McKenzie and North Umpqua from May through September.

GOLF

In the Cascades, where resort courses comprise most of the golf options, forested mountain sides, emerald meadows, rivers coursing through fairways, elk lingering on the perimeters and wild geese flying overhead add a unique dimension to the experience.

Northern Cascades Area

RESORT AT THE MOUNTAIN ✉*68010 East Fairway Avenue, Welches* ☎*503-622-2216* 🖱*www.theresort.com* This club has three nine-hole courses that are open to the public. The mountain setting makes all three scenic; the first nine is the longest, but fair and forgiving; the third nine, Fox Glove, is fairly narrow and the most challenging.

KAH-NEE-TA GOLF COURSE ✉*Off Route 26, Warm Springs* ☎*541-553-1112* 🖱*www.kahneeta.com* Located on an American Indian reservation, this championship 18-hole golf course is a fairly flat course, set in a valley. This location is often sunny, so the course is open year-round.

Central Cascades Area

BLACK BUTTE RANCH ✉*Route 20, eight miles west of Sisters* ☎*800-399-2322 (for tee times), 541-595-1500 (pro shop)* This resort has two award-winning 18-hole courses: Big Meadow (flat and open) and Glaze Meadow (hilly and narrow). Big Meadow is closed from late October to mid-March, while Glaze Meadow stays open until the snow flies.

WIDGI CREEK GOLF CLUB ✉*18707 Century Drive, five miles south of Bend* ☎*541-382-4449* 🖱*www.widgi.com* At this semiprivate golf club, an 18-hole championship course meanders beneath huge pine trees along the rim of the Deschutes River canyon. Closed in winter.

TOKATEE GOLF CLUB ✉*54947 McKenzie Highway, Blue River* ☎*541-822-3220, 800-452-6376* Probably the most famous course in the Cascades and certainly one of the most picturesque in the Northwest, Tokatee is set majestically in the McKenzie River Valley. "It's a walk with nature," says the pro. Tokatee, which is considered among the nation's top public courses, is closed December and January. Walk-ins are welcome.

Southern Cascades Area

CIRCLE BAR GOLF CLUB ✉*48447 Westoak Road, Oakridge* ☎*541-782-3541* The Circle Bar has a challenging public nine-hole course.

HARBOR LINKS GOLF COURSE ✉*601 Harbor Isles Boulevard, Klamath Falls* ☎*541-882-0609* 🖱*www.harborlinksgolf.net* The 18-hole public course here isn't near a harbor, but it is near a lake. It's a short course, fairly flat and narrow, with lots of water.

TENNIS

Many resorts in the Cascades have tennis courts available to guests; the public is permitted access sometimes as well.

Central Cascades Area

The Bend Metro Park and Recreation District (541-389-7275) maintains a number of tennis courts in the city. None of them are lighted, but they're free and available on a first-come, first-served basis (access to the courts at schools, however, may be restricted due to school-related activities).

JUNIPER PARK ✉*Franklin Avenue and Northwest 8th Street* Four courts.

SYLVAN PARK ✉Three Sisters Drive at Fairwell Drive, on the north side of Aubrey Butte Two courts.

SUMMIT PARK ✉Summit and Promontory drives Two courts

BEND HIGH SCHOOL ✉230 Northeast 6th Street Four courts.

MOUNTAIN VIEW HIGH SCHOOL ✉2755 Northeast 27th Street Four courts.

SUMMIT HIGH SCHOOL ✉2855 Clearwater Drive Four courts.

CENTRAL OREGON COMMUNITY COLLEGE ✉2600 Northwest College Way Four courts.

Southern Cascades Area

MOORE PARK ✉Lakeshore Drive, Klamath Falls ✆541-883-5351 Two courts.

HARBOR ISLES CLUB ✉Klamath Falls ✆41-884-3299 Four indoor courts.

CREST PARK ✉5801 Hilyard Avenue, Klamath Falls ✆541-884-5351 Four courts.

WIARD PARK ✉Wiard Street, Klamath Falls ✆541-884-5351 Four lighted courts.

SKIING

Skiing in July? It's possible in Oregon's endless winter and the Cascades offer a ton of alpine and Nordic opportunities.

Northern Cascades Area

TIMBERLINE LODGE AND SKI AREA  ✉Timberline ✆503-272-3311 ⌖www.timberlinelodge.com, info@timberlinelodge.com The best-known resorts in the area are found on the slopes of Mt. Hood. They include this venerable lodge, the only year-round ski resort in North America with six chairlifts serving an above-timberline snowfield and tree-lined runs. Three lifts operate on Friday and Saturday nights. From June to September, the resort has a summer season at the 8500-foot level.

MT. HOOD SKIBOWL ✆503-272-3206, 503-222-2695 (snowphone) ⌖www.skibowl.com Serving the Northern Cascades is this resort, with nearly 65 trails, 34 of which are lit for night skiing.

MT. HOOD MEADOWS ✆503-337-2222, 503-287-5438, 800-754-4663 ⌖www.skihood.com At this ski resort there are 11 chairlifts serving 87 trails, rated 15 percent beginner, 50 percent intermediate and 35 percent expert. They offer runs for the physically challenged in conjunction with area organizations.

Central Cascades Area

HOODOO SKI AREA ✆541-822-3799, 541-822-3337 ⌖www.hoodoo.com On Route 20's Santiam Pass west of Sisters, this ski area is a good bet for families looking for alpine or Nordic skiing.

474

MT. BACHELOR

☎800-829-2442 ✎www.mtbachelor.com, info@mtbachelor.com West of
Bend is Oregon's largest ski area offering dry powder and a season extending to mid-May. Ten chairs serve 3683 skiable acres,
with 1600 acres groomed daily.

SKJERSAA'S SPORTS SHOP ✉130 Southwest Century Drive, Bend ☎541-
382-2154 For full-service rental and repair of downhill skis and snowboards, try Skjersaa's.

EUROSPORTS ✉182 East Hood Avenue, Sisters ☎541-549-2471 A full selection of skis, snowboards and snowshoes can be rented at this shop.

Southern Cascades Area

CRATER LAKE NATIONAL PARK

☎541-594-3100 This national park has extensive Nordic trails with
views of the blue water beneath the snowcapped rim.

MT. BAILEY ☎800-733-7593 ext. 754 ✎www.catskimtbailey.com Diamond
Lake Resort also has Nordic trails, as well as snowcat skiing on this
mountain. Limited to just 14 people per run (approximately five to
seven runs), lifts transport skiers uphill to enjoy 6000 acres of deep-
powder terrain.

RIDING STABLES

Northern Cascades Area
KAH-NEE-TA HIGH DESERT RESORT ✉Warm Springs ☎541-553-1112
✎www.kahneeta.com From March to the end of September, guided hour-
long rides wind through the hills or scenic red-rock country at this
desert resort.

Central Cascades Area
EQUINE MANAGEMENT ✉Route 20, eight miles west of Sisters ☎541-480-
4394, 541-280-4892 ✎www.oregoncowboy.com In the Sisters area, guided
half-hour to all-day trail rides and overnight pack trips into the Cascades are operated by this company, which operates stables at Black
Butte Ranch.

SUNRIVER STABLES ✉Sunriver Resort ☎541-593-6995 Sunriver offers
rides anywhere in length from half an hour to a full eight-hour trip. Hay
rides and sleigh rides in the winter are also available.

Southern Cascades Area
DIAMOND LAKE CORRALS ☎541-793-3337 ✎www.diamondlakecorrals.
com Near Crater Lake, Diamond Lake is the place to go for one-hour,
three-hour and all-day rides; there are also pack trips and chuckwa-
gon rides.

Llamaland

One of the most singular sights you're likely to see while exploring the dry side of the Cascades is pastures full of llamas (pronounced "YA-mas"), those wooly long-necked South American cousins of camels. Llama ranching in the United States first appeared in central Oregon in the mid-1970s. The state now boasts about 170 llama ranches, of which more than half are located around Bend and the nearby towns of Sisters, Redmond and Prineville.

Llamas have been domesticated by the Inca people of the South American Andes for at least two thousand years. They have traditionally been raised there for wool and meat. Since they were imported to the United States, their main use has been as beasts of burden and companions, accompanying trekkers into mountain wilderness. Although a llama is not strong enough to carry a human rider, it can carry at least 40 pounds of backpacking and camping gear. Some outfitters rent llamas for independent hiking expeditions, while others organize guided trips. A growing number of outfitters use llamas to carry gear into the mountains in advance and await hikers with a fully set-up campsite.

Llamas also provide specialty wool, which is gathered by either frequent brushing or shearing. Llama wool has a higher warmth-to-weight ratio than sheep wool and comes in 22 natural shades of white, cream, beige, tan, brown, rust, gray and black. Although there is no organized commercial market for llama fiber, it is widely used by weavers and other craftspeople to make everything from scarves, ponchos, blankets and rugs to fishing flies. You'll find these products at galleries and arts-and-crafts shows throughout Oregon.

Perhaps the most unusual use of llamas is to guard livestock. Over the centuries they have developed instinctive behaviors for fighting off cougars and coyote-like Andean wild dogs. These behaviors, along with the llama's larger size and almost impenetrable wool coat, make llamas more effective than dogs for protecting sheep flocks. They are also used to guard deer, cattle, and ducks and geese.

CENTRAL OREGON LLAMA ASSOCIATION ✉P.O. Box 5334, Bend, OR 97701 ☎541-389-6855 ⌕www.centraloregonllamas.net, info@centraloregonllamas.org The economics of llama ranching is similar to horse ranching. Untrained llamas suitable as pets or guards sell for $250 to $1800. Llamas trained for trekking sell for up to $2000. Breeding males bring $2000 to $10,000 each, and breeding females $2000 to $12,000. For more information and to find out about llama ranch tours, contact the Central Oregon Llama Association.

BIKING

From easy town rides to mountain biking on rugged backcountry trails, the Oregon Cascades offer thousands of miles of scenic cycling.

Northern Cascades Area

ZIGZAG RANGER DISTRICT Among the best mountain biking trails is this one on 12-mile **Still Creek Road**. This rarely traveled route connects Trillium Lake with the town of Rhododendron. You might also try the ten-mile **Sherar Burn Road/Veda Lake** trail, which leads up to outstanding viewpoints.

Central Cascades Area

BEND AREA   Take **West Newport Avenue** for a six-mile trip to Shevlin Park or follow **O. B. Riley Road** five miles to Tumalo State Park. Another possibility is to take the road south 23 miles from Route 97 to **Newberry Volcano**.

BLACK BUTTE RANCH   Eighteen miles of bike paths traverse this area, including the **Lodge Loop** (5 miles), the scenic **Glaze Meadow Loop** (4 miles) and the **Aspen Loop** (1.6 miles).

SUTTLE LAKE   About ten miles from Sisters, this lake, with its "upsy-daisy" loop of about 13 miles, is a pleasant outing of moderate exertion for most people.

CASCADES LOOP   This popular trail begins in Bend, heads west on Century Drive to Mt. Bachelor and then continues on Cascades Lakes Highway to Route 58. Allow several days to enjoy these demanding 74 miles.

Southern Cascades Area

DIAMOND LAKE BIKE PATH   One of the most popular biking trails in the Southern Cascades is this 11.5-mile bike path. This level route is ideal for the whole family. The route takes cyclists from Thielsen View Campground to Silent Creek. Complete the loop on the highway returning to Thielsen View. A two-mile section of this route is wheelchair accessible.

CRATER LAKE   The ultimate biking experience at this lake is **Rim Drive**, offering the complete 33-mile overview of this volcanic landmark. Another excellent possibility is **Grayback Drive**, a scenic, unpaved route ideal for mountain bikes.

KLAMATH FALLS   In this area, **Nevada Avenue** and **Lakeshore Drive**, provide convenient bike-touring access to Upper Klamath Lake. The route continues west to Route 140 along the lake's west shore. **Kit Carson Way** also has a separated bike path.

Bike Rentals

EUROSPORTS   ✉*182 East Hood Avenue, Sisters*   ☎*541-549-2471* In Sisters, this shop rents mountain bikes in addition to children's bikes. The shop also has bike route maps as well as suggestions for rides in the area. Bikes are available in spring and summer.

PINE MOUNTAIN SPORTS   ✉*255 Southwest Century Drive, Bend*   ☎*541-385-8080* For mountain bike rentals or other sporting goods in Bend, stop by Pine Mountain. No rentals in the winter.

PAULINA PLUNGE INC.   ✉*P.O. Box 8782, Bend, OR 97708*   ☎*541-389-0562, 800-296-0562*   ✐*www.paulinaplunge.com* In the Bend area, **Paulina Plunge**, as it's known, is a six-mile downhill waterfall mountain-bike tour that descends 3000 feet on groomed trails, with two stops along the way at several waterfalls and two waterslides in the Newberry Crater region.

This tour company operates this activity from May to late September. Call ahead for availability.

HIKING

With hundreds of miles of trails, including many in wilderness areas, the Cascades are ideal for relaxed rambles or ambitious journeys. All hiking trails in the Cascades are best tackled in the warmer seasons and not recommended to try in the winter months. All distances listed for hiking trails are one way unless otherwise noted.

Northern Cascades Area

Many of Mt. Hood National Forest's trailheads are rather tricky to find. Stop by Clackamas' County Regional Visitors Center on Route 26, just before the 39-mile marker (before Welches), or at the Mt. Hood information center, 3 miles east of the Clackamas Center, on the right.

ZIGZAG TRAIL   This trail (2 miles) takes you across the Hood River's east fork via a drawbridge (closed in winter). You'll continue up the canyon to Dog River Trail, which leads to a viewpoint overlooking Mt. Hood and the Upper Hood River Valley.

TAMANAWAS FALLS LOOP   A 5.5 mile trek, this trail leads along the north bank of Mt. Hood National Forest's Cold Spring Creek. After hiking to scenic Tamanawas Falls, you'll return to the trailhead via Elk Meadows Trail.

CASTLE CANYON TRAIL   In Mt. Hood National Forest is this trail (.9 mile) climbing out of the rhododendron area to rocky pinnacles. Views of the scenic Zigzag Valley are your reward.

BONNEY MEADOW TRAIL   A relatively easy possibility is this trail, reached by taking Route 35 to Bennett Pass and then following Routes 3550 and 4891 to Bonney Meadows Campground. Take trail #473 (3.5 miles) east along the ridge to enjoy the views of Boulder and Little Boulder lakes. Return to the campground by turning right on trail #472.

Central Cascades Area

BLACK BUTTE TRAIL   Located 33.4 miles west of Sisters off Route 20 is this steady, moderate 2-mile climb to the top of a volcanic cone.

TUMBLE RIDGE TRAIL

In the Detroit Lake area, you might want to try this trail (5.3 miles), which begins on Route 22. The demanding trek heads up through second-growth forest, past Dome and Needle rocks to Tumble Lake.

LITTLE NORTH SANTIAM TRAIL

Built along the Little North Santiam River, this trail (4.5 miles) crosses eight tributaries with stringer bridges. Fishing and swimming holes are easily reached from this trail leading through some old-growth forests.

ROBINSON LAKE TRAIL   Return east on Route 20 and turn south on Route 126. Continue for eight miles to Forest Service Road 2664 and go east 4.4 miles to this lake trail (.3 mile). It's an easy family hike leading to a pleasant hideaway.

OLALLIE TRAIL   In the McKenzie Bridge area is this 9.7-mile all-day hike with memorable views of the Three Sisters, Mt. Washington, Mt. Jefferson and Bachelor Butte. Take this trail in summer and fall. The trailhead is three miles from Horse Creek Road.

LAVA RIVER TRAIL   For an easier hike off McKenzie Pass Highway (Route 242), take this trail (.5 mile). This interpretive trail beginning near the Dee Wright Observatory leads through lava flows. Signs add to your understanding of this moonscape's volcanic past. Wheelchair accessible.

FISHER CREEK TRAIL   To the south, the Willamette National Forest's Middle Fork Ranger District offers many fine hikes, including this 6.5 mile trek. A great way to see a primitive-forest region, you'll get a closeup view of old-growth trees. The silence is deafening.

WALDO LAKE TRAIL   Be prepared before you embark on this challenging 21.8-mile route around this incredibly pure lake.

LAVA RIVER CAVE TRAIL   This 1.2-mile trek is an easy, rather chilly trail through the state's largest lava tube. It's south of Bend off Route 97, one mile south of Lava Lands Interpretive Center, which is an excellent place to stop for some information on the area. Lanterns are available (seasonally) close to the parking lot.

LAVA CAST FOREST NATURE TRAIL   Fourteen miles south of Bend off Route 97, this nature trail (.9 mile) takes you through one of the Pacific Northwest's weirdest landscapes. You'll see tree molds created when molten lava destroyed a forest thousands of years ago.

Southern Cascades Area
ROGUE RIVER NATIONAL FOREST   Off Route 62, the road from Medford to Crater Lake, the **Upper Rogue River Trail** (6.5 miles) is an easy ramble. Begin at the Prospect Ranger Station in this national forest and make your way through sugar pines, pausing along the way to cool off in the stream. **Toketee Lake Trail** (.4 mile) runs parallel to the Upper Rogue River. Short spurs lead to the waterfront where you'll find otter, beaver, osprey and ducks complementing the scenery.

NORTH UMPQUA TRAIL   This trail (79 miles) offers a wide variety of hiking opportunities. Skirting both the Boulder Creek and Mt. Thielsen wilderness areas, this route ranges from easy to difficult. The last nine miles are in the Oregon Cascades Recreation Area and Mt. Thielsen Wilderness Area. Spur trails lead to waterfalls, fishing spots and campgrounds. Among the North Umpqua's most popular segments are **Panther Trail** (5 miles), beginning at Steamboat, and **Lemolo Trail** (6.3 miles), starting at Lemolo Lake.

MT. BAILEY TRAIL   A steep 5-mile route, this trail is located west of Diamond Lake. Your reward for climbing 3000 feet is a panoramic view of Diamond Lake, Mt. Thielsen and the Southern Cascades.

PACIFIC CREST SCENIC TRAIL   Running 2570 miles from Canada to Mexico, this trail is western America's back door to the wilderness, the kind of place John Muir lived for. Scenic, uncrowded, larger than life, it's worth a special trip. You can pick up a 30-mile segment at the North Crater Trailhead, a mile east of the Crater Lake National Park Trailhead on Route 138. Hike as much of this section as you care to. You can exit via the Tipsoo, Howlock Mountain, North Umpqua or Mt. Thielsen trails.

Crater Lake National Park

WATCHMAN PEAK TRAIL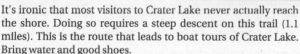

This .7-mile trail is a steep route up Watchman Peak. From the top you'll have a great view of Wizard Island.

CLEETWOOD COVE TRAIL

It's ironic that most visitors to Crater Lake never actually reach the shore. Doing so requires a steep descent on this trail (1.1 miles). This is the route that leads to boat tours of Crater Lake. Bring water and good shoes.

MOUNT SCOTT TRAIL   For a good workout, try this mountain trail (2.5 miles). Along the way you'll spot many small animals and birds. The gnarled whitebark pines make a good photographic backdrop. On top you'll have a 360-degree view of the park.

GODFREY GLEN TRAIL   To see some of the national park's impressive pinnacles, take this 1-mile loop. This route leads through a hemlock and red-fir forest to a view of Sand Creek Canyon.

GARFIELD PEAK TRAIL   Located east of Crater Lake Lodge, this trail (1.7 miles) is a fairly steep route offering views of the lake. Look for eagles and hawks along the way.

CASTLE CREST WILDFLOWER TRAIL   A short walk in the park is offered with this wildflower trail (.4-mile loop). This easy loop is the best way to sample Oregon wildflowers in mid-summer. An eden-like setting with small streams trickling down the hillside, the trail is one of Oregon's best-kept secrets.

SEVENMILE TRAIL/PACIFIC CREST TRAIL   West of Fort Klamath off Route 3334 West this 15-mile trail leads through the Sky Lakes Wilderness south of Crater Lake National Park. Sevenmile Trail hooks up with the Pacific Crest Trail for a 2.5-mile stretch and then cuts off to Seven Lakes Basin. You can also follow the Pacific Crest Trail to Devil's Pass and the steep ascent of Devil's Peak.

TRANSPORTATION

CAR

The Cascades are a 50-to-100-mile-wide band extending almost the entire length of the state. They begin on the eastern edge of the Willamette Valley and Ashland-Rogue River area and extend to the high-desert region of central Oregon.

Route 26 travels east from Portland to the Mt. Hood area. You can also reach Mt. Hood by taking **Route 35** south from the Hood River area.

From Salem, take **Route 22** east to the Detroit Lakes and Santiam Pass area. **Route 20** east of Albany leads to the same destination, while **Route 126** is Eugene's mainline east to the McKenzie Bridge and McKenzie Pass area. **Route 58** southeast of Eugene is convenient to the Deschutes National Forest, and **Route 138** takes you from Roseburg to the Umpqua River Canyon.

From Medford, take **Route 62** northeast to Crater Lake. An alternate route to Crater Lake is **Route 97** north of Klamath Falls. This same highway also provides access to the Bend area and the Central Cascades. If you're coming from the east, Routes 20 and 26 are the most convenient ways to reach the mountains.

AIR

REDMOND AIRPORT ✉*2522 Southeast Jesse Butler Circle, Redmond* 📞*541-548-0646* Sixteen miles north of Bend, this airport is served by Allegiant Air, Delta Connection, Horizon Airlines and United Express.

KLAMATH FALLS AIRPORT ✉*6775 Arnold Avenue, Klamath Falls* 📞*541-883-5372* ⌨*www.flykfalls.com* United Airlines exclusively serves this airport.

The **Portland International Airport**, **Eugene Airport** and **Rogue Valley International–Medford Airport** are also convenient to the Cascades.

REDMOND AIRPORT SHUTTLE 📞*541-382-1687* This shuttle provides service from the Redmond Airport to Bend and Cascades destinations like Sunriver, Mt. Bachelor, Sisters and Black Butte Ranch.

LUXURY ACCOMMODATIONS LIMOUSINE SERVICE 📞*503-668-7433* Limousine van service from the Portland airport to popular Northern Cascades recreation areas is provided by this agency.

BUS

GREYHOUND BUS LINES ✉*1555 Northeast Forbes Road* 📞*541-382-2151, 800-231-2222* ⌨*www.greyhound.com* Greyhound services Bend.

TRAIN

AMTRAK ☎*800-872-7245* ✐*www.amtrak.com* Amtrak's "Coast Starlight" is a scenic and comfortable way to reach the Cascades. It serves stations in Klamath Falls, Chemult, Eugene, Salem, Albany and Portland, all convenient starting points for the mountain resorts.

CAR RENTALS

Arriving passengers at the Redmond Airport are served by **Budget Rent A Car** (800-527-0700), **Hertz Rent A Car** (800-654-3131), **Avis Rent A Car** (800-230-4898) and **Enterprise** (800-261-7331).

Car-rental agencies at the Klamath Falls Airport are **Enterprise** (800-261-7331), **Budget Rent A Car** (800-527-0700), and **Hertz Rent A Car** (800-654-3131).

In Bend, you can rent from **Hertz Rent A Car** (800-654-3131).

PUBLIC TRANSIT

Lane Transit District (541-687-5555) serves McKenzie Bridge. **Basin Transit Service** (541-883-2877) operates in the Klamath Falls area.

TAXIS

For taxi service, contact **Redmond Taxi** (541-548-1182) in Redmond. In Klamath Falls, call **Classic Taxi** (541-885-8294).

HEART OF
OREGON

Heart of Oregon

McMinnville
22
18
18
99W
Willamette River
99E
★ Salem
Depoe Bay
101
22
Newport
20
Corvallis
226
22
5
Waldport
34
99W
Sweet Home
20
228
242
99
126
Florence
126
Eugene
Springfield
RANGES
Cottage
Grove
Lowell
Reedsport
38
Elkton
58
Umpqua River
101
138
North Bend
CASCADES
Coos Bay
Roseburg
Glide
138
Coquille River
Winston
OREGON
97
42
5
Port
Orford
Wolf Creek
227
230
Crater Lake
National
Park
COAST
Rogue River
62
Grants
Pass
Shady
Cove
Jackson-
ville
Medford
140
Upper
Klamath
Lake
101
238
Ashland
Klamath
Falls
KLAMATH
Cave
Junction
46
66
39
Brookings
199
Oregon
Caves
National
Monument
5
97
Crescent City
MOUNTAINS
CALIFORNIA

PACIFIC OCEAN

N

0   20 miles
0   20 kilometers

Drivers in a hurry barrel down Oregon's 280-mile Route 5 corridor in about five hours. Incredibly, that's the way many people see the region that lies at the end of the fabled Oregon Trail. Tempted by free land or the prospect of finding gold, the pioneers risked everything to get here. Today a new generation, rushing to reach Crater Lake, Mt. Hood or the Oregon Coast, speeds through, never knowing what they've missed.

That's progress. Fortunately, all it takes is a trip down a Route 5 offramp to get hooked on the Heart of Oregon, the 60-mile-wide region that extends from Salem to the California border. With the freeway left behind in the rearview mirror, you may understand why residents say God spent six days creating the Earth and on the seventh He went to Oregon.

Framed by the Klamath and Coast ranges on the west and the Cascades on the east, this is the place to find peaceful covered bridges and exciting rafting runs, the nation's oldest Shakespeare festival and a legislature that has made Oregon America's most environmentally conscious state. Home to two major universities, the center of Oregon agriculture and some of its most historic towns, the Heart of Oregon is where you'll find many of the state's best-known writers, poets, artists and artisans.

Just an hour from the state's famous mountain and seaside resorts, the Willamette Valley and the Ashland–Rogue River areas are the primary destinations in the Heart of Oregon. Fields of wildflowers, small towns with falsefront stores and gabled homes, businesses with names like "Wild and Scenic Trailer Park," pies made with fresh-picked marionberries—this is the Oregon found in the postcard rack. Soda fountains with mirrored backbars, jazz preservation societies, old river ferries, museums built out of railroad cars, music festivals and folk-art shrines— you'll find them all and even more here.

In many ways this area's heritage, touted by writers ranging from Washington Irving to Zane Grey, sums up the evolution of the West: American Indians followed by British fur traders, American explorers, missionaries, pioneer settlers, gold miners and the merchants who served them. The 19th-century nouveau riche tapped the hardwood forests to create Victorian mansions. As the mines were played out, lumber and agriculture became king. Strategically located on the main stage and rail lines to California and Washington, this corridor also became the principal gateway to most of Oregon's cities, as well as its emerging mountain retreats and coastal beaches.

But the Heart of Oregon story also has a special dimension, one told at local museums and historic sites. The fatal impact of American expansion on the American Indian culture began with the arrival of missionaries, who preached Christianity but left behind diseases that decimated their converts. In 1843 the promise of free land triggered a stampede as "Oregon or bust" pioneers sped west. Many became farmers who prospered in the California trade after gold was discovered in 1848 at Sutter's Mill. Three years later, after gold was found closer to home near Jacksonville, many settlers put down their plows and made a beeline for the mines. A new boom brought instant prosperity to this sleepy town as millions in gold dust poured through banks on California Street and miners dazzled their brides with mansions shipped in piecemeal from Tennessee.

Not sharing in this windfall were American Indians pushed from their ancestral lands by the settlers and miners. The Indians fought back in the Rogue River Wars between 1851 and 1856. But they were ultimately forced onto reservations, easing the path to statehood in 1859. Settled by Methodist missionaries in 1840, Salem was one of several towns that emerged as a regional supply center. Others included Eugene and Corvallis.

As the railroad improved access, businessmen discovered there was more to sell in Oregon than gold, lumber, dairy products and bountiful crops. Visitors began to explore the fishing streams, caves and forests. Chautauqua tents brought intellectuals and entertainers to Ashland, as Jacksonville offered a different kind of nightlife that gave preachers something to denounce on their pulpits. When

484 Zane Grey showed up to fish the Rogue and the Umpqua rivers, the entire country read about it in his articles. As the good word spread, more visitors began arriving to raft these and other rivers, to see the waterfalls and photograph the vernacular architecture.

Although it was a long way from Middle America, tourists loved the Main Street look and unspoiled countryside of the Heart of Oregon. Culturally it became a hub for social experiments and alternative lifestyles, happily exported by local celebrities like Ken Kesey, who took his famous traffic-stopping bus on a national tour with the "Merry Pranksters" in the 1960s.

Although the Heart of Oregon can be overcast and wet during the winter months, summers tend to be sunny and hot, particularly in the Ashland–Rogue River area. While Route 5 is the mainline, Route 99 is a pleasant alternative. Because the Willamette Valley is flat, it's ideal terrain for cyclists. South of Eugene, the Klamath mountains frame picturesque valleys and towns such as Medford, Ashland and Jacksonville. At the bottom of the state, the Siskiyous form the backdrop to the California border.

Because this is the state's primary transportation corridor, it's convenient to scores of popular attractions. Since you're only an hour from the beach or the Cascades, you can easily spend your days waterskiing or spelunking and your nights enjoying *King Lear*. Blessed with some of the state's finest resorts and restaurants, the Heart of Oregon also offers plenty of birdwatching thanks to several wildlife preserves found along the Willamette River. Here you're likely to spot great blue herons, red-tailed hawks, quails and woodpeckers. Deer, fox, opossums, coyotes and raccoons abound in the valley, while elk, bobcats, bear and flying squirrels are found in the southern mountains.

The region's highlands are pocketed by pristine lakes, hundreds of miles of remote hiking trails and resort lodges paneled in knotty pine. There's even downhill skiing on the highest peak here, 7533-foot Mt. Ashland. But there's little doubt that the signature attractions between Salem and Ashland are the river valleys. From the Willamette wetlands to the swimming holes of the Applegate River, it's hard to beat the streamside life. Rushing down from the Cascades, roaring through Hellgate Canyon, flowing through restaurants at the Oregon Caves, these tributaries define every area and delight every visitor.

One of the most attractive features is the proximity to the wilderness. You are seldom more than 15 or 20 minutes from the countryside, and even the bigger towns, such as Eugene and Salem, have major greenbelts within the city limits. Just north of Salem is Oregon's wine country. While the state capitol is the biggest draw, many historic homes and neighborhoods add to the charm of the central city.

Eugene's college-town status gives it the amenities you would expect in a larger community, while its central location makes the city an ideal base for visiting most of the state's popular destinations. And the city's Ecotopian fervor shows what can happen when environmentalists take control.

Jacksonville, a city that boomed during the rollicking gold rush days, is a delightful period piece, the kind of town where bed and breakfasts outnumber motels ten to one. The tree-lined streets, red-brick office blocks and dusty old bars make the town a favorite. Artists flock here and to Ashland, an Oregon mecca for the dramatic arts. Thoroughly gentrified, heavily booked and loaded with great restaurants, Ashland is the state's last temptation and a hard one to leave on the

SALEM AREA

Although best known as Oregon's capital, Salem is a desirable place to spend a day for many other reasons. A short drive from Oregon's wine country, Salem is also close to several historic Willamette Valley ferries. Near the Willamette, the downtown area is rich with restored buildings, museums, churches and a pioneer cemetery.

SIGHTS

Most travelers from Portland drive down the Willamette Valley to Salem via Route 5. But a far more scenic approach is to exit Route 5 in southern Portland and pick up **Route 99 West** through Tigard. Here you can continue through Oregon's wine country on 99 West, head through McMinnville and then cut east to Salem at Rickreall. Even better, turn off Route 99 West at the town of Dayton and pick up **Route 221**, a beautiful backroad paralleling the Willamette River. Near Hopewell it's fun to cross the river on the Wheatland Ferry.

MISSION MILL MUSEUM ✉1313 Mill Street Southeast, Salem ☎503-585-7012 ☎503-588-9902 🖳www.missionmill.org, info@missionmill.org In Salem, you'll find this historic restoration that turns back the clock to Oregon's pioneer days. Built in the 19th century, the Thomas Kay Woolen Mill is a factory-turned-museum. Adjacent are the Jason Lee House, the oldest residence standing in the Pacific Northwest, and the John Boon House, where you'll learn what family life was like in the mid-19th century. The 1841 Methodist Parsonage is open for tours. Enjoy a picnic here by the millstream. Closed Sunday. Admission. The **Salem Convention and Visitors Association** (503-581-4325, 800-874-7012, fax 503-581-4540, www.travelsalem.com, information@travelsalem.com) has an office in the complex. Closed Sunday.

DEEPWOOD ESTATE ✉1116 Mission Street Southeast, Salem ☎503-363-1825 🖳www.historicdeepwoodestate.org, historicdeepwoodestate@yahoo.com With its stained-glass windows, oak woodwork and solarium, this Queen Anne is a monument to turn-of-the-20th-century craftsmanship. A nature trail leads through the adjacent Bush's Pasture Park. Closed Saturday in summer; closed Monday, Tuesday and Friday in winter. Admission.

COURT-CHEMEKETA RESIDENTIAL HISTORIC DISTRICT ✉Court and Chemeketa streets, Salem ☎503-588-6173, 800-874-7012 ☎503-581-4540 🖳www.travelsalem.com This historic district showcases 117 historic Queen Anne, Italianate, Gothic, Craftsman and saltbox homes. On its mile-long walk you'll see many of these fine homes built by the city's founders.

OREGON STATE CAPITOL ✉900 Court Street Southeast, Salem ☎503-986-1388 ☎503-986-1131 🖳www.leg.state.or.us The capitol building is a four-story Greek-style structure boasting half a dozen bronze sculptures

Salem Area

LIVING ROCK STUDIOS
PAGE 490

Memorial to Oregon's past carved from 800 tons of rock and filled with pioneer and American Indian artifacts

AMADOR'S ALLEY
PAGE 492

Local favorite for huge portions of *huevos con chorizo*, chile colorado and enchiladas rancheros

WHITCOMB CREEK COUNTY PARK
PAGE 495

Campsites nestled beneath towering trees, deep in a stunning rainforest along Green Peter Reservoir

over the entrances. Built from Vermont marble, the state building is crowned by the 23-foot-high gilded statue *The Oregon Pioneer*. The tower and rotunda were damaged by the 1993 earthquake (the quake measured 5.5 on the Richter scale), but are repaired and open to the public today. Weekday tours up the 121 stairs of the tower run from the end of March through September. The surrounding Wilson Park has a pretty fountain and gazebo.

WILLAMETTE UNIVERSITY ✉*900 State Street, Salem* ☏*503-370-6300* ⏚*www.willamette.edu* Across from the capitol, Willamette University is the state's oldest institution of higher learning and the first university in the West (founded in 1842). On this shady campus you'll want to see the exhibit on the history of the school (which in many ways mirrors the history of Salem) at venerable **Waller Hall**. Cone Chapel (also in Waller Hall) is the place of worship for this one-time Methodist school. The campus is also home to an unusual formation of five giant sequoias known as the **Star Trees**; if you stand in the middle of them and look upward, you'll see the shape of a star. The trees are near the **Sesquicentennial Rose Garden**, a blooming place for a walk across State Street from the capitol.

The byways and secondary highways of the Willamette Valley north of Salem offer great possibilities for a day of sightseeing. Many of Oregon's best wineries are along Route 99 West—a rural and scenic alternative to Route 5.

North of Salem

SCHREINER'S GARDENS ✉*3625 Quinaby Road Northeast, Salem* ☏*503-393-3232, 800-525-2367* ⏚*503-393-5590* ⏚*www.schreinersgardens.com, iris@schreiners gardens.com* In the spring, don't miss Schreiner's Gardens, located five

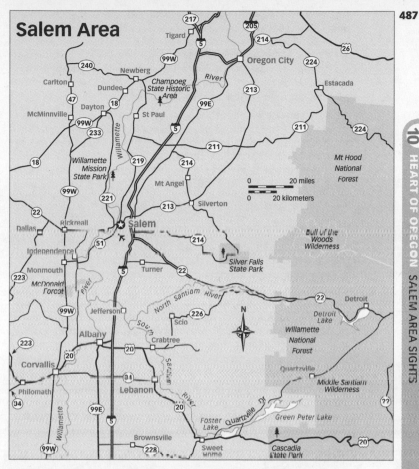

Salem Area

Tigard
217
205
214
26
5
240
Newberg
99W
Oregon City
224
Carlton
River
Dundee
Champoeg
State Historic
213
Estacada
47
Dayton
18
Area
McMinnville
St Paul
99E
211
224
99W
5
233
211
Mt Hood
National
Willamette
219
214
Forest
Mission
State Park
Mt Angel
99W
221
213
Silverton
0   20 miles
22
Rickreall
Salem
0   20 kilometers
Dallas
51
214
Bull of the
Woods
Independence
Wilderness
Monmouth
5
Turner
22
Silver Falls
State Park
223
McDonald
Forest
North Santiam River
22
Detroit
99W
Jefferson
226
Detroit
Lake
Scio
Willamette
223
Albany
Crabtree
National
20
20
Forest
Corvallis
20
Quartzville
Philomath
34
Middle Santiam
Wilderness
Lebanon
22
99E
20
5
Foster
Lake
Green Peter Lake
20
Brownsville
Cascadia
State Park
99W
228
Sweet
Home
N

miles north of Salem. Although there are over 200 acres here, only 10 of them are open to the public, and that is only during the May-to-June blooming season. Still, a visit to this photographer's dream is a must during those months; the rest of the year, the gardens are closed while Schreiner's ships irises all over the world through its catalog business.

MT. ANGEL ABBEY ✉ *1 Abbey Drive, St. Benedict* 📞 *503-845-3030* 📠 *503-845-3594* 🖥 *www.mountangelabbey.org, info@mountangelabbey.org* Mt. Angel Abbey is a 19th-century Benedictine monastic community 18 miles northeast of Salem. Visitors are welcome to take a walking tour of the Abbey, including the Romanesque church and retreat houses. A small museum focuses on the Russian Old Believer community, while another building emphasizes the natural history of the region. The beautiful library, designed by Alvar Aalto, features a display of rare books. Near the top of a 300-foot butte is the grotto of Our Lady of Lourdes. In July, the retreat hosts the Abbey Bach Festival.

Wineries are one of the true delights of the Salem area. Many are found along Route 99 West in the Willamette Valley north and west of the city.

REX HILL VINEYARDS ✉*30835 North Route 99W, Newberg* ☎*503-538-0666, 800-739-4455* 🖉*www.rexhill.com, info@rexhill.com* Rex Hill is a beautifully landscaped 25-acre winery with an inviting terraced picnic area. Furnished with antiques, the tasting room has a fireplace.

ERATH WINERY ✉*9409 Northeast Worden Hill Road, Dundee* ☎*503-538-3318, 800-539-9463* 📠*503-538-1074* 🖉*www.erath.com, info@erath.com* Set high above the Willamette Valley in the lovely Dundee Hills is this picturesque winery spread over 118 acres. You can sample the winery's wares in a rustic, wood-paneled tasting room. One-hour tasting tours (fee) are available at 1 p.m. daily.

ARGYLE ✉*691 North Route 99W, Dundee* ☎*503-538-8520, 888-427-4953* 🖉*www. argylewinery.com, tastingroom@argylewinery.com* Established in 1987 by an Australian vintner in a one-time hazelnut processing plant, Argyle specializes in champagne-like sparkling wines and pinot noirs. The inviting tasting room is in a restored Victorian farmhouse.

SOKOL BLOSSER WINERY ✉*5000 Sokol Blosser Lane, Dayton* ☎*503-864-2282, 800-582-6668* 📠*503-864-2710* 🖉*www.solkolblosser.com, info@solkolblosser. com* Established in 1971, Sokol Blosser was one of Oregon's first wineries. Here you'll enjoy great views of the Willamette Valley, along with a pleasant picnic area and contemporary tasting room offering not only the winery's fine pinot noir and pinot gris but also fruit preserves, gourmet mustards, salad dressings and candies. Tours (fee) are available Friday through Sunday at 10 a.m.

WINE COUNTRY FARM CELLARS ✉*6855 Breyman Orchards Road, Dayton* ☎*503-864-3466, 800-261-3446* 📠*503-864-3109* 🖉*www.winecountryfarm.com, jld@winecountryfarm.com* Four miles south of Dundee, this winery makes rare varietals such as Müller-Thurgau in addition to pinot noir and riesling. You'll find a picnic area and a B&B, and visitors can get acquainted with the resident Arabian horses. From here, it's a 20-mile drive back to Salem via Route 221.

YAMHILL VALLEY VINEYARDS ✉*16250 Southwest Oldsville Road (off Route 18), McMinnville* ☎*503-843-3100, 800-825-2450* 🖉*www.yamhill.com, info@ yamhill.com* These vineyards sit on a 150-acre estate. Try their pinot noir, pinot blanc and pinot gris wines in the elegant tasting room set in an oak grove. The cathedral ceiling and balcony overlooking the vineyard add to the charm. Closed Monday through Wednesday from March to May.

THE TASTING ROOM ✉*Main and Pine streets, Carlton; From McMinnville, take Route 47 north seven miles.* ☎*503-852-6733* 🖉*www.pinot-noir.com, info@pinot-noir. com* In the center of historic **Carlton** is this wine bar, which presents a selection of fine wines from around Oregon, with tastings each afternoon. Closed Tuesday and Wednesday and from January through March.

CARLO & JULIAN ✉*1000 East Main Street, Carlton* ☎*503-852-7432* 🖉*carlojul wine@yahoo.com* This winery is known for innovative viticulture techniques, including the use of frost for crop control and trained cats for gopher eradication. Producing fewer than 1000 cases of handcrafted pinot noir, tempranillo and nebbiolo annually, the winery is open for tastings and sales over Memorial Day and Thanksgiving weekends and by appointment.

LAUREL RIDGE WINERY ✉13301 Northeast Kuehne Road, Carlton ✆503-852-7050 ⌕www.laurelridgewinery.com If you continue east on Main Street as it becomes Northeast Hendricks Road, then turn left on Northeast Kuehne Road, you will arrive at Laurel Ridge. Set on 240 acres of farmland, the winery boasts a classic-style tasting room and gift shop. Tastings of their pinot noir, riesling and gewürztraminer are available Thursday through Sunday. Fee.

South of Salem

Heading south from Salem, you may want to skip Route 5 altogether. A fun loop drive, beginning in Albany (about 25 miles south of Salem), leads through Corvallis, home to one of Oregon's biggest universities, as well as through some accommodating rural towns and sights.

ENCHANTED FOREST ✉8462 Enchanted Way Southeast, Turner ✆503-371-4242 ⌕www.enchantedforest.com Take the kids to this magical playground, located in a park setting seven miles south of Salem on Route 5. The dream of creator Roger Tofte, this family fun spot has fairytale attractions like a crooked house, Seven Dwarfs' cottage, an Alice in Wonderland rabbit hole, old-lady's-shoe slide, haunted house and the Big Timber log ride. New additions include the Ice Mountain bobsleds and the interactive Challenge of Mondor ride. Plays are performed in an outdoor theater. Closed October to mid-March, and weekdays in September and April. Admission.

BUENA VISTA FERRY ✆503-588-7979 Heading southeast from Salem on Route 51, continue past the town of Independence and follow the signs seven miles south to the historic Buena Vista Ferry, which carries a handful of cars and cyclists across the Willamette in the time-honored manner. No trip to Oregon is complete without a ride on one of these old timers. Closed Monday and Tuesday, and from November through April.

Proceed south to Albany, where you can begin a circular drive of the area north of Eugene. South of Albany, Route 34 leads east to the town of Lebanon.

EAST LINN MUSEUM ✉746 Long Street, Sweet Home ✆541-367-4580 Continue east from Lebanon to Sweet Home and one of the Northwest's better pioneer museums. In a 1905 woodframe church, this museum's collection is big on logging equipment, antique dolls, quilts, butter churns, linotypes and saddles. There's also a full blacksmith shop here. Closed December through January; closed Monday from June through September, and Monday through Wednesday from September through April.

SWEET HOME CHAMBER OF COMMERCE ✉1575 Main Street, Sweet Home ✆541-367-6186 ⌕www.sweethomechamber.org, info@sweethomechamber.org This chamber of commerce provides information on the Cascades gateway. Closed Saturday and Sunday.

RESERVOIRS Perched in the foothills ten miles east of the town of Sweet Home are **Foster Reservoir** and the adjacent **Green Peter Reservoir** on Quartzville Road. Green Peter Reservoir offers the kind of views you'd expect to find in Switzerland.

LINN COUNTY HISTORICAL MUSEUM ✉*101 Park Avenue, Brownsville* ☎*541-466-5709* **Brownsville**, west of Sweet Home on Route 228, is one of the valley's most charming small towns. You can pick up a walking-tour brochure at this local history museum, which is housed in the town's original railroad depot.

MOYER HOUSE ✉*204 Main Street at Kirk Avenue, Brownsville* Built from lumber milled in John Moyer's own sash and door factory, this Italian-ate home features 12-foot ceilings. Landscapes are painted on the walls and window transoms.

LIVING ROCK STUDIOS _____

✉*Route 228, west of Brownsville* ☎*541-466-5814* 🖳*www.livingrockstudios. org, mackey@peak.org* Howard Taylor and his wife, Faye, devoted 20 years to the creation of this folk-art capital of central Oregon. Howard created this memorial to his pioneer ancestors with 800 tons of rock. The circular stone building is inlaid with pioneer wagon-wheel rims, an American Indian mortar and pestle, fool's gold, obsidian and coffee jars filled with crystals. A series of illuminated biblical pictures is displayed downstairs, while a circular staircase leads upstairs to a display of Taylor's carvings. Antiques and unique gifts are on display in the shop. Self-guided tours are available. Closed Sunday and Monday.

CORVALLIS A popular Oregon college town located on the west side of the valley at the edge of the coast range, Corvallis is also the seat of Benton County.

BENTON COUNTY COURTHOUSE ✉*120 Northwest 4th Street, Corvallis* A prominent landmark in Corvallis is this courthouse. The building, dating to 1887 and still in use, has an impressive clock tower. Closed weekends.

OREGON STATE UNIVERSITY ✉*Campus Way, Corvallis* ☎*541-737-0123* 🖳*541-737-0625* 🖳*www.oregonstate.edu/dept/arts* On the 500-acre Oregon State University campus in Corvallis, you'll find the OSU art department's **Fairbanks Gallery** in Fairbanks Hall (closed weekends, 541-737-5009), a small gallery space that usually features rotating exhibits, often by the university's students.

CORVALLIS TOURISM ✉*553 Northwest Harrison Boulevard, Corvallis* ☎*541-757-1544, 800-334-8118* 🖳*541-753-2664* 🖳*www.visitcorvallis.com, info@visitcorvallis. com* For information on other local attractions, contact Corvallis Tourism. Closed weekends in fall and winter.

MONTEITH HOUSE ✉*518 Southwest 2nd Avenue, Albany* ☎*541-967-8699, 800-526-2256* East of Corvallis on Route 20 is **Albany**, where you'll find nearly 500 Victorian homes. One of the best is the Monteith House, which is a frame residence with period 19th-century furnishings. Dressed in Victorian costumes, docents lead intriguing tours. You may learn such interesting historical facts such as that during the 1850s, when U.S. currency was scarce in the Northwest, Oregon Territory minted its own "beaver money" —$5 and $10 gold coins stamped with a beaver image. Closed Monday and Tuesday, and from mid-September to mid-June, except by appointment.

ALBANY REGIONAL MUSEUM ✉*136 Lyon Street South, Albany* ✆*541-967-7122* *www.armuseum.org* At this museum are an old-time general store, a shoe-shine shop and an exhibit on Camp Adair, a World War II Army training site. Closed Sunday.

ALBANY VISITORS ASSOCIATION ✉*250 Broadalbin Street Southwest, Suite 110, Albany* ✆*541-928-0911, 800-526-2256* *541-926-1500* *www.albanyvisitors. com, info@albanyvisitors.com* To arrange tours of the Monteith House or the Albany Regional Museum, contact this visitors association, where you can pick up a helpful walking-tour map.

LODGING

BEST WESTERN MILL CREEK INN
$$ 109 UNITS   ✉*3125 Ryan Drive Southeast, Salem* ✆*503-585-3332, 800-346-9659* *503-375-9618* *www.bestwestern.com/millcreekinn, bwmci@msn.com*
Convenient to Route 5, this Best Western has a variety of units, including junior suites with microwaves, refrigerators and wet bars. The large rooms have contemporary furniture and ample closet space. The rate includes breakfast at the nearby Denny's.

ECONOLODGE
$ 61 ROOMS   ✉*345 Northwest 2nd Street, Corvallis* ✆*541-752-9601, 541-752-0042* *hotelhelp@choicehotels.com*
This hotel offers lodging just 50 yards from the Willamette River. Clean, air-conditioned rooms are furnished in modern decor. The price is right for this hotel convenient to downtown.

SWEET HOME INN MOTEL
$$ 28 ROOMS   ✉*805 Long Street, Sweet Home* ✆*541-367-5137* *541-367-8859*
Rooms are clean here with white and pink brick walls and contemporary furniture. A small garden is located at the inn, which is a block away from the museums and shops of this gateway to some of the valley's best boating and fishing.

DINING

NICK'S ITALIAN CAFÉ
$$–$$$$ ITALIAN   ✉*521 Northeast 3rd Street, McMinnville* ✆*503-434-4471, 888-456-2511*
Just when you're about ready to give up on McMinnville as another franchise landscape, the chain stores of Route 99 give way to the town's well-preserved downtown. Tucked away in a storefront is Nick's, where the kitchen prepares memorable dishes such as smoked salmon with pinenuts, veal parmesan and homemade lasagna with pesto, mush-

rooms and Oregon filberts. The prix-fixe menu is standard, but all items can be ordered à la carte. Don't despair if you can't get a reservation because there's nearly always seating available at the counter. Seasonal hours; call ahead.

KWAN'S

$$ CHINESE   ✉835 Commercial Street Southeast, Salem   ☎503-362-7711
📠503-373-5818   🖥www.kwanscuisine.com

There's no MSG at this Chinese establishment with seating for more than 400. Specialties like imperial fried rice, curry lamb, Mongolian emu and mango chicken have won a loyal following. They offer five varieties of whole-grain rice as well as an assortment of fresh produce and meats. Entering this pagoda-style building, you'll find a 15-foot-tall redwood Buddha in the lobby.

MICHAEL'S LANDING

$$–$$$ STEAK/SEAFOOD   ✉603 Northwest 2nd Street, Corvallis   ☎541-754-6141
📠541-754-9578   🖥www.michaelslanding.com

Michael's serves prime rib and seafood salad in the restored Southern Pacific Station. One of the city's most popular restaurants, it has a great view of the Willamette. A full Sunday brunch is also available.

THE GABLES

$$–$$$ STEAK/SEAFOOD   ✉1121 Northwest 9th Street, Corvallis   ☎541-752-3364,
800-815-0167   🖥www.thegablessteakhouse.com

For steaks, prime rib and fresh seafood, try this restaurant, which offers generous portions. Parmesan-crusted Alaskan halibut, smoked ribeye and teriyaki chicken breast are all available, as are vegetarian options such as sun-dried tomato ravioli. There's also an extensive wine cellar. Dinner only.

AMADOR'S ALLEY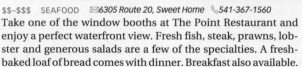

$–$$ MEXICAN   ✉870 North Main Street, Independence   ☎503-838-0170
📠503-838-1710

Located in a strip shopping center, this is one of the most popular Mexican restaurants in the area. Huge portions of *huevos con chorizo*, chile colorado and enchiladas rancheros are served up steaming. Diners are seated at plastic tables and chairs. Arrive early or be prepared to wait.

THE POINT RESTAURANT

$$–$$$ SEAFOOD   ✉6305 Route 20, Sweet Home   ☎541-367-1560

Take one of the window booths at The Point Restaurant and enjoy a perfect waterfront view. Fresh fish, steak, prawns, lobster and generous salads are a few of the specialties. A fresh-baked loaf of bread comes with dinner. Breakfast also available.

REED OPERA HOUSE MALL ✉ *189 Northeast Liberty Street, Salem* ✆ *503-391-4481* ⌕ *www.reedoperahouse.com* This opera house at Court and Liberty streets in Salem is a restored landmark that once presented plays by John Philip Sousa and speeches by Susan B. Anthony. Now the building is home to Salem's Repertory Theatre and is also a prime shopping area.

MISSION MILL STORE ✉ *1313 Mill Street Southeast, Salem* ✆ *503-585-7012* ⌕ *www.missionmill.org* The Mission Mill Museum's store sells the usual assortment of postcards, gifts and collectibles as well as blankets, clothes and hats. Closed Sunday.

BUSH BARN ART CENTER ✉ *600 Mission Street Southeast, Salem* ✆ *503-581-2228* ⌕ *www.salemart.org, cara@salemart.org* An excellent place for regional arts and crafts—pottery, sculpture, paintings, prints and jewelry, for example—is the Bush Barn. Closed Monday.

NIGHTLIFE

OREGON SYMPHONY ASSOCIATION ✉ *707 13th Street Southeast, Salem* ✆ *503-364-0149, 800-922-0422 (tickets)* This celebrated group offers classical concerts as well as a pops series.

PENTACLE THEATRE ✉ *324 52nd Avenue Northeast, Salem* ✆ *503-364-7200, 503-485-4300 (tickets)* ⌕ *www.pentacletheatre.org* A well-established community theater, the Pentacle produces eight plays each season.

MCMENAMIN'S BOON'S TREASURY ✉ *888 Liberty Street Northeast, Salem* ✆ *503-399-9062* 📠 *503-399-0074* For belly dancing, big band music, folk, reggae, rock or bluegrass, check out McMenamin's. This circa-1860 two-story brick building has live music Wednesday through Saturday nights. Artworks are frequently exhibited.

LENORA'S GHOST ✉ *114 Main Street, Independence* ✆ *503-838-2937* On Saturday night at this lively venue, a deejay will play songs by request. Friday nights, there's karaoke. Occasional cover.

PARKS

BUSH'S PASTURE PARK
✉ *600 Mission Street, Salem; The entry is off High Street Southeast.* ✆ *503-588-2410*
The Bush Collection of old garden roses is one of the highlights in this 89-acre park south of the capital. They were originally collected from pioneer homesteads to represent roses brought west on the Oregon Trail. Also here are natural wildflower gardens, a collection of flowering trees, the **Bush Barn Art Center**, featuring Northwestern artists, and the **Bush Conservatory**, the West's second-oldest greenhouse. Amenities include a picnic area, restrooms and tours of the **Bush House Museum** (fee), a playground and gardens.

WILLAMETTE MISSION STATE PARK

Wheatland Road, 12 miles north of Salem *503-393-1172* *503-393-8863*

Set in orchards and hop fields south of Wheatland's landing, this 1680-acre Willamette River park is the site of an 1830s Methodist Mission. A monument commemorates these early settlers. In the midst of the park are the historic Wheatland Ferry landings. This shady spot is a delightful retreat on a warm day. Fishing for bass and bluegill is popular with anglers. There are picnic tables, kitchen shelter areas, electricity, fire rings, restrooms, and bike and equestrian trails. Parking fee, $3.

SILVER FALLS STATE PARK

Route 214, 26 miles east of Salem *503-873-8681* *503-873-8925*

If you're addicted to waterfalls, look no further. Located in twin lava-rock gorges created by Silver Creek's north and south forks, the 8700-acre park has ten waterfalls. Also here are hiking, biking and equestrian trails leading through an old-growth fir forest with towering maples and quaking aspen ideal for fall-color buffs. South Falls, a seven-mile roundtrip hike from the highway, has the biggest drop, 177 feet, or 25 feet more than Niagara Falls. You'll find picnic tables, a snack bar, a playground, a swimming area, restrooms, rustic group lodging, a nature lodge, a jogging trail, bike trails and a horse camp. The park's lodge, home to the visitors center, was built by the CCC, which used native stone and logs in its construction. Parking fee, $3.

▲ There are 45 tent sites ($12 to $16 per night), 52 RV hookup sites ($16 to $20 per night), six horse-camp sites ($16 to $48 per night) and 14 cabins ($35 per night). Reservations: 800-452-5687.

MCDOWELL CREEK FALLS COUNTY PARK

hidden

Located 12 miles southeast of Lebanon via Fairview Road and McDowell Creek Drive *541-967-3917* *541-924-6915* *parks@co.linn.or.us*

This forested glen is a perfect refuge. An easy hike across the creek and up through a fir forest takes you to a pair of scenic falls. On a weekday you may have this park to yourself. There are picnic tables and vault toilets.

LEWIS CREEK COUNTY PARK

Three miles east of Sweet Home; Take Route 20 east to Foster Dam and turn left at Quartzville Road. At North River Drive turn left to the park. *541-967-3917* *541-924-6915* *www.co.linn.or.us/parks, parks@co.linn.or.us*

On the north shore of Foster Reservoir, this park is a good spot to swim and enjoy other water sports. Troll for bass and trout in the lake. The day-use park includes 20 acres of open space and 20 acres of brush and forest, as well as plenty of fine views of the Cascades. Picnic tables and a boat dock are the facilities here. Closed October through April. Parking fee, $3.

CASCADIA STATE PARK

Route 20, 14 miles east of Sweet Home *541-367-6021* *541-367-3757*

On the South Santiam River Canyon, this 253-acre park has a beautiful trail (.75 mile) leading to a waterfall. Largely forested with

Douglas fir, the park also has an open meadow on the north river bank. You can fish for trout in the river. Facilities include restrooms and picnic tables.

▲ There are 25 primitive sites ($14 per night). The campground is closed from October through April.

WHITCOMB CREEK COUNTY PARK _____ ⓗidden

✉ *From Sweet Home take Route 20 east to Foster Dam and turn left at Quartzville Road. Continue north 15 miles to the park.* ☎ *541-967-3917* 📠 *541-924-6915*

🚶 🚣 🚤 🎣 ⛵ With its stunning rainforest terrain on the shores of ten-mile-long Green Peter Reservoir, this 328-acre park in the foothills east of Sweet Home is a winner. It offers spectacular views of the Cascades and good trout fishing. The park is forested with fir and deciduous trees. You'll find picnic tables and restrooms. Boat ramps into the reservoir are located about a mile away. Closed October through April.

▲ There are 39 tent sites ($11 per night).

EUGENE AREA

College towns are often inviting and Eugene is no exception. Climb one of the town buttes and you'll find the city surrounded by rich farmland and beckoning lakes and streams. With the Cascades and the McKenzie River Valley to the east and the Coast Mountains to the west, Eugene has an ideal location. Eugene is at its best in the fall when maples, black walnuts, chestnuts and cottonwood brighten the landscape. The city, used for the filming of the movie *Animal House*, offers sidewalk cafés, malled streets and upscale shops.

SIGHTS

CONVENTION & VISITOR ASSOCIATION OF LANE COUNTY OREGON ✉ *754 Olive Street, Eugene* ☎ *541-484-5307, 800-547-5445* 📠 *541-343-6335* 🌐 *www.travellanecounty.org, info@cvalco.org* Pick up touring ideas at this visitor center. Closed Sunday in winter.

UNIVERSITY OF OREGON ☎ *541-346-3111, 800-232-3825* 🌐 *www.uoregon.edu* Stop by U of O's 250-acre campus. You'll find an arboretum with over 2000 varieties of trees; weekday tours for prospective students are offered from Oregon Hall at 13th and Agate streets.

MUSEUM OF NATURAL AND CULTURAL HISTORY ✉ *1680 East 15th Avenue, Eugene* ☎ *541-346-3024* 📠 *541-346-5334* 🌐 *www.natural-history.uoregon.edu, mnh@uoregon.edu* Among University of Oregon's campus highlights is this museum tracing the story of local land. The collection is a good way to orient yourself to the state's geology, flora, fauna and anthropology. Permanent exhibits cover Oregon's fossil history and archaeology. Closed Monday, Tuesday and during university holidays. Admission.

10 HEART OF OREGON EUGENE AREA SIGHTS

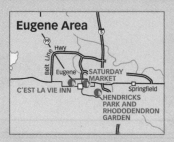

Eugene Area

C'EST LA VIE INN
PAGE 499

Over-the-top "painted lady" Victorian with lavish flower gardens and rooms with clawfoot soaking tubs

SATURDAY MARKET
PAGE 501

Open-air marketplace with live music, over 200 vendors selling handcrafted goods and the freshest produce

HENDRICKS PARK AND RHODODENDRON GARDEN
PAGE 503

Glorious spot where Oregon white oaks and Douglas firs tower over 6000 rhododendrons and azaleas

JORDAN SCHNITZER MUSEUM OF ART ✉ 1223 University of Oregon; Just east of 14th and Kincaid streets, Eugene ✆ 541-346-3027 ✎ 541-346-0976 ✐ jsma.uoregon.edu This colonnaded sculpture court with pool adjacent to the entrance is one of the campus's architectural highlights. The collection, one of the best in the state, displays American, European and a wide range of Asian artworks. Closed Monday. Admission.

5TH STREET PUBLIC MARKET ⓗidden

✉ 296 East 5th Avenue, Eugene ✆ 541-484-0383 ✎ 541-686-1220 ✐ www.5stmarket.com Eugene is big on adaptive reuse of commercial buildings. One great example is this public market, home to a distinctive collection of over 100 percent Oregon-owned retail shops, restaurants, international cafés and offices. It is located in the heart of Eugene's historic market district.

SPRINGFIELD MUSEUM ✉ 590 Main Street, Springfield ✆ 541-726-3677 ✎ 541-726-3688 ✐ www.springfieldmuseum.com, dgruell@ci.springfield.or.us The prime attraction in the neighboring town of Springfield is this museum, which has a section detailing the history of this timber-industry town (the first mill opened in 1853) and a gallery with changing exhibits of artwork, antique collections and Americana. Closed Sunday and Monday.

No trip to the Eugene area is complete without an excursion into the nearby countryside. You can head east on **Route 126** along the McKenzie River or southeast on **Route 58** to Lookout Point Reservoir, Oakridge and Salt Creek Falls. **Route 5** takes you south to Cottage Grove. Row River Road leads east past Dorena Reservoir and several covered bridges to the historic **Bohemia Mining District**. The mountainous district was the scene of a mid-19th-century gold rush that unfortunately proved to be a bust. Today, tourists roam the district by car and four-wheel-drive vehicles to see lost mines, ghost towns like Bohemia City and covered bridges.

COTTAGE GROVE RANGER STATION ☎541-767-5000 📠541-767-5075 Before setting out for the Bohemia Mining District be sure to check with this ranger station. Because there are active mining claims in the area, it is important not to trespass.

COTTAGE GROVE MUSEUM ✉Birch and H avenues, Cottage Grove ☎541-942-3963 This museum has a major exhibit on the Bohemia District, as well as displays on the *Titanic* and a covered bridge. The museum has seasonal hours, so call ahead.

ROSEBURG VISITORS CENTER AND CHAMBER OF COMMERCE ✉410 Southeast Spruce Street, Roseburg ☎541-672-9731, 800-444-9584 📠541-673-7868 ✐www.visitroseburg.com, info@visitroseburg.com Check with the local visitors center for a handy city tour guide. Closed Sunday in winter. Highlights include the **Roseburg Historic District** in the Mill Street/Pine Street neighborhood. You'll find many modest cottages built in the late 19th century.

FLOED-LANE HOUSE ✉544 Southeast Douglas Street, Roseburg This is a classic revival featuring a full-length, two-tier veranda with half a dozen square columns supporting each level. It's open for tours on Sunday or by appointment.

DOUGLAS COUNTY MUSEUM OF HISTORY AND NATURAL HISTORY ✉123 Museum Drive, Roseburg ☎541-957-7007 📠541-957-7017 ✐www.douglasmuseum.com, museum@co.douglas.or.us American Indian and pioneer artifacts are exhibited here, along with a 19th-century railroad depot and natural history wildlife dioramas. Admission.

WILDLIFE SAFARI ✉1790 Safari Road, Winston ☎541-679-6761 📠541-679-9210 ✐www.wildlifesafari.org This is Oregon's drive-through adventure, a 600-acre park where over 500 animals and birds roam freely. Visitors motor past Bactrian camels, hippopotamuses, lions, and scores of other species. In addition to the self-paced driving tour, the Safari Village has a petting zoo and a kid-friendly train. Elephant and camel rides are also available in the summer. Admission.

LODGING

VALLEY RIVER INN
$$$ 257 ROOMS ✉1000 Valley River Way, Eugene ☎541-743-1000, 800-543-8266 📠541-683-5121 ✐www.valleyriverinn.com, contact@valleyriverinn.com

This inn enjoys an enviable view of the Willamette River. Adjacent to the 140-store Valley River Center, the hotel features Indian quilts hanging over the big lobby fireplace that faces a conversation pit. Large rooms, decorated with either wicker furniture and impressionist prints or Laura Ashley designs, open onto small patios. Bicycling and jogging paths are adjacent to the inn, which rents bikes and has its own workout room. You'll also find a pool, sauna and jacuzzi as well as a full-service restaurant and lounge. All rooms are nonsmoking.

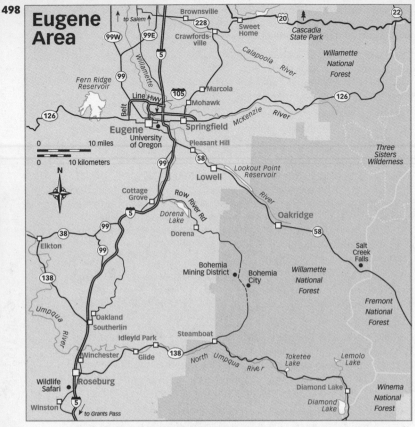

Eugene Area

to Salem

Brownsville

Crawfords-ville

Sweet Home

Cascadia State Park

Willamette National Forest

Calapoola River

Fern Ridge Reservoir

Willamette

Line Hwy

Marcola

Mohawk

McKenzie River

Eugene

Springfield

University of Oregon

Pleasant Hill

0   10 miles
0   10 kilometers

N

Lowell

Lookout Point Reservoir

Three Sisters Wilderness

Cottage Grove

Row River Rd

Dorena Lake

Dorena

River

Oakridge

Salt Creek Falls

Elkton

Bohemia Mining District

Bohemia City

Willamette National Forest

Fremont National Forest

Umpqua River

Oakland

Southerlin

Idleyld Park

Steamboat

Winchester

Glide

North Umpqua River

Toketee Lake

Lemolo Lake

Wildlife Safari

Roseburg

Diamond Lake

Winema National Forest

Winston

to Grants Pass

Diamond Lake

BEST WESTERN GREENTREE INN

$$ **65 UNITS** ✉ *1759 Franklin Boulevard, Eugene* 📞 *541-485-2727, 800-528-1234* 📠 *541-686-2094* ✐ *greentreeinn@aol.com*

This Best Western offers attractive, contemporary rooms with sitting areas and balconies, some with creek views. All units have refrigerators. Adjacent to the University of Oregon campus, this establishment has a pool, jacuzzi, exercise center, restaurant and sports bar. Continental breakfast is included.

SECRET GARDEN BED & BREAKFAST

$$$–$$$$ **10 ROOMS** ✉ *1910 University Street, Eugene* 📞 *541-484-6755, 888-484-6755* 📠 *541-431-1699* ✐ *www.secretgardenbbinn.com, innkeeper@secretgardenbbinn.com*

Tucked away in a quiet university neighborhood, the Secret Garden features unique rooms, each with a different garden theme. The Scented Garden room is furnished in sumptuous colors and Indian and Tibetan antiques, while the Apiary is decorated in French country style. A striking mural in the upstairs sitting room depicts the mythical Daphne in the middle of her metamorphosis into a tree. Naturally, the landscaped grounds are meticulous and lovely. Full breakfast included.

EXCELSIOR INN _____ hidden

$$$–$$$$ 14 ROOMS ✉ *754 East 13th Street, Eugene* ☎ *541-342-6963, 800-321-6963* ✍ *www.excelsiorinn.com, innkeeper@excelsiorinn.com*

Pick your favorite musician at this inn, where classical composers such as Beethoven, Strauss and Verdi lend their names to guest accommodations. Each of the musical rooms is distinctly decorated in dark cherry furniture, with elegant touches like writing desks, armoires, sleigh beds, arched windows and vaulted ceilings. Full breakfast from the inn's fine restaurant included.

THE CAMPBELL HOUSE _____ hidden

$$–$$$$ 18 ROOMS ✉ *252 Pearl Street, Eugene* ☎ *541-343-1119, 800-264-2519* ☏ *541-343-2258* ✍ *www.campbellhouse.com, campbellhouse@campbellhouse.com*

Overlooking Eugene, this inn offers peaceful and elegant accommodations within walking distance to both city center and outdoor pursuits. The rooms are individually decorated; all have a Victorian flavor with modern amenities. Some have fireplaces and jacuzzis. You'll also find a comfortable parlor and library. Full breakfast is served.

C'EST LA VIE INN _____ hidden

$$$ 4 ROOMS ✉ *1006 Taylor Street, Eugene* ☎ *541-302-3014, 866-302-3014* ☏ *541-302-3014* ✍ *www.cestlavieinn.com, contact@cestlavieinn.com*

The over-the-top architecture of this Queen Anne Victorian home—with its sunburst designs, elaborate roof shingle patterns, Gothic finials and scroll brackets—was the talk of the town when Eugene's local hardware and building supply dealer built it for his family in the 1890s. In 2004 it became a "painted lady," detailed in bright hues of blue, lavender and gold and surrounded with lavish flower gardens. Each guest room is individually decorated in a different theme—Casablanca, Monet, Matisse and Gauguin—and features queen-sized beds and private baths; some have clawfoot soaking tubs.

DINING

SWEETWATERS

$$$–$$$$ SEAFOOD ✉ *Valley River Inn, 1000 Valley River Way, Eugene* ☎ *541-743-1000, 800-543-8266* ☏ *541-683-5121* ✍ *www.valleyriverinn.com*

The emphasis here is on Oregon cuisine featuring locally grown veal, lamb, lettuce, herbs, mushrooms and fruits. Seafood entrées include grilled salmon, Dungeness crab chowder and fresh swordfish. This contemporary dining room overlooking the Willamette River is complemented by a deck ideal for drinks before or after dinner.

OREGON ELECTRIC STATION RESTAURANT AND LOUNGE

$$$–$$$$ AMERICAN   ✉️*27 East 5th Avenue, Eugene*   📞*541-485-4444*
📠*541-484-6149* 🖥️*www.oesrestaurant.com*

For a lively night on the town, I head to this historic building magnificently reborn as a club-like dining and entertainment venue with oak paneling, high-backed tapestry chairs and antique train cars serving as dining areas. On weekends, jazz and blues bands elevate the mood. Fresh grilled seafood and prime rib highlight the menu. No lunch on weekends.

AMBROSIA RESTAURANT AND BAR

$$ ITALIAN   ✉️*174 East Broadway, Eugene*   📞*541-342-4141*   📠*541-345-6965*
🖥️*www.ambrosiarestaurant.com, info@ambrosiarestaurant.com*

Ambrosia prepares Italian specialties in a red-brick building distinguished by leaded glass, a mirrored oak and mahogany backbar, Tiffany-style lamps and a tintype ceiling. You'll find pizzas and calzones made with a plum tomato sauce, pasta and entrées like grilled fresh lamb and fresh seafood. There are 325 vintages on the wine list, including 30 ports. Outdoor dining is available. No lunch on Saturday and Sunday.

EXCELSIOR INN AND RISTORANTE ITALIANO

$$–$$$ ITALIAN/PACIFIC NORTHWEST   ✉️*754 East 13th Avenue, Eugene*
📞*541-342-6963, 800-321-6963*   📠*541-342-1417*   🖥️*www.excelsiorinn.com,*
innkeeper@excelsiorinn.com

For pasta dishes, fresh salmon, lamb, steaks and generous salads, the Excelsior is a good choice. Located in a Victorian near the university, this pleasing restaurant also has an excellent Oregon and Italian wine list and a generous brunch on Sunday. Ask for a table on the terrace. Open for breakfast, lunch and dinner; but no lunch on Saturday.

MEKALA'S THAI CUISINE

$$ THAI   ✉️*1769 Franklin Avenue, Eugene*   📞*541-342-4872*
🖥️*www.mekalas.com, info@mekalas.com*

Mekala's serves authentic Thai recipes and boasts nearly 100 items, including traditional curries, noodle dishes, stir frys, soups and seafood. There is heated outdoor seating in summer only, and a full bar downstairs.

TOLLY'S SODA FOUNTAIN

$$–$$$ AMERICAN   ✉️*115 Locust Street, Oakland*   📞*541-459-3796*   📠*541-459-1833*
🖥️*tollys-restaurant.com*

Tolly's is one of the most inviting lunch counters in Oregon. Located in a brick building, Tolly's is an architectural landmark with a mirrored backbar, varnished mahogany counters and stools, brass footrests and Tiffany lamps. Enjoy a soda, milkshake or banana split. Also available

are breakfast potatoes and eggs, as well as Reuben sandwiches, crois-
sants, lasagna and fresh strawberry pie. The budget-priced breakfasts
and lunches are bargains; dinner brings a higher price tag. Dinner is
only available on Friday and Saturday.

SHOPPING

5TH STREET PUBLIC MARKET

✉ 296 East 5th Street, Eugene ☎ 541-484-0383 ✐ www.5stmarket.com
This market has an impressive collection of shops and galleries
in a charming indoor/outdoor setting. Boutiques boasting local
artwork and funky shops full of handmade items and clothing
make this a fabulous, eclectic shopping destination.

SATURDAY MARKET

✉ 76 West Broadway; Kitty-corner from 8th and Oak streets, Eugene ☎ 541-
686-8885 ℡ 541-338-4248 ✐ www.eugenesaturdaymarket.org, info@eugene
saturdaymarket.org Eugene's open-air marketplace is held weekly
from April through November, with more than 200 vendors selling handcrafted items, from clothing and jewelry to pottery and
more. There is also a farmer's market, an international food
court and live music. Holiday Market is held at the Lane County
Fairgrounds weekends from mid-November to Christmas Eve.

UNIVERSITY OF OREGON MUSEUM STORE ✉ 1680 East 15th Avenue, Eugene ☎ 541-346-3024 If you're searching for rocks and minerals,
American Indian art or books on Northwest natural history, head for
this store. Open Wednesday through Sunday afternoons.

NIGHTLIFE

HULT CENTER FOR THE PERFORMING ARTS ✉ Eugene Center,
corner of 7th Avenue and Willamette Street, Eugene ☎ 541-682-5000, 541-682-5746
℡ 541-682-2700 ✐ www.hultcenter.org The Hult Center is the home of the
summer Oregon Bach Festival, Oregon Mozart Players, Eugene Concert Choir, Eugene's symphony, opera and ballet, as well as visiting
artists from around the world. Performances take place in four different
venues, ranging from the 4000-seat Cathbert Amphitheater to the 225-
seat The Studio.

UNIVERSITY THEATRE ✉ Villard Hall, University of Oregon, Eugene ☎ 541-
346-4363 ℡ 541-346-1978 ✐ www.uoregon.edu/~theatre This theater stages full-
scale productions in the Robinson Theatre and smaller plays in the
Arena Theatre.

VERY LITTLE THEATER ✉ 2350 Hilyard Street, Eugene ☎ 541-344-7751
✐ www.thevlt.com Staging five productions a year, this "very little"
company is considered one of the best community theaters in the
Eugene area.

10 HEART OF OREGON EUGENE AREA NIGHTLIFE

ACTORS CABARET OF EUGENE ✉*996 Willamette Street, Eugene* ☎*541-683-4368* ✐*www.actorscabaret.org* The Actors Cabaret presents Broadway and off-Broadway comedies, dramas and musicals.

W.O.W. HALL ✉*291 West 8th Avenue, Eugene* ☎*541-687-2746* ✐*www.wow hall.org* An old standby for live reggae, rock, and folk shows is this 400-person venue and beer garden. Shows here are sponsored by the Community Center for the Performing Arts.

Bridging the Past

Oregon takes pride in the fact that it has more covered bridges (53) than any other state west of the Mississippi. Most of these wooden spans are found in the Willamette Valley, although a handful are scattered along the coast, in the Cascades, the Ashland–Rogue River area and around Bend. Although some have been retired and now serve only pedestrians and cyclists, all these bridges are worth a special trip.

Originally the idea of covering a bridge was to protect its plank deck and trusses from the elements. But aesthetics eventually proved as important as engineering, and Oregon's beautiful hooded spans became one of the state's signature attractions.

Highly recommended is the Calapooia River's **Crawfordsville Bridge** (Route 228) east of Brownsville. Clustered around the nearby agricultural communities of Crabtree and Scio are many other "kissing bridges" such as **Shimanek**, **Larwood** and **Hannah**. To the south, Lane County is home to 18 covered bridges, all listed on the National Register of Historic Places. The Lowell area, on Route 58 southeast of Eugene, has four spans, including the **Lowell Bridge**, which crosses a river later flooded to create a lake. Other bridges are at **Pengra**, **Unity** and **Parvin**. A highlight in the Cottage Grove area is **Chambers Bridge**, the only "roofed" railroad bridge on the West Coast. In the same region, south of Dorena Reservoir, is **Dorena Bridge**. Other covered bridges in the same area are found at **Mosby Creek** and **Currin**.

Douglas County has a number of fine spans. One is **Mott Bridge**, 22 miles east of Glide. Constructed in the 1930s, this on-deck wood-truss arch bridge may be the only bridge of its type in the country. The **Rochester Bridge** (County Road 10A) west of Sutherlin is also historic. After county highway workers burned down a bridge in the late 1950s, residents feared the beloved Rochester nearby was destined for the same fate. Armed with shotguns, they kept an all-night vigil and saved the span.

Take the time to visit **Weddle Bridge** in Sweet Home. In 1987, after 43 years of service, it was damaged but, thanks to strong protests, the county wisely decided to take the bridge apart piece by piece and put it in storage. Donations and promotions raised $190,000 to reassemble the bridge, originally built in 1937 for $8500.

Great guides include *Roofs over Rivers* (Oregon Sentinel Publishing) by Bill and Nick Cockrell and *Oregon Covered Bridges: An Oregon Documentary in Pictures* (Pacific Northwest Book Company) by Bert and Margie Webber. Or contact the **Covered Bridge Society of Oregon** (503-399-0436).

ALLANN BROTHERS COFFEE HOUSE

✉ *152 5th Street, Eugene* ✆ *541-342-3378, 800-926-6886* ✎ *541-342-4255*
🖰 *www.allannbroscoffee.com* Allann Brothers occasionally hosts live Friday or Saturday night performances, including zydeco, blues, salsa, jazz, folk and classical trios.

STEELHEAD BREWERY & CAFÉ ✉ *199 East 5th Avenue, Eugene* ✆ *541-686-2739* ✎ *541-342-5338* One of Eugene's premier brewpubs is the Steelhead, which has a handsome brick interior filled with large palms and ficus trees, marble tables and a mahogany bar. The pub offers cable sports stations, beers from the adjoining microbrewery and a casual menu.

JO FEDERIGO'S CAFÉ & JAZZ BAR ✉ *259 East 5th Avenue, Eugene* ✆ *541-343-8488* 🖰 *www.jofederigos.com* For jazz, try Jo Federigo's. An intimate cellar setting with hanging plants, fans and modern art provides the background for some of the region's finest musicians. Cover.

PARKS

BROWNSVILLE PIONEER PARK

✉ *Take Route 5 north from Eugene 22 miles to Route 228 and continue east four miles.*
An alternative scenic loop heads north from Springfield via Mohawk, Marcola and Crawfordsville. ✆ *541-466-5666* ✎ *541-466-5118* 🖰 *www.ci.brownsville.or.us/park*
🏃 🚶 ⛵ The forested, 26-acre city park along the banks of the Calapooia River is a short walk from the center of a historic Willamette Valley community. There are big playfields, horseshoe pits, shady glens and a spacious picnic area with picnic tables and restrooms.
▲ Permitted, though there are no formal sites; $10 per night for tents, $15 per night for RVs. Campgrounds are closed mid-October to mid-April.

HENDRICKS PARK AND RHODODENDRON GARDEN

✉ *Located at the east end of Summit Avenue, Eugene* ✆ *541-682-5324*
✎ *541-682-6834*
🏃 🚲 A glorious springtime spot when over 6000 rhododendrons and azaleas brighten the landscape. An expansive native plant garden is also on view. The 78-acre park is shaded by Oregon white oaks and Douglas fir. There are picnic tables, restrooms, trails and occasional Sunday tours year-round (call ahead).

ASHLAND– ROGUE RIVER AREA

If your vision of a good vacation is river rafting by day and Shakespeare by night, look no further. With the Klamath-Siskiyou mountains providing a rugged backdrop, this section of southern Oregon supports an

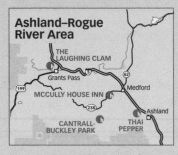

Ashland–Rogue River Area

THE LAUGHING CLAM
Grants Pass
MCCULLY HOUSE INN
Medford
Ashland
CANTRALL-BUCKLEY PARK
THAI PEPPER

THE LAUGHING CLAM
PAGE 510

Charming spot for classic clam chowder, or try the Seafood Mama—shrimp, scallops and clams on lemon linguine

MCCULLY HOUSE INN
PAGE 508

Immaculate 19th-century home where a grandfather clock sounds hourly and wine is served fireside

CANTRALL-BUCKLEY PARK
PAGE 515

Tucked-away park on a wooded hillside with picturesque views of farms along the Applegate River

THAI PEPPER
PAGE 511

Green and yellow curries served on a shady creekside patio, perfect on a warm summer evening

array of fun activities: river rafting, downhill skiing, and, yes, the West Coast's best Shakespeare festival. Home of the largest concentration of bed and breakfasts in Oregon, Ashland is also your gateway to backcountry famous for its hidden gems.

The wild and scenic Rogue River is one of Oregon's signature attractions. It is also convenient to wilderness areas, mountain lakes, thundering waterfalls, marble caves and popular resort communities.

SIGHTS

GRANTS PASS VISITORS CENTER ✉ *1995 Northwest Vine Street at 6th Street, Grants Pass* ✆ *541-476-5510* ✇ *541-476-9574* ✐ *www.visitgrantspass.org, vcb@visitgrantspass.org* A good place to orient yourself is this visitors center. Closed weekends from September through May.

WILDLIFE IMAGES

✉ *11845 Lower River Road, Grants Pass* ✆ *541-476-0222* ✇ *541-476-2444* ✐ *www.wildlifeimages.org, gifts@wildlifeimages.org* Each year more than 1500 injured animals are nursed back to health by veterinary staff and volunteers at this fascinating animal rehabilitation center. Among the creatures you can see being treated are owls, eagles, black bears and cougars. Highly recommended. Daily tours are offered by appointment.

POTTSVILLE POWERLAND ____ **h**idden

✉*Pleasant Valley Road west of Monument Drive, Pleasant Valley* ☎*541-479-2981* Pottsville Powerland has a vintage collection of tractors, farm and logging equipment, antique cars and fire trucks. A fair on Father's Day weekend features music, food, arts and crafts. It's five miles north of Grants Pass.

BRIDGEVIEW VINEYARDS ✉*4210 Holland Loop Road, Cave Junction* ☎*541-592-4688, 877-273-4843* ✒*541-592-2127* ✑*www.bridgeviewwine.com, bvw@bridgeviewwine.com* Although it's far from the core of Oregon's wine country, Bridgeview is attracting a loyal following. Situated on 74 acres in the Illinois Valley, this European-style winery offers tastings. Try the gewürztraminer, chardonnay, merlot, pinot gris, pinot noir or riesling.

OREGON CAVES NATIONAL MONUMENT ✉*19000 Caves Highway, Cave Junction* ☎*541-592-2100 ext. 262* ✑*www.nps.gov/orca* This is the Pacific Northwest's grandest spelunking adventure. Fifty miles southwest of Grants Pass, it's reached by taking Route 199 to Cave Junction and then turning south on Route 46. Hourly guided tours are led through the cave, which has over three miles of damp and dripping passageways lined with stalagmites, flowstone, translucent draperies and cave coral. Wear sturdy walking shoes that you don't mind getting muddy and a jacket—the caves are a constant 43°F. The tour is not recommended for those with respiratory or heart problems. To avoid the summer crowds at Oregon Caves National Monument, arrive when the park opens at 9 a.m. If you can't make it before 11 a.m., your best bet is to visit after 4 p.m. for a late afternoon tour. Closed December through March. Admission.

JACKSONVILLE Southeast of Grants Pass is this 19th-century mining town that has clung to its legendary frontier tradition. The entire town has been designated a National Historic Landmark with over 100 historic homes, stores and public buildings. Stop at the **Jacksonville Visitor's Center and Chamber of Commerce** (185 North Oregon Street, Jacksonville; 541-899-8118; www.jacksonvilleoregon.org, chamber@jacksonvilleoregon.org) to pick up a walking-tour map of the town's treelined streets. Closed Sunday in winter.

JACKSONVILLE MUSEUM OF SOUTHERN OREGON HISTORY ✉*206 North 5th Street, Jacksonville* ☎*541-773-6536* ✒*541-776-7994* ✑*www.sohs.org, publicrelations@sohs.org* Among the exhibits here are gold-mining artifacts and a large-scale exhibit about the life of Peter Britt, pioneer photographer and Renaissance man of Jacksonville. In the same complex is the **Children's Museum**. Kids, take your parents to this former jail filled with "please touch" exhibits, including a miniature kitchen, an 1890s general store and an American Indian lodge. Closed Monday and Tuesday.

Ashland–Rogue River Area

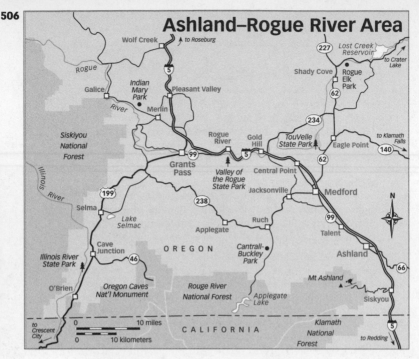

C. BEEKMAN HOUSE ✉ *Laurelwood and California Streets east of Beekman Square, Jacksonville* ✆ *541-773-6536* ✆ *541-776-7994* ✎ *www.sohs.org, info@sohs.org* **California Street**, the heart of Jacksonville, is a step back in time. The graceful balustraded brick buildings have been lovingly restored. Worth a visit is this gothic house. The living history tour re-creates the lifestyle of the rich and famous, circa 1876. Along the way you see banker Beekman's carved oak bedframe, overstuffed furniture, lap desk and summer kitchen. Nearby at California and 3rd streets, visit the **Beekman Bank**, one of the first buildings in Jacksonville to be restored. Open the first weekends of the month from June to September. Admission.

APPLEGATE VALLEY   Route 238, southwest of Jacksonville, leads to this picturesque valley, a two-mile-wide, fifty-mile-long canyon with memorable views and few tourists. After reaching the town of Applegate you can continue south on Applegate Road to the foot of the Siskiyous. Alternatively, Little Applegate and Anderson Creek roads loop back to Route 99.

HARRY AND DAVID'S ORIGINAL COUNTRY VILLAGE ✉ *1314 Center Drive, Medford* ✆ *541-864-2277, 877-322-8000* Located about ten miles east of Jacksonville via Route 238, **Medford** is by far the largest city in the vicinity of Ashland and the Rogue River. A much-frequented stop in the area is Harry and David's, famous for the gift packs it ships nationwide. The store has a fruit stand, gourmet pantry and gift shop. Weekday tours of the packinghouse depart from the gift store.

MEDFORD VISITORS & CONVENTION BUREAU ✉ *101 East 8th Street, Medford* 📞 *541-779-4847, 800-469-6307* 📠 *541-776-4808* 🖥 *www.visitmedford. org, vcb@visitmedford.org* This visitors bureau is an excellent source of information on southern Oregon.

SOUTHERN OREGON HISTORICAL SOCIETY'S HISTORY CENTER

✉ *206 North Central Avenue, Medford* 📞 *541-773-6536* 📠 *541-776-7994* 🖥 *www.sohs.org, publicrelations@sohs.org* This history center has an extensive collection of Jackson County artifacts as well as a large photography exhibit and research library. Nonmember admission.

BUTTE CREEK MILL ✉ *402 Royal Avenue North, Eagle Point* 📞 *541-826-3531* 📠 *541-830-8444* 🖥 *www.buttecreekmill.com, Info@buttecreekmill.com* Ten miles north of Medford off Route 62, this mill has been producing stoneground products since 1872. Occasionally you may see the miller grinding wheat, rye and corn on giant white stones quarried in France, assembled in Illinois, shipped around the Horn to California and finally brought over the Siskiyous by wagon.

ASHLAND While Ashland is best known for the Oregon Shakespeare Festival, theater is not the only thing here. From shopping to restaurants to biking, this city offers plenty of diversions. Home to more bed and breakfasts than any other city in the state, Ashland has strict zoning controls that protect the architectural landscape.

ASHLAND CHAMBER OF COMMERCE ✉ *110 East Main Street, Ashland* 📞 *541-482-3486* 📠 *541-482-2350* 🖥 *www.ashlandchamber.com, dana@ashlandchamber.com* To explore the possibilities, stop by the local chamber of commerce. A good place to begin your visit is the downtown plaza and verdant Lithia Park (see "Parks" below).

OREGON SHAKESPEARE FESTIVAL ✉ *15 South Pioneer Street, Ashland* 📞 *541-482-4331* 📠 *541-482-8045* 🖥 *www.osfashland.org, boxoffice@osfashland. org* Across the street from the chamber of commerce is the headquarters for this festival and its fascinating **Backstage Theatre Tour**. The excellent behind-the-scenes program is a helpful introduction to stagecraft and the history of the OSF. Members of the theater company guide you through this 90-minute look at the dramatic arts. No tours Monday. Closed November to mid-February. Admission.

MOUNTAIN LAKES Most people come to Ashland for the plays, but the mountain lakes east of town are a tempting day trip. Take Route 5 north and pick up Route 140 east to Dead Indian Road. Turn south to the first and most picturesque of these retreats, **Lake of the Woods**, an ideal place for a picnic, swimming or sunbathing. Continue southeast to **Howard Prairie Reservoir** and **Hyatt Reservoir**, both popular for water sports and fishing. Return to Dead Indian Road for the cliffhanging descent back into Ashland, an entrance that rivals anything you're likely to see on the Elizabethan stage.

WOLF CREEK INN

$–$$ 9 ROOMS   ✉*100 Front Street, Wolf Creek*   📞*541-866-2474*
📠*541-866-2692* ⌨*www.thewolfcreekinn.com, wolfcreek.info@state.or.us*

An 1880s stage stop, Wolf Creek now operates as a state historic property. The handsomely restored inn offers nine guest rooms with private baths. You'll find antiques, old photographs and brass beds in the medium-sized rooms. There's an on-site restaurant, and full breakfast is included in your stay. You can also see the room where Jack London stayed on his visit here. Closed Monday through Wednesday.

RIVERSIDE INN

$$–$$$ 63 ROOMS   ✉*986 Southwest 6th Street, Grants Pass*   📞*541-476-6873,*
800-334-4567 📠*541-474-9848* ⌨*www.riverside-inn.com, info@riverside-inn.com*

This is the largest motel in town with an enviable location on the Rogue River across from Riverside Park. Most of the 63 rooms have private balconies overlooking the river; some have fireplaces. There is a beauty salon and a full-service conference center, plus a swimming pool and spa. A Rogue jet-boat dock is next door, and there is some highway noise from the bridge traffic.

OREGON CAVES CHATEAU

$$–$$$ 23 ROOMS   ✉*20000 Caves Highway, Cave Junction*   📞*541-592-3400,*
877-245-9022 📠*541-592-5021* ⌨*www.oregoncavesoutfitters.com, caves@cavenet.com*

In a wooded glen surrounded by waterfalls, this chateau is an ideal place to spend the night after a visit to the Oregon Caves National Monument. Faced with cedar shakes, this National Historic Landmark has two big marble fireplaces framed with fir timbers in the lobby. Moderate-sized rooms with 1930s furnishings offer forest and pond views in this serene setting. Groups only from November through April.

JACKSONVILLE INN

$$$–$$$$ 12 UNITS   ✉*175 East California Street, Jacksonville*   📞*541-899-1900,*
800-321-9344 📠*541-899-1373* ⌨*www.jacksonvilleinn.com, info@jacksonvilleinn.com*

This historic red-brick inn offers eight nicely restored rooms with oak-frame beds, quilts, wall-to-wall carpets, antiques, gas-style lamps and floral-print wallpaper. The inn also has four honeymoon cottages, featuring king beds, fireplaces, jacuzzis and steam showers, located on a separate property. Full breakfast included.

MCCULLY HOUSE INN

$$$ 3 ROOMS   ✉*240 East California Street, Jacksonville*   📞*541-899-1942,*
800-367-1942 📠*541-899-1560* ⌨*www.mccullycountryhouseinn.com,*
ryan@mccullycountryhouseinn.com

Convenient to downtown Jacksonville, the McCully House is a charming 19th-century home where a grandfather clock sounds the hour and guests sip wine around the fireplace. This immaculate white house has hardwood floors, painted friezes on the walls and three rooms big on lace, walnut furniture and clawfoot tubs. The adjacent restaurant serves breakfast to all guests.

UNDER THE GREENWOOD TREE BED AND BREAKFAST INN

$$ 5 ROOMS   ✉ *3045 Bellinger Lane, Medford* ☎ *541-776-0000*
✍ *www.greenwoodtree.com, utgtree@quest.net*

Take an 1862 country estate, complete with a three-story barn, add a redwood deck, an English garden with 140 rose bushes and an orchard with hammocks and what do you get? Under the Greenwood Tree Bed and Breakfast Inn. Overfurnished with Persian rugs, Chippendale and chintz, this is the place for travelers who want to wind down with a full afternoon tea and pluck a truffle off their freshly ironed pillow before climbing into bed. Five rooms have queen beds and private baths. A gourmet three-course, farm-fresh breakfast is included.

ARDEN FOREST INN

$$$ 5 ROOMS   ✉ *261 West Hersey Street, Ashland* ☎ *541-488-1496, 800-460-3912*
🖨 *541-488-4071* ✍ *www.afinn.com, aforest@afinn.com*

Choose one of the Bard's works from the library and wander out to the lush gardens that surround this inn. Nestle into a secluded spot and catch up on the play you're about to see at the Shakespeare Festival. The inn also has fine views of Mt. Ashland and Grizzly Peak. Two rooms in the main house and three in the carriage house feature tasteful, comfortable furnishings; some have mountain or garden views, others have private patios. A heated pool rounds out the amenities. The two-course gourmet breakfast is a delight. Gay-owned and gay-friendly. Closed November through mid-February.

ASHLAND CREEK INN

$$$ 10 UNITS   ✉ *70 Water Street, Ashland* ☎ *541 482 3315*
✍ *www.ashlandcreekinn.com, reservations@ashlandcreekinn.com*

Tour the world at this inn, where you can "visit" New Mexico, Marrakesh or Japan, depending on which internationally themed suite you choose. All ten suites include private entrances, baths, kitchenettes and decks. Full breakfast included.

COLUMBIA HOTEL

$$ 24 ROOMS   ✉ *262-1/2 East Main Street, Ashland* ☎ *541-482-3726,*
800-718-2530 ✍ *www.columbiahotel.com*

Reached via a redwood staircase, the Columbia is a comfortable European-style inn. Rooms are furnished with brass beds, floral-print drapes, fans and wall-to-wall carpet. Some provide views of downtown and the surrounding mountains. Guests share a bathroom; suites with private baths are available.

THE VILLAGE SUITES AT ASHLAND HILLS

$$ 66 UNITS ✉2525 Ashland Street, Ashland ☎541-482-8310, 800-547-4747
📠541-488-1783 🖳www.windmillinns.com

The two-bedroom suites here are standard, but comfortable with floral prints and potted plants. A fitness room, free wi-fi and a continental breakfast delivered each morning are welcome amenities.

CEDARWOOD INN OF ASHLAND

$$–$$$ 59 ROOMS ✉1801 Siskiyou Boulevard, Ashland ☎541-488-2000,
800-547-4141 📠541-482-2000 🖳www.brodeur-inns.com/cedarwood

The Cedarwood is one of several modern motels found south of downtown. Choose between rooms with kings or queens and courtyard family units with kitchens and decks. All rooms have contemporary oak furniture. Pools, saunas and barbecue facilities are available.

For information on Ashland bed and breakfasts, and other inns across Oregon, check out **The Oregon Bed and Breakfast Guild** (www.obbg. org). You may also contact **Ashland's Bed and Breakfast Network** (800-944-0329; www.abbnet.com).

DINING

THE LAUGHING CLAM

$$–$$$ SEAFOOD ✉121 Southwest G Street, Grants Pass
☎541-479-1110

Clam chowder is the staple here. Stop by for lunch or dinner and choose from sandwiches, large salads, fresh seafood and pasta (including the Seafood Mama—shrimp, scallops and clams in a cream sauce over lemon linguine), and steak.

OREGON CAVES CHATEAU RESTAURANT

$$–$$$ AMERICAN ✉20000 Caves Highway, Cave Junction ☎541-592-3400
🖳www.oregoncavesoutfitters.com, caves@cavenet.com

Traversing a stream, this restaurant offers steaks, seafood, chicken and pasta dishes for dinner in the formal dining room. There's also a 1930s-style budget-priced soda fountain. Scores of patrons seated on red stools enjoy sundaes, omelettes, french toast, salads, deli sandwiches and hamburgers. Don't miss this knotty-pine-paneled classic. Closed November through mid-May.

JACKSONVILLE INN

$$$–$$$$ SEAFOOD/STEAK ✉175 East California Street, Jacksonville
☎541-899-1900 🖳www.jacksonvilleinn.com, info@jacksonvilleinn.com

Breakfast, lunch, dinner and Sunday brunch are served in this restored 19th-century Ryan and Morgan general-store building. The dimly lit, brick-walled dining room with red carpets and tablecloths creates a great setting for vast, seven-course dinners or à la carte dishes. A large menu features Oregon cuisine, including pan-seared prawns with feta cheese, razor clams, scallops, prime rib and vegetarian dishes. The wine list is endless. Open for Sunday brunch. No lunch on Monday.

GARDEN BISTRO AT MCCULLY HOUSE INN

$$–$$$ PACIFIC NORTHWEST ✉240 East California Street, Jacksonville
✆541-899-1942, 800-367-1942 ✎541-899-1560
⌨www.mccullycountryhouseinn.com, ryan@mccullycountryhouseinn.com

For patio dining, it's hard to beat the Garden Bistro. Seasonal entrées served outside or in one of the lovely dining rooms may include mango-glazed salmon, tequila lime prawns and whiskey-peppered New York steak. You'll find Oregon wildflowers on every table. Closed Sunday and Monday.

BELLA UNION

$$–$$$ AMERICAN ✉170 West California Street, Jacksonville ✆541-899-1770
✎541-899-3919 ⌨www.bellau.com, greatfood@bellau.com

Phoenix-like, this restaurant has risen from the ashes of one of Jacksonville's best-loved 19th-century saloons. Like its predecessor, this establishment is an important social center. On the menu you'll find pizza, seafood, pasta and sandwiches. You have your choice of several noisy dining rooms or the more serene heated patio out back. Open for Sunday brunch.

WINCHESTER COUNTRY INN

$$$ PACIFIC NORTHWEST ✉35 South 2nd Street, Ashland ✆541-488-1113,
800-972-4991 ⌨www.winchesterinn.com, innkeeper@thewinchesterinn.com

On a warm evening, the garden patio at the Winchester is an ideal place to enjoy a rich, leisurely meal. Temptations here include grilled wild salmon with corn and blueberry salsa, seared duck breast with huckleberry cream sauce, filet mignon and lamb *du jour*. For dessert, try the award-winning bread pudding. This opulent Victorian, surrounded by a colorful garden, also has gazebo seating and a dining room decorated in burgundy tones with accents of blue. Dinner and Sunday brunch.

GEPPETTO'S

$$ ITALIAN/AMERICAN ✉345 East Main Street, Ashland ✆541-482-1138
⌨www.geppettosrestaurant.com, dan@ashlanddirectory.net

Whether you choose a seat at the counter or one of the glass-paneled booths, you'll find this country-casual dining room a comfortable place to enjoy Italian and Ashland cuisine like linguine, five-spice chicken, steak, prawns and snapper. Try the fresh fruit pies. Breakfast, lunch and dinner.

THAI PEPPER

$–$$ THAI ✉84 North Main Street, Ashland ✆541-482-8058

Looking for Asian cuisine served at a creekside setting? Step into this romantic gray-walled dining room, take a seat on the wicker furniture and order such dishes as green chicken curry, yellow shrimp curry and crispy fish served with cold Singha beer. But your best bet, especially on a warm evening, is a seat on the shady patio next to the creek. Dinner only in winter.

CHATÊAULIN RESTAURANT

$$$–$$$$ FRENCH   ✉ 50 East Main Street, Ashland   ☎ 541-482-2264
🖳 www.chateaulin.com, doss@chateaulin.com

A French bistro with stained-glass windows and dark wood-booths illuminated by Tiffany-style lamps, Chatêaulin prepares such dishes as *crêpe Mediterranées*, pan-roasted duck breast and filet mignon *au poivre verte*. Closed Monday and Tuesday from October through June.

ALEX'S PLAZA RESTAURANT

$$–$$$ AMERICAN   ✉ 35 North Main Street, Ashland   ☎ 541-482-8818
🖳 www.alexsrestaurantandbar.com, info@alexsrestaurantandbar.com

Alex's has a good house pizza with your choice of two toppings. Also on the menu are a vegetarian pasta with portobello mushrooms, seafood stew, New York steak and rack of lamb. Located in the first brick building built following the disastrous 1879 downtown fire, this second-story dining room still has its original fir floors. It's flanked by patios.

GREENLEAF RESTAURANT — **h**idden

$$ MEDITERRANEAN   ✉ 49 North Main Street, Ashland   ☎ 541-482-2808
🖳 www.greenleafrestaurant.com, daniel@greenleafrestaurant.com

Mediterranean, Italian and vegetarian fare served in a creekside setting make this restaurant worth a visit. Specialties may include breakfast dishes like mushroom frittatas and tofu scrambles. For lunch or dinner, try pasta primavera, fruit salad or red snapper. An excellent choice for to-go fare, they will also prepare picnic baskets. Closed the month of January.

BROTHER'S RESTAURANT AND DELICATESSEN

$–$$ AMERICAN   ✉ 95 North Main Street, Ashland   ☎ 541-482-9671
🖳 www.brothersrestaurant.net

Brother's has an eclectic menu including shrimp omelettes, *huevos rancheros*, bagels and lox, and caesar and Greek salads. There's also a variety of vegetarian options. The carpeted, wood-paneled dining room with indoor balcony seating puts Brother's a cut above your average deli. Breakfast and lunch only.

SHOPPING

THREAD HYSTERIA ✉ 19 North Main Street, Ashland ☎ 541-488-3982 This shop stocks new name-brand clothing and accessories at discount prices.

BLOOMSBURY BOOKS ✉ 290 East Main Street, Ashland ☎ 541-488-0029 📠 541-488-2942 As befits a town dedicated to Shakespeare, Ashland's Main Street is lined with bookstores, including Bloomsbury, which is a good source for regional books and newspapers. Coffee and espresso drinks are served in an upstairs café.

TUDOR GUILD GIFT SHOP ✉ 15 South Pioneer Street, Ashland ☎ 541-482-0940 📠 541-488-4708 🖳 www.tudorguild.org, tudorguild@tudorguild.org Adjacent to the Elizabethan Theatre, this shop sells all the Bard's works, as well as

Oregon Shakespeare Festival merchandise, gifts, educational books, jewelry and toys with a dramatic flair. Limited hours during the festival's off-season, from November through early February; call ahead.

THE NORTHWEST NATURE SHOP ✉*154 Oak Street, Ashland* ☎*541-482-3241* This is a wonderful place to shop for birdhouses, minerals, wind chimes, hiking maps and nature and travel books. In a Craftsman-style house near downtown, this shop has a good selection of nature-oriented children's games.

NIGHTLIFE

BRITT FESTIVALS ✉*Britt Pavilion, Jacksonville* ☎*541-773-6077, 800-882-7488* ✍*www.brittfest.org, info@brittfest.org* This concert series offers classical, jazz, folk, dance, blues, bluegrass, world, pop and country music performances from mid-June to mid-September. Headliners such as Jewel, Brad Paisley and B.B. King make this event a worthy companion to the nearby Oregon Shakespeare Festival. At this outdoor theater, you can choose between lawn and reserved seating in the natural setting of the historic Britt estate.

THE OREGON SHAKESPEARE FESTIVAL ✉*15 South Pioneer Street, Ashland* ☎*541-482-4331, 800-219-8161* 📠*541-482-8045* ✍*www.osfashland.org, box office@osfashland.org* The nation's oldest and largest regional repertory theater, Oregon's Shakespeare fest attracts more than 120,000 people each season. The most popular venue is the **Elizabethan Theatre**, which stages plays from June through October. Prior to evening shows at the Elizabethan, the Green Show Renaissance Musicians and Dancers offer free half-hour performances in the Oregon Shakespeare courtyard. The indoor **Angus Bowmer Theatre** also presents Shakespearian performances, as well as classics by Shaw and Wilder and contemporary playwrights. Both new and classic works are presented at the **New Theatre**. The season runs from mid-February to late October. Advance reservations are strongly recommended in peak season.

OREGON CABARET THEATRE ✉*1st and Hargadine streets, Ashland* ☎*541-488-2902* 📠*541-488-8795* ✍*www.oregoncabaret.com, info@oregoncabaret.com* This cabaret theater holds professional productions, including musicals, revues and comedies in a renovated church with table seating on the tiered main floor and in the balcony. Dinner theater also available.

SISKIYOU PUB ✉*31-B Water Street, Ashland* ☎*541-482-7718* ✍*info@siskiyou pub.com* The Siskiyou features a deck overlooking Lithia Creek, 15 brews on tap and live entertainment. Bands of all kinds play on various nights. Occasional cover.

PARKS

VALLEY OF THE ROGUE STATE PARK
✉*Off Route 5, 12 miles east of Grants Pass* ☎*541-582-1118* 📠*541-582-1312*

🚶 🚴 ⚓ 🛶 🎣 This 316-acre park on the Rogue River is convenient to the Grants Pass Area. Near the interstate, it's central to many rafting operators. Trout, steelhead and chinook salmon are caught in the

Rogue River. The grassy, mile-long riverfront park is shaded by madrone, black locust and oak. Facilities include picnic areas and restrooms.

▲ There are 21 tent sites ($12 to $16 per night), 147 RV hookup sites ($16 to $20 per night) and 6 yurts ($27 per night). Showers are available. Reservations: 800-452-5687.

BEN HUR LAMPMAN WAYSIDE

✉ *Off Route 5, 16 miles east of Grants Pass* ☎ *541-582-1118* 🖷 *541-582-1312*

On the south bank of the Rogue River opposite Gold Hill, the 23-acre wayside park is named for the late Ben Hur Lampman, a popular Oregon newspaper editor, fisherman and poet laureate. Emulate his fishing prowess by angling for trout and steelhead in the Rogue. The river attracts swimmers as well, though no lifeguards oversee the area. Day-use only.

INDIAN MARY PARK

✉ *From Grants Pass take Route 5 north to the Merlin exit. Continue west ten miles on Merlin-Galice Road.* ☎ *541-474-5285* 🖷 *541-474-5288*

This half-mile-long park on the Rogue River west of Merlin is another ideal retreat for the entire family. Kids can play on the sandy beach or enjoy themselves at the playground. If you're towing a boat or raft, you can launch it here. You can also fish from the beach. You'll find picnic areas, restrooms, playgrounds and a sand volleyball court.

▲ There are 36 tent sites ($19 per night), 56 RV hookup sites ($20 per night) and two yurts ($30 per night). Reservations: 800-452-5687; www. reserveamerica.com.

LAKE SELMAC

✉ *Located 2.3 miles east of Selma via Upper Deer Creek Road* ☎ *541-474-5285* 🖷 *541-474-5288*

A large Illinois Valley lake convenient to the Grants Pass area, this is a popular summer resort. The 160-acre lake near Selma is a good choice for fishing (trout, bass and crappie), canoeing and sailing. The waters here tend to be warmer than the nearby rivers. Facilities include a playground, picnic area, day-use park, disc golf course and horse corrals.

▲ There are 53 tent sites ($17 per night), 36 RV hookup sites ($20 per night) and one yurt ($28 per night). Reservations: 800-452-5687; www. reserveamerica.com.

ILLINOIS RIVER STATE PARK

✉ *Route 199, one mile south of Cave Junction* ☎ *541-582-1118, 800-551-6949* 🖷 *541-582-1312*

The largely undeveloped 511-acre day-use park at the junction of the east and west forks of the Illinois River is a secluded spot perfect for trout and steelhead fishing and birdlife and wildlife viewing. You'll find picnic tables and restrooms.

▲ Permitted in nearby U.S. Forest Service campgrounds in the Illinois Valley. Among them are Grayback and Cave Creek campgrounds (541-592-4000), respectively 12 and 16 miles east of Cave Junction on Oregon

Caves Highway. Grayback has 39 tent sites ($16 per night); Cave Creek has 18 tent sites ($16 per night). Closed October through April.

TOUVELLE STATE RECREATION SITE

✉ *Take Route 62 nine miles north of Medford to Table Rock Road.* ☏ *541-582-1118, 800-551-6949* 📠 *541-582-1312*

🚶 ⚓ 🛥 🐟 ⚲ The 54-acre day-use facility is adjacent to Table Rock, an 1890-acre biologic, geologic and historic preserve forested with Pacific madrone, white oak and ponderosa pine. In the park you can swim or fish for salmon and trout. Facilities include picnic tables, restrooms and wildlife viewing platforms. Parking fee, $4.

CANTRALL-BUCKLEY PARK

✉ *Take Route 238 eight miles southwest from Jacksonville and turn left on Hamilton Road.* ☏ *541-774-8183* 📠 *541-774-6320*

🚶 ⚓ ⚲ Just eight miles southwest of Jacksonville on a wooded hillside above the Applegate Valley, Cantrall-Buckley extends half a mile along the inviting Applegate River and offers beautiful views of this farming region. Swimmers head to the small cove, while anglers try for trout in the river. There are picnic areas, barbecue pits, showers and restrooms. Parking fee, $4.

⚑ There are 30 primitive sites ($12 per night). Closed October 16 through April 14.

ROGUE ELK PARK

✉ *Route 62, eight miles north of Shady Cove* ☏ *541-776-7001* 📠 *541-774-6320*
✎ *parksinfo@jacksoncounty.org*

⚓ 🛥 🐟 ⚲ The nearly mile-long park on the Rogue includes a warm creek ideal for swimming, and the kids can swing out into the river Tarzan-style on a rope hanging from an oak limb. There's good rafting and fishing (steelhead and trout) in the Rogue. Shade trees make this park a good choice on warm days, and an ideal stopover en route to Crater Lake. You'll find picnic tables, restrooms and showers. Day-use fee, $4.

⚑ There are 22 tent sites ($18 per night) and 15 RV hookup sites ($22 per night). Closed mid-October to mid-April.

LITHIA PARK

✉ *59 Winburn Way; On the south side of the Ashland Plaza in Ashland* ☏ *541-488-5340, 800-735-2900* 📠 *541-488-5314*

🚶 ⚓ A beautiful place to walk or jog, this park was originally designed by John McLaren, the creator of Golden Gate Park in San Francisco. This 93-acre urban forest is filled with towering maples, black oaks, sycamore, sequoia, bamboo, European beech and flowering catalpa. Also here are a Japanese garden, rose garden and two duck ponds. Facilities include picnic tables, fire pits, a playground, a tennis court, a swimming hole, a band shell, a fountain and restrooms.

OUTDOOR ADVENTURES

FISHING

In a Northwest wonderland of sparkling lakes, rivers and mountain streams, it's no surprise that fishing is such a part of the scene. Even novice anglers should try casting a line; they're bound to catch something: fall salmon from coastal rivers and streams in October and November; winter steelhead, from December through March. Spring and summer bring trout (try Detroit Lake, or the McKenzie River for huge rainbow trout) and summer steelhead (the North and South Santiam rivers are the best spots).

Salem Area

BILL KREMERS ✉29606 *Northeast Pheasant Street, Corvallis* ☎541-754-6411, *541-602-8881* 🖉*www.oregonrivertrails.com* This company arranges daily fishing trips on the west side of the Cascades and longer excursions on the Deschutes River.

WHITE WATER WAREHOUSE ✉625 *Northwest Starker Avenue, Corvallis* ☎541-758-3150, 800-214-0579 🖉*www.whitewaterwarehouse.com, fun@whitewater warehouse.com* Camping and rafting trips on the Rogue River from May through October are available through this group. All levels of expertise are welcome.

Eugene River Area

WILDERNESS RIVER OUTFITTERS ✉1567 *Main Street, Springfield* ☎541-726-9471 📠541-726-6474 These outfitters run one-day and overnight fishing trips locally on the Willamette, Umpqua and McKenzie rivers and throughout Oregon. They also have a fly-fishing school, offering a four-day course on the river.

Ashland–Rogue River Area

ROGUE WILDERNESS ADVENTURES ✉325 *Galice Road, Merlin* ☎541-479-9554, 800-336-1647 🖉*www.wildrogue.com* For salmon and steelhead fishing, contact this adventure company, which has specialized in drift-boat fishing since 1970. Trips of one to four days can be arranged.

BRIGGS GUIDE SERVICE ✉1815 *Southwest Bridge Street, Grants Pass* ☎800-845-5091 For a day trip to fish for salmon and steelhead on the Chetco near Brookings, or in the Rogue estuary at Gold Beach, contact this guide service.

RIVER RUNNING

A rafting or kayaking adventure can take you from the wild and scenic whitewater ruggedness of the Rogue River (where some of the rapids are Class III and IV) to an outing on the more gentle Willamette River or one of the local lakes. With dozens of rivers in the foothills surrounding Salem, Eugene and Ashland, you're never far from an enjoyable stretch of river. The North Santiam River near Salem is popular for both its rapids and views of the surrounding woods, while the McKenzie and Willamette near Salem lean more toward the serene than the adventurous. But by far the most popular area is around Ashland. Here the Rogue River offers everything from casual floats to spectacular rapids, like those in Hellgate Canyon. In fact, the Rogue River's Hellgate Canyon—where sheer rock walls rise 250 feet—was the setting for the Meryl Streep film *The River Wild*.

Kayakers should look for a copy of the book *Soggy Sneakers*, a regional guide to kayaking published by the Willamette Kayak and Canoe Club.

OREGON GUIDES & PACKERS ASSOCIATION ✉531 Southwest 13th Street, Bend, OR 97702 ☎800-747-9552 ✐www.ogpa.org, info@ogpa.org One of the best regional resources for outdoor adventurers interested in fishing, hunting and rafting is this association in Eugene. The group publishes an extensive directory of guides and outfitters throughout the state.

Salem Area

WHITE WATER WAREHOUSE ✉625 Northwest Starker Avenue, Corvallis ☎541-758-3150, 800-214-0579 ✐www.whitewaterwarehouse.com This group can set you up with hardshell kayaks, sea kayaks, canoes and rafts. Instruction in whitewater kayaking is also available. The company also runs overnight camp and float trips locally on the Rogue River from May through October.

Eugene Area

WILDERNESS RIVER OUTFITTERS ✉1567 Main Street, Springfield ☎541-726-9471 These outfitters run a moonlit evening float along serene stretches of the Willamette.

Ashland–Rogue River Area

ORANGE TORPEDO TRIPS INC./GRANTS PASS FLOAT CO. ✉210 Merlin Road, Merlin ☎541-479-5061, 866-479-5061 ✐www.orangetorpedo.com Whether you paddle your own kayak or float with a guide, rafting is the ideal way to see the Rogue's wild and scenic sections. Choose between one-day trips and overnight trips. This group specializes in inflatable kayaking, with one-day and multiday whitewater trips on the Rogue, Klamath, Salmon and North Umpqua rivers.

ROGUE WILDERNESS ADVENTURES ✉325 Galice Road, Merlin ☎541-479-9554, 800-336-1647 ✐www.wildrogue.com Contact this company to set up for a one-day, 13-mile scenic adventure in an inflatable kayak or raft. They also arrange longer wilderness trips on the Rogue.

THE ADVENTURE CENTER ✉40 North Main Street, Ashland ☎541-488-2819, 800-444-2819 ✐www.raftingtours.com For a full- or half-day whitewater adventure led by a naturalist along the middle Rogue (water ratings range from Class I to IV), contact this adventure group. Multiday rafting and camping trips are also available on seven rivers. Food, lodging and gear are included.

HELLGATE JETBOAT EXCURSIONS ✉966 Southwest 6th Street, Grants Pass ☎541-479-7204, 800-648-4874 ✐www.hellgate.com, info@hellgate.com Hellgate Excursions will take you through the Rogue River's rugged Hellgate Canyon wilderness on one of several jet-boat tours it operates. They also offer dinner, lunch and brunch trips.

SKIING

Although most of the Heart of Oregon lies in a valley between the Cascades and the Coast Range, the southern section of the Route 5 corridor passes through the Klamath-Siskiyou Mountains.

MT. ASHLAND

✉ *Route 5, Exit 6* ☎ *541-482-2897* 🖱 *www.mtashland.com* Skiers in this area head for Mt. Ashland. At 7500 feet, it's the highest peak in the range and just 18 miles south of Ashland off Route 5. Facilities include a day lodge, rental shop, four lifts and 23 runs. You'll also find ungroomed cross-country trails here.

BALLOON RIDES

VISTA BALLOON ADVENTURES ✉ *Sherwood* ☎ *503-625-7385, 800-622-2309* 🖱 *www.vistaballoon.com, roger@vistaballoon.com* The quiet exhilaration of floating above it all—wine country, the river, rolling farmland—explains why ballooning is popular in the Salem area. From April to November, this company operates one-hour flights over the wine country of Newburg (about 25 minutes north of Salem), followed by a catered breakfast. The company has seven balloons and can fly six to ten passengers in each. If you're the participatory type, you can put on some gloves and help inflate the balloon. Closed Tuesday.

RIDING STABLES

Along the western slopes of the Cascades, within a 30-mile drive of the Willamette Valley, lie some of the most pristine wilderness areas in the state, much of them U.S. Forest Service land. One of the best ways to explore these alpine meadows, old-growth forests and scenic mountain peaks is on a guided day-long or multiday trail ride from a local outfitter. Even if you only have a couple of hours, Mt. Pisgah just outside Eugene provides a good opportunity for a casual ride.

Eugene Area
TRIANGLE 5 RANCH ✉ *39841 McKenzie Highway, Springfield* ☎ *541-747-7039* 🖱 *www.triangle5.com, info@triangle5.com* Rides through the beautiful McKenzie River Valley are available with this family-owned company about 16 miles east of Eugene. Traverse evergreens and oak meadows on a guided trek through these scenic foothills.

GOLF

Public courses in the area offer a variety of landscapes, course lengths, and difficulty ratings.

Salem Area

SALEM GOLF CLUB ✉️ *2025 Golf Course Road South, Salem* 📞 *503-363-6652* 🖥️ *www.salemgolfclub.com* Built in 1928, this is a lush, old-style Northwest course: 18 holes with meandering greens and big old fir trees.

SANTIAM GOLF COURSE ✉️ *8724 Golf Club Road, Aumsville* 📞 *503-769-3485* 🖥️ *www.santiamgolfclub.org* Near Stayton, this private 18-hole course has lots of water and trees and is fairly flat.

Eugene Area

FIDDLER'S GREEN ✉️ *91292 Route 99 North, Eugene* 📞 *541-689-8464* 🖥️ *www.fiddlersgreen.com* The relatively flat 18-hole course is famous for its pro shop.

HIDDEN VALLEY GOLF COURSE ✉️ *775 North River Road, Cottage Grove* 📞 *541-942-3046* The circa-1920 nine-hole golf course here is tucked away in a picturesque little valley and lined with mature fir and oak trees.

Ashland–Rogue River Area

OAK KNOLL GOLF COURSE ✉️ *3070 Route 66, Ashland* 📞 *541-482-4311* The nine holes here are regulation length, set on gently rolling greens.

CEDAR LINKS GOLF COURSE ✉️ *3155 Cedar Links Drive, Medford* 📞 *541-773-4373* This 18-hole, par-70 golf course is 6000 yards but an easy walk for the most part.

TENNIS

Salem Area

BUSH'S PASTURE PARK ✉️ *Mission and High streets* Four lighted courts.

HIGHLAND SCHOOL PARK ✉️ *Broadway and Highland Avenue Northeast* Two lighted courts.

ORCHARD HEIGHTS ✉️ *Orchard Heights Street and Parkway Drive* Four lighted courts.

HOOVER SCHOOL/PARK ✉️ *1104 Savage Road Northeast* Two courts.

WOODMANSEE PARK ✉️ *4629 Sunnyside Road Southeast* 📞 *503-588-6261* 📠 *503-588-6305* 🖥️ *www.cityofsalem.net/~parks* Two courts.

Eugene Area

WASHINGTON PARK ✉️ *2025 Washington Street* Two lighted courts.

CHURCHILL COURTS ✉️ *1850 Bailey Hill Road* Four lighted courts.

AMAZON COURTS ✉️ *Amazon Parkway and 24th Avenue* Four lighted courts.

SHELDON COURTS ✉️ *2445 Willakenzie Road* Four lighted courts.

ECHO HOLLOW COURTS ✉️ *501 Echo Hollow Road* Four lighted courts.

WEST MOORELAND COURTS ✉️ *20th and Polk streets* 📞 *541-682-4800* Four lighted courts.

U.S. SPORTS PLEX ✉️ *4540 Commerce Street, Eugene* 📞 *541-484-7451* Five courts.

Ashland–Rogue River Area

FICHTNER MAINWARING PARK ✉ *Stewart Avenue and Holly Street*
Four unlighted courts.

BEAR CREEK PARK ✉ *Siskiyou Boulevard and Highland Drive* Four lighted
courts.

NORTH MEDFORD HIGH SCHOOL ✉ *Keene Way Drive and Crater Lake
Road* Ten courts (five lighted).

HOLMES PARK ✉ *185 South Modoc Avenue* ✆ *541-774-2400* Two courts.

BIKING

For recreational bicyclers, there are hundreds of miles of relatively flat,
scenic bike trails that parallel beautiful rivers, parks and lakes
throughout the valley. Experienced, active riders will enjoy the more
challenging mountain trails or some of the longer loops in and around
the region.

Salem Area

OREGON TRANS-AMERICA TRAIL This trail begins in the Dallas area near Salem and heads south through the scenic wine country
to Corvallis.

WILLAMETTE MISSION STATE PARK ✆ *503-393-1172* Four miles
of bike trails traverse this state park, which is surrounded by orchards
and farm fields.

SILVER FALLS STATE PARK ✆ *503-873-8681* With its waterfalls and
gorges carved out of lava, this park has a popular four-mile paved bike
trail. There is also a 27-mile perimeter trail.

LYONS AND DETROIT LAKES East of the city, there are trails "all
over Lyons and Detroit lakes," according to one local enthusiast.

MCDONALD FOREST ✆ *541-737-4434* Near Corvallis, Oregon State
University has its own gated research forest. It's a hilly tract, but not
steep, and its 12-mile trail system is very popular. From the top of Dim-
ple Hill, which gains 800 feet in about four miles, you'll get a good view
of the surrounding area. The university maintains several trails and
outlines them in a map available at bike shops.

MARY'S PEAK The best part about ascending this peak, about 15
miles south of Corvallis, is that you can cheat. The summit rises over
4000 feet—it's the highest in the Coast Range—but you can drive to a
parking lot about three miles from the top. From there you can bike
along the pavement to the summit, from which you'll get great views of
the ocean and mountains to the east. When you're ready to descend,
you can can follow one of several trails down.

HOLMAN Bike trails can be found in state parks throughout the
area, including this town four miles west of Salem.

SALEM BICYCLE CLUB ✉ *P.O. Box 2224, Salem, OR 97308* ✎ *www.salem
bicycleclub.org* This club publishes a monthly newsletter that includes a

two- or three-page "Ride Sheet," which lists club-sponsored rides and is usually posted in bike shops around town. Club rides vary from beginner (15 to 20 miles) to expert (100-mile loops to the coast). Weekend rides are held year-round; in the summer, evening and overnight rides are held during the week.

Eugene Area

Eugene is one of the nation's top biking cities: more than 8500 people commute to school and work on bikes, and there are 200 miles of bike paths. All this in a city with a population of only 120,000.

WILLAMETTE RIVER RECREATION CORRIDOR Eugene's recreation corridor offers five bridges that connect the north and south bank bike trails. The flat 15-mile loop from Knickerbocker Bridge to Owosso Bridge takes you through or past parks and rose gardens, shops and restaurants in downtown Eugene, and the University of Oregon campus.

FOX SWALE AREA Eight miles south of Eugene, this area has eight miles of off-road trails ideal for mountain biking. Ride the Fox Hollow Road nine and a half miles over the summit and down into the valley to BLM Road 19-4-4. Note: The area gets muddy during the rainy season. Be sure to stay off private property in this area.

Ashland–Rogue River Area

EVANS VALLEY From the town of Rogue River, east of Grants Pass on Route 5, head north eight miles along Evans Creek to Wimer and this glorious valley. It's a scenic, relatively easy four-mile ride out Pleasant Creek Road to the covered bridge. Look for elk in the meadows alongside the road.

THE ADVENTURE CENTER ⊠40 North Main Street, Ashland ✆541-488-2819, 800-444-2899 ✆541-482-5139 ✍www.raftingtours.com If you'd like to join an escorted downhill bike tour on Mt. Ashland, contact this company. Beside bike rentals (and insider tips about the more pleasant route past small rural farms and ranches for a two-hour loop to Emigrant Lake), this outfitter offers several different off-road bike tours, all guided, with extras like picnic brunch.

Bike Rentals
SOUTH SALEM CYCLEWORKS ⊠4071 Liberty Road South, Salem ✆503-399-9848 Bike rentals in Salem are hard to come by. Try this shop for tandem, hybrid and road bikes.

PEAK SPORTS ⊠129 Northwest 2nd Street, Corvallis ✆541-754-6444 Pick up mountain and cruise bikes here. It's the only rental shop in the city. The shop also still has a few three-speeds, which are perfect for an easy afternoon ride around town.

EUGENE MOUNTAIN BICYCLE RESOURCES GROUP This group publishes *Mountain Bike Ride Guide*, available at bike shops in the Eugene area. Of the more than 14 bike shops in Eugene, there are only two places to rent.

HUTCH ✉ *960 Charnelton Street, Eugene* ✆ *541-345-7521* This shop rents out city bikes and is attached to the Rack and Roll sales/repair shop.

BLUE HERON BICYCLES ✉ *877 East 13th Avenue, Eugene* ✆ *541-343-2488* Blue Heron rents mountain and hybrid bikes in the spring and summer.

HIKING

Hiking does not necessarily mean huffing and puffing up steep mountain slopes. Several of the hikes mentioned here may be more aptly described as "walks." In any event, a hike or a walk along the river or through a park is a great way to get some exercise and to get to know the area. All distances listed for hiking trails are one way unless otherwise noted.

Salem Area

RIVERFRONT LOOP TRAIL In Willamette Mission State Park, this 4-mile loop trail offers a secluded stretch of river.

THE TEN FALLS LOOP TRAIL
This loop trail (7 miles) at Silver Falls State Park reaches all ten waterfalls along Silver Creek Canyon. Shorter hikes (less than 2.5 miles) can also be taken from roadside trailheads to the individual falls.

RITA STEINER FRY NATURE TRAIL This .3-mile trek in Salem offers a pleasant stroll through Deepwood Park, adjacent to the historic Deepwood Estate.

MINTO-BROWN ISLAND PARK On River Road South, a mile south of downtown, this park has around 15 miles of trails and paths.

Eugene Area

FALL CREEK NATIONAL RECREATION TRAIL Convenient to Eugene, this 13.7-mile trail is ideal for day hikes and overnight trips in the hardwood and conifer Willamette National Forest. Pristine Fall Creek is visible from most of the trail, which begins south of the Dolly Varden Campground.

MOUNT PISGAH ARBORETUM In Eugene, this arboretum has more than seven miles of hiking trails. You can enjoy a lovely walk through oak savanna, a Douglas fir forest or along a seasonal marsh.

PRE'S TRAIL This trail is a Eugene memorial to legendary Oregon runner Steve Prefontaine. This all-weather trail through the woods and fields of Alton Baker Park offers parcourse-style routes ranging from .5 to 1.5 miles.

KENTUCKY FALLS RECREATION TRAIL An 8.5-mile hike, this trail runs along Kentucky Creek through a forest of Douglas fir and western hemlock. Located 41 miles southwest of Eugene, it leads down 760 feet to the twin falls viewpoint.

ILLINOIS VALLEY RANGER DISTRICT   More than 30 trail systems, including 200 trails, are found in this district surrounding the Cave Junction/Oregon Caves area. Trails run from half a mile to almost 50 miles. Possibilities include **Tin Cup Mine**, the **Kalmiopsis Rim**, **Black Butte** and **Babyfoot Lake**.

BEAR CREEK GREENWAY TRAIL ☎ *541-774-6231* Try this Medford trail (5.5 miles), beginning at Bear Creek Park and running north through Medford to Pine Street in Central Point. The trail has two segments. One is near the Route 5 south interchange off Table Rock Road. A series of 18 interpretive stations points out more than 20 kinds of trees and berries as well as landmarks along the creek. The other trail segment (3.5 miles) is in the Talent area with the trailhead in Lynn Newbry Park. The trail runs south toward Ashland, passing wetland habitats and historical sites, with an interpretive guide available.

TRANSPORTATION

CAR

From Northern California, **Route 5** runs north over the border to Ashland and the Rogue River Valley. Route 5 also takes you southbound from Washington across the Columbia River into Portland. If you're arriving from the Northern California coast, pick up **Route 199**, which heads northeast through the Siskiyous into Southern Oregon and Grants Pass. Many other highways link the Willamette Valley with the Oregon Coast and central Oregon, including **Routes 126, 20** and **22**.

AIR

PORTLAND INTERNATIONAL AIRPORT ✉ *7000 Northeast Airport Way, Portland* ☎ *877-739-4636* 🖰 *www.fly.pdx.com* Two airports bring visitors to the Heart of Oregon: Eugene and Medford. In addition, this big international airport an hour north of Salem has convenient connections to all major cities and is serviced by Air Canada, Alaska Airlines, American Airlines, Continental Airlines, Delta Air Lines, Frontier Airlines, Hawaiian Airlines, Horizon Air, JetBlue, Lufthansa, Northwest Airlines, Southwest Airlines, United Airlines and United Express.

EUGENE AIRPORT This airport is served by Allegiant Air, Delta Connection, Horizon Air and United Express.

ROGUE VALLEY INTERNATIONAL–MEDFORD AIRPORT In Medford, this airport is served by Allegiant Air, Horizon Airlines, United Airlines and United Express.

AIRPORT CITY TAXI & LIMO ☎ *541-484-4142* For ground transportation to and from the Eugene Airport call this service.

YELLOW CAB ☎ *541-772-6288* In Medford, this company serves the airport and links the Shakespeare capital with the Medford Airport.

BUS

GREYHOUND BUS LINES ☎ *800-231-2222* ✐ *www.greyhound.com* Greyhound serves the Willamette Valley and Ashland–Rogue River area, with stations in Salem, Corvallis, Eugene, Grants Pass and Medford. **Salem:** (450 Church Street Northeast; 503-362-2428). **Corvallis:** (153 Northwest 4th Avenue; 541-757-1797). **Eugene:** (987 Pearl Street; 541-344-6265). **Grants Pass:** (460 Northeast Agness Avenue; 541-476-4513). **Medford:** (220 South Front Street; 541-779-2103).

TRAIN

AMTRAK ☎ *800-872-7245* ✐ *www.amtrak.com* Amtrak's "Coast Starlight" has daily service to the Willamette Valley, with stations in **Eugene** (433 Willamette Street), **Albany** (110 West 10th Avenue) and **Salem** (500 13th Street Northeast).

CAR RENTALS

You'll find many of the major agencies at the airports in Eugene and Medford. In Eugene, there are **Avis Rent A Car** (800-331-1212), **Budget Rent A Car** (800-527-0700) and **Hertz Rent A Car** (800-654-3131). In Medford, try **Avis Rent A Car** (800-331-1212), **Budget Rent A Car** (800-527-0700), **Hertz Rent A Car** (800-654-3131) and **National Car Rental** (800-227-7368).

PUBLIC TRANSIT

All the major Willamette Valley and Ashland–Rogue River cities have local public transit systems. While there are bus connections to many of the smaller towns, you'll need to rent a car to see many of the rural highlights.

The Salem area is served by **Cherriots** (503-588-2424). Contact the **Corvallis Transit System** (541-757-6998) in Corvallis. In Eugene, the **Lane Transit District** (541-687-5555) blankets the city. Medford, Jacksonville and Ashland are served by the **Rogue Valley Transportation District** (541-779-2877).

TAXIS

In Eugene, **Airport City Taxi** (541-484-4142) can take you downtown. In Medford, call **Yellow Cab** (541-772-6288).

VANCOUVER & THE SUNSHINE COAST

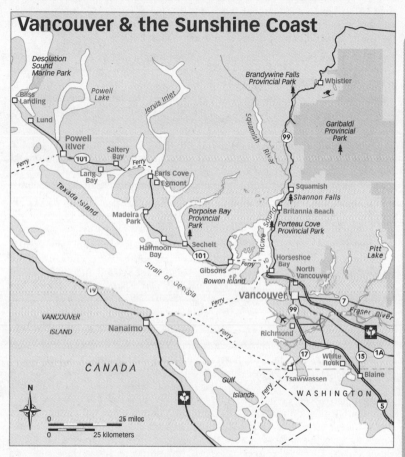

Vancouver & the Sunshine Coast

Mother Nature went all out in British Columbia, a Canadian province larger than California, Oregon and Washington combined. Stretched along the upper west coast of North America, the coastline is dotted by thousands of islands, only a few inhabited. Inland are thick forests, rugged mountain ranges and high deserts. The more remote northern regions contain vast, pristine wildernesses.

Bordered by the Pacific to the west, the United States to the south and the Coastal Range to the east, the southwestern corner of the province, including Vancouver, Whistler and the Sunshine Coast, contains unrivaled scenic splendors. The waters of the region, fed by heavy rains (45 inches annually in Vancouver, more at higher elevations), shape this land: the ocean, high lakes, mountain streams, broad rivers, inlets and fjords carve through alpine meadows and mold shorelines.

Nature has long provided for human needs here. Myriad indigenous tribes, living in peaceful coexistence with the earth, thrived in the mild climate of the region for centuries, hunting and camping in verdant forests, fishing salmon-filled waters and traversing the many streams and rivers. Europeans made an appearance in the 1770s, when Captain James Cook sailed through searching for the Northwest Passage and stopped to trade with the native inhabitants. Britain didn't lay claim to the area until Captain George Vancouver's visit in 1792.

Stories of the incredible abundance of wildlife brought in trappers and traders; a string of posts established by Hudson's Bay Company soon followed, with a steady flow of settlers not far behind. Friction arose when American settlers moved in and sought United States government authority. Eventually, the boundary between the United States and British Columbia was settled in 1846 by the Oregon Treaty.

As the fur trade began to wane, the Fraser Gold Rush of 1858 was just gaining speed, so the stream of settlers continued. Logging took off not long after the gold petered out. Gastown, the first settlement in what is now Vancouver, grew around an early saw mill. The city's future was ensured with the arrival of the transcontinental railroad in 1887 and, with its natural harbor, its importance as a shipping center soon became evident.

Industry in British Columbia is still largely based on what the land provides—logging, fishing and mining—with Vancouver as the processing and shipping center. Since the Vancouver World's Fair in 1986 focused worldwide attention on all the region had to offer, tourism has grown to become the second major industry in the province, after logging. Add to this mix Swiss-style banking regulations that attract investment from around the world and you have a truly dynamic city.

Canada's Pacific gateway in fact as well as image, Vancouver is one of the economic centers of the Pacific Rim, and a major North American shipping center. It's also a bustling cruise ship departure port. The city has long attracted immigrants from Asia, most recently from Hong Kong, although that tide has slowed now that control of the colony has reverted to China. Even so, Vancouver's Chinatown is second largest in North America, behind San Francisco. The city also has strong Italian, Greek, French, Indian, Japanese and Russian communities, and is a popular destination for European travelers. The West End (adjoining Stanley Park) is the most densely populated urban district in North America, much resembling a European city neighborhood with its residential towers, streetside shops and cafés. The Vancouver visitor can hear more than a dozen languages in a day's journey through the city, a reflection of its vital, cosmopolitan nature.

The combination of exceptional scenery, heady cultural life, economical production costs and attractive exchange rates has made Vancouver the third-largest film and television production center in North America, after Los Angeles and New York, with more than 200 movies filmed in B.C. in 2005 alone. *The X-Files* was taped here, along with a half-dozen other American TV shows and, sometimes, literally dozens of films a year. Aside from the cachet this brings the city, it's an economic boon—more than US$1.2 billion a year.

Whistler, 75 miles northeast of Vancouver, is close enough for a day trip from the city (though there's too much to see and do in just one day). With island-dotted Howe Sound to the west and the verdant Coastal Range to the east, there are enough sights along the picturesque Sea to Coast Highway to make driving the narrow, winding road slow but enjoyable. Parks and scenic pullouts along the way are perfect for a picnic or stretch.

The first settlers to arrive in Whistler in the early 1900s realized right away the potential in the area's beauty, so it comes as no surprise that some of the first structures were built as vacation retreats, most geared toward fishing and hunting. Skiing began in earnest in 1966 with the opening of the Garibaldi Lift Company in Whistler. A stylized European village resort was constructed 12 years and $550 million later at the convergence of the Blackcomb and Whistler mountains. In its short time, this ski destination has gained a strong international reputation and is now among the top attractions in North America. The resort is consistently rated number one in North America by *Ski Magazine*—ahead of such better-known destinations as Aspen, Vail and Sun Valley.

Although summer used to be the slow season at Whistler, an explosion of golf development is attracting a rapidly growing crowd of warm-weather visitors. Hiking, tennis, sailing, fishing, biking and horseback riding are among the other activities that occupy visitors; lodging and dining rates are still somewhat lower than in winter. Boutiques and eateries line the cobbled walkways of Whistler Village, which are often alive with street entertainers, from jugglers and clowns to dancers and musicians. The warmer months (June to September) are a favorite time to visit since crowds are minimal, prices for accommodations are drastically lower and there are so many outdoor activities to enjoy in the area's quiet alpine meadows, dense green forests and cool mountain lakes. However, even during ski season (November to May), you'll find no shortage of parking—a big problem at many resorts—because the main village of this carefully planned resort is built atop a massive underground garage.

With approximately 2400 hours of sunshine each year, the Sunshine Coast lives up to its well-deserved name. It is made up of small, quiet fishing and logging communities strung along a 90-mile coastline. These pleasant sights lie between Langdale, a short ferry ride from Horseshoe Bay in West Vancouver, and Lund, the gateway to Desolation Sound Marine Park. Another short ferry ride between Earls Cove and Saltery Bay connects the northern and southern sections of the coast. The ferry trips give visitors the sense that they are touring a series of islands, even though the Sunshine Coast is firmly attached to the mainland.

The region is a gem for anyone who loves the great outdoors, with mild weather and enough hiking, camping and water activities—fishing, diving, canoeing, kayaking, sailing or simply lounging on one of many beaches—to please one and all. The locals, mainly loggers, anglers and artists, are friendly and upbeat, willing to share recommendations for what to see and do in their neck of the woods. Except for warm summer weekends, the Sunshine Coast is not yet inundated by tourists and retains a rustic, provincial air.

Southwestern British Columbia offers something for everyone tucked into a neat package: the urbane and worldly pleasures of Vancouver, the bustle and excitement of resort life at Whistler and the undeveloped, uncrowded scenic beauty of the Sunshine Coast. Simply put, it is a vacationer's paradise in the Pacific Northwest.

WEST SIDE– GRANVILLE ISLAND

If museums are your passion, this is a good place to start your visit to Vancouver. A number of the city's leading facilities are found here. Marvelous Granville Island offers some cultural attractions as well.

SIGHTS

MUSEUM OF ANTHROPOLOGY — hidden

✉ *6393 Northwest Marine Drive* ☎ *604-822-5087* ✐ *www.moa.ubc.ca*
Begin your visit with a pleasant stroll through several of the city's leading museums. One of the finest is this one from the University of British Columbia that includes sunlit galleries of Northwest Coastal First Nation totems, chests, canoes, jewelry, ceremonial masks, clothing and contemporary native artwork. There's no charge to visit the true-to-life Haida longhouse and totems behind the museum; occasionally you may even find a carver at work on a totem there. Closed Monday from October through May. Admission.

VANCOUVER MUSEUM ✉ *1100 Chestnut Street* ☎ *604-736-4431* ✆ *604-736-5417* ✐ *www.vanmuseum.bc.ca* Further samples of First Nation artifacts along with intriguing collections of European costumes, tools, furniture and relics portraying the rapid colonization of the area are at this museum, located on a small green peninsula in English Bay known as Vanier Park. The **H. R. MacMillan Space Centre** (www.spacecentre.com) upstairs stages regular astronomy programs, live science presentations and hands-on exhibits. Closed Monday in winter.

VANCOUVER MARITIME MUSEUM ✉ *1905 Ogden Avenue* ☎ *604-257-8300* ✆ *604-737-2621* ✐ *www.vancouvermaritimemuseum.com* Documenting the maritime history of British Columbia, including the glory of international steamship travel, is this maritime museum. Housed in the connected A-frame is the Royal Canadian Mounted Police supply ship, the **St. Roch**, now a National Historic Site since it was the first ship to pass successfully through the Northwest Passage in both directions. Closed Monday from September to mid-May. Admission.

GRANVILLE ISLAND   Across a short bridge from downtown Vancouver lies this island. Refurbished by the federal government, Granville contains everything from parkland to craft studios to a cement factory. Once an industrial area, today it is a classic example of native funk gone chic. Corrugated metal warehouses have been transformed into sleek shops, while rusting cranes and dilapidated steam turbines have become decorative pieces. There are several **working studios** to view. The focal point is the **Granville Public Market**, a 50,000-square-foot collection of stalls selling fresh fish, fruits, vegetables and other goodies.

WRECK BEACH

PAGE 534

Secluded, undeveloped sandy stretch at the tip of the peninsula—the only *au naturel* spot in town

MUSEUM OF ANTHROPOLOGY

PAGE 528

Sunlit galleries filled with First Nations totems, jewelry, masks and a true-to-life Haida longhouse

BEAUTIFUL BED & BREAKFAST

PAGE 531

Spacious, attractive colonial-style home on a quiet side street just minutes from the city's best sights

VIJ'S

PAGE 532

Renowned Indian bistro serving innovative delights like cinnamon and red wine curry or lamb popsicles

FALSE CREEK FERRY ✆ 604-684-7781 🖅 www.granvilleislandferries.bc.ca
Getting to the Granville Public Market is half the adventure: You can walk, drive or catch this ferry from behind the Vancouver Aquatic Centre (under the Burrard Street Bridge).

AQUABUS ✆ 604-689-5858 🖅 www.theaquabus.com, mail@theaquabus.com This competing enterprise offers passage to the Granville Public Market across and along False Creek in small jitneys from various docks.

INFO CENTRE ✉ 1661 Duranleau Street, 2nd Floor ✆ 604-666-5784 🖅 www. granvilleisland.com, info@granvilleisland.bc.ca A quick stop here to pick up a map will help you focus on what you want to see and do.

GRANVILLE ISLAND BREWING COMPANY ✉ 1441 Cartwright Street ✆ 604-687-2739 🖅 www.gib.ca, info@gib.ca Leave time for an informal, one-hour tour of this brewing company, the first microbrewery in Canada and home of the popular Island Lager. Tastings are offered at the end of the tour. Admission.

RICHMOND OVAL ✉ 6111 River Road, Richmond ✆ 778-296-1400 🖅 www. richmondoval.ca Vancouver will host the Winter Olympic and Paralympic Games in 2010. Home of 12 speed-skating events during the games, along with an adjoining waterfront plaza and park, this will be the centerpiece of a major new City Centre community to be developed on 32 acres along the banks of the Fraser River.

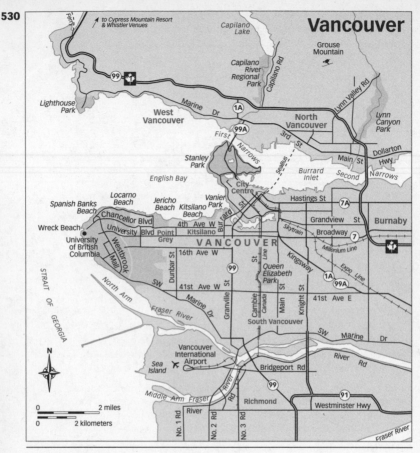

LODGING

HOSTELLING INTERNATIONAL—
VANCOUVER JERICHO BEACH

$ 252 BEDS ✉ 1515 Discovery Street ✆ 604-224-3208, 888-203-4303
✆ 604-224-4852 ✎ www.hihostels.ca

The second-largest youth hostel in North America, this property enjoys a prime setting on English Bay. Housed in what was once military barracks, there is space here for over 250 hostelers in the many dorm-style rooms with shared baths; the few couple/family rooms go quickly. With fully equipped communal kitchens, laundry facilities, a cafeteria and a lounge with a big-screen television, this is easily one of the fanciest hostels you could hope to visit. The hostel is open May through September.

EXECUTIVE AIRPORT PLAZA

$$$ 350 UNITS ✉ 7311 Westminster Highway, Richmond ✆ 604-278-5555, 800-663-2878 ✆ 604-278-0255 ✎ www.executivehotels.net, reservations@executivehotels.net

The welcoming glass lobby full of greenery bustles with businesspeople who form the the majority of the clientele here. This quiet, friendly hotel near the airport has 235 standard guest rooms and 115 suites in pastel tones with full kitchens and modern furnishings in separate seating and sleeping areas. Rooms with jacuzzis or kitchenettes are also available.

BEAUTIFUL BED & BREAKFAST

$$–$$$$ 4 ROOMS   ✉ *428 West 40th Avenue*   ✆ *604-327-1102*
📠 *604-327-2299*   🖳 *www.beautifulbandb.bc.ca, sandbbb@portal.ca*

Although it's on a back street in a quiet neighborhood, nearby public transportation makes this B&B accessible to Vancouver's main attractions, including downtown and the UBC, both of which are just minutes away by bus. Housed in a spacious, attractive Colonial-style home, the inn's four rooms include a honeymoon suite with marble fireplace and a balcony. Breakfast is served in a formal dining room with silver service. No children under 14 allowed.

CONFERENCES AND ACCOMMODATION AT UBC

$$–$$$ 3000 UNITS   ✉ *5961 Student Union Boulevard*   ✆ *604-822-1000, 888-822-1030*   📠 *604-822-1001*   🖳 *www.ubcconferences.com, reservations@housing.ubc.ca*

Throughout the year there are affordable rooms available through this budget alternative to Vancouver's pricey downtown hotels. Staying here makes me feel like a student again—without the inconvenience of attending class. Single and twin rooms in the dorm buildings are generally full of students during the school term but are available in the summer. Guests can get an inexpensive meal in the Student Union Building cafeteria.

DINING

The Kitsilano neighborhood, a long, narrow district that runs from around Burrard Street to Alma Street and features commercial corridors along 4th Avenue and Broadway, boasts many excellent, small restaurants.

SOPHIE'S COSMIC CAFÉ

$$–$$$ AMERICAN   ✉ *2095 West 4th Avenue*   ✆ *604-732-6810*
📠 *604-732-9417*   🖳 *www.sophiescosmiccafe.com*

The last time we stopped by Sophie's on a weekend, diners were lined up outside the door. Inside, people were piling into Naugahyde booths and gazing at the pennants, pictures and antique toys that line this quirky café. There are omelettes and Belgian waffles for breakfast, and falafel and veggie burgers later in the day. Dinner gets downright sophisticated as Sophie cooks up quesadillas, vegetarian pastas, wild salmon dishes, fresh oysters and nightly specials. There's a heated outdoor patio.

SHIJO JAPANESE RESTAURANT

$$ JAPANESE ✉ *1926 West 4th Avenue* ✆ *604-732-4676*
📠 *604-731-4589*

Atmospherically appointed with tatami, bronze lamps and black wood accents, this restaurant is popular with the downtown crowd. Sushi, vegetarian dishes and traditional Japanese fare are prepared with an innovative twist. Barbecued shiitake mushrooms are one of the standout dishes.

SEASONS IN THE PARK RESTAURANT

$$–$$$ SEAFOOD/PACIFIC NORTHWEST ✉ *Cambie Street at 33rd Avenue*
✆ *604-874-8008* 📠 *604-874-7101* ✐ *www.vancouverdine.com, info@vancouverdine.com*

Set near the conservatory at the peak of Queen Elizabeth Park, this elegant restaurant enjoys sweeping views of the Vancouver skyline and the mountains towering above the North Shore. The seafood and West Coast cuisine dishes are seasonal, and specials from the daily menu are always on a par with the outstanding view. Weekend brunch.

KIRIN MANDARIN

$$–$$$ CHINESE ✉ *1166 Alberni Street* ✆ *604-682-8833*
📠 *604-688-2812* ✐ *www.kirinrestaurant.com*

Spicy northern and southern Chinese cuisine is showcased brilliantly at this large, stylish restaurant handsomely adorned with creamy gold walls decorated with prints. An emphasis on fresh local seafood is evidenced by well-stocked fish tanks at the rear of the dining area. Shellfish dishes are especially noteworthy, including lobster and crab prepared with ginger sauce or chili-spiked sea scallops. Stop by for daily dim sum.

VIJ'S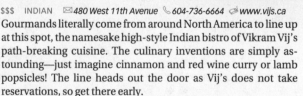

$$$ INDIAN ✉ *480 West 11th Avenue* ✆ *604-736-6664* ✐ *www.vijs.ca*

Gourmands literally come from around North America to line up at this spot, the namesake high-style Indian bistro of Vikram Vij's path-breaking cuisine. The culinary inventions are simply astounding—just imagine cinnamon and red wine curry or lamb popsicles! The line heads out the door as Vij's does not take reservations, so get there early.

BRIDGES

$$$–$$$$ SEAFOOD/AMERICAN ✉ *1696 Duranleau Street* ✆ *604-687-4400*
✐ *www.bridgesrestaurant.com*

For a fine view of the city lights from water level on the Granville Island Wharf, head to this happening eatery. The restaurant is one of the current hot spots of the dining elite who have the choice of the refined elegance of the dining room, the relaxed bistro, the fresh air on the deck or the convivial pub. The fare here ranges from nouvelle preparations of seafood and meats to basic pasta and finger foods. Be forewarned: Some readers claim it's too touristy.

GRANVILLE PUBLIC MARKET

$ INTERNATIONAL ✉ *1681 Johnston Street* ✎ *www.granvilleisland.com*

Inevitably you are going to end up on Granville Island. Should hunger strike while you're touring the shops and artist studios, check out the food stalls here You'll find a fish-and-chips shop, a souvlaki stand, a juice and salad bar, a deli and even a fresh soup outlet.

SHOPPING

4TH AVENUE   A strip of intriguing shops lies along this stretch between Burrard and Alma streets. Situated between Granville Island and the University of British Columbia campus, it is known as the Kitsilano neighborhood. Back in the 1960s and 1970s, "Kits," as it's lovingly called, was a center for Vancouver's counterculture. Since then, time and gentrification have transformed the area into a spiffy district of smart shops and comfortable homes.

T ⭕hidden

✉ *1568 West Broadway* ✆ 604-730-8390 ✎ *www.tealeaves.com, tearoom@ tealeaves.com* Along Broadway is one of the Kitsilano district's more intriguing shops, which also doubles as a tearoom. Devoted entirely to teas, T has over 250 varieties, ranging from common types such as Earl Grey to rarities such as a robust Tanzanian leaf. Fruit and pastries round out the offerings.

PUBLIC MARKET ✉ *1496 Cartwright Street* ✎ *www.granvilleisland.com* The main draw on Granville Island is this market, with rows of vendors selling fresh produce, flowers, pastas, wines, baked goods, seafood and meats, along with the section brimming with fast-food outlets proffering an international array of delectables. The **Kids Market** (604-689-8447; www.kidsmarket.ca) within the market is a mall full of toy stores, children's clothing shops and a tykes' beauty salon.

NIGHTLIFE

WATERFRONT THEATRE ✉ *1412 Cartwright Street* ✆ 604-685-6217 (box office), 604-669-3410 📠 604-669-3817 ✎ *www.carouseltheatre.ca* There is plenty of innovative theater to choose from on Granville Island. The **Carousel Theatre Company** offers family-oriented classical and contemporary productions at this venue. Recent productions include *Seussical, The Secret World of Og* and Shakespeare's *As You Like It.*

PLAYWRIGHTS THEATRE CENTER ✉ *1398 Cartwright Street* ✆ 604-685-6228 ✎ *www.playwrightstheatre.com* This center hosts the Annual Vancouver New Play Festival, showcasing the works of Canadian playwrights.

ARTS CLUB THEATRE ✉ *1585 Johnston Street* ✆ 604-687-1644 ✎ *www.arts club.com* The second-largest nonprofit theater in Canada is this one.

Arts Club produces a diverse range of plays on two stages on Granville Island: The Stanley Industrial Alliance Stage (2750 Granville Street) and Granville Island Stage (15858 Johnston Street). Recent productions include *Altar Boyz*, *Cyrano de Bergerac* and *Doubt*.

BRIDGES ✉ *1696 Duranleau Street* 📞 *604-687-4400* 🖥 *www.bridgesrestaurant.com*
A trendy bistro on Granville Island, this is a fairly quiet place to savor a glass of wine and the lights of the city dancing on the water of False Creek.

BEACHES & PARKS

QUEEN ELIZABETH PARK
✉ *Located at Cambie Street and 33rd Avenue* 📞 *604-257-8400* 🖥 *604-257-8427*
🚶 Taking the place of two stone quarries that once supplied building materials for the city, this 130-acre park now features various ornamental gardens showcasing the indigenous plants of the coast along with two rock gardens that reflect the land's past. At 505 feet above sea level, the park affords some of the best views of downtown Vancouver, crowned by the mountains of the North Shore. Bloedel Floral Conservatory rests at its peak. You'll find a restaurant, restrooms, picnic facilities, 18 tennis courts, lawn bowling lanes, frisbee golf and a pitch-and-putt golf course.

WRECK BEACH
✉ *Located south of Nitobe Garden and the Museum of Anthropology off Northwest Marine Drive; a steep, twisting trail opposite the university residences leads from the road to the beach.* 📞 *604-224-5739*
🖥 *wwww.pacificspiritparksociety.org*
🏖 Of the many beaches in and around Vancouver, this highly undeveloped (and unspoiled) sandy stretch across from the University of British Columbia on the tip of Point Grey Peninsula is the only *au naturel* spot in town. While proximity to the UBC campus has made this beach a traditional student hangout for generations, Wreck Beach has become an increasingly, though not exclusively, gay beach. The obvious problem the steep access trail poses for law enforcement has also made this beach a popular place to score the province's legendary "BC bud." Located within Pacific Spirit Regional Park, there are outhouses, seasonal concession services and a telephone at the top of the trail.

ENGLISH BAY BEACHES (SOUTHERN SHORE)
✉ *Kitsilano Beach is at Cornwall Avenue and Arbutus Street; Jericho, Lacarno and Spanish beaches are accessible off of Northwest Marine Drive* 📞 *604-665-3424*
🏖 Stretched around the north face of Point Grey Peninsula on the opposite side of the bay, Kitsilano Beach, Jericho, Lacarno and Spanish Banks beaches attract hordes of windsurfers, sunbathers, picnickers and swimmers, but are spacious enough not to feel overcrowded. There is a heated outdoor saltwater pool (open during the summer; fee) at

Kitsilano Beach in case the sea is too nippy. You'll find restrooms, life-guards (in summer), changing rooms and intermittent food stalls.

DOWNTOWN VANCOUVER

If your vision of downtown is an office world that rolls up the sidewalk at 6 p.m., get ready for a pleasant surprise. A beautiful harbor setting, intriguing historic districts, galleries and gardens set downtown Vancouver apart from most cities.

SIGHTS

VANCOUVER TOURIST INFO CENTRE ✉ *Plaza Level, Waterfront Centre, 200 Burrard Street* ☎ *604-683-2000* 🖷 *604-682-6839* 🖱 *www.tourismvancouver. com* Detailed visitor information is available through this agency.

GAY VANCOUVER ✉ *969 Richards Street* ☎ *604-682-0076* 🖱 *www.gayvancouver.net* As of July 2005, the Equal Marriage Act was signed into law, allowing same-sex couples to tie the knot legally throughout Canada. Some businesses, especially in the downtown area, are beginning to bill themselves as gay-friendly locales. This company has all the most up-to-date information on the best destinations.

GEORGIA STRAIGHT 🖱 *www.straight.com* The best guide to Vancouver dining, theater, music and other events is this free weekly with comprehensive coverage of the city's cultural life. It's available at most coffee shops, bookstores, hotels, restaurants and newsstands.

SCIENCE WORLD BRITISH COLUMBIA ✉ *1455 Quebec Street* ☎ *604-443-7440* 🖷 *604-443-7430* 🖱 *www.scienceworld.bc.ca, info@scienceworld.ca* The shining geodesic dome so prominent on the Vancouver skyline as you approach the city from the south was Expo Centre during the 1986 Exposition and is now home to this science center. Fascinating hands-on exhibits let you blow square bubbles, light up a plasma ball, dance on a giant synthesizer keyboard and more. The **OMNIMAX Theatre** (604-443-7443) upstairs features a variety of exciting films shown on one of the largest screens in the world. Separate admission to museum and theater.

B.C. PLACE ✉ *777 Pacific Boulevard* ☎ *604-669-2300* 🖱 *www.bcplacestadium. com* Since its completion in 1982, this ten-acre stadium in the heart of downtown is the home playing field of the B.C. Lions pro football team and the largest air-supported stadium in North America. In addition, it hosts trade shows, religious events, royal visits and rock concerts by the likes of David Bowie, the Beach Boys and the Rolling Stones. The domed roof is made of two layers of fiberglass-woven fabric, each only 1/30 inch thick and stronger than steel. Sixteen huge electric fans keep the air pressure inside the stadium higher than outside, holding the roof up without support beams. The removable synthetic turf floor used for sporting events is made of 32 rolls of nylon turf, weighing 72 tons and held together by zippers.

536

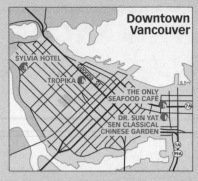

Downtown Vancouver

SYLVIA HOTEL
TROPIKA
THE ONLY SEAFOOD CAFÉ
DR. SUN YAT SEN CLASSICAL CHINESE GARDEN

SYLVIA HOTEL
PAGE 544

Ivy-covered historic landmark oozing with old-fashioned charm and an unbeatable waterfront location

TROPIKA
PAGE 550

Spicy red, green and yellow curries and tender, juicy satays—a prime introduction to Malaysian cuisine

THE ONLY SEAFOOD CAFÉ
PAGE 547

Vancouver's oldest family-owned restaurant, known for its outstanding clam chowder and pepper-stewed oysters

DR. SUN YAT SEN CLASSICAL CHINESE GARDEN
PAGE 537

Water, rock, plants and architecture blended in Taoist harmony for perfectly balanced urban serenity

LIBRARY SQUARE ✉ *350 West Georgia Street* ☎ *604-331-3600* ✐ *www.vpl. vancouver.bc.ca* Dedicated in 1995, this square is a stunning architectural highlight of Vancouver's decade-long building boom. Vancouver Public Library's Central Branch is the centerpiece: a fascinating oval building cast in reddish concrete, designed by famed Canadian architect Moshe Safdie to hint at the Roman Coliseum. Its many windows and unusual angles capture and reflect light like a prism. With nine floors of books and reference materials, the library is one of the largest in North America.

CHINATOWN There are numerous photo-worthy spots in this area, which stretches along Pender Street between Carrall and Gore streets. One of North America's largest Chinese communities, this crowded neighborhood is particularly festive during holiday periods.

SAM KEE BUILDING ✉ *8 West Pender Street* Among the most remarkable sites is this extremely narrow building listed in *Ripley's Believe It or Not!* as the skinniest building in the world at just six feet wide. Along the way you'll also see brightly colored, elaborately carved facades of buildings housing herbalists, bakeries, dim sum parlors, silk or souvenir shops and open-front produce stands.

CHINESE CULTURAL CENTRE ✐ *www.cccvan.com* Across the street from the Sam Kee Building, this cultural center offers slide show presentations on the history of Chinatown as well as guided tours of the neighborhood.

DR. SUN YAT SEN CLASSICAL CHINESE GARDEN ⓗidden

✉578 Carrall Street ☎604-662-3207 🖥www.vancouverchinesegarden.com
Take time to appreciate the urban serenity of this classical Chinese garden, secluded behind high white walls and designed to blend water, rock, plants and architecture in Taoist harmony. Every detail of the garden has a symbolic meaning. Pause to write a poem or simply meditate. Designed and constructed by craftsmen brought in from China, this Ming Dynasty–style garden is the first such garden to be built outside China. Many of the elements, including the architectural and artistic components, rocks and pebbles (but not the plants) were shipped in from China. Closed Sunday in winter. Admission.

Plunge back out onto teeming Pender Street, Chinatown's main street, where a three-block walk east to Gore Street will take you past exotic shops, apothecaries and restaurants. Then turn around and walk back up the other side of the street to Pender and Carrall.

MARKET ALLEY Be sure to check out this alley (aka Columbia Street), where street vendors sell exotic fruits, ginseng, seafood, baked goods, and assorted treasures and curiosities.

SUN TOWER BUILDING ✉100 West Pender Street ☎604-683-2000 🖥www.suntowerbuilding.com A bit farther on Pender Street from Market Alley is this building, which, at 272 feet, was once the tallest building in the British Empire and site of a daring escape stunt pulled off by Harry Houdini during the height of his career. Builder Louis Taylor, a newspaper publisher, deliberately intended the half-clad caryatids (maidens) atop the tower to offend Edwardian sensibilities.

GASTOWN 🖥www.seegastown.com This is where Vancouver got its start as a saloon-lined lumber mill port in 1870. Although the townsite was officially incorporated as Granville, it was locally known as Gastown after saloon keeper "Gassy" Jack Deighton. You'll find the **Gassy Jack Statue** near the oddly angled intersection of Water, Carrall, Powell

Vancouver's Hollywood

Yaletown, on downtown's south side roughly bounded by Richards and Smithe streets and Pacific Boulevard, was an industrial warehouse district as recently as the early 1990s. Today it is a neighborhood of sophisticated cafés, restaurants and exclusive galleries and boutiques. The change was brought about by Vancouver's fast-growing motion picture and TV industry, which made the low-rent district its headquarters during the rise of the independent film movement, when Canada offered tax incentives and a chance to avoid big-studio guild restrictions. Its reputation having been enhanced by the success of high-profile Vancouver-based productions such as *Smallville* and *Battlestar Galactica*, British Columbia has emerged as the third-largest film production community in North America, after Los Angeles and New York.

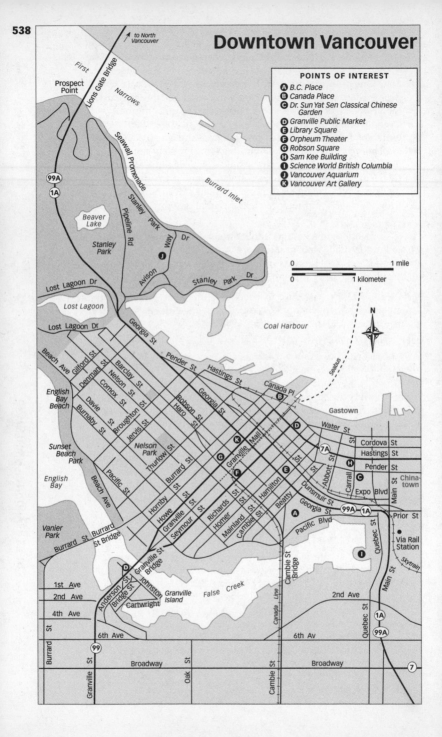

Downtown Vancouver

POINTS OF INTEREST

- **A** B.C. Place
- **B** Canada Place
- **C** Dr. Sun Yat Sen Classical Chinese Garden
- **D** Granville Public Market
- **E** Library Square
- **F** Orpheum Theater
- **G** Robson Square
- **H** Sam Kee Building
- **I** Science World British Columbia
- **J** Vancouver Aquarium
- **K** Vancouver Art Gallery

and Alexander streets. Since no one knows what Deighton actually looked like, the statue was made in 1986 from a century-old, randomly selected photo of an unidentified man who looked as if he could be Gassy Jack. Gastown's touristy heritage area of cobbled streets, Victorian street lamps and storefronts, charming courtyards and mews is chock-full of antique and souvenir shops and international eateries. On the corner of Cambie and Water streets is the **Gastown Steam Clock**, the first of its kind, wheezing out musical chimes on the quarter hour. It was built by the owner of a nearby shop, and over the years it has become Vancouver's trademark and most often photographed sight.

CANADA PLACE ✉ *At the foot of Howe and Burrard streets* ✍ *www.canadaplace.ca* On Carrall there's a great view of the harbor from this trade-convention center and cruise-ship terminal, complete with hotel and IMAX theater. From the bow of this landlocked behemoth you can scan the waterfront, taking in the broad sweep of North Vancouver and the spectacular mountains behind it. Bridges arch to port and starboard, ships lie at anchor in the harbor and an occasional ferry plies the narrow waterway.

LOOKOUT! ✉ *555 West Hastings Street* ☎ *604-689-0421* 🖷 *604-689-5447* ✍ *www.vancouverlookout.com, info@vancouverlookout.com* A glass elevator zips you up to this aptly named circular viewing deck high atop Harbour Centre. With a tremendous 360-degree view of Vancouver and environs, plaques pointing out all the major sights, guides present to answer all questions and a brief multimedia presentation on the highlights of the city, it is one of the best places to get your bearings. It's overpriced, though, and if you want the best view, try Grouse Mountain or Queen Elizabeth Park. Admission.

GRANVILLE MALL ✉ *Head west on Pender as it angles to the northwest for about five blocks, then southwest on Howe.* This is the modern urban heart of Vancouver, a popular shopping and nightlife area dedicated to pedestrians only.

VANCOUVER ART GALLERY ✉ *750 Hornby Street* ☎ *604 662 4700* ✍ *www.vanartgallery.bc.ca* Housed in what was once the central courthouse, this gallery has four floors of displays showcasing the works of international and Canadian contemporary artists; the Emily Carr Gallery, featuring many of her drawings and paintings of the coastal rainforests is a must-see. Admission.

BILL REID GALLERY OF NORTHWEST COAST ART

✉ *639 Hornby Street* ☎ *604-682-3455* 🖷 *604-682-3310* ✍ *www.billreidgallery.ca* Rivaling Emily Carr for recognition as British Columbia's greatest artist, Haida woodcarver, sculptor, goldsmith and painter Bill Reid (1920–1998) led the revival of interest in First Nations art and especially the carving of totem poles. His monumental works can be seen at the UBC Museum of Anthropology (where several of his golden pieces were recently stolen during Canada's most notorious art heist) and at other renowned art venues. But nowhere else will you find as many of his major works in one place as in this, Vancouver's newest art museum, which also exhibits his carving tools and other artifacts. Changing exhibits on other contemporary and 19th-century First Nations artists and craftspeople are also on display. Closed Monday and Tuesday.

ROBSON SQUARE ✉️*800 Robson Street* Below the current government offices and courts is this site of concerts and lectures with an outdoor skating rink. The various steps and plazas beside the multi-level fountain are popular with downtown workers for alfresco picnic lunches.

ROBSONSTRASSE Continuing north on Robson, between Burrard and Jervis streets, you'll find yourself in the city's chic shopping zone.

Stanley Park Area

STANLEY PARK ✉️*North foot of Georgia Street* 📞*604-257-8400* 🖱️*www.vancouver.ca/parks/parks/stanley* Easily ranked as one of the most outstanding city parks in the world, this 1000-acre park offers more recreational and entertainment options than you could imagine. Only the outer 20 percent of this green grove poking out into Burrard Inlet at the head of the downtown peninsula is developed for recreational use. On December 15, 2006, hurricane-force winds decimated Stanley Park's famous old-growth forests, blowing down some 3000 mature conifers and causing an estimated $9 million worth of damage. The park is now open again, but clearing, replanting and repairs to the damaged six-mile seawall will continue for the foreseeable future.

BROCKTON VISITOR CENTRE ___ **h**idden

Eight towering Kwakiutl and Haida totem poles guard the grounds near the park's visitor center. Composed of two pavilions covered by a floating roof, the center provides easily accessible restrooms and concessions and informational plaques about the impressive totem poles.

SEAWALL PROMENADE The best way to take in all the park's sights is to bike or hike along this divided five-and-a-half-mile seawall promenade (see "Outdoor Adventures" for more information). If you're pressed for time or just not up for the several-hour jaunt around the perimeter path, hop in the car and follow the one-way **scenic drive** signs from the park's main entrance off Georgia Street to hit most of the highlights.

Making your way around the promenade, you'll pass a statue of Lord Stanley, the rose gardens, the Royal Vancouver Yacht Club, Deadman's Island, the Nine O'Clock Gun, and the "girl in a wetsuit" statue next to the historic figurehead from the S.S. *Empress of Japan*.

PROSPECT POINT LOOKOUT 🖱️*www.prospectpoint.ca* If you continue along the promenade, you'll approach this lookout at the far northern tip of the park, which boasts a great view of the **Lions Gate Bridge**. One of the longest suspension bridges in the world, it stretches over Burrard Inlet to the slopes of West Vancouver. Siwash Rock, the hollow tree, and Second and Third beaches, extremely popular among sunbathers and water enthusiasts, finish out the seawall route. Second Beach has a heated outdoor pool.

ROSE GARDEN

✉ *Located near the park's entrance just off Georgia Street* ☎ *604-257-8400* Rose aficionados will want to stroll through this lovely rose garden, the crowning glory of the city's parks. The fragrant collection in this mid-sized formal garden is sure to contain one or two specimens you'd like to have in your own yard. Late summer is the best time to visit.

VANCOUVER AQUARIUM

✉ *845 Avison Way* ☎ *604-659-3474* ⊕ *www.vanaqua.org* Within the park you'll find this aquarium, where you can view dolphins and whales, as well as nearly 700 species of marine life in numerous exhibits. Then stroll through the Graham Amazon Gallery and listen to the birds chitter while peering at green anacondas or piranhas. An outdoor viewing deck on the west side of the compound allows free looks at the seal and beluga whale pools. Check out the brand new Canaccord Capital Exploration Gallery, with an expanded children's area and new gallery space. Admission.

CHILDREN'S FARM YARD

☎ *604-257-8531* You can enter this nearby farm yard to frolic with the potbellied pigs, goats and other little critters. You can also ride the miniature railway, a scaled-down version of the first train to cross Canada. Call for winter hours. Admission.

NATURE HOUSE

⊕ *www.stanleyparkecology.ca* To get to know the wild interior of the park, visit this interpretive center at the southeastern edge of Lost Lagoon where visitors learn about the flora and fauna in the park. Hikers will enjoy the miles of trails through thick coniferous forest while birdwatchers will probably prefer to perch quietly at the edge of **Beaver Lake** or **Lost Lagoon** to peer at Canadian geese, rare trumpeter swans and other waterfowl.

VARIETY KID'S WATER PARK

A wonderful, watery play area complete with slides, water cannons and a pint-sized, full-body blow drier, this park is great for kids. There's also a miniature steam locomotive, pony rides, Kids Traffic School and a fire-engine playground. Admission.

QUEEN ELIZABETH PARK

✉ *Cambie Street at West 33rd Avenue* The second-most visited Vancouver park is this beautiful, regally named recreation area. It boasts an arboretum, scenic pavilion and renowned gardens.

BLOEDEL CONSERVATORY

✉ *Queen Elizabeth Park, 30 30th Avenue East* ☎ *604-257-8570* This floral wonder is the star of Queen Elizabeth Park. Set at the crown of

Little Mountain, the conservatory houses over 500 tropical plant species under a 70-foot-high triodetic geodesic dome. Admission for the conservatory only.

VANDUSEN BOTANICAL GARDEN

✉ *5251 Oak Street* ☎ *604-878-9274* There are over 7000 species of plants from six continents divided into theme areas here. It takes a full day to make it through the 55-acre complex, but you can hit the major sites—the Elizabethan hedge maze, the hanging basket display, rock and stone gardens, Canadian Heritage garden, fragrance garden and herb garden—in two to three hours. Admission.

UNIVERSITY OF BRITISH COLUMBIA BOTANICAL GARDEN

✉ *6804 Southwest Marine Drive* ☎ *604-822-9666* ✐ *www.ubcbotanical garden.org* With over 16,000 species, the award for variety goes to this botanical garden. The 110-acre research facility is filled with exotic and familiar specimens separated into alpine, Asian, British Columbian natives and food gardens. Summer admission.

NITOBE MEMORIAL GARDEN

✉ *University of British Columbia Point Grey campus, 1895 Lower Mall* ☎ *604-822-6038, 604-822-9666* ✐ *www.nitobe.org* This is an authentic Japanese strolling garden with a teahouse. Narrow paths wind through two and a half acres of serene traditional Japanese plantings. Folks come here for the cherry blossoms in April, irises in June and flaming red Japanese maples in October. Closed weekends in winter. Summer admission.

LODGING

HELLO BC ☎ *800-435-5622* ✐ *www.hellobc.com* This company operates a free reservation hotline to assist visitors in arranging for accommodations in all price categories. It's expensive to stay in the city, especially in the downtown core, and especially in high season (June through August). If you bring your car, expect to pay an additional $10–$25 per day to park at most downtown hotels. You will also pay the Goods and Services Tax (16 percent) on all hotel accommodations; if 7 percent of this tax amounts to over C$7, you can claim a rebate for this percentage by filling out a form (available from your hotel) and mailing it to Revenue Canada.

TOURISM VANCOUVER ☎ *604-682-2222* ✐ *www.tourismvancouver.com* July, August and early September are the peak tourist times in the lower mainland of southwestern B.C., and that is indeed when the weather is most reliable. However, visitors would do well to consider off-season travel—that's when local hotels offer special packages that can be incredible bargains. Luxury accommodations are sometimes half-price—which, when you take into account the favorable exchange rate, can mean that a super-deluxe room can be had for less than US$100. For more information call this helpful agency.

SUTTON PLACE HOTEL

$$$$ 395 ROOMS   ✉ *845 Burrard Street*   ☏ *604-682-5511, 866-378-8866*
🖂 *604-682-5513*   ⌨ *www.suttonplace.com*

Located in the heart of the business and entertainment district of cosmopolitan Vancouver, this luxurious hotel offers five-star accommodations at prices comparable to (and in some cases lower than) other top hotels in town, while assuring guests more for their money in terms of space and personal attention. Rooms are elegant, with classical decor punctuated by a blend of antique reproductions and fine botanical prints; the suites have enormous marbled bathrooms with deep European-style tubs and separate showers. Personal service is the signature here.

FAIRMONT HOTEL VANCOUVER

$$$$ 556 ROOMS   ✉ *900 West Georgia Street*   ☏ *604-684-3131, 866-540-4452*
🖂 *604-662-1929*   ⌨ *www.fairmont.com, hvc.concierge@fairmont.com*

Home away from home for the British royal family since it opened in 1939, the Fairmont, peaked by a château-style oxidized copper roof, is a landmark. The calling card of this posh property is Old World elegance. Rooms are spacious and well appointed with polished antiques, plump chairs, large writing desks and tall windows that open to the surrounding scenery. Bathrooms are a bit small (typical of the period in which they were built) but elegant nonetheless.

FOUR SEASONS HOTEL VANCOUVER

$$$$ 345 ROOMS   ✉ *791 West Georgia Street*   ☏ *604-689-9333*   🖂 *604-689-3466*
⌨ *www.fourseasons.com/vancouver, res.vancouver@fourseasons.com*

There's a reason this hotel consistently shows up in top ten rankings for North America. The service here is incomparable, composed of dozens of tiny details that escape the average hotel. Head out the door to go jogging, for instance, and the doorman will greet your return with a dry towel. The location is superb and the spacious rooms are well equipped for business travelers. The extensive fourth-floor fitness center opens onto a remarkable waterfall garden, perfect for contemplation.

THE FAIRMONT WATERFRONT

$$$$ 489 ROOMS   ✉ *900 Canada Place Way*   ☏ *604-691-1991, 800-441-1414*
🖂 *604-691-1999*   ⌨ *www.fairmont.com/waterfront, thewaterfronthotel@fairmont.com*

The view from this hotel captures the essence of Vancouver: In the foreground is the commercial hub of Canada Place; beyond that is Burrard Inlet, with sailboats and container ships; beyond that, the Lion's Gate Bridge and Grouse Mountain. More than half the rooms in this deluxe business-class hotel are positioned to look out on this vista; be sure to ask for one. Amenities include flatscreen TVs with connectivity boxes for laptops. There's also an extensive herb garden on the patio adjoining the swimming pool.

COAST PLAZA HOTEL & SUITES AT STANLEY PARK

$$$$ 269 ROOMS ✉ *1763 Comox Street* ☎ *604-688-7711, 800-663-1144*
📠 *604-688-5934* ✎ *www.coasthotels.com, plazasuiteinfo@coasthotels.com*

The Coast Plaza is by far the best lodging near Stanley Park, just steps away from local beaches. With 269 airy, large rooms and suites looking out over the park and English Bay, its location is unsurpassed for West End visitors.

PACIFIC PALISADES

$$$$ 232 ROOMS ✉ *1277 Robson Street* ☎ *604-688-0461, 800-663-1815*
📠 *604-688-4374* ✎ *www.pacificpalisadeshotel.com,*
reservations@pacificpalisadeshotel.com

With a prime downtown location and lots of space, this hotel is conveniently located near shops, restaurants, English Bay beaches and Stanley Park. The well-furnished studios and suites are roomy with modern, bright decor; all are equipped with kitchenettes, and many have breezy patios with grand views of the harbor or mountains. An evening wine reception is just part of the pampering service that includes pluses like thick robes, French milled soaps and other extras. Check for off-season promotions.

THE WEST END GUEST HOUSE

$$$-$$$$ 7 ROOMS ✉ *1362 Haro Street* ☎ *604-681-2889, 888-546-3327*
📠 *604-688-8812* ✎ *www.westendguesthouse.com, info@westendguesthousecom*

A pink Victorian a block off bustling Robson Street, this accommodation offers a more personable alternative to the area's hotels and motels. Each of the guest rooms (one of which is hypoallergenic) is filled with a mixture of antiques and has a personality of its own. All have private baths and plush feather mattresses, duvets and luxurious linens. Meals here—from the afternoon sherry with nuts to the summertime iced tea on the sun deck to the multicourse morning repast—are a gourmand's delight. Free bike use. Gay-friendly.

BARCLAY HOTEL

$$ 85 ROOMS ✉ *1348 Robson Street* ☎ *604-688-8850* 📠 *604-688-2534*
✎ *www.barclayhotel.com, infos@barclayhotel.com*

It's not hard to tell from its layout that this three-story hotel was at one time an apartment building, though renovations have really spruced up the public areas. Rooms are a bit tight, with mix-and-match furniture, minuscule bathrooms and air conditioning. The suites provide an affordable (though not cheap) alternative for families. Facing Robsonstrasse near all the restaurants and boutiques, the location is its best attribute.

SYLVIA HOTEL

$$-$$$ 120 ROOMS ✉ *1154 Gilford Street* ☎ *604-681-9321*
📠 *604-682-3551* ✎ *www.sylviahotel.com*

Location is the main reason to stay at this ivy-covered historic landmark. It's set at the edge of Stanley Park, right across the road from the seawall. Built in 1912 as a luxury apartment complex and named after the original owner's daughter, the Sylvia experienced several transformations (including serving as Vancouver's first cocktail lounge in 1954) before arising as the boutique hotel it is today. The rooms have been thoroughly refurbished in gentle hues of beige and peach and have views of English Bay, Stanley Park or the downtown skyline.

BURRARD INN

$$ 71 ROOMS ✉ 1100 Burrard Street ☎ 604-681-2331, 800-633-0366
📠 604-681-9753 ⌂ www.burrardinn.com, burrardinn@burrardinn.com

The Burrard has standard, motel-style accommodations in a good central location. A crotchety old elevator takes guests to upper-level, medium-sized rooms arranged in a quadrangle around the carport hidden under a rooftop garden. Furnishings are run of the mill. There are a few kitchenette units available. There is a 7-Eleven and a coffee shop on the premises.

NELSON HOUSE

$$$–$$$$ 6 UNITS ✉ 977 Broughton Street ☎ 604-684-9793, 866-684-9793
📠 604 689 5100 ⌂ www.downtownbedandbreakfast.com,
Info@downtownbedandbreakfast.com

Offering one suite and five guest rooms, the Nelson is a three-story Edwardian located near Barclay Heritage Square. Each room is individually decorated to suggest a world travel destination. Lounge by one of three cozy fireplaces. Enjoy the full breakfast. Nonsmoking; children allowed by prior arrangement only. Gay-friendly.

KINGSTON HOTEL BED AND BREAKFAST

$$–$$$ 52 ROOMS ✉ 757 Richards Street ☎ 604-684-9024, 888-713-3304
📠 604-684-9917 ⌂ www.kingstonhotelvancouver.com

An unusual find in downtown Vancouver, this 1910 woodframe with the large green awning and red neon sign was recently renovated inside and out to look more like a European bed and breakfast. The tiny rooms are clean and offer the bare necessities—vanity sink, dresser, bed, small closet—and a shared bath down the hall; rooms with private bath and television are larger. The hotel has a restaurant with a sports lounge, and also a sauna.

HOSTELLING INTERNATIONAL—
VANCOUVER DOWNTOWN

$ 250 ROOMS ✉ 1114 Burnaby Street ☎ 604 684 4565, 888-203-4302
📠 604-684-4540 ⌂ www.hihostels.ca, info@hihotels.ca

This hostel is perfectly located—a 10 to 15 minutes' walk from Stanley Park, Granville Island, Gastown and the business district. With space for more than 200 hostelers, its rooms are clean and functional. Laundry, recreation, cooking, meeting and studying facilities with free wi-fi are available. Dozens of organized activities are offered every day, but wanderers will find almost limitless opportunities within easy reach. A free continental breakfast is included.

HOSTELLING INTERNATIONAL—VANCOUVER CENTRAL

$ 77 ROOMS ✉ 1025 Granville Street ☎ 604-685-5335, 888-203-8333
📠 604-685-5351 ⌂ vancouver.central@hihostels.ca

Located several blocks east on bustling Granville Street is this hostel, which offers private rooms with private baths in addition to four-bed dorm rooms. There's also a lively bar on-site.

O CANADA HOUSE _____ ⓗidden

$$$$ 6 ROOMS   ✉ *1114 Barclay Street*   📞 *604-688-0555, 877-688-1114*
📠 *604-488-0556*   🖰 *www.ocanadahouse.com, info@ocanadahouse.com*

Housed in a huge, exquisitely renovated 1897 Victorian home, O Canada's elegant, comfortable guest rooms all feature private bath and are furnished with period antiques. Guests are served a gourmet three-course breakfast in the morning and complimentary sherry in the afternoon. There's a pantry stocked with baked goods, teas and sodas. It's just a ten-minute walk to Granville Island, and 15 minutes to Stanley Park. Free parking. Gay-friendly.

Finding low-cost accommodations in downtown Vancouver can be a real challenge, especially since massive urban renewal in anticipation of the 2010 Winter Olympics has led to the destruction or upscale renovation of most older, cheaper hotels in the city center. One strategy for affordable lodging is to stay in the city's eastern suburbs, where hotels are fewer but room rates are much lower.

ROYAL TOWERS HOTEL _____ ⓗidden

$$ 92 ROOMS   ✉ *140 6th Street, New Westminster*   📞 *604-524-3777*

Though the hallways may look a little shabby, and you might catch a whiff of ancient cigar smoke, the rooms here are refurbished to the standards you'd expect of a midrange motor inn and many rooms have views of the Fraser River. There's wireless internet access, but only in the lobby, and a sports bar where incessant hockey games on TV are supplemented by live puck-shooting contests on what may once have been a hardwood dancefloor. The main virtue of staying at the Royal Towers, aside from rates that can dip into the budget category when the exchange rate is favorable, is that all the sightseeing highlights of downtown are about 13 miles away via freeway—a quick trip unless it's rush hour—and there's a SkyTrain station five minutes away.

DINING

PINK PEARL RESTAURANT

$$ CHINESE   ✉ *1132 East Hastings Street*   📞 *604-253-4316*   📠 *604-253-8525*
🖰 *www.pinkpearl.com*

Dining in Chinatown is spelled dim sum. And this restaurant is a dim sum emporium, a cavernous dining room where black-clad waiters and waitresses roll out dozens of steam-tray delectables on trundle carts. Dine on this finger food while enjoying the Chinese artwork adorning the walls.

HON'S WUN-TUN HOUSE

$ CHINESE ✉ *268 Keefer Street* ✆ *604-688-0871*

In the city with the largest Chinese-American population in the western hemisphere, locals agree that Hon's is the best Chinese restaurant in Vancouver—not because of its atmosphere or decor (with its bright lights and big green blackboard filled with daily specials to augment the already-huge menu), but because of the authentic Cantonese food and incredibly reasonable prices. Here you can try marinated jellyfish, deep-fried bean curd in spicy rock salt or something as normal as sautéed shrimp. Be sure to try some of Hon's celebrated appetizers, such as lettuce wraps, potstickers and Chinese broccoli in oyster sauce.

THE ONLY SEAFOOD CAFÉ

$ SEAFOOD ✉ *20 East Hastings* ✆ *604-681-6546*

Miraculously, while just about everything else along Vancouver's old skid road has been renovated beyond recognition for the 2010 Winter Olympics, the longest-surviving family-owned restaurant in the city, established in 1912, endures with all its traditional charm intact—and its landmark neon seahorse sign still twinkling. Though mirrored walls make "The Only" look rather spacious, there are only 18 counter stools and two booths, so expect a wait. It is known for its outstanding clam chowder. Other good bets include buttered crab, pepper-stewed oysters and fried halibut. Portions are large and prices are phenomenally low.

C

$$$$ SEAFOOD ✉ *1600 Howe Street (on the False Creek Pier)* ✆ *604-681-1164*
✆ *604-605-8263* ✎ *www.crestaurant.com, info@crestaurant.com*

The decor at this snazzy seafood restaurant overlooking False Creek is flashy—lots of wood, metal and glass, exposed pipes and modern furniture, along with kitschy touches such as fishing lures on the restroom doors. The food is equally inventive, including entrées such as salmon with grand fir emulsion. Fish dishes are cooked to perfection, with only the freshest of seafood used, and you can round off dinner with one of C's 15 types of tea. Seasonal lunch.

BLUE WATER

$$$–$$$$ SEAFOOD/SUSHI ✉ *1095 Hamilton Street* ✆ *604-688-8078*
✎ *www.bluewatercafe.net*

I find that seafood is rarely executed as expertly as it is at this sensational centerpoint of Yaletown dining. The signature appetizer tower features a dozen delights, ranging from crab cakes to sushi; the entrées take peerless ingredients such as salmon and cod, fancy them up a bit (pumpernickel crust) and leave the flavor intact. Desserts include handmade sorbets and a sensational key lime cheesecake. Lots of glitz and glamour here, with black-clad young professionals hugging the sushi bar. The wood-decor and open ceiling are a delight, and the service is matchless.

THE WILLIAM TELL

$$$$ SWISS/FRENCH   ✉ *Georgian Court Hotel, 765 Beatty Street*   📞 *604-688-3504*
📠 *604-683-8810*   🖰 *www.thewmtell.com, info@thewmtell.com*

When the wallet is plump and it's time to indulge the taste buds, head for this longtime favorite, poshly appointed with fine European art and a few antique crossbows in keeping with its name. Your gastronomic experience might start with smoked BC salmon tartar or escargot, followed by seared veal with morel mushrooms or Fraser Valley duck breast with cherry compote in a terragon *jus*. Try the extraordinary set meals presented in conjunction with shows at the Queen Elizabeth Theatre or other local playhouses. Reservations recommended. Closed Monday.

IL GIARDINO

$$$–$$$$ ITALIAN   ✉ *1382 Hornby Street*   📞 *604-669-2422*   🖰 *www.umberto.com,*
ilgiardino@umberto.com

If you're in the mood for Italian food, you can't go wrong by heading to one of the region's five restaurants in the Umberto dynasty. The service and decor are impeccable and the food always tasty: Caprese salad, antipasti and pasta are reliable choices. Specials included rack of lamb, venison and Chilean sea bass. For alfresco dining on sunny days, we recommend the villa-style, terracotta courtyard of Il Giardino. Check their website or the phone book for addresses and phone numbers of other Umberto locations. No lunch on Saturday. Closed Sunday.

PRESTO PANINI

$–$$ ITALIAN   ✉ *859 Hornby Street*   📞 *604-684-4445*
🖰 *www.prestopanini.ca*

This place is inconspicuous, but not hard to find—right in the heart of downtown—no doubt the reason it's hard to get a table here at lunch. The menu is simple—Italian soups, salads, pastas and panini sandwiches. The list of sandwiches is extensive—with two dozen concoctions scooped onto toasted focaccia—and excellent. Service is efficient, portions filling. Closed Sunday.

FLEURI RESTAURANT

$$$ CONTINENTAL   ✉ *Sutton Place Hotel, 845 Burrard Street*   📞 *604-642-2900*   📠 *604-682-5513*   🖰 *www.suttonplace.com, fleuri@suttonplace.com*

Well-known for outstanding Continental cuisine, Fleuri also serves an incredible Chocoholic Bar from 6 to 10 p.m. each Thursday, Friday and Saturday night that attracts hordes of sweet-toothed locals. There are 12 to 16 different chocolate items on the buffet (crêpes, fondues, cakes, covered fruits) that change daily. They also feature a Sunday jazz brunch (be sure to try the croissant bread pudding), monthly winemakers dinners and afternoon tea daily. Reservations highly recommended.

LE CROCODILE

$$$$ FRENCH ✉909 Burrard Street ☎604-669-4298 📠604-669-4207
🖱www.lecrocodilerestaurant.com

Success can be a dangerous thing. Long cited as the premier French restaurant in Vancouver, Le Crocodile shows the signs of complacency: Service is a bit snotty, the bread can be stale, portions are shrinking. Champagne glasses are not much larger than thimbles, but the prices aren't equally minuscule! However, the Alsatian main dishes, such as veal sweetbreads with black truffle foie gras cream sauce or roasted lamb in a mustard sabayon, remain hearty and rich. The nightly specials are inviting, and the crowded buzz of the place creates an energizing, cosmopolitan air. No lunch on Saturday. Closed Sunday.

VILLA DEL LUPO

$$$–$$$$ ITALIAN ✉869 Hamilton Street ☎604-688-7436 📠604-688-3058
🖱www.villadellupo.com

Chef Julio Gonzalez-Perini practices food as art. Each dish served here is not only exquisitely flavorful, it's visually striking—swirls of sauce, artfully layered dashes and splashes of ingredients. The pastas, all handmade, are especially fine. The basement wine cellar (which guests can sometimes use for very intimate private parties) is extensive. Dinner only.

WHITE SPOT

$–$$ CANADIAN ✉718 Drake Street ☎604-605-0045

Ask any Vancouverite where you can find an authentic Canadian restaurant, and chances are they'll direct you to the nearest White Spot. Once there, you'll discover that there's really no such thing as distinctively Canadian cuisine, but residents are quite fond of regional enterprises that have been around for long enough to style themselves as legends, and no restaurant in British Columbia is more legendary than the White Spot. The huge menu, developed by some of Vancouver's top chefs, runs the gamut from classics like bacon burgers and fish and chips to Cajun chicken, chipotle quesadillas, Indian naan and Thai red curry prawns.

TREES _____ hidden

$ COFFEEHOUSE/BAKERY ✉450 Granville Street ☎604-684-5060
📠604-684-5026 🖱www.treescoffee.com

Vancouver's explosion of coffee shops has become, if anything, greater than Seattle's. There are many fine local purveyors; the best downtown is this small enclave in the financial district just a couple of blocks from Canada Place. They roast their own all-organic coffees; even better, the very best cheesecake muffins in town are baked in the kitchen out back.

BOJANGLES

$ COFFEEHOUSE/DELI ✉785 Denman Street ☎604-687-3622 📠604-687-3613
🖱www.bojanglescafe.com, denman@bojanglescafe.com

Of the dozens of cafés and small eateries along Denman, near Stanley Park, Bojangles is a bit snazzier than most, but still offers an economical lunch for visitors who've spent the morning in the park. The deluxe sandwiches are exceptionally good; soups and salads are dependable. A small outdoor seating area faces south, into the sun, along a side street.

SEQUOIA GRILL AT THE TEAHOUSE

$$$–$$$$ PACIFIC NORTHWEST ✉*Ferguson Point, Stanley Park Drive*
📞*604-669-3281, 800-280-9893*

Five fireplaces—including one that heats an outdoor patio—chase away the chill and mist at this teahouse. Diners might begin with an appetizer of mushrooms stuffed with crab, shrimp and mascarpone (a cream cheese made from the milk of cows fed on a special diet of herbs and flowers). For the main course, try the braised lamb shank with figs or an elaborate cioppino served with fresh-baked focaccia bread. In place of dessert, you might sip one of British Columbia's legendary, explosively flavorful ice wines.

CIN CIN

$$$–$$$$ ITALIAN/MEDITERRANEAN ✉*1154 Robson Street* 📞*604-688-7338*
⌨*www.cincin.net, info@cincin.net*

Its entrance is right on Robson, but this spot would be easy to miss if you weren't looking. The restaurant itself is upstairs, a surprisingly large and spacious dining room whose Mediterranean decor and cuisine have long been among the city's most popular. The fresh-baked bread, rich soups and grilled meats and seafoods here are all highly flavored and imaginatively conceived. Dinner only.

TROPIKA

$$ MALAYSIAN ✉*1128 Robson Street* 📞*604-737-6002*
⌨*www.tropika-canada.com*

This restaurant offers a fine introduction to Malaysian cuisine. If you really don't know what you're getting into, order satay (marinated meat skewered and grilled over charcoal); if you've had some exposure, you'll appreciate the spicier starred selections. They specialize in curries.

FOGG 'N' SUDS

$–$$ INTERNATIONAL ✉*1323 Robson Street* 📞*604-683-2337* 📠*604-669-9297*

A just-for-fun diner is this fancified hamburger joint with a relaxed atmosphere and a friendly crowd. Their menu includes Thai noodle salad, steaks and a variety of pastas. You probably won't have time to try each of the 150 beers from around the globe, but regulars get a chance to fill out a stylized passport of brews.

TAPASTREE

$$ MEDITERRANEAN ✉*1829 Robson Street* 📞*604-606-4680* 📠*604-682-6509*
⌨*www.tapastree.ca, tapastree@gmail.com*

Unlike most tapas cafés, the menu here is not so long you need a lengthy perusal to satisfy your curiosity. The two dozen small Mediterranean plates here vary from duck confit and sautéed wild mushrooms to braised beef short ribs. It's just two blocks from Stanley Park, perfect after a trek around the seawall.

ELBOW ROOM CAFE

$–$$ DINER   ✉ *560 Davie Street*   ☎ *604-685-3628*   📠 *604-685-4338*
💻 *www.theelbowroomcafe.com*

Generous breakfasts and lunches attract a mixed clientele to this café, which is decorated with autographed photos of movie stars. Start your day with the lumberjack or English breakfast, eggs Benedict, pancakes or an omelette. For lunch try a Monte Cristo, clubhouse or shrimp and crab sandwich. Hamburgers are big and popular. The owners say you have to have personality to fit in. If a customer fails to finish the food ordered at the Elbow Room Cafe, he or she is required to give a donation to a local charity. How much? Past donations have ranged from 50 cents to $50. Weekend breakfasts are popular.

STEPHO'S

$ GREEK   ✉ *1124 Davie Street*   ☎ *604-683-2555*

Local office workers line up on the sidewalk at lunchtime to get a table at this fairly traditional Greek taverna that serves up souvlakis as well as heaping platters of excellent roast lamb. One platter is a huge meal at a most reasonable price—about US$9.

DELILAH'S

$$$ PACIFIC NORTHWEST   ✉ *1789 Comox Street*   ☎ *604-687-3424*
💻 *www.delilahs.ca, info@delilahs.ca*

With its bordello decor and prime Northwest haute cuisine, funky Delilah's in the West End is one locals usually prefer not to share. As you arrive, you'll be handed a seasonal menu—perhaps bacon wrapped pork tenderloin, tagliatelle pasta tossed with roasted potatoes and seared artic char with a sweet caper oil. Next, sidle up to the bar for one of their famous martinis to keep you happy during the wait to be seated and served. Dinner only. Closed Monday.

SHOPPING

There are enough shops in Vancouver to overwhelm even the most serious of the "I'd-rather-be-shopping" crowd. Here are a few in the most popular shopping districts.

BEIJING TRADING COMPANY   ✉ *89 East Pender Street*   ☎ *604-684-3563*
In Chinatown, this trading company carries an intriguing selection of herbs, teas and food products.

INUIT GALLERY

✉ *206 Cambie Street*   ☎ *604-688-7323, 888-615-8399*   💻 *www.inuit.com*
Gastown teems with souvenir shops full of T-shirts, totems, maple sugar, smoked salmon and other regional items. This gallery has high-dollar Northwest Coast First Nation and Inuit art.

SIKORA

✉432 West Hastings Street ✆604-685-0625, 866-685-0625 ⌂www.sikoras classical.com Located on the edge of Gastown, this is a modern oddity, a store with just one type of merchandise—classical music. But what a selection! With close to 25,000 CDs, classical music lovers will find artists and versions of standards that you'll never see in mainstream American music stores, no matter how large.

SALMAGUNDI WEST

✉321 West Cordova Street ✆604-681-4648 It seems like there are a zillion antique and curio shops in the Gastown area; this is one of the best, with an engaging collection of clothes, jewelry and greeting cards. The owner has a fetish for horns, so if you need an antique trumpet or other heraldic instrument, this is the place.

KIL SLI NATIVE GIFT SHOP

✉Bill Reid Gallery of North Coast Art, 639 Hornby Street ✆604-682-3455 ✆604-682-3310 ⌂www.billreidgallery.ca This new gift shop within the Bill Reid Gallery of North Coast Art is discreetly tucked away in an upper-level courtyard beside the museum and sells perhaps the finest modern-day First Nations artworks in the city. Closed Monday and Tuesday.

LUSH

✉1020 Robson Street ✆604-687-5874 ⌂www.lush.ca Lush is exactly what its name implies—a redolent profusion of lotions, emollients, soaps, oils and other cosmetics and body-care products. It's an outpost of a popular European chain; all its products are natural and fresh.

ROBSONSTRASSE

Vancouver's trendiest shopping area is this Germanization of Robson Street that reflects the influx of European luxury shops, designer outlets and see-and-be-seen sidewalk cafés in recent years. The heart of Robsonstrasse is a six-square-block area along Robson bounded by Burrard, Haro, Jervis and Alberni streets, northwest of Robson Square. Along this fashionable strip you'll find famous-name stores like Armani, Bebe, Body Shop, Club Monaco and Saatchi side-by-side with little specialty shops selling handcrafted jewelry, clog shoes, Belgian chocolates and art glass.

CANADIAN CRAFTS

✉1045 Robson Street ✆604-684-6629 You'll find a wide selection of handmade regional gift items at this local shop.

NORTHERN ART COMPANY

✉1026 Robson Street ✆604-683-3773 This company specializes in fine handcrafted regional items, including British Columbia jade, American Indian masks and other Canadiana.

SILVER GALLERY ___ **h**idden

✉ *1226 Robson Street* ✆ *604-681-6884* ✐ *www.silvergallery.ca, mail@silver talks.com* Offering contemporary native American jewelry hand-crafted in British Columbia, this shop is a worthwhile stop for authentic souvenirs.

ROBSON FASHION PARK ✉ *1131 Robson Street* At this locale, you'll find a number of boutiques selling high fashion.

ROBSON PUBLIC MARKET ✉ *1610 Robson Street* ✆ *604-682-2733* ✆ *604-682-2776* ✐ *www.robsonpublicmarket.com* There are several souvenir shops scattered along the strip, in addition to some fun places such as this public market, with over two dozen retail stores.

DANIEL'S LE CHOCOLAT BELGE ✉ *4447 West 10th Avenue* ✆ *604-224-3361* ✐ *www.danielchocolates.com* Vancouver is a chocoholic's paradise, with an unusual number of fine chocolate shops throughout the city. A favorite is Daniel's, which uses top-quality Belgian chocolate to create truffles and other confections.

BOBOLI ✉ *2776 Granville Street* ✆ *604-257-2300* A high-style boutique on the west side of town, this shop features imported European clothing for men and women.

NIGHTLIFE

GEORGIA STRAIGHT ✐ *www.straight.com* There are hundreds of clubs, discos, cabarets, lounges, pubs and taverns in Vancouver; we touch on only a few popular selections here. A complete listing of all the acts at all the clubs, bars and taverns appears every Thursday in this helpful paper.

QUEEN ELIZABETH THEATRE AND PLAYHOUSE ✉ *Hamilton Street between Georgia and Dunsmuir streets* ✆ *604-665-3050* The Vancouver Opera Association (604-682-2871; www.vancouveropera.ca, tickets@vancouveropera.ca) stages productions several times a year at this playhouse, also home to **Ballet British Columbia** (604-732-5003; www.balletbc.com) as well as major theater productions and visiting musicals.

VANCOUVER SYMPHONY ORCHESTRA ✉ *884 Granville Street* ✆ *604-876-3434* ✐ *www.vancouversymphony.ca* This orchestra provides first-rate entertainment at **The Orpheum**, a multilevel Vaudeville theater built in the mid-1920s that's worth a visit in itself.

RICHARD'S ON RICHARDS ✉ *1036 Richards Street* ✆ *604-687-6794* ✐ *www.richardsonrichards.com, info@richardsonrichards.com* Richard's, with its refined wood, brass and stained-glass decor, has live music on weekdays and deejays on weekends. It attracts a mixed crowd, predominantly upscale businesspeople.

SHARK CLUB ✉ *180 West Georgia Street* ✆ *604-687-4275* ✐ *www.sharkclubs.com* If you don't like hockey, don't venture into this club, where dozens of TV monitors are tuned to Canada's national madness. During the in-

frequent breaks in hockey, other sports manifest themselves. As sports bars go, this one is a bit more refined than most.

THE ROXY

✉932 Granville Street ☎604-331-7999 ⌕www.roxyvan.com The hub of Vancouver's lively rock scene since 1988, the Roxy has become the place where Canadian celebrities come to see and be seen. By celebrities, we mean hockey players, not movie stars. While new and established guest bands sometimes perform here, the entertainment mainstay is a string of house bands—Joe's Garage on Monday and Troys R Us on Thursday, Friday and Saturday.

GÉRARD LOUNGE ✉Sutton Place Hotel, 845 Burrard Street ☎604-682-5511

For an unhurried drink and quiet conversation, your best bet is this genteel gentlemen's-style club; it is the place to spot visiting celebrities as well.

COASTAL JAZZ AND BLUES SOCIETY HOTLINE ☎604-872-5200, 888-438-5299 ⌕www.coastaljazz.ca This hotline lists what's going on in the numerous jazz clubs around town.

CELEBRITIES NIGHT CLUB ✉1022 Davie Street ☎604-681-6180 ⌕www.celebritiesnightclub.com Of the local gay haunts, Celebrities is open to both men and women.

LOTUS SOUND LOUNGE ✉The Lotus Hotel, 455 Abbott Street ☎604-685-7777 The Lotus offers Top-40 music played by a deejay. A mixed gay and lesbian crowd frequents the dancefloor at this contemporary lounge.

GREAT CANADIAN CASINO ✉709 West Broadway ☎604-872-5543 Casino gambling is legal here, with half the profits going to local charities; for a little roulette, sic bo or blackjack action, try the Great Canadian.

BEACHES & PARKS

ENGLISH BAY BEACHES (NORTHERN SHORE)

✉Off Beach Avenue on the southwest side of town ☎604-257-8400 ⊠604-257-8427

🏊 Connected by Stanley Park's seawall promenade, silky English Bay Beach and broad Sunset Beach Park are prime candidates for a long sunset stroll. Within walking distance of the city center, they are a favorite of businesspeople out for a lunch break or there to catch the last rays after work during the week. There are restrooms, as well as changing rooms and intermittent food stalls in summer.

STANLEY PARK

✉Follow Georgia Street heading west through downtown to the park entrance ☎604-257-8400 ⊠604-257-8427

🏃 🚴 🏊 This beautiful park is a green oasis in downtown Vancouver. Highlights include the aquarium, children's farmyard, seawall promenade, children's water park, a miniature railway, scenic lighthouses, totem poles and statues, pitch-and-putt golf, tennis courts, an evening gun salute (each day at 9 p.m.), an open-air theater, a swan-filled lagoon, nature house and miles of trails through thick coniferous forest. Second and Third bathing beaches are extremely popular among sun lovers and water enthusiasts. Second Beach boasts a heated outdoor pool. Facilities include restaurants and concession stands, restrooms, showers and picnic facilities.

NORTH SHORE

One of Vancouver's best features is its proximity to nature. Just a few minutes from the heart of town is this lush, green slope with scenic beaches, ecology centers and campgrounds. Easily reached by transit, this area also offers a great bird's-eye view of the metropolitan district.

SIGHTS

CAPILANO SUSPENSION BRIDGE AND PARK ✉3735 Capilano Road, North Vancouver ☎604-985-7474 ☏604-872-3055 ✎www.capbridge.com There are several sights of interest on the North Shore, beginning with this swaying footbridge stretched over the chasm 230 feet above the Capilano River; you will pass through a park complete with totem poles and souvenir-filled trading post to reach the bridge. The Treetops attraction takes visitors through the rainforest canopy on rope bridges. Admission.

CAPILANO SALMON HATCHERY ✉4500 Capilano Park Road, North Vancouver ☎604-666-1790 ☏604-666-1949 ✎capilano@pac.dfo-mpo.gc.ca Up the road a bit from the suspension bridge and park is this salmon hatchery, where the public can take a self-guided tour and learn about the life cycle of this important fish.

GROUSE MOUNTAIN ——— **h**idden
✉6400 Nancy Greene Way, North Vancouver ☎604-984-0661 ☏604-984-6360 ✎www.grousemountain.com, info@grousemountain.com This mountain at the top of Vancouver is where visitors catch the Skyride gondola to the mountain peak complex to ski, hike and snowshoe. The incredible high-tech mythology and history presentation about Vancouver in "The Theatre in the Sky" is also here. Admission.

LODGING

GROUSE INN
$$–$$$ 80 ROOMS ✉1633 Capilano Road, North Vancouver ☎604-988-7101, 800-779-7888 ☏604-988-7102 ✎www.grouseinn.com, stay@grouseinn.com
Near the north end of the Lions Gate Bridge not far from shopping, dining and sightseeing spots, this inn offers tidy but plain, motel-style rooms decorated in earth tones. Standard rooms have the basics—full bath, queen-sized bed, cable television, small table and chairs—

HIDDEN LISTINGS

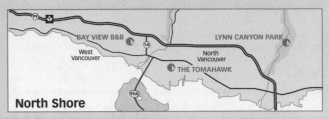

North Shore

BAY VIEW B&B

PAGE 557

Panoramic views of English Bay and the city skyline from a classic home set in a beautifully landscaped garden

LYNN CANYON PARK

PAGE 558

Lush rainforest threaded with hiking trails and a rope bridge stretched 240 feet above the rapids

THE TOMAHAWK

PAGE 557

Vintage American diner chock-full of Northwest Indian artifacts and knickknacks, serving sandwiches and homemade pie

though a few are set up as family suites and others are equipped with kitchenettes. There's a playground and heated pool. Continental breakfast included.

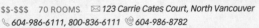

LONSDALE QUAY HOTEL

$$-$$$ 70 ROOMS ✉ 123 Carrie Cates Court, North Vancouver
📞 604-986-6111, 800-836-6111 📠 604-986-8782
🖥 www.lonsdalequayhotel.com, sales@lonsdalequayhotel.com

If you weren't looking for it, you'd hardly notice this gracefully aging little waterfront hotel. Guest units are exceptionally spacious, though configurations and quality vary because of ongoing room-by-room renovation. All have air conditioning and wi-fi, while premium rooms boast leather-upholstered furniture, luxury bedding and marble bathrooms. Most rooms have small private balconies; reserve one that faces west, both for the great view of the downtown Vancouver skyline and the relative peace and quiet (rooms facing the nearby shipping dock facility can be noisy all night). Facilities include a swimming pool and exercise room. Pet-friendly.

CAPILANO RV PARK

$ 208 SITES ✉ In North Vancouver at 295 Tomahawk Avenue 📞 604-987-4722
📠 604-987-2015 🖥 www.capilanorvpark.com, info@capilanorvpark.com

Located under the north end of Lions Gate Bridge, this RV park is the closest camping option you will find. While it's primarily set up for recreational vehicles, there are eight grassy tent sites; reservations can be made for 125 hookup sites only, and are essential during the busy summer months. There are restrooms, showers, picnic tables, a playground, a lounge, laundry facilities, a pool and a whirlpool.

BAY VIEW B&B

$$$ 5 UNITS ✉1270 Netley Place, West Vancouver ☎604-926-3218, 800-208-2204 ✆604-926-3216 ✍www.bayview-bb.com, bayview@bayview-bb.com

If you're looking for quiet, Bay View's perch—an exclusive residential neighborhood above West Vancouver—is the place. A spacious, neat home at the end of a little-traveled cul-de-sac, Bay View has elegant suites decorated with Canadian art and European antiques. All offer panoramic views of English Bay, Stanley Park, the city skyline and the Lion's Gate Bridge. Guests are greeted with a plate of steaming fresh cookies and a scrumptious four-course breakfast is served. Its grounds are equally stunning, with beautifully landscaped gardens and a quaint gazebo. Despite its bucolic locale, it's just 15 minutes from downtown Vancouver.

DINING

BLACK BEAR

$$ BRITISH ✉1177 Lynn Valley Road, North Vancouver ☎604-990-8880 ✆604-990-8860 ✍www.blackbearpub.com, alastair@blackbearpub.com

Neighborhood pubs are a much-loved part of life in Canada, and this one is the most popular in North Vancouver. Housed in a handsome Craftsman building, the restaurant offers 24 different draught ales and beers, as well as an outstanding menu you'll be hard-pressed to find in any other pub: peppercorn steak with an Irish whiskey sauce, pulled pork sandwiches, chicken *roti*, Indonesian curry pasta. There are also burgers, but you can opt for chicken, ostrich or salmon instead of ho-hum beef. Closed Monday.

THE TOMAHAWK

$–$$ AMERICAN ✉1550 Philip Avenue, North Vancouver ☎604-988-2612 ✆604-988-5262 ✍www.tomahawkrestaurant.com, info@tomahawkrestaurant.com

Packed to the gills with Northwest Indian artifacts, this spot is more than a small diner-style eatery that has been pleasing locals since 1926. It's an archaeological treat, one that came to be when the original owner allowed the exchange of knickknacks for food during the Depression. Nowadays, you'll have to pay for your meal: egg dishes, french toast and pancakes at breakfast, sandwiches and burgers at lunch, and steak, meatloaf and chicken potpie at dinner. If you can, save room for homemade pie for dessert.

THE SALMON HOUSE

$$–$$$ SEAFOOD ✉2229 Folkestone Way, West Vancouver ☎604-926-3212 604-926-8539 www.salmonhouse.com, dinner@salmonhouse.com

For that million-dollar view of the city and outstanding seafood to match, this restaurant, perched on a West Vancouver hill, fits the bill. The specialty here is fresh Alder salmon grilled over alderwood, but the prawns and scallop brochettes and rack of lamb are also worth trying. Lunch, dinner and Sunday brunch; reservations recommended.

VILLAGE FISH

$ SEAFOOD ✉1482 Marine Drive, West Vancouver ☎604-922-4332

This is a traditional seafood store much favored by locals. There's fresh crab, prawns and salmon among the many selections. Ask for some Indian candy (honey-cured salmon) to take with you as you leave.

BEAN AROUND THE WORLD

$ COFFEEHOUSE ✉1522 Marine Drive, West Vancouver ☎604-925-9600 www.cowboycoffee.ca

Right across the street from Savary Island Pie Shoppe, this coffeehouse offers much better coffee—roasted on-site—and friendlier service. The adjacent bakery turns out a rich selection of muffins, breads and pastries every morning; it's hard to find a seat here around 8 a.m., but it's worth a few minutes' wait. Breakfast and lunch only.

SHOPPING

LONSDALE QUAY MARKET ✉123 Carrie Cates Court, end of Lonsdale Avenue ☎604-985-6261 www.lonsdalequay.com, e-comments@lonsdalequay.com

Across Burrard Inlet in North Vancouver, this market is a tri-level atrium mall on the waterfront. In addition to postcard views of the Vancouver skyline, this bustling shopping center combines hotel rooms, trendy stores and a fresh fish market. A great place to spend money, people watch and survey the shoreline.

BEACHES & PARKS

LYNN CANYON PARK

✉In North Vancouver at the end of Peters Road ☎604-981-3103

Though it's much shorter but slightly higher than the Capilano Suspension Bridge, there is no charge to venture out onto this park's high-rise rope bridge stretched 240 feet above the rapids of Lynn Canyon. The pretty 617-acre park boasts a lush rainforest threaded by numerous hiking trails. There is also a fine ecology center. Facilities include restrooms, picnic facilities, nature trails, a concession stand and an ecology center. Please heed the signs warning of the dangers on nearby cliffs. Admission.

WHISTLER

One of Vancouver's best day trips leads to Whistler, a resort area famous for its skiing and après-ski life. Snow lovers are drawn to the region's crystalline lakes and lofty mountains as well as its alpine trails and cosmopolitan ski village. Located 79 miles northeast of Vancouver, the Whistler area has a number of British Columbia's best-known provincial parks that make the area ideal for fishing, windsurfing, swimming and, of course, loafing.

SIGHTS

GAY WHISTLER ☎604-288-7218 ✎www.gaywhistler.com, dean@gaywhistler.com In recent years, Whistler has begun to promote itself as an ideal locale for gay and lesbian travelers. For up-to-date events and information, including dining and lodging recommendations, visit this experienced group's site.

B.C. MUSEUM OF MINING ✉Route 99, Britannia Beach ☎604-896-2233, 800-896-4044 ✎www.bcmuseumofmining.org, general@bcmuseumofmining.org On your way up to Whistler, stop for an underground tour through this mining museum, which takes you deep into the workings of what was once the highest-yielding copper mine in the British Empire. The kids will enjoy panning for gold and exploring the large museum area. Closed weekends, except in spring and late December through early January. Admission.

SHANNON FALLS As you're cruising farther up the Sea to Coast Highway, you'll pass this beautiful sight worth a detour near the town of Squamish. It is a high, shimmering ribbon of tumbling water immediately off the highway.

STAWAMUS CHIEF This monument is often called, incorrectly, the second-largest monolith in the world after the Rock of Gibraltar. At 2300 feet, it's actually the second-largest in the British commonwealth. On a fine day, there will be climbers dangling all about the face of this mountaineer's dream.

RAINBOW PARK ✉Alta Lake Road One of the more interesting heritage sites in Whistler is at this park, the site of the area's first vacation retreat. This is also the best spot for a view of the valley and the Blackcomb and Whistler mountains.

WHISTLER MUSEUM AND ARCHIVES SOCIETY ✉4333 Main Street ☎604-932-2019 ☎604-932-2077 ✎www.whistlermuseum.org, info@whistlermuseum.org For an in-depth look at the history of the area, visit this quaint museum next to the public library in Whistler Village that houses relics, artifacts, documentary videos and an interesting slide presentation (which must be booked for viewing). Call ahead for hours. Admission.

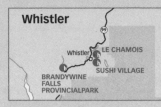

BRANDYWINE FALLS PROVINCIAL PARK

PAGE 565

Charming little park where nature trails wind past a 230-foot cascading waterfall

LE CHAMOIS

PAGE 561

Luxury hotel boasting impeccable service and bay windows overlooking the snowy slopes

SUSHI VILLAGE

PAGE 563

Bustling local favorite with serene atmosphere, tasty tempura and mouth-watering à la carte sushi

MEAGER CREEK HOT SPRINGS

📞604-898-2100 📠604-898-2191 North of Whistler past the logging and farming town of Pemberton is this series of pools, each varying in temperature, set in a pristine grove of evergreens. To get there, take Route 99 to the Pemberton Meadows Road and follow it north to Hurley River Road. After 45 minutes on this logging road, you'll come to the springs. If the road's not washed out (and it often is), it's possible to drive all the way through in summer, but it's closed during winter. Call ahead for road conditions.

LODGING

HOSTELLING INTERNATIONAL—WHISTLER

$ 32 BEDS ✉5768 Alta Lake Road 📞604-932-5492 📠604-932-4687
💻www.hihostels.ca, whistler@hihostels.ca
Located on Lake Alta, this hostel is only ten minutes from Whistler Village. Accommodations are basic here, with men's and women's dorms and a private room upstairs, and a kitchen, dining room and game room downstairs overlooking the lake. There's also a sauna.

UBC WHISTLER LODGE

$ 42 BEDS ✉2124 Nordic Drive 📞604-822-5851, 877-932-6604 📠604-822-4711
💻www.ubcwhistlerlodge.com, whistler@ams.ubc.ca
You still need to provide your own food and bedding and will share cubicles with other hostelers, but this rustic lodge set above a quiet residential section offers lots of pleasant extras like a sauna and jacuzzi, barbecue and fire pit off the large deck, ski equipment/bike storage

locker, kitchen, laundry, game lounge, separate television room and internet access. Bedding can be rented for a nominal fee. Book well in advance for ski season.

HOLIDAY INN SUNSPREE WHISTLER

$$–$$$$ 115 ROOMS   ✉ 4295 Blackcomb Way   📞 604-938-0878, 800-229-3188   📠 604-938-9943   ✍ www.whistlerhi.com

If you're planning a stay in Whistler during ski season, and student hostels aren't your cup of tea, let's face it—you're going to pay dearly for a roof over your head. That said, this château-style resort centrally located in Whistler Village offers the most reasonable winter rates in town (though still in the $200 range). All the bright, contemporary guest units have fireplaces, microwaves and jetted soaking tubs, and many also have pull-down Murphy beds and full kitchen facilities, washers and dryers. There's plug-in high-speed internet access and a fitness center with a large hot tub.

FAIRMONT CHÂTEAU WHISTLER

$$$$ 550 ROOMS   ✉ 4599 Château Boulevard   📞 604-938-8000, 888-540-4424   📠 604-938-2291   ✍ www.fairmont.com/whistler, chateauwhistlerresort@fairmont.com

Lifestyles of the Rich and Famous dubbed this luxurious destination, located at the base of Blackcomb Mountain, "Whistler's premier address" with good reason. The property is strikingly elegant and brimming with Old World charm. Guests enjoy inspiring alpine views from smartly furnished rooms with country-style wood furniture, queen- or king-sized beds, mini-bars and large bathrooms. They also have an 18-hole golf course designed by Robert Trent Jones, Jr.

LE CHAMOIS

$$$$ 50 ROOMS   ✉ 4557 Blackcomb Way   📞 604-932-8700, 888-560-9453   📠 604-932-4486   ✍ www.leschamoiswhistlerhotel.com, res@wildflowerlodge.com

A full-service luxury hotel, this place shares the same prime ski-in, ski-out location at the base of the Blackcomb runs as the Fairmont Château. However, its smaller proportions (only 50 rooms) allow for a high degree of personal attention. The guest rooms are spacious, with big bathrooms, kitchenettes and designer touches evident throughout the decor; some of the studio rooms are especially wonderful, with two-person jacuzzi tubs in the living room area set before bay windows overlooking the slopes and lifts.

WHISTLER ACCOMMODATION   ✉ 103-4573 Chateau Boulevard   📞 604-905-4607, 866-905-4607   📠 604-905-4656   ✍ www.whistleraccommodation.com, info@whistleraccommodation.com

A viable lodging option for family and small-group ski trips to Whistler is a rental condominium or townhouse. Many private owners of condos derive tax advantages as well as supplemental income by turning their units over to a property management service for short-term rental when they're not using them. For these in-

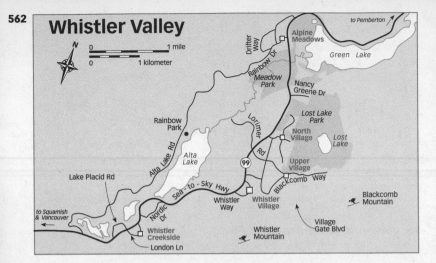

Whistler Valley

dividually decorated two- to four-bedroom units with fireplaces, full kitchens and other luxury amenities, you can expect to pay around $500–$600 a night in ski season. While there are half a dozen such management companies in town, this agency specializes in ski-in, ski-out townhomes in relatively private settings. Minimum stays of as much as a week may be required. Discount lift tickets are available.

DINING

BEARFOOT BISTRO

$$$$ PACIFIC NORTHWEST ✉4121 Village Green ☎604-932-3433 ✎604-932-8383 ⌨www.bearfootbistro.com, info@bearfootbistro.com

Polished wood paneling and high-backed leather dining chairs strike a contrast with cut crystal stemware and handpainted china to create a rich, warm ambience here. Most starters are small seafood plates such as Vancouver Island black cod or stone crab; main courses include such exotica as Japanese waygu beef and a wild game trio. When it comes to wine pairings, the bistro's vast wine cellar contains 20,000 bottles and has won the *Wine Spectator* Award of Excellence for 12 consecutive years. Bargain-hunting bon vivants take note: Prices are $50 per person lower outside of ski season. Dinner only.

ARAXI

$$$$ PACIFIC NORTHWEST ✉4222 Whistler Village Square ☎604-932-4540 ✎604-932-3348 ⌨www.araxi.com, info@araxi.com

A bright and airy restaurant with congenial staff, Araxi has been a dependable favorite in town since its beginning. The menu features creative Pacific Northwest–style cuisine, including poached free-range chicken with golden beets and carrot purée. Breads, sausages and pasta are all house-made. The dining room is often overflowing with customers, while the bar is best for a rousing drink with your friends.

INGRID'S VILLAGE CAFÉ ⓗidden

$ DINER   ✉*4305 Skiers Approach #102*   ☏*604-932-7000*   ☞*604-932-2930*
🖳*www.ingridswhistler.com*

At Ingrid's the tradition of savory home cooking continues in this family-owned tiny bistro on the village plaza a few minutes from the central lift base. Soups and bulging sandwiches are fresh-made daily; breakfasts are heaping platters of eggs, potatoes, toast and sausage. It's hard to find a better value in Whistler.

SUSHI VILLAGE ⓗidden

$$–$$$ SUSHI/JAPANESE   ✉*4272 Mountain Square*   ☏*604-932-3330*
☞*604-932-2594*   🖳*www.sushivillage.com, info@sushivillage.com*

Amazingly, there are five Japanese restaurants in little Whistler Village, and of those five, this is the one the locals most often visit. This place is busy, so service can be slow to a fault, but the atmosphere is serene, the decor clean-cut and the food quite good, especially the tasty tempura and à la carte sushi items.

CARAMBA!

$–$$ AMERICAN   ✉*4314 Main Street #12*   ☏*604-938-1879*   ☞*604-938-1856*

This place may sound Mexican, but it's really not. It's comfort food—black bean soup, roast chicken, grilled salmon, pizzas from an alder wood–fired oven. Yes, there's even macaroni and cheese.

THE WILDFLOWER

$$$$ PACIFIC NORTHWEST   ✉*Fairmont Château Whistler, 4599 Château Boulevard*
☏*604-938-2033*   🖳*www.fairmont.com/whistler*

When I want to escape from the bustling activities of the central village, I book a table at this dining room, a perfect destination for a romantic dinner. This elegant restaurant's decor echoes the Old World charm of its setting in the Fairmont Château Whistler. The award winning chef focuses on fresh Pacific Northwest cuisine featuring organically grown regional herbs, veggies, fruits, eggs and meat. Seafood is also a specialty of the house. The Sunday brunch is a bargain, considering the quality, as is the daily breakfast buffet.

SHOPPING

ESCENTS AROMATHERAPY OF WHISTLER ✉*Town Plaza, 4314 Main Street #20* ☏*604-905-2955* 🖳*www.escentsaromatherapy.com* Most of the great shopping in Whistler is done in the Town Plaza, at shops like this one. It offers a variety of essential oils—rosemary, lavender and such—as well as a dizzying array of lotions, oils, soaps, scents, potions and emollients.

THE PLAZA GALLERIES ✉*4314 Main Street #22* ☏*604-938-6233* 🖳*www.plazagalleries.com* These galleries have a unique distinction: among their artists are celebrities such as Tony Curtis and the late Anthony Quinn.

Keep your eyes open for the occasional Rembrandt or Picasso, too. It's all very ritzy.

ROCKY MOUNTAIN CHOCOLATE FACTORY ✉ *4190 Springslane* ☎ *604-932-4100* Chocoholics will be in seventh heaven at this deliciously dangerous spot.

NIGHTLIFE

LONGHORN SALOON ✉ *Carleton Lodge, 4284 Mountain Square* ☎ *604-932-5999* 📠 *604-932-6124* ⌨ *www.longhornsaloon.ca* You'll find a good selection of lounges, taverns and discos in Whistler Village (not surprising for a resort destination). The après-ski scene is big everywhere, though one of the most popular spots is this saloon, with a deejay nightly and one of Whistler's largest dancefloors.

GARFINKEL'S _____ ⓗidden

✉ *4308 Main Street #1* ☎ *604-932-2323* ⌨ *www.garfswhistler.com, info@ garfswhistler.com* This rustic and rowdy tavern (known to locals as Garf's) offers a wide variety of music, including reggae and rock. Thursday through Sunday nights feature all-out party themes with special acts. Cover on weekends.

SAVAGE BEAGLE ✉ *4222 Village Square* ☎ *604-938-3337; info@savagebeagle. com* An eclectic mix of sounds (hip-hop, house, classic rock and salsa) can be found in this venue's upstairs lounge and the danceclub down below.

MALLARD LOUNGE ✉ *Fairmont Château Whistler, 4599 Château Boulevard* ☎ *604-938-8000* This refined lounge, with a large fireplace, soft piano music and expansive views of the Blackcomb Mountain base, is infinitely suitable for a quiet drink with friends.

BEACHES & PARKS

PORTEAU COVE PROVINCIAL PARK
✉ *Located off Sea to Sky Highway 15 miles north of Horseshoe Bay* ☎ *604-986-9371* ⌨ *www.seatoskyparks.com, info@seatoskyparks.com*

🚣 🐟 ⛵ 🏊 This is a favorite among scuba enthusiasts because of its sunken ships and concrete reefs full of marine life located not far off the rocky beach. Porteau Cove is a long, narrow park stretched along the B.C. Rail tracks on the east shore of picturesque Howe Sound. Swimmers and kayakers are also welcome. Restrooms, showers, picnic facilities, an amphitheater, and a divers' changing room are available. Parking fee, $3.

▲ There are 44 developed tent/RV sites (no hookups); $24 to $29 per night; and 16 walk-in sites; $10 per night. Very popular; reservations recommended (800-689-9025; www.discovercamping.ca).

GARIBALDI PROVINCIAL PARK
✉ *Located 40 miles north of Vancouver off the Sea to Sky Highway (Route 99), north of Squamish* ☎ *604-898-3678* 📠 *604-898-4171*

🚶 🚴 ⛺ 🚣 ⚓ Named for Mt. Garibaldi, its crowning point, this awe-inspiring park is made up of 480,000 acres of intriguing lavaland, glaciers, high alpine fields, lakes and dense forests of fir, cedar, hemlock, birch and pine. Thirty-six miles of developed trails lead into the five most popular spots—Black Tusk/Garibaldi Lake, Diamond Head, Singing Pass, Cheakamus and Wedgemont Lake. You can try for rainbow trout in Mamquam Lake (Diamond Head area), but swimming is very cold throughout the park. You'll find restrooms, picnic tables, shelters and nature, bike and cross-country ski trails (biking is restricted to the Cheakamus area). Parking fee, $3.

▲ There is a hike-in shelter with propane stoves (seven-mile hike) at Diamond Head; you must bring your own gear, including toilet paper; C$10 per night. There are two hike-in campgrounds at Garibaldi Lake (six-mile hike) with propane stoves; C$5 per night. Elfin Lakes has a shelter with bunks for 33 people; C$10 per night or C$25 per family.

BRANDYWINE FALLS PROVINCIAL PARK

⌨Located approximately 60 miles north of Vancouver on the Sea to Sky Highway (Route 99) ☎604-986-9371 ⌁www.seatoskyparks.com, info@seatoskyparks.com

🚶🚲 The highlight of this small park is its 230-foot waterfall; winding nature trails are also close at hand. There are restrooms, picnic facilities, fire pits and nature and hiking trails. Day use only. Parking fee, $3.

SUNSHINE COAST

With a 100-mile shoreline that stretches along the northeast side of the strait of Georgia, the Sunshine Coast is bordered by sandy beaches, secluded bays and rugged headlands. It reaches from Howe Sound in the south to Desolation Sound in the north. This area is rustic, even a bit worn around the edges, but don't let that stop you. There are pleasant sites, plus a good number of artists in residence whose work is worth checking out.

SIGHTS

GIBSONS As you leave the ferry at Langdale and begin to wind your way up the Sunshine Coast along Route 101, one of the first areas of interest is this port town.

MOLLY'S REACH ⌂647 School Road, Gibsons ☎604-886-9710 Be sure to stop at this restaurant, which for years was the setting for a popular Canadian television series, *The Beachcombers*.

SUNSHINE COAST MUSEUM AND ARCHIVES ⌂716 Winn Road, Gibsons ☎604-886-8232 ⌁www.sunshinecoastmuseum.ca, curator@sunshinecoast museum.ca This museum maps the history of the area. The first floor exhibits cover the region's maritime history, while the second floor displays explore the First Nations and early European pioneers, along with the area's natural and industrial history. Closed Sunday and Monday.

HOUSE OF HÉWHÎWUS ✉*5555 Route 101, Sechelt* ☎*604-885-2273* 📠*604-885-3490* Also known as the House of Chiefs, this is the center of government, education and entertainment for the self-governing Sechelt Indian band. Photographs and artifacts relating the history of the tribe are on display in the **Tems Swîya Museum** (604-885-6012). Ask for directions to the totems and grouping of carved figures behind the complex. Closed some Sundays (call ahead).

PICTOGRAPHS

If you have an interest in archaeology, rent a boat and head north up the inlet from Porpoise Bay to view ancient Indian pictographs on the faces of the cliff walls looming above the water. The pictographs are very difficult to see; local guidance is essential.

SKOOKUMCHUK NARROWS From the trailhead near the town of Egmont, it takes approximately an hour to stroll the well-posted trail to see this natural phenomenon of rapids, whirlpools and roiling eddies created by massive tidal changes pushed through the narrow inlet. If you arrive at low tide, you can view the fascinating marine life trapped in tidal pools near Roland Point.

LANG CREEK SALMON SPAWNING CHANNEL

✉*Route 101* Taking the ferry hop from Earls Cove to Saltery Bay brings you to this salmon spawning channel about midway to Powell River. During the peak spawning season (September to November), you can get a close look at pink or chum salmon making the arduous journey upstream.

POWELL RIVER HISTORICAL MUSEUM ✉*4798 Marine Avenue, Powell River* ☎*604-485-2222* 📠*604-485-2327* 🖥*www.powellrivermuseum.com, museum@powellrivermuseum.com* An octagonal building just across from Willingdon Beach, this museum houses a fine collection of regional memorabilia. Displays include furniture, utensils and hand tools of pioneers and Sliammon First Nation people, along with a photo and print archive with material dating back to 1910. Closed weekends from September to mid-June. Admission.

HERITAGE WALK For a further lesson in the history of the area, take the heritage walk through the Powell River Townsite to view the early-1900s homes, churches and municipal buildings of this old company town. Maps are available from the **Powell River Info Centre** (Joyce Avenue, Powell River; 604-485-4701; www.discoverpowellriver.com, info@discoverpowellriver.com).

MILL VIEWPOINT ✉*Route 101* At this viewpoint there's a great hilltop view of the "Hulks," a half-moon breakwater of ten cement ships protecting the floating logs waiting to be processed in the mill. Interpretive signs give a bit of history about the ships and the mill.

There are no big resorts or major chain hotels yet. Motels, inns and lodges are sometimes a shade worn but generally are friendly and inexpensive—part of the coast's unique charm.

BONNIEBROOK LODGE

$$$ 7 UNITS   ✉ 1532 Ocean Beach Esplanade, Gibsons   ☎ 604-886-2887, 877-290-9916   ✆ 604-886-8853   ⌨ www.bonniebrook.com, info@ bonniebrook.com

A bed and breakfast since 1922, this is a charming yellow clapboard house overlooking the Strait of Georgia. Guest suites feature Victorian-style furnishings, jacuzzi tubs, fireplaces and patios. A fine dining restaurant is on-site.

ROYAL REACH MOTEL AND MARINA

$$ 32 ROOMS   ✉ 5758 Wharf Road, Sechelt   ☎ 604-885-7844   ✆ 604-885-5969

The Royal Reach offers clean, basic accommodations in simple rooms that are pretty much the same. Nondescript furnishings include one or two double beds, a long desk/TV stand, plain bedside table and lamps, a mini-fridge, electric kettle and a small bathroom. Ask for one of the waterfront rooms that looks out over the marina and Sechelt Inlet. You can also book a bay cruise, on a sailboat or powerboat, with the proprietors. Rowboats and paddle boats also for rent.

BEACH GARDENS MOTEL AND MARINA

$$ $$$ 18 ROOMS   ✉ 7074 Westminster Avenue, Powell River   ☎ 604-485-6267, 800-663-7070   ✆ 604-485-2343   ⌨ www.beachgardens.com, beachgardens@shaw.ca

All of the oceanfront rooms here feature private decks. There are also cabins and kitchenette units available. Extra amenities include the private marina, dining room and weight room.

BEACON B&B AND SPA

$$$ 2 ROOMS   ✉ 3750 Marine Avenue, Powell River   ☎ 604-485-5563, 877-485-5563   ✆ 604-485-9450   ⌨ www.beaconbb.com, stay@beaconbb.com

Within moments of arriving at this charming B&B and getting settled into one of the two inviting upstairs bedrooms, you'll begin to unwind and feel right at home. It's hard to tell whether to attribute this to the genuine hospitality or the cozy, down-home decor. Whatever the case, the congenial hosts, great ocean view, proximity to the beach and thoughtful touches like on-site massage and healthy, hearty breakfasts make this one of the most delightful lodging options in the region.

OLD COURTHOUSE INN

$$–$$$ 8 ROOMS   ✉ 6243 Walnut Street, Powell River   ☎ 604-483-4000, 877-483-4777   ⌨ www.oldcourthouseinn.ca, oldcourt@telus.net

This Powell River inn is in the middle of the historic townsite, not far from the lower end of Powell Lake and its popular canoe route. The heritage building, handsomely refurbished, holds very comfy private rooms, with an on-site café, cable TV and ready access to outdoor activities. The inn is nonsmoking.

DINING

GIBSONS FISH MARKET

$ SEAFOOD   ✉*294 Gower Point Road, Gibsons*   ☎*604-886-8363*
Gibsons, a smallish outlet on the main drag above the landing, does a booming business with tasty takeout fish-and-chips. It may not look like much, but there's usually a crowd lined up on the front sidewalk. Closed Sunday.

BLUE HERON INN

$$$ CONTINENTAL   ✉*5591 Delta Road, Sechelt*   ☎*604-885-3847, 800-818-8977*
⌨*www.blueheronrestaurant.ca*
A delightful waterfront home-turned-restaurant on picturesque Porpoise Bay, this restaurant is home to masterful creations. The daily menu uses fresh regional produce and seafood in the dishes. Reservations are recommended. Dinner only. Closed Monday and Tuesday.

THE SEA HOUSE

$$ MEDITERRANEAN   ✉*4448 Marine Avenue, Powell River*   ☎*604-485-5163*
For homemade Mediterranean and Greek cuisine, try this cozy eatery. Entrées include seafood, souvlaki, steak, focaccia and brick-oven pizza. No lunch on Saturday or Sunday.

SHINGLE MILL BISTRO AND PUB

$$–$$$ STEAK/SEAFOOD   ✉*6233 Powell Place, Powell River*   ☎*604-483-2001*
☎*604-483-9413*
The Shingle Mill, situated at the tip of Powell Lake, has large windows on three sides so you can enjoy views of this beautiful, pine-trimmed lake while you eat. It's no surprise that they serve grilled B.C. salmon in this waterfront eatery, but the steak *au poivre*, chicken in puff pastry and fusilli primavera are unexpectedly good. Items from the dinner menu are available in the relaxed bistro.

SHOPPING

SUNSHINE COAST ARTS COUNCIL ✉*5714 Medusa Street, Sechelt* ☎*604-885-5412* ⌨*www.suncoastarts.com* There is an abundance of artists living in small communities all along the Sunshine Coast, many willing to open their studios to tours. Brochures are available through this arts agency. Closed Monday and Tuesday.

CULTURAL CENTER GIFT SHOP

✉*5555 Route 101, Sechelt* ☎*604-885-4592* For arts and crafts of Northwest First Nations, including masks, drums, totems and baskets, visit this gift shop. Closed some Sundays (call ahead).

WESTWIND GALLERY ✉ *292 Gower Point Road, #14, Gibsons* ☎ *604-886-*
9213 🖱 *www.westwindgallery.net* You'll find fine representations of local art
(serigraphs, pottery, woodwork, watercolors, jewelry, sculpture) at this
gallery. Closed Sunday.

CRANBERRY POTTERY idden

✉ *6729 Cranberry Street, Powell River* ☎ *604-483-4622* 🖱 *www.cranberry*
pottery.bc.ca A working studio, this shop offers functional and
affordable handmade stoneware in varying designs and glazes.
Closed Sunday.

NIGHTLIFE

Along the Sunshine Coast you'll find slimmer after-hours pickings, limited primarily to friendly, no-airs local taverns and pubs that occasionally have a dance space, live music and great water views.

THE BLACKFISH PUB ✉ *966 Venture Way, Gibsons* ☎ *604-886-6682*
🖱 *www.blackfishpub.com* A popular hangout, this pub has occasional live
music. On other nights, enjoy the game room or heated deck.

SHINGLE MILL BISTRO AND PUB ✉ *6233 Powell Place, Powell River*
☎ *604-483-2001* Powell River has an amiable establishment in which to
spend a comfortable evening after canoeing the lakes. Kick back with
a brew and a view overlooking Powell Lake at this comfortable spot.

BEACHES & PARKS

PORPOISE BAY
PROVINCIAL PARK idden

✉ *Located northeast of Sechelt off Porpoise Bay Road* ☎ *604-898-3678*
📟 *604-898-4171*

🏃 🚣 🛶 ⛵ One of the prettiest parks along the coast, this 150-
acre recreation site has a broad, sandy beach anchored by grass
fields and fragrant cedar groves. This is a favorite base for canoeists who come to explore the waterways of the Sechelt Inlets
Marine Recreation Area. You'll also find excellent sportfishing.
The park has restrooms, showers, picnic tables, an adventure
playground, an amphitheater, nature trails, visitor programs and
a fall salmon run. Parking fee, $3.
🏕 There are 84 tent/RV sites (no hookups); C$24 per night. They
also have cyclist campsites with showers; C$10 per night.

SALTERY BAY
PROVINCIAL PARK idden

✉ *Located off Sunshine Coast Highway 17 miles south of Powell River*
☎ *604-898-3678* 📟 *604-898-4171*

🚣 🦅 🛶 🚤 ⚓ ⛵ Named for the Japanese fish-saltery settlement located in this area during the early 1900s, this lovely

170-acre oceanside park with twin sandy beaches enjoys grand views of Jervis Inlet, where sharp-eyed visitors often catch glimpses of porpoises, whales, sea lions and seals. Swimming and offshore salmon fishing are excellent. Scuba divers flock here to visit the nine-foot bronze mermaid resting in 60 feet of water not far offshore from the evergreen-shrouded campground. There are restrooms, picnic sites, fire pits and disabled diving facilities.

▲ There are 42 developed tent/RV sites (no hookups); C$10 to C$24 per night.

POWELL FOREST CANOE ROUTE

✉ *Jumpoff point for the canoe route is Lois Lake, accessed by the Canoe Mainline* ☎ *604-485-4701, 877-817-8669* 📠 *604-485-2822*
🖥 *www.discoverpowellriver.com, info@discoverpowellriver.com*

🚶 🛶 There are 8 fjordlike lakes interconnected by rivers, streams and miles of hiking trails making it possible to make portage canoe trips of anywhere from three days to a week in this beautiful Northern Sunshine Coast recreational area. There are over 200 miles of hiking trails around Powell River. Best time to make the trip is between March and November; lakes at upper elevations tend to freeze, and roads are inaccessible during winter months. Facilities include outhouses, picnic tables and hiking trails (the Inland Lake trail is wheelchair accessible).

▲ Permitted at any of the 12 recreation sites. Prices vary from free (at forestry-run campgrounds) to C$20 at some of the municipal and provincial campsites around the area.

WILLINGDON BEACH MUNICIPAL CAMPSITE

✉ *4845 Marine Avenue in the Westview section of Powell River*
☎ *604-485-2242* 🖥 *www.willingdonbeach.ca*

🚶 🛶 The sandy, log-strewn, crescent beach bordered by wooded acres of campsites draws a big summertime crowd to this comfortable municipal site in Powell River. Some of the camp-

---

Trading Places

It seems as if most of British Columbia's historic figures came from the United States. They include founding father Simon Fraser (New York), eight-term Vancouver mayor L. D. Taylor (Michigan), timber tycoon Sewell Moody (Maine), B.C. Sugar Refinery founder Benjamin Tingley Rogers (Pennsylvania), and Canadian Pacific Railway builder William Cornelius Van Horne (Illinois), who gave the city of Vancouver its present-day name. British Columbia, in turn, has provided more than its share of American movie and TV stars—among them Raymond Burr, Michael J. Fox, Pamela Anderson, Jason Priestley, Jennifer Tilly, Mike Myers and James Doohan (Scotty from the original *Star Trek*).

sites are right up on the beach, while others in a grove of cedar are more secluded. The site has great, though unsupervised, swimming. You'll find restrooms, showers, a laundry, a barbecue area, playgrounds, a nature trail and a seasonal food stall.

▲ There are 81 sites, half with full hookups; C$17.50 to C$24 per night. Monthly winter rates are available.

DESOLATION SOUND MARINE PARK

✉ *Boat access only from the coastal towns. Easiest access is from Powell River*
☎ *604-898-3678*   📠 *604-898-4171*

🛶 ⛵ 🚣 🚤 ⚓ This park is made up of 37 miles of shoreline and several islands. The waters here are very warm and teem with diverse marine life, making the area ideal for fishing (excellent for cod or salmon), swimming, boating and scuba diving. The park is wild and undeveloped, with magnificent scenery at every turn. There are a few onshore outhouses and numerous safe anchorages. Be sure to bring your own water as there is none provided in the park.

▲ There are several walk-in wilderness campsites; no charge.

WHITE ROCK

Perhaps because it is so close to the border that they whiz right on by, U.S. travelers overlook White Rock, a peaceful seaside town about 40 minutes from downtown Vancouver that claims Canada's best climate and has a couple of palm trees growing right along the main drag for proof. Canadians and European visitors to Canada flock to White Rock's small inns, motels and B&Bs; on summer weekend afternoons the town is astir with people using the beachside promenade, or strolling the avenue of small shops, cafés and restaurants behind it.

There isn't anything particularly glamorous about White Rock. In fact, it seems ever so much like the small British beach towns from which it drew its inspiration. That's what makes it charming—no big resorts, no famed sights, no fancy shops. Facing south into the sun, with a Mediterranean cast to the houses climbing the slope that fends off northerly storms, it does offer a balmier clime than most of the rest of B.C. Innumerable places offer fish and chips, and lots of happy couples stroll hand in hand along the promenade. For a tourist destination, it's charmingly low-key.

SIGHTS

WHITE ROCK PROMENADE ✉ *Along Marine Drive in downtown White Rock. Please note that White Rock's parking meters are enforced until midnight along the promenade.* Built in 1986 with assistance from the national and provincial governments, this promenade spans one and a quarter miles of the town's gray-sand beach. Paved in brick, with numerous benches, it's a great place for a walk or a run; the sun keeps it warm, but the harbor breeze prevents excess warmth. When the tide's out, a truly vast expanse of gray sand beach lies exposed, attracting many sandcastle builders young and old. A pier leads a quarter-mile out into deeper water; you can toss crab pots in the water here if you're interested in hand-caught seafood. Not far south of the pier, the White Rock that lent the city its name sits on the slope above the beach. At 486 tons, it's staying put. If it was not truly white historically, liberal coats of paint ensure that it is now.

WHITE ROCK MUSEUM AND ARCHIVES ✉ *14970 Marine Drive* 📞 *604-541-2222* 📠 *604-541-2223* 🖳 *www.whiterock.museum.bc.ca, whiterockoffice@ telus.net* Built into the handsome, restored 1912 railroad depot, this museum offers revolving exhibits focused on regional cultural and natural history. There's an on-site gift shop and a visitor information booth located just east of the depot. Closed Monday from January through April. Admission.

LODGING

FAIRMONT VANCOUVER AIRPORT

$$$–$$$$ 392 UNITS ✉ *Vancouver International Airport, 3111 Grant McConachie Way* 📞 *604-207-5200, 866-540-4441* 📠 *604-248-3219* 🖳 *www.fairmont.com*
Seasoned travelers ordinarily avoid airport hotels, but this Fairmont boasts a remarkable property that's worth a stop if you're heading out of Vancouver on a morning flight. Built right in the terminal's east end, the hotel is a high-tech marvel with computerized gadgets galore— lights flick on automatically when you enter a room. The room decor is discreetly luxurious, with plum fabrics and maple-burl desks, and vast baths that include tiled showers and a soaking tub. Substantial insulation keeps jet noise to a minimum (not zero, though), and the reception area has an intriguing space-age look (hotel staffers stand at solo terminals). Prices are deluxe, but off-season the hotel offers some remarkable bargain packages.

DINING

CIELO'S TAPAS AND OYSTER BAR

$$–$$$ MEDITERRANEAN ✉ *15069 Marine Drive* 📞 *604-538-8152* 🖳 *www.cielosrestaurant.com, info@cielosrestaurant.com*
Tapas are the fare at Cielo's, one of the Mediterranean-style eateries on Marine Drive, White Rock's main drag. The chefs prepare creative plates such as fresh basil and oven-roasted beet risotto, Argentinian lamb sirloin and chorizo sausage. There are plenty of seafood options as well, in addition to oysters on the half-shell. Three plates is an ample amount for two, and the atmosphere is a bit more elegant than the typical pub eatery found on Marine.

HOLLY'S POULTRY IN MOTION

$ AMERICAN ✉ *15491 Marine Drive* 📞 *604-538-8084*
If it's a full-scale breakfast you're after, grab a table at Holly's and order "The Big One." The plate comes piled high with eggs, hash browns, toast and ham or bacon. Lunch entrées, sandwiches and burgers are similarly generous.

$ DESSERT ✉ *14909 Marine Drive* 📞 *604-538-0030*

As a quasi-beach resort, White Rock has at least a dozen ice cream stands along its waterfront drive. The best of them all is undoubtedly White Mountain, where they advertise homemade product, and deliver the best you can imagine. The acid test is vanilla—it's practically perfect. In fact, it's almost cause to visit the town just for the ice cream.

OUTDOOR ADVENTURES

HELICOPTER TOURS

WHISTLER HELI-SKIING ✉ *4154 Village Green, Whistler* 📞 *604-932-4105, 888-435-4754* 🖥 *www.whistlerheliskiing.com* Quick trips to the backcountry for hiking, fishing, skiing or other activities are possible via helicopters. This company will arrange skiing trips to the Sea-to-Sky Corridor near Whistler.

BLACKCOMB HELICOPTERS 📞 *604-938-1700, 800-330-4354* 🖥 *www. blackcombhelicopters.com* This outfitter arranges fishing and hiking trips, glacier sightseeing and even mountaintop picnics year-round.

HELIJET 📞 *604-270-1484, 800-987-4354* 🖥 *www.helijet.com* Contact this group if you want a company that specializes in drop-off service to the Tantalus Range, a rugged area with glaciers, lakes and the highest concentration of bald eagles in North America.

WATER SPORTS

With 5000 miles of sheltered water within easy reach, Vancouver and southwestern British Columbia afford many opportunities to get out on the water. You can rent a powerboat or a sailboat and head north to the Sunshine Coast, where Desolation Sound has the warmest waters north of Mexico, or you can hop into an inflatable raft and paddle the Chilliwack River whitewater.

Downtown Vancouver Area
BLUE PACIFIC ✉ *1519 Foreshore Walk, Granville Island* 📞 *604-682-2161, 800-237-2392* 🖥 *www.bluepacificcharters.com, info@bluepacificcharters.com* Although Canada does not require a license to operate either a powerboat or a sailboat, Blue Pacific requires that you prove your expertise before you rent one of its vessels. Otherwise, Blue Pacific will set you up for a three- to five-day "cruise-and-learn" excursion with a qualified instructor.

North Vancouver Area
CANADIAN OUTBACK ADVENTURES ✉ *657 Marine Drive #100, West Vancouver* 📞 *604-921-7250, 800-565-8735* This adventure company offers five-day guided kayak trips into Desolation Sound.

Whistler Area

WHISTLER OUTDOOR EXPERIENCE CO. ✉*8841 Highway 99* ✆*604-932-3389, 877-386-1888* ✑*www.whistleroutdoor.com* Canoeing and kayaking are very popular on Whistler's five beautiful lakes. Rentals and tours are available through this group from mid-May to mid-October. Rent a canoe or kayak and take a self-guided tour of the Serene River of Golden Dreams, where you'll see plenty of wildlife.

Sunshine Coast Area

DESOLATION SOUND MARINE PARK AND POWELL FOREST CANOE ROUTE ✑*www.env.gov.bc.ca/parks* This marine park and 50-mile canoe route, which includes eight breathtaking lakes and lush, interconnecting forests, are ideal spots for canoeing and swimming. "Powell Forest Canoe Route is as beautiful as the more popular Bowron Lake Route in northern British Columbia, but it's less populated by people in canoes," explains a local outfitter.

MITCHELL'S CANOE, KAYAK AND SNOWSHOE ✉*8690 Route 101, Powell River* ✆*604-487-1609* ✑*www.canoeingbc.com* To rent a canoe for one or eight days, contact Mitchell's in Powell River. They also rent kayaks and provide transportation to Desolation Sound.

SUNSHINE KAYAKING LTD. ✉*Molly's Lane, Gibsons, BC V0N 1V0* ✆*604-886-9760* ✑*www.sunshinekayaking.com* Experienced kayakers can rent craft for the day from this group in Gibsons, on Howe Sound. Longer tours and kayaking classes are also offered.

RIVER RUNNING

Scenic floats and whitewater rafting are also immensely popular around Vancouver, especially on the Chilliwack River, 65 miles east of the city. Near Whistler, the Green and Birkenhead rivers are popular, as are the Thompson, Squamish and Elaho rivers.

Greater Vancouver Area

HYAK WILDERNESS ADVENTURES ✉*3823 Henning Drive #203, Burnaby* ✆*604-734-8622, 800-663-7238* ✑*www.hyak.com* Contact these guides for whitewater-rafting trips on the Chilliwack River in the spring, when snow still caps surrounding mountains. By summer, focus shifts to the Thompson River, with its desert scenery. Rapids along these rivers range from Class II to Class V. You can actively participate by paddling, or go the lazy route and let the guides do the work.

Whistler Area

WHISTLER RIVER ADVENTURES ✉*P.O. Box 202, Whistler, BC V0N 1B0* ✆*604-932-3532, 888-932-3532* 📠*604-932-3559* ✑*www.whistlerriver.com* There are mountains, glaciers and waterfalls to observe on guided raft trips on several local rivers, including the Green and Squamish. Jet boat trips (on the Green and Lillooet rivers) and guided fishing trips can be arranged through this company from late May to September.

The tremendous variety of fish in southwestern British Columbia waterways affords an array of exciting challenges for the angler. In the mountain country, you can flyfish or spin-cast in high alpine lakes and streams for rainbow trout, Dolly Varden, steelhead or kokanee salmon. On the coast, you'll find chinook, coho, chum, pink and sockeye salmon and bottom-dwelling halibut, sole and rockfish. Licenses for both fresh- and saltwater fishing are required (charter operators usually can provide them); regulations change frequently.

DEPARTMENT OF FISHERIES AND OCEANS ✉ *401 Burrard Street, Vancouver, BC V6C 354* ☎ *604-666-0566, 800-663-1660* 📠 *604-666-5835* 🖃 *www.pac. dfo-mpo.gc.ca* **Saltwater licenses** are issued by this federal agency. Closed Saturday and Sunday.

Freshwater licenses are issued through the provincial government and can be bought at most sporting goods stores. **The Ministry of Environment, Lands and Parks (B.C. Environment)** maintains a list of licensed **freshwater fishing guides.** For a copy, call 604-582-5200.

SCUBA DIVING

A thick soup of microscopic plant and animal life attracts and feeds an abundance of marine life that in turn attracts divers in numbers that continue to grow. This area is home to the largest artificial reef in North America, a 366-foot destroyer that sank and is now a diver's paradise. Add to this the array of wrecks and underwater sights (such as a nine-foot bronze mermaid in the Powell River) and it's easy to understand the popularity of scuba diving around Vancouver and the Sunshine Coast.

GREAT PACIFIC DIVING ✉ *1236 Marine Drive, North Vancouver* ☎ *604-986-0302* 🖃 *www.greatpacific.net* Dive charters to local waters, the Gulf Islands and Howe Sound are arranged by this dive group. Rentals and lessons are also available.

SKIING

The majestic range crowning Vancouver's North Shore offers three fine ski areas within minutes of the city.

North Shore Area
CYPRESS MOUNTAIN ☎ *604-926-5612* 🖃 *www.cypressmountain.com* With 35 runs on two lift-serviced mountains, Cypress boasts the longest vertical run of the local Vancouver resorts. Snowboarders share the runs with downhill skiers. A third area features 10 miles of groomed cross-country trails tracked for both classic and skate skis. Night skiing and backcountry skiing trails are available in the provincial park.

GROUSE MOUNTAIN

✉6400 Nancy Greene Way, North Vancouver 📞604-984-0661 🖱www.grousemountain.com The glittering string of lights visible each night on the North Shore across the inlet from downtown Vancouver marks the arc-lit runs of this mountain, where residents head after work to get in some slope time. The resort has 25 runs, a variety of lifts, a snowboard park and a snowshoeing park. There's also outdoor skating on a pond.

MT. SEYMOUR

✉1700 Mt. Seymour Road, North Vancouver 📞604-986-2261 🖱www.mountseymour.com On a clear, fogless day, Burnaby and Richmond are visible from the 21 ski runs at Mt. Seymour. Good novice runs make this a best bet for beginners or those who want to avoid hot doggers. Downhill runs are serviced by a network of chairlifts and tows and are open for night skiing. Though the skiing here is mainly beginning and intermediate (80 percent of the runs), Mt. Seymour attracts international professional snowboarders who come for the natural terrain in its three parks. Hilly cross-country trails run through the adjacent Mt. Seymour Provincial Park.

Whistler Area

WHISTLER-BLACKCOMB

✉4545 Blackcomb Way, Whistler 📞604-904-7060, 888-403-4727 🖱www.whistler-blackcomb.com Whistler is considered by many to be one of North America's top ski areas. Located 75 winding miles northeast of Vancouver at the base of Whistler and Blackcomb mountains is this world-class resort and one of the top ski destinations in the world. The resort offers over 200 marked runs and the longest lift-serviced ski runs in North America, with a drop of one vertical mile. The official season runs from late November to late May, then starts again for glacier skiing in mid-June.

RIDING STABLES

Whistler Area

WHISTLER OUTDOOR EXPERIENCE CO. ✉8841 Route 99 📞604-932-3389, 877-386-1888 🖱www.whistleroutdoor.com This outfitter leads guided rides in the summer through the Pemberton Meadows and along Ryan Creek and the Lillooet River. Winter sleigh rides provide views of glacier-fed Green Lake and a ring of mountains.

Golf in Vancouver is bound to involve water in some way. Even if there isn't much of it on the course, the location or the view will likely encompass a body of water—English Bay, the Strait of Georgia, one of the rivers.

Downtown Vancouver Area

FRASERVIEW GOLF COURSE ✉ 7800 Vivian Street, Vancouver ✆ 604-257-6923 🖰 www.fraserviewgolf.ca Near the Fraser River, this is a par-72, 18-hole public course.

MAYFAIR LAKES GOLF AND COUNTRY CLUB ✉ 5460 Number 7 Road, Richmond ✆ 604-276-0505 🖰 www.golfbc.com The semiprivate Mayfair course has lots of water—14 out of 18 holes have water, including the heavily bunkered 18th with water right up to the green.

Whistler Area

WHISTLER GOLF COURSE ✉ 4001 Whistler Way ✆ 604-932-3280, 800-376-1777 🖰 www.whistlergolf.com In Whistler, you can tee off amid the splendid terrain at this 18-hole public course.

CHÂTEAU WHISTLER GOLF CLUB ✉ 4612 Blackcomb Way ✆ 604-938-2097 You can swing and putt at this 18-hole course. The narrow, mountainous course is surrounded by trees and has scenic views of Blackcomb and Whistler mountains.

Sunshine Coast Area

MYRTLE POINT GOLF CLUB ✉ C-3 McCausland Road, RR #1, Powell River ✆ 604-487-4653 🖰 www.myrtlepointgolfclub.com Open year-round, the 18 holes here have splendid views of Texada and Vancouver Islands.

PENDER HARBOR GOLF CLUB ✉ Sunshine Coast Highway, Pender Harbor ✆ 604-883-9541 This golf club has nine holes, surrounded by lush vegetation and breathtaking scenery.

SUNSHINE COAST GOLF AND COUNTRY CLUB ✉ 3206 Sunshine Coast Highway, Roberts Creek ✆ 604-885-9212, 800-667-5022 🖰 www.sunshinecoast golf.com An 18-hole semiprivate course with challenging greens, this well manicured, treelined, par-71 links isn't too long and is good for the average golfer.

TENNIS

There are over 80 locations in the Vancouver area with tennis courts: most are free and first-come, first-served; all are open for play year-round, weather permitting. Call the Park Board (604-257-8400) for a list of locations other than those listed here. Of course, many of the area's resorts provide tennis facilities for guests as well.

West Side/Granville Island Area

KITSILANO BEACH PARK ✉*Cornwall Avenue and Arbutus Street* Ten public courts. Fees only during warm weather months.

Other parks with courts include **Queen Elizabeth Park**, just off Cambie Street, and **Jericho Beach Park**, off Northwest Marine Drive.

Downtown Vancouver Area

STANLEY PARK Of the 21 courts in Stanley Park, six charge minimal fees for reserved playing times; the rest are free.

BIKING

West Side/Granville Island Area

To avoid busy streets, try the shoreside paths at **Jericho Beach** and **English Bay** and the pathways that parallel Chancellor and University boulevards and 15th Avenue on the scenic campus of the **University of British Columbia**.

Downtown Vancouver Area

STANLEY PARK Because of heavy traffic in Vancouver, cyclists are better off sticking to the protected 5.5-mile seawall path around the perimeter of this park.

Whistler Area

Biking is popular in Whistler, especially mountain biking on rough alpine trails or paved trails around **Lost Lake** and along the **Valley Trail**, which connects the village with the nearby residential areas, parks and lakes. Daredevils go for the **mountain descents**, often taking a helicopter or gondola to the peaks so that they don't expend the energy needed for zooming down the dry ski runs. At ungodly speeds, they follow an experienced trail leader who knows how to run the slopes safely.

WHISTLER OUTDOOR EXPERIENCE CO. ✉*8841 Highway 99* ☎*604-932-3389, 877-386-1888* 🖰*www.whistleroutdoor.com* This company offers a guided descent on Blackcomb Mountain as well as slower-paced bike tours of parks and lakes.

WHISTLER BACKROADS MOUNTAIN BIKE ADVENTURES ✉*P.O. Box 643, Whistler, BC V0N 1B0* ☎*604-932-3111* 🖰*www.backroadswhistler.com* For a "heli-biking" adventure (a helicopter will fly you into a wilderness area for single-track mountain biking), contact these adventure experts.

Sunshine Coast Area

There is no protected bike path along **Route 101**, the main artery of the Sunshine Coast, and the rocky shoulder drops off entirely at times, forcing bikers onto the highway. However, the moderately challenging trip from Langsdale to Earls Cove is popular nonetheless. The backcountry of the entire coast is laced with marked and unmarked **logging trails** leading off Route 101 just waiting to be explored by intrepid mountain bikers; a detailed map of the trails between Jervis Inlet and

Lund is available from the Powell River Travel InfoCentre (604-485-4701; info@discoverpowellriver.com).

Bike Rentals & Tours

SPOKES BICYCLE RENTALS ✉*1798 West Georgia Street, Vancouver* 📞*604-688-5141* 📞*604-681-5581* 🖱*www.vancouverbikerental.com* This shop has a large selection of bike rentals; they arrange group tours to nearby Stanley Park.

WHISTLER BACKROADS MOUNTAIN BIKE ADVENTURES ✉*Westbrook Hotel Base* 📞*604-932-3111* 🖱*www.backroadswhistler.com* During the warm months you can rent a bike from this group.

TAWS CYCLE AND SPORTS ✉*4597 Marine Avenue, Powell River* 📞*604-485-2555, 877-481-2555* 🖱*www.tawsonline.com* On the Sunshine Coast, this is a reliable shop to rent bikes.

HIKING

All distances listed for trails are one way unless otherwise noted.

West Side/Granville Island Area

PACIFIC SPIRIT REGIONAL PARK

This park (30 miles) crisscrosses 1000 acres of parkland on Point Grey Peninsula, offering easy-to-moderate hikes of varying length through this largely unmarked ecological reserve. Here you're more likely to run into a blacktail deer or bald eagle than another hiker. A map is available from the Greater Vancouver Regional Parks office (604-432-6350).

Downtown Vancouver Area

STANLEY PARK SEAWALL PATH A 5.5-mile path, this hike is carefully divided to accommodate both cyclists and pedestrians and is easily the most popular hike in town. There are also numerous paths that plunge into the thickly forested acres of the park.

North Shore Area

CAPILANO PACIFIC TRAIL

In North Vancouver's Capilano River Regional Park, this 4.5-mile trail passes from massive Cleveland Dam to Ambleside Park through sections of coastal rainforest and offers great views of the Lions, the twin mountain peaks soaring majestically above the dam.

LYNN HEADWATERS REGIONAL PARK 📞*604-985-1690 (trail conditions)* Also in the North Shore area, **Norvan Falls** (9.5 miles) offers a more rugged backcountry trek for the experienced hiker through the wilderness areas of this regional park. The shorter **Lynn Loop Trail** (3 miles) affords views of Lynn Valley and passes an abandoned cabin.

Whistler Area

VALLEY TRAIL   There are trails in Whistler for all levels. This trek (15 miles roundtrip) is a bustling paved walkway/bike path/cross-country ski trail that winds through town, connecting Alpha, Nita, Alta, Lost and Green lakes, the village and the various residential areas.

LOST LAKE TRAILS   All together this 9-mile set of hikes serves as the cross-country ski trails during the winter and make for fairly level summer hiking paths (with some paved areas) through the forested area between Lost and Green lakes.

GARIBALDI PARK   **Singing Pass-Russet Lake** (6.75 miles), an alpine hiking trail just behind Whistler Village, and the graded **Garibaldi Lake Trail** (5.5 miles), located off Route 99 south of town, are prime options for experienced hikers interested in heading into the steep fringes of incredible Garibaldi Park.

Sunshine Coast Area

SOAMES HILL MOUNTAIN TRAIL   This mountain trail (1.5 miles) is a brisk stair climb to an elevation of 800 feet followed by expansive views of Howe Sound, the surrounding mountains and villages. The trail is also known as "The Knob" because of its appearance to passengers on ferries approaching Langdale.

SMUGGLER'S COVE MARINE PARK TRAIL   An easy walk (.5 mile), this trail leads from the parking lot off Brooks Road approximately six miles north of Sechelt to the cove once used to smuggle in Chinese immigrants and other contraband and is now home to an array of seabirds.

MT. VALENTINE TRAIL   Approximately 1 mile in length, this trek offers a short walk up a gravel path followed by a steep climb up a stone staircase leading to panoramic views of Malaspina and Georgia straits, Vancouver Island and the surrounding town of Powell Lake.

INLAND LAKE TRAIL   Just north of Powell River, this 8-mile trail offers a longer hike over a well-maintained circuit of boardwalks and bridges through scenic swamp areas and skirting lovely Inland Lake. The entire trail is wheelchair accessible, and several handicap shelters and fishing wharfs are along the way.

TRANSPORTATION

CAR

From the West Coast of the United States, **Route 5** turns into **Route 99** after crossing the Canadian border at Blaine and proceeds northwest through Vancouver's suburbs and into the city core where the name changes once again, this time to **Granville Street**. The **Trans-Canada Highway (Route 1)** connects Vancouver with points east in Canada.

Route 99, referred to as the **Sea to Sky Highway** from Horseshoe Bay northward, picks up again in North Vancouver, hugs the rugged coastline and continues north into the mountains to Whistler. Fog, snow, wind, flooding and landslides have frequently hampered travel to Whistler. A major highway improvement project is underway, and the road will have 50 miles of new passing lanes, plus median barriers, bike lanes, weather monitoring stations and reinforced bridges in time for the 2010 Winter Olympics. Meanwhile, inquiring about road conditions before starting a drive to Whistler is still a good idea.

Route 101, the only major thoroughfare through the Sunshine Coast, connects Langdale to Earls Cove and Saltery Bay to Lund, the northernmost point of this long, transcontinental highway with southern terminus in Chile.

AIR

VANCOUVER INTERNATIONAL AIRPORT ✑ www.yvr.ca This international airport services domestic charters and flights by Harbour Air and Whistler Air Service. International airlines include Air Canada, Air China, Air New Zealand, Alaska Airlines, American Airlines, British Airways, Cathay Pacific Airways, Continental Airlines, Delta Air Lines, Horizon Air, Japan Airlines, KLM, Korean Air, Lufthansa, Northwest Airlines, Qantas, Singapore Airlines and United Airlines.

THE AIRPORTER ✆ 604-946-8866, 800-668-3141 ✑ www.yvairporter.com Airport express buses operated by this company depart every 20 to 30 minutes or so from the arrivals level of the Main Terminal building and stop at the bus station and most major hotels in downtown Vancouver.

TRANSLINK ✆ 604-953-3333 ✑ www.translink.bc.ca These buses serve the airport; catch #424 from the airport and then transfer to #98 at Airport Station, which will take you right into downtown Vancouver.

BOAT

CANADA PLACE ✉ 999 Canada Place, Vancouver ✆ 604-775-7200 ✑ www.canadaplace.ca Between May and October, cruise ships call regularly at the terminal at this architectural stunner under Teflon-coated white "sails."

BUS

GREYHOUND BUS LINES ✉ 1150 Station Street, Vancouver ✆ 800-231-2222 from the U.S., 800-661-8747 from Canada ✑ www.greyhound.com Greyhound offers service to and from the United States.

TRAIN

VIA RAIL CANADA ✉ 1150 Station Street, Vancouver ✆ 800-561-8630 (within Canada) ✑ www.viarail.com This Vancouver company provides rail service throughout Canada and connects with **Amtrak** (800-872-7245; www.amtrak.com) to points within the United States.

WHISTLER MOUNTAINEER ☎604-606-8460 Offering one of the most scenic train trips in Canada, this locomotive runs daily between the North Vancouver Rail Depot and Whistler, a three-hour, $179 round-trip. Call for information.

CAR RENTALS

Rental agencies at Vancouver International Airport include **Alamo Rent A Car** (800-462-5262), **Avis Rent A Car** (800-879-2847), **Budget Rent A Car** (800-299-3199), **Dollar Rent A Car** (800-800-3665), **Hertz Rent A Car** (800-263-0600), **Thrifty Car Rental** (800-847-4389).

Discount Car Rentals (604-207-8180) has an office in the neighboring suburb of Richmond and offers free airport pickup.

PUBLIC TRANSIT

TRANSLINK ☎604-953-3333 ✐www.translink.bc.ca This agency governs Vancouver's expansive transit system, with buses, the SkyTrain and the SeaBus, covering all the main arteries within the city and fanning out into the suburbs. Running on a 16-mile, mostly elevated track between Canada Place downtown and the suburb of Surrey, the SkyTrain is a good way to see some of the major sights of the city. You can also get a great view of the skyline from the water aboard the SeaBuses that cross Burrard Inlet between downtown and the North Shore. The handy "Transportation Services Guide for Greater Vancouver" tour guide, day passes and timetables are available from Travel Info Centres.

WHISTLER TRANSIT ☎604-932-4020 The local operator for B. C. Transit, this group runs buses connecting Whistler Creek and Whistler Village every fifteen minutes. Translink is also responsible for transit service along the Sunshine Coast; for more information dial 604-953-3333.

TAXIS

Cab companies serving the airport include **Black Top and Checker Cabs** (604-731-1111), **Vancouver Taxi** (604-255-5111) and **Yellow Cab** (604-681-1111).

VICTORIA & SOUTHERN VANCOUVER ISLAND

Victoria & Southern Vancouver Island

I say, do you want a taste of veddy proper Britain without having to fly across the Atlantic? Then step into Victoria, a city of stately government buildings, picture-perfect lawns and fascinating glimpses of the British influence. Shorn, manicured and embellished, Victoria is called more British than Britain itself.

But have no fear: This is not stiff-upper-lip territory. Travel out of Victoria and you will find the rest of Vancouver Island an untamed land. Stretching 280 miles along the rugged Pacific coastline of Canada and the United States, it occupies some 12,400 square miles and is North America's largest Pacific island. Most of this mass protects the lower mainland of British Columbia from torrential rains and gale-force winds of the open ocean. However, the island does cross the 49th parallel, the general boundary between the United States and Canada, and its southern fifth, including the city of Victoria, is on the same latitude as parts of Washington State.

Much of the island lies in its natural state with beaches, forests, mountains and meadows. Rains nurture thick, sometimes ancient forests, and over centuries the ocean has carved out sandy beaches. The area is a stunning contrast of the rugged, mountainous and relatively uninhabited west coast to sleepy seaside villages, farms and provincial islands on the southeastern shore. Not all of Vancouver Island is so bucolic. The west coast is rugged with craggy mountains, a rugged coastline and often dramatic weather. In fact, in the early 19th century, during the era of sailing ships, the West Coast of Vancouver Island was dubbed "Graveyard of the Pacific" for the number of shipwrecks that occurred there. Starting in September, the winter rains start to pour, and blustery winds are not uncommon. On the west coast, winds and rains can be brutal. Mountains drop right into a raging Pacific Ocean. Many remote settlements or camps—too small even to be called villages—have scant road access and rely on freighters, boats or float planes to deliver everything from apples to asphalt.

Geography and the elements have conspired to make the southern part of the island a relative haven where farming, tourism and commerce thrive. In fact, more Canadians retire to Greater Victoria than anywhere else in the country, thanks to its relatively mild climate and fairy-tale Olde English character. A number of picturesque villages and towns are perched on the coast. The Malahat Drive offers fabulous views of Washington's Olympic Mountains, the Gulf Islands and the Saanich Peninsula, which is dotted with small farms, orchards and gardens.

For the most part, the island's climate is gentle, thanks to the warmth from the Japanese current. A majestic range of mountains divides the island into a dense rainforest on the west coast and the drier lowlands on the east coast. The eastern summers can be blissful with long, sunny days. The climate of Victoria and the southeastern part of the island is akin to that of the Mediterranean—dry, cool summers and mild winters. It is no accident that many Canadians choose to retire there.

In contrast to the rugged side of Vancouver Island, Victoria emerges gracious and genteel. On the island's southern shore, this is the seat of the provincial government, but there is also a cozy and quaint look to the place. It overflows with flowers, the lawns graced with tulips, rhododendrons and roses, the window boxes and hanging planters filled with geraniums and lobelia. Victoria's economy rests on the shoulders of government and tourism. Although heightened in summer, tourism is a year-round activity in this city.

Unfortunately, the Victoria area's development has not come without some cost. The Saanich Peninsula once held large tracts of an ecosystem known as oak savannah, very similar to terrain a thousand miles south in California. Today the savannah, the rarest ecosystem in Canada, is almost gone, replaced by housing and farms. (You can see hints of what it looked like on Rockland Hill east of downtown Victoria, where a number of beautiful old oaks remain, and in Beacon Hill Park.)

Prior to settlement by white explorers, the island's people lived in harmony with nature. Natives lived in bands of the Nootka or Nuu-chah-nulth on the west, the Coast Salish to the south and east and the Southern Kwakiutl to the north. These people lived off the bounty of the land, principally the salmon, cedar and wild berries. Spanish explorers first came to the island in 1592, followed by Captain

James Cook in 1778. Vancouver Island is the namesake of George Vancouver, **585** British naval captain, who negotiated the island away from Spain in 1795.

In 1843 James Douglas, a representative of the Hudson's Bay Company and an explorer (the Douglas fir was named for him), established a fort. He named it after the British queen, Victoria, where Bastion Square sits on Wharf Street today, just above the Inner Harbour, an admirably protected anchorage. Coal mining, fishing, logging and fur trading brought settlers to other parts of the island.

Fortunately, the island's wealth of wildlife has not all been hunted away. Home to several species of salmon, the waters surrounding the island make for excellent fishing and offer a supply of natural food for orcas or killer whales, sea lions and seals. These waters also contain a wide variety of seabirds. The mountains and highlands contain Roosevelt elk, black bears, black tail deer, marmots, wolves and cougars.

It's all waiting for you. Ta-ta!

DOWNTOWN VICTORIA

The City of Gardens combines a rich, British heritage with a relaxed lifestyle and climate of the North American West Coast. Winsome, gracious and colorful, the city comes alive with sights that illustrate its history, customs and ties with the sea. Sightseeing in Victoria veers in the direction of its British influence, its natural history and the residents' passion for gardening.

SIGHTS

TOURISM VICTORIA VISITOR CENTRE ✉812 Wharf Street ✆250-953-2033, 800-663-3883 ✐www.tourismvictoria.com, info@tourismvictoria.com This is the place to get information about the Inner Harbour.

SCENIC MARINE DRIVE The drive along the coast is the best route to see views of the water, the coast, the Olympic Mountains and some of Victoria's most elegant homes. Starting at Mile 0, the end of the Trans-Canada Highway, (at the intersection of Dallas Road and Douglas Street), follow the signs as the drive winds along the coast. You pass through Oak Bay, around part of Cadboro Bay, to Mount Douglas Park and the Saanich Peninsula. At Elk Lake, you can turn left onto Route 17 to head back to Victoria.

TALLY-HO SIGHT SEEING ✉Under the red umbrella at the corner of Belleville and Menzies streets, Inner Harbour ✆250-514-9257, 866-383-5067 ✉250-652-0143 ✐www.tallyhotours.com, info@tallyhotours.com Visitors get a good overview of the city by taking a horse-drawn tour with this group, whose steeds have been clip-clopping their way through the streets since 1903.

VICTORIA CARRIAGE TOURS ✉Under the green umbrella at the corner of Belleville and Menzies streets ✆250-383-2207, 877-663-2207 ✉250-383-2097 ✐www.victoriacarriage.com Horse-drawn outings are available from this respected tour group.

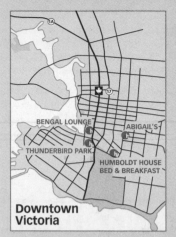

FAIRMONT EMPRESS ✉721 Government Street ☏250-384-8111, 866-540-4429 📠250-381-4334 ⌨www.fairmont.com/empress, theempress@fairmont.com The Empress is Victoria's unofficial central landmark and faces the Inner Harbour. Opened in 1908, it reflects the gentility of an earlier time. Tea is served in the elegant Empress Tea Lobby, which overlooks Inner Harbour. A dress code is enforced; no shorts or tanktops.

MINIATURE WORLD ✉649 Humboldt Street ☏250-385-9731 📠250-385-2835 ⌨www.miniatureworld.com On the ground floor of the Empress hotel, you will find this gallery, with more than 80 miniaturized illustrations of history and fantasy. Miniature World includes the world's smallest operational sawmill, two of the world's largest dollhouses and one of the world's largest model railways. Admission.

VICTORIA CONFERENCE CENTRE/CRYSTAL GARDEN ✉720 Douglas Street ☏250-361-1000, 866-572-1151 ⌨www.victoriaconference.com, sales@victoriaconference.com In 2007–08 this convention center was expanded by annexing the Crystal Garden, which had long been one of the Inner Harbour area's key attractions. Built in 1925, the Crystal Garden was roofed with glass windows that let in light even on the most dismal days. For decades, it housed the largest public swimming pool in the British Empire, along with a poolside tearoom and dancefloor—mass leaps into the pool during formal black-tie balls became a Victoria tradition. In 2008 the Crystal Garden reopened once more as an atrium of the conference centre, allowing the public to enter the newly renovated interior of the landmark building once more. Some members of city government are presently lobbying to supplement the municipal coffers by opening a casino in the Crystal Garden.

ROYAL BRITISH COLUMBIA MUSEUM ✉ *675 Belleville Street* 📞 *250-356-7226, 888-447-7977* 📠 *250-387-5674* 🖳 *www.royalbcmuseum.bc.ca, reception@royalbcmuseum.bc.ca* Walk across Belleville Street, just south of the Fairmont Empress, to a complex anchored by this major museum. One of the best on the continent, the museum focuses on the history of British Columbia—its land and people from pre historic times to the present—in a personal and evocative way. Visitors sit among totem poles, walk inside a longhouse and learn stories of native people and the changes they encountered once white settlers arrived. The museum's spectacular collection of First Nations ceremonial masks is probably the finest in the world. Museum guests also can stroll down the streets of Old Town, plunge into the bowels of a coal mine and walk through the Discovery, a replica of the ship used by Captain Vancouver. In the Ocean Station exhibit you can peer through portholes and a periscope at kelp beds, fishes, sea stars, sea urchins and other B.C. ocean life in a 95-gallon aquarium. There is also an IMAX theater on-site. Admission.

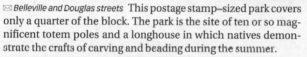

THUNDERBIRD PARK ✉ *Belleville and Douglas streets* This postage stamp–sized park covers only a quarter of the block. The park is the site of ten or so magnificent totem poles and a longhouse in which natives demonstrate the crafts of carving and beading during the summer.

HELMCKEN HOUSE ✉ *10 Elliott Street* 📞 *250-356-7226* 🖳 *www.royalbcmuseum.bc.ca, reception@royalbcmuseum.bc.ca* Just behind Thunderbird Park and adjacent to the Roytal British Columbia Museum is this house, built in 1852 for pioneer doctor J. S. Helmcken. It is British Columbia's oldest residence on its original site. Rooms decorated in the style of the period are furnished with pieces brought around Cape Horn from England by Victoria's founding families. The library includes Dr. Helmcken's medicine chest and medical instruments. Call for winter hours. Admission.

EMILY CARR HOUSE ✉ *207 Government Street* 📞 *250-383-5843* 🖳 *www.emilycarr.com, ecarr@shaw.ca* A couple blocks south of the Helmcken House is this Victorian Italianate cottage where Canada's most famous female artist, British Columbia landscape painter Emily Carr, was born in 1871 and lived her girlhood years. Carr was a contemporary of Georgia O'Keeffe in the U.S. and Frida Kahlo in Mexico. Historians have restored the home with period wall coverings and furnishings to look as it did when she lived there. Carr was also an author, and her gardens have been re-created from her books, excerpts of which are inscribed on plaques among the vegetation. Closed Sunday and Monday and from October to May, except the month of December. Admission.

PARLIAMENT BUILDINGS ✉ *501 Belleville Street* 📞 *250-387-3046* 📠 *250-356-5876* 🖳 *www.leg.bc.ca, tours@leg.bc.ca* These legislative buildings are

Downtown Victoria

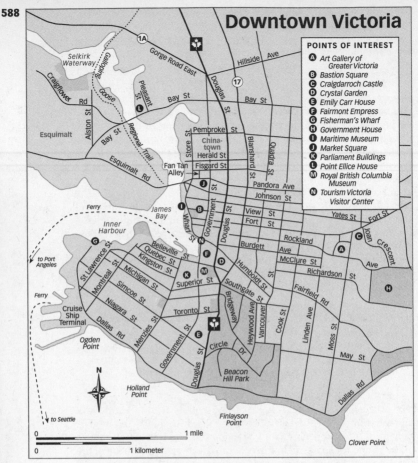

POINTS OF INTEREST

- Ⓐ Art Gallery of Greater Victoria
- Ⓑ Bastion Square
- Ⓒ Craigdarroch Castle
- Ⓓ Crystal Garden
- Ⓔ Emily Carr House
- Ⓕ Fairmont Empress
- Ⓖ Fisherman's Wharf
- Ⓗ Government House
- Ⓘ Maritime Museum
- Ⓙ Market Square
- Ⓚ Parliament Buildings
- Ⓛ Point Ellice House
- Ⓜ Royal British Columbia Museum
- Ⓝ Tourism Victoria Visitor Center

Francis Rattenbury's creation, dating back to 1898, and feature 33 copper domes. At night they are outlined with more than 3000 twinkling lights. A statue of Queen Victoria stands in front of the buildings, and many others are located in the buildings themselves. Guided tours explain historic features and the workings of the provincial government. Closed weekends from late May through Labor Day.

ROYAL LONDON WAX MUSEUM ✉470 Belleville Street ✆250-388-4461, 877-929-3228 🖨250-388-4493 🖳www.waxmuseum.bc.ca, info@waxmuseum.bc.ca Across the street from the Parliament Buildings is this museum, also designed by Rattenbury as the Victoria terminal for the Canadian Pacific Steamships. The Acropolis-style building now contains wax sculptures of the Princess of Wales, President George W. Bush and some 300 other Josephine Tussaud figures. The likenesses of the American figures are lacking, but the Royal Family is very lifelike. You will want to keep young children out of the Horror Chamber with its gruesome depictions of decapitations and other methods of torture, but adolescents love it. Admission.

PACIFIC UNDERSEA GARDENS ✉490 Belleville Street ☎250-382-5717 ☎250-382-5210 🖳www.pacificunderseagardens.com, pug@obmg.com On the water side of the Wax Museum is this salute to British Columbia life below water. At regularly scheduled intervals, divers swim behind huge windows in the enclosed aquarium tanks to show and tell visitors information about sea creatures within the province. Admission.

FISHERMAN'S WHARF ✉Corner of Dallas Road and Erie Street You can continue out Belleville Street by car, cab, bus or bicycle to this picturesque working fishing pier. Moorage allows for up to 400 boats, but the little bay often is jammed with many more, tied up to one another. If the fishing fleet is in, visitors can buy fresh fish from the docks.

JAMES BAY NEIGHBORHOOD A walk in this neighborhood, one of the city's more fashionable areas, takes you past several restored Victorian and Edwardian homes.

BASTION SQUARE ✉Off Wharf Street between Fort and Yates streets Continue back around the Inner Harbour past the Empress and the Travel Info Centre heading north on Wharf Street to Bastion Square. In 1843–44, James Douglas established Fort Victoria here, but the buildings there now, including warehouses, offices, saloons and waterfront hotels, were constructed in the late 1800s, the city's boom period. The buildings, many of them red brick, have been restored and now house restaurants, shops and art galleries. The square itself is home to a couple dozen craft and gift booths during good weather.

MARITIME MUSEUM OF BRITISH COLUMBIA ✉28 Bastion Square ☎250-385-4222 ☎250-382-2869 🖳www.mmbc.bc.ca, info@mmbc.bc.ca This museum is housed in a large, turreted building that was originally the Provincial Court House. The museum depicts British Columbia's maritime history from its early days to the present. It includes nautical charts, an extensive model ship collection, brassware from old ships, Navy uniforms and an incredible vessel—Tilikum, a 38-foot dugout canoe that sailed from Victoria to England at the turn of the 20th century. Admission.

MARKET SQUARE ✉Government and Johnson streets Walk over to Government Street and continue north to Johnson Street. Here you will find Market Square, which incorporates the original Occidental Hotel, the choice of many Klondike gold miners in 1898, now a favorite area for shopping and dining.

CHINATOWN Take Fan Tan Alley north another block to this neighborhood at Government and Herald streets. In the late 19th century, Victoria's Chinatown was second largest on the continent, only trailing that of San Francisco. The Chinese immigrants headed to British Columbia to work on the railroad and to mine for coal and gold. Approaching Chinatown from Government Street, you see the ceramic-tiled Gate of Harmonious Interest with two hand-carved stone lions standing guard. Fan Tan Alley, dubbed Canada's narrowest street, contains boutiques and artists' studios.

LODGING

The problem with lodging in Victoria is the same as elsewhere in popular cities—it's expensive. Several luxurious hotels line the Inner Harbour. Several others charge luxurious prices for mediocre to shoddy rooms. Budget prices can be found, but those accommodations are often farther from downtown.

Like Vancouver's, Victoria's high season is from the end of June to October. And like Vancouver's, the city's hotels offer superlative offseason lodging packages that often bring room rates down to near 50 percent of the summer tariff. The weather isn't as dependable, but the streets aren't thronged with crowds of bus-borne tourists.

TOURISM VICTORIA ✉ *812 Wharf Street* ☎ *800-663-3883* 📠 *250-382-6539* 🖥 *www.tourismvictoria.com, info@tourismvictoria.com* This accommodation line provides current rates and availability at a full range of places.

ABIGAIL'S

$$$–$$$$ 23 ROOMS ✉ *906 McClure Street* ☎ *250-388-5363, 800-561-6565* 📠 *250-388-7787* 🖥 *www.abigailshotel.com, innkeeper@abigailshotel.com*
Just four blocks east of downtown, this Tudor inn has a European ambience with colorful, well-kept gardens and a light, bright interior. The foyer features marble floors and an open oak staircase to the guest rooms. The sitting room is luxurious, with hardwood floors, a leather sofa, fireplace and fresh flowers. Each of the rooms features down comforters and antiques, and some have jacuzzi tubs, fireplaces and vaulted ceilings. In a spa treatment room, guests can receive a massage, manicure or facial. Included in the room rate are evening hors d'oeuvres in the library and a gourmet breakfast served in the dining room.

BEDFORD REGENCY HOTEL

$$ 40 ROOMS ✉ *1140 Government Street* ☎ *250-384-6835, 800-665-6500* 📠 *250-386-8930* 🖥 *www.bedfordregency.com, frontdesk@bedfordregency.com*
Located in an ideal location downtown, across from Victoria Bay Centre, is the Bedford. The large open lobby is furnished with traditional pieces. Invoking the charm of early Victoria, the hotel's individually decorated guest rooms feature comfortable beds complete with down comforters and pillows, cotton sheets, window boxes overflowing with colorful flowers; some have wood-burning fireplaces. A full breakfast is served in the hotel's Belingo Lounge and fresh coffee or tea is placed outside each room in the morning.

FAIRMONT EMPRESS

$$$–$$$$ 477 ROOMS ✉ *721 Government Street* ☎ *250-384-8111, 800-441-1414* 📠 *250-381-5959* 🖥 *www.fairmont.com/empress, theempress@fairmont.com*
The dominant sight in Victoria's Inner Harbour is this stately, neo-Gothic hotel. Canadian Pacific Railways commissioned architect

Francis Rattenbury to design this magnificent hotel. Amenities include a swimming pool, sauna, health club, spa, lobby and lovely grounds. This grande-dame hotel is known throughout the world for its British-style elegance and wonderful afternoon teas. Make reservations one to two weeks in advance.

JAMES BAY INN

$$ 45 ROOMS ✉270 Government Street ☎250-384-7151, 800-836-2649
☎250-385-2311 🖥www.jamesbayinn.com, info@jamesbayinn.com

Even after renovating its rooms, the James Bay still fills the bill for price-minded travelers. It's located in a residential area among heritage homes and small cafés but is pretty convenient to downtown. The hotel, which opened in 1911, features light-oak paneling and period furnishings in the lobby. Guest rooms are small but comfortable. A few travelers have found the service here a bit gruff.

HOTEL GRAND PACIFIC

$$–$$$ 304 UNITS ✉463 Belleville Street ☎250-386-0450, 800-663-7550
☎250-380-4475 🖥www.hotelgrandpacific.com, reserve@hotelgrandpacific.com

For luxury accommodations along the Inner Harbour near the Parliament Buildings, this hotel is one of the city's finest. The lobby and other public areas are airy and lavish affairs. The rooms and suites feature private balconies with views of the harbor or downtown; the west wing offers one of the city's best views of the Inner Harbour. Amenities include an indoor swimming pool, sauna, whirlpool, health and fitness facilities, a European-style spa, restaurants and a lounge.

COAST HARBOURSIDE HOTEL & MARINA

$$–$$$ 132 UNITS ✉146 Kingston Street ☎250-360-1211, 800-716-6199
☎250-360-1418 🖥www.coasthotels.com, Info@coasthotels.com

Just a brisk walk, shuttle or ferry ride from the downtown attractions, this hotel faces a 42-slip marina. Marine colors of teal blue, dark mahogany, original art and watery motifs are found throughout the hotel. The rooms and suites, each with private balcony, come with all the amenities of a top-rate hotel, including a bar and computer hookups. Pick your view: the harbor or the Olympic Mountains. The hotel features an indoor/outdoor pool and deck, with whirlpool, sauna and exercise room. They also offer free parking and a courtesy van to downtown.

VICTORIA HOSTEL

$ 100 BEDS ✉516 Yates Street ☎250-385-4511, 888-883-0099 ☎250-385-3232
🖥www.hihostels.ca, victoria@hihostels.ca

The place for basic accommodations is this hostel, sandwiched between historic buildings and offices downtown. The hostel features two kitchens, a gameroom, a lounge, an eating area, a library, a bicycle storage area, laundry facilities and hot showers. There are 108 beds, dormitory-style, and five small family rooms. Private double-occupancy rooms are available with reservation.

OCEAN ISLAND BACKPACKERS INN

$$–$$$ 200 BEDS ✉791 Pandora Avenue ☎250-382-1788, 888-888-4180
☎250-385-1780 🖥www.oceanisland.com, info@oceanisland.com

This inn is a funky but very economical property in the west end of downtown Victoria, near Chinatown. Facilities include a licensed pub, kitchen, internet access, storage and parking. There are some private rooms and there is no curfew. Rates start as low as C$28 to C$94 (US$23 to $75).

SWAN'S SUITE HOTEL

$$–$$$ 29 UNITS ✉506 Pandora Avenue 📞250-361-3310, 800-668-7926
📠250-361-3491 ⌨www.swanshotel.com, info@swanshotel.com

A small, all-suite hotel in a restored brick heritage building along the harbor in downtown Victoria, Swan's offers a colorful pub and restaurant. Each contemporary unit, ranging from studios to two-bedroom suites, features designer decor and includes a full kitchen, dining area and original art on the walls.

HUMBOLDT HOUSE
BED & BREAKFAST

$$$ 6 UNITS ✉867 Humboldt Street 📞250-383-0152, 888-383-0327
📠250-383-6402 ⌨www.humboldthouse.com, rooms@humboldthouse.com

A truly hidden discovery for couples seeking a romantic getaway is this bed and breakfast, which looks like a private residence. A Victorian home built in 1893 and renovated in 1988, it includes six suites. The library offers walls full of books and a fireplace. Guests are served sparkling wine and chocolate truffles on arrival. The rooms are individually decorated and have jacuzzis and fireplaces. Guests have breakfast delivered to their room via a two-way compartment.

BEACONSFIELD INN

$$$–$$$$ 9 ROOMS ✉998 Humboldt Street 📞250-384-4044, 888-884-4044
📠250-384-4052 ⌨www.beaconsfieldinn.com, info@beaconsfieldinn.com

A large, 1905 Edwardian-style home, this inn has an early 1900s ambience with antique pieces, stained glass, oak fireplace, 14-foot beamed ceiling and the original, dark paneling. Millionaire R. P. Rithet built it in 1905 as a wedding present for his daughter, Gertrude. The nine guest rooms vary in charm, but all include down comforters and antiques. Many feature canopy beds, jacuzzis and fireplaces. Guests also can enjoy sherry hour in the library and a full gourmet breakfast in the original dining room or sunroom, all included in the room rate.

DASHWOOD MANOR
BED AND BREAKFAST

$$$ 11 ROOMS ✉1 Cook Street 📞250-385-5517, 800-667-5517 📠250-383-1760 ⌨www.dashwoodmanor.com, frontdesk@dashwoodmanor.com

A gracious Tudor mansion built in 1912, the Dashwood sits next to Beacon Hill Park and offers views of the Strait of Juan de Fuca and the Olympic Mountains. All of the rooms are decorated with antiques and feature fireplaces and jacuzzis. A full breakfast is served in the oceanview diningroom. The grounds are impeccable and the rooms are clean.

DINING

BENGAL LOUNGE

hidden

$$–$$$ INDIAN ✉ *Fairmont Empress, 721 Government Street*
📞 *250-384-8111* 📠 *250-389-4334* 🖥 *www.fairmont.com/empress,*
theempress@fairmont.com

How can anything at the Fairmont Empress be hidden? Easy: So much attention focuses on the hotel's lobby, tea service and upscale shops that visitors overlook this curry bar par excellence. Once the hotel's library, the lounge is decorated with curios reflecting the British Empire's colonial era—a tiger-skin wallhanging, Indian ceiling fans. The curry is served buffet-style at lunch and dinner; a centennial indulgence dessert bar is available Friday and Saturday nights. A word to the wise: The Bengal Lounge serves an all-day à la carte menu. If you want to experience tea at the Empress, but haven't made a reservation, you can order tea and scones here. It's a welcome contrast to the monotony of British pub fare that tends to overwhelm Victoria dining.

JAMES BAY TEA ROOM AND RESTAURANT

$ DINER ✉ *332 Menzies Street* 📞 *250-382-8282* 📠 *250-389-1716*
🖥 *www.jamesbaytearoomandrestaurant.com jamesbaytearoom@shaw.ca*

This is a homey place with photographs of English royalty overlooking tables set close together with hand-crocheted tea cozies insulating every teapot. This place is popular with the older set and families. Breakfast, lunch and tea service available all day.

YOKOHAMA

hidden

$$ JAPANESE ✉ *980 Blanshard Street* 📞 *250-384-5433* 📠 *250-384-5438*

With its large sushi bar and an extensive menu, this charming and graceful Japanese restaurant is deemed the best place in town for such fare. The restaurant features authentic Japanese entrées as well as familiar favorites of tempura, sukiyaki and ginger pork in the main dining area or in private tatami rooms.

THE KEG STEAKHOUSE AND BAR

$$–$$$ STEAK ✉ *500 Fort Street* 📞 *250-386-7789* 📠 *250-386-5201*
🖥 *www.kegsteakhouse.com*

The Keg is an informal restaurant, one of the most popular, reasonably priced places downtown. Its dining room offers great views of the Inner Harbour. Entrées include prime rib and grilled shrimp. Try the Classic Meal, a sirloin or New York steak served with seasonal vegetables, caesar salad and a baked potato. Dinner only.

CAMILLE'S RESTAURANT

$$$ WEST COAST/PACIFIC RIM   ✉45 Bastion Square   ☎250-381-3433

📠250-381-3403   🖱www.camillesrestaurant.com, info@camillesrestaurant.com

Historic Bastion Square is home to one of Victoria's best restaurants. Camille's is romantic and elegant with brick walls, balloon curtains and linen tablecloths. This intimate restaurant prepares delicious West Coast and Pacific Rim cuisine, such as local Muscovy duck with orange and lavender demi glace, and spice-crusted venison on beet and barley risotto. The breads and desserts are heavenly. Camille's also has an extensive wine cellar. Dinner only. Closed Sunday and Monday.

SIAM THAI RESTAURANT

$$ THAI   ✉512 Fort Street   ☎250-383-9911   📠250-380-2220
🖱www.siamthai.ca

Siam Thai serves up some of the best Thai food in Victoria. The atmosphere is dark and quiet, with soft lighting lending a bit of mystery to this ethnic eatery. Only fresh ingredients are used in the entrées, such as *larb gai*, diced chicken in spicy lime juice, onions and vegetables, or *kung phad prik paow*, sautéed prawns with green-red peppers, onions, mushrooms and chili paste. No lunch on Sunday.

BLUE FOX

$ AMERICAN   ✉919 Fort Street   ☎250-380-1683

Crowds line up outside this small Fort Street café to get in on weekend mornings. They've come for heaping platters of breakfast—huge omelettes, piles of hash browns and toast, or redolent huevos rancheros—and equally filling lunch, including that endangered rarity: handmade hamburgers. Breakfast is available all day, of course.

BEAN AROUND THE WORLD

$ COFFEE SHOP   ✉533 Fisgard Street   ☎250-386-7115   🖱www.cowboycoffee.ca

This is a cozy, friendly and top-quality coffee shop in Chinatown. The coffee is custom roasted, and the muffins and pastries are fresh and filling. It also serves light lunches.

DON MEE

$$ CHINESE   ✉538 Fisgard Street   ☎250-383-1032   📠250-383-8387
🖱www.donmee.com

Go through the door under the neon sign and walk up a long, burgundy-carpeted staircase to the large dining area in this traditional Chinese restaurant in the heart of Chinatown. The food here is good, portions are ample and the presentation is upscale. People come for the Cantonese-style seafood dishes like lobster in ginger sauce or crab with black beans. Favorites include

Szechuan chicken and fresh vegetable dishes. The dim sum, served for lunch daily, is especially good.

WILD SAFFRON BISTRO

$$$–$$$$ PACIFIC NORTHWEST   ✉Swan's Suite Hotel, 506 Pandora Street
☎250-361-3310 ✆250-361-3491 ☞www.swanshotel.com, info@swanshotel.com

A brick-walled dining room illuminated by a bright lemon-colored ceiling and original artwork, this bistro in the Swan's Suite Hotel delivers fresh, local cuisine five nights a week. The creative menu features entrées such as pan-seared trout with saffron tomato cream and oven-roasted duck breast with port fig jus, along with a variety of steak, free-range chicken and game dishes. Dessert is just as delectable, and the wine list is extensive. Closed Sunday and Monday.

IL TERRAZZO

$$–$$$ ITALIAN   ✉555 Johnson Street ☎250-361-0028 ✆250-360-2594
☞www.ilterrazzo.com, ilterrazzo@shaw.ca

Outdoor dining made warm and cozy by fireplaces and overhead heaters is offered here, where they serve sophisticated Northern Italian cuisine on a brick plant-filled terrace off Waddington Alley. Daily specials yield such possibilities as grilled lamb chops seasoned with garlic and fresh mint or baked halibut with blackberries and asiago cheese. No lunch on weekends in winter.

SHOPPING

Victoria's downtown is chock full of fascinating shops. Best buys are locally made candies, Indian-made sweaters, carvings and silver, British Columbia jade, weavings and pottery, books on Canada and goods imported from Britain. Shopping starts with tiny shops in the Empress Hotel and extends north on Government Street.

ROGER'S CHOCOLATES ✉913 Government Street ☎250-384-7021, 800-663-2220 ✆250-384-5750 ☞www.rogerschocolates.com, info@rogerschocolates.com

Roger's is the place for connoisseurs of fine chocolates. Roger's started offering chocolates to Victorians in 1885, and ever since then fans have been returning for the hugely popular "Victoria Creams." Housed in a 1903 building with a tiled floor, dark-oak paneling and oak-and-glass display cases, the shop is full of Dickensian charm. Some of the sinfully luscious confections include Empress Squares (caramel and roasted almonds in semisweet chocolate), classic truffles (filled with orange, raspberry, mocha and coconut) and traditional chocolate almond brittle.

MUNRO'S BOOKS ✉1108 Government Street ☎250-382-2464, 888-243-2464 ✆250-382-2832 ☞www.munrobooks.com, service@munrobooks.com Even if you brought all your reading with you, stop at Munro's to see this neoclassical heritage building with high ceilings and carved details, formerly the head office of the Royal Bank. It is one of the finest bookshops in western Canada. The shop holds more than 50,000 titles of Canadian, British and American works.

MURCHIES ✉1110 Government Street ☎250-383-3112 ✆250-383-3255 ☞www.murchies.com Check out this purveyor of fine teas and coffees, where

you can also pick up some delectable pastries and enjoy lunch or afternoon tea.

IRISH LINEN STORE ✉ *1019 Government Street* ✆ *250-383-6812, 877-966-6868* 🖰 *www.irishlinenvictoria.com* For Irish linen tablecloths, fine handkerchieves, linen blouses and embroideries, visit this shop, a family operation since 1910.

THE BAY CENTRE ✉ *Government and Fort streets* ✆ *250-952-5690* 🖷 *250-381-5285* 🖰 *www.thebaycentre.ca* This multilevel shopping mall located in the heart of Victoria has more than 90 shops and opens to an interior courtyard under skylights and arches. Bay Centre offers goods from all over the Commonwealth, especially china and woolen products.

HUDSON'S BAY COMPANY ✉ *1150 Douglas Street* ✆ *250-385-1311* 🖷 *250-385-9247* 🖰 *www.hbc.com* Located within Bay Centre, this is the Canadian company that pioneered settlement of the West. It still carries the famous Hudson's Bay point blankets and top brands of English china and woolens. It also houses a gallery featuring bay history art.

ANTIQUE ROW Fort Street between Blanshard and Cook streets is filled with stores offering antique maps, stamps, coins, estate jewelry, rare books, crystal, china, furniture and paintings.

NIGHTLIFE

BENGAL LOUNGE ✉ *Fairmont Empress, 721 Government Street* ✆ *250-384-8111* 🖰 *www.fairmont.com/empress* In the Fairmont Empress, this lounge, with its high ceilings, potted plants and rattan furnishings, is fit for the raj. It is a comfortable, old-money place for a drink.

HUSH ✉ *1325 Government Street* ✆ *250-385-0566* 🖰 *www.hushnightclub.ca* A gay-friendly danceclub, this hot nightlife destination features house music. Deejays provide music Wednesday through Sunday until 2 a.m. Cover.

For a more cultured evening, Victoria offers several options.

PACIFIC OPERA VICTORIA ✉ *Royal Theatre, 805 Broughton Street* ✆ *250-385-0222, 250-386-6121* 🖰 *www.pov.bc.ca, boxoffice@pov.bc.ca* This well-respected opera performs at the Royal Theatre.

VICTORIA SYMPHONY ✉ *620 View Street* ✆ *250-385-9771 (information), 250-385-6515 (tickets)* 🖷 *250-385-7767* 🖰 *www.victoriasymphony.ca, boxoffice@victoriasymphony.ca* The symphony here offers concerts featuring international conductors and artists. On the first weekend in August it holds the celebrated "Symphony Splash," a free, open-air concert where the orchestra plays from a barge in the harbor.

Victoria's pubs offer an alternative to the expensive price of having a drink in the hotel lounges. Some of these pubs feature beers made on the premises, while others stock a wide variety of local and imported beers and ales. Whether in historic buildings or cottage breweries, you also are apt to find a game of darts and a number of skilled competitors.

SWAN'S SUITE HOTEL ✉ *506 Pandora Avenue* ✆ *250-361-3310, 800-668-7926* 🖰 *www.swanshotel.com* One of the liveliest pub crowds is found at

Swan's, where you can hear great live music every night and see a changing and colorful collection of local and international art.

MCPHERSON PLAYHOUSE ✉*Government and Pandora streets* ✆*250-386-6121, 888-717-6121* ✐*www.rmts.bc.ca* Centennial Square includes the original City Hall (1878) and this restored baroque and Edwardian-style theater seating 772. It hosts stage plays, classical and pops concerts, dance performances, films and touring lectures. The Gallery at the MAC, located in the lobby, showcases local visual artists.

DARCY'S WHARFSIDE PUB ✉*1127 Wharf Street* ✆*250-380-1322* ✐*www.darcyspub.ca* Darcy's is a comfy, old-fashioned pub with pool tables, a patio and live music every night. Cover on weekends.

SOPRANOS KARAOKE & SPORTS BAR ✉*30 Caledonia Street* ✆*250-382-5853* ✐*www.sopranoskaraoke.com* A favorite spot for karaoke singalongs is Sopranos. They also boast 25 TVs (two of them big screens), so if being a rock star isn't your thrill, you can relax and catch up on sports.

PARKS

BEACON HILL PARK
✉*Along Douglas Street, only a ten-minute walk from the Empress hotel* ✆*250-361-0600* ✇*250-361-0615* ✐*www.beaconhillpark.com*
This sedate park near downtown, founded in 1882, contains forest, open grassy areas, ponds and Goodacre Lake, a wildfowl sanctuary. Among gardens blooming nearly year-round, you also will find one of the tallest totem poles in the world (160 feet), lawn bowling, an 1850s cricket pitch, the Mile 0 marker of the Trans-Canada Highway and a children's petting zoo in the summer, all at the southwestern corner where Dallas Road and Douglas Street meet. Facilities include rest rooms, picnic areas, tennis courts, playground, lawn bowling, baseball and soccer fields, a children's wading pool and water play area.

VICTORIA NEIGHBORHOODS

Beyond the heart of Victoria are some of the city's most important landmarks, including a castle fit for a queen and the house where Her Majesty actually stays on her visits. Your itinerary also features Victoria's major art gallery and a leading museum of Victoriana. If you have half a day at your disposal, just follow our lead.

SIGHTS

CRAIGDARROCH CASTLE ✉*1050 Joan Crescent* ✆*250-592-5323* ✇*250-592-1099* ✐*www.thecastle.ca, info@thecastle.ca* You'll need your own or public transportation to head out east on Fort Street to this historic structure. Robert Dunsmuir had the house built for his family after he made his fortune mining coal on Vancouver Island in the mid-1800s, making him one of the richest men in British Columbia. Sadly, Dunsmuir himself died before the castle was completed in 1890. Today, visitors can tour Craigdarroch, furnished in turn-of-the-20th-century style featuring 22,000 square feet on five floors with stained-glass windows, intricate woodwork, period furniture and turrets. Exploring the castle requires some agility; there is no elevator and there are 87 steps throughout the self-guided tour. Closed weekends. Admission.

ART GALLERY OF GREATER VICTORIA ✉1040 Moss Street ☎250-384-4101 🖶250-361-3995 ⌨aggv.bc.ca Just a couple of blocks southwest of Craigdarroch Castle is this featured art gallery. One of Canada's finest art museums, this gallery features Canadian art, European pieces from the 15th through 20th centuries and the only authentic Shinto shrine outside Japan, plus a large Asian art collection. A portion of the gallery is housed in Spencer Mansion, built in 1890, which features a dramatic staircase, a Jacobean ceiling and a dollhouse with many intricate details. Admission.

GOVERNMENT HOUSE ✉1401 Rockland Avenue ☎250-387-2080 🖶250-387-2078 ⌨www.ltgov.bc.ca The Queen of England and her family stay here when they visit Victoria. It is the official residence of the Lieutenant Governor, the Queen's representative in British Columbia. When royalty is not visiting, the public can stroll through the formal lawns and gardens, complete with a lilypond, waterfall and extensive collection of roses. It's a pleasant, uncrowded (and free) contrast to the frenzy of Butchart Gardens.

ROCKLAND AVENUE Take a few minutes to explore this street, which is home to many mansions, ranging from late Victorian to Craftsman-style, built during the 1880s and 1890s.

POINT ELLICE HOUSE ✉2616 Pleasant Street off Bay Street ☎250-380-6506, 250-389-1211 (in winter) ⌨www.pointellicehouse.ca, reservations@pointellicehouse.ca If you enjoy Victorian furnishings, you will want to see this house, which contains British Columbia's most comprehensive collection of Victorian furnishings and art in its original setting. The house was built around 1862. Visitors also can stroll through a wonderful 19th-century garden where afternoon tea is served daily (reservations required) throughout the summer. The house can be reached by a ten-minute ferry ride from Victoria's Inner Harbour (ferry information, 250-708-0201). Limited hours; call ahead. Admission.

FORT RODD HILL NATIONAL HISTORIC SITE ✉Ocean Boulevard off the Old Island High way, Esquimalt ☎250-478-5849 🖶250-478-2816 ⌨www.pc.gc. ca/fortroddhill, fort.rodd@pc.gc.ca Swing west of Victoria along Esquimalt Harbour to visit one of the region's most important landmarks, a 44-acre park of rolling hills; an open, parade-grounds area; woods; and beach. The fort was built in 1895 to protect the entrance to the Royal Navy Yards in Esquimalt Harbor. It became a park in 1962. Visitors can see restored gun batteries and the restored Fisgard Lighthouse, the oldest lighthouse on the Pacific Coast, which features exhibits on shipwrecks and navigation. A film is shown at the entrance of both sites. Admission.

IFANWEN
BED AND BREAKFAST

hidden

$$ 2 ROOMS ✉ 44 Simcoe Street ☎ 250-384-3717 🖥 www.ifanwen.com,
ifanwen@telus.net

The Ifanwen is in the quiet residential area of James Bay, but downtown shopping and attractions are only a leisurely stroll away. The full breakfast is cooked to order and guests can enjoy the sundeck or the secluded garden, depending upon the weather. Gay-friendly.

AMETHYST INN

$$$ 13 ROOMS ✉ 1501 Fort Street ☎ 888-265-6499 📠 250-595-2054
🖥 www.amethyst-inn.com, innkeeper@amethyst-inn.com

Many of the furnishings here were shipped around Cape Horn in barrels of protective molasses—they and this exquisite 1885 Victorian mansion remain in pristine condition today. The decorative frieze girdling the high walls of the public rooms is incredibly intricate, and the European tilework on the fireplaces is priceless. Every room has a soaker tub, spa or antique clawfoot tub.

OAK BAY BED AND BREAKFAST GUEST HOUSE

$$ 11 ROOMS ✉ 1052 Newport Avenue ☎ 250-598-3812, 800-575-3812 📠 250-598-0369 🖥 www.oakbayguesthouse.com, stay@oakbayguesthouse.com

Oak Bay is a 1912 B&B furnished with period antiques. The rooms offer garden views and private baths, some with clawfoot tubs. Relax by the livingroom fireplace or enjoy a book in the sunroom. Gay-friendly.

UNIVERSITY OF VICTORIA HOUSING SERVICES

$ 800 ROOMS ✉ P.O. Box 1700, Sinclair Road, Victoria, BC V8W 2Y2 ☎ 250-721-8395
📠 250-721-8930 🖥 housing.uvic.ca, housing@uvic.ca

If you don't mind student housing without frills, this service, 20 minutes north of downtown, offers over 800 rooms, and breakfast in the residence dining room, from May 1 to August 30.

TRAVELODGE

$$$ 73 ROOMS ✉ 229 Gorge Road East ☎ 800-565-3777 or 800-578-7878
📠 250-388-4153 🖥 www.travelodgevictoria.com, info@travelodgevictoria.com

The Gorge Waterway extends northwest from the Inner Harbour. Here you will find a number of less expensive motels. Hidden among the many motels lining Gorge Road, this lodging offers the most quality and service for your money. The hotel appeals to families because of its indoor pool, twin saunas, full-service restaurant and lounge. Just a few minutes drive from downtown, the motel has 73 rooms that are clean, are decorated in cool colors and feature oak trim. Some units feature kitchenettes.

THE AERIE

$$$ 35 UNITS ✉ 600 Ebedora Lane, Malahat ☎ 250-743-7115, 800-518-1933
📠 250-743-4766 🖥 www.aerie.ca, resort@aerie.ca

This resort is one of Canada's most conspicuous inns, an over-the-top Mediterranean-style complex resting astride Malahat Mountain. With a dizzying array of levels, angles and perspectives, it sprawls along the hill like a Greek resort; but inside the decor and ambience aim for Roman Empire opulence, with columns and canopy-draped beds, whispering baths and neoclassic statuary. The air of sensuous decadence is bolstered by the restaurant's legendary multicourse dinners (see "Dining" below). The six-bedroom villa (groups only) is closed from November through March. The resort is closed for two weeks in January.

DINING

PAPRIKA BISTRO

$$$–$$$$ CONTINENTAL   ✉2522 Estevan Avenue   ✆250-592-7424
📠250-592-7425   ✍www.paprika-bistro.com

A warm contemporary room with local artwork on the walls forms the interior of Paprika. George and Linda Szasz pay homage to generations of recipes with classic bistro fare. The tiger prawn curry and the half-roasted duckling with sour cherry and ginger sauce show off the kitchen's varied talents. Desserts include homemade ice cream and sorbet. Dinner only. Closed Sunday and Monday.

BLETHERING PLACE

$–$$ BRITISH   ✉2250 Oak Bay Avenue, Oak Bay   ✆250-598-1413, 888-598-1413
📠250-592-9052   ✍www.thebletheringplace.com, tearoom@thebletheringplace.com

What is the difference between afternoon tea and high tea? Afternoon tea consists of a pot of tea and a selection of delicate finger sandwiches, scones, cakes, fruit, cookies or petit fours served anytime after noon, while high tea is more substantial, served in the early evening in place of dinner. For a truly English dinner or afternoon tea, meander out to this restaurant in Oak Bay. You will find the silver-haired set gossiping over hours-long tea, and families stopping by for supper. The fare includes crumpets, tarts, scones, Welsh rarebit, bangers, steak-and-kidney pie and decadent desserts. You'll find live music and entertainment on weekends.

MARINA RESTAURANT

$$$–$$$$ SEAFOOD   ✉1327 Beach Street   ✆250-598-8555   📠250-598-3014
✍www.marinarestaurant.com

This restaurant not only has a smashing view of Oak Bay and the Lower Mainland in the distance, it also offers excellent seafood and pastas, along with house-made breads. There's also a fine sushi bar making good use of local fish and shellfish. It's extremely popular with residents.

BEACON DRIVE-IN

$ AMERICAN   ✉126 Douglas Street   ✆250-385-7521

The Beacon is a Victoria institution, offering all the usual drive-in items—hamburgers, fries, shakes, ice cream and hearty breakfasts—made the old-fashioned way. Be sure to try an island favorite, the oyster burger.

SIX MILE PUB

$$ BRITISH   ✉494 Island Highway at Six Mile Road   ✆250-478-3121   📠250-478-8765
✍www.sixmilepub.com, info@sixmilepub.com

To experience an off-the-beaten-path aspect of Victoria's unique merry olde England character, I head out to an 1855 carriagehouse six miles from downtown, one of the oldest buildings in the Pacific

Northwest. It is the picture of an old English pub with hanging lamps, oak moldings, dartboards, pool and poker tables, and stained-glass windows. At lunch expect traditional pub fare such as fish and chips or steak-and-mushroom pie. Changing specials at dinner may include charbroiled salmon or New York steak.

THE AERIE

$$$$ PACIFIC NORTHWEST/FRENCH ✉ *600 Ebedora Lane, Malahat*
📞*250-743-7115, 800-518-1933* 📠*250-743-4766* 🖱*www.aerie.ca, resort@aerie.ca*

One of Victoria's most elegant restaurants, this resort sits atop the Malahat summit. Located outside greater Victoria on the way to Duncan, the eatery's dining room has a 23-carat-gold-leaf ceiling, with panoramic views stretching from the Gulf Islands to the Olympic Mountains. The menu changes, depending on availability of the very freshest local ingredients. Entrées such as seaweed-wrapped Salt Spring Island lamb or roasted venison loin with a matsutake mushroom sauce attract enough high-flying guests that a helicopter pad was added to the restaurant and 35-room guesthouse.

SHOPPING

OAK BAY AVENUE The municipality of Oak Bay offers an array of boutiques and specialty stores on Oak Bay Avenue featuring designer clothing, English toffees, New Age toys and games, crafts and jewelry. **Avenue China & Chintz** (2225 Oak Bay Avenue; 250-595-1880) typifies the district, with a pleasing and eclectic array of elegant housewares and decor items. Closed Sunday.

MAYFAIR SHOPPING CENTER ◻*A mile from downtown near Douglas Street and Finlayson Avenue* 📞*250-383-0541* 📠*250-381-0542* 🖱*www.mayfairshopping centre.com* This shopping center is one of the largest and most upscale shopping centers on the island. It contains more than 120 shops specializing in men's and women's fashions.

NIGHTLIFE

THE SNUG PUB ✉*1175 Beach Street, Oak Bay* 📞*250-598-4556* 📠*250-598-6180* 🖱*sales@oakbaybeachhotel.bc.ca* In Oak Bay, east of downtown Victoria, this pub at the Oak Bay Beach Hotel attracts locals and visitors alike. It has a warm, British atmosphere with plaster walls, dark-wood beams, a large bar and fireplace. During the summertime, the balcony overlooking the ocean is popular.

BEACHES & PARKS

THETIS LAKE REGIONAL PARK

✉*Off Route 1, about five miles northwest of downtown Victoria* 📞*250-478-3344* 📠*250-478-5416*

🚶🚴🐎♨🛶⛷ Just five miles from the city center, this park offers opportunities for walking, hiking and solitude on more than 1900 acres of rolling hills, fir and cedar forest and lake frontage. You can swim and fish in the lake during the summer. There are picnic areas and restrooms.

MT. DOUGLAS MUNICIPAL PARK

✉ *Located about five miles northeast of downtown Victoria off Route 17 and Royal Oak/Cordova Bay Road* ☎ *250-475-5522*

🚶 On the east side of the Saanich Peninsula is this 475-acre park with forests of arbutus, fir and cedar, a beach and Mt. Douglas peak. Visitors can drive a one-and-a-half-mile paved route to a parking area and then hike a short distance to the peak where the view stretches in all directions. You'll find picnic areas and restrooms.

SAANICH PENINSULA

One of Vancouver Island's leading tourist attractions, Butchart Gardens, is the Saanich Peninsula's primary draw. This area also offers a host of other garden retreats featuring exotic fauna from all over the world.

SIGHTS

BUTCHART GARDENS

✉ *800 Benvenuto Drive* ☎ *250-652-5256, 866-652-4422* 📠 *250-652-3883* 🌐 *www.butchartgardens.com, email@butchartgardens.com* Traveling north on Route 17 from Victoria toward Sidney, signs direct you to this must-see for anyone who has ever dreamed of having a green thumb. Dating back to 1904, the industrious wife of a manufacturer of Portland cement turned a quarry pit created by her husband into a fabulous sunken garden. Today, Jennie Butchart's project (still run by the Butchart family) is a 55-acre display garden, which includes the Rose Garden, the Italian Garden, the Japanese Garden, the Star Pond and the Ross Fountain. The gardens are now a National Historic Site of Canada. Joined by a series of walkways, the gardens display masses of color and rare and exotic plants. See fantastic fireworks displays every Saturday night in July and August. In summer the bus-borne crowds can be a bit much (some of the paths are rather narrow) so it's a good idea to come early in the day to avoid the masses of tourists who arrive by bus. Christmastime features an extensive lighting display and open-air ice skating rink. Admission.

VICTORIA BUTTERFLY GARDENS ✉ *1461 Benvenuto Avenue, Brentwood Bay* ☎ *250-652-3822, 877-722-0272* 📠 *250-652-4683* 🌐 *www.butterflygardens.com, info@butterflygardens.com* Near the entrance to Butchart Gardens, this enchanting attraction is one of the largest butterfly conservatories in Canada. Its indoor rainforest habitat is designed for the breeding of tropical species imported from throughout the world. More than 35 rare species are bred, hatched and raised here—including the Atlas moth, the world's largest moth—with roughly 2000 butterflies taking wing among the banana trees, hibiscus, bougainvillea and coconut palms. Flamingos, South African turacos, koi and tropical ducks also grace the gardens. There's also an orchid display. Closed in January. Admission.

GLENDALE GARDENS AND WOODLAND

PAGE 603

Vibrant displays of lilies, dahlias and fruit trees amid serene forest paths and babbling creeks

COMPASS ROSE CABINS & MARINA

PAGE 604

Light and airy cabins built right over Brentwood Bay—the ultimate waterfront accomodations

ISLAND VIEW BEACH REGIONAL PARK

PAGE 606

Views of Mt. Baker and the San Juan islands from rolling dunes of fine, white sand strewn with driftwood

SIDNEY HISTORICAL MUSEUM ⊠2423 Beacon Avenue, Sidney ☏250-655-6355 ⌨www.sidneymuseum.ca, info@sidneymuseum.ca This museum, in what was once a ferry customs building, offers a glimpse of turn-of-the-20th-century Saanich Peninsula through photographs, dioramas and even a fully re-created Depression-era kitchen and historic barn. Admission.

NEW MARINE CENTRE ⊠9811 Seaport Place, Sidney ☏250-665-7511 ⌨www.newmarinecentre.ca, angus@newmarinecentre.ca Whale fans will be lining up to tour this state-of-the-art marine center when it opens in 2010. Conceptualized in cooperation with the Vancouver Aquarium, it will offer visitors an undersea tour of the nearby gulf, from its depths to its beaches, along with tide-touch pools and a killer whale skeleton that seems to come to life. Admission

GLENDALE GARDENS AND WOODLAND _____

⊠505 Quayle Road ☏250-479-6162 ☏250-479-6047 ⌨www.hcp.bc.ca, info@hcp.bc.ca Returning south on Route 17, you can stop at these gardens where displays are cultivated year-round. You walk on forest paths through a rhododendron vale to see a fabulous display of Asian lilies, a creek flanked with ferns and hostas and collections of fuschias and dahlias. They have a winter garden of fruit trees and a fuchsia arbor, giving the center flowers year-round. Admission.

CENTRE OF THE UNIVERSE ⊠Little Saanich Mountain, 5071 West Saanich Road, Victoria ☏250-363-8262 ⌨www.hia.nrc.ca/cu Farther south on Route 17, on a hilltop overlooking Elk Lake, stands a white dome that houses what in 1918 was the largest telescope in the world, a 65-inch optical masterpiece that still offers a stunning view of the heavens—tour visitors get to turn the massive instrument. On Saturday night, visitors can hear nontechnical talks about astronomy. The nearby interpretive center offers exhibits on Canadian contributions to space exploration, and lots of interactive displays for kids. Closed Sunday and Monday from November through March.

CRAIGFLOWER MANOR AND SCHOOLHOUSE ⊠*110 Island Highway, corner of Craigflower and Admirals roads* ☏*250-479-8053* ✆*250-744-2251* ✎*craigflower@conservancy.bc.ca*

When Route 17 intersects with Route 1, head west on Route 1 and follow the signs to this charming sight. Craigflower grew out of the requirement that in order to have a lease on Vancouver Island, the Hudson's Bay Company had to colonize it. Craigflower is one of four farms planned by the company. Some 25 families arrived from Scotland in 1853 to live on and work the farm. Visitors can tour the Georgian-style farmhouse built for bailiff Kenneth McKenzie in 1856, which contains furnishings and articles brought from Scotland. Craigflower School house is the oldest school building in western Canada. There is also a heritage garden with heirloom plants and farm animals. Open Wednesday through Sunday. Closed mid-September to mid-May. Admission.

LODGING

BEST WESTERN EMERALD ISLE MOTOR INN

$$$ 65 ROOMS ⊠*2306 Beacon Avenue, Sidney* ☏*250-656-4441, 800-315-3377* ✆*250-655-1351* ✎*www.bwemeraldisle.com, bestwesternemeraldisle@shaw.ca*

Near Butchart Gardens, ferries and the airport, this Best Western appeals to families because it is convenient and rooms have kitchenettes. No decorator interiors here, but the decor is functional. The rooms (including 12 two-room suites), some of which are nonsmoking, are clean. Amenities include a restaurant, whirlpool baths, a sauna, and laundry and exercise facilities.

COMPASS ROSE CABINS & MARINA

$$$ 3 UNITS ⊠*799 Verdier Avenue, Brentwood Bay* ☏*250-544-1441* ✆*250-544-1015* ✎*www.compassrosecabins.com, compassrosecabins@shaw.ca*

The three cabins here are not only waterfront: They are over the water on pilings, facing south on Brentwood Bay just north of Butchart Gardens. Each cabin is a clean, light and airy space with a loft bedroom, and sitting, dining and cooking areas downstairs. Full meal service is available at an adjoining restaurant. Guests can rent canoes and kayaks on-site, either for a leisurely cruise on the bay or a crowd-free quick trip to the back entrance at Butchart Gardens.

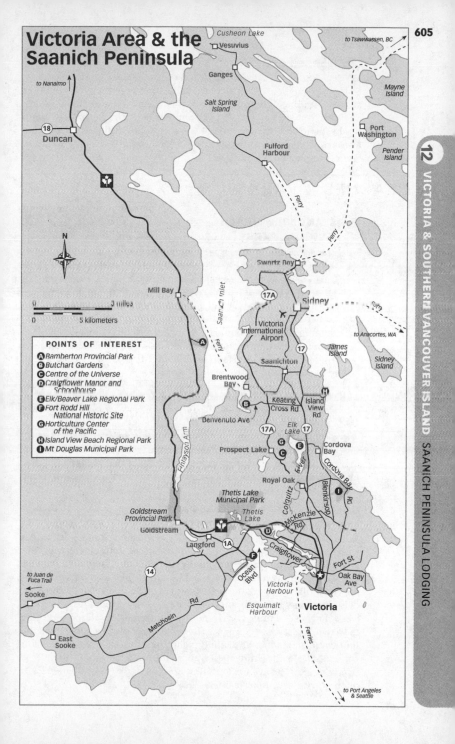

Victoria Area & the Saanich Peninsula

Cusheon Lake

Vesuvius

to Tsawwassen, BC

Ganges

Mayne Island

Salt Spring Island

Port Washington

to Nanaimo

18 Duncan

Fulford Harbour

Pender Island

Ferry

N

Mill Bay

Swartz Bay

Ferry

0   5 miles
0   5 kilometers

17A

Sidney

17A

Victoria International Airport

17

to Anacortes, WA

James Island

Sidney Island

POINTS OF INTEREST

A Bamberton Provincial Park
B Butchart Gardens
C Centre of the Universe
D Craigflower Manor and Schoolhouse
E Elk/Beaver Lake Regional Park
F Fort Rodd Hill National Historic Site
G Horticulture Center of the Pacific
H Island View Beach Regional Park
I Mt Douglas Municipal Park

Saanichton

Brentwood Bay

B

Keating Cross Rd

Island View Rd

H

Benvenuto Ave

17A

Elk Lake

17

Cordova Bay

Prospect Lake

G

C

E

Royal Oak

Colquitz

Blenkinsop

Cordova Bay Rd

I

Finlayson Arm

Thetis Lake Municipal Park

Thetis Lake

McKenzie Rd

Goldstream Provincial Park

Goldstream

D

Langford

1A

Craigflower

Fort St

to Juan de Fuca Trail

14

F

Ocean Blvd

Victoria Harbour

Oak Bay Ave

Sooke

Esquimalt Harbour

Victoria

Metchosin Rd

Ferries

East Sooke

to Port Angeles & Seattle

DINING

SEAHORSES CAFÉ

$$ SEAFOOD   ✉799 Verdier Avenue, Brentwood Bay   ✆250-544-1565

Seahorses is right on the water next to the Brentwood Bay ferry dock—a suitably marine environment for this lovely little seafood bistro. Shellfish, prawns and fish dishes dominate, with the fresh sheet menu the best choice. A variety of salads, sandwiches and pasta dishes are also available. The outdoor deck is a great choice in nice weather. Hours vary in winter; call ahead.

BEACHES & PARKS

ISLAND VIEW BEACH REGIONAL PARK

✉Located northeast of Victoria on the Saanich Peninsula off Route 17 and Island View Road   ✆250-478-3344   ✆250-478-5416   ✐crdparks@crd.bc.ca

🚶 ⛱ 🏊 On the eastern shore of the Saanich Peninsula, the weather has molded this relatively flat park with rolling sand dunes at the north end and a long, accretion beach at the water's edge. The beach, full of fine, white sand, is strewn with sculpture-like driftwood. The water, however, is cold, although some do swim in it. The park offers views of Mt. Baker, Haro Strait and the San Juan and Gulf islands. Facilities include picnic areas, hiking and restrooms.

ELK/BEAVER LAKE REGIONAL PARK

✉Located north of Victoria off Route 17 and Beaver Lake Road   ✆250-478-3344   ✆250-478-5416   ✐crdparks@crd.bc.ca

🚶 🚴 🏇 ⛱ 🛶 🚣 🏊 Lush wetlands, tranquil forests and hilltop vistas surrounding Elk and Beaver lakes (good trout and bass fishing) provide more than 1000 acres of habitat at this regional park for many birds, including owls, woodpeckers and ducks. There are picnic areas and restrooms.

GOLDSTREAM PROVINCIAL PARK

✉Off Route 1, ten miles northwest of Victoria   ✆250-474-1336   ✆250-478-0376

🚶 ⛱ This park provides two distinct vegetation zones—dry ridges with dogwood, lodgepole pine and arbutus, and wetter areas with 600-year-old Doug las fir, western red cedar, western hemlock, western yew, black cottonwood and big-leaf maple, as well as many wildflowers. A salt marsh, where the Goldstream River flows into Finlayson Arm, contains many salt-tolerant plants such as sea asparagus and gumweed. Each November, the river draws thousands of salmon returning to spawn. The river got its name after gold was discovered there, but the find was a small one. You'll find picnic areas, restrooms and a visitor center that provides information about the area's natural history.

⛺ There are 173 sites for tents and RVs (no hookups available); C$24 per night. Reservations: 800-689-9025.

SOUTHEAST ISLAND

Vancouver Island's southeast region is a great place to learn about the area's native heritage and logging industry as well as swim at surprisingly warm beaches such as those on Qualicum Bay.

SIGHTS

DUNCAN   The towns on the island's protected southeastern shore tend to be more low key than the proper British Victoria. This logging town is the site of a collection of some 60 totem poles, ten of which are along the highway and the others scattered about town.

BRITISH COLUMBIA FOREST DISCOVERY CENTRE ✉*2892 Drinkwater Road, Duncan* ☎*250-715-1113, 866-715-1113* 📠*250-715-1170* ⬧*www.discoveryforest.com, info.bcfdc@shawlink.ca* Duncan is the site of this center, where you ride the rails on a steam locomotive or a gas-powered train through a typical Northwest forest, across a trestle over Somenos Lake to the train station. Once there you can walk around the 100-acre park to see early logging equipment, the Log Museum exhibiting logging artifacts and dioramas explaining the history of logging. There's also a picnic area and playground. Closed December through March. Admission.

QUW'UTSUN' CULTURAL AND CONFERENCE CENTRE idden

✉*200 Cowichan Way, Duncan* ☎*250-746-8119, 877-746-8119* 📠*250-746-4143* ⬧*www.quwutsun.ca, shelia@quwutsun.ca* Visitors have an opportunity to experience authentic traditions of the Cowichan people at this cultural and conference center in Duncan. Today, the Cowichan Band, with about 3300 members, is the largest group of native peoples in British Columbia. During the summer you can see carvers at work and watch women as they spin and knit authentic Cowichan sweaters. Call to make a reservation for the midday salmon barbecue with two shows of interpretive dancing. Guided tours are available and an audiovisual presentation gives a sense of the Cowichan spiritual traditions so closely tied with the earth and nature. The center also includes a fine-art gallery and a smaller gift shop. Closed weekends in October and November and from January through March. Admission.

CHEMAINUS   North of Duncan, this community is known as the little town that did. Instead of allowing unemployment to turn Chemainus into a ghost town when the local mill closed, residents hired well-known artists to paint murals all over the town. Yellow footprints on the sidewalks direct visitors past images of native chiefs, loggers felling huge trees and locomotives hauling logs through the forest. The murals have drawn tourists from around the world, creating a new industry there.

QUW'UTSUN' CULTURAL AND CONFERENCE CENTRE

PAGE 607

In-depth look at the fascinating cultural and spiritual traditions of BC's largest First Nations group

PACIFIC SHORES INN

PAGE 609

Charming private suites, like the romantic Fairy Tale Cottage with its unique storybook design

STRATHCONA PROVINCIAL PARK

PAGE 613

Endless hiking trails, like the trek up the 1443-foot Della Falls, one of the world's highest cascades

BAMBERTON PROVINCIAL PARK

PAGE 611

Campsites nestled amid twisting arbutus trees beside a sandy beach with warm water perfect for a swim

NANAIMO

With a population of 75,000, this town is a hidden destination right under the noses of visitors who pass through it on their way from the ferry landing. The city's name grew out of its native title, "Snenymo," meaning both "great and mighty people" and "gathering place." White pioneers came to the area after large deposits of coal were discovered in 1851. The city was incorporated in 1874, and today its economy rests on fishing, forestry, port business and tourism.

NANAIMO MUSEUM

✉ *100 Cameron Road, Nanaimo* 📞 *250-753-1821* 📠 *250-740-0125* 🖱 *www. nanaimomuseum.ca, info@nanaimomuseum.ca* This museum gives visitors an experience of the city's past by taking them through a coal-mining tunnel, a blacksmith's shop, a general store, and a barbershop in a turn-of-the-20th-century town; a restored miner's cottage; dioramas depicting the history and culture of the Nanaimo First Nations people; and an area focusing on Chinatown. Closed Sunday and Monday during the winter. Admission.

TOURISM NANAIMO INFO CENTRE ✉2290 Bowen Road, Nanaimo ☎250-756-0106, 800-663-7337 📠250-756-0075 🌐www.tourismnanaimo.com, info@ tourismnanaimo.com There's a self-guided, historical walking tour of Nanaimo detailed in a map available at this center. Closed Sunday.

HUDSON'S BAY BASTION ✉Just south of the Seaplane Terminal along the harbor This 30-foot-tall building was built on the waterfront in 1852, ostensibly to protect white settlers from the natives. But because the Indians proved to be peaceful, the fort really didn't protect anything. Since 1910 it has been a museum depicting Nanaimo's heritage.

ST. ANNE'S ANGLICAN CHURCH ✉407 Wembley Road, Parksville ☎250-248-3114 📠250-248-3295 ✉pelican407@shaw.ca In the Parksville–Qualicum area, you can visit one of the oldest churches on the island. A group of 45 farmers in the area used oxen to haul the logs for building it. The log church features stained-glass windows. Closed weekends.

CRAIG HERITAGE PARK AND MUSEUM ✉1245 East Island Highway, Parksville ☎250 248 6966 This complex displays artifacts from the local area, including an old schoolhouse, post office, church, fire engine and period cottages. Very limited winter hours; call ahead.

BIG QUALICUM FISH HATCHERY ✉Off the East Island Highway north of Qualicum Beach ☎250-757-8412 📠250-757-8741 ✉barbara.dunsmore@pac.dfo-mpo. gc.ca The name of Qualicum is derived from a native word that means "where the dog salmon run," and if you visit this fish hatchery during the fall spawning season, you can watch the salmon thrashing their way upstream to lay their eggs. After the staff spawn the salmon eggs that have been held for brood, the eggs are placed under controlled conditions for hatching and are eventually released back into the wild. There are hiking trails and a picnic area on the grounds.

COOMBS Located just a few miles west of Parksville is this little town with its Old West look of boardwalks and hitching posts. In the summer, goats graze on the thatched roofs of some of the shops.

BUTTERFLY WORLD AND GARDENS ✉Route 4A ☎250 248 7026 📠250-752-1091 🌐www.nature-world.com West of Coombs is this whimsical "world" where visitors can see all stages of butterfly life, including egg laying and caterpillar rearing. The most colorful area is the tropical indoor garden where butterflies sip nectar, court and flit among colorful blossoms. Also check out the new orchid garden, aviary, koi pond and gift shops. Closed November to mid-March. Admission.

LODGING

PACIFIC SHORES INN _____ ⓗidden

$$–$$$ 3 UNITS ✉9847 Willow Street, Chemainus ☎250-246-4987 📠250-246-1051 ✉pacificshoresinn@shaw.ca
This Victorian inn offers three suites (sleeping two to four people) with kitchens and private entrances. Two of the suites feature washers and dryers, making them ideal for families. For a roman-

tic getaway, rent the Fairy Tale Cottage with its unique stonework and wood detailing, fireplace, and private deck and yard.

COAST BASTION INN

$$–$$$$ 177 ROOMS   ✉ 11 Bastion Street, Nanaimo   ☎ 250-753-6601, 800-716-6199
📠 250-753-4155   🖃 www.coasthotels.com, coastbastion@coasthotels.com

The Coast Bastion is one of the most luxurious hotels in the area with 177 air-conditioned rooms whose balconies offer views of the harbor. The inn has a sauna, whirlpool and exercise room, restaurant, café and lounge.

BEST WESTERN DORCHESTER HOTEL

$$$–$$$$ 70 ROOMS   ✉ 70 Church Street, Nanaimo   ☎ 250-754-6835, 800-661-2449
📠 250-754-2638   🖃 www.dorchesternanaimo.com, info@dorchesternanaimo.com

Oceanfront views are the standard for almost all of the guest rooms and suites here. Built on the former site of the old Windsor Hotel and Opera House near the Bastion, the hotel also has a restaurant and lounge.

BEACH ACRES RESORT

$$$–$$$$ 53 UNITS   ✉ 1051 Resort Drive, Parksville   ☎ 250-248-3424, 800-663-7309
📠 250-248-6145   🖃 www.beachacresresort.com, reservations@beachacresresort.com

Surrounded by woods on three sides, this resort opens onto a large, secluded beach. The beachfront or forest cottages or oceanview condominiums with kitchens are clean, comfortably furnished and all feature fireplaces. Amenities here include an indoor pool, whirlpool, sauna, tennis courts, a playground, laundry and a restaurant.

PARKSVILLE BEACH RESORT

$$ 43 ROOMS   ✉ 161 West Island Highway, Parksville   ☎ 250-248-6789, 888-248-6789
📠 250-248-4789   🖃 www.parksvillebeachmotel.com, info@parksvillebeachmotel.com

Wood paneling, plush carpets and water views mark the rooms at this resort, right on the beach in this sunny resort town north of Nanaimo. Rooms have either two queen or two double beds, and some include kitchenettes. The resort itself has two beach volleyball courts, a whirlpool and sauna, an indoor pool, horseshoe pits and tennis courts. A playground and water park are next door.

DINING

LIGHTHOUSE BISTRO AND PUB

$$$–$$$$ AMERICAN   ✉ 50 Anchor Way at the Sea plane Terminal, Nanaimo   ☎ 250-754-3212   📠 250-753-1299   🖃 www.lighthousebistro.ca, lighthousebistro@telus.net

This place is designed to look like a lighthouse built into a green, Cape Cod–style building with light cream-colored trim. The restaurant offers great harbor views, especially from the large deck. Fresh local fish and juicy steaks dominate the menu along with traditional chicken and pork dishes. The pub upstairs offers a more casual atmosphere.

KALVAS

$$$ FRENCH/GERMAN   ✉ 180 Moilliet Street, Parksville   ☎ 250-248-6933
📠 250-947-9844

In Parksville, visit this large, log-beam building for fine French and German fare. You can feast on East Coast lobster, fresh local crab and oysters. Dinner only.

QUW'UTSUN' CULTURAL AND CONFERENCE CENTRE — hidden

✉200 Cowichan Way, Duncan ☎250-746-8119 📠250-746-4143 🌐www. quwutsun.ca, askme@quwutsun.ca In Duncan, this cultural center offers one of the largest selections of authentic native arts and crafts on the island, including original paintings, jewelry, carvings and Cowichan knitted items. Closed Saturday and Sunday in October and November and from late December through April.

HILL'S NATIVE ART — hidden

✉76 Bastion Street, Nanaimo ☎250-755-7873 📠250-755-7873 🌐www. hills nativeart.com, info@hillsnativeart.com Housed in a 1908 brick building, this shop features Cowichan sweaters, handcarved totem poles of all sizes, carvings, jewelry and prints. Fine leathers, First Nations masks, instruments and baskets are all showcased as well.

NIGHTLIFE

Nightlife isn't plentiful outside Victoria, but that doesn't mean you can't have an enjoyable time in some of the island's southeastern communities.

DINGHY DOCK PUB ✉8 Pirate's Lane, Protection Island ☎250-753-2373 📠250-741-8244 🌐www.dinghydockpub.com Reached by a ten-minute ferry ride (250-753-8244 ferry information), this pub offers locally brewed beers and other spirits and spectacular views of Nanaimo, its harbor and Newcastle Island. There is live music Friday and Saturday nights.

TOURISM NANAIMO INFO CENTRE ✉2290 Bowen Road, Nanaimo ☎250-756-0106, 800-663-7337 🌐www.tourismnanaimo.com Nanaimo also has a handful of theater companies, including the Nanaimo Theatre Group, Yellow Point Drama Group and Malispina College Drama Group. For information on all groups, call this information office.

BEACHES & PARKS

BAMBERTON PROVINCIAL PARK — hidden

✉Located northwest of Victoria off Route 1 at the northern foot of Malahat Drive ☎250-474-1336 📠250-478-0376

The warm waters of the Saanich Inlet make this park, with a 750-foot sandy beach, attractive to swimmers. The park contains many arbutus trees in a second-growth forest. The Saanich Peninsula, Mt. Baker and the Gulf Islands form the backdrop to water and mountain views from this park. Picnic areas and restrooms are the only facilities.

▲ There are 50 tent/RV sites (no hookups); C$15 per night. Reservations: 800-689-9025.

NEWCASTLE ISLAND PROVINCIAL MARINE PARK

✉ *In summer, scheduled foot passenger ferry service departs from Maffeo-Sutton Park next to Front Street and Comox Road.* 📞 *250-754-7893*
🖋 *www.newcastleisland.ca, admin@newcastleisland.ca*

🚶 🚴 ⛵ 🛶 ♨ 🚤 🛥 ⛴ ⚓ Over 750 acres of woods and sandy beaches on an island in Nanaimo Harbor afford views of Vancouver Island and the mainland's Coast Mountains. The park features sandstone ledges and sandy, gravel beaches. The area was a site for coal mining and sandstone mining in the mid- to late 1800s. Cast a rod for salmon. There are picnic areas, a playground, restrooms, over 130 feet of docks, a visitors center and a small bistro in the summer. Cars cannot access the island.

▲ There are 18 tent sites available on a first-come, first-served basis; C$15 per night.

RATHTREVOR BEACH PROVINCIAL PARK

✉ *It's about two miles south of Parksville off Route 19* 📞 *250-474-1336*
📠 *250-478-0376*

🚶 🚴 ⛵ 🎣 ♨ 🛥 ⚓ Located between Nanaimo and Parksville, this park's popularity lies within its sandy beach. There are also a wooded upland area, excellent birdwatching during the spring herring spawn and views of Georgia Strait. There are picnic areas, restrooms and showers. Parking fee, C$3.

▲ There are 150 tent/RV sites (no hookups), C$24 per night; and 15 walk-in sites, C$15 per night. Reservations (mandatory in July and August): 604-689-9025, 800-689-9025; www.discovercamping.ca.

ENGLISHMAN RIVER FALLS PROVINCIAL PARK

✉ *Located west of Parksville off Route 4* 📞 *250-474-1336* 📠 *250-478-0376*

🚶 🚴 🏇 ⛵ 🛶 ⛷ 🎣 ⚓ Forests of huge cedar trees surround two large, crashing waterfalls in this lush 240-acre park. Large groves of hemlock and fir also can be found in the park. A good time to visit is in autumn when the maple trees offer a colorful contrast to the evergreens. You'll find picnic areas and restrooms. Parking fee, C$3.

▲ There are 105 tent/RV sites (no hookups); C$12 to C$30 per night. Reservations: 604-689-9025, 800-689-9025.

LITTLE QUALICUM FALLS PROVINCIAL PARK

✉ *Located 11 miles west of Parksville off Route 4* 📞 *250-474-1336* 📠 *250-478-0376*

🚶 ⛵ ⚓ Although a neighbor to Englishman River Falls Park, this park is much drier. Consequently, visitors see more pine, Douglas fir and arbutus trees in this park that straddles the Little Qualicum River. A must-see are the impressive waterfalls splashing down a rocky gorge. Fish for salmon and take a dip in Cameron Lake. Picnic areas and rest rooms are the only facilities. Parking fee, C$3.

⚠ There are 91 tent/RV sites (no hookups); C$17 per night. Reservations: 604-689-9025, 800-689-9025 ✉www.discovercamping.ca.

STRATHCONA PROVINCIAL PARK

✉ *The park is 40 minutes west of Camp bell River on provincial Route 28* ☎ *250-337-2400* 🖷 *250-337-5695* ✉ *www.strathcona.bc.ca, info@strathcona.bc.ca*

🚶 🚵 This is British Columbia's oldest provincial park, a half-million-acre enclave in the middle of Vancouver Island four hours north of Victoria. It offers popular day hikes from Paradise Meadows on the Forbidden Plateau and Buttle Lake; both can also serve as the starting point for extensive backcountry pack trips. Intrepid hikers might want to try for 1443-foot Della Falls, one of the ten highest waterfalls in the world, accessible only by boat and foot on the Port Alberni side of the park. Less determined visitors can just relax in the Buttle Lake campground.

⚠ Campsites at Buttle Lake (86 sites) or Ralph River (60 sites) are on a first-come, first-served basis; C$12 and C$15 per night from Memorial Day through September, free the rest of the year. The nearby Strathcona Park Lodge (250-286-3122, fax 250-286-6010) offers simple rooms ($$–$$$) and cottages ($$$).

SOUTHWEST ISLAND

Whether you come by land or sea, southwest Vancouver Island is one of the Pacific Northwest's most accessible wilderness regions. With its national parks, wildlife and snow-capped peaks, this is a favorite getaway.

SIGHTS

M. V. LADY ROSE ✉ *Argyle Pier, Port Alberni* ☎ *250-723-8313, 800-663-7192* 🖷 *250-723-8314* ✉ *www.ladyrosemarine.com* Board the *Lady Rose* for a unique experience traveling the Alberni Inlet aboard a freighter, the likes of which have served the hidden, remote communities on the island's west coast for over 50 years. Passengers on the day-long trips can see deliveries of fish food to commercial fish farms, asphalt shingles to individuals re-roofing their homes and mail to residents of communities such as Bamfield and Kildonan. Kayakers can be dropped off at the Sechart Lodge at the Broken Group Islands. Tourists should be forewarned that the boat is primarily a freighter, so don't expect a naturalist or interpretive guide with fascinating commentary.

COULSON FLYING TANKERS

✉ *4890 Cherry Creek Road* ☎ *250-724-7600* 🖷 *250-723-7766* ✉ *www.martin mars.com* Just outside Port Alberni at Sproat Lake, take the time to view this hidden attraction, a private fire protection service. The sight of the largest firefighting aircraft in the world dropping

7200 gallons of water on the lake in a test run is almost too impressive for words. The facility is open to the public from the end of June through August. Admission.

PACIFIC RIM NATIONAL PARK ☎250-726-3500 📠250-726-3520 ⬦www.parkscanada.gc.ca/pacificrim, pacrim.info@pc.gc.ca Comprising three units, this national park protects the windswept and jagged west coast of Vancouver Island. The three parts of the park are distinctly different. The West Coast Trail should be traveled only by experienced hikers. The Broken Group Islands unit can be reached by boat, canoe or kayak. The Long Beach unit, the most accessible, includes a six-mile-long sandy beach. There, between Ucluelet and Tofino, you will find the Wickaninnish Centre, an interpretive center that displays exhibits on Pacific Ocean history. Here visitors can see powerful waves rolling up on the beach, watch nature presentations, participate in day hikes and view seals and sea lions. The most popular wildlife of Pacific Rim National Park is the Pacific gray whale, seen during spring migration between mid-March and mid-April. There's also a restaurant with views of the surf and spectacular sunsets. The center is closed from October to mid-March.

Most of the park includes a rocky shoreline that supports tidepools with barnacles, mussels, starfish, hermit crabs and anemones. Sitka spruce thrive just behind the pockets of sandy beaches and the rocky outcroppings. Farther inland are cedar, hemlock, fir and areas of bog and muskeg with pine and laurel. The forest floor is redolent with moss, ferns, huckleberry and salmon berry. The park also offers sightings of sea lions, harbor seals, river otter, mink and a vast array of resident and migrating birds (see "Beaches & Parks" below for more information).

EAGLE AERIE GALLERY

✉350 Campbell Street, Tofino ☎250-725-3235, 800-663-0669 📠250-725-4466 ⬦www.royhenryvickers.com, tofino@royhenryvickers.com This gallery is as much a cultural experience as it is an art gallery. The building was designed and constructed by native artist Roy Henry Vickers and his brother Arthur. The gallery is built in the longhouse style with adzed cedar paneling and massive totem houseposts. Effective lighting, evocative subject material and background music of taped native chanting and flute playing inspire a spirit of reverence unlike almost any other place. The gallery sells Vickers' art, as well as jewelry made by other local artisans.

LODGING

OCEAN WILDERNESS INN

$$–$$$ 9 ROOMS ✉9171 West Coast Road, Sooke ☎250-646-2116, 800-323-2116 📠250-646-2317 ⬦www.oceanwildernessinn.com, info@oceanwildernessinn.com

A bed and breakfast that started as a 1940s log cabin and grew to include a cedar addition with nine guest rooms, this inn offers

Southwest Island

EAGLE AERIE GALLERY

PAGE 614

Local art showcased in a longhouse-style building made with cedar paneling and totem houseposts

CHESTERMAN BEACH BED AND BREAKFAST

PAGE 616

Private beachside cottages with fireplaces, oceanfront decks and amazingly warm, welcoming hosts

SOOKE HARBOUR HOUSE

PAGE 617

Fresh, local ingredients like fresh skate with cranberry vinegar served in a handsome dining room on a bluff

EAST SOOKE REGIONAL PARK

PAGE 619

Small pocket beaches perfect for beachcombing and tidepooling tucked along the windswept coast

travelers a secluded seaside retreat. Set on five oceanfront acres just outside Sooke, the inn boasts contemporary-style rooms, some with bright, bold fabric, other with pale, calming decor. Decks overlook the water or garden. A Japanese gazebo houses a hot tub.

THE BEST WESTERN BARCLAY HOTEL

$$$ 86 ROOMS ✉4277 Stamp Avenue, Port Alberni ☎250-724-7171, 800-563-6590 📠250-724-9691 🖥www.bestwesternbarclay.com, info@bestwesternbarclay.com

This Best Western is the largest hotel in town. It features an attractive lobby, a coffee shop, dining room, sports bar and lounge. Accommodations are clean, fairly standard rooms and suites. Amenities include a heated outdoor pool, whirlpool, fitness center, and sauna.

THE HOSPITALITY INN

$$–$$$ 49 ROOMS ✉3835 Redford Street, Port Alberni ☎250-723-8111, 877-723-8111 📠250-723-0088 🖥www.hospitalityinnportalberni.com, info@hospitalityinnportalberni.com

All of your needs will be met at this cozy inn with a new, heated saltwater swimming pool and exercise room. The lobby features comfortable seating in front of a fireplace and rooms are decorated in soft, attractive colors with firm beds and standard motel furniture. A private liquor store is on-site.

CANADIAN PRINCESS RESORT

$$ 74 ROOMS ✉Ucluelet Harbor, Ucluelet ☎250-726-7771, 800-663-7090
📠250-726-7121 💻www.canadianprincess.com, info@obmg.com

The Canadian Princess is unique in that 30 of its 74 rooms are aboard the ship of the same name (which serviced from 1932 to 1975 as a hydrographic survey vessel). Consequently, these moderately priced staterooms are small, and many share a bath. Three buildings contain 46 spacious, contemporary rooms and loft suites with fireplaces, decks and views of the ship and the harbor. The resort also includes ten fishing boats and a nautical-themed restaurant and lounge for guests. Closed mid-September to June.

THORNTON MOTEL

$$–$$$ 16 UNITS ✉1861 Peninsula Road, Ucluelet ☎250-726-7725
📠250-726-2099 💻www.thorntonmotel.ca, inquiries@thorntonmotel.com

Just a block from the Ucluelet marina is this motel with rooms and suites that include standard furnishings and private baths; some boast kitchenettes. It's popular with the fishing crowd.

WEST COAST MOTEL

$$–$$$ 21 ROOMS ✉247 Hemlock Street, Ucluelet ☎250-726-7732
💻www.westcoastmotel.com, info@westcoasthotel.com

At this motel, views of the harbor from some of the rooms make up for the rather standard motel decor. Nonsmoking rooms are available. Added advantages are an indoor swimming pool, gym and sauna.

PACIFIC SANDS BEACH RESORT

$$$–$$$$ 54 UNITS ✉1421 Pacific Rim Highway, Tofino ☎250-725-3322,
800-565-2322 📠250-725-3155 💻www.pacificsands.com, info@pacificsands.com

When I feel the need to really get away from it all, my favorite writer's hideaway in all of Canada is a shorefront suite at this beach resort, adjoining the Long Beach section of Pacific Rim National Park. Located on Cox Bay, it's one of the best resorts on the West Coast, offering 54 housekeeping suites with contemporary furnishings, fireplaces and views of the beach and the ocean, as well as 22 beachfront villas. Three of the suites have hot tubs.

CHESTERMAN BEACH BED AND BREAKFAST

$$$$ 3 UNITS ✉P.O. Box 72, Tofino, BC V0R 2Z0 ☎250-725-3726
💻www.chestermanbeach.net, surfsand@island.net

If you want a more personal experience, try the Chesterman, which offers a charming cottage, a spacious suite and a cozy honeymooner's room, on the beach by the same name. All private units include fireplaces and two have oceanfront decks. Kayaks and bikes are available for guests' use. After a visit to the island's west coast, owners Todd and Lynda fell in love with the place. Their hospitality and tasty breakfasts match their enthusiasm.

DUFFIN COVE RESORT

$$$–$$$$ 13 UNITS ✉215 Campbell Street, Tofino ☎250-725-3448, 888-629-2903
📠250-725-2390 💻www.duffin-cove-resort.com, duffin@duffin-cove-resort.com

The best thing about Duffin Cove is that it offers views of the ocean from a rock bluff a block away from downtown. Eleven suites and kitchen units and two cottages with fireplaces on the beach are a winter storm–watcher's delight. Ask about their whale-watching tours

OCEAN VILLAGE BEACH RESORT

$$–$$$ 51 UNITS ✉555 Hellesen Drive, Tofino 📞250-725-3755 📠250-725-4494
🖥www.oceanvillageresort.com, info@oceanvillageresort.com

A nest of comfortably rustic duplex and single cedar chalets, this resort is on McKenzie Beach, a quarter-mile of safe, sandy beach facing the Pacific Ocean. The units feature an eating area with table and benches, sitting area and a sleeping area or separate bedroom and bath. The resort also includes an indoor swimming pool, hot tub, laundromat and wireless internet.

WICKANINNISH INN
hidden

$$$$ 76 ROOMS ✉Osprey Lane at Chesterman Beach, Tofino
📞250-725-3100, 800-333-4604 📠250-725-3110 🖥www.wickinn.com, info@wickinn.com

Perched on a rocky point thrusting out into the Pacific, not far from Pacific Rim National Park and Clayoquot Sound, this inn has a spectacular setting under any circumstances. During the West Coast's sometimes phenomenal winter storms, it's an unparalleled natural experience. Each of the 76 spacious rooms faces the ocean, and includes a soaking tub, large-screen television, refrigerator, fireplace, and furniture made from recycled old-growth fir, cedar and driftwood. A spa at the inn offers massage and other treatments. A new state-of-the-art fitness center, as well as full communications technology, including high-speed dual-line phones, makes it possible to use the inn as an executive retreat.

DINING

SOOKE HARBOUR HOUSE
hidden

$$$$ PACIFIC NORTHWEST/SEAFOOD ✉1528 Whiffen Spit Road, Sooke 📞250-642-3421, 800-889-9688 📠250-642-6988
🖥www.sookeharbourhouse.com, reservations@sookeharbourhouse.com

Some of the finest dining in British Columbia is offered at this white clapboard inn surrounded by colorful, organic gardens on a bluff above Sooke Harbour's Whiffen Spit. In a setting of handsomely refinished pine and maple furnishings with whimsical folk art accents, the dining room offers a changing menu. There's an emphasis on fresh seasonal ingredients and local seafood that might include such unusual delicacies as sea urchin roe or fresh skate served with cranberry vinegar. Suckling kid, duck and rabbit are among the possible meat choices. Winter closures, call ahead.

LITTLE BAVARIA

$$–$$$$ GERMAN ✉3035 4th Avenue, Port Alberni ☏250-724-4242
✆250-724-4242, 800-704-2744 ✎www.littlebavariarestaurant.com,
info@littlebavariarestaurant.com

It would be hard to leave hungry after a meal at this place, which seduces local appetites with huge plates of traditional German favorites such as schnitzel, homemade bratwurst and a variety of seafood dishes. The Bavarian Platter offers meat, sausage, potatoes, noodles, bread and vegetables for two at about $39. No lunch on weekends.

COMMON LOAF BAKE SHOP

$ BAKERY ✉180 1st Street, Tofino ☏250-725-3915

Everybody needs a cup of coffee and a muffin in the morning. The best place to get them in Tofino is this bake shop, where the espresso makers are capable and the baked goods are filling. You'll also find calzones, pizzas and curries. The bulletin board is also the news center for the counterculture community in Clayoquot Sound, if you want to find out who's protesting what this month.

SHOPPING

HOUSE OF HIMWITSA

✉300 Main Street, Tofino ☏250-725-2017 ✆250-725-2361 ✎www.himwitsa.com, tofino@himwitsa.com In Tofino, this gallery offers an excellent selection of native art including limited-edition prints, silver jewelry, weavings, carvings, beaded items and pottery. The shop is owned and operated by First Nations artists.

WILDSIDE BOOKSELLERS ✉320 Main Street, Tofino ☏250-725-4222

Wildside is fairly small, but as the name implies it has an excellent selection of natural history and outdoor recreation books geared toward the West Coast. Summer reading selections and social activism books round out the book fare.

EAGLE AERIE GALLERY

✉350 Campbell Street, Tofino ☏250-725-3235 Featured works here are by Roy Henry Vickers, a native artist who has found international acclaim for his pieces that integrate the contemporary and traditional.

NIGHTLIFE

SHELTER RESTAURANT ✉601 Campbell Street, Tofino, 250-725-3353

✎www.shelterrestaurant.com You won't find nightclubs on the rugged West Coast. Some bars and lounges offer sunset views. This restaurant has an extensive wine list designed to complement its organic and locally grown appetizers and entrées, such as Cortez Island mussels and Tofino Dungeness crab.

BEACHES & PARKS

A note about using parks and beaches in the Sooke area: Do not leave valuables in your car, as the region has been plagued by gangs of thieves that prowl the trailhead and picnic area parking lots. It's best to leave valuable items in your hotel room, but if you can do nothing else, make sure they're locked in the trunk.

EAST SOOKE REGIONAL PARK

✉ *Located about 25 miles southwest of Victoria off East Sooke Road on Becher Bay Road* ☎ *250-478-3344* 📠 *250-478-5416*

🚶 🚗 🚤 This regional park is where the west coast begins. The 3500-acre park encompasses beautiful arbutus trees clinging to the windswept coast. You'll find small pocket beaches, rocky bays and islets for beachcombing and tidepooling. It features six miles of rugged coast trails and 30 miles of trails through forest, marsh and field with opportunities to view orca whales, sea lions, harbor seals, Columbian black-tailed deer and cougar. In September, check out the large number of bald eagles, hawks and other raptors that stop here during their migration. The park has views of the Strait of Juan de Fuca and the Olympic Mountains. You'll find picnic areas and restrooms.

FRENCH BEACH PROVINCIAL PARK

✉ *Located west of Sooke off Route 14 near Jordan River* ☎ *250-474-1336* 📠 *250-478-0376*

🚶 🚗 🚤 ⛵ 🎣 🚣 🚤 Visitors have the opportunity to see whales in the spring from this mile-long, sand-and-gravel beach on the Strait of Juan de Fuca. The park also contains second-growth forest. There are picnic areas and restrooms.

▲ There are 69 tent/RV sites (no hookups); C$15 per night. Reservations: 800-689-9025 🖱 www.discovercamping.ca.

PACIFIC RIM NATIONAL PARK

☎ *250-726-7721* 📠 *250-726-4720* 🖱 *www.pc.gc.ca/pacrim, pacrim.info@pc.gc.ca*

Cliffs, islands, bog and beach are just some of the topography visitors discover at this vast, 158,400-acre park. The reserve is divided into three units: Long Beach, the Broken Group Islands and the West Coast Trail. During the park's low season, from mid-October to mid-March, expect most park facilities to be closed. Fee.

LONG BEACH

✉ *Route 4 (Pacific Rim Highway), 62 miles west of Port Alberni* ☎ *250-726-3500*

🚶 🚴 🐎 🚶 🚗 🚤 🚣 🚤 🚤 ⛵ The most accessible section of the reserve, Long Beach is a six-mile stretch of sand and surf between rocky outcroppings. Beach hiking is excellent. Nine marked trails traverse old-growth rainforest. Facilities include picnic areas, restrooms and a restaurant. Parking fee, C$7.80.

▲ Green Point Campground has 18 primitive walk-in sites above the beach and 94 inland tent/RV sites with beach access; C$17.80 to C$23.75 per night. Closed November to mid-March. To reserve a drive-in site, call 800-689-9025.

BROKEN GROUP ISLANDS

✉ *The M. V. Lady Rose (250-723-8313), a mail boat that also takes passengers and kayaks, makes trips to Bamfield, Sechart Lodge at Sechart Bay and Ucluelet.* ☎ *250-726-3900*

🚶 ⛵ 🛶 🏕 ⛵ 🚣 With more than a hundred islands and islets in Barkley Sound, this is kayak and sailboat territory. Accessible only by boat, these remote islands offer up wildlife ranging from sea lions to eagles; diving is excellent. There are First Nations sites here, many of spiritual significance, so be aware; boaters are asked not to tie up on the southeast side of Nettle Island. Composting toilets are available in the camping areas.

▲ There are primitive campsites on eight of the islands; C$9.80 per night, per adult.

WEST COAST TRAIL

✉ *Land access to the Bamfield and Port Renfrew trailheads is by logging roads only. The M. V. Lady Rose (250-723-8313, 800-663-7192) drops hikers at Bamfield. For reservations and permits, call 800-663-6000.*

🚶 This demanding 47-mile stretch between Bamfield and Port Renfrew follows a turn-of-the-20th-century trail constructed to aid shipwrecked mariners. Only experienced backpackers should undertake this grueling five- to eight-day trek. Expect to see coastal rainforests, the remains of early settlements, shipwrecks and a plethora of marine life. The number of hikers on the trail is regulated. Reservations and permits are required. Closed October through April.

MACMILLAN PROVINCIAL PARK

✉ *Located west of Parksville, about 11 miles east of Port Alberni off Route 4* ☎ *250-474-1336* 🖥 *250-478-0376*

🚶 On the shores of Cameron Lake, this 336-acre park, available for day-use only, provides access to Cathedral Grove, a large stand of giant, old-growth Douglas fir. Some of the trees are 800 years old, and the largest are nearly 250 feet tall and nearly ten feet in diameter. The Douglas firs here are believed to have survived a fire some 300 years ago because of their fire-resistant bark, nearly a foot thick on some of the trees now. Walking through this ancient forest can be a spiritual experience, but the area is so popular it is being "loved to death" by tourists. Parking fee, C$3.

SPROAT LAKE PROVINCIAL PARK

✉ *Eight miles northwest of Port Alberni off Route 4* ☎ *250-474-1336* 🖥 *250-478-0376*

🚶 🚴 🎣 🏕 🛶 ⛵ 🚣 On the north shore of Sproat Lake just west of Port Alberni, this park is a water enthusiast's paradise. The lake is warm and sunny, perfect for summer swimming. Fishing is excellent for steelhead, trout and salmon. Visitors can walk a short distance through the woods to see prehistoric petroglyphs. Facilities are limited to picnic areas and pit toilets. Parking fee, C$3.

▲ There are 59 tent/RV sites (no hookups); C$19 to C$22 per night. Reservations: 604-689-9025, 800-689-9025; www.discovercamping.ca.

STAMP FALLS PROVINCIAL PARK

✉ *Located about eight and a half miles north of Port Alberni off Route 4 on Beaver Creek Road* ☎ *250-474-1336* ⌨ *250-478-0376*

🏃 ⛵ 🚣 🎣 This park offers pleasant walks among the stands of cedar and fir, and an area for contemplation near the waterfall. Visitors can view salmon jumping up the fish ladders in summer and fall. Steelhead and cutthroat trout also invite anglers. Picnic areas are the only facilities.

▲ There are 23 tent/RV sites (no hookups); C$15 per night. Reservations: 604-689-9025, 800-689-9025; www.discovercamping.ca.

THE GULF ISLANDS

Ready for some island-hopping? Whether you're into beaches, arts and crafts, birdwatching, dining or just plain looking around, there is something here for everyone. The Gulf Islands provide plenty of activities—swimming, wind surfing, scuba diving, beachcombing, boating, bicycling, hiking and horseback riding—to suit families and outdoor enthusiasts of all abilities.

These islands are isolated places where residents enjoy a bucolic lifestyle. At sunset, basking like a group of sea turtles in the water, the islands appear like shadows, amorphous shapes in muted shades of blue, mauve and gray stacked up behind one another. The islands, sisters of the San Juan Islands in Washington State, include mountain peaks, sandy beaches, and pastoral farms. The climate is Mediterranean-like—mild and dry. The archipelago includes almost 200 islands, but only five have a population of more than 250—Salt Spring, Pender, Galiano, Mayne and Saturna.

B.C. FERRIES ☎ *250-386-3431, 888-223-3779* ⌨ *250-381-5452* 🖱 *www.bcferries. com* These ferries ply the waterways between Tsawwassen, just south of Vancouver, and the Gulf Islands and Vancouver Island's Swartz Bay and the islands.

HARBOUR AIR ☎ *250-537-5525, 800-665-0212* 🖱 *www.harbour-air.com* Scheduled floatplane service to several of the islands from Vancouver is offered by this company.

SIGHTS

SALT SPRING ISLAND Named for a series of briny springs at the island's north end, this island is the largest, with a population of about 9500. The first nonnative settlers were blacks escaping slavery in the United States in 1859. Once supported by an agrarian economy, the island now thrives on tourism and the arts. In fact, the Gulf Islands are believed to be home to more artists per capita than most other regions in Canada.

GANGES   This is the largest village on Salt Spring, a pedestrian-oriented, seaside hamlet, where visitors flock to a summer-long arts and crafts fair, art galleries and the Saturday morning market. Mid-June to mid-September, a dozen of the galleries stay open late Friday evenings for visitors to browse.

CUSHEON LAKE   A popular, freshwater lake with a large swimming area—the water is warm—is Cusheon. The island also offers popular oceanside beaches; Vesuvius and Bader's beaches on the island's west side have the warmest water. Because it sits at the edge of the forest, Bader offers much more privacy, but the sandy beach is small.

PENDER ISLAND   With a population of 1500, this island is really two islands connected by a narrow, wooden bridge that affords splendid views of Browning and Bedwell harbours. Medicine Beach in Bedwell Harbour and Hamilton Beach in Browning Harbour are popular picnic spots. The Driftwood Centre and Port Washington are locations of several galleries.

Birdwatching is a prime activity on the Gulf Islands. Cormorants, harlequin ducks, gulls, oyster catchers, turkey vultures, ravens and bald eagles are commonly seen. Other birds include tanagers, juncos, bluebirds, flycatchers, black birds and sparrows. Many of these birds can be seen in the island's parks.

PROVINCIAL PARKS   On Salt Spring Island is **Mouat Provincial Park** (Seaview Avenue, Ganges), a pleasant, wooded park with camping and picnicking facilities. **Prior Centennial Provincial Park** is near Bedwell Harbour on Pender Island. It features good fishing, swimming, a boat launch, picnic areas and restrooms.

BEAUMON MARINE PARK   The islands also are sites of several marine parks. One of the largest is Beaumon on South Pender Island and sheltered by Bedwell Harbour. It includes upland forest, picnic areas, campsites and hiking trails.

LODGING

THE INN ON PENDER ISLAND

$$ 12 UNITS   ✉ *4709 Canal Road*   ☎ *250-629-3353, 800-550-0172*
📠 *250-629-3167*   🖱 *www.innonpender.com*

This inn, with nine rooms, three cabins and a hot tub, sits on seven acres of wooded tranquility near Prior Centennial Provincial Park, where hiking, bicycling and beachcombing are in abundance. There is a restaurant on the premises.

CUSHEON LAKE RESORT

$$$ 16 UNITS   ✉ *171 Natalie Lane, Salt Spring Island*   ☎ *250-537-9692, 866-899-0017*
📠 *250-537-9692*   🖱 *www.cusheonlake.com, resort@cusheonlake.com*

Cusheon Lake has fully equipped log and A-frame chalets on four forested acres, all with kitchens and water views, some with fireplaces, and an outdoor jacuzzi. Fishing, swimming and boating are available.

OUTDOOR ADVENTURES

FISHING

Victoria has incredible sportfishing for salmon, primarily, but also for bottom fish like rock cod and red snapper and the occasional halibut. Besides the great angling possibilities, there's the unsurpassable natural backdrop of scenery and wildlife: snowcapped mountains, old lighthouses, sea lions, whales, bald eagles, herons and other water birds.

FISHERIES AND OCEANS CANADA ✉*401 Burrard Street, Vancouver, BC V6C 3S4* ✆*604-666-0566* ✐*pflu@dfo-mpo.gc.ca* **Saltwater licenses** are issued by the federal government. Charter operators will usually sell the license to you.

Freshwater licenses are issued through the provincial government and can be bought at most sporting goods stores. The Ministry of Environment, Lands and Parks (B.C. Environment) maintains a list of licensed **freshwater fishing guides**. For a copy, call 604-582-5200.

Downtown Victoria Area
ADAM'S FISHING CHARTERS ✉*Inner Harbour* ✆*250-370-2326* ✐*www. adamsfishingcharters.com, gethooked@shaw.ca* Adam's has a standard charter package for a minimum of five hours for up to four people, as well as more customized trips.

Southwest Island Area
DAY'S INN WEIGH WEST MARINE RESORT ✉*634 Campbell Street, Tofino* ✆*250-725-3277, 800-665-8922* ✐*www.weighwest.com* Located right next to the Pacific Rim National Park, this resort offers charters for fishing trips and whale watching.

WHALE WATCHING

The southern part of Vancouver Island is known for orca (or killer) whales, porpoises, harbor seals, sea lions, bald eagles and many species of marine birds. Watch also for the occasional minke whale, gray whale or elephant seal. Whale-watching season extends from April through September. June is the best time to see the orcas. By July and August, cruise operators are very busy, so try to call a day or two ahead for reservations.

Look for little black-and-white Dall's porpoises that play off the bow or follow behind in the wake when you're out on one of these whale-watching excursions.

Downtown Victoria Area
SEACOAST EXPEDITIONS ✉*Coast Victoria Harbourside Hotel, 146 Kingston Street* ✆*250-383-2254, 800-386-1525* ✐*www.seacoastexpeditions.com* This company can accommodate 12 people per boat (for a total of up to 36 people) on its whale-watching cruises, which begin in May. The cruises last about three hours.

FIVE-STAR WHALE WATCHING ✉*651 Humboldt Street, off Douglas Street* ☎*250-388-7223, 800-634-9617* ⌨*www.5starwhales.com* Five-star offers three-hour cruises with naturalists, departing from the Inner Harbour.

SEA KAYAKING

Kayaking is an up-close way to explore the coastal inlets of Vancouver Island, where there's plenty of sea mammals, birds and other wildlife to keep you company.

Downtown Victoria Area

OCEAN RIVER SPORTS ✉*1824 Store Street* ☎*250-381-4233, 800-909-4233* ⌨*www.oceanriver.com* This group will rent single or double kayaks to individuals, but only to those with kayaking experience. Check out their three-hour day tours to the southern Gulf Islands or inquire about customized trips to other locales. Overnight trips are also available.

Southwest Island Area

TOFINO SEA KAYAKING CO. ✉*320 Main Street, Tofino* ☎*250-725-4222, 800-863-4664* ⌨*www.tofino-kayaking.com* No experience is necessary to join one of these guided day trips or overnight excursions into Clayoquot Sound, along the island's west coast. Longer excursions, lasting six days, head farther into Clayoquot Sound.

SCUBA DIVING

There are several popular and worthwhile dive spots around Victoria and Sidney. Easily accessible from downtown Victoria, Ogden Point Breakwater on Dallas Road is a marine park where diving depths range from 20 to 100 feet. Not the best dive spot, but one that's great for snorkeling and exploring tidepools is East Sooke Park, between Victoria and Sooke. For advanced deep-sea diving, try Race Rocks, also a marine park, where high-current activity stirs up much marine life.

Between Victoria and Sidney, on the Saanich Peninsula, there's good shore access at 10-Mile Point, the ecological reserve, although it has strong currents and is not for beginners. Saanich Inlet is several hundred feet deep with a sharp 200-foot drop and little tidal exchange, so there's no current.

If you are a diver, the Gulf Islands provide a number of good locations. Divers often see octopi, wolf eels, sea cucumbers, sea stars, sea urchins and sea pens. Shore dives include Vesuvius Bay on Salt Spring Island for sighting octopus and ling cod; Fulford Harbour opposite the ferry terminal with a shallow area perfect for seeing crabs and starfish; and Tilley Point on North Pender Island for viewing interesting kelp beds. Near Thetis Island, the Miami, a steel- and coal-carrying freighter that sunk in 1900, is covered with interesting vegetation and marine life. The *Del Norte*, a 190-foot side-wheel passenger steam ship that sank in 1868, is between Valdez and Galiano islands and appropriate only for more advanced divers.

Downtown Victoria Area

FRANK WHITE'S DIVE STORE ✉1620 Blanshard Street, Victoria ☎250-385-4713, 800-606-3977 ✐www.frankwhites.com Frank White's rents equipment and can provide information and directions for you and your diving buddy or buddies. The shop sponsors group shore dives every Saturday at 10 a.m. and monthly night dives on every second Thursday. You can also arrange a private dive trip with a dive master.

BEYOND DEEP DIVING ✉1636 Cedar Hill Crossroad, Victoria ☎250-475-2202 ✐www.divinginvictoria.ca This company rents gear and runs full-day trips to the lower Gulf Islands, Race Rocks and wreck dives along the artificial reefs off Sidney.

BOATING

Boating and sailing are popular all around Victoria, the southeastern side of Vancouver Island and in the waters surrounding the Gulf Islands. The waters off the west coast are often too rough for relaxed boating, but some pleasure charters are available.

GOLF

Golf is very popular in Canada, and Vancouver Island is no exception.

Downtown Victoria Area

CEDAR HILL MUNICIPAL GOLF COURSE ✉1400 Derby Road ☎250-475-7151 ✐www.golfcedarhill.com There's a "mean" 16th hole at this golf course. It's a par-four downhill, with a two-tiered elevated green.

HENDERSON PARK GOLF COURSE ✉2291 Cedar Hill Road ☎250-370-7200 The nine hole, par three course here is fun for beginners. You'll only need three clubs to play this course, and you can rent them there. Closed in winter.

OLYMPIC VIEW GOLF CLUB ✉643 Latoria Road ☎250-474-3673 Just as the name suggests, this course offers views of the Olympic Peninsula from its 18 holes. It's cut right out of the wilderness, situated about 25 minutes from Victoria.

PROSPECT LAKE GOLF CLUB ✉4633 Prospect Lake Road ☎250-479-2688 ✐www.golfprospect.com This challenging 32-par, nine-hole course is set on the shore of Prospect Lake.

ROYAL OAK GOLF COURSE ✉540 Marsett Place ☎250-658-1433 ✐www.royaloakgolfclub.com The executive nine-hole course here is just minutes from the ferry.

Saanich Peninsula Area

GLEN MEADOWS GOLF AND COUNTRY CLUB ✉1050 McTavish Road, Sidney ☎250-656-3136 ✐www.glenmeadows.bc.ca Glen Meadows is a semiprivate 18-hole championship course that has hosted the World Lefthanders Golf Tournament. Also available are three tennis courts and a curling rink.

Southeast Island Area

EAGLECREST GOLF CLUB ✉2035 *Island Highway West, Qualicum Beach* ✆ *250-752-9744, 800-567-1320* For some beautiful views of southeast Vancouver Island, try this 18-hole course in the Parksville-Qualicum neighborhood.

MORNINGSTAR INTERNATIONAL GOLF COURSE ✉525 *Lowry's Road, Parksville* ✆ *250-248-2244, 800-567-1320* Morningstar hosts one of the events on Canada's professional golf tour. The holes have four sets of tees, so this course can provide a challenge to most golfers.

BIKING

Downtown Victoria Area

Although Victoria's terrain is perfect for cycling, the city's streets and walkways are often very crowded; there are no official bike paths, and many walking paths prohibit bicycles. One of the best bets for great views of the water and the Olympic Mountains is Victoria's Beach Drive, a six-mile route that passes through lovely Victorian neighborhoods near the ocean. It's an easy ride, with only a few low hills. But use caution on Beach Drive; it is winding and there is often considerable motor traffic.

GALLOPING GOOSE TRAIL ✉*Capital District Regional Parks* ✆*250-478-3344* ⊘*www.gallopinggoosetrail.com* This trail is a multi-use section of the Trans-Canada Trail. You can pick it up in downtown Victoria and head west toward Sooke and beyond into the mountains.

GREATER VICTORIA CYCLING COALITION ✉706 *Yates Street* ✆*250-480-5155* ⊘*www.gvcc.bc.ca* For a map of bike routes in the area, contact this agency.

Bike Rentals

SPORTS RENT ✉1950 *Government Street #3* ✆*250-385-7368* ⊘*www.sportsrentbc.com* This shop rents bikes and inline skates, as well as equipment for camping and water sports.

CYCLE BC RENTALS ✉707 *Douglas Street* ✆*250-380-2453, 866-380-2453* ✉950 *Wharf Street* ✆*250-380-2453* ⊘*www.cyclebc.ca* Cycle BC has several locations that rent bikes and scooters.

HIKING

All distances listed for hiking trails are one way unless otherwise noted.

Downtown Victoria Area

CAPITAL REGIONAL DISTRICT ✉490 *Atkins Avenue, Victoria, BC V9B 2Z8* ✆*250-478-3344* ⊘*www.crd.bc.ca/parks* A good hiking resource is this district, with helpful information about trails in Victoria (see below). For information on trails outside the Greater Victoria area, call B.C. Parks (250-391-2300; www.env.gov.bc.ca/bcparks).

WESTSONG WAY WALK For an easy stroll (just over 2 miles) around the Inner Harbour take this walk. From here you can watch all kinds of water vessels, including float planes, passenger catamarans, fishing boats and yachts.

Victoria Neighborhood Areas

THETIS LAKE PARK   There is a maze of trails in this lake park. Paths loop around Upper Thetis and Lower Thetis lakes and along Craigflower Creek.

MT. DOUGLAS MUNICIPAL PARK   The **Norn Trail** (less than 1 mile) at this park is an easy walk on a well-marked route with plenty of trees. It joins the **Irvine Trail** to reach the summit of Mount Douglas. Hikers can access the Norn Trail from the parking lot at the intersection of Cordova Bay Road and Ash Road.

Saanich Peninsula Area

ISLAND VIEW BEACH REGIONAL PARK LOOP   On this park loop (1.5 mile roundtrip), visitors can take an easy hike from the parking lot at Island View Park that loops through fragile sand dunes and provides views of the beach and Haro Strait.

LAKESIDE ROUTE   This 6.3-mile trek located at Elk/Beaver Lake Regional Park is a shaded and well-groomed trail of wood chips and wooden bridges through the beaches surrounding Elk and Beaver lakes.

JOHN DEAN PROVINCIAL PARK   The trail system within this park (total of 6 miles of trails) provides views of Saanich Inlet, fertile farmland and orchards. Take East Saanich Road to Dean Park Road.

GOLDMINE TRAIL   A 1-mile trail at Goldstream Provincial Park, this hike is on a dirt pathway that travels past a miner's spring and out to Squally Reach Lookout.

Southeast Island Area

HARBOURSIDE WALKWAY   For an easy walk in Nanaimo, take this walkway (2.5 miles) around the harbor with views of Protection Island and the Coast Mountains.

GALLOPING GOOSE REGIONAL TRAIL   This trail (37 miles) is a popular multi-use path. Favored by hikers, bicyclists and horses, it begins in downtown Victoria, winds through farmland of Metchosin, then into the semi-wilderness of the Sooke River Valley and up the hills providing ocean views. As a former railroad bed, most of it's perfect for long bike rides but a bit monotonous for walking.

Southwest Island Area

GOLD MINE TRAIL   Beginning just west of the Pacific Rim National Park information center on Route 4, this trail (approximately 1 mile) is a nonstrenuous hike through a forest of amambilis fir, red cedar, hemlock, Douglas fir and red alder.

SOUTH BEACH TRAIL   This trail (approximately .5 mile) starts behind the Wickaninnish Centre and winds through a stand of Sitka spruce. Side trails lead to rocky or sandy coves surrounded by headlands. At the far end of Lismer Beach, a boardwalk climbs over a bluff to

South Beach. At the top of this bluff, the Wickaninnish Trail leads to the left, but continuing to the right takes hikers past groves of moss-enshrouded Sitka spruce and western hemlock.

WICKANINNISH TRAIL   A 1.5-mile trail, the Wickaninnish links Long Beach to Florencia Bay. The trail is a part of the early Tofino-Ucluelet land route that used beaches, forest trails and sheltered inlets to link the two towns before a road was built farther inland. Hikers have access via the South Beach Trail or from the Florencia Bay parking lot.

**JUAN DE FUCA
MARINE TRAIL**

✉ *Off Route 14, Km. 8.7 to Km. 30.2 northwest of Jordan River* While this trail hugs the sometimes rugged coastline for about 14 miles, winding through tall fir forest between driftwood-strewn gravel beaches, the most popular section for day hikes is the fairly gentle northern part between Chin Beach (not to be confused with China Beach at the south trailhead) and Botanical Beach, a distance of about six miles. Other beaches along this portion of the trail include legendary Sombrio Beach, a good surfing spot with wilderness camping areas ($5 per night in summer, free in winter), where flower children and their offspring have been congregating and living off the land since 1993, when squatters were run out of Pacific Rim National Park following environmental protests.

WEST COAST TRAIL   The most arduous trek on Vancouver Island is this coast trail (47 miles), stretching along the west coast. Hikers need to be prepared for five to eight days traveling on an irregular slippery trail. There are tidepools, fjordlike cliffs, opportunities to see Pacific gray whales, sea lions, harbor seals, shorebirds and sea birds. Access to the southern trailhead is at Port Renfrew. The northern trailhead access is at Bamfield.

TRANSPORTATION

CAR

Vancouver Island lies across the Strait of Juan de Fuca from the state of Washington and west of mainland British Columbia. Victoria and the southeastern communities are accessible from either. Route 14 runs from Victoria through Sooke to Port Renfrew on the west coast. The Trans-Canada High way (Route 1) goes from Victoria to Nanaimo. Route 4 goes from the Parksville-Qualicum area west to Port Alberni, leading to the west coast communities of Ucluelet and Tofino.

AIR

VICTORIA INTERNATIONAL AIRPORT ✐ *www.victoriaairport.com*
This international airport is 20 minutes from Victoria in Sidney.

Carriers include Aeromexico, Air Canada, Alpha Executive Air, Horizon Air, Orca Airways, Pacific Coastal Airlines, United Express and WestJet.

AKAL AIRPORT SHUTTLE BUS ✆250-386-2525 ✑www.victoriaairport shuttle.com Airport bus service between downtown Victoria and the Victoria International Airport is provided by this company.

HELIJET AIRWAYS ✆800-665-4354 ✑www.helijet.com Helijet has helicopter service into downtown Victoria from downtown Vancouver, and from Victoria Harbour to Vancouver Airport.

NANAIMO AIRPORT ✑www.nanaimoairport.com This small airport is served by Air Canada.

KENMORE AIR HARBOR ✆425-486-1257, 866-435-9524 ✑www.kenmore air.com Floatplanes offer a unique experience as they take off on the water and land directly in Victoria's Inner Harbour. This company has a daily schedule to Victoria and the San Juan Islands from the Seattle area and also goes to Nanaimo in the summer.

HARBOUR AIR ✆604 274 1277, 800 665 0212 ✑www.harbour-air.com The B.C. coast's major operator, this service flies from Victoria to the Gulf Islands, Vancouver and other coastal destinations.

FERRY

Ferries provide daily, year-round sailings to Victoria and Nanaimo. The number of sailings daily usually increases in the summer, but it is advisable to call for up-to-date schedules and rates.

Travelers wishing to depart from the U.S. can take Black Ball Transport, Washington State Ferries or Victoria Clipper to Victoria.

BLACK BALL TRANSPORT ✉101 East Railroad Avenue, Port Angeles, WA; 430 Bellville Street, Victoria, BC ✆360-457-4491 (Port Angeles), 250-386-2202 (Victoria) ✑www.cohoferry.com Black Ball takes vehicles and foot passengers from Port Angeles to Victoria's Inner Harbour.

WASHINGTON STATE FERRIES ✉Seattle, WA ✆206-464-6400 ✑www.wsdot.wa.gov/ferries This agency takes vehicles and foot passengers on a scenic route through Washington's San Juan Islands between Anacortes, WA, and Sidney, BC, and buses take foot passengers to downtown Victoria from Sidney.

CLIPPER VACATIONS ✆800-888-2535 (U.S.), 206-448-5000 (Seattle, WA), 250-382-8100 (Victoria, BC) ✑www.clippervacations.com These ships are 300-passenger, high-speed catamarans that run year-round between Seattle's Pier 69 and Victoria's Inner Harbour with separate trips to the San Juan Islands from May through September.

B.C. FERRIES ✆250-386-3431 (Victoria, BC), 888-223-3779 (within BC) ✑www. bcferries.com This company travels year-round from Tsawwassen, just south of Vancouver, to Swartz Bay, a scenic, half-hour drive by car or bus from Victoria. Long, long lines in summer suggest trying out B.C.'s ferry reservations system; call the main ferries number. You can also sail from Tsawwassen or Horseshoe Bay to Nanaimo.

TRAIN

VIA RAIL ☎ *888-842-7245* ✎ *www.viarail.ca* Contact this company for Vancouver Island rail service between Victoria and Courtenay, with stops at Nanaimo.

CAR RENTALS

Agencies in downtown Victoria and at the Victoria airport include **Avis Rent A Car** (800-879-2847), **Budget Rent A Car** (800-668-9833), **Hertz Rent A Car** (within the U.S., 800-654-3001; within Canada, 800-263-0600), **National Car Rental** (800-227-7386).

PUBLIC TRANSIT

ISLAND COACH LINES ☎ *250-385-4411* Island Coach has bus service between Victoria and other points on Vancouver Island, connecting with B.C. Ferries routes as well.

B.C. TRANSIT *250-382-6161* ✎ *www.bctransit.com* This agency provides local bus service throughout the greater Victoria area.

HANDY DART ☎ *250-727-7811* B.C. Transit and Victoria Regional Transit Commission offer public transit service to the disabled called Handy DART.

TAXIS

In the Victoria area, you will find **Bluebird Cabs** (250-382-4235, 800-665-7055), **Empress Taxi/Yellow Cabs** (250-381-2222, 800-808-6881) and **Victoria Taxi** (250-383-7111, 888-842-7111).

INDEX

642

LODGING INDEX

HOSTELS

LODGING SERVICES

DINING INDEX

h DINING INDEX

HIDDEN GUIDES

Adventure travel or a relaxing vacation?—"Hidden" guidebooks are the only travel books in the business to provide detailed information on both. Aimed at environmentally aware travelers, our motto is "Where Vacations Meet Adventures." These books combine details on unique hotels, restaurants and sightseeing with information on camping, sports and hiking for the outdoor enthusiast.

PARADISE FAMILY GUIDES

Ideal for families traveling with kids of any age—toddlers to teenagers—Paradise Family Guides offer a blend of travel information unlike any other guides to the Hawaiian islands. With vacation ideas and tropical adventures that are sure to satisfy both action-hungry youngsters and relaxation-seeking parents, these guides meet the specific needs of each and every family member.

Ulysses Press books are available at bookstores everywhere. If any of the following titles are unavailable at your local bookstore, ask the bookseller to order them.

You can also order books directly from Ulysses Press
P.O. Box 3440, Berkeley, CA 94703
800-377-2542 or 510-601-8301
fax: 510-601-8307
www.ulyssespress.com
e-mail: ulysses@ulyssespress.com

HIDDEN GUIDEBOOKS

____ Hidden Arizona, $16.95
____ Hidden Baja, $14.95
____ Hidden Belize, $15.95
____ Hidden Big Island of Hawaii, $14.95
____ Hidden Boston & Cape Cod, $14.95
____ Hidden British Columbia, $18.95
____ Hidden Cancún & the Yucatán, $16.95
____ Hidden Carolinas, $17.95
____ Hidden Coast of California, $19.95
____ Hidden Colorado, $15.95
____ Hidden Disneyland, $13.95
____ Hidden Florida, $19.95
____ Hidden Florida Keys & Everglades, $15.95
____ Hidden Hawaii, $19.95
____ Hidden Kauai, $14.95
____ Hidden Los Angeles, $14.95
____ Hidden Maine, $15.95
____ Hidden Maui, $15.95
____ Hidden Miami, $14.95

____ Hidden Montana, $15.95
____ Hidden New England, $19.95
____ Hidden New Mexico, $15.95
____ Hidden Oahu, $14.95
____ Hidden Oregon, $15.95
____ Hidden Pacific Northwest, $19.95
____ Hidden Philadelphia, $14.95
____ Hidden Puerto Vallarta, $14.95
____ Hidden Salt Lake City, $14.95
____ Hidden San Diego, $14.95
____ Hidden San Francisco & Northern California, $19.95
____ Hidden Seattle, $14.95
____ Hidden Southern California, $19.95
____ Hidden Southwest, $19.95
____ Hidden Tahiti, $19.95
____ Hidden Tennessee, $16.95
____ Hidden Walt Disney World, $13.95
____ Hidden Washington, $15.95
____ Hidden Wine Country, $14.95

PARADISE FAMILY GUIDES

____ Paradise Family Guides: Kaua'i, $17.95
____ Paradise Family Guides: Maui, $17.95

____ Paradise Family Guides: Big Island of Hawai'i, $17.95

Mark the book(s) you're ordering and enter the total cost here ⇨ [   ]

California residents add 8.75% sales tax here ⇨ [   ]

Shipping, check box for your preferred method and enter cost here ⇨ [   ]

❑ BOOK RATE   FREE! FREE! FREE!

❑ PRIORITY MAIL/UPS GROUND   cost of postage

❑ UPS OVERNIGHT OR 2-DAY AIR   cost of postage

Billing, enter total amount due here and check method of payment ⇨ [   ]

❑ CHECK   ❑ MONEY ORDER

❑ VISA/MASTERCARD _____ EXP. DATE_____

NAME_____ PHONE _____

ADDRESS_____

CITY_____ STATE_____ ZIP _____

MONEY-BACK GUARANTEE ON DIRECT ORDERS PLACED THROUGH ULYSSES PRESS.

ABOUT THE
CONTRIBUTORS

Richard Harris, the update author for this edition, has written or co-written more than 35 other guidebooks, including *Hidden Puerto Vallarta*, *Hidden Cancún and the Yucatán*, *Hidden Colorado* and the best-selling *Hidden Southwest*. He has also served as contributing editor on guides for John Muir Publications, Fodor's, Birnbaum and Access guides and has written for numerous magazines, including *Four Corners*, *Ritz-Carlton*, *Southwest Photographic* and *Southwest Profile*. He is past president of PEN New Mexico and an officer and director of the New Mexico Book Association.

John Gottberg Anderson has traveled and worked all over the world. The former chief editor of the Insight Guide series and the travel news and graphics editor for the *Los Angeles Times*, he has written eight travel guides, including *Hidden Seattle* and *Hidden Montana*, and been published in *Travel & Leisure* and *Island* magazines. He lives in Bend, Oregon.

Eric Lucas is a freelance writer and editor who has been a newspaper editorial columnist, travel writer, magazine editor and business journalist. Author of Ulysses Press' *Hidden British Columbia*, he is also an avid gardener, fisherman, backpacker and runner.

Stephen Dolainski, a regular contributor to *Westways* and *Avenues*, is a freelance travel editor and writer living in Southern California. He has written about travel and business for magazines, and has contributed to several travel guidebooks, including *Hidden Southern California*.